T0161477

Yeki bud, yeki nabud

ESSAYS ON THE ARCHAEOLOGY OF IRAN IN HONOR OF WILLIAM M. SUMNER

Edited by Naomi F. Miller and Kamyar Abdi

The Cotsen Institute of Archaeology, University of California, Los Angeles
published in association with
The American Institute of Iranian Studies and
The University of Pennsylvania Museum of Archaeology and Anthropology

2003

Library of Congress Cataloging-in-Publication Data

Yeki bud, yeki nabud : essays on the archaeology of Iran in honor of
William M. Sumner / edited by Naomi F. Miller and Kamyar Abdi.
     p. cm. -- (Monographs series ; 48)
Includes bibliographical references and index.
  ISBN 1-931745-05-6
  1. Iran--Antiquities. 2. Iran--Civilization--To 640. 3.
Archaeology--Iran--Methodology. I. Miller, Naomi Frances. II. Abdi,
Kamyar. III. Sumner, William M. IV. Monographs series (Cotsen Institute
of Archaeology at UCLA) ; 48
  DS261 .Y45 2003
  935--dc21
                              2002012656

Cover illustrations: Qashqa'i migration from the upper Kur river basin to winter pastures (autumn, 1976). Wild almond and pistachio trees grow at the bottom of the mountain pass, and oak grows up the slopes. The "Kaftari bird" is the most recognizable motif on the pottery of the Kaftari phase (see *The Birds of Anshan* [Sumner 1999]).

CONTENTS

CONTENTS

LIST OF FIGURES

LIST OF TABLES

PREFACE

WILLIAM M. SUMNER referred to the beginning of many a Persian tale, "Yeki bud, yeki nabud," in the concluding section of his 1986 article, "Achaemenid Settlement in the Persepolis Plain." Best translated as "Once upon a time...," he used the phrase to "emphasize the importance of attempts to push beyond the bare bones of archaeological and textual data to a deeper understanding of ancient life, even if our first efforts are later shown to be fairy tales" (Sumner 1986b: 28, n. 124). This creative, yet skeptical, intelligence characterizes his intellectual contribution to archaeology, especially that of Iran.

This volume honoring William M. Sumner was conceived independently by its two editors. Bill mentored both of us at very different points in his career—during his days as a Professor at The Ohio State University (Miller) and as Director of the Oriental Institute (Abdi). We joined forces after Henry Wright informed us that the other was organizing a festschrift. The response to our call for papers from Bill's students and colleagues was overwhelming, and we hope the finished product lives up to Bill's high standards.

It is our wish that Bill continue to produce first-class scholarship for many years to come in good health and in high spirits. In the meantime, we hope he will find this volume a sign of our gratitude towards him.

Acknowledgments. The publication subvention was generously provided by the American Institute of Iranian Studies and the University of Pennsylvania Museum of Archaeology and Anthropology.

We would particularly like to thank Stuart J. Fleming, Scientific Director of the Museum Applied Science Center for Archaeology (MASCA) at the University of Pennsylvania Museum for supporting the production of publishable maps and illustrations. Under his guidance, John (Mac) Marston, Lindsay Shafer, and Zachary Christman created, improved, and standardized many of the computerized maps and illustrations. Unless otherwise indicated, ancient sites appear as dots and modern towns appear as circled dots. Cuyler Young was kind enough to donate the title of this volume.

Note on transliteration. Archaeological sites, modern geographic place names, and other Persian words are written as they appear in English language publications. If they have no standard English designation, we have used authors' spellings for archaeological sites and simplified direct transliteration from Persian for places and words. Diacritical marks and other special characters are used only in the two chapters that focus on ancient texts.

— *Naomi F. Miller*
Kamyar Abdi

1.1 William M. Sumner. *Photograph by N.F. Miller*

CHAPTER 1

INTRODUCTION

NAOMI F. MILLER AND KAMYAR ABDI

THIS VOLUME is a collection of essays by colleagues, friends, and students of William M. Sumner (figure 1.1) in appreciation of his outstanding contribution to Iranian archaeology, especially to our archaeological knowledge of Fars, a center of Iranian civilization. Besides sharing a long friendship with Bill, contributors to this volume mostly share a not-too-distant history of working in Iran, either at Malyan or at other sites. As systematic archaeological fieldwork in Iran by foreign expeditions has been halted for the past two decades, some authors, eager to take part in this jubilee, contributed chapters on their current research dealing with geographical areas beyond modern Iranian borders, that nonetheless demonstrate the breadth of cultural interaction in the ancient Near East of which Iran was an important part.

WILLIAM M. SUMNER

Bill Sumner's interest in archaeology developed while he was a supply officer for the US Navy, improbably stationed in land-locked Tehran from 1960 to 1962. On his overland trips to southern Fars and the Persian Gulf, he took the opportunity to visit archaeological sites; he even discovered a Middle Paleolithic knapping site near Jahrom. These visits were essential in forming his decision to become an Iranian specialist. During his tour of duty he also took Ezat O. Negahban's evening classes on Iranian archaeology at Tehran University (see chapter 27). Upon resigning his commission in 1964 with the rank of lieutenant commander, Supply Corps, he embarked on his new career by enrolling in the graduate anthropology program at the University of Pennsylvania as a student of Robert H. Dyson, Jr. After first excavating at Kithera, Greece (1965), he quickly focused on his original goal: Iran. Bill chose the Kur river basin in Fars province for his dissertation study for several reasons. It met the intellectual requirement of archaeological interest—not only did the remains of Persepolis provide an immediate touchstone for research but also the plain clearly had a long history of occupation worthy of an intensive survey project. In addition, earlier work in the area by Louis Vanden Berghe provided a foundation upon which he could build his more comprehensive study.

The Kur river basin is only about 40 km by paved highway from Shiraz. Ever practical, with a wife and children to take care of, Bill found it convenient to be based in that "city of roses and nightingales" (Sumner 1972). During the period he spent in Iran conducting the survey of the Kur river basin (1967–1969), Bill found time to hone his already fine excavation skills helping fellow Penn graduate student Mary Voigt (at Hajji Firuz in 1968) and working with Robert H. Dyson, Jr. (at Dinkha Tepe in 1968) and T. Cuyler Young, Jr. (at Godin Tepe in 1969). It never hurts to make a living, and in 1971, the American Institute of Iranian Studies hired Bill as its first director in Tehran. With his first wife, Frances, he organized the hostel, library, and associated facilities at 9 Khiaban-e Moshtaq.

By the time Bill began excavations in 1971 at Malyan, the largest site in the Kur river basin, he already had quite a bit of experience, both organizational and archaeological. After the first two exploratory field seasons of 1971 and

1972, he assembled a varied crew for the major excavations of 1974, 1976, and 1978. It is now considered normal, if not necessary, to have a zooarchaeologist and an archaeobotanist involved in an excavation from the very beginning. When M.A. Zeder and N.F. Miller joined the project in 1974, not only was it a novel concept to look *systematically* for plant remains from Bronze Age sites (Helbaek's 1969 archaeobotanical report on Ali Kosh had gone a long way toward persuading archaeologists to look for plants on Neolithic sites) it was also very unusual to involve the faunal and botanical specialists in determining sampling strategies. But Bill fully supported that work, despite the kicking and screaming of the excavators that it was too much trouble to screen deposits for bones and other items, to take soil samples, and most difficult of all, to actually record the volume of the sampled deposits! Other specialists, like M.J. Blackman (geologist) and M.W. Stolper (epigrapher), were similarly integral to Bill's plan for a large, multidisciplinary project. The Malyan crew (archaeologists and local workers) were a dedicated lot, however, and the high quality of the work is a testament to Bill's archaeological and directorial skills.

Meanwhile, back at the dig house... After an episode of hepatitis in 1972, Bill made certain that in subsequent field seasons the highest standards of cleanliness were maintained. By 1974, at least, when Miller joined the project, Malyan was one of the best fed and healthiest digs around, thanks to the superb Iranian cook Bill knew from his time in the Navy. When leavened bread was a rarity even in town, visitors marvelled when offered a choice of eggs (any way) and toast or French toast for breakfast, with bread freshly baked at 3 A.M. by the cook. For several of the crew, Malyan was their first exposure to village life in the Near East. The mix of old hands and neophytes made for an interesting and rewarding experience.

Relations with the village were generally cordial. (Well, we did once suffer some minor vandalism to our excavation trenches, but Bill solved the problem. He held hostage a sheep that strayed into our courtyard. Before returning it, he extracted a promise from the shepherd boys' parents that the kids would stay out of the excavation trenches.) The team was always a bit of an American enclave at the edge of the village, but it did have a place. In 1976, Bill donated some money towards building a mosque in the village; that same year he served as the head of our highly unusual household for purposes of the Iranian census. Bill's vision for the Malyan project was always more than just his own excavation. With a multiyear commitment to the project, he set up the dig house so that it could support satellite studies during the regular excava-

tion season (M. Rosenberg). He also had the foresight to make arrangements so that in the off-season people could use the dig house as a base for survey and other work (L. Jacobs, J.R. Alden, N.F. Miller). Had the Americans not been, however temporarily, part of the community, that would not have been possible.

As the excavation season ended in August 1978, the Iranian Revolution was gaining momentum. Although fieldwork at Malyan came to a halt, the next decade saw the completion of a number of Malyan project dissertations (see below). It had not been possible to use computers in the field (the project pre-dated both the personal computer and the Internet), but Bill foresaw the value a computerized database would have for a big project like Malyan. His second wife, Kathleen J. Sumner, was a registrar during the 1976 and 1978 field seasons. The team depended on her organizational skills back in the United States, too, where she mediated access to information on the new computerized database on the mainframe at the Ohio State University and cheerfully answered queries that allowed research to proceed. During this period, Bill continued to give generously of his time as an advisor, and he obtained grants to help support students working on their dissertations. He also wrote a number of articles synthesizing his ideas about cultural development in the Kur river basin.

Although it was not possible to return to Iran, Bill missed archaeological fieldwork. So when Mary Voigt proposed that he join the University of Pennsylvania Museum project at Gordion, Turkey, to conduct preliminary regional survey in 1987 and 1988, he quickly accepted. He put many miles on his new motorbike and the old 1960 Gordion pickup truck, visiting prominent mounded sites (and non-sites!). Surveying more intensively on foot immediately around the Gordion Citadel Mound, he made the dramatic discovery that the settlement had an extensive outer town.

In addition to Bill's contributions to archaeology, especially in Iran, he has had a significant career as teacher, mentor, and administrator. The Ohio State University Department of Anthropology appointed Bill assistant professor while he was finishing his dissertation. He followed a fairly traditional academic path, becoming an associate and then full professor. In 1989, he retired from OSU to take on the next challenge—directorship of the Oriental Institute of the University of Chicago.

The Oriental Institute benefited more from Bill's extensive administrative experience than from his archaeological knowledge. In addition to bureaucratic tasks the director of such a prestigious and complex institution must carry out, Bill was also faced with the mammoth responsibility of fund-raising, building a new wing to the Oriental Institute, and renovating the storage and gallery space of the museum, projects that were well under way by the time he retired in 1997. Abdi had the privilege of studying with Sumner during his later years at the Oriental Institute. Despite his busy schedule, Bill took the time to mentor Abdi through a number of independent study courses including the archaeology of Fars and survey methodology. In the summer of 1995, when everybody else had taken refuge next to an air-conditioner to avoid the intolerable heat that killed nearly seven hundred people in the Chicago area, Bill and Abdi sat in the office, drank gallons of water, and went through sample sherds from each and every pottery tradition in Fars. Abdi has vivid memories of how Bill was trying hard to explain details of stylistic variation in Bakun IA and IB pottery or the significance of concave rank-size distribution to this confused student fresh out of Iran.

WILLIAM M. SUMNER
AND IRANIAN ARCHAEOLOGY

Bill Sumner has influenced archaeology and archaeologists in Iran over his entire career, both directly and indirectly. Through his institutional positions at the American Institute of Iranian Studies, Ohio State University, and the Oriental Institute, he has always encouraged young scholars. The influence of his scholarly work is reflected in the range of topics discussed in this volume. Although a number of researchers had both excavated and conducted surveys in Iran, Bill was among the first anthropologically-trained archaeologists to pursue a regional approach aimed at answering broader questions about demography and land use. Furthermore, when many of his peers were working in the already crowded Susiana plain in Khuzestan, he chose to focus on an equally important region, namely, the Kur river basin in Fars. In the 1970s, one of the main topics discussed by American archaeologists working in Iran was the development of complex societies and the origins of the state. With its long cultural sequence, the Kur river basin provided data for evaluating that question, as well as data concerning the somewhat less popular subject of subsequent cycles of development and collapse. Sumner's survey was one of the first regional studies of cultural and demographic cycles in an important cultural area focusing on both sedentary and nomadic populations. His project provided much of the basic data and interpretive approach for answering questions about the evolution of societies in Fars from the Neolithic period to the Bronze Age and about the nature of the Proto-Elamite, Elamite, and Achaemenid worlds.

Perhaps one of Sumner's most important contributions to Iranian as well as Near Eastern archaeology was his rediscovery of Malyan on March 27, 1968. Subsequent confirmation of the identification of the site as ancient Anshan ended nearly eighty years of speculation about the location of the highland capital of Elam. With Malyan identified as the city of Anshan, we gained a whole new view on the long-known, if poorly understood, relations between the highlands and the lowlands—a key to understanding the course of Elamite history. It is therefore no surprise that Bill's contributions are valued by those interested in contemporary developments in Susiana and Mesopotamia.

Some of Bill's innovative studies have broader application. One can readily think of articles about archaeological survey methodology (1990b), the use of ethnographic analogy for developing plausible population estimates (1979, 1989b), and his already classic attempt to correlate the survey data with textual references of the Achaemenid period in the Persepolis area (1986b). Bill Sumner's ongoing scholarly legacy includes not only his own publications but also the dissertations, theses, and articles of the Malyan project members (see partial list following Sumner bibliography).

THE SCOPE OF THIS VOLUME

This book focuses on two of the main geographical areas studied by archaeologists in Iran: the southwest and the northwest. The chapters concern primarily the fifth to second millennia BCE in the southwest and the first millennium BCE in both areas. In southwestern Iran, the fifth to third millennia BCE witnessed the development of complex societies. Elamite culture and society prevailed for about two thousand years (2600–600 BCE); towards the end of that period, cultural developments in northwestern Iran came to bear on those to the south. Assyrians impinged on the Elamites in the lowlands of Khuzestan and on the Urartians in the northwest; Iranian-speakers migrated, or at least came to the highlands of Fars from points north, and in a few centuries established the Achaemenid empire.

The attentive reader will notice several recurrent themes in this volume: the relations between mobile and sedentary peoples; the difficulty of identifying political or cultural boundaries; the importance of geographical factors for understanding sociocultural phenomena. Even as our field work necessarily deals with individual sites or regions, the populations we study did not live in isolation from each other. We hope this volume adequately addresses the complexity of the archaeology of Iran.

On the edge of the Near East but near the center of Eurasia, Iran has seen the movement of materials, people, and ideas over vast distances from earliest times. Such large geographical units are difficult to study, in part because it may not be possible to define ancient cultural and social boundaries. The regions examined may be separated by archaeologically unstudied areas; for example, stone tools of Epipaleolithic Fars have parallels with the Zarzian tools first recognized in the northern Zagros (chapter 8). The ancient social reality itself may have been characterized by fuzzy or permeable boundaries—a consideration for the later periods, which saw the movement of the first crops and obsidian in the arc of the Fertile Crescent (chapter 2). Given the difficulty of recognizing culturally and/or geographically distinct groups in the archaeological record, it is hard to frame questions concerning the relationships among them, whether social (nomad and farmer, or elite and commoner) or spatial (highlands and lowlands, or mobile, rural, and urban [for the latter, see chapter 26]). Even so, many topics, such as the development of agriculture and village life and the beginning of social complexity, have been usefully examined at the fairly local level of site or watershed (for example, chapter 5).

With all the uncertainties of archaeology, ethnographic and historical studies provide useful models, especially for the later periods. One of the most influential models is that of the thirteenth-century political philosopher, Ibn Khaldun, who emphasized the alternating dominance of tribes and states (see Khouri and Kostiner 1990; chapter 3). There are more specific regularities and continuities that link the ancient and modern Near East, too. For example, we can note that the distribution of fifth millennium BCE Bakun pottery coincides with the territory occupied by the present-day mobile pastoral populations (chapter 7) or look to ancient Mesopotamia for origins of the *waqf,* the Muslim pious endowment (Zettler 1992:211–213).

It is not environmental determinism to point out that the historical and ethnographically known pattern of pastoral nomadism is one of the most efficient ways to utilize the landscape of southwestern Iran (chapter 28). The herds of sedentary farmers can graze only part of the year, so the farmers have to store at least some fodder, whether collected or cultivated. By moving between lowland winter pastures and upland summer pastures, pastoral nomads can take full advantage of seasonally luxuriant grazing lands. Consequently, more people and animals can live in the same territory when mobility is part of the subsistence system. Ecological and ethnographic models cannot, however, fully address questions about the origin and early development of tribes and states, nor can they tell us exactly how the institutions analogous to those observable today operated in the past. The farther back in time we consider, the more our information comes from archaeology and related disciplines; the social context in which the earliest interactions between mobile pastoralists and sedentary folk took place surely differed from any in recorded history.

Southwestern Iran includes the highlands of Fars and lowlands of Khuzestan. Writing systems, which appeared at the end of the fourth millennium, mark one of the most important cultural boundaries of the time. Mesopotamians began keeping records in an archaic symbol system that developed into cuneiform. In Susa (in the plain of Susiana, the eastern extension of Mesopotamia in Khuzestan) as well as in settlements further to the east and north, people used a different system, as yet undeciphered, called Proto-Elamite (chapter 11). Although Potts (1999) proposes that the language referred to as Proto-Elamite was not necessarily ancestral to that of the later Elamites, there is no evidence for population replacement, and the Proto-Elamite phenomenon does include a highland and lowland component, much as in later times.[1]

Miroschedji (chapter 3, see table 3.1) considers periods of integration, expansion, and collapse in southwestern Iran. One key issue is the alternating connection between Susiana and Mesopotamia, and between Susiana and Fars. The nature and causes for this cyclical (but not exacly repeating) pattern may relate in part to the basic geography of the region, and people's cultural response to it. Demographically the pattern is expressed in part by movement between the urban, rural, and nomadic components of the population (chapter 4). For example, Wright and Carter (chapter 6) note that during several periods, population grew in the Ram Hormuz plain in response to excess population in neighboring Susiana. In the highlands, despite the archaeological problem of finding traces of mobile populations, regional survey data support baseline demographic inferences for the Kur river basin. In this context, excavation results from Banesh phase (circa 3000 BCE) Malyan shed light on urban organization in a nomad-dominated setting (Sumner 1986a; chapter 9; chapter 10).

Sometimes, identifying contact with evidence of exotic materials or foreign technologies is the first step toward evaluating the limits of cultural or political influence—an Early Dynastic Mesopotamian style statue found on Khark Island in the Persian Gulf (chapter 12), Kaftari and Middle Elamite (second millennium BCE) artifacts found on the Oman peninsula (chapter 13), a shift from arsenical to tin bronze alloys at Kaftari phase Malyan (chapter 14). Unfortunately, it is hard to distinguish the quality of an interaction from the quantity. In the absence of recognizable exotic goods and relevant texts, "foreign" influences are even harder to document.

The late third/early second millennium BCE saw renewed urban development in the Kur river basin centered initially at Kaftari phase Malyan (Anshan). Texts and other material remains show connections between the Elamite highlands and lowlands, reflected in one of the royal titles, "king of Anshan and Susa." The ruling dynasty of the time is conventionally referred to by another royal title, Sukkalmah, which was borrowed from Mesopotamia (Sumerian sukkal.mah, Akkadian *sukkalmahhu*) (see also chapter 3; chapter 15; chapter 17). The archaeological site of Tall-i Qaleh is of particular importance for the Kur river basin ceramic sequence, as it has sherds of all the phases of that urbanizing period—Kaftari, Qaleh, Shogha/Teimuran (chapter 16). A gap in that sequence at the beginning of the first millennium BCE reflects a gap in continuous settlement on the plain.

At some point in the late second or early first millennium, pastoral peoples, probably Iranian speakers, moved into the region from the north, mixing with the local population (Sumner 1994a; chapter 3; chapter 22; chapter 23). Persians were probably in the Kur river basin by the time Late Plain Ware appeared, a marker for the Achaemenid period in Fars (chapter 24). Evidence for the early imperial Achaemenid period in Fars is, however, elusive. As Boucharlat (chapter 24) notes, "beyond a radius of about 25–30 km [from Persepolis and the Kur river], the pastoral way of life remained undisturbed" by the political and economic developments of the empire, even at its height. One may well wonder what multicultural political reality is reflected in the trilingual inscriptions at Persepolis, written in Babylonian, Elamite, and Old Persian (chapter 25).

Much of our historical information from the early part of the first millennium BCE is filtered through Assyrian accounts of devastation wrought on Urartu in the northwest and Elam in the southwest. Fortresses dating to this period are common in the archaeological record (chapter 18), as well as in the iconography of the time (chapter 19; chapter 20). The military activity of the ninth and eighth centuries, a dramatic example of which is seen in Hasanlu's destruction (Dyson 1989a), may be both cause and effect of the population movements of the time. Stylistic similarities between objects from Mesopotamia and eastern Anatolia/northwestern Iran are common, such as those described by Dyson and Voigt (chapter 20). Yet similarity in styles is not always evidence of contact, as Rubinson (chapter 21) points out in her comparison of the iconography on the Hasanlu gold "bowl" with that on objects of the Trialeti culture of Armenia, dated at least five hundred years earlier; Hurrian influence is seen independently on both.

Landscape, in the sense of the physical features of land and climate as used and perceived by people, is one of the major forces shaping society. As people moved around—Iranian speakers perhaps in the second millennium BCE and Turkic speakers in the first millennium CE—they entered a territory with its own history and constraints to which they had to adjust. Both continuity and change, so basic to the archaeologist's world view, are exemplified by Alizadeh's mapping of the distribution of Bakun pottery (fifth millennium BCE) onto the territory of the present-day mobile pastoralists of southwestern Iran (chapter 7), and by Rothman's comment, "the heartland of the Urartian empire coincides almost exactly with the distribution of groove and circular groove and dimple and groove wares [of the Early Transcaucasian culture], yet Urartu rose to prominence almost two millennia later" (chapter 18).

There are many ways to look at the history of Iranian civilization. Southwestern Iran, with its early use of writing, dominates the historical record. Archaeological data support and extend some of the text-based interpretations. Both data sets show long-term demographic cycles and alternating cultural dominance between highlands and lowlands and between nomads and sedentary folk, and may suggest a kind of timelessness for the study of Iran's past. But even during the more than two millennia of Elamite presence, internal development and interchange with the wider world promoted change. Migrations of Iranian speakers, the introduction of Islam, and the movement of Turkic tribes each added to and changed Iranian culture.

Acknowledgment. We thank Mary Voigt, Matt Stolper, Cuyler Young, and Richard L. Zettler for their helpful comments, most of which we took to heart.

NOTE
1. Most of the authors in this volume completed their chapters before Potts's (1999) comprehensive book became available.

PUBLICATIONS BY WILLIAM M. SUMNER

1972a Cultural Development in the Kur River Basin, Iran, an Archaeological Analysis of Settlement Patterns. Ph.D. dissertation, Department of Anthropology, University of Pennsylvania, Philadelphia.

1972b Tall-i Malyan. *Iran* 10:176.

1973a Malyan. *Iran* 11:199–200.

1973b Tall-i Malyan and the Chronology of the Kur River Basin, Iran. *American Journal of Archaeology* 77:288–290.

1973c Excavations at Ancient Anshan. *Archaeology* 26(4):304.

1974 Excavations at Tall-i Malyan, 1971–72. *Iran* 12:155–180.

1975a Excavations at Tal-e Malyan: A Summary of Three Seasons' Results. In *Proceedings of the 3rd Annual Symposium on Archaeological Research in Iran,* edited by F. Bagherzadeh, 157–162. Tehran: Iranian Centre for Archaeological Research.

1975b An Investigation of Uruk Settlement Patterns in Susiana. *Reviews in Anthropology* 2(1):55–60.

1975c Malyan, Survey of Excavations. *Iran* 13:186–187.

1976a Analysis of Material from Tal-e Malyan: 1975. In *Proceedings of the 4th Annual Symposium on Archaeological Research in Iran,* edited by F. Bagherzadeh, 85–88. Tehran: Iranian Centre for Archaeological Research.

1976b Excavations at Tall-i Malyan (Anshan) 1974. *Iran* 14:103–115.

1977a Early Settlements in Fars Province, Iran. In *Mountains and Lowlands: Essays in the Archaeology of Greater Mesopotamia,* edited by L.D. Levine and T.C. Young, Jr., 291–306. Bibliotheca Mesopotamica 7. Malibu: Undena.

1977b Tal-e Malyan (Anshan). *Iran* 15:177–179.

1979 Estimating Population by Analogy: An Example. In *Ethnoarchaeology: Implications of Ethnography for Archaeology,* edited by C. Kramer, 164–174. New York: Columbia University Press.

1982 Ancient Civilization in the Near East. (review of *An Early Town on the Deh Luran Plain,* edited by H.T. Wright) *Science* 218:671–672.

1983 More on Proto-Elamite Iran. (comment on Alden, *Current Anthropology* 23:613–640) *Current Anthropology* 24:531–532.

1983/84 Tal-e Malyan (Anshan) *Archiv für Orientforschung* 29/30:304–306.

1984 Excavations at Tal-e Malyan, Iran. *National Geographic Research Reports* 17:335–339.

1985 The Proto-Elamite City Wall at Tal-e Malyan. *Iran* 23:153–161.

1986a Proto-Elamite Civilization in Fars. In *Gamdat Nasr: Period or Regional Style?,* edited by U. Finkbeiner and W. Röllig, 199–211. Beiheft zum Tübinger Atlas des Vorderen Orients, Reihe B, Nr. 26. Wiesbaden: Dr. Ludwig Reichert Verlag.

1986b Achaemenid Settlement in the Persepolis Plain. *American Journal of Archaeology* 90:3–31.

1988a Maljān, Tall-e (Anšan). *Reallexikon der Assyriologie* 7/3–4:306–320.

1988b Prelude to Proto-Elamite Anshan: The Lapui Phase. *Iranica Antiqua* 23:23–43.

1988c Review of *The Archaeology of Western Iran,* edited by Frank Hole. *Paléorient* 14(1):177–179.

1989a Anshan in the Kaftari Phase: Patterns of Settlement and Land Use. In *Archaeologia Iranica et Orientalis: Miscellanea in Honorem Louis Vanden Berghe,* edited by L. De Meyer and E. Haerinck, 135–161. Gent: Peeters Press.

1989b Population and Settlement Area: An Ethnoarchaeological Example from Iran. *American Anthropologist* 91:631–641.

1990a An Archaeological Estimate of Population Trends Since 6000 B.C. in the Kur River Basin, Fars Province, Iran. In *South Asian Archaeology 1987,* edited by M. Taddei, 1–16. Rome: Istituto Italiano per il Medio ed Estremo Oriente.

1990b Full-coverage Regional Archaeological Survey in the Near East: An Example from Iran. In *The Archaeology of Regions: A Case for Full-coverage Survey,* edited by S.K. Fish and S.A. Kowalewski, 87–115. Washington DC: Smithsonian Institution Press.

1990c Introduction. *The Annual Report of the Oriental Institute of the University of Chicago for 1988–1990:*2.

1991a Ceramics vi: Uruk, Proto-Elamite, and Early Bronze Age in Southern Persia. In *Encyclopaedia Iranica,* Vol. 5, Fasc, 3, edited by E. Yarshater, 284–288. Costa Mesa, CA: Mazda Publishers.

1991b Review of *The Archaeology of Western Iran,* edited by F. Hole. *American Journal of Archaeology* 95:546–547.

1991c Introduction. *The Annual Report of the Oriental Institute of the University of Chicago for 1989–1990:*2–8.

1992 Introduction. *The Annual Report of the Oriental Institute of the University of Chicago for 1990–1991:*2–4.

1993a Introduction. *The Annual Report of the Oriental Institute of the University of Chicago for 1991–1992:*2–3.

1993b Introduction. *The Annual Report of the Oriental Institute of the University of Chicago for 1992–1993:*2–4.

1994a Archaeological Measures of Continuity and the Arrival of the Persians in Fars. In *Achaemenid History 8: Continuity and Change,* edited by H. Sancisi-Weerdenburg, A. Kuhrt, and M.C. Root, 97–105. Leiden: Instituut voor het Nabije Oosten.

1994b The Evolution of Tribal Society in the Southern Zagros Mountains, Iran. In *Chiefdoms and Early States in the Near East: The Organizational Dynamics of Complexity,* edited by G.J. Stein and M.S. Rothman, 47–56. Madison: Prehistory Press.

1994c Introduction. *The Annual Report of the Oriental Institute of the University of Chicago for 1993–1994*:3–4.

1995 Introduction. *The Annual Report of the Oriental Institute of the University of Chicago for 1994–1995*:2–4.

1996 Introduction. *The Annual Report of the Oriental Institute of the University of Chicago for 1995–1996*:3–5.

1997 Introduction. *The Annual Report of the Oriental Institute of the University of Chicago for 1996–1997*:3–5.

1999 The Birds of Anshan. In *The Iranian World: Essays on Iranian Art and Archaeology Presented to Ezat O. Negahban,* edited by A. Alizadeh, Y. Majidzadeh, and S.M. Shahmirzadi, 85–100. Tehran: Iran University Press.

2003 *Early Urban Life in the Land of Anshan: Excavations at Tal-e Malyan in the Highlands of Iran.* Malyan Excavation Reports, Vol. 3. With contributions by John Alden, Annette Ericksen, P. Nicholas Kardulias, Samuel K. Nash, Vincent C. Pigott, Holly Pittman, David Reese, Harry C. Rogers, and Massimo Vidale. Philadelphia: University of Pennsylvania Museum.

Sumner, William M., and Donald Whitcomb

1999 Islamic Settlement and Chronology in Fars: An Archaeological Perspective. *Iranica Antiqua* 34:309–324.

MALYAN PROJECT DISSERTATIONS AND BOOKS

Alden, John R.

1979 Regional Economic Organization in Banesh Period Iran. Ph.D. dissertation, Department of Anthropology, University of Michigan, Ann Arbor.

Carter, Elizabeth

1996 *Excavations at Anshan (Tal-e Malyan): The Middle Elamite Period.* Malyan Excavation Reports, Vol. 2. University Museum Monograph 82. Philadelphia: University Museum, University of Pennsylvania.

Jacobs, Linda K.

1980 Darvazeh Tepe and the Iranian Highlands in the Second Millennium B.C. Ph.D. dissertation, Department of Anthropology, University of Oregon, Eugene.

Miller, Naomi F.

1982 Economy and Environment of Malyan, a Third Millennium BC Urban Center in Southern Iran. Ph.D. dissertation, Department of Anthropology, University of Michigan, Ann Arbor.

Nicholas, Ilene M.

1980 A Spatial/Functional Analysis of the Late 4th Millennium Occupation at the TUV Mound, Tal-e Malyan, Iran. Ph.D. dissertation, Department of Anthropology, University of Pennsylvania, Philadelphia.

1990 *The Proto-Elamite Settlement at TUV.* Malyan Excavation Reports, Vol. 1. University Museum Monograph 69. Philadelphia: University Museum, University of Pennsylvania.

Nickerson, John L.

1983 Intrasite Variability During the Kaftari Period at Tal-e Malyan (Anshan), Iran. Ph.D. dissertation, Department of Anthropology, The Ohio State University, Columbus.

Pittman, Holly

1990 The Glazed Steatite Glyptic Style: The Structure and Function of an Image System. Ph.D. dissertation, Department of Art History and Archaeology, Columbia University, New York.

1994 *Glazed Steatite Glyptic Style: The Structure and Function of an Image System in the Administration of Protoliterate Mesopotamia.* Berliner Beiträge zum Vorderen Orient. Berlin: D. Reimer.

Rosenberg, Michael

1988 Paleolithic Settlement Patterns in the Marv Dasht, Fars Province, Iran. Ph.D. dissertation, Department of Anthropology, University of Pennsylvania, Philadelphia.

Stolper, Matthew W.

1984 *Texts from Tall-i Malyan, I: Elamite Administrative Texts (1972–1974).* Occasional Publications of the Babylonian Fund, 6. Philadelphia: University Museum.

Sumner, William M.

1972 Cultural Development in the Kur River Basin, Iran, an Archaeological Analysis of Settlement Patterns. Ph.D. dissertation, Department of Anthropology, University of Pennsylvania, Philadelphia.

2003 *Early Urban Life in the Land of Anshan: Excavations at Tal-e Malyan in the Highlands of Iran.* Malyan Excavation Reports, Vol. 3. Philadelphia: University of Pennsylvania Museum.

Zeder, Melinda A.

1985 Urbanism and Animal Exploitation in Southwest Highland Iran, 3400–1500 B.C. Ph.D. dissertation, Department of Anthropology, University of Michigan, Ann Arbor.

1991 *Feeding Cities: Specialized Animal Economy in the Ancient Near East.* Washington DC: Smithsonian Institution Press.

2.1   Sites mentioned in text. *Prepared at MASCA*

CHAPTER 2

ARCHAEOBOTANY IN IRAN, PAST AND FUTURE

NAOMI F. MILLER

THE TWO MOST IMPORTANT SOURCES of evidence for vegetation and land use in ancient Iran are plant remains found on archaeological sites and pollen from lake cores. The former more directly reflect plant use by ancient people, for they are remains of plants used for food, fodder, fuel, construction, and other purposes, brought into settlements by people and animals. They consist primarily of seeds and wood remains, usually preserved in charred form, and also include some archaeological pollen. In contrast to remains from archaeological sites, lake sediment pollen records regional vegetation. It is important both for reconstructing the environment in which people lived and for identifying human impact on the vegetation.

From the beginning of modern archaeobotanical studies in the 1960s, plant remains from Iran have provided important information about a variety of topics. Collaboration among botanists, archaeobotanists, and other archaeologists has been affected by intellectual trends in the rest of the Near East and elsewhere. An early example is Hans Helbaek's (1969) work on the Deh Luran plain, which was part of one of the earliest and most influential projects concerned with early agriculture—Hole, Flannery, and Neely's (1969) *Prehistory and Human Ecology of the Deh Luran Plain*. Hans Helbaek pioneered the study of the development of agricultural economies and technology and was the first person in Iran to use flotation to obtain plant remains. As an archaeologist, Henry Wright's broad-based interest in the early civilizations prompted him to take flotation samples (he was probably the first to

measure soil volume) from Farukhabad and Sharafabad (see Wright et al. 1981). William Sumner's unstinting support of archaeobotanical research at Malyan provided the material for one of the first large archaeobotanical studies of an early city (Miller 1982). Setting the environmental scene for all this was basic work by Willem van Zeist and colleagues on pollen cores from the central Zagros mountains that documented the harsh conditions of the last Ice Age and the gradual return and spread of trees to the Zagros (van Zeist and Bottema 1977, 1991).

After a brief outline of the major vegetation zones of Iran, this chapter discusses some of the issues that archaeobotanical data are well-suited to address: human impact on the environment that accompanied the development of agricultural and pastoral economies starting about ten thousand years ago, the impact of the early civilizations on the landscape, and the spread of new crops and technologies from and to neighboring regions (figure 2.1).

All the members of the basic Near Eastern crop complex—the wheats (emmer, einkorn, hard wheat, and bread wheat) and barleys (the two-row and hulled and naked six-row types), lentil and other pulses, and flax, whether for oil or fiber—have been grown in Iran for more than seven thousand years. With the possible exception of grape, fruit-growing began later. After the Bronze Age, we know a variety of other crops that came to Iran, such as millets, sesame, rice, cotton, and sugar cane, but the introduction of these crops is not always attested archaeobotanically (see Zohary and Hopf [2000] for overviews of the different crops) (table 2.1). The long span of human settlement in Iran led inevitably to changes in the landscape, and this too can be traced in the archaeobotanical record.

PHYTOGEOGRAPHY

Iran can be divided into five major vegetation provinces: Caspian, Zagros, central Iranian Plateau, Khorasan, and Laro-Baluchestan (this section is based primarily on Zohary [1963]). The influence of the Mediterranean climate regime is manifested by moisture-bearing winds that predominate in the winter. Trade winds associated with high pressure are a significant factor for the extreme summer aridity in most of Iran. Generally speaking, precipitation increases with altitude and decreases with latitude. Although archaeological and archaeobotanical research has favored some regions over others, this overview is provided as background to this and subsequent chapters, and to encourage future archaeobotanical research. A number of surveys of the climate and vegetation history in the Near East are available that include discussions of pollen and macroremain evidence for Iran (for example, Miller 1997a; van Zeist and Bottema 1991; Willcox 1991).

CASPIAN REGION

The Caspian region includes the Caspian Sea lowlands and Elburz mountains to the south. The mountains run in an east–west direction and reach a maximum elevation of 5670 m. There is a pronounced rain shadow on the southern slopes facing the central Iranian Plateau. The coastal plain and northern slopes are favored with more than 1000 mm annual precipitation, and the lower altitudes experience mild winters. The climax vegetation is described by Zohary (1963) as thermophilous and temperate forest. Despite the agricultural richness of this area today, there are no archaeobotanical reports published for any site in this region. One area that may prove fruitful is the southern slopes of the Elburz, a possible route for agriculture into Turkmenistan (Harris and Gosden 1996; see below).

ZAGROS REGION

The Zagros region incorporates the highlands of western Iran. The mountains run in a northwest–southeast direction. The rain shadow on the eastern slopes can be quite pronounced, but the western slopes are influenced by winter moisture from the Mediterranean. Interspersed among the 3000- to 4800-m peaks are intermontane valleys, the location of most of the settlements in this region. Precipitation varies from 200 to 1000 mm, so dry farming can be practiced in most of the region. The dominant vegetation in the wetter north and west is xerophilous oak forest,

with a general trend toward the drier south and east to a pistachio or pistachio-almond steppe-forest. Susiana, with its cool moist winter and hot dry summer can be considered part of this region, though it lies just at the edge of the dry-farming zone. Most of the archaeobotanical research in Iran has been done in this area.

During the last glacial period, cold, dry conditions could not support forests. In the central Zagros, pollen from Lake Zeribar shows that the vegetation was mainly cold dry steppe dominated by *Artemisia* and members of the Chenopodiaceae family (van Zeist and Bottema 1991). With warming in the Holocene, trees repopulated the Zagros, though vegetation change followed climate change. It took some time for oak to reach its present distribution. For example, oak had not yet reached the site of Tepe Abdul Hosein, occupied during the Neolithic (Willcox 1990:226). Even as late as the Proto-Elamite period, small quantities of oak in the archaeobotanical record of Malyan may indicate its absence in a region that today is at the edge of the oak forest (Miller 1990a).

CENTRAL IRANIAN PLATEAU

The central Iranian Plateau, almost completely surrounded by mountain ranges, has a very dry continental climate. Elevation is about 1300 m, though the land rises to 4000 m in some places. Steppe and desert (including the Dasht-e Kavir in the north and the Dasht-e Lut in the south), sand dunes, salt deserts (*kavir*), gravelly and pebbly steppes are common. Some spots are unvegetated, due to annual precipitation that ranges from 200 mm down to 0 mm. At the higher elevations there are some remnant forests, but mostly the region is characterized by *Artemisia* or *Astragalus* steppe, with psammophilous (sand-loving) and halophilous (salt-loving) species being common. Very little archaeobotanical research has come out of this region. Tepe Yahya lies at its southern edge, and Shahr-i Sokhta is on the east, but the environment is so harsh in most of the region that there has never been much human occupation there.

KHORASAN REGION

The Khorasan region in northeastern Iran is an upland area that reaches an elevation of 3000 m. Annual precipitation ranges from 100 to 500 mm. Consequently, the vegetation is primarily steppe or desert, with forest remnants in the upper elevations. The natural vegetation in much of the area would be juniper steppe-forest. Archaeobotanical remains from Hissar have been investigated—in addition to staple cereals and pulses, some native wild olive and also grape seeds were encountered (Costantini and Dyson 1990).

Table 2.1 Crop plants

	Barley		Wheats			Pulses		Fiber/oil	Fruit		Millet	Other
	2-row	6-row	einkorn	emmer	bread/hard	lentil	bitter vetch	flax	grape	date	(broom-corn)	
Neolithic												
Ali Kosh (1)	•	+	+	•	.	+	.	w	.	.	.	
Tepe Sabz (1)	•	•	+	+	•	•	.	•	.	.	.	
Musiyan (1)	+	?	+	+	+	+	.	+	.	.	.	
Jaffarabad (2)	b	.	+	•	.	•	+	.	.	.	.	
Bendebal (2)	b	.	cf.	.	.	.	.	.	.	.	.	
Ganj Dareh (3)	b	.	.	.	.	+	.	.	.	.	.	
Hajji Firuz (4)	+	+	.	+	.	.	.	+	.	.	.	Wine residue
Jeitun (5)	b	.	•	+	.	.	.	.	.	.	.	
Chalcolithic, Bronze Age												
Farukhabad (6)	•	+	+	+	+	+	.	.	.	.	.	
Sharafabad (7)	.	•	.	•	.	+	.	.	.	.	.	
Malyan (8)	•	•	+	•	+	•	+	.	•	+	.	
Godin (9)	.	•	+	.	•	•	.	.	.	.	.	Wine, beer residues
Shahr-i Sokhta (10)	+	+	+	+	+	+	.	+	•	.	.	
Yahya (11)	+	+	+	+	+	+	.	+	+	+	?	*Pistacia vera*
Gijlar (12)	+	•	•	.	•	+	.	+	+	.	.	
Hissar (13)	+	+	.	+	+	+	.	+	•	.	.	*Olea* cf. *cuspidata*
Anau North (14)	.	•	.	.	•	.	.	.	.	.	.	
Anau South (14)	.	•	.	.	•	.	.	.	•	.	.	
Iron Age and later												
Bastam (15)	.	•	.	+	•	+	.	.	+	.	+	*Sesamum indicum*
Nush-i Jan (16)	+	.	.	•	•	+	+	.	+	.	.	
Hasanlu (17)	+	•	+	+	•	•	+	.	+	.	•	
Ville Royale II (Susa, 1st cent. CE) (18)	+	.	.	.	+	+	.	.	.	+	.	
Q. Ismail Aqa (12)	+	+	+	+	+	+	.	+	.	.	+	

+: present; • present in relatively substantial quantity; b: barley unspecified; w: wild; cf.: uncertain determination

1-Helbaek 1969; 2-Miller 1983; 3-van Zeist et al. 1984(1986); 4-Michel et al. 1993, Voigt 1983; 5-Harris et al. 1996; 6-Miller 1981a; 7-Wright et al. 1981, Miller unpublished data; 8-Miller 1982, 1996a; 9-Badler et al. 1990, Miller 1990b; 10-Costantini 1977; 11-Costantini and Costantini Biasini 1985, Lamberg-Karlovsky and Tosi 1989; 12-Costantini and Biasini 1985; 13-Costantini and Dyson 1990; 14-Miller 1999; 15-Hopf and Willerding 1989; 16-Kyllo and Hubbard 1981; 17-Tosi 1975, Costantini 1988; 18-

LARO-BALUCHESTAN REGION

The Laro-Baluchestan region lies between the central Plateau and the southern coasts. It has a hot, dry climate. The results of archaeobotanical research at Siraf, one of the first sites in the Near East on which flotation was employed (Williams 1973), unfortunately remain unpublished.

ESTABLISHMENT OF AGRICULTURE AND PASTORALISM

The best evidence for the initial domestication of plants comes from the "Levantine corridor" (the Jordan valley to the middle Euphrates). Farming spread from that region, probably through a combination of natural population increase with subsequent emigration and "stimulus diffusion" (Bar-Yosef 1998; van Zeist 1986). That is, Pre-Pottery Neolithic B (PPNB) and PPNB-related archaeological cultures seem to have expanded along the Taurus-Zagros arc. These early farmers did not, however, domesticate all of the important early crops in the same time and place. For example, the original homeland of domesticated einkorn may be somewhere near Diyarbakir, Turkey, and

bitter vetch would also seem to be Anatolian. In contrast to several of the other early domesticates, the wild ancestor of barley, *Hordeum spontaneum,* may have been taken under cultivation more than once; DNA analyses of modern plant populations may help locate where that might have happened (Zohary 1999).

In one of the first substantial archaeobotanical reports about the Near East, Hans Helbaek set many of the terms of discussion on this topic (1969). He pointed out that cultivation (that is, modifying the soil to grow plants) and domestication (manipulation of plants that results in genetic changes) are different processes. In this context, one might define agriculture as a system in which reliance on cultivation is so strong that it is no longer possible to revert to a foraging way of life, perhaps because population increase requires the high productivity of domesticated plants or because cultivation has changed the landscape itself (for example, through the destruction of habitat or over-hunting). In any case, the origins of agriculture, domestication, and cultivation are three different problems.

Helbaek used macroremains to investigate ancient farming, nutrition, ecology, and landscape change, and he recognized the importance of taking into account the archaeological context of the plant remains. At Ali Kosh, in the rainfall agriculture zone of Khuzestan, he found domesticated plants in the earliest levels, dating to about ten thousand years ago. They included emmer, a grain that was most likely domesticated first in the Levantine corridor. Other material, particularly obsidian, shows that there was contact down the Taurus-Zagros arc, so the routes of contact do not require us to assume large movements of population. The other cultigens were hulled two-row barley, naked barley, lentil, and a trace of einkorn. Most remarkable, however, were large numbers in the category "endemic legumes," clover-like plants that include *Astragalus, Trigonella,* and *Medicago,* all of which are preferred forage plants for grazers. Although Helbaek believed that the inhabitants of Ali Kosh collected them to eat, and that they also ate cereal chaff, it seems more likely that many of the remains actually came from animal dung burned as fuel (Miller 1996b), or perhaps from crop-processing (see Hillman 1984).

ENVIRONMENTAL CONSEQUENCES OF AGRICULTURE AND PASTORALISM

Helbaek's work as part of the Prehistory and Human Ecology on the Deh Luran Plain project was one of the earliest to raise the question of environmental change and human impact on the landscape:

> Left to itself, the terrain would have changed even if, as here presumed, the climatic conditions remained more or less stable. Exposed to man's exploitation, nothing would be untouched. (1969:412)

Both macroremains and pollen evidence from the early farming site of Ali Kosh (Woosley and Hole 1978) suggest a decline in sedges (generally plants of moist ground), but no other evidence for moisture change; that is, there was some localized shift in drainage, but not overall climate change. In addition, the seed evidence suggests that there was no straight-line development in agriculture, for in several important respects, the Bus Mordeh (7500–6750 BCE) and Mohammed Jaffar (6000–5600 BCE) assemblages are more similar to each other than either is to the intervening Ali Kosh phase (Miller 1996b). In particular, if the seeds of the steppe legumes originated in dung burned as fuel, their high proportion in the Bus Mordeh and Mohammed Jaffar phases argues for an economy based on pastoral pursuits. In contrast, the shrub legume *Prosopis* may have been introduced as a weed and would therefore be an

indicator of cultivation. That would explain why it becomes common in the Ali Kosh phase (Helbaek 1969), when farming may have become more important relative to herding, and why it declines in relative importance by Mohammed Jaffar times. Even though the subsistence pursuits of Bus Mordeh and Mohammed Jaffar phases were similar, a comparison of the assemblages suggests that there was some degradation of pasture over time, as high quality fodder, represented by the steppe legumes, declined. Note that this long-term process has been observed along the Syrian Euphrates at Abu Hureyra as well (Moulins 1997; Miller 1998).

The archaeobotanical assemblage of another early agricultural site, Ganj Dareh, provides an informative contrast to the steppe site of Ali Kosh. Pollen and macroremain evidence suggest that when Ganj Dareh was occupied, open pistachio forest (with almond and other types) prevailed; the modern Zagros oak forest had not yet established itself (van Zeist et al. 1984[1986]:216). People at both Ali Kosh and Ganj Dareh herded animals (Hole at al. 1969; Zeder and Hesse 2000). For Ali Kosh, Helbaek (1969:387) reports no carbonized wood but tens of thousands of seeds in fewer than fifty samples. At Ganj Dareh, van Zeist et al. (1984[1986]) report for more than one hundred samples at least some wood charcoal in most, but fewer than twenty seeds per sample. We cannot compare charred seed and wood densities, because these sites were excavated before it became routine to report volume of soil floated. Nevertheless, the assemblages of charred material seem to reflect fuel use. Wood was a more important fuel in forests than on the steppe. Thus, Ganj Dareh has relatively few seeds compared to Ali Kosh, where dung appears to have been burned (as evidenced by the absence of wood, but presence large numbers of seeds) (see Miller 1984, 1996b).

AFTER THE NEOLITHIC

As farming economies became established, human impact on the environment increased. Cultivation, by constantly disturbing the soil, allowed domesticated plants to thrive, but also expanded the weed habitat. As domesticated flocks became a more significant factor in the environment, the vegetation of the natural pastures changed, too. Food preservation techniques helped even out the food supply from year to year. Where practiced, irrigation stabilized and also helped increase yields, especially after the introduction of summer crops allowed two plantings annually. As the pastoral component became an integral part of the agricultural system, whether through transhumance of some portion of a farming population or the development of specialized nomadic pastoralism, more people (and animals) could be supported on the land, and the potential for overuse was realized—evidence for several kinds of land degradation appear in the archaeobotanical record: lower quality pastures and deforestation (apparent at Ali Kosh, see above, and at Malyan, see below).

The archaeobotanical record is particularly thin at the end of the Neolithic, and does not really pick up again until the fourth millennium in the Kur river basin of Fars, at Malyan, and to a lesser extent in Khuzestan in Susiana and Deh Luran. William Sumner documented the long settlement history of the Kur river basin (Sumner 1972). The excavations he directed at Malyan during the 1970s yielded archaeobotanical evidence of environment and land use primarily during Banesh (3400–2800 BCE) and Kaftari (2400–1600 BCE) times (Miller 1982, 1984, 1985). Despite the several hundred year gap in settlement in the middle of the third millennium, the settlement survey allows us to imagine some of the influences on the landscape that go beyond the evidence from the Malyan excavation. In particular, Malyan started out as a small center, in a valley characterized by a relatively low population density. In the Kaftari phase, Malyan had grown to its maximum extent and served or exploited, depending on your point of view, a populous hinterland. On these grounds alone, one might expect the archaeobotanical record to show changes in the landscape and land use patterns, and indeed it does. In particular, wood charcoal suggests that Malyan was established in the zone of pistachio-almond forest, which at the time also had juniper. In the Kaftari phase, under conditions of higher population density and correspondingly higher demand for agricultural products and fuel, this nearby forest was thinned, and the somewhat more distant (20 km or so) oak forest was tapped for more fuel. Ethnoarchaeological work at Malyan established the likelihood that many charred seeds found on Near Eastern archaeological sites originated in dung fuel; it is sufficient to note here that the argument was supported by a large increase in the proportion of seeds to charcoal that corresponded to the proposed deforestation.

The Khuzestan material does not allow the same sort of discussion, at least not yet, as samples are fewer and smaller. Almost any generalization one makes could be overturned with the analysis of relatively few additional samples. Nevertheless, there do seem to be some small differences between Farukhabad on the Deh Luran plain and Sharafabad and Susa in Susiana that may reflect differences between rain-fed and irrigation agriculture, in terms of crop choice for people and fodder for animals.

For example, Farukhabad and other Deh Luran assemblages generally have more small-seeded legumes, where lentil is relatively more common in Susiana (Miller 1981a, 1981b, and unpublished laboratory notes).

NEW TECHNOLOGIES, NEW CROPS

As agriculture replaced the foraging way of life, new farming practices and food-processing techniques were invented. When we find evidence for new crops in archaeobotanical assemblages they may reflect new technologies as well.

IRRIGATION

On the Deh Luran plain, irrigation improves crop security and productivity. The earliest farmers did not irrigate, but Helbaek (1969) suggested several indicators of irrigation at sixth-millennium Tepe Sabz. Where Ali Kosh had a few flax seeds that were similar in size to the wild type, Sabz had larger ones comparable to later archaeological examples known to have been irrigated. An overall increase in the amount of six-row barley, which generally requires more water than the two-row type, suggested irrigation, as did a single spikelet fragment and a grain of free-threshing wheat. These three crops appear to have been domesticated earlier elsewhere, but there is no need to propose newcomers to the region brought the crops—they could have spread through a series of local trade contacts along the edge of the Zagros.

In the Zagros region and northern Khuzestan, irrigation is an option that reduces risk and improves yields. In lowland Susiana and the arid interior where rainfall is under 250 mm per year, agriculture cannot be practiced without it. We can infer irrigation at Shahr-i Sokhta from an increase in the size of flax seeds (Costantini 1977). Costantini found a similar assemblage in earlier levels at Tepe Yahya, also located in a very arid region where irrigation was practiced (Lamberg-Karlovsky and Tosi 1989). The very plump seeds of free-threshing wheat found both at Shahr-i Sokhta and Tepe Yahya are further indicators of irrigation (see Miller 1999).

FERMENTATION

Although the primary reason people consumed fermented beverages may well have been for their psychotropic effects, fermentation has nutritional and storage consequences as well. Wine, for example, extends the availability of grapes (raisins do, too). It would be hard to distinguish intentional production of vinegar in the archaeological record because it is a pickling agent as well as evidence that wine has spoiled. As of this writing, the earliest evidence for wine production has come not from macroremains but from residues of grape wine resinated with terebinth pistachio in a pottery vessel found at the Neolithic site of Hajji Firuz in northwestern Iran (McGovern et al. 1996). The site lies within the range of wild grape, so we do not know if the grapes fermented were cultivated. In the Near East generally, and Iran in particular, large numbers of grape seeds do not appear until the third millennium BCE. It is not possible to distinguish wild (*Vitis vinifera* subsp. *silvestris*) and domesticated (*V. vinifera* subsp. *vinifera*) grape based on shape, but Helmut Kroll (1999) observes that it is only in the domesticated variety that underdeveloped seeds occur in the ripe fruit. This criterion is new, so older reports do not mention whether underdeveloped grape seeds were encountered. It is nonetheless probable that vines were coming under cultivation during the fourth millennium. At Malyan, for example, there are a few Banesh grape seeds, but quite a bit more in the Kaftari phase, including a few hundred mineralized ones from a latrine deposit (Miller 1982). Many grape seeds were found at Shahr-i Sokhta, which is a further indication that grape cultivation had become widespread by the third millennium (Costantini 1977). Wood of the vine would be hard to cut, so its presence may best be interpreted as trimmings from cultivated plants. Never common, the first appearance of grape wood fragments at Malyan (Miller 1982) and Mehrgarh, Pakistan (Thiebault 1989) dates to the mid-third millennium, further supporting the view that significant grape cultivation is a relatively late phenomenon.

Once begun, the tradition of wine-making was never lost, judging from residue analysis on some jar sherds from fourth millennium levels at Godin. By about 3500 BCE, people were drinking beer there, too (Michel et al. 1993). In contrast to grapes, which can ferment naturally from yeasts that grow on the fruit, barley beer has a more complex manufacturing process that involves sprouting the barley to create the malt on which the yeasts work.

SUMMER CROPS: MILLET, RICE, SESAME

The dry summers that prevail over most of Iran do not permit summer cropping without some form of irrigation. Several exotic crops probably arrived in western Iran as domesticates. For example, Lorenzo Costantini reported the surprising presence of broomcorn millet (*Panicum miliaceum*) as early as the fifth millenium BCE at Tepe Yahya (Lamberg-Karlovsky and Tosi 1989), along with some *Pistacia vera*. The presumed homeland of the wild ancestors of both these food plants is Central Asia (Zohary and Hopf 2000). The earliest really secure evidence of broom-

corn millet as a crop, however, comes from Haftavan (1900–1550 BCE) in northwestern Iran (Nesbitt and Summers 1988), and the best evidence for *Pistacia vera* dates to about the same time and comes from Djarkutan in Uzbekistan (Miller 1999). Assuming the identifications to species hold up, the geographically and temporally isolated Yahya finds may be evidence of trade rather than the spread of the cultivation of those crops. Rice from Parthian period (about 210 BCE–225 CE) deposits at the Ville Royale II excavation at Susa is the earliest attested to date for the Near East (Miller 1981b). Whether by sea or overland, rice most probably arrived in Iran from south or east Asia, but it is difficult to trace, as there are no reports from coastal sites and few from the interior. Sesame, which may have been originally domesticated in India, first appears in the archaeobotanical record of Iran in Iron Age Bastam (Hopf and Willerding 1989).

QUESTIONS AND CHALLENGES FOR ARCHAEOBOTANY IN IRAN

At this point, the single most important goal for archaeobotanical research in Iran must be continued documentation for all regions to trace changes in landscape and land use. Of particular interest is the spread of agriculture and the history of individual crops.

THE SPREAD OF AGRICULTURE BEYOND IRAN

The Near Eastern crop complex, which developed and spread over much of southwest Asia during the PPNB, was adopted by people in neighboring regions. Wheat and barley occur as early as the seventh millennium BCE at Mehrgarh in Pakistan (Costantini and Costantini-Biasini 1985). At Jeitun, a Neolithic site in Turkmenistan, connections based on material culture can be traced along the Caspian coast or the northern edge of the Iranian Plateau along the Elburz mountains (Harris and Gosden 1996), but einkorn is the main crop plant (Harris et al. 1996). It is hard to imagine that einkorn, having evolved in Anatolia, would thrive in the moist Caspian lowland forest. Therefore, based on the plant evidence, perhaps the southern route is the more likely. Excavation of suitable sites in both regions would certainly help answer this question.

ORIGIN AND SPREAD OF BREAD WHEAT

Hexaploid bread wheat (*Triticum aestivum*) evolved after initial wheat domestication. It has the genes of a tetraploid domesticated emmer, *Triticum dicoccum,* and a diploid wild type, *Aegilops squarrosa*. It could not have evolved until people brought the domesticated wheat into contact with the wild *Aegilops,* most probably southwest of the Caspian (Zohary and Hopf 2000). Since the grains of bread wheat are indistinguishable from those of the tetraploid free-threshing wheat, *Triticum turgidum,* it has not been possible to trace the evolution of this crop. Grains tentatively identified by Costantini as bread wheat at Hajji Firuz date to the early sixth millennium (Voigt 1983:275–277).

NEW CROPS

Throughout history, territorial conquest has provided a mechanism for the transfer of crops and other plants. As early as the eighth century BCE, we know that Assyrian rul-ers were bringing exotic plants and animals back to their gardens and parks, both self-consciously as a sign of mastery but also for their potential use and interest. Alexander the Great's exploits exposed the Greek world to new ideas, as well as plants, some of which presumably came from Iran or crossed it (for south and east Asian plants known to the Hellenistic world, see discussions of Zohary and Hopf [2000]). Two crops that are associated with the coming of Islam are cotton and sugar cane (Watson 1983); others, like maize and tomatoes, had to await European contact with the New World. Unfortunately, these contacts have not yet been documented in the archaeobotanical record of Iran.

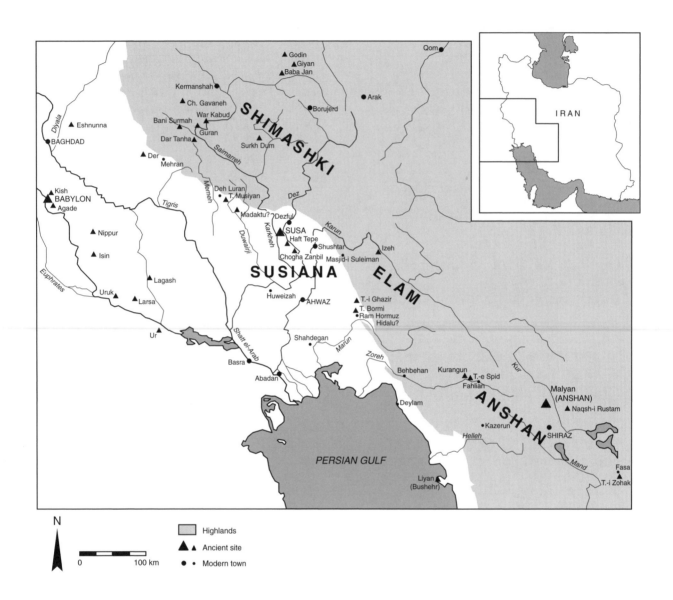

3.1 Southwestern Iran, showing sites mentioned in text. *P. de Miroschedji*

CHAPTER 3

SUSA AND THE HIGHLANDS

Major Trends in the History of Elamite Civilization

PIERRE DE MIROSCHEDJI

IN THE FIELD OF ELAMITE STUDIES, one line of inquiry, especially in the last two decades, has been to elaborate a conceptual framework for understanding the civilizations of Susa in antiquity. This search goes back to the dawn of the twentieth century and the beginning of Elamite studies. In 1901 the famous epigrapher Vincent Scheil wrote in the foreword of the third volume of the *Mémoires de la Délégation en Perse*:

> *Le dualisme ethnique en Élam est un fait certain. À ce dualisme correspondent sous les plus grands règnes, dans le protocole royal, le double nom de Anzan-Suse, et dans la littérature deux sortes de documents.*
>
> [Ethnic dualism in Elam is an unquestionable fact. Under the major reigns, this dualism is reflected in the royal protocol by the double name *Anshan-Suse,* and in the written records by two kinds of documents.]

Scheil proceeded to distinguish between the Elamite inscriptions, which he called *anzanites,* and the Akkadian inscriptions, which he called *susiennes,* arguing that Susa was originally a Semitic city (Scheil 1901:vii). With this statement, Scheil actually set the terms of discussion concerning the history of Susa, which, in its cultural and ethnic orientations, appeared to be both Semitic (that is, Mesopotamian) and Elamite (that is, linked to the Iranian Plateau).

The implications of this statement could not be fully understood as long as the archaeological sequence of Susa remained unknown and the Elamite hinterland unexplored. As a result, Scheil's observations were largely ignored and Susa was often described as a sort of provincial satellite of Mesopotamia.

After 1945, Roman Ghirshman's excavations at Susa and Chogha Zanbil, Ezat Negahban's work at Haft Tepe and William Sumner's research at Malyan revealed other aspects of Elamite civilization and completely changed this picture. In 1979, relying on a vastly increased knowledge of Elamite archaeology, Pierre Amiet published an influential article in which he added to Scheil's concept of ethnic duality that of cultural alternation, thus reinstating the Elamite hinterland to its historical role (Amiet 1979a, 1979b). Amiet endeavored to show that throughout its history, Susa had been alternately under the influence of Mesopotamia and of the Elamite highlands. Amiet's thesis, however, was largely descriptive because it was difficult at this stage of research to attempt a comprehensive explanation.

A year later, François Vallat published a short monograph entitled "Suse et l'Élam" (Vallat 1980) in which he concluded that Susa and Elam need to be sharply distinguished, and that Susa is not in Elam because Elam is actually Anshan, more precisely the Kur river basin of central Fars, where Malyan (the ancient city of Anshan) and Persepolis are located. Vallat's conclusions implied that the history of Susa was essentially the result of a balance between Susiana and Anshan, two areas separated by some 500 kilometers.

Also in 1980, I published a paper on the Elamite god Napirisha (Miroschedji 1980), analyzing the dual structure of the Elamite empire throughout history both in political and religious terms on the basis of royal titles. My subsequent researches were mostly concerned with the Late Elamite period (Miroschedji 1976, 1981a, 1981b, 1981c), focusing on the process of collapse of the Elamite civilization in the first half of the first millennium BCE, and stressing in particular the demographic, social and political consequences of the development of nomadic pastoralism in southwestern Iran during the second and first millennia (Miroschedji 1982, 1985, 1986, 1990a).

In this chapter, I would like to elaborate on my previous arguments and on those of my predecessors, using more evidence pertaining to a longer period of time in order to reach a more comprehensive view of Elam's historical trajectory and of Susa's relations with the highlands. The first part will be deliberately theoretical. Its aim is to examine the various natural and sociopolitical constraints which have shaped the historical development of southwestern Iran and to show their systemic functioning in the perspective of a historical *longue durée*. The second part will be a short review of the history and archaeology of Elam intended to illustrate the validity of the proposed theoretical framework. The goal is not simply to observe various historical phenomena but rather to integrate them into an overall conceptual framework and, ultimately, to explain them as much as possible.

A THEORETICAL APPROACH

A first task is to delineate the various constraints which have determined the development of Elamite civilization and to understand how they interrelated.

SPATIAL DIVERSITY

It is appropriate to begin with an understanding of the geographical frame in which the historical phenomena under review have taken place. Both the extent and the diversity of the geographical landscape should be emphasized. The geographical area that can be considered as forming the hinterland of Susiana in antiquity covers both the eastern part of the Mesopotamian plain and the entire southwestern Iranian highlands, comprising the modern provinces of Khuzestan and Fars and partly those of Lurestan up to southern Kurdestan (figure 3.1). For modern historians, these territories together constitute "Greater Elam" or the "Elamite confederacy" because, at one time or another and to varying degrees, they were subject to the domination or direct influence of Elamite kings, and for that reason were called "Elamite" by the Mesopotamians.

As an integrated political unit, however, "Greater Elam" existed only during relatively short periods of time. It was composed of various political entities repeatedly mentioned in historical texts as major components of the empire. Their location is often problematic but considerable progress has been made in the course of the last two decades to identify them geographically (see figure 3.1):

- *Susiana* occupies the northern part of the plain of Khuzestan, which represents a simple geographical extension of the Mesopotamian plain.
- *Elam* had come to designate for the Mesopotamians all Elamite territories, including Susiana, whenever they were ruled by an Elamite king. But *sensu stricto,* it may have corresponded to the mountainous area extending an unspecified distance to the east of the plain of Khuzestan. This is precisely the area occupied in the first century BCE by the kingdom of Elymais, which was historically the heir and successor of ancient Elam (Amiet 1979b:197). The Old Elamite kingdom of Awan may have been part of this territory.
- *Anshan* is Fars *sensu lato*, but more specifically the large plain of the Kur river basin where the city of Anshan (Malyan) was located. Originally an autonomous polity, it was an essential part of Greater Elam in the late third and early second millennium BCE, but should not be confused with nor used as an interchangeable designation of Elam *sensu stricto* (contra Vallat 1980).
- *Shimashki* extended over parts of Lurestan and southern Kurdestan (R.C. Henrickson 1984, 1986, 1987; Stolper 1982:45). In the Late Elamite period, part of this territory was occupied by the principality of Ellipi, a close ally of the Elamite kings.

In addition, there were other, less important territorial entities (Ayapir, Huhnur, Bashime, Rashi, and others) that may have been districts of the above-mentioned major provinces and which can be located with more or less confidence (see Carter 1984:187 [Ayapir]; Duchêne 1986 [Huhnur and Bashime]; Miroschedji 1986:212 [Rashi]).

In geographical, economic, and social terms, the Elamite territories present a considerable variety. Only the plain of Khuzestan and some valleys of the highlands (for example, the Kur river basin, the valleys of Behbehan and Khorramabad, and a few other areas) were large and fertile enough to permit irrigated agriculture and a centralized political organization based on the presence of a large sedentary population. Elsewhere, along the piedmont of the Zagros and in most of the high valleys and plains of the Plateau, the fragmented topography and uncertain agricultural returns have always precluded political unity and encouraged pastoral nomadism as a more reliable subsistence strategy.

This situation has introduced in southwestern Iran an essential measure of ethnic, political, and cultural diversity which explains both the loose unity and the fragile nature of the Elamite confederacy and the varying degree of integration of these areas according to changing historical situations. The basic contrast is between the mountainous highlands in general, where pastoral nomadism was always the dominant subsistence strategy, and the alluvial lowlands of Khuzestan, which are well suited to irrigation agriculture and welcomed seasonally transhumant pastoralists.

DIACHRONIC DISCONTINUITIES

While the historical trajectory of the Elamite civilization encompasses almost three millennia between the Proto-Elamite and Late Elamite periods, there are gaps during this considerable span of time when Elam as a whole, or some parts of it, suffered eclipses and vanished from the historical scene, and sometimes even from the archaeological landscape (table 3.1). For example, it seems that the entire Kur river basin—the most fertile area of Fars—had no permanent settlement at all between circa 2800 and 2400 BCE and again between circa 1000 and 550 BCE; the fabled city of Anshan yields no historical information after the eighteenth century BCE except for a short interlude in the late twelfth century BCE. Similarly in Susiana, very little is known historically of the sixteenth-fifteenth and the thirteenth centuries and almost nothing for the period between circa 1100 and 750 BCE. These historical fluctuations are well expressed by the two best known population curves for southwestern Iran, that of the Kur river basin in Fars (Sumner 1972, 1988a, 1990a, 1990b) and that of the Khuzestan plain (Miroschedji 1990a).

The settlement history of the Kur river basin shows three cycles of population growth and decline (figure 3.2). The first one, from Neolithic through Late Chalcolithic times, ended with the Banesh phase or Proto-Elamite period, around 2800 BCE. As stated above, the latter period was followed by a Dark Age, during which there is no evidence of sedentary settlement for about four centuries, until about 2400 BCE. The second settlement cycle began circa 2400 BCE with the massive sedentarization of pastoralists at the outset of the Kaftari phase, the Golden Age of historic Anshan. After about six centuries of prosperity, the disaggregation of the Kaftari state is indicated from the early centuries of the second millennium BCE onward by a steady decline in settlement. It is marked by

the progressive abandonment of towns, and eventually of villages in the first half of the first millennium BCE. The corollary of this decline was the strong development of pastoral nomadism from the mid-second millennium BCE onward, reaching a peak in the Late Elamite period. A third settlement cycle began in the sixth century BCE and lasted until medieval times. Its initial phase is marked again by a massive sedentarization process which I have interpreted as marking the ethnogenesis of the Persians (Miroschedji 1985:292–296).

The demographic curve of Susiana also presents three major cycles of population growth and decline, although they are more complex as each shows some fluctuations (figure 3.3). The first cycle took place between the Chalcolithic and the end of the Proto-Elamite period, circa 3000 BCE. The second cycle started in the early third millennium BCE, culminated toward the middle of the second millennium and reached its minimum in the Late Elamite II period in the seventh-sixth century BCE. The third cycle began with the Achaemenid period and ended in medieval times.

These two curves thus show overall similarities which are probably indicative of trends affecting the entire southwestern Iran. They both reveal the existence of three major cycles of population growth and decline. The first began in the Neolithic and ended with the Proto-Elamite period at the beginning of the third millennium. The second cycle started in the course of the third millennium, culminated in the second millennium and ended during the Late Elamite period in the second quarter of the first millennium. The third cycle began with the Achaemenid period and ended in medieval times.

But these curves are not exactly synchronous and show also differences in the magnitude of the cyclic variations. At least in the second and first millennia BCE, settlement density and complexity were higher—and the state apparatus accordingly more developed—in the lowlands than in the highlands, where urban centers had existed for a comparatively shorter period of time. Urban life was also more resilient in the lowlands, even during the Dark Age of the early first millennium BCE, than in the highlands, where population decline started earlier and was much more marked, leading twice to the virtual disappearance of the settled population. Consequently, from the middle of the second millennium BCE onward, urban society and state organization continued to exist in the lowlands while the highlands had already reverted to nomadic pastoralism, a change which brought a dramatic shift of the center of gravity of the Elamite empire from the highlands to the lowlands. The corollary of this observation is a fact of cardinal historical importance: demographically and politically,

Table 3.1 Chronological chart (for comments, see "Excursus" on p. 37)

Date	KHUZESTAN				Elamite System	Irano-Mesop. System	FARS	
	Historical Periods	Archaeol. Periods	Susa Sequence	Susa Stratigr.*			Archaeol. Periods	Malyan Sequence**
500	Achaemenid	Achaemenid		*Ville Royale II* 5-4		Late Assyrian to Achaemenid	Achaemenid	
	Final Elamite	Late Elamite II	Susa X	7-6	*Collapse*		*Gap*	
	Late Elamite			*Ville Royale A*	*Late Elamite Phase*			*EDD*
1000	Late Elamite "Dark Age"	Late Elamite I	Susa IX	9-8 Pits in A IX	*Collapse*	*Collapse*		IIIA
	Late"Shutrukids"			10 A IX			Shogha / Teimuran	IVA Middle Elamite
	"Shutrukids"	Middle Elamite II	Susa VIII	11 A X	Middle Elamite Phase	Kassite		IVB
	Late "Igihalkids"			12 Gap				
	"Igihalkids"			13 A XI			Qaleh	*GHI*
1500	"Kidinuids" ?	Middle Elamite I	Susa VII	A XII sup.	*Collapse*	*Collapse*		I II
	Late Sukkalmahs	Old Elamite III	Susa VI	*Ville Royale B* A XII B VI réc.inf. A XV				III
	Middle Sukkalmahs							IV
	Early Sukkalmahs	Old Elamite II	Susa V	B V B VI *Ville Royale I*			Kaftari	
2000	Shimashki Dyn.							
	Ur III Period			B VII 6	Old Elamite Phase	Early Dynastic to Old Babylonian		
	Akkad Period / Awan Dynasty	Old Elamite I	Susa IV	B 7 8 9			*Gap*	
2500	Early Dynastic			A 12				
		?	Susa III	C 13	*Collapse*	*Collapse*		*TUV* I
	P R E H I S T O R I C	Proto-Elamite Period		B *Acropole I* 14B 18 14A		Uruk to Jemdet-Nasr	*ABC* II III IV	II III
3000				A 16	Proto-Elamite Phase		Banesh	
		Uruk Period	Susa II	17				
3500				22 23				
		Susa I	Susa I				Lapui	
4000				27			Bakun	

* *References:* Acropole I : Lebrun 1978; Ville Royale A & B : Gasche 1973, Steve et al. 1980; Ville Royale I : Carter 1980; Ville Royale II : Miroschedji 1981a, 1987.
** *References:* General : Sumner 1988a; TUV : Nicholas 1990; and EDD : Carter 1996.

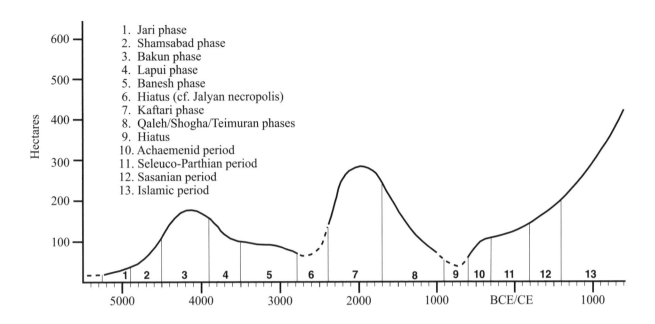

1. Jari phase
2. Shamsabad phase
3. Bakun phase
4. Lapui phase
5. Banesh phase
6. Hiatus (cf. Jalyan necropolis)
7. Kaftari phase
8. Qaleh/Shogha/Teimuran phases
9. Hiatus
10. Achaemenid period
11. Seleuco-Parthian period
12. Sasanian period
13. Islamic period

3.2 Variations of the sedentary population of the Kur river basin according to occupied surfaces. *Adapted from Sumner 1990a*

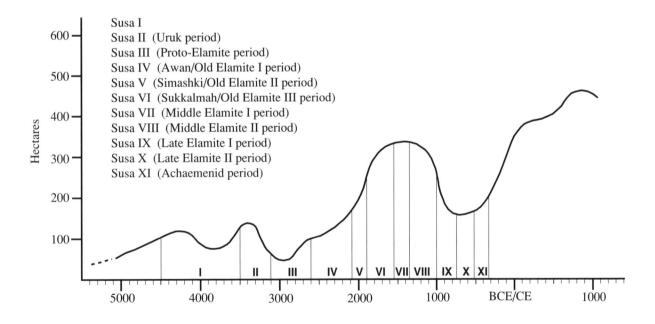

Susa I
Susa II (Uruk period)
Susa III (Proto-Elamite period)
Susa IV (Awan/Old Elamite I period)
Susa V (Simashki/Old Elamite II period)
Susa VI (Sukkalmah/Old Elamite III period)
Susa VII (Middle Elamite I period)
Susa VIII (Middle Elamite II period)
Susa IX (Late Elamite I period)
Susa X (Late Elamite II period)
Susa XI (Achaemenid period)

3.3 Variations of the sedentary population of Susiana according to occupied surfaces. *After Miroschedji 1990a*

Table 3.2 Aspects of the collapse taking place with the transition from the Middle to the Late Elamite periods

Middle Elamite Period (14th–11th century BCE)	Late Elamite Period (9th–6th century BCE)
▶ Important sedentary population	▶ Strong decline of sedentary population
▶ Pastoral population not important	▶ Strong increase of pastoral nomadic elements
▶ Developed urbanization	▶ Disurbanization, many villages and hamlets
▶ Ethnic homogeneity	▶ Ethnic heterogeneity
	- Regression of the Elamite component
	- Installation of Arameans, Persians, etc. at the periphery of Elam
▶ Social homogeneity	▶ Social heterogeneity
	- Extension of areas inhabited by pastoral nomads
	- Development of tribal organizations
▶ Political centralization	▶ Political fragmentation
- Unity of Greater Elam	- Disintegration of "Greater Elam" (decline and separation from Anshan)
- One single capital	- Several capitals, decentralized government
- Regional administrative centers	- Administration weak or absent

the bipolarity between Anshan and Susa within the Elamite confederacy existed only during the Proto-Elamite and the beginning of the Old Elamite periods. During the Middle and Late Elamite periods, the hegemony of Susa over the highlands was complete and the notion of a bipolarity between Susa and Anshan survived merely through the use of a royal title evoking the Golden Age of a distant past rather than the political realities of the time.

Historical and settlement discontinuities were the result of complex processes of collapse. These were not specific to southwestern Iran. Similar processes have been identified and analyzed by several scholars in different parts of the world (Tainter 1988; Yoffee and Cowgill 1988), notably in Mesopotamia (Adams 1981; Yoffee 1979, 1988) and in the southern Levant (Finkelstein 1995). Their most articulate analysis was presented by Colin Renfrew, who has listed the following features as general characteristics of systemic collapses (Renfrew 1979:482–485):

Four main features characterize the collapse itself:

▶ Collapse of central administrative organization (for example, disappearance or reduction in number of levels of central place hierarchy, abandonment of palaces, eclipse of major religious centers, loss of literacy)

▶ Disappearance of the traditional class elite

▶ Collapse of centralized economy (for example, reduction or cessation of external trade and of craft-specialist manufacture)

▶ Settlement shift and population decline (for example, abandonment of many settlements; reduction in population density).

Two other features typify the aftermath of a collapse:

▶ Reduced socioeconomic integration (for example, emergence of segmentary societies showing analogies with those seen centuries or millennia earlier in the

"formative" level in the same area; fission of realm into smaller territories whose boundaries may relate to those of earlier polities)

▶ Development of romantic Dark Age myth (for example, attempts by new power groups to establish legitimacy in historical terms with the creation of genealogies seeking to find a link with the "autochthonous" former state).

Amongst the diachronic aspects of a systemic collapse, Renfrew has listed these additional features:

▶ The collapse may take around 100 years for completion.

▶ Dislocations are evident in the earlier part of the period.

▶ Boundary maintenance may show signs of weakness during this time, so that outside pressures leave traces in the historical record.

All these features can be observed several times in the fluctuating history of Elamite civilization. One significant example is given on table 3.2, where the two columns contrast the main characteristics of the Middle and Late Elamite periods (see Miroschedji 1990a).

SYSTEMIC HIERARCHY

As collapses are usual consequences of the functioning of systems, they are quite often cyclic in nature, because as long as the system operates in a similar way, it basically has the same effects. Indeed, the spatial and diachronic discontinuities observed in Elam are amenable to systemic analysis. Depending on the scale at which the phenomena are viewed, two major systems can be considered, which differ in their *modus operandi* and in their chronology, but which could at times function in conjunction: the Irano-Mesopotamian System and the Elamite System.

At a large scale, the changing political and economic interaction between the highland resource areas of the Iranian Plateau and the lowland alluvial plains of Greater

Mesopotamia constitute a system which, for the purpose of this essay, can be conveniently called "the Irano-Mesopotamian System." I believe that this system was ultimately responsible for the emergence of the Elamite civilization. Its cyclic variations seem to involve three phases:

1. Expansion of Mesopotamia toward the Zagros highlands and the Persian Gulf, stimulating the establishment of trade routes and the development of international exchanges;
2. Emergence by a process of secondary state formation of highland polities which benefit from the international trade and tend to control the import of essential commodities. After their eventual unification, these polities may finally take advantage of a Mesopotamian weakness or collapse to gain control of the lowlands, and even of Mesopotamia itself; and
3. Cessation of the international trade and subsequent collapse of the peripheral highland polities, leading to political fragmentation and a strong resurgence of pastoral nomadism in the highlands.

These cyclic variations recurred at least three times between the mid-fourth and the late second millennium BCE (table 3.1): first in the Uruk and Proto-Elamite periods, between circa 3500 and 2800 BCE; again with the flourishing of the trans-Iranian trade, between circa 2600 and 1750 BCE; and once more in Kassite times, between the fourteenth and the twelfth centuries BCE. It is likely that the trans-Iranian trade was revived in the Late Assyrian/Late Elamite period, introducing a fourth cycle from the eighth century BCE onward.

At a regional scale, the relationship between the plain of Khuzestan and the various districts of its mountainous periphery constitute another system, which can be called "the Elamite System" because it concerns the relationship between the Elamite highlands and lowlands. Its appearance was linked to the introduction of transhumant pastoralism in the highlands from the fourth millennium onward BCE (Gilbert 1983; E. F. Henrickson 1985; Hole 1978; Zagarell 1982). Thus, this system was also in operation before and after the existence of an Elamite civilization, probably until the nineteenth century of our era (see below). It was mainly governed by two variables: the nature and fluctuations of the Irano-Mesopotamian contacts throughout history, and the development of pastoralism which, at certain periods in the mountainous areas, brought a sharp decrease in the number of permanent settlements and a correlative dominance of the nomadic elements en-

gaged in seasonal movements. The need to control the winter pastures, economic complementarity between nomads and agriculturists and kinship ties between them explain the emergence of an ethnic, social and cultural continuum between the highlands and the lowlands. In periods of pastoralist expansion, it led to the rule of nomadic khans of the highlands over the settled agriculturists of the lowlands. When the movement was reversed, kings based in the lowlands could exercise their suzerainty over the highland tribes.

THE ELAMITE PARADIGM OF GROWTH AND DECLINE
Hence the functioning of the Elamite System resulted in a paradigm of growth and decline involving schematically three successive phases:

- *Integration.* The impetus for the political integration of the highlands and the lowlands may usually have come from the Elamite heartland in eastern Khuzestan.
- *Expansion.* The control of the agricultural resources of Susiana and of the capital city of Susa gave kings enough power and prestige to eventually unite under their authority the highland tribes of the entire southern and central Zagros, from Fars to Lurestan or southern Kurdestan; and in some favorable circumstances it could even give them the strength to intervene briefly in Mesopotamia.
- *Collapse.* The excessive extension of the Elamite confederacy, its weak administration, and the instability of its political organization led to the loss of the most peripheral provinces (for similar processes in Mesopotamia, see Adams 1965, 1981; Yoffee 1977, 1979, 1988) and eventually to a more or less advanced state of political fragmentation. Each component of the confederacy reverted then to independence and isolation. In the case of Susa, this situation implied increased relations with its Babylonian neighbors (that is, Amiet's *alternance*).

The next phase marks the beginning of a new cycle: Susa's political weakness and economic dependence on the highlands made it an easy prey for an enterprising mountain khan who took control of Susiana, recreated a powerful kingdom and then reembarked on an expansionist policy.

This Elamite paradigm of growth and decline has repeated itself with variations several times from the fourth to the first millennium BCE (table 3.1). The remainder of this essay is devoted to illustrations of this cyclic phenomenon.

CYCLES OF GROWTH AND DECLINE

THE FIRST CYCLE: PROTO-ELAMITE (SUSA II-III)

INTEGRATION: THE URUK PERIOD (SUSA II)

The Irano-Mesopotamian System started to operate when Greater Mesopotamia began to desire various commodities which could be obtained only from the Iranian Plateau (table 3.1). This need arose sharply in the Uruk period and by around 3500 BCE led to the incorporation of the plain of Khuzestan into the Mesopotamian economic sphere (Algaze 1989, 1993a, 1993b; Johnson 1973). This shift is dramatically expressed in the archaeological sequence of Susa with the transition from the Susa I phase, with its magnificent painted pottery typical of the Zagros piedmont area, to the Susa II phase, when Susiana became part and parcel of the Mesopotamian civilization of the Uruk period (Algaze 1993a, 1993b; Amiet 1988; Le Brun 1978). The latter expanded in the western Zagros, where it established colonies in a local, non-Uruk cultural environment, as in Godin Tepe V (E.F. Henrickson 1994; Young 1986). These colonies were intended to tap preexisting exchange networks, which were then considerably developed, mostly toward the central and northern Plateau.

EXPANSION: THE PROTO-ELAMITE PERIOD (SUSA IIIA)

This network of Uruk settlements lasted for several centuries. Its collapse toward the end of the fourth millennium gave way to the emergence on the periphery of the Uruk-held territories of Proto-Elamite polities as a result of a secondary urbanization process. In Khuzestan, the main polity was established in Susa where the shift from the Uruk to the Proto-Elamite periods took place with the transition from the Susa II to the Susa III phases. It is marked by the disappearance of Mesopotamian-related cultural features and their replacement by new cultural features with distinctly highland affinities, such as a new glyptic style and the first tablets with Proto-Elamite script (Amiet 1986a, 1988). The other major Proto-Elamite polity of southwestern Iran had its seat at Malyan in the Kur river basin, where the settlement grew rapidly by the Middle Banesh phase and eventually reached, in the Late Banesh phase, an occupied area of about 50 ha, although 200 ha were enclosed by a city wall (Alden 1982a; Nicholas 1990; Sumner 1985, 1986a, 1988a:317; Stolper 1985) (figure 3.2). It would be anachronistic, however, to deduce from the *de facto* bipolarity between Malyan/Anshan and Susa the existence at such an early period of a political link between these two emerging cities. But direct contacts between them are reasonably certain and this configuration foreshadows the complementary relationship that will determine the characters of the Elamite confederation during part of the third and second millennium BCE.

The Proto-Elamite cities of Khuzestan and Fars were engaged in the control of the flow of products from the Plateau. They imported a large variety of metal and stone artifacts, or produced them from imported raw materials (Carter 1990:90–93) and stimulated the growth of a chain of settlements with more or less strong Proto-Elamite affinities across the entire Plateau (Amiet 1986a:105–119; Glassner 1998a). However, no Proto-Elamite settlement *sensu stricto* is known east of Fars, where archaeology has revealed only sites with Proto-Elamite enclaves (as in Sialk IV and Tepe Yahya IVC) or sites with evidence of contacts with the Proto-Elamite culture (such as Shahr-i Sokhta IV).

COLLAPSE (SUSA IIIB-C)

These Proto-Elamite polities collapsed around 2800 BCE. The consequences of the collapse were different in the highlands and in the lowlands. On the Iranian Plateau, all the Proto-Elamite related settlements were abandoned. At the same time, the southern and central Zagros reverted to pastoral nomadism and plunged into a Dark Age for several centuries. In Fars, Malyan was deserted and no settlement has been identified in the Kur river basin between the Late Banesh and the early Kaftari phases (Sumner 1988a:315–316, 1990a, 1990b) (figure 3.3). In western and southern Lurestan, mostly cemeteries are known, although it is probable that some of them at least were connected with permanent settlements (Carter 1984:141–142, 1986; Haerinck 1986), while in eastern Lurestan and southern Kurdestan contemporary sites are few (R.C. Henrickson 1986, 1987). The resemblances between the painted wares found in cemeteries of western and eastern Lurestan, in contemporary tombs at Musiyan and at Susa and in the graves of the Jalyan cemetery in eastern Fars (Carter 1984:Fig. 9; Miroschedji 1974) suggest the existence, toward the middle of the third millennium BCE, of strong cultural affinities between the central and southern Zagros range, from southern Kurdestan to eastern Fars, resulting presumably from similarities in ways of life and seasonal movements of nomads. This basic unity shaped the foundation for the forthcoming rise of the Elamite kingdoms of Awan, Shimashki, and Anshan. A much later but striking historical analogy is that of the Medo-Persian *koine* which developed in the same area in the eighth-seventh centuries BCE as a prelude to the emergence of the Achaemenid Persians (see below).

During this Dark Age, the lowlands of Khuzestan were left to themselves and developed a local culture which owed its originality to the close relationships with the peoples living along the piedmont of the Zagros range and to the Mesopotamian environment. Toward the middle of the third millennium BCE, Susa had actually become just another Mesopotamian city, and it remained such for several centuries. Art objects of this time are Sumerian in character (see Harper et al. 1992:83–85 [nos. 50–52]). Presumably, it was then that Susa's patron deity, Inshushinak, acquired its Sumerian name and that Elam received its pictographic writing NIM, meaning "the High Land," and adopted the cuneiform script.

THE SECOND CYCLE: OLD ELAMITE (SUSA IV-VI/VII)
The second cycle in Elamite history was dominated by the functioning of the Irano-Mesopotamian System (table 3.1). From the mid-third millennium until the beginning of the second millennium BCE, a triangular exchange network linking the three major centers of civilization of the time—Mesopotamia, the Indus valley, and the Central Asian principalities (Turkmenistan, Margiana, Bactria)—developed on an unprecedented large scale, stimulating an intense maritime trade in the Persian Gulf and an active overland trade across the Iranian Plateau, where it gave rise to several oasis settlements (Amiet 1986a:121–207; Hiebert and Lamberg-Karlovsky 1992; Lamberg-Karlovsky 1985; D.T. Potts 1982, 1993a; T.F. Potts 1994). The reestablishment of Malyan/Anshan and its new phase of prosperity, corresponding in Fars with the Kaftari phase (Sumner 1988a:317–318, 1989a), were to a large extent coincidental with the floruit of the trans-Iranian trade, of which Susa was also a major recipient.

INTEGRATION: THE OLD ELAMITE I PERIOD (SUSA IV)
The resources of this trade increasingly attracted the Mesopotamians who, toward the middle of the third millennium BCE, were engaged in a process of political unification. It was presumably because the nascent Elamite principalities of the Zagros controlled the resources of the trans-Iranian trade that the first Sumerian kings engaged in an active Elamite policy, alternatively diplomatic and hostile (Moorey 1993; D.T. Potts 1982; T.F. Potts 1994:90–96; Stolper 1984a:10–12). Their goal was clearly to secure access to the goods travelling across the Iranian Plateau. Thus the Sumerian epic tale of "Enmerkar and the Lord of Aratta" alludes to a commercial embassy sent to a distant Iranian polity (in Kerman?) in order to obtain exotic commodities and mentions that this practice goes back to earlier times (Komoróczy 1982; Moorey 1993; T.F. Potts 1994:12–14). The kings of Agade exercised more or less direct control over Susiana and campaigned against highland polities, including Anshan and Marhashi (Kerman?)

(Amiet 1976a:24; Steinkeller 1982; Stolper 1984a:11–15). Later, Gudea of Lagash made a similar claim (Stolper 1984a:16). This policy was continued by kings of the Third Dynasty of Ur who annexed Susiana and devoted much effort to the administrative organization of the piedmont area, resorting to both military campaigns and diplomatic exchanges to secure the cooperation of the highland polities, mainly Anshan (McNeill 1978; T.F. Potts 1994; Sigrist and Butz 1986; Stolper 1984a:16–19; Steinkeller 1987).

In a much more sophisticated way, this Mesopotamian domination echoes the Uruk presence of the fourth millennium. A major difference, however, is that the Mesopotamians had from the outset encountered an autochthonous opposition, which rapidly grew in strength and organizational capabilities. Thanks to the ethnic and cultural homogeneity of these territories (see above), a state formation process took place in the Zagros uplands as a result of the Mesopotamian pressure on the nascent polities. This process escapes historical analysis because it is documented only by occasional references to Elamite "kings of Awan" in Sumerian and Akkadian inscriptions (see Stolper 1984a:14). It is reminiscent of the process which had given birth to the Proto-Elamite polities a millennium earlier as a result of the Uruk activities. Its culmination is suddenly revealed when, following the collapse of the empire of Akkad, Susa fell briefly under the power of Puzur-Inshushinak, the last king of the Elamite highland kingdom of Awan, probably located in the central Zagros (see Glassner 1996:26).

This event is of considerable historical importance. On the one hand, Puzur-Inshushinak is historically the *first* Elamite king to have taken control of Susa, where he engaged in lavish constructions for the city's patron god (Amiet 1976b:36ff.; B. André-Salvini [in Harper et al. 1992:87–91]; André and Salvini 1989; Salvini 1998). The devotion to Inshushinak on the part of a highlander suggests that Susa had begun to assume its historical role of a lowland metropolis upon which the highlanders looked with admiration and respect, and whose control gave to their leader much prestige and legitimacy.

This state formation process was not limited to Awan and affected other areas of the Zagros. Ultimately, it brought the formation of the Elamite kingdoms of Shimashki in the central Zagros and of Anshan in the southern Zagros (Stolper 1982:49–54). At the end of the twentieth-first century BCE, these two highland polities annexed Susiana and led the onslaught on Mesopotamia, which brought the end of the Third Dynasty of Ur (Stolper 1982:54–56)

The annexation of Susiana represents a watershed in the history of southwestern Iran. Until then, the Elamite kingdoms of the Zagros highlands were shadowy figures on the fringe of the Mesopotamian world of which Susa was part. Now, they emerged on the scene of history as main performers and from then on, Susa's fate would remain linked to theirs.

EXPANSION: THE SHIMASHKI DYNASTY AND THE EARLY AND MIDDLE SUKKALMAHS (SUSA V- EARLY VI)

Territorial extent and political organization. The newly-born Elamite confederacy controlled the entire southwestern Iran. It was composed of several principalities or kingdoms more or less tightly united: Shimashki itself, Susiana, and Anshan, to which correspond archaeologically three major cultural provinces: that of the Godin III:4 and III:2 phases in the central Zagros (R.C. Henrickson 1984, 1986:23–26, 1987:51–56); that of the Susa V, and subsequently Susa VI phases in Susiana (see Carter 1984:146–151 and Fig. 10:1-20); and that of the Kaftari phase in central Fars (Carter 1984:151–154; Sumner 1972, 1989a). Contacts between these areas are archaeologically attested: the wide distribution of the white-filled black incised ware and that of the often associated Attahushu-type of axes, for example, are good indicators of Elamite presence both in the Zagros piedmont and in the mountain range from Kermanshah to Anshan (for references see Carter 1990:96); the occasional presence in the lowlands of Kaftari painted vessels (especially pilgrim flasks: see Carter 1984:Fig. 10:10, 19, 25) and the discovery in Susa of many cylinder-seals of the so-called "Popular Elamite Style" (see Amiet 1972:239–242), well attested at Malyan/Anshan (Carter 1984:Fig. 10:32; Sumner 1974:172, Fig. 12:i), confirm the contacts between Khuzestan and central Fars.

The great cultural and social diversity of the Elamite realm explains the complicated rules adopted for the division and transmission of power between the members of an extended family and the personal ties which had to be maintained between rulers at different levels (Stolper 1982:54, 1984a:24–25). These rules express not only peculiar kinship ties based on matriarchy (see Glassner 1994, 1998b; contra Vallat 1990a, 1994, 1998) but also a complex social organization, with a pyramid of potentially autonomous groups which had to be integrated into a single power structure.

Dynastic shift to Anshan? Around the middle of the twentieth century BCE, power shifted from the Shimashki to the Sukkalmah dynasty (thus called because most of its rulers used as a royal title this old Sumero-Akkadian title, meaning approximately "grand regent"). The smooth transition between the two may have been a simple shift of

power between two branches of an extended ruling family, which controlled essentially the same territories (Stolper 1982:55–56, 1984a:27). A later historical analogy for this situation would be the transmission of power from the Medes to the Persians in the mid-sixth century BCE.

The early sukkalmahs possibly originated from Anshan (Miroschedji 1980:132–140; Stolper 1982:54), as suggested by their title of "King of Anshan and Susa," and further by the stylistic affinities of royal cylinder seals (see W.G. Lambert 1979:no. 42; 1992). This proposition, however, is not certain because similar seals are also attested in Susa (Amiet 1972:239–242, 1986a:Figs. 113–114; Aruz in Harper et al. 1992:115f. [nos. 74–75]). Furthermore, no texts from Malyan/Anshan give evidence of a control of this city by Shimashkian kings or by early sukkalmahs, while the presence of eighteenth-century BCE sukkalmahs is well attested there (see table 3.3). Around 2000 BCE, Malyan covered some 130 ha and sheltered about 30,000 inhabitants, nearly half of the total population of the plain (Sumner 1988a:317–318, 1989a, 1990b:106–110) (figure 3.2). Aside from Susa, it was the largest city of southwestern Iran. The sukkal of Susa was next in line to succeed the sukkalmah and devoted much building effort on the sacred area of the city. Thus the title of "King of Anshan and Susa," introduced at that time, appropriately expressed the demographic and political bipolarity of the empire.

Another dynastic shift? The considerable territorial extent of the Elamite confederation, the diversity of its components and the shifting nature of its power structure imply a certain fluidity in the rules of succession (see Stolper 1982:54). Reconstructions of "dynastic" lists by recent scholarship (Grillot and Glassner 1991, 1993; Vallat 1990a, 1994) remain uncertain because they imply very strict rules of succession, whose application may have been actually hampered by political circumstances. More importantly, these reconstructed lists leave the misleading impression of a continuity between the early sukkalmahs (the "kings of Anshan and Susa") and their apparent successors, a group of six sukkalmahs who reigned one after another from Siruktuh to Kuk-Nashur (II) son-of-the-sister of Temti-Agun. In reality, a gap of about one century separates these two groups: the first group dates to the second half of the twentieth and the early nineteenth century BCE (Miroschedji 1980:134, n.35; Stolper 1984a:27; Vallat 1989a); the chronology of the second group is firmly anchored in the eighteenth century BCE.

The chronology of this latter group of sukkalmahs is based on two observations. First, Mesopotamian synchronisms allow the dating of the first three sukkalmahs of this group (Siruktuh, Siwe-palar-hupak and Kuduzulush) to the first half of the eighteenth century BCE (Stolper 1984a:28ff.); second, a letter from Susa published by Scheil and recently discussed by Grillot and Glassner (1991:88) implies that the reigns of the six sukkalmahs of this group had altogether the duration of three generations. The third generation, contemporary with Kuk-Nashur (II) son-of-the-sister of Temti-Agun, can thus be dated to the last third of the eighteenth century. Therefore, the synchronism between this sukkalmah and the first year of Ammisaduqa (1646 BCE), recently advocated by Vallat (1997, 1998:303; see also Gasche et al. 1998), cannot be upheld, and the sukkalmah contemporary with Ammisaduqa was more likely Kuk-Nashur (III) son of Tan-Uli, as previously held by scholars (for example, Harper et al. 1992:xviii; Vallat 1990a:127).

These conclusions have important consequences for a better understanding of an otherwise confused picture. Although ignored by recent historians, the gap of nearly a century in the so-called "dynastic" list between the first and the second group of sukkalmahs could well indicate a period of turmoil following the reign of the last documented "king of Anshan and Susa." Archaeologically, this gap corresponds to the cultural break taking place in Susa at circa 1800 BCE with the transition from levels B V to A XV of the Ville Royale A and B excavations, that is from the Old Elamite II to the Old Elamite III periods or (in the scheme followed here) from the Susa V to the Susa VI phases (see Steve et al. 1980:72; Tallon 1987:66, 69) (table 3.1). Historically, it can be correlated with a change in the titles used by the sukkalmahs who, from the eighteenth century BCE onward, no longer called themselves "king of Anshan and Susa" and often claimed descent from "the sister of Shilhaha," in an apparent effort to affirm their legitimacy through a link with the prestigious line of the early sukkalmahs.

These observations raise the possibility that from circa 1800 onward, after a period of disorder for which no historical sources are available, another branch of sukkalmahs had come to power, originating from an area other than Anshan, perhaps from Elam *sensu stricto,* or even from Susiana itself (see also Miroschedji 1981d:22–23). This could explain why these sukkalmahs had changed the royal titles, and why they left so few inscriptions in Fars, and all of them in Akkadian instead of Elamite (see table 3.3).

Territorial expansion. It is under these eighteenth-century BCE sukkalmahs, especially under the reigns of Siruktuh, Siwe-palar-hupak and Kuduzulush, that Elam reached the zenith of its might. The two fragmentary victory stelae known from this period, one anonymous (Amiet 1966a:Fig. 308), the other one possibly to be ascribed to Siruktuh (Farber 1975), commemorate an Elamite expansion which

apparently took place both within and outside the limits of the Elamite realm.

Outside of Elam, these sukkalmahs struggled for the control of the High Road linking Mesopotamia to the central Zagros via the city-state of Eshnunna. After the capture of this city and the conquest of the northern Jazira in the time of Siwe-palar-hupak, the Elamites briefly became the major power in an area stretching from Babylonia to northern Syria (Charpin 1986; Charpin and Durand 1991; Durand 1986, 1994; see also the contemporary Cappadocian seals found in Susa: Amiet 1985:11). Until Cyrus the Great, no other ruler of southwest Iran would achieve such large conquests.

At the same time, the eighteenth-century BCE sukkalmahs manifested their control over their own territory by establishing outposts, constructing temples and carving rock reliefs (table 3.3, figure 3.4). An Elamite outpost may have existed at Chogha Gavaneh in southern Kurdestan, where various lowland-related objects were found in a large building compound (Kordevani 1971). The royal building activities concerned not only Susa, but also Susiana and Fars, in both the cities of Anshan and Liyan (Bushehr). It should be stressed that in the present state of knowledge, only these sukkalmahs have engaged in building activities outside of Susa.

In view of this evidence of political strength and presence in Fars, it seems only logical to ascribe to the sukkalmahs of the eighteenth century BCE the Old Elamite rock reliefs of Fars, which presumably were part of open-air cultic places. The most famous is at Kurangun (Seidl 1986:7–13; Vanden Berghe 1986), where it may have been connected to an ancient Elamite settlement (Kleiss 1993a). This relief seems to be unfinished. It shows a king and an acolyte standing in front of a god seated on a coiled snake with a human head, with waters flowing out of his hand. Behind him stands his consort, seated on a low podium. I interpret this relief as representing a scene of investiture of the king by the god, who extends to him the rod and the ring, symbols of divine power (Miroschedji 1980, 1981d). The location of the relief at the top of a prominent cliff not far from the road leading to Anshan and Fahliyan may have symbolized the great god's blessing to the king's domination over all of this territory. Whether this relief represents the great god of neighboring Anshan, Napirisha, and his consort Kiririsha is merely a logical inference, since on the stela of Untash-Napirisha the same male deity is identified as Inshushinak (see below).

The same divine couple was represented not far from Anshan, on the cliff at Naqsh-i Rustam, a place sacred from the Old Elamite to the Sasanian periods (Seidl

Table 3.3 Provenience of Elamite royal building inscriptions from the Old to the Late Elamite periods

PERIOD	SOVEREIGN*	KHUZESTAN		FARS		
		Susa [1]	Outside of Susa	West	Central	South
Old Elamite II	DYNASTY OF SHIMASHKI					
	Kindattu	(Susa)				
	Tan-Ruhuratir	Susa				
	Idadu II	Susa				
	EARLY SUKKALMAHS					
	Eparti	(Susa)				
	Shilhaha	(Susa)				
Old Elamite III	MIDDLE SUKKALMAHS					
	Siruktuh	(Susa)				?Bushehr [2]
	Shimut-wartash					Bushehr [3]
	Siwe-palar-hupak	(Susa)			Malyan [4]	
	Kutir-Nahhunte	(Susa)				
	Temti-Agun	Susa	Ch. Pahn West [5]			
	Kuk-Nashur II	Susa				
	LATE SUKKALMAHS					
	Kuk-Kirwash	Susa				
	Temti-halki	Susa				
Middle Elamite I	KIDINUIDS					
	Tepti-ahar	Susa	Haft Tepe [6]			
	Inhushinak-sunkir-nappipir	Susa				
	IGIHALKIDS					
	Igi-halki		Deh-i Now [7]			
	Humbanumena	Susa				Bushehr [8]
	Untash-Napirisha	Susa	Ch. Zanbil [9]			
			Ch. Pahn East [10]			
			T. Deylam [11]			
			T. Gotwand [12]			
			T. Bormi [13]			
Middle Elamite II	SHUTRUKIDS					
	Shutruk-Nahhunte I	Susa	Ch. Pahn West [14]			Bushehr [15]
			Deh-i Now [16]			
	Kutir-Nahhunte	Susa	Deh-i Now [17]			Bushehr [18]
	Shilhak-Inshushinak I	Susa	Deh-i Now [19]	Tul-e Spid [20]		Bushehr [21]
			Ch. Pahn West [22]			
			Dezful ? [23]			
			Shushtar ? [24]			
			T. "Pomp" [25]			
			T. Bormi [26]			
			Izeh [27]			
	Hutelutush-Inshushinak	Susa	Shaluliki [28]		Malyan [29]	
Late Elamite II	Shutruk-Nahhunte II	Susa	T. Bormi [30]			
	Hallutush-Inshushinak	Susa				
	Tempt-Huban-Inshushinak	Susa				

Note: No Elamite building inscription is known from Luristan/Kurdistan nor from northern and eastern Fars.

* Only the kings and sukkalmahs are mentioned. The Susian rulers who did not accede to the supreme power are omitted.

1. References to royal building inscriptions from Susa are to be found in Malbran-Labat 1995, s.v. Brackets indicate that the building activity of the sovereign is referred to by Shilhak-Inshushinak I in one of his own inscribed bricks: see Malbran-Labat 1995 : no. 38.
2. cf. König 1965: no. 1 and Miroschedji 1980: 135, n.49.
3. cf. Sollberger and Kupper 1971: 262 (IVO7a).
4. Stolper 1982: 57, 59-61.
5. Steve 1987: no. 1.
6. Reiner 1973b; cf. Negahban 1991.
7. Steve 1987: no. 2.
8. König 1965: no. 4B-C; Vallat 1984b.
9. Steve 1967.
10. Stolper and Wright 1990.
11. Vallat 1983.
12. Steve 1987: no. 5.
13. Carter 1971: 277.
14. Steve 1987: no. 9J.
15. König 1965: no. 19.
16. Steve 1987: no. 9.
17. Steve 1987: no. 14.
18. König 1965: no. 31.
19. König 1965: no. 42 = Steve 1968: 299.
20. König 1965: no. 41A.
21. König 1965: no. 57-59.
22. Stolper 1978.
23. Steve, Gasche and De Meyer 1980: 80.
24. Steve, Gasche and De Meyer 1980: 81.
25. Steve, Gasche and De Meyer 1980: 82.
26. Vallat 1981a.
27. Walker 1981: no. 213; and cf. Stolper 1978: 93.
28. Steve 1987: no. 20.
29. Reiner 1973a.
30. cf. Vallat 1981a (actually not Shutruk-Nahhunte II but an unspecified Late Elamite king).

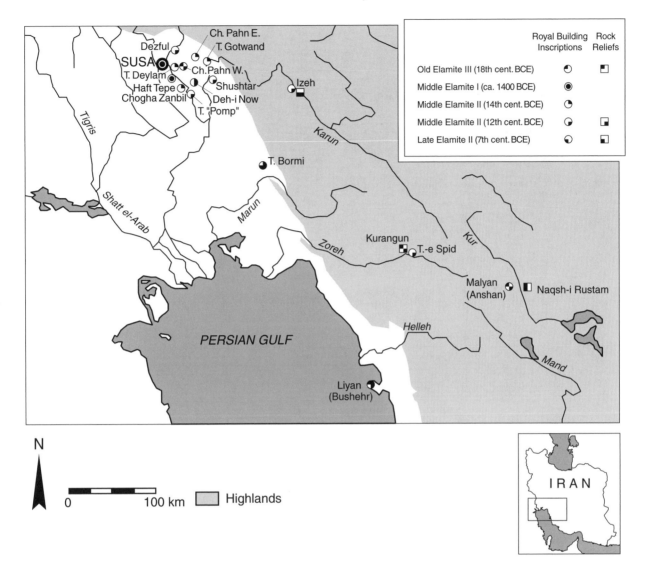

3.4 Distribution of Elamite royal building inscriptions and rock reliefs from the Old to the Late Elamite periods.
   P. de Miroschedji

1986:14–19). The central part of the Elamite relief, which was partly erased by the addition of a Sasanian relief, shows the faint traces of two deities, a god and a goddess behind him, both seated on a throne in the shape of a coiled snake with a human head. Two figures, probably a king and an attendant, stood in front of the deities.

Stylistic and iconographic comparisons suggest that two other rock reliefs located in the plain of Izeh at Hong-i Nowruzi and at Shah Savar could possibly also date from this time (Calmeyer 1988:281; Vanden Berghe 1963:Pls. XXV–XXVII). As in Fars, these reliefs inaugurate a local tradition of relief carving which will be followed up in the Middle and Late Elamite periods.

The reliefs of Kurangun and Naqsh-i Rustam usually have been dated to the seventeenth century BCE on the

basis of iconographic and stylistic comparisons with cylinder seal impressions representing the great god seated on a coiled snake with human head (summary of discussions in Seidl 1986:11–12, 17–18, who dates the Old Elamite relief at Naqsh-i Rustam to the sixteenth century BCE; see also Miroschedji 1989). Indeed, at least two of these impressions date to the seventeenth century BCE since they are inscribed with the name of the sukkalmah Tan-Uli (Amiet 1972:no. 2330; Miroschedji 1981d:Pl. I:5), or with that of "Kuk-Nashur sukkalmah, son-of-the-sister of Shilhaha" (Amiet 1973a:No. 49, 1980a:138–139; Miroschedji 1981d:Pl. I:3; also referred to in Steve 1994:26), probably to be identified with Kuk-Nashur (III) son of Tan-Uli (see Vallat 1997:103) who, as we have seen above, was a contemporary of Ammisaduqa in circa 1646

BCE. But another very similar imprint—so similar that it was previously not distinguished from the above-mentioned two imprints—is inscribed with the name of "Kuk-Nashur son-of-the-sister of Temti-Agun" (Amiet 1972:no. 2015; Miroschedji 1981d:Pl. I:4), that is, Kuk-Nashur II, whose reign can be dated, as we have seen above, to the last third of the eighteenth century BCE. Therefore there is no reason to compare the Old Elamite rock reliefs of Fars with seventeenth rather than with eighteenth-century BCE cylinder seals, especially when considering that their iconography already existed in the twentieth and nineteenth centuries BCE (Miroschedji 1981d:Pl. I:1–2). Actually, the eighteenth-century BCE dating of these reliefs is the only one which makes sense historically since there is ample proof of the might of the sukkalmahs of this time and of their presence in Fars, while there is no testimony that their seventeenth to sixteenth-century BCE successors retained a comparable power (see below).

Economic prosperity. There is little doubt that the rise of Anshan and that of the Shimashkian and Sukkalmah states was made possible thanks to the prosperity derived from the control of the trans-Iranian trade. In Mesopotamia, textual evidence testifies to the importation of materials and objects which reached the alluvial plains through Shimashkian territories. Most important among them was tin; in the time of Zimri-Lim, Elam was the source of Mesopotamian tin, which was trans-shipped via Eshnunna, reached Larsa in Babylonia or Mari on the middle Euphrates, and then beyond the Mediterranean shore. A letter of Zimri-Lim mentions the equivalent of 485 kg of tin which were distributed to his allies of Aleppo, Hazor, Ursum and Ugarit (Charpin 1986; Charpin and Durand 1991; Durand 1986; Joannès 1991). Excavations at Susa have shown the remarkable development of the local metallurgy (Carter 1990:93–97; Tallon 1987:340–352) and revealed substantial evidence of contacts with the southern and eastern Iranian Plateau (Amiet 1986a:141ff.; Miroschedji 1973a). At the same time, Elam was engaged in the sea trade in the Persian Gulf, as suggested by the discovery at Susa of late third-early second millennium BCE chlorite objects and seals originating from the Gulf area (Amiet 1986a:171–180; Miroschedji 1973a; see also chapter 13). Mercantile interest in the seafaring trade probably explains also the building activities of sukkalmahs of the eighteenth century BCE at the coastal city of Bushehr (ancient Liyan) (see table 3.3), a site where archaeological remains of the Kaftari culture were also found (Miroschedji 1980:137, n. 51). Between circa 2200 and 1900 BCE, Susa was actually the only city within the limits of Greater Mesopotamia which received goods and objects originating from the Persian Gulf, the Iranian Plateau (Lurestan, Kerman, Seistan), the lands located beyond (the Indus valley, Afghanistan, Central Asia) and possibly also Syria (for Syrian contacts, see Amiet 1985:9–10; Beyer 1989).

COLLAPSE: THE LATE SUKKALMAHS AND THE BEGINNING OF THE MIDDLE ELAMITE I PERIOD (SUSA VI FINAL-VII)

There are many indications that the eighteenth-century BCE acme of the Sukkalmah state was followed by a slow process of disintegration that lasted for more than two centuries, at least until the second half of the fifteenth century BCE. After the victory of Hammurabi of Babylon over Kuduzulush in 1765 BCE, Elam withdrew from Mesopotamia and the historical sources fall almost silent. After about 1700 BCE, there is no evidence of Elamite royal building activities outside Susa, a situation which implies a withdrawal to the Susiana home-base. This Elamite disengagement was probably not a historical accident. Significantly, it occurred together with the collapse of the seafaring trade and that of the trans-Iranian exchange network in the eighteenth century BCE. No exotic items appear to have been in circulation over the Iranian Plateau and in the Persian Gulf from this time onward. The oasis cities of the Iranian Plateau were then more or less deserted in a short lapse of time (Amiet 1986a:171–207) and the entire area reverted once more to nomadic pastoralism, depriving Elam of the economic hinterland on which its prosperity was based.

Thus ended the first Golden Age of Elam. The consequences were almost immediate and far-reaching. Comparative analysis of the population curves of Fars and Khuzestan suggests that the highland areas were affected first and much more profoundly (figures 3.2, 3.3). In Fars, the Kur river basin—the heartland of Anshan—entered a phase of steady demographic decline by the seventeenth century. Between about 1600 and 1300 BCE, Malyan lost about two-thirds of its population and the number of settlements in the plain decreased radically. At the same time, imported products disappeared, cylinder seals and writing were no longer in use and the cultural unity of the plain was broken (Jacobs 1980; Sumner 1972, 1988a, 1990a, 1990b, 1994a; see also Overlaet 1997). This sharp decline of the Kaftari polity is almost a textbook example of collapse. Similar tendencies were in evidence in the central Zagros, where the end of the Godin III:2 phase in the seventeenth century BCE is marked by the virtual disappearance of settlements and a widespread development of transhumant pastoralism (R.C. Henrickson 1986, 1987). This phenomenon suggests that by this time the old Shimashkian polity had disappeared.

Thus the period of Anshan's political power seems to be restricted to the twentieth to nineteenth centuries BCE, after which the city seems to have lost a great deal of its political significance. After circa 1800 BCE, the center of gravity of Elam shifted to the lowlands where most of the sedentary population was then concentrated. This represents a second turning point in Elamite history.

In Khuzestan, little is known historically of the seventeenth and sixteenth centuries BCE, to which few building inscriptions can be ascribed (table 3.3). The decline of Elam's power did not have the same consequences in the lowlands as in the highlands. Susa remained a prosperous city mostly engaged in agricultural exploitation of its hinterland, living in a cultural milieu which was mainly Mesopotamian. After Kuk-Nashur (II), son-of-the-sister of Temti-Agun, textual evidence is less frequent and the succession of rulers becomes uncertain (Vallat 1998:303). As a result, it is not known exactly when the Sukkalmah period came to an end, possibly sometime during the sixteenth century BCE. If indeed Kuk-Nashur III is the last sukkalmah known, there is a gap of 50 to 100 years for which no ruler is attested. This gap, however, can be narrowed if one chooses to retain the low chronology (by dating Hammurabi to 1696–1654 BCE) recently advocated on very solid grounds by Gasche et al. (1998). Note, however, that Gasche's chronological scheme for the stratigraphy of Level A XIII to Lower Level A XII of Susa's Ville Royale A excavations is based on Vallat's doubtful contention that the synchronism with Ammisaduqa's first year concerns Kuk-Nashur II instead of Kuk-Nashur III.

The stratigraphy of Susa suggests a smooth transition to the following Middle Elamite I period (Susa VII) (Gasche et al. 1998:22–24; Steve et al. 1980; Steve 1994). The latter period remains obscure. The names of five rulers are known, regrouped into the so-called "Kidinuid Dynasty." They probably cover the fifteenth century BCE, but except for the last one, Tepti-Ahar, nothing is known of them, and even their order of succession is uncertain (Steve et al. 1980:92–98; the chronology has been corrected by Steve and Vallat 1989).

As the contemporary strata in Susa's Ville Royale A excavations were poorly represented, the period is illuminated mainly by the excavations at Haft Tepe, ancient Kapnak, a city largely built by Tepti-ahar in the latter part of the fifteenth century BCE and virtually abandoned after the king's death (Negahban 1991). Tepti-ahar's constructions at Haft Tepe and the results of the archaeological surveys (Carter 1971; Miroschedji 1981c) testify that the period was quite prosperous in Susiana.

Tepti-Ahar and the other rulers of this period had resumed the old title of "King of Susa and Anshan" (for in Akkadian inscriptions the names of the two cities were inverted in the royal title: "King of Susa and Anshan," instead of "King of Anshan and Susa," as was customary in Elamite inscriptions). As it is very doubtful that the authority of these kings extended to Fars, the revival of this old title had no territorial significance and probably meant simply that they considered themselves heirs of the glorious kings of the twentieth century BCE. Actually, they may have exerted their authority on rather limited territories. Allusions in the Haft Tepe tablets suggest a situation of political fragmentation marked by the coexistence of other kings in Khuzestan and its eastern border (Glassner 1991:126 has shown that one king existed at Huhnur, another one at Halisrat(i) [location unknown]).

The corollaries of this political fragmentation were the extensive relationships with Kassite Babylonia and the increasing similarities between the material culture of both countries (see Amiet 1986b, 1996). The art of this time, especially the glyptic, implies few contacts with the outside world and shows the survival of the Old Elamite/Old Babylonian tradition (Amiet 1996:142). Despite a stylistic evolution, this is illustrated by Tepti-Ahar's own seal: it shows the king standing in front of the god seated on a coiled snake with human head (Miroschedji 1981d:Pl. VII).

THE THIRD CYCLE: MIDDLE ELAMITE (SUSA VII–IX)

The third cycle of growth and decline in the history of Elamite civilization started around 1400 BCE and lasted until the eighth century BCE (table 3.1). It includes the Middle Elamite II period, which represents a period of considerable expansion, the second Golden Age of Elam, and the Late Elamite I period, which marks a phase of deep disintegration, a typical Dark Age (see table 3.2). The Middle Elamite II revival took place in a context of widespread international exchanges, which in the Amarna period (fourteenth century BCE) involved the entire Near East, from Egypt to Iran. It was achieved by kings, the so-called "Igihalkids," who were probably not originally from Susiana and who perhaps came from the eastern margin of the Khuzestan plain. They were responsible for accelerating the process of "Elamitization" of Susiana, which became then *de facto* the Elamite heartland given the continuing decline of Fars.

INTEGRATION: THE END OF THE MIDDLE ELAMITE I PERIOD

It is difficult to decide when the decline of Elam came to an end because the evidence of history and archaeology is quite confused. A convenient dividing line can be drawn with the reign of Tepti-Ahar. His achievements at Haft Tepe imply a certain amount of wealth and some objects from his time suggest the establishment of an exchange network with the area of Marlik in northern Iran (Amiet 1977, 1989). This situation heralds the beginning of a new era.

The kings of the following "dynasty," the so-called "Igihalkids," also titled themselves "King of Anshan and Susa." In addition, Humbanumena resumed the old sukkalmah title of "son-of-the-sister (that is, descendant) of Shilhaha," the founder of the Sukkalmah dynasty nearly five centuries earlier, in an effort to increase his legitimacy through a connection with a glorious past. Humbanumena rebuilt the temple of Kiririsha in Bushehr (Liyan) (see table 3.3), indicating thereby, on the one hand, the beginning of a process of political integration which gave him the capability to control distant territories and, on the other hand, Elam's renewed involvement in the seafaring trade of the Persian Gulf, which was reactivated with the advent of the Kassite period.

But this nascent prosperity was not accompanied immediately by a change in the material culture, and a sharp distinction must be drawn between historical and archaeological periodizations. Archaeologically, the Middle Elamite I period *sensu stricto* extends until circa 1350. The following archaeological period, the Middle Elamite II, is not attested before the development of the new city of Chogha Zanbil, ancient Dur-Untash (or al-Untash Napirisha), built by the son of Humbanumena, Untash-Napirisha, in the second half of the fourteenth century BCE (see also Carter 1998:319–320; for the dating of Untash-Napirisha's reign, see Steve and Vallat 1989; Van Dijk 1986). Then started a new phase of expansion.

EXPANSION: THE MIDDLE ELAMITE II PERIOD (SUSA VIII)

Economic prosperity. The wealth of the Middle Elamite empire was derived again from the control of extensive trade networks. There is ample evidence for widespread connections that Elam maintained in the fourteenth century BCE with several distant countries, especially in the Persian Gulf area (see table 3.3 for the list of Middle Elamite II builders in Bushehr), the Levant via Mitanni-held northern Mesopotamia (Amiet 1985:11–12; and compare Porada 1970:22, Pl. XIV:Fig. 10 for an Elamite cylinder seal from the city of Assur), and the Iranian Plateau at large, including Marlik, via Lurestan (Amiet 1980b, 1989, 1990). As in the early second millennium BCE, the wealth of the kingdom may have been based chiefly on the control of Iranian copper and tin. The statue of queen Napir-Asu, the wife of Untash-Napirisha, weighing nearly two tons of bronze, and the sacrificial table with two snakes, found at Susa but probably originating from the *Siyan-kuk* (sacred precinct) of Chogha Zanbil/Dur-Untash, testify to the Elamite kings' extensive access to metals at this time

(Amiet 1966a:Figs. 280, 291; Tallon in Harper et al. 1992:132–135). This conclusion probably applies as well to the kings of the Shutrukid dynasty in the twelfth century BCE, as suggested by a fragmentary bronze relief (Amiet 1966a:Fig. 305).

The wealth resulting from the trade across the Iranian Plateau and the agricultural resources of the plain of Khuzestan, together with the prestige derived from the control over Susa, gave the Elamite kings the means to rule the entire highlands, from Lurestan to Fars. However, the marked development of pastoral nomadism in these areas from circa 1700 onward made this task difficult. To impose their authority over the highland tribes, the Middle Elamite kings had to devise new methods of political management. The data at hand suggest that these methods differed in the fourteenth and in the twelfth century BCE.

Empire management in the the fourteenth century BCE. To demonstrate their political presence, the kings of the Igihalkid "dynasty" did as their sukkalmah predecessors: they undertook pious constructions in various parts of their empire. We have already mentioned that Hubanumena rebuilt Kiririsha's temple in Bushehr on the coast of Fars. His son Untash-Napirisha undertook several constructions in the eastern plain of Khuzestan, even dedicating a ziggurat at Chogha Pahn East to the local goddess, Upurkupak (table 3.3, figure 3.4).

Untash-Napirisha's ultimate solution was the creation of a new capital, distinct from Susa, which could therefore be claimed on an equal footing by all members of the empire (Ghirshman 1966; Miroschedji 1980:142–143, 1981d:13–15, 1997). The sacred precinct (*Siyan-kuk*) of Chogha Zanbil/Dur-Untash was a federal sanctuary regrouping the great gods of the major cities and districts of the empire. With its concentric structure—the sacred precinct with the ziggurat in its center being surrounded by a religious city and the latter by a royal city—the site appeared as a sort of symbolic representation of Elam. The fact that the ziggurat at the center of this Elamite microcosm was initially dedicated to the god of Susa, Inshushinak, clearly shows that Susiana was then perceived as the center of the whole empire.

Only later did Untash-Napirisha change his construction program and rededicate the ziggurat jointly to Inshushinak *and* to the god of Anshan, Napirisha. The reason for this change can only be guessed. A logical assumption is that Untash-Napirisha was the first Middle Elamite king who had effectively reintegrated Anshan into the Elamite realm. Although there is no archaeological proof of Untash-Napirisha's presence at Anshan, an indirect indication is provided by a twelfth-century inscription of Shutruk-Nahhunte I who mentions the return to Susa of statues from both Anshan and Dur-Untash (König 1965:nos. 20–21). This fact is confirmed by the discovery at Susa of several monuments which, according to their inscription, had been initially erected in the *Siyan-kuk* of Dur-Untash (see Grillot and Vallat 1978:82, n.3). We have seen that Humbanumena, Untash-Napirisha's father and immediate predecessor, had already annexed the coastal region of Bushehr. Presumably, Untash-Napirisha had achieved control of the uplands of Fars and decided to manifest the new state of affairs with a rededication of the sacred precinct of Chogha Zanbil/Dur-Untash, then brought under the joint tutelage of the patron deities of both Susa and Anshan. The new scheme implies that the empire was then conceived as the union of the highlands and the lowlands.

As demonstrated elsewhere, there are good reasons to believe that the famous stela of Untash-Napirisha was dedicated during the first phase of construction of the ziggurat, when the sacred precinct was under the sole tutelage of the god of Susa, who is indeed mentioned alone in the associated inscription (Miroschedji 1981d:14f., 1989:359f; contra Amiet 1988:78, 93).

A failure. Untash-Napirisha's grandiose political enterprise seems to have ended in failure. The construction of Chogha Zanbil/Dur-Untash was never completed. Although historians have recently tried their utmost to ascribe to the thirteenth century BCE the shadowy figures of three kings (see Steve and Vallat 1989:228), there is a gap in the historical record during most of this century. Presumably Untash-Napirisha's death was followed by a period of turmoil, lasting three or four generations and marked by occasional confrontations with Kassite Mesopotamia.

When Elamite kings reappeared on the scene of history in the twelfth century BCE with the dynasty of the Shutrukids, drastic changes were introduced. Chogha Zanbil/Dur-Untash was abandoned in favor of Susa and Inshushinak was promoted to the rank of the major deity of the empire. Various monuments initially set up in temples of other Elamite cities, notably Chogha Zanbil/Dur-Untash (now mostly desacralized) and Anshan, were assembled on the Acropolis of Susa and dedicated to the city's patron deity (König 1965:Nos. 20–21). Susa's Acropolis became a sort of national shrine (cf. Heim in Harper et al. 1992:123–126).

Empire management in the twelfth century BCE. But at the same time, while exalting Susa's position, the Shutrukid kings decentralized the cult of Inshushinak through the multiplication of royal monuments throughout the empire (table 3.3, figure 3.4).

Religious constructions were built in the plain of Khuzestan on at least seven sites beside Susa, in its mountainous eastern periphery at Izeh, and in Fars on at least three sites, including Anshan. Several of these temples were dedicated to a local divinity or to a local divine couple in addition to Inshushinak. These double dedications imposed each time the notion of an *alliance* between the local deities and Inshushinak, that is, between the local people and the Elamite king residing in Susa.

Malyan/Anshan offers an exemplary case of the creation of such a royal enclave. A temple dedicated to Napirisha, his consort Kiririsha, and to Inshushinak was built there (M. Lambert 1972; Reiner 1973a) as well as a large administrative building whose administrators were concerned with transfers of metal, hides and foodstuffs (Stolper 1984b). The building was adorned in a Susian manner with glazed knobs and plaques (Carter 1996). The administrators were lowland Elamites using a pottery of lowland type, in particular a kind of "Elamite goblet," rather crude but almost interchangeable with their Susian counterparts (Carter 1996:Figs. 21:9–15, 40:9, 42:7). The contemporary local pottery was completely different, as it belonged to the so-called Qaleh ware (Jacobs 1980). This difference in material culture emphasizes the alien character of this lowland enclave at Malyan.

Malyan was probably not the only Middle Elamite outpost in the highlands. Discoveries of objects and pottery, especially at Tepe Guran (Thrane 1999a, 1999b) and at Surkh Dum in central Lurestan (Schmidt et al. 1989), suggest a Middle Elamite II presence up the Saimarreh valley, possibly reaching as far as the Mahidasht plain in southern Kurdestan (Carter 1984:177–179).

As their eighteenth-century predecessors had done, the Elamite kings of the twelfth century BCE may have also commissioned the carving of rock reliefs in Fars. At Kurangun, it is probably at this time that rows of worshippers were added to the initial Old Elamite relief (Seidl 1986:12). In the area of Izeh, two groups of rock reliefs are known (Calmeyer 1988; de Waele 1972, 1973; Vanden Berghe 1959, 1963). The four reliefs of Shikaft-i Salman can be dated to the twelfth century BCE on stylistic grounds (Amiet 1976a); they were part of an open-air sanctuary focused on a spring and a cave dedicated to the goddess Mashti, well attested in eastern Khuzestan at Tepe Deylam. On the other side of the valley, the contemporary reliefs of Kul-i Farah were also part of an open-air sanctuary dedicated to the god Tirutir, perhaps a warrior god. Most interesting is the relief III, showing on its southern face a long procession represented on four registers and led by a man standing on a podium carried by four kneeling figures. The other side shows a similar procession led by a man walking on foot. Pierre Amiet (1992:89) has supposed that the two men do not walk side by side but are actually meeting, while the late Peter Calmeyer (1973:149) has suggested that the podium carriers are representatives of *ethnica* or provinces, forerunners of those represented on the Achaemenid royal tombs. Amiet's and Calmeyer's explanations actually complement each other: the relief Kul-i Farah III could represent the alliance between a king and a lower-ranked tribal chief. The subject of the relief IV, a banquet scene, could well illustrate a ceremony held periodically and during which tribal chieftains presented their allegiance to the king. If these interpretations are valid, these rock reliefs would illustrate the existence in the highlands of a tribal society subjected to the suzerainty of the Elamite king. Such a sociopolitical structure would have been essentially fragile.

COLLAPSE: THE LATE ELAMITE I PERIOD (SUSA IX)

The powerful Middle Elamite empire collapsed in 1115 BCE in the wake of Nebuchadnezzar I's campaign in Susiana. But Elam's crucial defeat was probably more the signal of the collapse of the Middle Elamite empire than its real cause. The empire had reached such an extent that it was difficult to maintain given the low level of administrative control and the instability of tribal allegiances. But internal causes can be only a part of a more global explanation, for at the same time, the overland and maritime international trade came to a sudden end, while Babylonia and the Persian Gulf entered also a phase of long term depression between about 1100 and 750 BCE (Miroschedji 1990a:81–83). Hence the events affecting Elam were part of a more general phenomenon resulting from a multi-secular evolution and marked by deep ethnic, social and economic changes.

Elam's collapse was profound and enduring. It was marked by a general breakdown of the Elamite confederation, whose individual components reverted to isolation and engaged in particular developments determined by local conditions (Miroschedji 1990a). In the Kur river basin of central Fars, the depopulation process begun after the Kaftari phase continued and became more severe in the early first millennium (figure 3.2). The area then plunged into a total Dark Age, to the point that archaeologists are unable to identify with certitude settlements dating to the first half of the first millennium BCE (Sumner 1972, 1988a, 1990a, 1990b, 1994a). The same applies to the entire Fars province, where nomadic pastoralism had clearly become the dominant way of life. The crisis was severe but less drastic in Khuzestan, the only area of southwestern Iran which managed to preserve an urban network.

But the latter was considerably downgraded, with a marked decline in the number and the size of the settlements, implying a sharp decrease in the amount of settled population (Miroschedji 1990a) (figure 3.3). Here too the corollary of this situation was a development of pastoralism and a strong political fragmentation. Notably, all written documents disappeared and there is no evidence of administrative management. This situation is another typical example of collapse (table 3.2).

THE FOURTH CYCLE: LATE ELAMITE (SUSA X)
INTEGRATION AND EXPANSION: EIGHTH TO SEVENTH CENTURIES BCE

By the late eighth century BCE, Elam reemerged on the stage of history, but in a very different political, social and ethnic environment (Miroschedji 1985, 1990a) (table 3.1). In Mesopotamia, the Late Assyrian kings represented then a formidable power whose imperialist policy had stimulated the establishment of new exchange networks, especially across the Iranian Plateau, the Arabian peninsula and the Persian Gulf. The competition for the control of these trade routes forms the background of the Assyro-Elamite conflicts. In southwestern Iran, major changes had taken place. In the central and southern Zagros, from the outset of the first millennium BCE onward, the Elamite ethnic element had regressed as a result of the expansion of the Iranian tribes (Miroschedji 1990a:69). After several centuries of Dark Age in a nomadic environment, the political landscape was completely altered through tribal recomposition. In Khuzestan, the newly arrived Aramean and Chaldean tribes had also modified the old ethnic fabric of the population (Miroschedji 1990a:70). Coupled with a sharp development of pastoralism and a severe decline in urban settlement, this evolution had weakened the administrative basis for the management of the empire and modified the traditional networks of tribal allegiances.

To cope with this situation, the Late Elamite kings resorted to a decentralized political organization, with three capitals: Susa, Madaktu and Hidalu (Miroschedji 1986) (figure 3.1). Susa remained the symbolic capital of the kingdom, where the kings dedicated many stelae and statues, later destroyed or carried away by the Assyrians. But the kings resided at Madaktu, possibly to be identified with Tepe Patak in the Deh Luran plain (Miroschedji 1986), and at Hidalu, probably to be located in eastern Khuzestan or in western Fars, perhaps in the area of Behbehan (Carter 1994a:74–76; Miroschedji 1985:273). Hence, the center of gravity of the empire was clearly in the lowlands and their eastern margin.

Consequently, the authority of the kings extended only nominally to the highlands. Close contacts were maintained with the Lurestan area, as suggested both by textual evidence and by discoveries in the sanctuary of Surkh Dum in Lurestan and in Iron Age II tombs of the Pusht-i Kuh range (Miroschedji 1990b:184–185; Schmidt et al. 1989). One possible evidence of royal Elamite presence in Fars is the addition, on both sides of the Old Elamite relief at Naqsh-i Rustam, of the figures of a queen and a king (Seidl 1986:Tf. 14–15, Abb. 2b). The headdress of the queen dates this addition to the seventh century BCE (Amiet 1966a:560; Miroschedji 1985:279; contra Seidl 1986:19, who prefers a ninth-century date), and that of the king is comparable to the headdress of Adda-hamiti-Inshushinak, one of the last Late Elamite kings of Susa (compare Muscarella in Harper et al. 1992:198. Miroschedji [1989:360] erroneously dated this image to the twelfth century, while Seidl [1986:18] ascribed it to the original Old Elamite relief). Another relief which could be dated to this time is that of Kul-i Farah I, but it is not a royal monument; it was carved by Hanni, a local chieftain, who also usurped the four twelfth century BCE reliefs of Shikaft-i Salman (Calmeyer 1988; de Waele 1972, 1973; Stolper 1988; Vanden Berghe 1959:Pl. 90:b, 1963). This suggests that the Elamite kings did not maintain a tight control over the entire Elamite territory and that local rulers could achieve a large measure of autonomy from the central power.

Although less glorious than its Old and Middle Elamite predecessors, the Late Elamite kingdom was nevertheless powerful enough to engage in a protracted armed confrontation with the Assyrians over the control of Babylonia and the Sea Land, where the overland and maritime trade routes from Arabia converged, and possibly also over the control of the highways crossing the central Zagros. Hence, in preparation for the battle of Halulê in 691 BCE, they managed to unite against the Assyrians all the people of southwestern Iran, from Fars to Lurestan (Miroschedji 1985:271). The Assyro-Elamite confrontation ended in 646 BCE with a victorious campaign of Assurbanipal and the thorough destruction of Susa, crystallizing Mesopotamian hatred accumulated over two millennia of hostile contacts.

COLLAPSE: AFTER THE ASSYRIAN CAMPAIGNS
Susa's destruction was a severe blow that signalled the collapse of the Late Elamite political configuration. Although the short period that follows until Cyrus the Great's conquest of the city in circa 539 has been interpreted by Pierre Amiet and myself as a short-lived renaissance (Amiet 1973b:24; Miroschedji 1982, 1990a:78–81), I rather believe today that it should be understood as just another instance of Elamite political disintegration marked by the resurgence of several principalities, which had formed the fabric of the Elamite confederacy in the preceding pe-

riod. This assumption is sustained by inscriptional evidence on tablets and cylinder seals which imply the existence of several kings in different areas of Khuzestan and its eastern margin, including western Fars (Miroschedji 1990a:79; Vallat 1996a:391). The Susa tablets mention local kings whose reigns can be dated to the late seventh to early sixth century BCE, including a Shutur-Nahhunte II who was the father of Hupan-kitin, whose cylinder seal is known (Amiet 1973; Miroschedji 1982; Steve 1986). A contemporary bronze plaque found at Persepolis names a king called Huban-Shuturuk in an area situated presumably not far from Izeh and Behbehan. Several inscribed silver vessels acquired on the antiquity market and tablets from Susa refer to a line of "kings of Samati," of unknown location (western Fars?) (W.G. Lambert in Mahboubian 1995; Caubet 1995; Demange 1996; Vallat 1996b), while other Susian tablets allude to a "king of the Zareans" (Vallat 1996a:391, n.43). Some of these "kings" may have been sovereigns of real states while others were probably only tribal chieftains who simply used a more prestigious title. Presumably, the king controlling Susa was the most powerful of them.

This period of political fragmentation was propitious to political and cultural realignments. The pure Neo-Babylonian style of Hupan-Kitin's cylinder seal and of many imprints on contemporary tablets from Susa (Amiet 1973b; Bollweg 1988; Miroschedji 1982) shows that Susa's material culture was again closely linked to that of Mesopotamia, a fact borne in mind by evidence of close contacts between Susiana and Babylonia (see Zadok 1976). Other observations point to sustained economic intercourse with the highlands of eastern Khuzestan and Fars. But these territories were then increasingly subjected to Iranian influence. As contended elsewhere (Miroschedji 1985:292–296), the ethnogenesis of the Persians can be recognized archaeologically in the Kur river basin from the mid-seventh century BCE onward (compare Sumner 1986b, 1994a, and chapter 24; see also Amiet 1992:92). The influence of the late seventh to early sixth century BCE Elamito-Persian kings of Fars spread rapidly and soon may have reached western Fars. A tomb recently discovered at Arjan, near Behbehan, illustrates the wealth of a local prince of that time (Alizadeh 1985; Majidzadeh 1992; Tohidi and Khalilian 1982; chapter 23) and exhibits distinct Persian stylistic characters which herald the Achaemenid period (on the Late Elamite-Achaemenid transition, see also Miroschedji 1985:296ff.; Boucharlat 1994). The same remark applies to the objects inscribed by the "kings of Samati" referred to above.

LATER CYCLES

The Late Elamite II period represents the last instance of the functioning of the Elamite paradigm of growth and decline in an Elamite cultural and ethnic context. We may imagine that a new phase of political integration and expansion would have followed. But it did not, because the geopolitical and ethnic situation of the entire Near East had dramatically changed in the seventh and early sixth century BCE. In southwestern Iran, the newly emerged Medes and Persians had rebuilt the unity of the highlands, from Kurdestan to Fars, in a way reminiscent of the Shimashkian and Anshanite principalities of the early second millennium BCE. This is suggested historically by the Greek historiographic tradition on Persian origins which stresses the close ties between Medes and Persians (see Tuplin 1994), and archaeologically by the fact that the earliest Achaemenid pottery of Fars and Khuzestan derives from the Median sphere and owes nothing to the Elamite pottery tradition. But this Medo-Persian cultural *koine* of the Zagros area was achieved around an Iranian node, not an Elamite one. Deprived of the highland territories of the central and southern Zagros, the political configuration of Greater Elam could never be restored. Elam thus became a marginal polity, eventually restricted to the limits of the modern province of Khuzestan. Its incorporation as a satrapy into the Persian Empire sealed its final historical disappearance.

Smaller political configurations, limited to the lowlands and uplands of Khuzestan, and sometimes including western Fars, reappeared periodically afterwards until the dawn of the twentieth century of our era. These polities have been briefly reviewed elsewhere (see Miroschedji 1990a:88–89) and need here only a brief reminder. The kingdom of Elymais, which still preserved the name of Elam in the Hellenistic and Parthian periods, the polity of the Great Lur, centered at Izeh in the twelfth–early fifteenth century CE, and that of the Bakhtiari confederation in the nineteenth century CE, all represent to some degree blueprints of antique Elam. They show more or less the same geographical extent and the same pattern of rise and collapse: a rise starting in the mountainous hinterland of Khuzestan—the traditional Elamite territory—culminating with the control of the plain of Khuzestan and its capital (Susa, or later Dezful), and a final collapse marked by a general disaggregation and a return to isolation for each territorial component. This implies that the history of the Elamite civilization is indeed inscribed in the *longue durée* of southwestern Iran, and that the latter was determined for more than five thousand years by the operation of an essentially similar system of rise and collapse, based ultimately on the sociopolitical interplay between the inhabitants of the lowlands (mainly agriculturalists) and those of the highlands (chiefly pastoralists).

CONCLUSION

The conclusion of this survey can be summarized by four main statements. First, the fate of Elam has always been closely linked to that of Mesopotamia, the ups and downs of Elamite history being to a large extent determined by the development of an international exchange network stimulated or enhanced by Mesopotamian needs. The collapse of this trade was usually followed by the collapse of Elam, whose prosperity was linked to the control of the riches of the Iranian Plateau.

Second, Elam's history appears as a series of rises starting in the eastern margin of the lowlands and collapses beginning in the highlands. Politically and territorially, Greater Elam was a unified entity for only short periods of time. In periods of strength or integration, it was a more or less tight confederacy of ethnically and culturally related principalities. In periods of weakness or disintegration, it was an aggregate of independent principalities with ties based on shifting allegiances between tribal chiefs around an Elamite heartland reduced to eastern Khuzestan and Susiana.

Third, in the course of Elam's history, the center of gravity of southwestern Iran shifted from the highlands to the lowlands when most of the southern Zagros area converted to nomadic pastoralism. This shift was accomplished in the mid-second millennium BCE and gave to Susiana a central role in the empire.

Thus, Elamite royal titles should not be interpreted literally. In particular, the title of "King of Anshan and Susa" does not necessarily mean that the king who used it came from Anshan, or even controlled the area of central Fars—just as the king of Elymais did not control the area of the former Achaemenid empire because he used its traditional title, "Great King." It is also clear that Elam and Anshan should neither be equated nor confused. Anshan was an essential component of Greater Elam for about six centuries only, between circa 2400 and 1750 BCE. Its inclusion into the Elamite confederacy was afterwards intermittent and came to a final end in the mid-seventh century BCE at the latest.

Finally, in Elam's history, the major element of political, religious and cultural continuity is indeed represented by Susa. Actually, the cycles of rise and collapse of the Elamite confederacy were possible only with Susa. The city was at the core of Elam's existence. It is the city where the Elamite kings invested the most because it was for them and for their Mesopotamian counterparts, as it is for us today, the symbol of Elamite civilization.

EXCURSUS: NOTES ON PERIODIZATION AND TERMINOLOGY IN ELAMITE HISTORY AND ARCHAEOLOGY

The chronological table (table 3.1) deserves some brief comments concerning the historical and archaeological periodization of Lower Khuzestan (Susiana), which determines to a large extent the terminology used to designate the phases of Elamite civilization as a whole.

A first remark concerns the distinction between historical and archaeological periodizations. Recent proposals use a historical periodization but designate its phases with an archaeological terminology (see Steve 1986, 1991; Vallat 1984a, 1996a, 1996b, 1996c, 1998). Actually, the two sequences are not interchangeable. Textual data allow a rather detailed historical periodization, defining dynasties which sometimes lasted less than a century, a degree of chronological refinement which cannot be achieved with archaeological data. Moreover, the correspondance between historical and archaeological periods exists only in broad terms. For example, the transitions from the Shimashki to the Sukkalmah dynasties and, later, from the Kidinuid to the Igihalkid dynasties probably took place about a century earlier than, respectively, the Old Elamite II/III and the Middle Elamite I/II transitions. Since the individual phases are usually not coterminous, archaeological and historical periodizations should be clearly distinguished in the terminology.

A second remark concerns the archaeological sequence of Susa. It is based on a series of pottery assemblages whose sequence was recognized in several stratigraphic soundings excavated between 1969 and 1979. The chronological overlap between the soundings "Acropole I" and "Ville Royale I" established a sequence of five periods numbered Susa I to Susa V (see Amiet 1988; Carter 1984). As the second millennium strata had not yet been subjected to a stratigraphic reexamination, the two Late Elamite periods identified in the sounding "Ville Royale II" were not originally numbered in the Susa sequence. However, since the publications, final or preliminary, of the pottery and architecture of Ghirshman's excavations "Ville Royale A" and "Ville Royale B," the broad lines of the second millennium sequence are now reasonably clear. Thus, there is no reason to delay further the numbering of the entire Susa sequence, as was done in table 3.1. Accordingly, the pre-Achaemenid archaeological sequence comprises ten periods numbered Susa I to Susa X.

A third remark concerns the periodization of the end of the Middle Elamite and Late Elamite periods. It has been suggested that we define the eleventh century as a Middle Elamite III period (Vallat 1996c, 1998, followed by Carter 1998). Historically, after the continuous and glorious line of the Shutrukids, the existence of some kings can indeed be identified, or surmised, in the eleventh century, although nothing is known otherwise about this lapse of time. Archaeologically, however, the eleventh century can hardly be defined, in the present state of knowledge, beyond the mere observation that some pottery shapes, notably the "Elamite goblets," may show typological changes toward the end (the eleventh century?) of the Middle Elamite II period (Carter 1996:29; Miroschedji 1981a:37). Such a discrete evolution is, I believe, insufficient to warrant the introduction of a Middle Elamite III period in the sequence, especially since these changes, if they exist, are not of the same magnitude as those affecting the pottery assemblages with the transition of the Middle Elamite I/II periods.

It has also been proposed that we call Late Elamite III (with two subphases, IIIA and IIIB) the period between Susa's destruction by Assurbanipal in 646 BCE and its conquest by Cyrus the Great in 539 BCE (Vallat 1984a, 1996a, 1996b, 1998; Steve 1986). This period is indeed a viable historical construct (see Miroschedji 1982, 1985, 1990a). But archaeologically, a Late Elamite III period (let alone IIIA and IIIB) simply does not exist. The archaeological sequence of the first half of the first millennium BCE was established on the basis of careful stratigraphic excavations at Susa's Ville Royale II sounding and corroborated by other excavations and surveys at Susa (Miroschedji 1981b; Steve et al. 1980:58) and elsewhere in Khuzestan (Carter 1994a; Miroschedji 1981c). It includes only three pottery assemblages: a Late Elamite I pottery assemblage represented by strata 9–8 of the Ville Royale II excavations, followed by a Late Elamite II pottery assemblage corresponding to strata 7–6 of the same excavations, and the third assemblage, Achaemenid, illustrated by the next strata 5–4. Only the glyptic allows one to draw a chronological distinction between the seventh and the first half of the sixth century BCE (Amiet 1973b; Bollweg 1988; Miroschedji 1982). The chronological limits of the Late Elamite II period are uncertain; the upper limit at circa 750 BCE is conjectural and the lower limit at circa 520 BCE is an inference based on the supposition that Susa's urban layout and material culture remained unchanged until the reign of Darius I. Thus, the archaeological period called Late Elamite II corresponds historically to both a Late Elamite phase (pre-646 BCE) and a Final Elamite phase (circa 646–539 BCE).

Dedication. These pages are offered to William Sumner as a token of esteem and friendship, and also in remembrance of an afternoon in Spring, 1971, when, while surveying together at Malyan, Bill picked up the first inscribed brick, which established the identification of the site as the fabled city of Anshan. This discovery and the subsequent excavations, which Bill directed on the site in such a masterly fashion, have set the archaeology of southwestern Iran on entirely new tracks. The present essay is an attempt to integrate into an overall archaeological and historical picture some results of Bill's research in the Kur river basin. (An earlier and shorter version of this chapter was delivered on 29 January 1993 at the International Symposium on "The Royal City of Susa," organized by the Metropolitan Museum of Art in New York City.)

CHAPTER 4

ARCHAEOLOGICAL SURVEY AND LONG-TERM POPULATION TRENDS IN UPPER MESOPOTAMIA AND IRAN

T.J. WILKINSON

The estimation of settlement density and of population density on the basis of survey data from prehistoric sites is one of the most perilous exercises in prehistoric archaeology.

— Renfrew (1972:383)

ALTHOUGH THE ABOVE STATEMENT IS TRUE, archaeologists still must attempt to make basic estimates of population from archaeological survey data. We should therefore be extremely grateful to Bill Sumner who contributed so significantly to this field, not only by the use of archaeological survey data (Sumner 1972, 1990a) but by assembling ethnographic information as well (Sumner 1979, 1989b). Sumner has argued persuasively that demographic estimates should be derived from archaeological survey data, but he is equally aware of the pitfalls, both in evaluating the primary field data and in producing the final synthetic curve (Sumner 1990a). In this chapter I examine recent developments in the estimation of population from archaeological survey data for northern Iraq and Syria (hereafter Upper Mesopotamia) and briefly compare these results with some of Sumner's conclusions concerning the Kur river basin as well as other results from western Iran.

Some knowledge of long-term trends in population is crucial to any understanding of issues such as the processes of urbanization, state formation and collapse, the development of agriculture, human effect on the environment, and population migration. Significantly, archaeologists appear to belong to the only academic community that has the data at hand suitable for reconstructing quantitative demographic estimates for the duration of thousands of years. In certain instances archaeological data have been employed by those who construct long-term demographies (Whitmore et al. 1990), but because they have neither knowledge nor control over the field records, it is the responsibility of the archaeologist to present the data so that they can be assessed critically by demographers and geographers. Furthermore, archaeological surveys, which supply the field data for the demographic curves discussed here, also provide an essential record of the rapidly diminishing resource of archaeological sites, which are being removed by recent urban growth, civil engineering projects, and extension of agriculture. In the past, archaeologists have not always considered ancient populations in terms of the full range of demographic variables, but if long term demographic curves are to be used we need to interpret them in the context of changes in fertility levels, family size, migration (both local and long-distance), biological data, and mortality patterns. Although we cannot recognize all of these entities in the archaeological record directly, we need to give them appropriate consideration in order to evaluate the curves (Paine 1997).

METHODOLOGY AND PROBLEMS INTERPRETING SURVEY DATA

Archaeological surveys should be viewed critically because, as with any methodology, survey data have their limitations and ambiguities. Ironically, in the Near East, the

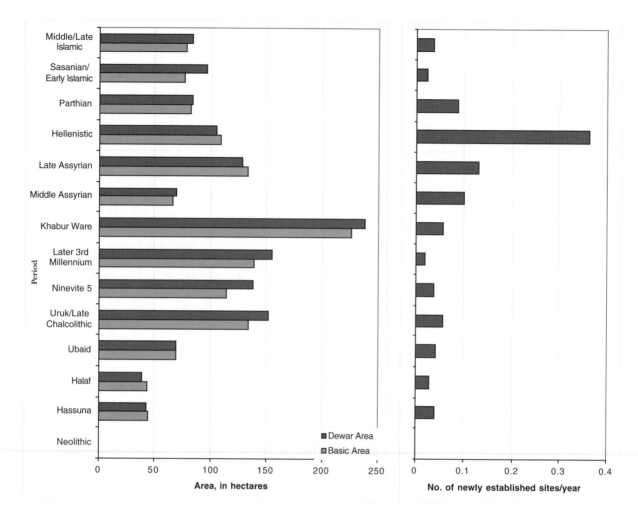

a

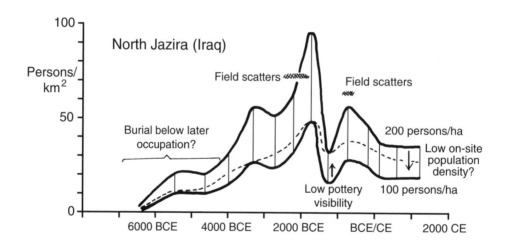

b

4.1 Various methods of presenting long-term population estimates from the north Jazira (Iraq): *a (left)*, light bars, basic aggregate site area per ceramic period of variable length; dark gray bars, application of Dewar's algorithm to the same data set; *a (right)*, rate of newly established settlements using Dewar's methodology (note how the number of newly established sites increases in the Late Assyrian, and especially the Hellenistic periods, when there was a significant colonization in the form of the dispersal of small, rural settlements); *b*, trends in population showing possible adjustments that could be made to the raw aggregate site data. Population estimates assume on-site densities of 100 and 200 persons per ha. *Sources: a (left), Wilkinson and Tucker 1995; a (right), after Dewar 1991; data analysis by Ben Diebold, Yale University; b) T.J. Wilkinson*

very conspicuousness of archaeological sites such as tells has discouraged the development of intensive survey. Consequently, techniques have lagged behind those in the Mediterranean basin or Mesoamerica where the site record is more subtle. Nevertheless, it would be folly to neglect the large sites to concentrate on only the minor elements of the survey record. If possible, it is expedient for the surveyor to provide a record of both the structural components of settlement pattern and the subtleties of the minor sites and off-site activity, the latter contributing to a knowledge of pastoral nomadic communities and land use.

Occupational area can be estimated for each phase of a complex site by dividing the site area into sub-units, whether larger topographic divisions or sample squares (Wilkinson and Tucker 1995) or circles (Whallon 1979). By summing the settlement area for each period, a curve of aggregate settlement area can be constructed that can then be adjusted or normalized, as will be discussed below.

Through time there may be a significant attrition of the archaeological record, by burial of sites beneath alluvial sediments (Adams 1981; Brookes et al. 1982) or by cultural processes. This attrition commonly results in underestimation of the early part of the archaeological record because earlier occupations are obscured by later occupation phases that overlie them. As a result of such burial, the older rising part of a demographic curve may always be suspect (see below). Only if settlements consistently occur in the form of low single-phase sites will earlier occupation phases in a region remain visible. Furthermore, when survey data is plotted according to the duration of ceramic periods of varying length it should not be assumed that every site was occupied for the entirety of each period (Dewar 1991; Schacht 1984; Sumner 1990a:7–10; Weiss 1977). To compensate for this factor it is possible to make arithmetic adjustments or iterative compensations that allow for both the different lengths of ceramic periods and the rate of growth and extinction of settlements (Dewar 1994a; for example figure 4.1b). Nevertheless, if the period that is subjected to Dewar's (1991) algorithm falls within the prehistoric period, that is, within the rising limb of the aggregate settlement area curve, then the low quality of the surface area data may result in spurious accuracy despite the sophisticated nature of the algorithm applied (see also chapter 5, on Dewar's method).

The calculation of actual population figures from excavated areas can provide a wide range of estimates (Postgate 1994). Because population density per unit area of the site may be variable across large areas or long time spans, application of a single population density such as 100 persons per ha might seem simplistic. Nevertheless a recent study of preindustrial and later urban populations has shown that population densities in the range of 100 to 200 persons per ha do predominate (Storey 1997), which agrees with estimates reported for the Near East (Kramer 1980; Sumner 1989b). That within any given cultural or geographical area consistent relationships do exist between settlement area and population is also supported by recent ethnographic studies in lowland South America and the Caribbean (Curet 1997). Nevertheless, to allow for higher population densities that could exist on certain sites it is probably expedient to apply a range of population densities to the estimated site area: 100, 200, or even 300 persons per ha, so that estimates can be arrived at in terms of a probability range. Calculation of the population of any site by the application of a single "magic number" is liable to error, but when applied to large numbers of settlements over large areas, the individual site variations can be evened out to produce more reliable estimates of total population at the scale of the region (De Roche 1983:190). This further underlines the value of survey data, as opposed to excavations of single sites, for estimating past populations. Another issue is that of so-called frame dependence (Bronson 1975:68), in which the size of the study area influences the perceived degree of population flux. Thus, for large areas, long-term population fluctuations may appear to be much less than within smaller areas.

FULL-COVERAGE SURVEY VERSUS INTENSIVE SURVEY

A major issue in archaeological survey is the relative merit of broad full-coverage versus partial but intensive sampling (Sumner 1990b). Full-coverage survey takes as its limits the boundary of the natural region so that, in principle, all site locations within the designated area may be noted. Such a top-down approach, which continues to be practiced almost exclusively in greater Mesopotamia, has the distinct advantage of providing structural patterns that can then be analyzed by spatial analysis and location models (Falconer and Savage 1995; Sumner 1990b:109). In practice, however, only obvious sites are recorded, because it is very difficult to find and record every single site within an area that may be greater than 300 km². Even when carried out diligently, the full-coverage approach tends to underrepresent the smallest sites. Yet such "minor" sites can be fundamental to understanding the processes of settlement change, especially for the later periods of territorial empires (that is, after about 1000 BCE).

In contrast, a partial sample survey makes generalizations about an entire region by sampling only a part

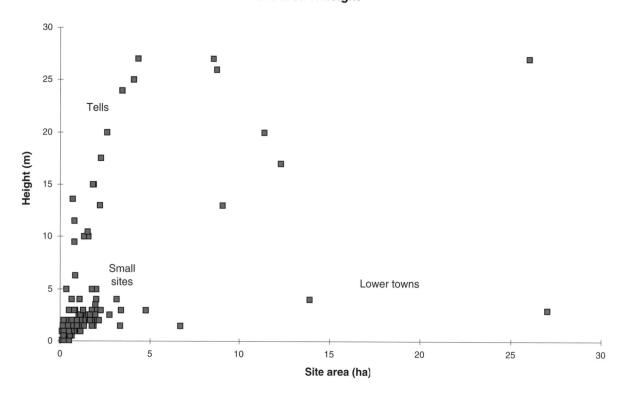

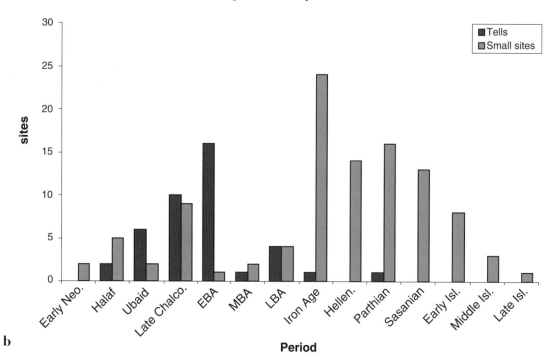

4.2 Tell Beydar area, western Khabur basin: *a*, scatter plot showing morphology of tells, small sites, and lower towns; *b*, long-term change in tells versus small sites in the area of Tell Beydar. *T.J. Wilkinson*

of it. Techniques include intensive walking transects across strips of terrain, which may be employed to provide estimates of the full distribution of site sizes as well as the lower end of the settlement size range.

The most expedient approach for Mesopotamian archaeology is to first use full-coverage methods to recover the basic settlement structure and then develop a strategy for a more intensive sample survey. Such a two-stage procedure is not new, however (Redman 1973). In the Marvdasht the broad pattern of settlement was initially outlined by Sumner (1972) and then more detailed intensive pedestrian surveys and random sampling were undertaken (Alden 1979; Rosenberg 1988, this volume). Despite the early introduction of on-site sampling techniques (see Whallon 1979), they are not frequently applied in the Near East. In part this is because on the large areas required for survey, a small team or even an individual is spread very thinly. As a result it is perceived to be counterproductive for the surveyor(s) to expend the large amount of time that is required to perform such sampling schemes, both at the collection and the analysis stage. More important, however, is that there is sometimes more utility in spending the available time carefully evaluating the greater site area (including apparent "off-site" areas) in order to determine whether subtle traces of outlying settlements remain in the immediate site periphery. In other words it can be more effective to cover the entire area of a 10-ha lower town than to neglect such a feature and elegantly subdivide a one- to two-ha tell into smaller subunits that may fall between the main size classes employed in statistical analysis. Ideally, of course, one should attempt both strategies.

OFF-SITE SURVEY

Although in recent years advances have been made in the recovery of off-site data (Wilkinson 1982), buried sites (Banning 1996), landscape features such as canals and quarry sites (chapter 24), and pastoral camps (Bernbeck 1993; Hole 1991), such components of the record continue to be overlooked and the research agenda of many surveys continues to focus on the more visible elements of sedentary sites. Since the 1970s it has been recognized that the archaeological landscape does not simply consist of discrete points of activity (sites) with extensive areas of zero activity between, but rather there is a virtually continuous record of off-site material, archaeological features, and other activity areas (Cherry 1983). Such off-site material can be either relegated to nuisance value (that is, off-site sherd scatters as "background noise") or used to supply hints about the intensity of cultivation (Wilkinson 1982), or conversely pastoral nomadic activities or hunter-

gatherers (Cribb 1991; Foley 1981). Unfortunately, in Iran by 1979, when surveys by European and American archaeologists effectively came to an end, such techniques were relatively new. In contrast, since the mid-1970s off-site surveys in Upper Mesopotamia have continued to contribute to the survey database, primarily by providing indications of land use practice. Further west in Syria and the Amuq area of southern Turkey where there was a significant increase in small dispersed settlements in the Roman period, off-site surveys are also proving to be of value in recognizing the smallest end of the site size spectrum.

In Iran, off-site field scatters have been recognized on early Islamic fields behind Siraf, where they relate to the application of settlement-derived refuse to fields as fertilizer (Wilkinson 1982) and also in the Tepe Yahya area where similar processes have resulted in site areas appearing to be significantly enlarged (Prickett 1986:646, 745–746). "Off-site" sherd scatters extending for some 500 m from the main mound at Tepe Yahya have also been interpreted as forming the remains of lower towns (Vidali et al. 1976), a reasonable explanation, given that lower towns have often been overlooked by conventional mound surveys elsewhere in the Near East. Nevertheless, that the scatters were lower town occupations was not demonstrated unequivocally by the off-mound survey because transects were not taken sufficiently far from the site. If transects had been one or even several kilometers in length, as is normally the case for off-site survey, they would have demonstrated whether the scatters were discrete bounded occupations characteristic of sedentary occupations or simply faded out into the distance at progressively lower densities as is more characteristic of off-site "field scatters."

Unfortunately, future off-site surveys may be rendered worthless by the practice of the application to fields of earth excavated from mounds for fertilizer (see chapter 7). Although it is possible to distinguish such intrusive soils from ancient field scatters, this can be laborious, and such dumping may still result in the false appearance of sites. For example, in the case of field scatters, which tend to belong to a limited time range, taphonomic processes operating over long spans of time can result in the wearing down of pottery into small abraded sherds. Earth removal for fertilizer results in larger sherds and more on-site material on the surface (such as querns and foundation stones) as well as a wider range of ceramic types, because soils from a cultural matrix are rarely taken from a single ceramic horizon. Consequently, it will be increasingly necessary in the future for field surveyors to ascertain what the modern agricultural practices are before embarking on intensive survey.

LONG-TERM POPULATION CURVES: ALTERNATIVE APPROACHES

Although visually satisfying, long-term demographic curves should be used with caution. Here I will only briefly consider the use of long-term population estimates (but see Wilkinson 1999 for further details) and instead will discuss alternative approaches to the problem. Having constructed a curve, and potentially adjusted the aggregate site area statistics using Dewar's algorithm, long-term data can then be presented with appropriate adjustments as follows (figure 4.1): sedimentation, burial of early levels beneath later ones, underrepresentation of certain periods where the ceramics are little known, variations in population densities (where sites appear as straggling, low density mound complexes), and other factors. Such curves, although suspect in detail, provide a valuable illustration of gross rises and falls of population and settlement. Minor rises and falls within such curves, however, must be treated with considerable caution. In the future, rather than making estimates of specific population levels, it may therefore be more productive to address demographic questions with qualitative but more robust concepts such as:

- Structural changes in the settlement pattern
- Spatial dynamics of population and settlement "patchiness"
- The use of off-site data to supply cross-checks on population size estimates using estimates of feasible land use configurations and water supply.

Additional issues that would benefit from both qualitative and quantitative analysis include:

- Interactions between population and environmental change
- Relationships between estimated population levels and proxy indicators of intensification such as irrigation or applications of manure
- The concept of population "reservoirs" that illustrate interactions between urban, rural and nomadic populations.

STRUCTURAL CHANGES IN SETTLEMENT

In much of the Jazira of Upper Mesopotamia, Bronze Age settlement is primarily in the form of nucleated tells, whereas earlier Chalcolithic and Neolithic as well as post Late Bronze Age settlement mainly occurs in the form of smaller, dispersed settlements. These morphological changes can be recognized simply by plotting site height versus site area on a scatter diagram (figure 4.2a) or alternatively by assessing changes in settlement size according to urban-rural settlement sectors.

For example, in the Tell Beydar area of the western Khabur, Syria, tells were mainly occupied within the Chalcolithic and Early Bronze Age, after which lower towns and dispersed rural settlement were the norm (figure 4.2b). A similar trend is recognizable in the Balikh valley, northern Syria (Wilkinson 1998:Fig. 7), as well as in the north Jazira, Iraq.

In the north Jazira structural change was recognized because each ceramic phase could be broken down into aggregate occupied areas for large, rural, and medium-sized settlements (figure 4.3). Urbanization, in the form of large settlements on tells, is clearly an Early and Middle Bronze Age phenomenon, whereas rural settlements (defined here as sites smaller than 2.5 ha) were more significant either before about 3000 BCE or after 1000 BCE. It is probably significant that there is a decline in rural settlement at approximately that point when centers were expanding in the earlier part of the third millennium BCE, although the coarse resolution of the survey record provides only a rough impression of this process. This rural decline at the onset of urbanization implies that urban growth was at the expense of the rural sector which therefore declined in overall size. Such a differential flux may represent underlying demographic trends in which population growth in rural areas may exceed that in urban areas whose inhabitants are more likely to contract or transmit infectious diseases than those in rural settlements (Grigg 1982). Thus for urban growth to be maintained it is often necessary for a significant reservoir of rural population to exist to supply potential immigrants. In addition, immigrants may be expected to come from outside the area, and can include population drawn from both sedentary populations and pastoral nomadic communities. When population increases are particularly large, as in the Kur river basin, then such distant populations are much more likely to provide the population reservoirs for urban growth (Sumner 1989a).

The decay of urban centers that occurred in the north Jazira during the second millennium BCE, although appearing to represent a demographic collapse, may also be explained by differential demographic growth rates. Published reports (Wilkinson and Tucker 1995) probably exaggerate the difference between settlement in the early and mid-second millennium BCE because Khabur ware has a longer time range than was originally appreciated

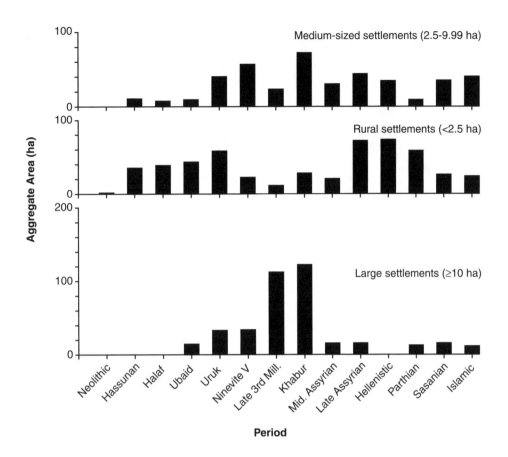

4.3 Large, rural, and medium-sized settlement in the north Jazira (Iraq) through time. *T.J. Wilkinson*

(Postgate et al. 1997:54). As a result, the peak of Khabur ware use (that is, earlier second millennium BCE) should be extended so that aggregate settlement area for this phase continues to perhaps the early fourteenth century BCE. The gradual dwindling of the size of centers that occurred during the second millennium BCE may therefore result in part because the rural population reservoir did not exist to re-supply the centers with population, which therefore progressively dwindled in size.

The trend from nucleated tells towards rural settlement, which is presumably recognizable in much of the Jazira, thus represents a major structural shift in the pattern of settlement during the second millennium BCE. It is tempting to see such a shift as representing adjustments to the settlement system that stem from a shift from Bronze Age city-states to a territorial empire initially under the Middle Assyrian and then the Neo-Assyrian empires, but the elaboration of this point is beyond the scope of this chapter.

Similar structural changes can be observed in the Kur river basin where small rural settlements predominate in the later periods, whereas earlier settlements have a more

even balance between rural and urban (figure 4.4). This changeover to a dominantly rural settlement pattern occurs in the Qaleh phase around 1400 BCE. The recognition of changes in settlement structure is particularly useful because, unlike the quantitative demographic approach, it is less burdened by assumptions concerning site population densities.

SPATIAL DYNAMICS OF SETTLEMENT AND POPULATION
In northern Iraq and Syria the comparison of data from a number of surveys conducted over a very large area shows that settlement density does not necessarily rise and fall in a consistent and synchronous pattern over the entire Near East. Rather, in certain cases a settlement rise in one area may be associated with periods of sparse settlement elsewhere. There is thus a degree of complementarity in the survey record that can be sketched from relative population shifts in adjacent areas (table 4.1) (see chapter 6).

For example, in the later third millennium BCE both surveys and excavations indicate a significant growth of settlements in dry-farmed areas along the Syrian Euphrates at a time when major centers farther east in the Khabur

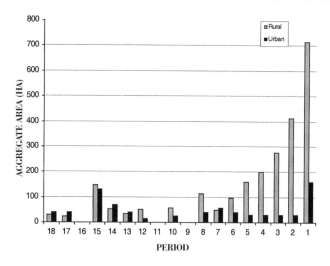

4.4 Kur river basin settlement, Iran, classified according to rural and urban components by period: *1*, Modern (based on census); *2*, Islamic; *3*, Islamic 3/2; *4*, Islamic 2/1; *5*, Islamic 2/1; *6*, Islamic 1; *7*, Islamic 1/Sasanian; *8*, Sasanian; *9*, missing data; *10*, Achaemenid; *11*, hiatus?; *12*, Shogha, Teimuran; *13*, Qaleh; *14*, Late Kaftari; *15*, Kaftari; *16*, hiatus; *17*, Late Banesh; *18*, Middle Banesh. *After Sumner 1990b: Table 2*

valley were apparently in decline (Weiss et al. 1993). Thus, Tell es-Sweyhat, in a dry-farmed area about 3 km from the Euphrates in the Tabqa area, grew significantly in size and was enclosed with an outer wall during the final quarter of the third millennium BCE (Holland 1976, 1977; Zettler 1997). Furthermore, settlements such as Selenkehiye, also in the Tabqa area, maintained their size until approximately the turn of the millennium, and in the Carchemish area to the north of the Turkish border, surveys by Guillermo Algaze demonstrate a distinctive late third millennium BCE peak in settlement (Algaze et al. 1994). Still further north in the area of Kurban and Titriş along the Turkish Euphrates, urbanization in the third quarter of the millennium was followed by a shift to a dispersed rural settlement. The late third millennium BCE ruralization phase probably therefore represents a migration out from the declining urban centers, although alternatively additional factors may be involved. For example, the collapse of a center could result in its desertion by the inhabitants, some of whom could have been incorporated into nomadic communities. Subsequent re-sedentarization could have taken place into a new generation of dispersed farming communities.

Unfortunately, the long time spans of the ceramic periods employed can inhibit the matching of curves. For example, in the Kur river basin, following the Late Banesh phase of the first quarter of the third millenium BCE (Voigt

and Dyson 1992), the valley was entirely abandoned for some 500 to 600 years, after which there was a renewal of sedentary occupation on a large scale in the Kaftari phase, beginning around 2200 to 2100 BCE or shortly thereafter (Sumner 1989a:135). This record is virtually the converse of the record for parts of northern Syria such as the Khabur basin, where urbanization was really under way during the post-Banesh hiatus (roughly equivalent to Susa IV and Va [Voigt and Dyson 1992]). A similar decline around the mid-third millennium BCE in the Cizre region of southeastern Turkey (Algaze et al. 1991) contrasts with what is clearly a period of growth in both the north Jazira (Iraq) and the Leilan area (Syria). In the Cizre case it can be argued that this large well-watered plain may have been deserted because growing centers to the south (for example, Tells al-Hawa or Leilan) were absorbing population from areas to the north. In the Kur river basin, on the other hand, settlement abandonment appears to have been associated with increased pastoral activity, while the emergent Kaftari phase that followed was built upon a combination of immigration of craft specialists and the settlement of nomadic pastoralists on vacant farmland (Sumner 1989a:136).

Long-term demographic curves often blur the rise and fall in aggregate settled areas, with the result that gaps, such as the post-Banesh hiatus, can be obscured. In part this is because of the considerable compression of the time scale that erodes the finer chronological distinctions. Thus, in figure 4.5, the Kaftari settlement peak (c) for the Kur river basin can be seen to fall between the "later third millennium" and Old Babylonian (Khabur ware) points in the north Jazira (a and b respectively). Whereas on the one hand there may be a significant break between (a) and (b) (the Khabur hiatus; Weiss et al. 1993), other sites such as Tell Brak provide a continuous record of occupation in post-Akkadian times (Oates and Oates 1994). Such ambiguities cannot, at present, be satisfactorily distinguished by survey data, which is more valuable for presenting broad long wavelength trends in settlement.

SETTLEMENT, POPULATION, AND CLIMATE CHANGE
From at least the Early Bronze Age in northern Mesopotamia, episodes of low population densities in one area are sometimes contemporary with rises elsewhere, which suggests that population and settlement were very heterogeneous. Many of these shifts presumably relate to changes in socioeconomic or political conditions, but because Holocene climate fluctuations appear often to have been significant, these may also have influenced settlement. It is therefore instructive to compare long-term

Table 4.1 Complementary survey areas in the Syrian-Iraqi Jazira showing areas of dense versus sparse settlement of the same archaeological period

Period	Dense settlement	Sparse or absent settlement
Late Chalcolithic	Beydar survey (1)	Abd al-Aziz survey (2)
Mid-3rd millennium BCE	North Jazira, Leilan (3)	Cizre-Silope, Upper Tigris (4)
Mid-3rd millennium BCE	Kurban/Titriş Höyüks (5)	Carchemish/Birecik (6)
Late 3rd millennium BCE	Carchemish/Birecik, Tabqa (7)	Kurban/Titriş Höyüks; Leilan, Brak area (8)
Early 2nd millennium BCE	Eastern Khabur, North Jazira, Cizre-Silopi (9)	Western Khabur, Beydar area (10)
Early Islamic	Balikh valley (11)	Kurban Höyük, Carchemish (12)

Sources: 1-Wilkinson (N.D.); 2-Hole (1997, 1998), Kouchoukos (1998); 3-Wilkinson and Tucker (1995), Stein and Wattenmaker (1990); 4-Algaze et al. (1991:182, 196), Rosenberg and Togul (1991:245); 5-Wilkinson (1990), Algaze et al. (1992); 6-Algaze et al. (1994); 7-Algaze et al. (1994); Zettler (1997), Holland (1976); 8-Wilkinson (1990), Algaze et al. (1992), Weiss et al. (1993); Eidem and Warburton (1996); 9-Meijer (1986), Wilkinson and Tucker (1995), Algaze et al. (1991: 197); 10-Lyonnet (1996), Wilkinson (N.D.); 11-Bartl (1994); 12-Wilkinson (1990), Gerber (1996), Algaze et al. (1994: 23)

trends in settlement and population to recent high resolution evidence for climate change in the region.

The above-mentioned "Khabur hiatus" has been suggested as a period of intense aridity that precipitated a widespread demographic collapse (Weiss et al. 1993). Here I will compare the nearest proxy record of climatic phases from Lake Van with settlement trends at Malyan and in the north Jazira, the two closest population proxy curves (figure 4.5) to see whether similar relationships might be evident. The Lake Van record, based on lake geochemistry and oxygen isotope data sampled from annually deposited varves in the lake floor, shows an early to mid-Holocene moist period followed by significant late Holocene atmospheric drying (Lemcke and Sturm 1997, based on core taken in 1990). The development of Chalcolithic settlement in both the Kur river basin and north Jazira therefore occurred against a background of atmospheric moisture that was slightly greater than the average for the Holocene. Although the survey data is rather coarse to be meaningfully compared with the Van data, it does appear that the later third millennium BCE phase of settlement growth in the north Jazira, as well as perhaps even higher peaks in the early second millennium BCE (that is, Khabur ware for the north Jazira, and Kaftari for the Kur river basin) occurred in the face of a significantly drying climate so that in a rain-fed farming regime, as prevailed in the north Jazira, communities would have experienced significantly greater food stress through the second millennium BCE.

This situation can be illustrated by a simple supply and demand model: population can be expressed in the form of a demand for staple foods in tons per year (dominantly rain-fed cereals, but also pulses which ultimately depend upon rainfall); supply can be expressed in the first approximation as cereal production (and also potentially expressed in tons per year); assuming constant sown area, supply would then be proportional to annual rainfall. Thus a simple ratio of population to moisture index should provide a secondary index for food stress. Here for this preliminary estimate, population for the north Jazira is expressed in the form of population per km^2 and the moisture index from Lake Van on a scale of 2 (moist) to 6 (dr y) (based on Lemcke and Sturm 1997:Fig. 2). The food stress index (FSI) is simply:

$$FSI = \frac{Estimated\ Population}{Moisture\ Index}$$

The values of this food stress index suggest that during the early to mid-Holocene not only was rainfall sufficient for successful crops in most years but also population was sufficiently low that the stress index was low. Through the period 6000 to 3750 BP (roughly later Chalcolithic to Middle Bronze Age), the ratio of population to moisture index increased as potential production declined (as a result of atmospheric drying), and demand increased due to population increase. This inclement combination climaxed around 3750 years BP, that is in the period when Khabur wares were the primary diagnostic ceramic, when the stress index reached its maximum and food stress must have been considerable. After this point it declined again simply because demand declined faster than potential supply.

A trough in population numbers that occurred around the mid to late second millennium BCE and which is evident in a number of demographic curves (see Wilkinson 1999) appears to fall within this period of declining rainfall. Again it might be suggested that this trough was a result of population decline in the face of crop failures as a result of a steadily drying climate. It should be noted that although such drying atmospheric conditions increase the likelihood of crop failure, it does not mean that rain-fed cultivation became impossible. Significantly both Tells Brak and Rimah, both in very marginal positions near the limit of rain-fed cultivation, show every sign of having been supported by rain-fed cultivation, and also having been occupied continuously through most of the second

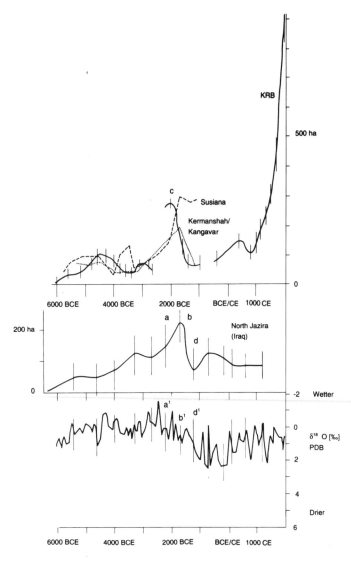

4.5 *Top*, Population estimates for the Kur river basin, Susiana plain, and Kermanshah/Kangavar survey areas, western Iran. Vertical lines for top and middle graph indicate the chronological mid-points of ceramic class in question. *Based on Sumner 1990b:Fig. 4; Susiana and Kermanshah/Kangavar data from Schacht 1987:Fig. 45*

Middle, Aggregate settlement area for north Jazira plain, Iraq, at approximately the same scale as top graph. See text for details. *Redrawn from Wilkinson and Tucker 1995:Fig. 50*

Bottom, Aridity/moisture index based on oxygen isotope data for varved sediments from Lake Van, Turkey, plotted as deviations of the isotope ratio of the sample from the international belemnite standard (PDB). *Lemcke and Sturm 1997:Fig. 2*

millennium until at least the thirteenth century BCE. The eventual abandonment of both sites in the thirteenth or perhaps twelfth century could, of course, be blamed on the continued drying that apparently took place in the centuries around the turn of the millennium, but it is noteworthy that the food stress index (figure 4.6) was low during the late second millennium, probably because low yields were nevertheless sufficient to supply the diminished population. Because the resolution of the cultural and chronological record for the dark age that followed remains poor, it is difficult to make a convincing case even for this phase of climatic drying having contributed to the demographic decline, although certainly there must have been many years when food stress was experienced.

In summary, long-term demographic estimates, by supplying a rough but moderately continuous record, do enable us to frame problems with greater clarity and make comparisons with high resolution records such as that from Lake Van. Nevertheless, alternative approaches can be fruitfully explored.

When population peaks or troughs in adjacent areas do not coincide it is possible that there will have been some population shifts from one area to another. Although this might have been simply in the form of a direct movement of population, a compelling case can be made for the medium of exchange being the pastoral nomadic community with their annual migratory routes or transhumance cycles that would have absorbed excess population from urban decline in one area and (eventually) have contributed them to areas where conditions were more propitious for settlement elsewhere (see below). Although climatic drying would certainly have stressed crop and pastoral production systems, because these systems exploit territories of different scales often in somewhat different climatic zones, it is unwise to assume that climatic stress would have been felt uniformly by all communities.

POPULATION TRENDS ESTIMATED FROM CULTIVATED AREA OR IRRIGATION SUPPLY

In addition to providing a proxy record of long-term population trends, demographic estimates based on settlement survey data can be tested against off-site data. For example around Tell al-Hawa in northern Iraq, evidence for off-site field scatters has been combined with estimates of total cultivated areas, the latter being derived from when linear hollow routes "fade out" near the assumed limit of cultivation (Wilkinson 1994). These combined estimates result in a synthetic map of land use zones characterized by a dense sherd scatter zone indicative of the inner zone of most intensive land use, and a limit of the fields which is indicated approximately by the linear hollows. These two estimates can then be compared to the expected food demand from the settled population estimated from the site area. By arriving at land use estimates from two directions (that is, off-site data and site area), it is possible to roughly cross-check the two data sets. Such comparative studies demonstrate that the sustaining area calculated from estimated site population approximately matches the cultivated area estimated from off-site data. Although the match between the two data sets is by no means close, this approach does provide support for the methods employed for estimating site populations.

Eventually it may be possible for population estimates to be stated in terms of a mathematical probability of their falling in a specified range of say 100 to 300 persons per ha (or even more). In other words, if the higher site population density figures are applied, sustaining areas will increase in size to such a point where they will exceed the available cultivable land. The point that such a threshold was crossed would then provide the best estimate of the local population. An alternative dynamic exploratory approach is to compare regional population estimates with estimates of available irrigation water to test whether available water supply would be sufficient to support the settlement system in question. Such analyses applied to the settlement record of the Balikh valley, Syria, suggest that in the early second millennium sedentary population in the lower Balikh had risen to such a point that water competition was likely, a point echoed by cuneiform records from Mari (Wilkinson 1998).

LONG-TERM POPULATION TRENDS AND INTENSIFICATION
Any attempt to relate increased levels of population density with intensification of land use in a Boserupian relationship is often deemed controversial (Thomas 1990:xi) or even an intellectual "albatross" (Morrison 1996:605), and to posit linkages is certainly less popular today than twenty years ago (see Smith and Young 1972, 1983; Young 1972, 1977). At a more general level, where population proxy curves are available, as in for example Upper Mesopotamia or western Iran, population levels often appear to decline after attaining a peak, usually sometime in the third millennium BCE (figure 4.1a, b, c, early second millennium BCE; see also Sumner 1990a:Fig. 4, ca. 2000 BCE; Young 1977:Fig. 2, between 1600 and 1800 BCE), which implies that after a certain point, be it for social, economic, political or environmental reasons, conditions were not conducive for continued population increase.

In Upper Mesopotamia, as in the Deh Luran plain, there is little evidence that land use intensification and high population pressure were present to any significant

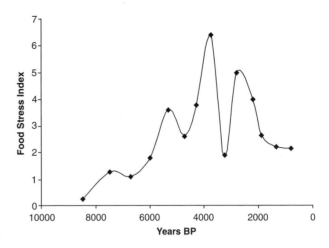

4.6 Food stress index for the North Jazira Project, Iraq, calculated from estimated population and atmospheric moisture. For methods of calculation, see text. NOTE: FSI rises as demand for staple foods increases and atmospheric moisture declines. *Based on Wilkinson and Tucker 1995 (population); Lemcke and Sturm 1997 (atmospheric moisture)*

degree before the mid-third millennium BCE (Johnson 1987:284). Before this, in the Ubaid period, the north Jazira plain of Iraq was approaching the point of being fully settled, and it exhibited a three-level settlement hierarchy with most of its land area potentially under cultivation (Wilkinson et al. 1996:18–21). That the Kur river basin was also approaching significant population pressure is hinted at by the middle Bakun settlement distribution (within the range 4600 and 4000 BCE), which suggests that the amount of agricultural land available to support each inhabitant might have dropped to as little as 0.8 to 1.1 ha per person (Sumner 1994b:52).

Nevertheless, when potential indicators of land use intensification and manuring are available in the form of off-site sherd scatters, their presence coincides approximately with peaks of settlement on the long term demographic curves (Wilkinson 1999). This strengthens the notion that increases in population density may, other things being equal, force the introduction of technologies that allow for improvements in agricultural production. Although around a few sites, such as Tell es-Sweyhat and Tell al-Hawa, it appears that both population density and intensification had peaked by the mid-late third millennium, in many cases this peak came much later. For example, dense and well attested off-site sherd scatters that demonstrably do not belong to *in situ* occupation have been recorded for the Partho-Roman to Early Islamic periods in the Balikh valley (Syria); around Kurban Höyük

(Turkey); Abu Duwari and Abu Salabikh (southern Iraq); and near Daulatabad (Prickett 1986) and Siraf (Wilkinson 1974) (Iran). Although these scatters appear to coincide with phases of increased population, they could also result from the introduction of the use of household waste fertilizer as a culture-specific practice alone. In areas with a demonstrated settlement decline in these late periods (for example, the North Jazira Project or the Tell Beydar survey areas), the scatters are absent, whereas they can be recognized for the third millennium. This, albeit negative, evidence suggests there might indeed be a relationship between population levels and land use intensity, but clearly much more empirical data is needed to test this. From the above evidence it can therefore be argued that land use intensification, perhaps resulting from increased population pressure, has occurred occasionally in association with third-millennium BCE urbanization but is more likely a late feature associated with the development of dense rural settlement systems from the late first millennium BCE.

Whether a similar increase in population led to the development of the large scale canal systems is less clear. For example, in the Balikh and Khabur valleys, it appears that the construction of canals at a regional scale coincides with the development of large territorial empires such as those of the Neo-Assyrians and Seleucids. By enlarging the basic administrative unit empires made it possible for region-wide canal systems to be built, a situation that would have been difficult when land was administered by small-scale polities engaging in local territorial disputes. Perhaps more fundamental, however, were the high levels of investment that were being made by the later empires in major canal and irrigation systems that ultimately resulted in massive increases in regional populations in key areas (Adams 1965; Wenke 1987).

When field scatters are employed as indicators of manuring they often can be seen to coincide with a population peak, but such correlations still require further investigation. On the other hand, large-scale irrigation as an indicator of intensification can often more readily be shown to be related to major imperial investments as well as changes in land availability as a result of the development of territorial empires; it appears to be much more difficult to demonstrate that population pressure initiated canal construction.

POPULATION RESERVOIRS AND THE QUESTION OF NOMADS
Because Near Eastern archaeological surveys have mainly concentrated on plains dominated by the remains of sedentary settlements, the more mobile elements of the population continue to be underestimated. Consequently, despite the large number of enthusiastic references to the importance of the nomadic element, they continue to be

underrecognized in the survey record (Alden 1979; Alizadeh 1992; Cribb 1991; Hole 1991; Wright 1987; Zagarell 1982). Although considerable advances have been made in recent years in locating nomadic settlements, it is still extremely difficult to recognize, estimate, and date these with any precision (Alden 1979; Sumner 1990a:Fig. 4 dashed line) (see also chapter 7). Thus most statistics on survey continue to refer to what is primarily the sedentary component of the population that lived in communities ranging in size between farmstead/hamlets and larger urban scale settlements.

Adams (1981) has likened the nomadic and sedentary spheres of Mesopotamia to "reservoirs," and it is possible to extend this analogy further by viewing populations in the ancient Near East as belonging to a series of linked population reservoirs that comprised urban, rural, and nomadic communities, each characterized by different demographic growth rates. Both rural and nomadic population reservoirs may have been necessary at different times to supply the growing urban centers. One can therefore envision that population in the ancient Near East must have been constantly in flux, with urban centers growing as a result of population movements from rural areas and pastoral communities, as well as other urban centers, but in varying degrees. Similarly, urban decline would result in the growth of either the rural sector, as along the Turkish Euphrates at the end of the third millennium BCE (Wilkinson 1990), or of nomadic communities. Furthermore, a nomadic or transhumant population "reservoir" probably formed a potential pathway that allowed regions to be interlinked so that growth in one area was matched by decline elsewhere. During times of agricultural stress, the nomadic population could absorb spare population from the sedentary reservoirs, and then ultimately, when conditions were again suitable for sedentary settlement, some of the mobile population would be contributed to the sedentary sphere. Such concepts of demographic fluidity have been discussed before (for example, Adams 1981; Marfoe 1979), but as a result of archaeological surveys conducted over the past twenty years the evidence for such patterns is becoming clearer (see chapter 6).

CONCLUSIONS
From a current perspective, the 1960s and 1970s appear to have been a golden age of survey in Iran and southern Mesopotamia. Since that time some advances have been made, although undoubtedly some wheels have been reinvented. Furthermore, demographic curves are still with us. It is clear that they must be used with due caution, and moreover, despite the progress that has been made in the use of algorithms to adjust for site growth and extinc-

tion as well as differences in the length of particular ceramic phases, these adjustments cannot be applied to all parts of the long-term demographic curves. Despite these caveats, demographic curves make useful statements about broad trends in population, and they also should enable us to compare the record of human settlement with the emerging high-resolution environmental proxy records.

A good case also can be made for the use of more qualitative records; these can be at least as useful, and are potentially less misleading than the demographic curves. For example, the plotting of structural changes in the record, such as tells versus low rural settlements, can be especially valuable in providing a clear impression of changing settlement which, in turn, can be related to shifts in the political economy.

From the survey record, both quantitative and qualitative, we are therefore getting an impression that "spatial dynamics in settlement and population are manifest" (Johnson 1987:291). To this I would add that settlement in Upper Mesopotamia has been subject to considerable transitions that result in a very patchy record with rises and falls occurring asynchronously in different areas. These fluctuations and shifts, although difficult to sort out, must be understood if we want to be able to understand the development and trajectory of complex societies.

Acknowledgment. This chapter is dedicated to Bill Sumner, who deserves many thanks for providing sustained encouragement for my research while he was Director of the Oriental Institute. In addition I must thank Naomi F. Miller and Kamyar Abdi for their help in tidying up this chapter, and their patience during the editorial process.

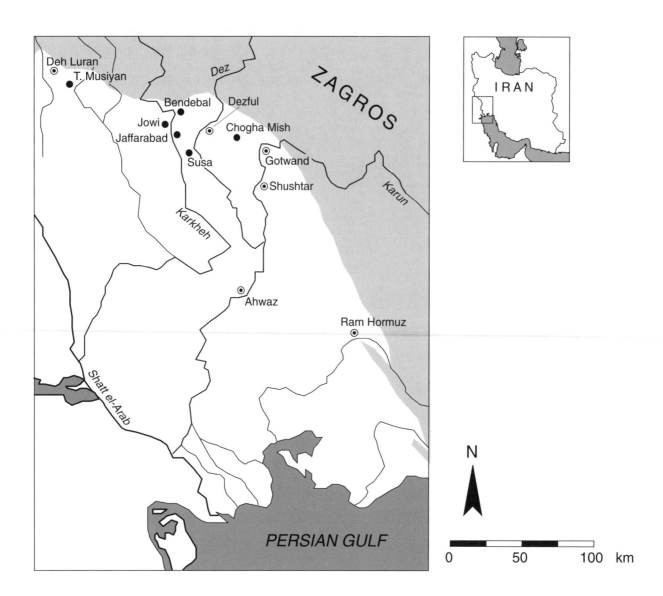

Deh Luran
⊙
● T. Musiyan

Dez

ZAGROS

Bendebal   Dezful
Jowi ●   ⊙ Chogha Mish
Jaffarabad ●
● Susa   ⊙ Gotwand
Karkheh   ⊙ Shushtar

Karun

⊙ Ahwaz

Ram Hormuz
⊙

Shatt el-Arab

PERSIAN GULF

IRAN

N

0   50   100   km

5.1 Khuzestan, Iran. *Prepared at MASCA*

CHAPTER 5

CHANGING ESTIMATES OF SUSIANA'S PREHISTORIC SETTLEMENT

NICHOLAS KOUCHOUKOS AND FRANK HOLE

I T IS FITTING to honor Bill Sumner with a short article on a topic close to his interests: the analysis and interpretation of archaeological survey data (Sumner 1979). Along with others (Schacht 1981; Weiss 1977), Bill worked toward developing a rational approach to understanding the spatial and temporal dynamics of prehistoric populations. As he well knows, there are three inescapable problems faced by all archaeologists studying ancient landscapes. The first is a matter of chronology. How many and which of the sites dated to a given archaeological period were occupied at once? The second concerns survey methodology and taphonomy. What proportion of these sites has been discovered? What proportion has been destroyed by geomorphic process or land use change? And the third problem is demographic. What is the relationship—if indeed there is one—between the area of a site and the number of its inhabitants? In this short contribution, we review progress toward solving these problems in the context of a short history of archaeological survey of the Susiana plain in southwest Iran.

Research by western archaeologists in Iran ceased at the time of the 1979 revolution and has not resumed since—a hiatus of more than twenty years. One might expect, therefore, that there is nothing new to report, that summaries such as are contained in *The Archaeology of Western Iran* would remain current. This is only partly true, for while fieldwork has ceased, the data recovered by previous work in the form of pottery, lithics, maps and measurements are still rich sources for investigation. More

important, however, new approaches and analytical tools have emerged that allow us to revisit old data and wring from them new insights.

The interval of Susiana's prehistory we are concerned with here is known generally as the Village period (Hole 1987b). This period began at approximately 7000 BCE with the appearance of the first clearly sedentary villages throughout southwest Iran and continued until roughly 4000 BCE, when village populations began to coalesce into larger and larger settlements. The accumulated evidence from excavation shows that the Village period was a time of great change in social organization throughout the region (Alizadeh 1992; Hole 1987a; Kouchoukos 1998:59–72; Pollock 1983; Wright 1984). Among the most significant developments were: the emergence of central places such as Susa and Chogha Mish, distinguished from other settlements by their size, monumental architecture, and well-furnished burials; the refinement and elaboration of pottery, metalworking, and the glyptic arts; the development of irrigated agriculture and the intensification of sheep and goat herding; and the intensification of interaction and exchange between the societies of the Susiana plain and those of the Zagros highlands to the east. These changes are widely believed to represent the growing centralization and stratification of economic and political power within Susiana society, though there has been some debate about the ways in which this power was organized and the contexts in which it was exercised (see Hole 1983; Pollock and Wright 1987). Much of our understanding of these changes depends on knowledge of population dynamics and spatial relationships, factors that can only be determined through regional survey.

ARCHAEOLOGICAL SURVEYS
OF THE SUSIANA PLAIN

Occupying much of the oil rich province of Khuzestan, the Susiana plain is home to the major cities of Dezful, Ahwaz and Shushtar (figure 5.1). Unlike most of Iran, this plain, lying between the foothills of the Zagros mountains and the lower Tigris-Euphrates valley, ranges in elevation from less than 200 m at the base of the mountains to 20 m at Ahwaz. Today the northern part of the plain receives rainfall barely adequate for the subsistence cultivation of winter crops, and summer crops are supported by irrigation from surface water and shallow wells. Although heavily cultivated today—largely with supplementary irrigation—in recent history there were few settlements outside the cities, and the plain was seasonal home to Luri and Bakhtiari pastoralists. This was the landscape seen by Rawlinson (1839) who visited Susa (biblical Shushan) and the tomb of Daniel, and W.K. Loftus (1857), who excavated there between 1850 and 1853. In 1884 the French engineer-historian, Marcel-Auguste Dieulafoy resumed excavations at Susa, establishing a French presence at the site that lasted until the Iranian revolution in 1979 (Dieulafoy 1893). It is to the subsequent Mission Scientifique en Perse led by the French mining engineer and archaeologist Jacques de Morgan that we owe the first rigorous historical and geographic reconnaissance of the Susiana plain and of the neighboring plain of Deh Luran (Morgan 1900a; Gautier and Lampre 1905). It was de Morgan's successor, Roland de Mecquenem, who first recorded the locations of prehistoric sites on the Susiana plain and carried out small-scale excavations at them (Mecquenem 1943). The ceramics recovered from these small soundings formed the basis for Louis LeBreton's (1947) chronology of the prehistoric period, which he divided into five phases lettered Susiana a to Susiana e (the latter period also called Susa A). Collectively, these works established the sequence of prehistoric cultures as reflected in painted pottery but made no attempt to describe changes in settlement, population or land use.

Such issues were first addressed explicitly by Robert McC. Adams who carried out a survey on the Susiana plain in advance of major agricultural development that threatened to destroy sites. With LeBreton's chronology in hand, Adams attempted to assign periods of occupation at each site and to estimate its size. His reconnaissance and subsequent analysis made use of tools previously unavailable to

archaeologists: topographic maps, aerial photographs and detailed studies of soils and geomorphology. Following one intense season of exploration in 1960–1961, Adams produced a short paper that outlined the entire settlement history of the plain in relation to the local environment, social and political changes, and agricultural innovation—raising questions that guided much subsequent research in the region (Adams 1962).

To refine Adams's assessment of settlement changes, Frank Hole revisited all of the sites of the Village period that had been identified by Adams and surveyed several unrecorded sites. Over the next ten years additional surveys were carried out by Henry Wright (1969), Elizabeth Carter (1971), Gregory Johnson (1973), Robert Wenke (1975–76), Robert Schacht (1976), John Alden (1987), Hassan Tala'i (1978) and Pierre de Miroschedji (1981c). During the 1950s and 1960s, Dr. F. G. L. Gremliza, a German medical doctor, collected painted sherds from sites in Khuzestan, a collection that has been studied and published by Abbas Alizadeh (1992; see table 5.1).

Although each of these surveys was oriented toward a particular time period or geographic region of the Susiana plain and was conducted separately by many different individuals, well over one thousand sites dating from the early Village period to the classical Islamic period have been recorded. The resulting data set is unparalleled in the Near East for its comprehensive coverage of a large coherent agricultural plain and has been augmented by smaller scale surveys to the north and east. Though there are problems raised by the range of methods used by different teams pursuing different goals, the surveys have resulted in many useful advances in our knowledge. It is fortunate that most of the ceramics recovered from the prehistoric sites exist in collections in the United States, providing an opportunity to carry out technical analyses and reassessments of earlier conclusions in light of new information.

APPROACHES TO THE ANALYSIS
OF SURVEY DATA

The first attempt to infer the population dynamics of the Village period from analysis of archaeological survey data was by Henry Wright and Gregory Johnson (Wright and Johnson 1975; Wright et al. 1975). They argued that the later Village period, when social changes appear to have been most rapid, was a time of precipitous population decline and concluded that population pressure could be ruled out as a driving force of political and economic centralization. Instead, they suggested that centralization may have been a response to population growth in the adjacent Zagros highlands and to a consequent increase in interregional

Table 5.1 Surveys of the Susiana plain

Surveyor	Date of survey	Area of interest	Periods of interest	#of sites	Collections
R. McC. Adams (1962) F.G.L. Gremliza	1960–1961	Susiana	all	about 275	None
(Alizadeh 1992)	1959–1966	Susiana	prehistoric	43	Oriental Institute, U of Chicago
E. Carter (1971)	1968–1969	Susiana	Elamite	n/a	Susa
F. Hole (1969, 1985)	1969	Susiana	prehistoric	99	Peabody Museum, Yale
H.T. Wright (1969)	1969	Gotwand	all	30	Susa
G.A. Johnson (1973)	1970–1971	Susiana	Uruk	65	Museum of Anthro., U of Michigan
R. Wenke (1975–76)	1973–1974	Susiana	all	about 1000	Iranian Centre for Arch. Research
J.R. Alden (1987)	1977	Susiana	Proto-Elamite	29	unknown
R. Schacht (1976)	1974	Mianab	all	47	Museum of Anthro., U of Michigan
H. Tala'i (1978)	1978	Dimceh	all	42	unknown

Table 5.2 Radiocarbon chronology

Regional period	Local period	Site(s)	^{14}C dates	Interval (years BCE)	Length (years)
Terminal Susa A	Susa A1	Susa, Jaffarabad	2	4000–3900	100
Late Susiana 2 (Susa A)	Susa A2	Susa, Jaffarabad	9	4200–4000	200
Late Susiana 1 (Susiana d)	Farukh	Farukhabad	1	4700–4200	500
Middle Susiana 3 (Susiana c)	Bayat	Tepe Sabz	6	5100–4700	400
Middle Susiana 2 (Susiana b)	Mehmeh	Tepe Sabz	1	5500–5100	400
Middle Susiana 1 (Susiana b)	Khazineh	Tepe Sabz	1	5700–5500	200
Early Susiana (Susiana a)	Sabz	Tepe Sabz	1	6000–5700	300

Table 5.3 Tabulation of sites by geomorphic unit

Geomorphic unit	Area (km²)	% of plain	# of sites	% of total sites	sites/km²
Old alluvium	1287	33	175	67	0.136
Younger alluvium	385	10	21	8	0.055
Young alluvium	481	12	10	4	0.021
Flood plain	404	10	4	2	0.001
Anticlinal ridge	390	10	3	1	0.001
Colluvial soils	600	15	32	12	0.053

conflict and violence, attested perhaps by destruction levels at sites such as Susa and Chogha Mish. This ran counter to some interpretations that saw population increase as a prime mover in the evolution of social complexity (Smith and Young 1983; Weiss 1977).

In a rebuttal to Wright and Johnson, Harvey Weiss (1977) calibrated radiocarbon measurements from sites on the Susiana and Deh Luran plains to support an argument that the later Village period lasted much longer than previously supposed. He thus found it very unlikely that all of the sites assigned to this period by Wright and Johnson were occupied at once and worried that populations were being overestimated. Attempting to correct this bias, Weiss divided the total settled area recorded for each of the subperiods making up the Village period and the Uruk by his reckoning of the period's length to arrive at a standardized estimate of settlement intensity (hectares/year) during successive periods. From this exercise, he concluded not only

that later Village period populations were significantly smaller than those estimated by Wright and Johnson but also that they increased steadily throughout this period and into the subsequent Early Uruk period. On this basis, Weiss reintroduced population pressure as a causal factor in the social changes of the later Village period, hypothesizing that this growth resulted from the emergence of a dependent labor class.

More recent analysis of the still very thin radiocarbon evidence from the Susiana and Deh Luran plains using updated calibration curves and statistical methods has confirmed many of Weiss's observations about period lengths (Kouchoukos 1998:72–78). This evidence, together with published evidence from stratigraphic excavations at Susa (Perrot 1978), Chogha Mish (Delougaz and Kantor 1996), and the smaller sites of Jaffarabad, Bendebal, and Jowi (Dollfus 1971, 1983a) has provided the basis for an integrated archaeological chronology of the Village period.

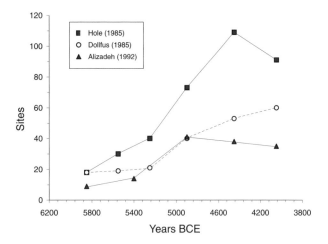

5.2 Graph of different periodizations. *N. Kouchoukos*

Though separate projects have tended to develop their own chronological nomenclature, attempts to relate and reconcile these different schemes are largely in agreement (Hole 1985, Dolfus 1985, Alizadeh 1992). Based on these sources, table 5.2 presents a synthetic chronology of the Village period.

Though archaeologists have worked productively toward the integration of different archaeological periodizations, there has been little consensus on the criteria used to assign surveyed sites to these periods. The magnitude of this problem and its implications for the interpretation of the survey data are clear from examining the results of four different attempts to assign periods to sites based on their pottery collections. Studies by Geneviève Dollfus (1985) and Frank Hole (1985) focused on large collections of Susiana material at Yale University and the University of Michigan, while Abbas Alizadeh (1992) looked exclusively at the Gremliza collection at the Oriental Institute. When the results of these studies, each of which used a different chronological scheme, are mapped onto the unified chronology presented above, it is clear that differences between them are large and not easily reconciled (figure 5.2). In Hole's analysis (based on both raw and normalized counts of sites by period), populations rise steadily throughout the Village period, culminating in the Middle Village period (=Susiana d) and declining slightly in the following Susa A and Terminal Susa A periods (Hole 1985:Fig. 1; Hole 1987a:Table 10). Dollfus's analysis is similar, although it differs slightly in the timing of maximum population. Dollfus and Hole divided time somewhat differently and Hole's normalization took into account the estimated lengths of the ceramically defined periods. Alizadeh's analysis of the smaller Gremliza collection, to which neither Hole nor Dollfus had access, presents yet another assessment of the changing number of occupied sites, which reached a

maximum in the Susiana c (=Middle Susiana 3) period. In an attempt to resolve these contradictions, Kouchoukos (1998:86–89) conducted a systematic restudy of the entire corpus of Susiana material in the United States and Europe using statistical methods to seriate surface collections of pottery. The results of this analysis closely resembled Alizadeh's but are based on nearly three times as many sites. Thus it appears from raw site counts that prehistoric populations on the Susiana plain reached a maximum during the Susiana c period and either declined slightly or remained more or less stable throughout the remainder of the Village period.

All of these assessments of settlement dynamics used as a working assumption that surveys could locate most of the sites that once had existed or, that sites discovered on survey constituted a representative sample of what had existed. Nevertheless, as geomorphological studies have shown, the plain surface is dynamic and has been subject to prolonged cycles of deposition and erosion (Kirkby 1977). Rivers and streams have migrated in their channels, and there has been extensive modification of the land through agriculture and canalization over the millennia (Hansman 1967). With growing knowledge of these processes, our assumptions have become increasingly untenable.

Kirkby's geomorphological study of the Deh Luran and Susiana plains characterized their modern state and inferred changing conditions for settlement in the past. Most relevant to our understanding of settlement history is that during the Village period the plain was aggrading through a series of braided distributaries rather than through the incised channels now present. According to his analysis, it "appears likely that braided patterns once covered the whole of the Deh Luran and Khuzestan plains, depositing 5 m or more of sediment since the last glaciation" (Kirkby 1977:281). Under such a regime the sediments deposited on the upper stretches of the plain would have been coarser than those deposited lower or in depressions. Given low precipitation, the latter situations would have been favored for agriculture because of their higher water retention. Such a sedimentary regime would, however, have been favorable to small-scale agriculture supported by flood water.

Some estimate of the number of sites that have been destroyed by geomorphic process, however, can be inferred from an analysis of maps produced prior to the expansion of irrigation works in the 1950s and 1960s (Veenenbos 1958). These maps classify different regions of the Susiana plain into one of six major geomorphic units: 1) anticlinal ridges, 2) colluvial soils, 3) old alluvial terraces, 4) younger alluvial terraces, 5) young alluvial

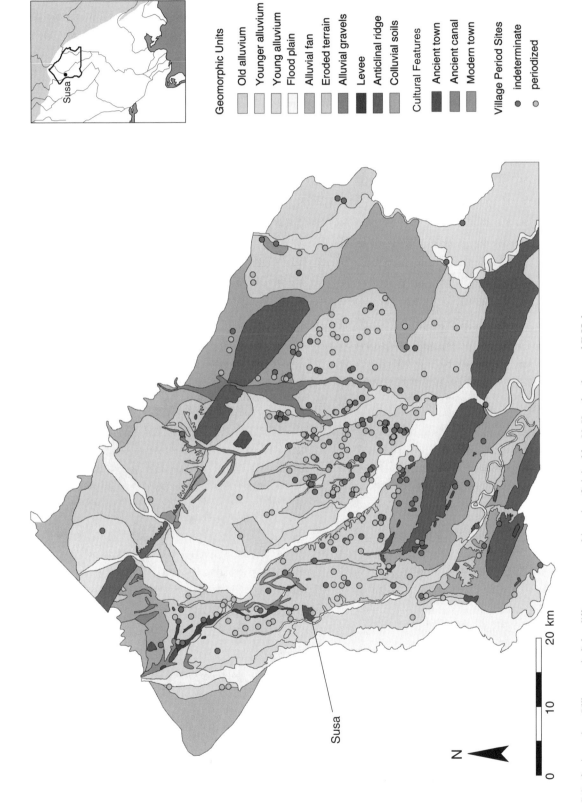

Geomorphic Units

Old alluvium
Younger alluvium
Young alluvium
Flood plain
Alluvial fan
Eroded terrain
Alluvial gravels
Levee
Anticlinal ridge
Colluvial soils

Cultural Features

Ancient town
Ancient canal
Modern town

Village Period Sites

● indeterminate
○ periodized

Susa

N

0   10   20 km

5.3 Susiana sites (Village period) by different geomorphic units. *Original by N. Kouchoukos and F. Hole*

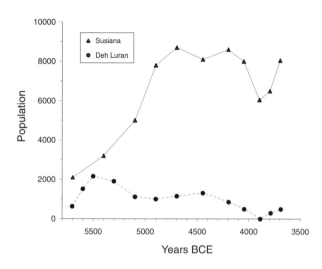

5.4 Graph of population curves and rates of population growth. *N. Kouchoukos*

terraces, and 6) active flood plains. From a tabulation of the distribution of Village period sites across these units, it is clear that nearly 70% of all known Village period sites are located on the "old alluvium," which accounts for less than one-third of the total area of the plain (table 5.3, figure 5.3). These areas, along with the colluvial soils and anticlinal ridges have been less affected by alluvial process and hence preserve a greater number of Village period sites. Sites located on the younger alluvium, young alluvium, and flood plains, on the other hand, have narrowly escaped erosion or deep burial and hence represent only a small fraction of the original number of sites in these areas. It is possible, therefore to arrive at a crude estimate of the original number of Village period sites on the plain by multiplying the total area of later alluvial landforms (1270 km²) by the density of sites recorded on the old alluvium (0.136 sites/km²). The resulting figure of 173 sites, minus the 35 sites preserved on the later alluvium, may be added to the 210 sites on the old terraces, colluvial soils, and anticlinal ridges to arrive at a total of 348 sites, or roughly 30% more sites than the 264 recorded by survey. This figure is still, however, an underestimate, as the density of sites on the old alluvium is suppressed by large areas in the Vale of Andimeshk, the Gotwand plain, and the Mianab plain that have been only partially surveyed. At the same time, intensive irrigation since the Village period has covered much of the old alluvium with thick silt deposits that mask much early settlement in these comparatively undisturbed areas.

ESTIMATES OF POPULATION

Once issues of chronology and taphonomy have been addressed explicitly, it is possible to turn to conceptually and methodologically more complex questions concerning the number of sites that were occupied at any one time and the number of individuals who lived at these sites. An ingenious solution to this problem has been developed recently by Robert Dewar (1991, 1994b) and applied to the analysis of data from James Neely and Henry Wright's survey of the Deh Luran plain. Dewar's method involves dividing the number of sites founded or abandoned during a given period by that period's length in years to obtain rates of occupation and abandonment. A simple simulation model can then be constructed that begins with the number of sites occupied at the beginning of the period (estimated from the number of sites occupied in both the preceding period and the period in question) and steps yearly through the length of the period, using the probabilities given by these rates to determine whether a site is founded or abandoned in each year. At the end of the period, the number of settlements occupied in each year is averaged and a standard deviation taken to estimate the mean number of sites occupied at once. The simulation can be repeated many times to arrive at a grand mean.

When applied to the Susiana survey sites that can be dated reliably from surface collections (n=139), Dewar's technique yields interesting results (figure 5.4). In the Susiana b period, roughly twenty-eight settlements were occupied at any one time, but by the Susiana c period, this number had more than doubled to sixty sites. This growth continued into the Susiana d period when the number of contemporary settlements peaked at seventy-seven. This was followed by a slight decline in the Susa A period to fifty-eight sites, and this decline continues into the Early Uruk period. This reconstruction thus contradicts the common assumption that the Susiana d period was the time of maximum population growth during the Village period and confirms Wright and Johnson's hypothesis of a population decline between the Susa A and early Uruk periods (see chapter 6).

Though Dewar's technique estimates how many sites were occupied at once, it does not tell us which ones. This limitation, combined with the fact that we are only treating 139 of at least 348 prehistoric sites on the Susiana plain makes it difficult indeed to arrive at reliable estimates of the population of the plain during any given period—even if we were able to arrive at a robust figure for the average number of people per settled hectare (see Wenke 1975–76). Thus any population curve we were to construct would be off by a factor of at least two and perhaps five. But what is important to realize is that Dewar's technique provides a firm basis from which to calculate *rates* of population change. These are arguably more informative than raw counts based on a palimpsest of sites.

CONCLUSIONS AND PROSPECTS

This short resumé of the history of settlement analysis on the Susiana plain illustrates the importance of collecting and curating both sherds and the records of their discovery in the certainty that new approaches and techniques will allow them to speak more clearly in the future. Because these collections are in accessible locations, it is possible for scholars to continue to mine their data. These archives are literally irreplaceable inasmuch as many of the sites have been destroyed by industrial agricultural developments and new settlements. At the same time it should also be acknowledged that *because* the sites have been collected, one could never recover exactly the same range of material. Indeed, Bernbeck (1995) has argued that it is unconscionable to remove sherds. In an ideal world where we had free access to sites this might be true, but we know all too often that most visible sites will eventually fall victim either to the forces of nature or to the depredations of humans seeking to improve their landscapes.

The collections of Susiana sherds will continue to inform us, particularly through technical analyses. Neutron activation analysis (NAA) has been carried out on a sample of Susiana material (Berman 1994) and such work could be extended to different data sets. NAA, along with petrographic and electron microprobe analyses, can be used to investigate sources, manufacturing techniques, and compositions of pigments as well as trade or exchange. Chemical analyses might also identify residues revealing the contents of pots and thereby patterns of local production, consumption, and ex-

change. Finally, there still remains one of the most accessible, yet neglected avenues, stylistic analysis. Detailed, meticulous studies of the type common in art history are waiting to be done, and the study of formal attributes of composition and design could be more widely applied (Hole 1984). Such analyses as these may inform on issues of site contemporaneity, local exchange patterns (Johnson 1973), and changing methods of production and use.

Our understanding of the setting of the archaeological sites is still in its infancy, but the work of geomorphologists (Kirkby 1977), coupled with historic accounts (Hansman 1967) and the interpretation of current satellite imagery, provide hints of what might be learned. An accurate understanding of the plain's history will require coring and dating of sedimentary episodes, tasks beyond those traditionally carried out in archaeology but of potentially great significance. The fact is we have only a couple of small windows into the early plain surface where it has been exposed during archaeological excavation. Potentially much more data lie in well logs and contractors' studies in preparation for the digging of canals. Satellite imagery, including the recently released Corona intelligence photographs, provide broad geographic overviews of the plain and relatively high resolution views of particular locales that make clear the differences in land quality and its concomitant uses. Such studies have the potential to greatly enrich our understanding of the early settlement of Susiana.

Despite two decades of archaeological inactivity on the Susiana plain, we continue to gain new insights into its prehistory by making use of old collections and new methods. For the future of archaeology in this region there is both a firm foundation and an agenda. We are delighted to be able to present such an affirmation on the occasion of Bill Sumner's retirement, recognizing that the future builds importantly on the foundations that he himself laid.

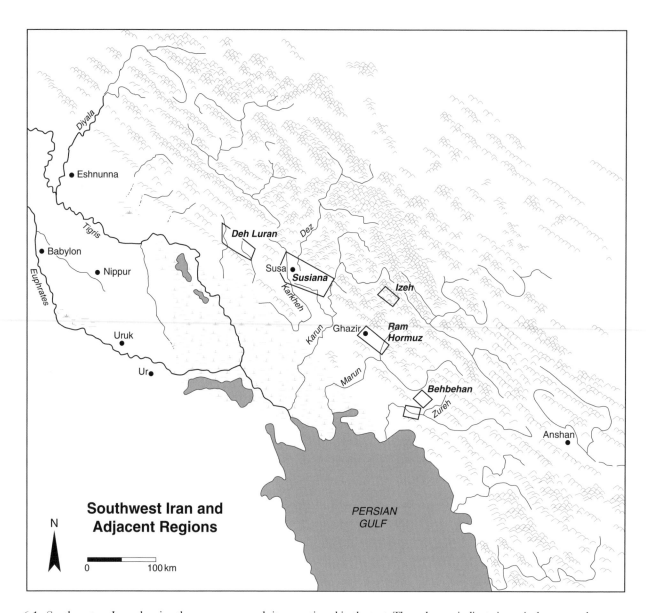

6.1 Southwestern Iran, showing the survey area and sites mentioned in the text. The polygons indicate intensively surveyed areas.
Illustration by K. Clahassey

CHAPTER 6

ARCHAEOLOGICAL SURVEY ON THE WESTERN RAM HORMUZ PLAIN

1969

HENRY T. WRIGHT AND ELIZABETH CARTER

ARCHAEOLOGICAL SURVEY has had a long history in Iran. Though many have thought of it as a technique simply to find sites worthy of excavation, it is has been developed into a precise tool for the study of ancient land use and settlement organization. Even some of the earliest efforts—from those of Jacques de Morgan (1894) in the Talesh region west of the Caspian to those of Aurel Stein (1940) throughout the Zagros—had broader geographical purposes. Erich Schmidt (1940) first demonstrated the value of air photography, and Robert McC. Adams (1962) made the use of air photographs an integral part of his problem-oriented surveys in central Khuzestan. In his surveys of the Marvdasht and adjacent areas, William Sumner has shown us the mature and judicious use of this approach (1972, 1986b, 1988b, 1990b), and it is appropriate that this report on a survey of one of the valleys linking his own research area in central Fars and the plains of central Khuzestan be dedicated to him.

The initial purpose of the 1969 survey program in Khuzestan was to elucidate ancient settlement on the peripheries of the well-known area around Susa. At about the same time William Sumner discovered the site of ancient Anshan (modern Malyan), the historically attested highland capital of the Elamite state in northwestern Fars (Sumner 1974). One of the most characteristic features of the ancient Elamite state in the third and second millennia BCE was the political union between Susa and Anshan. Thus, once Anshan's location was known, the data from the Ram Hormuz survey took on increased historic importance. It was now possible to investigate the patterns of highland-lowland interaction over the *longue durée* in an intermediate zone between the two ancient Elamite capitals, Susa and Anshan (see chapter 3).

The Ram Hormuz plain is on the most accessible line of communication linking lowland Khuzestan and the highlands of central Fars (figure 6.1). It lies at the edge of the lowlands,160 km southeast of Susa and 310 km northwest of Anshan. The location of the plain suggested that the population might well have grown as a result of increased exchange between lowland Susiana and highland Fars. The Ram Hormuz plain and the Behbehan and Zuhreh plains to the southeast of Susiana are the easternmost extensive areas of cultivable land in lowland Khuzestan. It therefore also seemed likely that these plains became more prosperous when the nearby central Susiana plain required an "overflow" for excess population, regardless of whether or not exchange activity intensified. It is also possible that neither or both of these propositions will be supported by the evidence. In the end, a more complex pattern emerged than we had originally predicted.

The specific period of interest was the fourth and third millennia BCE, the time of the first development of urban economies and state polities. Central Khuzestan between the Karun and Karkheh rivers had been surveyed by Robert McC. Adams of the University of Chicago (Adams 1962). It had been reexamined by the Mission Archéologique Française under the direction of Jean Perrot and by Frank Hole, then of Rice University. Further surveys by Gregory Johnson (1973, 1987), and by Robert Wenke (1975–76) were already being planned. Therefore, further landscape coverage was not necessary and examination of notes and collections at Chicago and Susa supplemented our own much smaller surveys. Similarly, the Deh Luran area to the northwest of the central Susiana plain was surveyed by Frank Hole and Kent Flannery in 1961 and was intensively resurveyed by James Neely in 1969 (Neely and Wright 1994). Once again further fieldwork was not necessary; comparative information on this area peripheral to central Khuzestan was available in notes and collections at Deh Luran.

The 1969 surveys were therefore concentrated in two other peripheral areas not previously surveyed. One was the Ram Hormuz plain. The other was the east bank of the Karun river near Gotwand and Shushtar (see chapter 5). The Ram Hormuz survey (see figure 6.1), which produced much evidence of settlement development during the past seven millennia, is the focus of this report. The report is based entirely on notes made in 1969 and on published reports, without access to the sites, to better maps, or to the ceramic collections.

The Ram Hormuz plain is centered on a large and still active alluvial fan in the first major synclinal valley at the foot of the Zagros mountains. The river, termed the "'Ala river" on most maps, the "Ramuz river" on others, drains the front ranges of the mountains and carries a heavy load of boulders of Mesozoic limestones and Tertiary sandstones and gypsums. While the river may at one time have flowed westward—and in recent times canals have certainly carried its waters in that direction—the present course runs southward and joins the Marun or Agha Jarri river flowing from the east.

A traveler can easily move northwestward toward the Susiana plain or eastward toward Behbehan. From this point it was easy to reach the Persian Gulf, and, although Ram Hormuz is near the midpoint of the route between Fars and Susiana, it was not much farther from southern Mesopotamia than Susa. The Ram Hormuz plain also has easy access to the mountains and the town is a traditional trading and administrative center for the Bakhtiari tribe (Layard 1894 [1971]:92–313; Zagarell 1982:97–125).

The water of the 'Ala is relatively fresh. In 1969 the fields around the town of Ram Hormuz sustained such annual crops as wheat, barley, clover, alfalfa, and lentils as well as perennial orchard crops such as dates, citrus, and pomegranates.

The Ram Hormuz plain was surveyed once before, between 1947 and 1948, by Donald McCown of the Oriental Institute of the University of Chicago, prior to his excavations at Tal-i Ghazir. His notes and a rough sketch map of site locations were available to us, and we have integrated them where possible in the following survey report. We

also had access to J.R. Caldwell's brief report on the early periods at Tal-i Ghazir (1968a), and Carter (1994a) was able to restudy the later material from this important site.

The plain was crisscrossed by jeep, and all sites noted were recorded, regardless of period. Pace and compass maps were made and sherds were collected when possible. In the following pages all this information is presented in condensed form. The ceramics later than the seventh century BCE were examined in the field by John Hansman, and his datings are presented in the site catalogue. Most of the collections were left at the Muzeh-ye Shush for future examination by others interested in the area. A type collection of fourth millennium sherds was prepared for the Muzeh-ye Iran-e Bastan in Tehran.

Our thanks are due to all the people mentioned above, to the Archaeological Service of Iran, the late Alan Craig of the Development and Resources Corporation, and the many people of the Ram Hormuz area, without whose assistance the project would never have been completed.

GEOGRAPHICAL NOTES
ON THE RAM HORMUZ PLAIN

All the area of the Ram Hormuz plain west of the 'Ala river was examined in detail. Survey was begun on the east bank, but it was not possible to complete this work because of flooding of the river. Several efforts to return to Ram Hormuz during the 1970s and finish the survey met with failure because of floods, vehicle breakdown and other problems. The intensive survey on the west side of the river was facilitated by the availability of excellent soil and land-use maps prepared by the Food and Agriculture Organization of the United Nations for the Khuzestan Water and Power Authority.

Our survey area covered about 400 km^2 (see figure 6.2). More than forty sites of various periods were examined within the intensively investigated area. We believe we located most of the mounded sites greater than one hectare. Some small farmhouse sites of the Parthian or Sasanian periods were not examined, and one mound about 2 km north of RH-22 could not be reached. The areas covered by the McCown's survey and ours are as follows:

- Our survey area overlapped with that of McCown to the east, north, and south of Ram Hormuz, and along the northwest edge of the plain on the road to Tal-i Ghazir. With the exception of three small sites apparently destroyed by the growth of the modern town of Ram Hormuz, we believe we have located all of the sites recorded in McCown's notes. We have included his site numbers and other useful information in the "Comments" on sixteen

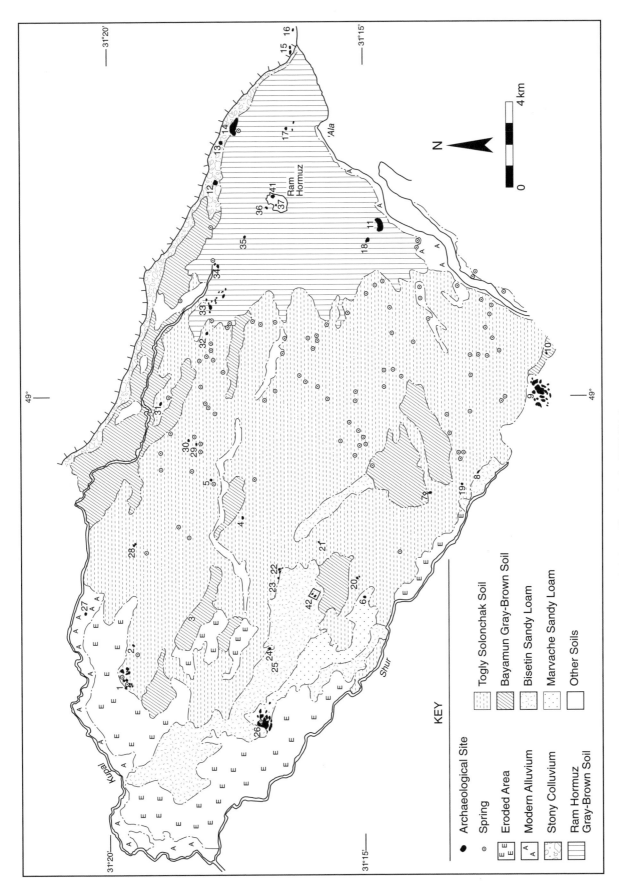

6.2 The western Ram Hormuz plain—soil types and all recorded sites. *Illustration by H.T. Wright*

KEY

Archaeological Site

Spring

	Eroded Area
	Modern Alluvium
	Stony Colluvium
	Ram Hormuz Gray-Brown Soil
	Togly Solonchak Soil
	Bayamun Gray-Brown Soil
	Bisetin Sandy Loam
	Marvache Sandy Loam
	Other Soils

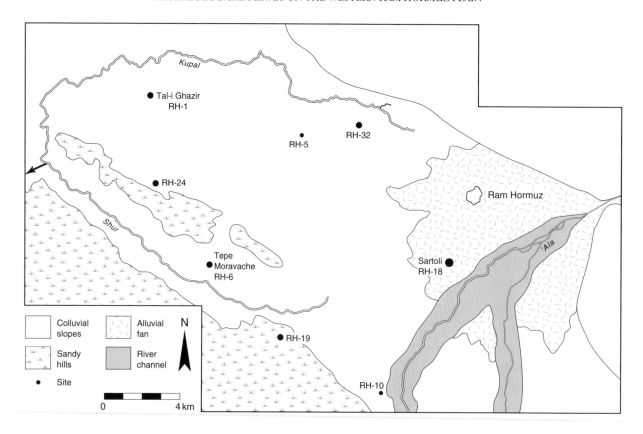

6.3 Sites of the Late Susiana phase on the western Ram Hormuz plain. *Illustration by K. Clahassey*

sites in the site catalogue, in the hope that his sherd collections still exist and can some day be restudied.

▸ We did not examine the area on the extreme northwestern corner of the plain, north and west of Tal-i Ghazir, surveyed by McCown, and we do not include his information on seven undated sites there.

▸ We were able to ford the flooded 'Ala river on our last day of survey, and visit three sites on horseback (sites 38–40, not shown on figure 6.2). Many others were visible, and it is clear that further survey is warranted east of the 'Ala and along the right bank of the Marun toward Behbehan.

There are five different kinds of land within the survey area, indicated on the maps of ancient settlement patterns (figure 6.3; also 6.6 and 6.8):

1. The Colluvial Slopes covered in places with thin, gravelly colluvial soils. This is primarily an area for grazing sheep and goats and a source of stones, particularly gypsum for plaster and alabaster for vessels.

2. The Alluvial Fan of the 'Ala, an area of well-drained silts and clays resting on gravels, termed the Ram Hormuz

soil series (figure 6.2; Subramanian and Van Osten 1959). These areas can be easily irrigated with small canals from the 'Ala river.

3. The Saline Plain, an area of varied but often salt-encrusted soil that can be irrigated with the waters of the many small springs in this area or of longer canals from the 'Ala. On figure 6.2, it is the area covered by Togly solonchak soils. The source for the springs is probably the 'Ala and surface runoff during the season of intermittent rains between November and April. Each is surrounded by marshes. Their waters collect in the saline Kupal river along the north edge of the plain and Shur river, along the southwest edge of the plain, which join near the west extremity of the plain and flow southward. The leached phase of this Togly solonchak soil and the Bayamun gray-brown leached clayey soils (figure 6.2; Subramanian and Van Osten 1959) are both adequate for dry farming grain.

4. River Channel along the 'Ala river. This is today of value only for grazing and cutting fire wood.

5. The Sandy Hills, an area of easily tilled soil southwest of the plain, but one very difficult to irrigate. The Bisetin sandy soils (figure 6.2; Subramanian and Van Osten 1959) can be dry farmed.

Parts of the (2) Alluvial Fan, (3) Saline Plain, and (5) Sandy Hills can be cultivated with rainfall alone, but the risk of crop failure is great. The distribution of settlements in these different area can inform us about ancient agricultural economies.

In addition to agricultural resources of land and water, the occupants of the plain had access to several other resources useful in traditional technologies. First, on the slopes northeast of the plain are massive deposits of gypsum or alabaster, including fine varieties tinted green and other colors. On the surface of Tal-i Ghazir (RH-1) are partly worked fragments of this material, showing that vessels were locally made, and tinted fragments are known from other parts of Khuzestan (Wright 1987). Second, at Mamatain-e Bala, 10 to 15 km west northwest of Ram Hormuz, are major sources of bitumen (Conan and Deschene 1996:58–59). This bitumen was used at Susa during the Achaemenid period, and could have been important earlier (Conan and Deschene 1996:75). Both the bitumen and alabaster are products that were exchanged with central Khuzestan and Fars.

The site catalogue, general map (figure 6.2), and site maps give full information on the sites discovered on both sides of the 'Ala. These data have been be used in several articles by Wright and others (Wright and Johnson 1975, Wright 1987) and by Carter (1971) in her monograph on Khuzestan in the second millennium BCE. All records have been reassessed and sites remeasured for this report, and the more detailed data here take precedence over earlier reports.

SETTLEMENT DEVELOPMENT ON THE RAM HORMUZ PLAIN

No sites of Pleistocene or Early Holocene age were found. It seems likely that the still active aggradation on the plain has deeply buried most sites of these periods. The oldest recorded site was a Tol es-Suwada (RH-3), a small mound on the Saline Plain covering only 0.3 ha. Thick, gritty Susiana buff sherds were found there, including an example with zigzag incising over a vertical painted stripe (figure 6.4a), most similar to those of Susiana a or Early Susiana times (Dollfus 1975:Fig. 18:1; 1978:Figs. 16, 20).

During the Middle and Late Susiana periods, there was a general increase in the number of settlements. During the Middle Susiana period, only four small hamlets with a total area of only 2.1 ha are known. None has an adequate ceramic assemblage, but incurved bowls with exterior bold zigzags (figure 6.4b) and bowls with ladder motifs (figure 6.4c) are distinctive. Even if these sites were all occupied during the same span of time and at a high density, they

would not have contained enough people to sustain a human population. We must, however, keep in mind that 80 km to the east, up the Marun in the Behbehan area and 90 km southeastward in the Hindijan-Zuhreh valley, are large settlements of this period (Dittmann 1984:69–71, Maps 6–10). The small communities of the Ram Hormuz plain may well have been dependent on these larger social units.

During the Late Susiana period, unprecedented numbers of settlements were occupied (figure 6.3). Our larger assemblages have a full range of jars with plain and banded necks (figure 6.5n,o), bowls with dot motifs (figure 6.5a, d, j, k), gridded rectangles (figure 6.4d; 6.5a, h), oblique lines (figure 6.4e, 6.5g), and small goats or birds (figure 6.5l, m) similar to earlier Later Susiana (Susiana d or Bendebal phase) assemblages from Bendebal (Dollfus 1978, 1983b). However, the fine-line motifs (figure 6.5b) and checkerboard motifs (figure 6.5j, k) and heavy vertical lines (figure 6.5i) are also characteristic of later Late Susiana assemblages (compare Susa A [LeBreton 1957]) or Suse Phase from Jaffarabad (Dollfus 1971) and Susa (Le Brun 1971), and the larger Ram Hormuz sites may have continued into the late fifth millennium BCE. The Ram Hormuz assemblages also have close parallels in the later Bakun phase assemblages of central Fars, in particular the leaping animals in a field of dots (figure 6.5a; cf. Langsdorf and McCown 1942:Pl. 70). It seems likely that with study of larger samples from more sites, there may not prove to be a distinct style border between Khuzestan and Fars but rather a gradual change in the frequencies of design elements and the application of rules for the organization of such elements.

During the earlier Late Susiana period, ten settlements covering 11 ha are known to have been occupied on the plain west of the 'Ala river (figure 6.3). Many smaller sites are near springs on the saline areas of the plain. Though rainfall cultivation would have predominated, some irrigated gardening would have been possible. The larger settlement of Boneh Sartoli (RH-18) is located on the Alluvial Fan, where successful canal irrigation has been practiced in recent times with minimal effort. There are few known Late Susiana small settlements near Boneh Sartoli, but the central plain has received much more alluvial sediment as a result of irrigation and flooding than the margins of the plain. Moreover, the alluvial plain has been intensively cultivated to sustain the larger towns of recent times, perhaps leveling smaller sites. A program of canal-walking, coring, and backhoe-trenching may be needed to locate small settlements in this area.

Boneh Sartoli (RH-18) covers at least 2.5 ha (and perhaps 4.0 ha if the Susiana sherds on nearby Tepe Bormi

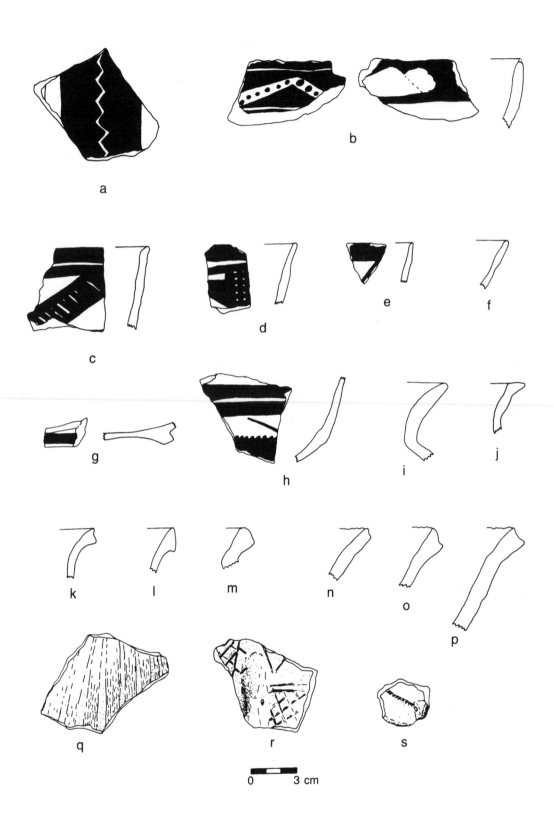

Opposite:

6.4 Susiana and Uruk ceramics from various Ram Hormuz
      sites: *a*, RH-3 Body sherd of deep bowl. Medium sand
      inclusions. Diam 23 cm. Yellowish brown body. Reddish
      brown paint; *b*, RH-2 Rim of incurved bowl. Fine body.
      Diam 25 cm. Overfired pale brown body. Greenish brown
      paint; *c*, RH-10 Rim of large bowl. Fine inclusions. Diam
      30 cm. Pale yellowish green body. Greenish brown paint;
      d, RH-10 Rim of bowl. Fine inclusions. Diam 15 cm. Pale
      green body. Greenish brown paint; *e*, RH-10 Rim of bowl.
      Fine inclusions. Diam 16 cm. Pale green body. Dark
      greenish brown paint; *f*, RH-10 Rim of bowl. Fine
      inclusions. Diam 25 cm. Pale green body; *g*, RH-10 Ring
      base. Fine inclusions. Base diam 11 cm. Pale green body.
      Dark greenish brown paint; *h*, RH-10 Body sherd of
      carinated bowl. Fine inclusions. Pale green body. Dark
      greenish brown paint; *i*, RH-10 Rim of flared jar. Fine
      inclusions. Diam 18 cm. Pale green body; j, RH-10 Rim of
      ledge rim jar. Fine inclusions. Diam 12 cm. Pale brown
      body; *k*, RH-32 Rim of flared expanded rim jar. Angular
      calcite and vegetal inclusions. Diam 12 cm. Light red
      body. Grayish surface; *l*, RH-32 Rim of band rim jar.
      Vegetal inclusions. Diam 10 cm. Light red body; *m*, RH-32
      Rim of heavy expanded jar. Medium sand and vegetal
      inclusions. Diam 16 cm. Gray body; *n*, RH-32 Rim of
      beveled rim bowl. Diam 14 cm. Light brown body; *o*, RH-
      32 Rim of beveled rim bowl. Diam 15 cm. Light brown
      body; *p*, RH-32 Rim of beveled rim bowl. Diam 18 cm.
      Light brown body; *q*, RH-32 Reserved slip body sherd.
      Medium sand and vegetal inclusions. Light gray body; *r*,
      RH-32 Jar shoulder with nose lug and cross-hatch incised
      bands and triangles. Medium sand and vegetal inclusions.
      Grayish green body; *s*, RH-32 Small jar shoulder with
      punctates and nose lug. Fine inclusions. Gray body.
      Illustration by H.T. Wright

[RH-11] represent occupation, rather than sherds moved
in mud bricks). On the western plain, there were two
village-sized settlements to the northeast along the Kupal
(RH-1 and RH-32), and three to the southwest along the
Shur (RH-6, RH-19, RH-24). Small hamlets of a half hectare or less are spaced between these larger settlements. We
can expect a similar pattern of small settlements in the
unsurveyed areas of the eastern plain. At this time, around
4400 BCE, when settlement had diminished along the
Marun and the Hindijan rivers, Ram Hormuz seems to
have emerged as a larger and more integrated settlement
unit. There may have been some continued occupation into
the succeeding later Late Susiana period at Tal-i Ghazir and
Boneh Sartoli, but the area occupied at the end of the fifth
millennium is unclear.

During the Uruk period, which comprises the early and
middle fourth millennium, only Tal-i Ghazir and two other
small settlements on the western plain were inhabited. Chronological details suggest a small fourth millennium settlement
cycle, peaking during Middle Uruk times. Tal-i Ghazir (RH-
1) and Bayamun (RH-32), with a total area of 2.1 ha, were
occupied during the Early Uruk phase, as indicated by
neckless ledge rim jars and tapered rim (proto-) beveled rim
bowls. These two, plus Moravache (RH-6), covered an estimated total area of 3.9 ha during the Middle Uruk phase, as
indicated by high expanded band-rim jars (figure 6.4l), heavy
expanded rim jars (figure 6.4m) and grayware jars with nose
lugs (figure 6.4s). Tal-i Ghazir and Moravache continue into
the Late Uruk phase, as indicated by bottles with droop spouts
and jars with cross-hatch triangles (figure 6.4r). These cover
a settled area of perhaps 3.0 ha.

Only Tal-i Ghazir survived into the late fourth millennium as a small Banesh phase center. Some administrative
specialization is also indicated by a tablet with Proto-Elamite
numbers (Caldwell 1968a; Whitcomb 1971). The tablet has
close parallels to an example from Sialk (Ghirshman 1938:cf.
Pl. XCII, S1619) and is probably the record of a grain transaction (Robert Englund, pers. comm. to E. Carter 1996).
It is unclear why such a center was sustained, but two possibilities would be to protect trading parties passing from
the Iranian highlands to the Susiana and Mesopotamia
(Alden 1982a; Wright and Johnson 1975:278, Table V) or
nomad groups using winter pastures on the Ram Hormuz
plain (Wright 1987). Surprisingly, no evidence of occupation during the middle or later third millennium was
recognized in our survey. The ceramics of these periods
were poorly understood in the late 1960s, and it is possible
that restudy of the surface collections or excavations would
reveal unrecognized traces.

Settlement was reestablished during the second millennium. There are only two small Sukkalmah Elamite sites of
the early second millennium, Tal-i Ghazir (RH-1) covering
only 1.2 ha, and Moravache (RH-6) covering 1.8 ha. These
sites are recognized through the occurrence of types well
known from later Sukkalmah levels at Susa, specifically vats
and jars with overhanging rims; band-rim jars; button,
stump and disc bases; and incised jar and basin sherds
(Caldwell 1968a:Figs. 35–38; Carter 1971:259–263, 275–
276, Figs. 54–56). Expansion onto the Ram Hormuz plain
under the later Sukkalmahs after about 1700, when population on the central Susiana plain was high (Carter and Stolper
1984; Schacht 1987), is reasonable.

During the later second millennium, Middle Elamite
settlement expanded to unprecedented levels (figure 6.6;
see chapter 3). These sites are marked by a distinctive local
ceramic assemblage with vegetal tempered buff and reddish wares, including bowls with overhanging rims with

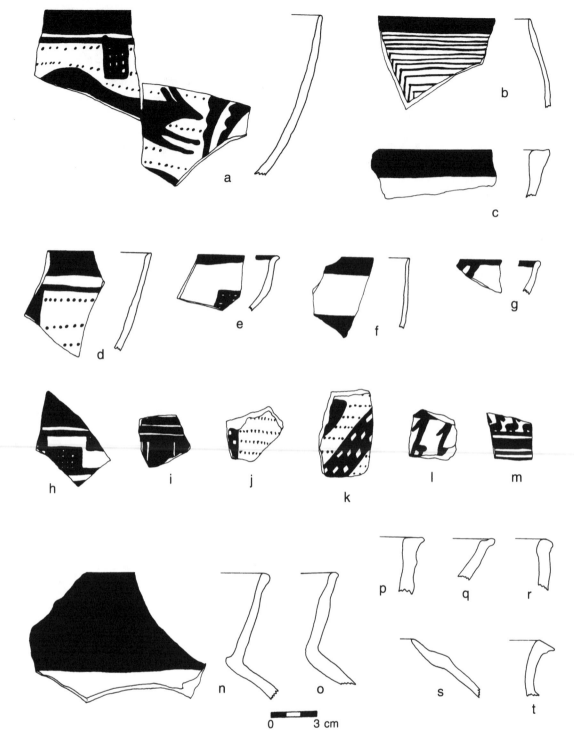

6.5 Susiana ceramics from Tepe Sartoli (RH-18). All have fine sand inclusions and light gray "buff" bodies unless noted: *a*, Rim of large bowl. Diam 30 cm. Dark greenish brown matte paint; *b*, Rim of large bowl. Diam 30 cm. Some vegetal inclusions. Dark greenish brown paint; *c*, Rim of large bowl. Diam 44 cm. Reddish-brown paint; *d*, Rim of small bowl. Diam 20 cm. Reddish-brown paint; *e*, Rim of small bowl. Diam 25 cm. Dark greenish brown paint; *f*, Rim of small bowl. Diam 16 cm. Reddish-brown paint; *g*, Rim of small bowl. Diam 19 cm. Dark reddish-brown paint; *h*, Bowl sherd. Diam 19 cm. Some vegetal inclusions. Dark reddish-brown paint; *i*, Bowl sherd. Diam 14 cm. Dark reddish-brown lustrous paint; *j*, Bowl sherd. Diam 16 cm. Dark reddish-brown paint; *k*, Bowl sherd. Diam 19 cm. Light grayish-green body. Dark greenish brown paint; *l*, Bowl sherd. Diam 24 cm. Dark greenish brown paint; *m*, Bowl sherd. Diam 20 cm. Dark reddish-brown paint; *n*, Jar rim. Diam 17 cm. Reddish-brown paint; *o*, Jar rim. Diam 17 cm; *p*, Large basin rim. Diam 34 cm. Greenish-brown paint on rim top; *q*, Large basin rim. Diam 40 cm. Light gray body; *r*, Large basin rim. Diam 34 cm. Light gray body; *s*, Hole mouth jar rim. Diam 21 cm. Reddish-brown body; *t*, Ledge rim jar rim. Diam 15 cm. Some vegetal inclusions. Reddish body. *Illustration by H.T. Wright*

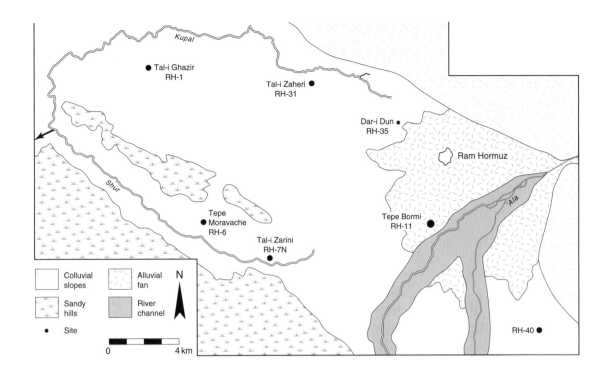

6.6 Sites of the Middle Elamite period on the western Ram Hormuz plain. *Illustration by K. Clahassey*

painted ticking (figure 6.7g, h) and globular jars with straight necks and disc bases, decorated horizontal painted bands (figure 6.7a–f). The painted ware assemblage found in Ram Hormuz was used along with lowland related buff wares (Carter 1994b). The latter (Elamite goblets, conical bowls, band-rim jars and vats) find their closest parallels in Anshan (Malyan, at EDD IV) and Susa (at Ville Royale II) and are similar to the lowland ceramic styles of Mesopotamia and central Khuzestan (Carter 1996). The painted wares from the survey find parallels with the Izeh valley to the north (compare Wright 1979:106–113), with the Qaleh wares of Anshan to the southeast (Carter 1996), and with various sites in Lurestan to the northwest (Henrickson 1986:Fig. 17; Schmidt et al. 1989:Pls. 109e, i, k; 115b). The distribution of these painted ceramics suggest a shared craft tradition in the central-western Zagros during the late second millennium.

More than 28 ha of Middle Elamite settlement existed on the intensively surveyed western plain (figure 6.6). Much of this population lived in the central nucleated town at Tepe Bormi (RH-11, figure 6.9) with its area of public buildings and domestic areas, covering 18 ha. This town contrasts sharply with the smaller dispersed settlement at Tal-i Ghazir (RH-1, figure 6.10), where a number of discrete mounds total 6 ha in area. There are four village-sized settlements—two near the Shur, Moravache (RH 6) and Zarini (RH-7N), one near the Kupal, Zaheri (RH-31), and one east of the 'Ala (RH-40)—covering a total area of 5.5 ha. There is one

small hamlet site covering only 0.2 ha on the central plain, Dar-i Dun (RH-35). Repeated searches in the central plain revealed no other second millennium sites, though remains could be hidden by the houses and gardens of modern Ram Hormuz. While it is possible that major canal construction began in this period, the distribution of sites closely matches those of the Late Susiana period, and it seems more likely that the same strategies of land use were pursued: small-scale canal irrigation on the central plain around the 'Ala river and dry farming with limited irrigation from springs and small streams on the western plain.

Neo-Elamite ceramics have been recognized on only two sites, Tepe Bormi (RH-11), which seems to have been extensively occupied, and Tal-i Ghazir (RH-1), of which only the northwestern group has evidence of occupation. We tentatively estimate a total settlement area of 21.6 ha. It must be emphasized, however, that at the time of our survey, Miroschedji's studies of Neo-Elamite ceramics at Susa had not yet been undertaken, and though Carter suggested Neo-Elamite occupation at Tal-i Ghazir and Tepe Bormi, it was only with Miroschedji's 1977 resurvey that this occupation was well defined (Miroschedji 1981c). It is possible that restudy of the ceramics from some of the smaller Elamite sites would demonstrate Neo-Elamite occupations.

The archaeological record offers some evidence of Neo-Elamite prosperity in eastern Khuzestan in the eighth to seventh centuries BCE (Alizadeh 1985; Carter 1994a, 1999; Stolper and Wright 1990). If we assume that Arjan, northwest of modern

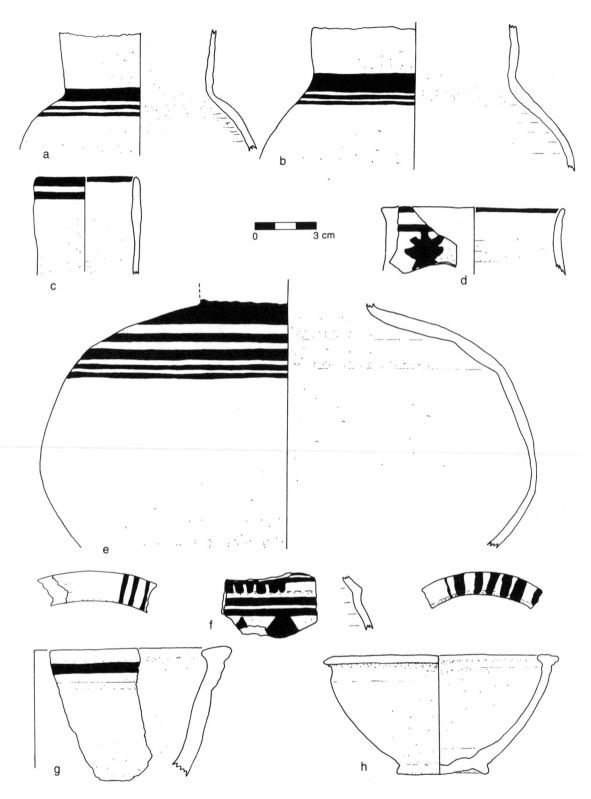

6.7 Middle Elamite ceramics from Ram Hormuz sites: *a*, RH-11 Jar neck. Vegetal inclusions. Light gray body. Light gray surface. Brown paint; *b*, RH-11 Jar neck. Vegetal inclusions. Light gray body with dark core. Light pinkish gray surface. Eroded brown paint; *c*, RH-11 Jar neck. Vegetal inclusions. Light reddish gray body with dark core. Light gray surface. Eroded brown paint; *d*, RH-7N Jar neck. Vegetal inclusions.Light reddish gray body with dark core. Light gray surface. Brown paint; *e*, RH-11 Jar body. Vegetal inclusions. Light greenish gray body. Light gray surface. Brownish black paint; *f*, Jar shoulder. Vegetal inclusions; *g*, RH-7N Bowl rim. Vegetal inclusions. Light pinkish gray body with gray core. Light pinkish gray surface. Light red paint; *h*, RH-11 Bowl. Vegetal inclusions. Reddish body with dark core. Red paint. Disc base added with a daub of heavily straw-tempered clay. *Illustration by E. Carter*

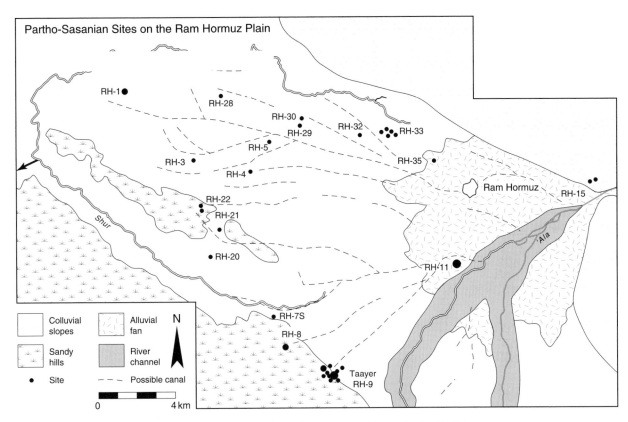

Partho-Sasanian Sites on the Ram Hormuz Plain

RH-1
RH-28
RH-30
RH-32 RH-33
RH-29
RH-5
RH-3
RH-4
RH-35
Ram Hormuz
RH-15
RH-22
RH-21
Shur
Ala
RH-20
RH-11
RH-7S
RH-8
Taayer
RH-9

Colluvial slopes
Alluvial fan
Sandy hills
River channel
Site
Possible canal
N
0   4 km

6.8 Sites of the Partho-Sasanian period on the western Ram Hormuz plain. *Illustration by K. Clahassey*

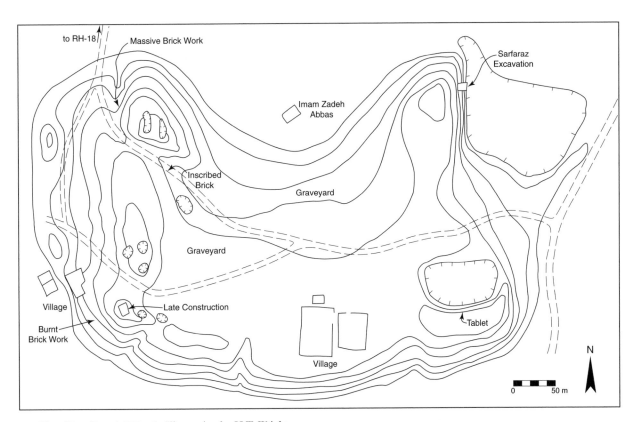

to RH-18
Massive Brick Work
Sarfaraz Excavation
Imam Zadeh Abbas
Inscribed Brick
Graveyard
Graveyard
Village
Late Construction
Tablet
Burnt Brick Work
Village
N
0   50 m

6.9 Plan, Tepe Bormi (RH-11). *Illustration by H.T. Wright*

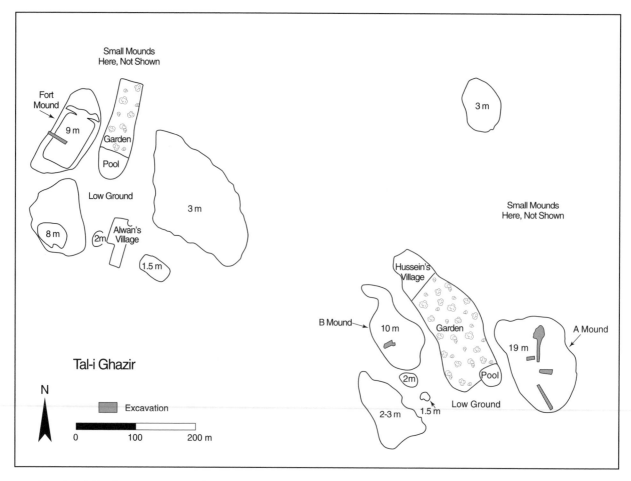

6.10 Plan, Tal-i Ghazir (RH-1). Height of each mound is indicated in meters. *Illustration by E. Carter*

Behbehan, was ancient Huhnur (Duchêne 1986), then neighboring ancient Hidalu might well have included the Ram Hormuz region within its boundaries in Neo-Elamite times (Carter 1994a:74–76; Vallat 1993). Southeast of Behbehan, the valleys leading to Fars tend to be small and lack enough good agricultural land to support significant populations. Pressured on the west by the Assyrians, on the north by the Medes, and on the east by the Persians, the Elamites may well have sought refuge in the Ram Hormuz and Behbehan valleys. These areas were more sheltered than Susiana, had adequate agricultural land, and had easy access to the sea and thus to southern Babylonia—Elam's ally in resisting Assyria for more than a century (circa 743–646 BCE).

After the Neo-Elamite period, evidence of settlement is limited. During the Achaemenid period and perhaps later there is some continued occupation at the two Middle Elamite and Neo-Elamite centers at Tepe Bormi (RH-11) and Tal-i Ghazir (RH-1). However, during the Parthian period, there is unprecedented change and expansion (figure 6.8). It is likely that many of the sites labeled simply as "1st millennium CE" in the catalogue are Parthian or early

Sasanian in age. The total area of settlement occupied during this period is at least 52 ha. A large and impressive system of canals appears to have been in use when the town marked by Taayer (RH-9) grew to cover 28 ha of settled area.

Following the Sasanian and early Islamic periods yet another phase of development occurs during the ninth to thirteenth centuries CE. A total of at least 39 ha of settlement are recorded from the ninth to tenth centuries under the Abbasids, and 53 ha are recorded from the eleventh to thirteenth centuries under Il Khanid rulers, even without estimates for Ram Hormuz and Tal-i Ghazir (RH-1). Ram Hormuz itself (RH-36, RH-37, RH-41), in the center of the Alluvial Fan, was an important town, no doubt using canals from the 'Ala to sustain its gardens. Large towns (RH-25 earlier and RH-26 later), however, emplaced in or near the Sandy Hills imply an emphasis on rainfall agriculture.

Finally there is much settlement in the immediate area of Ram Hormuz dating during the seventeenth to nineteenth centuries. Not only did Ram Hormuz itself become

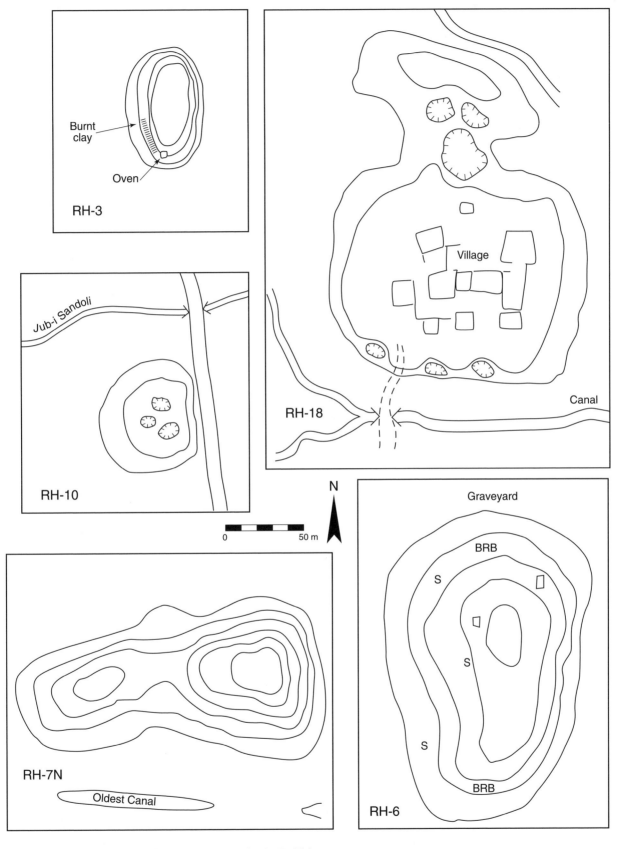

6.11 Small sites on the Ram Hormuz plain. *Illustration by K. Clahassey*

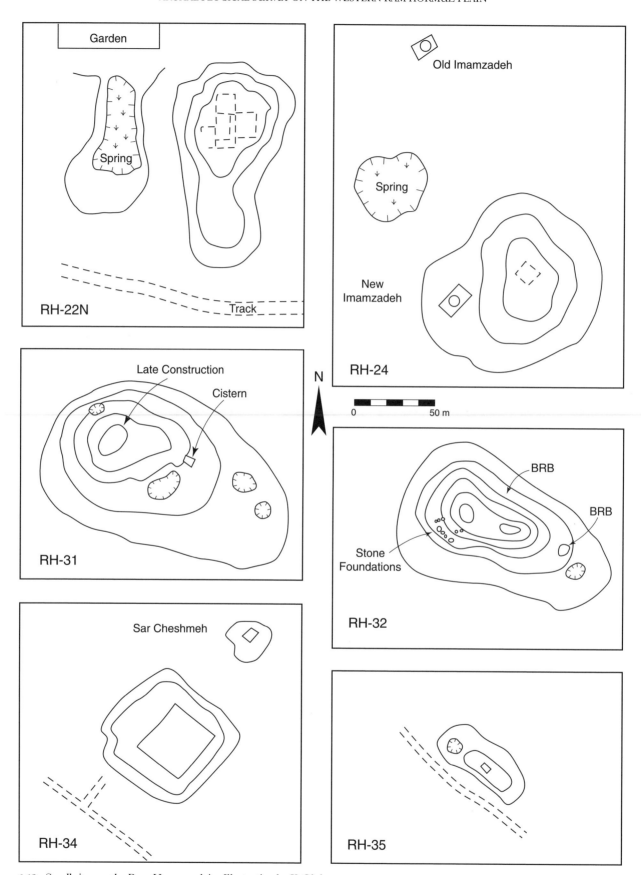

6.12   Small sites on the Ram Hormuz plain. *Illustration by K. Clahassey*

a substantial town but also villages, rural estates, mills, tombs, and forts were established around the town.

CONCLUDING REMARKS AND FUTURE PROSPECTS

At the outset we presented two propositions about the western Ram Hormuz plain: that growth occurred during times of increased exchange relations between lowland Susiana and highland Fars, or alternatively, when people moved in from the nearby central Susiana plain because of excess population there. Given our results, what, then, can we say about the correlation of periods of prosperity with times of either increased exchange or of population growth in the adjacent area? We can examine the five pre-Islamic phases of growth on the western Ram Hormuz plain to evaluate the implications of these propositions. The settlement patterns indicate local growth, from which we infer prosperity, during the later Susiana period of the mid-fifth millennium BCE, the Uruk period of the mid-fourth millennium BCE, the Middle Elamite period of the late second millennium BCE, the Neo-Elamite period of the first half of the first millennium BCE, and the Partho-Sasanian period of the early first millennium CE.

- Of these, only the Middle Elamite and Partho-Sasanian periods are generally recognized periods of increased exchange in Iran. During other periods of increased exchange—Proto-Elamite Banesh phase and subsequent Early Dynastic period of early and middle third millennium BCE, the Sukkalmah Elamite period of the early second millennium BCE, and the Achaemenid and Seleucid periods of the middle to late first millennium there is no notable growth on the Ram Hormuz plain.

- The phases of pre-Islamic settlement growth on the Ram Hormuz plain do correspond with periods of growth on the central Susiana plain—with the exception of the Neo-Elamite period, when the Susa area was subject to Assyrian attacks.

Thus, our evidence sustains the proposal that regional demographic conditions in southwestern Iran led to the need for new, albeit somewhat marginal, lands as population grew on the Susiana plain. Our evidence further suggests that this marginal area may have on occasion served as a refuge from attack. It does not support the suggestion that interregional exchange leads to growth in the areas along the exchange routes. Nevertheless, these issues merit more research in other valleys along the route.

Our brief survey on the western Ram Hormuz plain itself is not definitive, and further survey is warranted there.

- The geological complexities of the plain make it particularly important that future work be conducted with geoarchaeologists undertaking a program of coring and trenching.

- Within the western part of the plain, the 1969 survey sites must be precisely relocated using a Geographical Positioning System (GPS) and precisely mapped.

- Our program of mound survey undoubtedly missed smaller or more deeply buried sites, traces of which might be found by field-walking and coring.

- Sections exposed by road cuts, borrow pits, and other disturbances should be cleaned and sampled to better date sites. In addition, the larger grass-covered mounds which produced little or no ceramics should be cored to document their earlier occupations.

- The areas north and west of Tal-i Ghazir, surveyed in part by McCown but not by ourselves, should be reexamined with this more intensive approach. The higher ridges overlooking the plain should also be examined.

- The improved survey procedures outlined above should be applied to the eastern portions of the Ram Hormuz plain.

This consideration of the settlement evidence from the Ram Hormuz plain points to a number of historically interesting periods which merit further research. Among these are the following:

- The Middle and Late Susiana periods of the fifth millennium BCE, which saw the growth of a local settlement unit in Ram Hormuz, whose economic and political organization merits further study.

- The Uruk and Banesh periods of the fourth millennium BCE appear to be a time of growth, conflict, and change in the southern Zagros, processes whose impact can best be monitored with more detailed survey and excavation.

- The Middle and Neo-Elamite periods of the late second and early first millennia BCE witnessed a poorly understood renaissance of Elamite communities in the southern Zagros foothills of eastern Khuzestan. Investigations at Tepe Bormi will doubtless produce not only archaeological evidence of economic and social organization but also additional tablets with useful parallel information.

- The Parthian and Early Sasanian periods of the earlier first millennium CE present an opportunity to study a Parthian agricultural system with minimal late Sasanian overlay.

SITE CATALOGUE
RH-1: TAL-I GHAZIR (figures 6.10, 6.14a)
This site is a complex of seven major mounds in three groups:

1. Three mounds to the southeast—including the high oval mound 'A' to the east, the lower oval mound with north extension 'B' to the northwest, and a low triangular mound to the southwest—are grouped around a spring with pool and walled garden. To the north of the garden is a walled village occupied at the time of both McCown's excavation and our survey;
2. Three mounds to the northwest—including the rectangular "Fort" mound to the northwest, the semicircular southwest mound, and a large, low irregular mound to the east—also surround a spring with pool and walled garden. To the south is a walled village occupied at the time of McCown's excavation and our survey;
3. One mound to the northeast, a low oval mound, has no special features.

There are a number of smaller mounds, most of Islamic times.
Dimensions (Taken from McCown's map, copied in Carter 1971): SE Group:Mound 'A': 160 m NW-SE, 100 m NE-SW, ht. 19 m; Mound 'B': 90 m NW-SE, 70 m NE-SW, ht. 10 m; SW mound: 140 m NW-SE, 70 m NE-SW, ht. approx. 3 m
NW Group: Fort mound: 160 m NE-SW, 60 m NW-SE, ht. 9 m; SW mound:130 m N-S, 80 m E-W, ht. 8 m; East mound:250 m NW-SE, 140 m NE-SW, ht. 3 m; NE mound: 90 m NW-SE, 60 m NE-SW, ht. 3 m
Location: Northeast side of the western plain, 2 km south of the Kupal river
Soil: Togly solonchak, leached phase
Features: In the SE group, excavation on the high mound 'A' revealed pre-Islamic fortification walls, perhaps Neo-Elamite. In the NW group, the rectangular form of the "Fort" mound suggested major architecture, and McCown's trench here produced evidence of a large wall of the Islamic period, resting in deposits of what he termed the "Neo-Babylonian and Achaemenid" periods. The two large permanent springs appear to have an influence on the site's disposition since the late 2nd millennium if not before.

Periods: Late Susiana, Uruk, Banesh, early–late 2nd millennium BCE, Neo-Elamite, 1st millennium BCE, 1st millennium CE, 14th–16th centuries CE
Comment: In McCown's survey, this was recorded as site 55 under the spelling "Tol-i Ghasir." We use his excavation map, rather than his survey notes, to derive the above description. Only the 1.2 ha of mound 'A' was occupied in the 5th to early 3rd millennia and during the Sukkalmah period of the early 2nd millennium, as far as we now know. During the late 2nd millennium, surface sherds and excavated material indicate that all the mounds were occupied, a total of at least 6 ha. Occupation during the Neo-Elamite and Achaemenid periods of the early 1st millennium BCE was concentrated in the 3.5-ha northwest group, and with some evidence from a sounding by McCown in mound B (Carter 1994a). Occupation during the 1st millennium CE is not clearly delineated, but occupation was extensive during the fourteenth to sixteenth centuries CE, including most of the mounds and many small outliers, and perhaps reached 10 ha.

RH-2: NAME UNKNOWN
Dimensions: Mound diameter approx. 40 m, sherd scatter approx. 60 m, ht. approx. 2.5 m
Location: Northeast side of the western plain, 2.5 km south of the Kupal river
Soil: Togly solonchak, leached phase
Periods: Middle Susiana II; Late Islamic
Comment: This may be McCown site 102, for which notes are lacking. We attribute a size of 0.4 ha to both periods.

RH-3: TOL ES-SUWADA (figure 6.11)
Dimensions: 80 m N-S, 50 m E-W, ht. approx. 5 m
Location: On the western plain, 4 km southwest of the Kupal river, and 5 km northeast of the Shur river
Soil: Bayamun gray-brown leached clay
Features: A layer of reddish burnt clay and the remains of an oval oven are visible eroding from the lower southwest slope of the mound, about a meter and a half above plain level.
Periods: Middle Susiana I, 1st millennium CE
Comment: This site may be McCown site 103, for which notes are lacking. We

attribute a size of 0.3 ha to both periods.

RH-4: TEPE QOWAILEH
Dimensions: 180 m E-W, 100 m N-S, ht. approx. 6 m
Location: On the western plain, 5 km southwest of the Kupal river, and 6 km northeast of the Shur river
Soil: Togly solonchak, leached phase, with Bayamun gray-brown leached clay to north
Features: Occupied houses are on the northwest, southwest, and southeast flanks of the mound.
Periods: 1st millennium CE
Comment: Approx. 20 m south of the mound is a spring. There must be earlier material on this large mound, but only a brief examination was possible. We attribute a size of 1.4 ha to this site.

RH-5: TEPE GHAZU
Dimensions: Outer mound: 160 m N-S, 140 m E-W, ht. approx. 1 m. Central mound: Diameter 85 m, ht. approx. 4 m
Location: Northeast side of the plain, 3.5 km southwest of the Kupal river
Soil: Togly solonchak, leached phase, but weakly saline phase to north
Features: Spring approx. 30 m to south
Periods: Late Susiana, Early Sasanian
Comments: We attribute a size of 0.5 ha to both periods.

RH-6: TEPE MORAVACHE (figures 6.11, 6.14b)
Dimensions: 190 m N-S, 140 m E-W, ht. approx. 7 m
Location: On the southwest edge of the plain, half a km north of the Shur
Soil: Mosaic of Togly solonchak, leached phase and Bayamun gray-brown leached clay
Features: Susiana sherds are found on the west slope from 1 to 5 m above plain level. Uruk beveled rim bowls (BRBs) were noted about 3 m above plain level at both the north and south ends of this mound.
Periods: Late Susiana; Uruk; early and late 2nd millennium BCE
Comments: There is a recent graveyard just north of the mound, and farther to the north a modern village covers a slightly larger mound at which no sherd collection was made. We attribute a size of 1.0 ha to the Susiana occupation and 1.8 ha to later ones. The soil scientists transcribe this name as "Marvache."

RH-7 SOUTH: TOL-I ZARINI (figure 6.11)
Dimensions: 170 NW-SE, 95 m NE-SW, ht. approx. 9 m

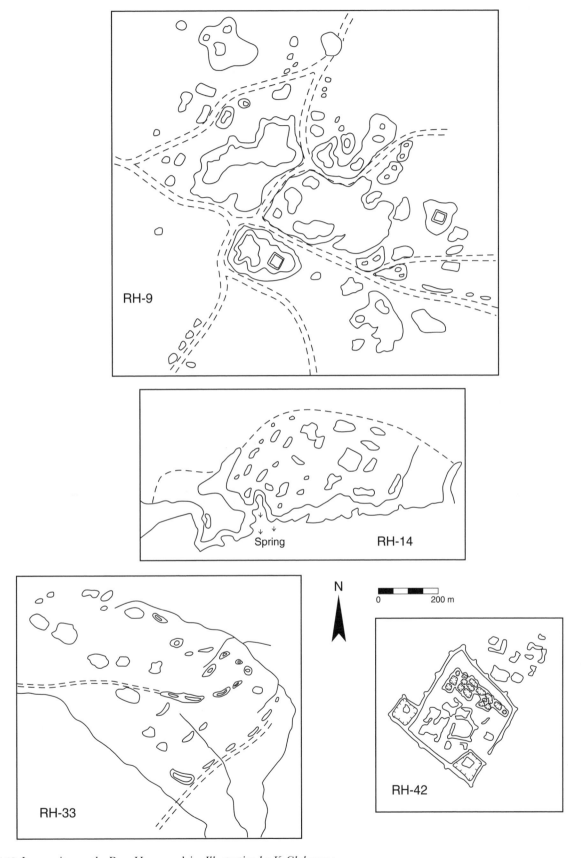

6.13 Larger sites on the Ram Hormuz plain. *Illustration by K. Clahassey*

6.14 *a*, RH-1 (Tal-i Ghazir) from west;
b, RH-6 (Tepe Moravache); *c*, RH-
22. *Photographs by E. Carter*

Location: Southwest edge of the plain, just south of the head stream of the Shur river
Features: There is modern grave on the summit.
Soil: Mosaic of Togly solonchak, leached phase and Bayamun gray-brown leached clay to south and west
Periods: Sasanian. There may be earlier material on this large mound, but careful examination revealed no evidence of it.
Comments: This site may be McCown site 71. He gives the name 'Zahariyah' and reports dimensions of 30 by 50 yards and 8 feet in height, much smaller than we recorded. He found few sherds and did not suggest a date. We estimate 1.4 ha for this site.

RH-7 NORTH: ALSO TOL-I ZARINI
Dimensions: 200 m E-W-SE, 90 m N-S, ht. approx. 6 m to west, 10 m to east
Location: Southwest edge of the plain, just north of the head stream of the Shur river
Soil: Bayamun gray-brown leached clay to north and east; eroded phase of Togly solonchak to west
Features: Immediately south of this mound is the trace of an early canal oriented E-W. Southwest of the mound is a ruined trapezoidal complex, probably fairly recent, which was not examined.
Periods: Late 2nd millennium BCE, possibly 9th–13th centuries CE also.
Comment: This is probably McCown site 72, which he reports as 200 by 100 yards N-S and 50 feet high. He found few sherds, and did not suggest a date. We attribute a size of 1.4 ha to both periods.

RH-8: NAME UNKNOWN
Dimensions: 270 m N-S, 170 m E-W, ht. 3 m with a larger south summit, and a small north summit
Location: Southwest edge of the plain, 2 km south of the headwaters of the Shur river
Soil: Togly solonchak to north and east; Bisetin sandy loam to west and south
Periods: probably Parthian
Comment: This is probably McCown Site 70, which he reported as 100 yards in diameter and approx. 12 feet high with probable northern extension. He identified it as Sasanian-Parthian. We estimate a size of 3.4 ha.

RH-9: TAAYER (figure 6.13)
Dimensions: approx. 1000 NW-SE, approx. 700 m NE-SW, ht. approx. 5m
Location: Southwest edge of the plain

Soil: Togly solonchak to north; soil to south not recorded
Features: This was a large settlement composed of six larger mounds, two of which have traces of rectangular buildings and at least thirty smaller mounds separated by linear features, perhaps roads or canals.
Periods: Early Parthian with possible earlier and later material as well
Comments: This site is McCown site 57. He notes plaster floors and walls on one mound but has no comments on ceramics. Mapped from 15 August 1957 air photo no. 9534 at the Iranian Organization for Cartography (IOC), we attribute a size of 28 ha of mounded settlement to the Parthian period.

RH-10: TEPE MAL-I SANDOLI (figure 6.11)
Dimensions: Diameter 60 m, ht. 2.5 m
Location: Southwest edge of the plain, near the right bank of the 'Ala river
Soil: Togly solonchak to north; same with leached phase to south
Features: Several recent graves on top
Periods: Middle–Late Susiana
Comment: This site is McCown site 56. He records it as 30 yards in diameter and 3 feet high and notes pebbles but makes no remarks about ceramics. The west edge was cut by the road. We estimate an area of 0.4 ha.

RH-11: TEPE BORMI (figure 6.9)
Dimensions: 540 m E-W, 340 m N-S, ht. approx. 10 m
Location: Near the center of the plain on the right bank of the 'Ala river
Soil: Ram Hormuz gray-brown clays and brown silts
Features: The higher west end of the site has massive mud brick construction exposed on both its northern and southern extremities. Baked bricks are common. Two inscribed bricks, one in the name of the Middle Elamite ruler Untash ᵈNapirisha (Carter 1971:280, Fig. 58) and one a Neo-Elamite copy of brick dedicating a restoration of a temple built by the Middle Elamite ruler Shilhak-Inshushinak I (Vallat 1981a) were found here. In a recent borrow pit on the southeast end, we recovered half of an unbaked clay tablet, probably 2nd millennium BCE. This is too small to be read but is possibly of Neo-Elamite date on the basis of the sign forms (Matthew W. Stolper, personal communication) There are occupied houses on the southwest and

south sides of the site, there are several groups of recent graves on the summit, and a tomb, Imamzadeh Abbas, is just north of the site.
Periods: Late Susiana, 2nd millennium BCE, Neo-Elamite, Parthian, Sasanian
Comments: This site is McCown site 68, which he calls "Tul-i Burmi." He gives somewhat smaller dimensions of 400 yards E-W and 250 yards N-S and 35 feet high. He makes no remarks about date. During the mid-1960s, the northeast end of the site was damaged by bulldozers and was tested by Ali Akbar Safaraz of the Archaeological Service. Subsequent to our survey, the site was reexamined by Pierre de Miroschedji, who retrieved additional inscribed bricks on the west end (Miroschedji 1981c:170, n.10; Vallat 1981a). We attribute a size of 1.5 ha to the Late Susiana occupation, 18.0 ha to the later Middle Elamite and Neo-Elamite periods, and an arbitrary 10 ha to the diminished Achaemenid and Partho-Sasanian occupations, of which we found evidence on the central and eastern parts of the site.

RH-12: NAME UNKNOWN
Dimensions: Diameter 180 m, on a sloping hillside
Location: Northeast slope overlooking the plain
Soil: Baqdak stony colluvial soil to north; Ram Hormuz gray-brown alluvial silt to south
Features: Many foundations of gypsum blocks, much disturbed
Periods: Late 19th–early 20th centuries CE
Comment: This is probably McCown site 53, which he reports as 125 by 50 yards with reddish baked bricks and gypsum, without hazarding an assessment of the date. There are recent pits, probably to recover gypsum to make plaster. We estimate 3.4 ha.

RH-13: NAME UNKNOWN
Dimensions: 160 m E-W, 100 m N-S on sloping hillside
Location: Northeast slope overlooking the plain
Soil: Baqdak stony colluvial soil to north; Ram Hormuz gray-brown alluvial silt to south
Periods: Late 18th and 19th centuries CE
Comment: Similarly pitted. We estimate 1.2 ha.

RH-14: IMAMZADEH ALI ABBAS (figure 6.13)
Dimensions: 550 m E-W, 350 m N-S

Location: Northeast slope overlooking the plain
Soil: Baqdak stony colluvial soil to north; Ram Hormuz gray-brown alluvial clays to south
Features: Many small low mounds, a majority oriented NE-SW or NW-SE, probably individual buildings. A spring is on the south edge of site.
Periods: 9th–13th centuries CE
Comments: This site is probably McCown site 50, which he estimates as 220 yards in length and reports simply as "Islamic." Mapped from 29 October 1960 air photo no. 8183 (Film 11, Run 46, Area A, RC5A) at the IOC, we attribute a size of 3.0 ha of mounded settlement to the Early Islamic period.

RH-15: DAR-I CHEHEL
Dimensions: About 300 m E-W, 50 m N-S over looking the plain. ht. approx. 30 m to east, 10 m to east
Location: On a natural ridge on the northeast slope overlooking the plain, 2 km north of the right bank of the ʿAla river
Soil: Baqdak stony colluvial soil thinly developed on gravels
Features: Standing walls and other traces of buildings on higher east eminence; similar traces on lower west ridge
Periods: 1st millennium CE throughout, 17th-century CE standing structure to east; 19th century CE to west
Comment: McCown reports the name of the fort as "Dua Dukhtar" but did not give it a number. We attribute 0.8 ha to the early occupation, 0.3 ha to the 17th century occupation and 0.4 ha to the 19th century.

RH-16: NAME UNKNOWN
Dimensions: Small sherd scatter on a natural hill
Location: Northeast slope overlooking the plain and the right bank of the ʿAla river
Soil: Baqdak stony colluvial soil thinly developed on gravels
Period: Late Islamic
Comments: This may be McCown site 51, which he reported to have evidence of two structures with masonry walls. We attribute no size to this small, badly disturbed site.

RH-17: IMAMZADEH KHAURI NAʿAMAT
Dimensions: North mound: 70 m NW-SE, 50 m NE-SW, ht. approx. 3 m. South mound: 40 m E-W, 20 m N-S, ht. approx. 3 m

Location: On the northeast side of the plain 1.5 km north of the right bank of the ʿAla river
Soil: Ram Hormuz gray-brown alluvial silts and clays
Features: The north mound has clear stone house foundations; the south mound has many graves. Between the two is a tomb, the eponymous imamzadeh. To the west is a well-preserved undershot mill with drop tower. The 15 x 9–m masonry mill building has six domes. Traces of an older canal go east from the south mound to the mill.
Periods: All elements appear to be 18th century CE
Comments: This is may be McCown site 52, which he termed "Imamzadeh Abbas," where a pit revealed reddish baked bricks set in lime mortar. We estimate a size of 0.3 ha for the north mound and 0.1 ha for the south mound.

RH-18: TEPE SARTOLI (figure 6.11)
Dimensions: 206 m N-S, 165 m E-W, ht. approx. 5 m.
Location: On the center of the plain on the right bank of the ʿAla river
Soil: Ram Hormuz gray-brown alluvial silts and clays
Features: Composed of a higher, roughly square southern mound and a smaller northern extension, much pitted for brick clay. Clay pits around the south edge of the mound have revealed various middens and ash beds containing sherds and bones.
Periods: Late Susiana, 15th–16th centuries CE
Comment: This site is McCown site 67, who reports it as 100 x 300 yards with a maximum height of 15 feet. He notes the occurrence of "buffwares," by which he meant Susiana or Bakun buffware. Largely covered by a modern village. It seems likely that the steep southern edge of the mound has been cut by canals and perhaps by Elamite brick pits, perhaps accounting for the occurrence of a few Late Susiana sherds at Tepe Bormi (RH-11), only 300 m to the south. We attribute a size of 2.5 ha of mounded settlement to both periods.

RH-19: NAME UNKNOWN
Dimensions: Diameter 140 m, ht. approx. 2 m
Location: On the southwest side of the plain, 4 km southwest of the Shur river
Soil: Mosaic of Togly solonchak to east and

Bayamun gray-brown leached clay to west
Periods: Late Susiana
Comment: Badly eroded. We attribute a size of 1.4 ha to this site.

RH-20: NAME UNKNOWN
Dimensions: West mound: 120 m E-W, 100 m N-S, ht. approx. 0.5 m. East mound: Diameter 80 m, ht. approx. 2 m
Location: Southwest side of the plain, 1 km northeast from the Shur river.
Soil: Mosaic of Togly solonchak, leached phase and Bayamun gray-brown leached clay
Features: East mound has a recent structure of mud brick set in gypsum mortar.
Periods: 1st millennium CE
Comment: We attribute a size of 1.4 ha to this site.

RH-21: NAME UNKNOWN
Dimensions: Diameter 90 m, ht. approx. 4 m
Location: On the southwest side of the plain, 3 km northeast of the Shur river
Soil: Togly solonchak to west and south, with leached phase to north and east
Periods: 1st millennium CE
Comment: We attribute a size of 0.6 ha to this site.

RH-22 NORTH: NAME UNKNOWN (figures 6.12, 6.14c)
Dimensions: 120 m N-S; 80 m E-W, ht. approx. 5 m
Location: On the southwest side of the plain, 4 km northeast of the Shur river
Soil: Eroded Togly solonchak to north; Bisetin sandy loam to south
Features: A ruined structure, perhaps a fortified *qaleh* (fortress), on the summit
Periods: Late Susiana, 18th century CE
Comment: We attribute a size of 0.6 ha to the Susiana occupation and 0.2 ha to the recent occupation.

RH-22 SOUTH: NAME UNKNOWN
Dimensions: Diameter: 60 m, ht. approx. 4 m
Location: On the southwest side of the plain, 4 km northeast of the Shur river
Soil: Eroded Togly solonchak to north; Bisetin sandy loam to south
Features: Modern graves on the summit
Periods: Late Sasanian
Comment: We attribute a size of 0.3 ha to this small disturbed site.

RH-23: NAME UNKNOWN

Dimensions: NE mound: Diameter: 50 m N-S, 25 m E-W, ht. approx. 5 m. SW mound: Diameter 20 m N-S, 15 m E-W, ht. approx. 1 m

Location: Southwest side of the plain, 4 km northeast of the Shur river

Soil: Eroded Togly solonchak to north; Bisetin sandy loam to south

Periods: The northeast mound is Middle Susiana. Its area is estimated at only 0.1 ha.

RH-24: NAME UNKNOWN

Dimensions: Diameter 100 m, ht. 5 m

Location: Southwest side of the western plain, 2 km northeast of the Shur river

Soil: Eroded Togly solonchak to north; Bisetin sandy loam to south

Features: There is a new imamzadeh on the site and an older one to the northwest, with a spring between them.

Periods: Middle Susiana, Late Susiana, 13th century CE

Comment: We attribute an area of 0.9 ha to the Susiana occupation. The 13th century sherds are probably associated with the tomb, and we therefore attribute no occupational area to that period.

RH-25: NAME UNKNOWN

Dimensions: approx. 750 m NE-SW, approx. 600 m NW-SE

Location: Southwest side of the western plain, 1 km from the Shur river

Soil: Bisetin sandy loam to east and west; Marvache sandy loam to south

Features: Composed of many low, small mounds

Periods: 9th–10th centuries CE

Comments: A large short-lived town composed of many small mounds like RH-14. Unfortunately, not covered by our air photos and therefore not mapped. We attribute a size of 22 ha of mounded settlement to the Early Islamic period.

RH-26: BISETIN

Dimensions: approx. 800 m NE-SW, approx. 550 m NW-SE

Location: Southwest side of the western plain, 1 km from the Shur river

Soil: Bisetin sandy loam and Marvache sandy loam to north and east; eroded badlands to south

Features: Composed of low mounds, both large and small

Periods: 10th–14th centuries CE

Comments: A large town, similarly not

covered by our air photographs and therefore not mapped. We attribute a size of 34 ha of mounded settlement to the Early Islamic period.

RH-27: NAME UNKNOWN

Dimensions: 90 m E-W, 70 m N-S, ht. approx. 1 m, except knoll

Location: Northeast side of the western plain, half a km from the Kupal river

Soil: Kupal valley bottom clays and silts

Features: Small high knoll on northwest corner reaches 3 m; recent graves on lower southeast terrace

Periods: 1st millennium CE

Comment: This site is estimated to cover 0.6 ha

RH-28: NAME UNKNOWN

Dimensions: 150 m E-W, 110 N-S, ht. approx. 1 m

Location: Northeast side of the western plain, 3 km southwest of the Kupal river

Soil: Togly solonchak to north, with Togly solonchak, leached phase, to south

Periods: 1st millennium CE

Comment: This site is estimated to cover 1.3 ha.

RH-29: NAME UNKNOWN

Dimensions: 120 m NW-SE, 80 m NE-SW, ht. approx. 2 m

Location: Northeast side of the plain, 2 km southwest of the Kupal river

Soil: Togly solonchak to north, with Togly solonchak, leached phase, to south

Features: Recent graves on summit, spring 30 m to southwest, spring 50 m to south

Periods: 1st millennium CE

Comment: This site is estimated to cover 0.5 ha.

RH-30: NAME UNKNOWN

Dimensions: Diameter 50 m, ht. approx. 1 m

Location: Northeast side of the plain, 2 km southwestof the Kupal river

Soil: Togly solonchak to north, with Togly solonchak, leached phase, to south

Features: Spring 200 m to east

Periods: First millennium CE

Comment: This site is estimated to cover 0.2 ha.

RH-31: TOL-I ZAHARI (figure 6.12)

Dimensions: 160 m NW-SE, 80 m NE-SW, ht. of higher knoll to northwest approx. 8 m

Location: Northeast side of the plain, 1 km south of the Kupal river

Soil: Mosaic of Bayamun gray-brown leached clay and Darvish poorly drained saline humic soils

Features: Traces of late construction on summit and possible cistern on southeastern side of knoll. Several recent pits on low terrace to southeast.

Periods: Late 2nd millennium BCE, Late Islamic

Comment: We attribute the full area of 1.1 ha to the 2nd millennium but only 0.2 ha to the Late Islamic period.

RH-32: TEPE BAYAMUN (figure 6.12)

Dimensions: 130 m NW-SE, 65 m NE-SW, ht. approx. 10 m

Location: Northeast slope of the plain, near the head springs of the Kupal river

Soil: Mosaic of Togly solonchak and Bayamun gray-brown leached clay

Features: Stone footings eroding out on southwestern slope about 5 m above plain level. Sherds of beveled-rim bowls noted on northeast and southeast slope also about 5 m above plain level

Periods: Late Susiana, Uruk, 1st millennium CE

Comment: We attribute the full area of 0.9 ha to the Late Susiana period, 0.6 ha to the Uruk period, and 0.2 ha to the 1st millennium CE.

RH-33: NAME UNKNOWN (figure 6.13)

Dimensions: approx. 650 m NW-SE, approx. 300 m NE-SW

Location: Northeast slope of the plain, near the head springs of the Kupal river

Soil: Mosaic of Togly solonchak and Bayamun gray-brown leached clay to northwest; Ram Hormuz gray-brown clay to south and east

Features: A few small low mounds with many crosscutting canal banks making the site appear overly large and complex.

Periods: 1st millennium CE

Comments: We hazard no estimate of the occupied area of this site. Mapped from 2 November 1960 air photo no. 9159 (Film 17, Run 48, Area A, RC5a) at the IOC

RH-34: SAR CHESHMEH (figure 6.12)

Dimensions: 75 m square, oriented NW-SE by NE-SW, ht. approx. 2.5 m

Location: Northeast slope of the plain, near the head springs of the Kupal river

Soil: Ram Hormuz gray-brown clay, some poorly drained

Features: Traces of square building on flat summit

Periods: 16th–17th centuries CE
Comment: This structure is estimated to cover 0.4 ha.

RH-35: DAR-I DUN (figure 6.12)
Dimensions: 60 m NW-SE, 20 m NE-SW, ht. approx. 2.5 m
Location: Near the center of the plain, 6 km north of the 'Ala river
Soil: Ram Hormuz gray-brown clay and silt
Features: Recent shrine on top. Recent borrow pit in southeast end was the find spot of the 2nd millennium sherds.
Periods: Late 2nd millennium BCE, possible Sasanian
Comments: This very small mound is estimated to cover 0.1 ha.

RH-36: RAM HORMUZ CEMETERY
Dimensions: 120 square oriented NS-EW, ht. approx. 1.5 m
Location: Near the center of the plain, 4 km north of the 'Ala river
Soil: Ram Hormuz gray-brown clay and silt
Features: Many recent graves
Periods: 11th–13th centuries CE
Comments: We attribute 1.4 ha to this mound.

RH-37: NAME UNKNOWN
Dimensions: Diameter 35 m, ht. approx. 4 m
Location: Near the center of the plain, 4 km north of the 'Ala river
Soil: Ram Hormuz gray-brown clay and silt
Features: A heap of ceramic kiln wasters
Periods: Early 13th century CE
Comment: It would be senseless to ascribe an occupational area to this small special purpose area in a large site covered by the modern town.

RH-38: NAME UNKNOWN
Dimensions: Diameter 40 m, ht. approx. 2 m
Location: Near the center of the plain, 4 km south of the left bank of the 'Ala river
Soil: Not recorded.
Features: Trace of stone footing on summit
Periods: 1st millennium CE
Comments: This site covers 0.1 ha. Since it is on the partially surveyed eastern plain, however, we do not include it in any settlement size analysis.

RH-39: TOL-I SORKHI
Dimensions: Diameter 90 m, ht. approx. 8 m
Location: Near the center of the plain, 6 km south of the left bank of the 'Ala river
Soil: Not recorded
Periods: Early 19th century CE. There is probably earlier material on this briefly examined large site.
Comments: This site covers 0.6 ha. Since it is on the partially surveyed eastern plain, however, we do not include it in any settlement size analysis.

RH-40: NAME UNKNOWN
Dimensions: 150 m NE-SW; 100 m NW-SE, ht. approx. 7 m
Location: Southeast part of the plain, 8 km south of the left bank of the 'Ala river
Soil: Not recorded
Periods: Late 2nd millennium BCE; possible Achaemenid, and a few sherds and glass fragments of the 11th century CE on summit
Comments: This site covers 1.2 ha. Since it is on the partially surveyed eastern plain, however, we do not include it in any settlement size analysis.

RH-41: RAM HORMUZ AB ANBAR
Dimensions: Size unclear
Location: Near the center of the plain, 4 km north of the 'Ala river
Soil: Ram Hormuz gray-brown clay and silt covered with occupied urban housing
Periods: Late 18th century CE and perhaps earlier
Comment: It would be senseless to ascribe an occupational area to this small area of a large site covered by the modern town.

RH-42: NAME UNKNOWN (figure 6.13)
Dimensions: 310 m NE-SW, 300 m NW-SE, with 80 m square extension on north side of west corner
Location: On the southwest edge of the plain, 2 km north of the Shur
Soil: Bisetin sandy loam to east and west; Marvache sandy loam to south
Features: A roughly trapezoidal walled site, with opening to southeast. Wall has corner bastions, two bastions on southwest side, and three on both the northwest and northeast sides. Inside the south corner, there is a walled area with a small rectangular mound inside; the west extension is similar. In the center and east are irregular mounds, and to the northeast is a complex of well-defined rectangular units. To the northeast of the wall are some more irregular mounds.
Periods: Unknown. The good preservation suggests a relatively recent Islamic site.
Comment: Surprisingly, no ceramics were found.

CHAPTER 7

SOME OBSERVATIONS BASED ON THE NOMADIC CHARACTER OF FARS PREHISTORIC CULTURAL DEVELOPMENT

ABBAS ALIZADEH

AS PART OF MY INTEREST in the possible role of the ancient mobile pastoralists in the development of complex societies in Iran, in 1995 I conducted a regional survey in the valleys northwest of the Marvdasht plain, the locus of Persepolis. The development of mobile pastoralism as a subsistence economic system is linked primarily to the Near Eastern topography and climate which created regions with varying degrees of resource disparity that can only be exploited through regulated seasonal movements of people and animals. In the valleys northwest of the Marvdasht I sought a settlement pattern of the Bakun A phase (late fifth millennium BCE) similar to the existing pattern of spatial distribution exhibited by the numerous villages inhabited by either the settled Qashqa'i or by a mixture of the Qashqa'i tribesmen and members of the local population (figure 7.1).

ETHNOGRAPHIC MODELS FOR MOBILE PASTORALISM IN FARS

In areas where mobile pastoralism has flourished for millennia, much insight can be gained from ethnographic data. The ethnography and history of the Near East attest to the political and economic importance of the region's mobile pastoralist tribal confederacies. Mobile pastoralist communities in highland Iran have had a high degree of interaction with the urban and to a lesser degree with village communities. This interaction is fostered by the ecological niches and geographic features that force mutually dependent, territorially bound, and autonomous entities to share regions that provide the matrix for a myriad of social,

economic, and political interactions. Rowton (1973a, 1973b, 1974, 1981) considered economic interdependence and territorial coexistence of mobile pastoralists and sedentary agriculturists for part of the year an important factor for this high level of integration.

Historically, Fars has been favored by many mobile tribes for its vast multitude of natural resources. The tribes of the Bakhtiari confederacy roamed in the region stretching from west of Isfahan to southeastern Khuzestan; the Mamasani and Boyr Ahmadi tribes occupied the areas between north and southeastern Khuzestan and northwestern Fars. The tribes of the Qashqa'i confederacy swung from the area southwest of Isfahan well into southern Fars, near the Persian Gulf, covering a distance of more than seven hundred kilometers in their annual migration. Other mobile tribes of the Khamseh confederacy and Arabic-speaking tribes also exploited Fars, sharing it with numerous other mobile tribes and the sedentary farming population (Barth 1959, 1961; Beck 1986; Garthwaite 1983; see chapter 28).

It is probably no accident that the locations of the summer and winter pastures of the Qashqa'i, Khamseh, Mamasani, and Boyr Ahmadi confederacies correspond to the pattern of geographical distribution of the Bakun A painted pottery (see site catalogue). Clearly the political configurations and the ethnic makeup of these mobile tribes are the outcome of later historical and political developments (Beck 1986:41–95; Garthwaite 1983:4–16). Nevertheless, since the geographical and ecological features of this region impose certain migration patterns between summer and winter pastures, particularly in the case of

7.1 Southwestern Iran—geographic distribution of mobile pastoralist tribes and Bakun painted pottery (shaded area). *Prepared at MASCA based on draft by A. Alizadeh*

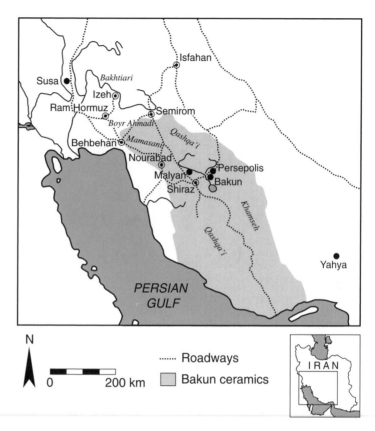

SURPLUS PRODUCTION AND TRADE

The creation of surplus in traditional agricultural societies depends on social and economic variables. The former include obligations to kin, acquisition of resources through marriage, ritual/religious duties, and chiefly tributes. The latter include labor, irrigation technology, storage facilities, market availability, and incentive (Boserup 1965, 1981). Of these, market availability and incentive are crucial in the absence of a state-regulated economy. To produce a surplus, a farmer needs a market to absorb his excess production and to provide him with material goods in exchange, such as pottery, tools, and cloth, that he may not be able to produce on his own for technological or economic reasons, or both.

In contrast, a mobile pastoralist needs no incentive to produce a surplus. Animals reproduce themselves without the difficulties involved in the production of agricultural surplus; in fact in the course of several years of favorable environmental conditions, a mobile pastoralist would have more animals than needed for a subsistence economy (Balikci 1981; Boonzajer Flaes 1982:87–95; Swift 1979). There are, however, cultural (Galaty 1981:72–80) and economic-environmental limitations to the production of

surplus among mobile pastoralists. For example, Clark (1984:67–74) discusses the dangers of having large flocks in a time of drought (see also Khazanov 1980:8–13). The most important limiting factor is the problem with internalization of the surplus (that is, increasing the size of the herd) in a basically undiversified economy. There is always the danger of overgrazing, a potential shortage of manpower to tend the herd (Gilles and Jantgaard 1982:1–10), and certain sociocultural inhibitions. One solution to this problem (invented by the Baseri tribe in Fars) is for the wealthier individuals to sublet part of their herds to less fortunate members of other camps, ignoring the like individuals of their own camp. This practice helps spread economic risks in time of natural calamities and minimize the loss, see Barth (1961:13–14, 28).

Animal surplus can be externalized without damaging the production possibilities of the remaining herds (Boonzajer Flaes 1982; Bourgeot 1981). Externalization of surplus among modern Iranian mobile pastoralists has been done through the purchase of luxury goods such as jewelry, carpets, or a second wife from a wealthy family, or by acquisition of agricultural land, with some individuals becoming landlords as well as herd-owners (Barth 1961:110; Balikci 1981:154; for a different approach to this aspect of the pastoral mode of economic adaptation, see Botte [1979]). Mobile pastoralists are therefore more interested in trade (either exchanging their own products or serving as intermediaries in long-distance trade) than sedentary people, because of their specialized and one-sided economy. Self-sufficient villages by definition, however, are not a viable market for tribesmen and mobile pastoralists cannot trade among themselves because of their undiversified economy. So we know historically, and expect prehistorically, an association between the crystallization of mobile pastoralist societies and the rise of towns.

FIFTH AND FOURTH MILLENNIA IRAN: THE CRYSTALLIZATION OF MOBILE PASTORALISM

In the late fifth and early fourth millennia BCE, some sites in the Near East grew much larger than their neighbors. These sites exhibit features considered manifestations of socioeconomic complexity that eventually led to the formation of early states. Prominent among these features are monumental buildings; planned architecture designed to segregate residential, administrative and production quarters; and the use of sealings, particularly door sealings, to regulate the flow of goods and to limit access to resources. Such early regional centers (for example, Chogha Mish, Susa, and Uruk) were usually large, with populations several degrees of magnitude greater than other settlements in the surrounding regions.

Explanations to support theories on the development of state organizations centered in such prominent sites may vary slightly, but a large population is an undeniable factor in the development of socioeconomic complexity. A number of sites, however, exhibit most of the characteristics of the larger regional centers but are nevertheless too small for large population to be a factor in their development. Prominent among these special sites are Tepe Gawra (Tobler 1950; Rothman 2001), Tell Abada (Jasim 1985), Kheit Qasim (Forest-Foucault 1980; Margueron 1987), possibly Tell Madhhur (Roaf 1982, 1987), and Tall-i Bakun A, the focus of this chapter. As we will see later, no similar sites have been reported from lowland Susiana and southern Mesopotamia, although this does not mean that small late prehistoric sites with evidence of administrative technology and monumental buildings do not exist in those areas. But if our assumptions about the demographic base of such sites are correct, we would be unlikely to find them in prime agricultural regions.

The sites just mentioned constitute a category of settlements that does not fit our current models of early urban development in which large, circumscribed populations play a fundamental role in creating socioeconomic and political complexity. In such models, the number of sites determines the size of a regional population, and the population of

each site is determined by its size. Such estimates, their uncertainties notwithstanding, obviously account for the settled-farming population of a given region. For good reason, however, such models do not account for the ancient mobile pastoralist communities, though they seem to have coexisted for thousands of years with settled communities as separate socioeconomic and political entities.

FOURTH TO FIFTH MILLENNIUM IN FARS: TALL-I BAKUN A

Mobile pastoralist populations rarely leave tangible archaeological remains. But a region's pastoral community, though archaeologically invisible, must have some indirect material manifestations that can be inferred archaeologically. Such manifestations, however, must not violate our intuitive understanding of human societies or be diametrically opposed to what we already know about such societies. For purposes of this discussion, I suggest that Tall-i Bakun A, with its evidence that anticipates later state organizations, serve as a *footprint* and material expression of the archaeologically invisible mobile pastoralist population of Fars in the late fifth millennium. In considering Bakun's archaeological evidence relevant to our discussions of ancient mobile pastoralism, we recognize that regional populations as a whole, not just residents of villages, towns, and cities, can create administrative demands and spur processes that might lead to further social complexity.

In the study of regional cultural development, particularly in highland Iran, it is important to take into account the ancient mobile pastoral population, even though they left little direct archaeological evidence. Nevertheless, the mobile pastoralist groups that might have wintered in lowland Mesopotamia and Susiana in the late fifth and early fourth millennia would have generated internal reorganization in the lowland farming communities. Indirect evidence pertaining to the presence of pastoral groups in late prehistoric Iran (late fifth and fourth millennia) includes isolated highland cemeteries (Vanden Berghe 1970, 1973), the presence of flat mounds, and the specific location of a large number of late prehistoric highland sites on mountain slopes instead of valley beds. Elsewhere I have also argued that the westward shift of the late fifth millennium settlements in lowland Susiana may possibly be linked to the influence of the mobile pastoralist population (Alizadeh 1992, N.D.; Delougaz and Kantor 1996).

Indirect evidence to study the problem is reported in the final publication of Tall-i Bakun A (Alizadeh N.D.). One line of evidence results from testing the hypothesis that distribution of the Bakun A painted pottery correlates with the geographic extent of the modern mobile pastoralist tribes of Fars. The 1995 survey was conducted primarily to test this hypothesis. Moreover, most of the villages in the valleys northwest of the Marvdasht are occupied by the Qashqa'i tribes, who abandon them in the harsh winter months, a situation that could account for a number of small and low sites in the region. This hypothesis can be tested by excavation at such sites through a comparative study of the spatial-functional composition of the architecture with that of the modern nomadic villages and campsites.

While we consider mobile pastoralists the core of Fars regional population that gave rise to the complexity we see at Tall-i Bakun A, the invisible population that created demands for administrative features seen at the small Mesopotamian sites mentioned above may have resided in their hinterlands. Through secular or religious factors, or most likely a mixture of both, the hinterland population led to demands for regulating mechanisms and to regional elite who resided within these nodes of population interaction. In such contexts, the hierarchy of social order does not physically manifest itself in specific locations or in large regional elite centers that can readily be seen in archaeological surface surveys. In these regions, evidence for socioeconomic features and for industrial production can be obtained only through excavations.

Although Tall-i Bakun A, with its small size and a population perhaps under two hundred, can hardly be considered a town, we cannot ignore the other characteristics it shares with the large late fourth millennium urban centers of the ancient Near East. Long before the appearance of administrative technology and physical segregation of administrative, production, storage, and residential units in urban centers of the second half of the fourth millennium, the Bakun A culture stands as one of the precursors to the complex societies of the early urban centers.

The 1995 archaeological survey in the valleys northwest of the Marvdasht shows that the geographic distribution of the Bakun A sites roughly corresponds to the territories the mobile pastoralist Qashqa'i cover in their annual migrations. Other archaeological surveys record sparse settled populations during the Bakun A phase in Fars. In this study, such evidence and formal interpretation of the excavated and survey data are woven together to suggest a mobile pastoralist base for the Bakun A society that prevailed in the region at least until the Islamic period.

THE 1995 SURVEY

We began the archaeological survey on May 1, 1995. Our project was designed to seek answers to a number of questions concerning the geographical extent and settlement patterns of the Bakun A culture in Fars during the fifth and early fourth millennia. The area we chose to investigate lies to the northwest of the Marvdasht, which had already been surveyed some twenty-five years ago by William Sumner (1972). Although the southern parts of the survey area overlapped with the region Sumner covered in his survey, the northern parts had not been surveyed.

The 1995 survey was conducted as part of a more comprehensive study of the nature of Tall-i Bakun A in its regional context. The archaeological surveys in northwestern Fars were conducted with three specific objectives. First, we wanted to map the distribution of sites in the previously unknown remote and mountainous regions northwest of the Marvdasht. Second, the northwest-southeast parallel valleys in this region are still used by the Qashqa'i tribes as migratory routes, and as such we were interested in the nature of the archaeological sites and their spatial relations to each other and to natural resources. Third, we were interested in the geographic extent of the Bakun A ceramics and whether it corresponded with the Qashqa'i territories. Thus, the most important part of the survey was the information I gathered on the modern demographic makeup of the Qashqa'i territory and the interaction between the nomadic tribes and farming villages in the valleys northwest of the Marvdasht.

All of the archaeological materials collected in the survey are in Tehran. A final analysis of the survey data can be done only after the material is studied in detail. Sherds representing each attested phase should have been illustrated, but because no archaeological materials (except bones and carbonized seeds) are allowed out of the country, and because I could not prolong my stay in Tehran, the time-consuming illustration task must wait. The following are general remarks and should be considered tentative until the final publication of the survey data.

As we expected, pre-Islamic settlements were sparse and relatively small. In particular, Bakun A settlement was sparse outside of the Marvdasht plain, the most fertile region in Fars. As in the Bakhtiari mountains (Zagarell 1982), most of the pre-Islamic sites were located on the slopes of the mountains bordering narrow and broad intermontane valleys, as are most of the modern villages in the survey area. At least three factors may account for this spatial pattern. First, some of these valleys, such as the one in Dasht-e Bakan, northwest of the Marvdasht, are inundated during the rainy seasons, a situation that makes it impossible to reside in the flat areas. Second, most of these valleys were traditionally part of the pasture of the mobile tribes of the Qashqa'i. Finally, in most of the areas we visited, valley beds were the only available good arable and fertile land (considering the technology). Thus, the settlement location was dictated by the necessity to avoid the seasonally flooded valley floors, to maximize land use, and to reduce conflicts between the settled communities and the mobile pastoralists, a situation also observed in the Bakhtiari mountains (Zagarell 1975, 1978, 1982). Moreover, because of the fluid nature of mobile pastoralism some segments of the tribes settle periodically in small villages and towns in their territories to pursue farming by acquiring farmland. Such centers are usually small and preserve their tribal allegiance to the tribal chief.

GENERAL RESULTS OF THE 1995 SURVEY
In the course of the survey, we discovered seventy-seven sites, ranging in date from the early Neolithic to the Safavid periods (see site catalogue). Most of the sites were small, between 0.5 and 2.0 to 3.0 ha but both larger and smaller ones did exist. Unfortunately, we found no late fifth millennium site that resembled Tall-i Bakun A and was comparatively large and, relative to other sites, centrally located.

After a day of work it became apparent that the site dimensions had been heavily affected by local farmers as well as by natural forces. Most of the sites had been virtually destroyed for fertilizer; the soil of the cultivated lands surrounding the mounds was almost always mixed with potsherds. There were even small fertile valleys occupied by a number of modern villages but with no visible sign of ancient mounds. Therefore, the statistics that our survey produced do not represent the actual settlement pattern and population density in the region. Nevertheless, a simple walk across the cultivated fields with scattered potsherds would reveal the remnants of the mounds that once existed in such valleys. Therefore, the general picture during the period of our interest, that is, late prehistory (4500–3600 BCE), is one of seemingly random distribution of small sites with a barely recognizable two-tiered hierarchy.

To ascertain the degree of destruction of archaeological sites since 1979, we also visited all the known sites we could locate in the Marvdasht. The following is a description of the various cultural phases attested in the course of the survey. The dating of the sites discovered in the course of the survey is based on the pottery.

The region to the northwest of the Marvdasht consists of a number of parallel valleys that lead to the inner Zagros mountains through Semirom, the boundary between the Qashqa'i and the Bakhtiari confederacies. These valleys vary from less than 1 km to more than 5 km in width. They are also different in the quality, quantity, and distribution of natural resources, including spring water, freshwater rivers, firewood, and arable land. On the whole, narrower valleys have fewer modern villages and ancient sites. In the large intermontane valleys, both modern villages and ancient sites tend to be situated on the slopes of the mountains, as expected in valleys dominated by mobile tribes and/or subject to flooding. Dasht-e Bakan (about 120 km to the northwest of the Marvdasht), which was still inundated by the spring rains, clearly demonstrated the reason for this spatial distribution of both ancient and modern sites.

The following is a brief description of each attested period; a comprehensive list of all the surveyed sites is provided for future reference. Question marks following a period indicate uncertainty. For example, in the absence of specific diagnostic sherds, it is difficult to separate Sasanian from early Islamic, Shogha from Teimuran, and Bakun B2 from Gap. Also, when crude, straw-tempered sherds were collected on sites with clear absence of other diagnostics, the period is simply designated "Neolithic." A number of types of Iron III gray ware seem to continue into the Achaemenid period. Thus, the sites that did not produce strong diagnostics for either period are marked uncertain as well.

PERIODS ATTESTED IN THE SURVEY
The literature on prehistoric Iranian archaeology is filled with site names that designate cultural sequences. The proliferation of names is nevertheless useful, and perhaps unavoidable, for prehistoric cultural sequences in the Zagros mountains, where a myriad of contemporary cultures with regional characteristics developed. The cultural sequence designation developed by Delougaz and Kantor for the Susiana sequence is simple, neutral, and inclusive (see also Alizadeh 1987:803, 1992:19). It is also flexible in the sense that newly discovered cultural phases can be incorporated into the chronological framework without introducing new names. Although these names are not standard for use in Fars, equivalents are Archaic Fars 1 (Mushki), Archaic Fars 2 (Jari), Middle Fars 1 (Bakun B2), Middle Fars 2 (Gap), Late Fars (Bakun A), Proto-Banesh (Lapui). See also chapter 16 for later periods in the region.

THE MUSHKI PHASE
Except for the type-site of Mushki, in the Marvdasht, we found no site of this phase in our survey; nor did we find any site with comparable early Neolithic pottery.

THE JARI PHASE
As with the Mushki phase, Jari phase sites are found only in the Marvdasht, not in the survey area, with the remote possibility at Tall-e Nourabad.

THE BAKUN HORIZON
This period can be divided into at least three phases: Early, Middle, and Late. The Early phase was discovered on only

four sites and is represented by a soft, straw-tempered plain pottery. This type of pottery continues into the Bakun B2 and Gap phases alongside a distinct Susiana-related black-on-buff pottery, resembling most closely the late Middle Susiana pottery of lowland Susiana (Alizadeh 1992, N.D.). The sites that have both the straw-tempered red ware and the black-on-buff ware create a problem in that it is almost impossible without excavation to know with any degree of certainty whether these sites have one or two phases of occupation.

Bakun B2 and Gap phases. These phases (Middle Bakun) are known from Tall-i Bakun B (Bakun B2 phase) and Tall-i Gap. Only seven sites in our survey area are dated to this phase.

Bakun A phase. This phase (Late Bakun) was attested on only ten sites in our survey area. Most of the sites were located in the valleys northwest of the Marvdasht, scattered all the way to Yasuj, the northernmost part of our survey. Most of the sites belonging to this phase are small. But, with two exceptions, they are primarily located not at the bottom of the valleys but on hillsides, a characteristic of settlements in predominantly mobile pastoralist territories. Almost all the Bakun A sites also contained sherds of the following Lapui phase, indicating a degree of continuity in the late prehistoric period.

THE LAPUI PHASE
This last prehistoric period in Fars is represented by twenty-two sites scattered almost evenly in the valleys.

THE BANESH PHASE (PROTO-ELAMITE)
The two sites dating to this phase indicate a drastic depopulation in the region. Both sites are small and one also had Lapui pottery.

THE KAFTARI PHASE
Fifteen sites are dated to this phase, clearly a marked increase in the population of these valleys after the decline in the Banesh phase.

THE QALEH, SHOGHA, AND TEIMURAN PHASES
Only one site is dated to the Qaleh phase, while the Shogha/Teimuran phase is represented by eight sites.

IRON AGE III
The presence of a distinct gray ware, similar to the pottery from the corresponding phase in the Zagros and at Chogha Mish (Delougaz and Kantor 1996:13–18), on twenty sites is indicative of this period. This type of pottery, which may be associated with the Iranian tribes who migrated into Fars, has not been reported from the Marvdasht or the nearby Beiza district. If this is not an accident of discovery, then this can be taken as evidence of the gradual penetration of these tribes into Fars. These sites are almost evenly distributed in the valleys that are traditionally traversed by the mobile pastoralist tribes of Fars.

THE ACHAEMENID PERIOD
The assignment of thirty-nine sites to this period is based on the similarity of their pottery to that found along the fortification walls at Persepolis. Most of the sites dated to the Achaemenid period were small in area but tall, an indication of fortified outposts rather than settlements.

THE PARTHIAN PERIOD
No sites could be assigned to this period with any degree of certainty.

THE SASANIAN PERIOD
Nineteen sites are dated to this period. However, some of these could be dated to the early Islamic period, since Sasanian pottery outlasted the period by at least a few generations.

THE ISLAMIC PERIOD
Most of the sites (fifty-five) discovered in the survey date to this period. The majority of the sites were large in area but low in height, so it is likely that smaller ones were completely missed by our survey. The sites that were larger than ten hectares had a topography with associated materials (kilns, slag, burnt soil, and wasters) that indicated industrial quarters.

ROLE OF MOBILE PASTORALISM IN FIFTH TO FOURTH MILLENNIUM FARS
I have proposed that mobile pastoralism might have been a crucial variable in socioeconomic and political development of highland Iran, particularly in Fars, as early as the late fifth and early fourth millennium BCE. Direct archaeological evidence for the presence of mobile pastoralists in Fars is limited (see Sumner 1986a:200). However, the small size, the location, apparent lack of architecture, and midden deposits of ash and debris indicate that at least some of Bakun A mounds were occupied seasonally (Alizadeh 1988a, 1988b, N.D.). More important is the existence of flat sites located by Aurel Stein in his survey of southern Fars (Stein 1936:161, 163, 175, 180) and my own survey in 1995. In addition, in the upper Kur river valley (the Ujan plain) a number of flint sites were found (Sumner 1972:251). This area is traditionally used as summer pasture by the mobile

tribes of the Qashqa'i. It must be noted, however, that although it seems obvious that hunters or sedentary herders may have used these sites, it is equally possible that they had been occupied by mobile groups.

Thus, known Bakun A sites can be assigned to three categories: 1) permanent villages represented by mound sites with architecture, 2) seasonal villages represented by mound sites without architecture, and 3) campsites represented by flat areas covered with potsherds and flint blades. While there is little doubt about the nature of the sites of the third group, the nature and function of the first two groups can be understood only by a detailed analysis of their components, which should reflect the material needs of their occupants. Beginning with Arrian (Anabasis III.17.1–5), historical documents and early travelers make it clear that moving to more favorable areas for part of the year has been customary for centuries among many highland pastoralist groups (for example, Bishop 1891; Stack 1882). Before the introduction of modern technology, the inhabitants of many villages in the Zagros valleys moved to the lowlands in the winter. Also, some of the intermontane plains become flooded and freeze during the winter, a situation that we should keep in mind surveying in the region. In the absence of modern roads and technology, year-round occupation of sites in harsh environment is almost impossible and even mounded sites may not have been permanent settlements. These observations must be factored into the interpretation of regional and interregional population density.

The Bakun A type ceramics have the widest geographic distribution in late prehistoric Iran. Bakun A is a homogeneous culture in Fars and is represented by widespread painted pottery. Outside Fars this pottery has been found in the Bakhtiari mountains (Zagarell 1975, 1982), the Behbehan and Zuhreh regions (Dittmann 1984; Stein 1940), and the Ram Hormuz area (Caldwell 1968a:348–350). No doubt Tall-i Bakun A and some other sites were major centers for manufacturing various goods in Fars; it is, however, unlikely that the vast geographical distribution of the Bakun A painted pottery was the result of long-distance trade. First, it would have been difficult to transport the fragile Bakun pottery over long distances and through mountainous regions, making a trade of this sort neither feasible nor economical. Second, the Bakun A painted pottery outside Fars is of limited shapes and designs, as would be expected of peripheral regions. Thus, Bakun cultural influence outside Fars in regions traditionally under the sway of numerous mobile tribes may have been the outcome of common cultural and perhaps ethnic backgrounds which the settled Fars population shared with the mobile tribes who

dispersed Bakun A culture over vast areas (see chapter 6). (A similar situation has been noted for distribution of the Neolithic Urfirnis pottery in Greece, Jacobson 1984.)

Archaeological investigations in the Behbehan-Zuhreh area (Dittmann 1984), the Dasht-e Susan (Wright 1975:50), and particularly in the Bakhtiari mountains (Zagarell 1979, 1982) have indicated that in the fifth to fourth millennia BCE these regions were utilized by mobile communities. The fifth millennium was a period of major change in the Bakhtiari mountains, when there began to be an increase in the number of seasonal and cave sites. The absence of Susa A pottery and the presence of Bakun A and Sialk III related ceramics there implies a connection between Fars and the Iranian Plateau in the region, perhaps a shift in regional alliance. This situation seems more important considering that in the late fifth and early fourth millennia the amount of luxury items such as copper, lapis lazuli and turquoise increased sharply in Mesopotamia, lowland Susiana, and Fars. Moreover, archaeological data from the Bakhtiari mountains suggest a parallel development during the first half of the fourth millennium in Fars, culminating in the abandonment of some sites and the displacement of the Bakun A painted pottery by a plain red ware (Zagarell 1982:44–50). The situation is less clear in the Behbehan and Zuhreh plains and in upper Susiana. Nonetheless, the appearance and disappearance of the Bakun A painted pottery in Fars is paralleled in Susiana, the Behbehan/Zuhreh region, and the Bakhtiari mountains. These circumstances are indicative of parallel developments in both the lowland and highland and require interregional explanation.

The areas cited have been traditionally exploited as summer and winter pastures, even today, by the mobile pastoralists of the Zagros. Attribution of the Bakun A society to a mobile pastoral base does not explain how and why a pastoral based economy would shift to another mode of economic production. The known Bakun A sites of the Late Fars phase (Bakun A phase) are small with one hundred to two hundred inhabitants who presumably practiced subsistence agriculture, an assumption that only comparative floral analysis can support. Even if future botanical analysis indicates the inhabitants of Bakun A sites were engaged in subsistence agriculture, the low density of the population as well as the absence of any clear evidence for canal irrigation agriculture argues against any large-scale agricultural activity that might support industrial activities. Nevertheless, it is unlikely that most Bakun A sites were engaged in manufacturing and distribution of various commodities as the inhabitants of Tall-i Bakun A were. Thus, a source other than agriculture must have supported the administrative and manufacturing community at Tall-i Bakun A and similar small sites.

The available archaeological data are the basis for our inference that non-agricultural production at Tall-i Bakun A was supported through externalization of surplus generated by the pastoral communities. It can be hypothesized that the surplus by which the Bakun craftsmen and traders could maintain their economy was basically related to a pastoral mode of production (see Boonzajer Flaes 1982). Conversion of the wealth of herds into land and other items of exchange requires some kind of currency. In the case of the Bakun A society, to convert mobile pastoralist surplus into other currencies of exchange that would have provided the economic power to maintain a body of full-time craft specialists would have required mutual demands for grains, wool, intestine, meat, various tools, pottery, and textiles which both settled and mobile populations of the highlands created as a result of their interdependence, population increase, and the rise of a nascent elite group. The emergence of small manufacturing/administrative centers such as Tall-i Bakun A coincided with the rise of late prehistoric urban centers in both southern Mesopotamia and lowland Susiana.

The available data do not indicate a large settled population during the Bakun A phase. If in a pre-state society the development of institutions of a higher level to deal/control/organize consumer goods is related to the size of the consumer potentialities, as suggested by Nissen (1983:336), it is possible that a mobile pastoral population, being economically more flexible and more adaptive than the agriculturists, would affect this relationship and would add to the potential consumers regardless of the size of the settlement system. This observation may explain why settlement patterns of the Bakun A sites in Fars differ from those in Susiana, where there is a marked settlement hierarchy, with large centers such as Chogha Mish, Abu Fandowa, Musiyan, and Susa dominating smaller sites.

Given that all known Bakun A sites in Fars are too small to be considered towns in the sense that their inhabitants engaged in non-subsistence economy, Tall-i Bakun may have emerged in response to material demands of Susiana, and perhaps to some extent of southern Mesopotamia. Viewing the problem from this angle, Tall-i Bakun A seems to have been the residence of some of the wealthier and higher-ranking individuals whose economic strength and social status allowed them to engage in sedentary trade economy. A common ethnic background and perhaps kinship ties between the ancient settled and mobile communities in Fars and the Zagros mountains may have facilitated processes of economic and sociopolitical development in Fars. The small cadre of individuals at Tall-i Bakun A, who controlled the resources and production of crafts, may have easily procured raw materials from faraway regions, and traded the finished products through their mobile pastoralist kinsmen (see Hjort 1981:50–67). In this fashion, they not only enjoyed the support and protection of the mobile pastoralists, but also a steady flow of valuable information needed to conduct their inter- and intraregional trade in material goods such as pottery, stone vessels, stone, semi precious stones, tools, ornaments, and possibly textiles.

LATER CYCLES OF MOBILE PASTORALISM

Tall-i Bakun A enjoyed a brief period of prosperity and was apparently suddenly abandoned some time in the early fourth millennium. Some of the Bakun sites were deserted some time before the middle of the fourth millennium. The following Lapui phase is poorly known, except for its settlement patterns and its characteristic red ware; not a single Lapui site in Fars has yet been excavated. This phase is seen by Sumner as a period of shifting emphasis from field crops to sheep and goat herding. The shift is assumed to be evidenced by spatial patterns of the Lapui as opposed to the Bakun A settlements. Sumner (1990b:17–18) reports that by the end of the Bakun A phase, the number of sites drops from 156 to 108, of which 52 are new settlements while the remaining 56 rest on Bakun A sites. He argues that pastoralism "is a response to rapidly decreasing productivity in the Soon district caused by salinization and other adverse consequences of agricultural intensification. The initial success of the herding strategy sets in motion a process that leads to nomadic pastoralism." Sumner's conclusion is based on the number of settlements assigned to the period dominated by the black-on-buff pottery of the Bakun B2, Gap, and Bakun A phases. The 156 sites that Sumner assigned to this period cover a span of perhaps one thousand years and represent three distinct phases: Bakun B2, Gap, and Bakun A. Lumping settlements dating to these distinct phases creates an inflated figure against which the number of Lapui sites suggests a decrease in population. Whereas once 156 settlements are divided into three phases, the Lapui phase actually represents an increase in the settled population, or at least an increase in mounded sites.

Furthermore, although the soil salinity and its attendant consequences may have had some influence on the socioeconomic and political developments of the fourth millennium, the gradual depopulation of the countryside, shifting of settlement patterns, and rise of large urban centers in regions where complex societies developed were universal phenomena in the Near East that cannot be satisfactorily explained by single environmental causes.

The outcome of the socioeconomic and political

development of early fourth millennium Fars is by no means clear. We know little about the period between the end of Bakun A and the beginning of the Banesh phase, when Malyan emerges as the regional center with state organization. Perhaps the socioeconomic and political developments that began in the fifth millennium did in fact continue after the disappearance of its elaborate painted pottery. Indeed, the Bakun A society may represent a case in which the sociopolitical situation became complex and mature enough to develop state organizations. Or perhaps Bakun A represents a pre-state community in which administrative problems were changing into political ones as a result of internal competition among the small cadre of individuals who controlled and redistributed resources (Wright 1977). The emergence of an impressive urban center at Malyan (historic Anshan), much larger than the contemporary Susa, and the concomitant development of Proto-Elamite civilization dominating both the lowland and the southern highlands may well have had their roots in earlier, Bakun A, times.

Following the decline of Kaftari phase Malyan, Sumner (1972:252) considered his later phases VI and VII (Shogha and Teimuran) a period of major nomadization, noting that the radical drop in number of sites and unprecedented increase in settlement size are indicative of the appearance of a mobile pastoralist population. While there is no reason to assume a link between either phenomenon, there are basic theoretical and archaeological problems that would suggest an alternative interpretation. First, if mobile pastoralism is not an indigenous development, then there must be a quantitative correlation between the total area of large sites and the earlier smaller sites. If this correlation exists, then we may reasonably assume that an external factor (namely, migration of mobile pastoralist groups into Fars, or an increase in mobile pastoralist population) forced the inhabitants of small settlements into larger aggregates to defend themselves better, which seems to be Sumner's underlying assumption. Moreover, we must be able to account for the difficulties involved in the transition from extensive to intensive farming, which requires large-scale canal irrigation. This in turn imposes a linear spacing of settlements. However, the assumption that desertion of the early sites and emergence of large ones was caused by salinization fails to explain how in such regions with saline soil the intensive agriculture necessary for large centers was possible.

Contrary to the idea that equates depopulation to the rise of mobile pastoralism, a decrease in the settled population of an area and the proportional increase in the existing mobile population may disturb the equilibrium in a region

with such mixed subsistence economies. The ethnographic and historical records show that "pure" mobile pastoralists do not exist and that they depend on farmers for the bulk of the cereal they need. In fact, it has been demonstrated that in southwestern Iran, during the fifth/fourth millennia, the growth of population in the lowland was concomitant with the increase in transhumant activities (Wright 1987:141–55). A parallel development can be suggested for the Bakhtiari mountains (Zagarell 1982).

Historical and ethnographic data, including my own observations, indicate that the major trading partners of pastoral productions involve urban centers, not traditional villages. Farmers living in villages all over Iran rarely consume meat in their daily diet and are self-sufficient in dairy production. Urban dwellers buy or exchange for meat, dairy products, wool and skin. The urban demand for such products cannot possibly be met by self-sufficient villages with a subsistence economy. If the same situation existed in prehistory, we would expect to see the tandem development of and interaction between the highland mobile pastoralist communities and the emergence of urban centers, particularly in lowland Susiana and southern Mesopotamia.

CONCLUSION

The archaeological data for the late fifth and early fourth millennia from Fars and the neighboring regions discussed above suggest the following proposals: The plain of Susiana suffered a decline in population by the end of the Middle Susiana period (Adams 1962:61–70; Alizadeh 1992). During the Middle Susiana period, a black-on-buff pottery much like the ceramics of the Late Middle Susiana phase appeared in Fars. At this point it is a matter of conjecture whether some of the inhabitants of Susiana migrated into Fars as farmers or adopted a mobile pastoralist way of life, or both, and whether this situation in Susiana was due to new socioeconomic and political developments that eventually resulted in the formation of state societies there.

Whatever factors contributed to demographic developments in Fars by the late fifth and early fourth millennia, it seems that the population increase in both mobile pastoralists and farming communities created new demands for material goods and incentive for the wealthy mobile pastoralists to externalize their economy by engaging in manufacture of goods and trade. Sites such as Tall-i Bakun A, where a cadre of well-to-do and privileged individuals had organized inter- and intra-regional networks of exchange of various exotic goods and pottery, rose to the occasion. Such centers were by no means mere manufacturing settlements. Judging by the evidence for administrative technology (stamp seals, sealings, tokens, for example) at Tall-i Bakun A and perhaps other sites, namely Vakilabad and Rigi (see Stein 1936), such settlements were at once manufacturing sites and centers for the administration of production and trade. The spatial distribution of warehouses and sealings as well as certain symbolic painted motifs, such as humans, lizards, and large-horned animals in what we call Bakun administrative quarters[1] indicates internal socioeconomic segregation in a pre-state community (see Alizadeh N.D.). This observation in turn suggests that the elite segment of the Bakun A society resided in and had control over these centers (Pollock 1983:354–390). The existence at some sites of such items and motifs may be a result of exchange of marriage gifts restricted to some prominent families.

After the disappearance of the Susa A painted pottery, material culture at the two major centers in Susiana (Susa, levels 18–17, and Chogha Mish) exhibits strong similarities with that of southern Mesopotamia, though there are a number of features (apparent absence of temple economy and stylistic aspects of glyptic, among others) that set the two regions apart. The number of sites increased in Fars and though surface surveys have revealed evidence of the existence of some forms of Protoliterate ceramics there, the local Lapui culture with its distinct red pottery continued. Whether spurred by the growing socioeconomic and political complexity in Mesopotamia, central Zagros, southwestern and southern Iran entered a new era by the end of the fourth millennium BCE. Around 3200 BCE, the Proto-Elamite civilization, quite different in material culture from its Mesopotamian neighbors, developed in Iran, most probably in Fars, centered at Malyan rather than at Susa. The following Banesh period (Proto-Elamite), most likely of highland origin, dominates both lowland and highland.[2] The foregoing pattern of cultural development in both lowland and highland repeats itself for millennia. A glance at the historical development in these regions and the "tug-of-war" between Mesopotamia and Iran, with Susiana as the bone of contention and theater of war, reveals how archaeological and historical developments in southwestern Iran go hand in hand (see Carter and Stolper 1984; Henrickson 1984:98–122; Steinkeller 1982; Stolper 1982; also chapter 3).

As I have suggested, and as the historical and archaeological evidence would indicate, political developments in Iran were shaped to a considerable degree by the mobile population of the highland. Moreover, it seems to be this segment of the highland and lowland population that provided a durable political base and continuity for various dynasties, not only in ancient times but also in historical times until the end of the eighteenth century CE, when the Luri Zand dynasty was replaced by the Qajars. Rowton's terms "dimorphic chiefdom" and "dimorphic state" for

political systems where an urban-based nomadic chiefly or royal family controls regions with mixed populations of farmers (as its economic base) and pastoralists (as its military base) appears an apt description for most of the political history of Iran (Rowton 1973b). Similarly, Lambton (1953:283) argues that "The power of the khans derives from two sources: on the one hand, from the tribe of which they are leaders, and, on the other hand, from land, which they own. In their capacity as landowners they collect their share of the produce of the land or their rents and dues as other landowners, while in the capacity as tribal leaders they collect certain levies from their followers."

Consistent with our characterization of pre-Islamic Iranian society, the dearth of literary and historical documents in Iran prior to the rise of the Sasanians, an urban-based dynasty, is not surprising. Compared with Mesopotamia and Egypt, a century of archaeological research in southwestern Iran, particularly in lowland Susiana, has yielded precious few written documents of historical and literary value. If the rarity of such documents in pre-Islamic Iran is not an accident of discovery, a point difficult to maintain given the volume of archaeological research in southwestern Iran, then we may attribute this lack to the strong oral tradition of mobile pastoralist societies.

No doubt, we have raised more questions than we have answered, owing to the paucity of both textual and archaeological materials, particularly from Fars and the Zagros mountains. We believe that a non-Susa/Susiana-centered approach is helpful in shedding more light on the important role the ancient mobile pastoralist communities played in the development of state organizations in southwestern Iran. This study remains for the most part heuristic, in the hope of encouraging similar studies and specifically designed researches that may offer new insights to analysis of socioeconomic organization in pre-state societies in highland Iran.

Acknowledgment. When he was the director of the Oriental Institute, Bill Sumner dropped by my office almost every day to, as he put it, "badger" me; he kept me on my toes. Bill had a vested interest in what I was doing and relentlessly hammered my ideas, thereby opening my eyes and mind to a number of unbaked or half-baked proposals I was trying to formulate. I thank Bill Sumner for discussing his archaeological and anthropological insights with me and I dedicate this "locust leg" as a token of my appreciation for his friendship.

NOTES

1. Sumner (1972:40) reports, for example, that out of 3000 sherds only twenty had naturalistic motifs such as dancing men, animals, snakes, and birds.
2. Vallat (1983) argues that when Elamite districts were united into one realm, its capital was Anshan with Susa as a dependency.

SITE CATALOGUE

Sites discovered or revisited in the Kur river basin in 1995.

DK 101: TALL-E CHARKHU

Geographic position: 52° 32' 00" N, 30° 07' 45" E
Elevation: 1620 m
Size: 65 x 50 x 1 m
Periods attested: Bakun A, Lapui, Achaemenid?, Islamic
Observations: Used traditionally by a mobile pastoralist family who keep their animals in the cave above the site.

DK 102: JASHNYIAN

Geographic position: 52° 31' 50" N, 30° 08' 30" E
Elevation: 1610 m
Size: 45 x 30 x 3 m
Periods attested: Achaemenid
Observations: Next to an irrigation canal and mostly destroyed by road and irrigation canal constructions.

DK 103: BIZJAN CAVE

Geographic position: 52° 27' 30" N, 30° 11' 05" E
Elevation: 1640 m
Size: n/a
Periods attested: Neolithic?
Observations: Still used by the Qashqa'i as animal shelter. The presence of a few crude, friable sherds indicate Neolithic settlement.

DK104: QADAMGAH

Geographic position: 52° 25' 40" N, 30° 15' 30" E
Elevation: 1635 m
Size: 60 x 47 x 2.30 m
Periods attested: Jari?, Lapui
Observations: Used by the nearby villagers as cemetery. Just to the northeast of a large natural spring.

DK 105: TALL-E BALANGOON

Geographic position: 52° 26' 50" N, 30° 13' 00" E
Elevation: 1653 m
Size: 116 x 85 x 5.95 m
Periods attested: Jari?, Bakun B1/2, Bakun A, Lapui, Achaemenid
Observations: Much of the site has been dug away and scattered in the surrounding farms.

DK 106: TALL-E ASHKI

Geographic position: 52° 26' 50" N, 30° 13' 20" E
Elevation: 1635 m
Size: 146 x 45 x 3.80 m
Periods attested: Bakun A, Lapui, Iron III, Achaemenid, Islamic
Observations: Two-thirds of this mound is destroyed and mudbrick architecture, presumably of the Lapui period, is exposed.

DK 107: ROCK SHELTER

Geographic position: 52° 18' 05" N, 30° 24' 00" E
Elevation: 1685 m
Size: 17 x 8 x 7m
Periods attested: Neolithic?
Observations: The site is used by the Qashqa'i for animal shelter. A few flint cores indicate a Neolithic occupation of uncertain phase.

DK 108: TALL-E BAKAN

Geographic position: 52° 24' 00" N, 30° 24' 10" E
Elevation: 2165 m
Size: 77 x 59 x 4.95 m
Periods attested: Lapui, Kaftari, Iron III
Observations: Situated in the middle of wheat field on the bed of an extensive valley.

DK 109A+B: TALL-E MANJQULI

Geographic position: 52° 19' 55" N, 30° 38' 40" E
Elevation: 2152 m
Size: 50 x 45 x 1.6 m/56 x 48 x 2.7 m
Periods attested: Iron III, Achaemenid, Islamic
Observations: Twin site, a and b. Both are cultivated and destroyed by farmers for fertilizer. Several pieces of iron slag were found.

DK 110: TALL-E CHAR

Geographic position: 52° 49' 30" N, 29° 58' 09" E
Elevation: 2110 m
Size: 134 x 94 x 3.70 m
Periods attested: Sasanian, Islamic (Seljuq) Trishi
Observations: Brick architecture is exposed. Bricks measure 36 x 25 x 6 cm; saddle shaped mound. Height = 2.30 m (east), 3.70 m (west), 1.0 m (middle).

DK 111: TALL-E JALALI

Geographic position: 52° 49' 07" N, 29° 58' 04" E
Elevation: 2125 m
Size: 149 x 146 x 2.60 m
Periods attested: Lapui, Kaftari, Iron III, Achaemenid
Observations: Mostly destroyed, with artifacts and pottery scattered in the surrounding fields.

DK 112: TAPPEH EMAMZADEH SHAH GHEIB

Geographic position: 52° 41' 35" N, 29° 57' 10" E
Elevation: 1620 m
Size: 266 x 162 x 3.70 m
Periods attested: Islamic (Safavid)
Observations: Traces of a large brick kiln and wasters still visible.

DK 113: TALL-E RASHTI

Geographic position: n/a
Elevation: 1590 m
Size: 392 x 181 x 3.20 m
Periods attested: Lapui, Banesh, Kaftari, Qaleh?
Observations: This low mound is located on the right side of the highway from Marvdasht to Zarqan and cannot be seen during the growing season. The main settlement dates to the Kaftari and Middle Elamite period.

DK 114: TALL-E SOOZ/SABZ A

Geographic position: 52° 47' 20" N, 29° 51' 40" E
Elevation: 1599 m
Size: 108 x 81 x 5.60 m
Periods attested: Lapui, Kaftari, Iron III, Achaemenid?, Islamic
Observations: The site is located in the modern town of Marvdasht and surrounded by residential buildings. Seemingly Achaemenid bricks of two sizes (34 x 34 x 8 and 20 x 20 x 7 cm) are scattered on the mound.

DK 115: TALL-E SOOZ/SABZ B

Geographic position: 52° 47' 15" N, 29° 51' 30" E
Elevation: 1599 m
Size: 119 x 40 x 1.30 m
Periods attested: Kaftari, Iron III, Achaemenid, Sasanian, Islamic
Observations: This mound is also located in the town of Marvdasht, next to DK 114. Traces of rectangular stone architecture (4 rooms) are still visible on the mound. It is possible this and DK 114 originally formed one large mound.

DK 116: RASHMIJAN

Geographic position: 52° 51' 50" N, 29° 52' 40" E
Elevation: 1595 m

Size: 82 x 83 x 3.60 m
Periods attested: Bakun B1/2?, Achaemenid? Islamic
Observations: The mound is the site of a modern cemetery.

DK 117: TALL-E HALQEH A
Geographic position: 52° 51' 45" N, 29° 52' 10" E
Elevation: 1590 m
Size: 79 x 58 x 3.30 m
Periods attested: Iron III, Achaemenid? Islamic
Observations: It is possible that this mound is the extension of DK 118.

DK 118: TALL-E HALQEH B
Geographic position: 52° 51' 40" N, 29° 52' 15" E
Elevation: 1590 m
Size: 62 x 51 x 0.90 m
Periods attested: Achaemenid?
Observations: Perhaps once connected to DK 117.

DK 119A: QADAMGAH A
Geographic position: 52° 50' 25" N, 29° 51' 20" E
Elevation: 1590 m
Size: 107 x 70 x 5.10 m
Periods attested: Achaemenid, Sasanian, Islamic

DK 119B: QADAMGAH B
Geographic position: 52° 50' 20" N, 29° 51' 20" E
Elevation: 1590 m
Size: see observations
Periods attested: Achaemenid?, Sasanian, Islamic
Observations: The site consists of a central and a number of little mounds numbered 1–5; no. 1 = 88 x 76 x 3.0; no. 2 = 54 x 48 x 2.7; no. 3 = 54 x 32 x 2.7; no. 4 = 43 x 40 x 3.0; no. 5 = 125 x 73 x 2.9 m.

DK 120: TALL-E MORAD
Geographic position: 52° 52' 20" N, 29° 50' 50" E
Elevation: 1600 m
Size: 51 x 50 x 6.20 m
Periods attested: Iron III, Achaemenid
Observations: Scattered ashlars on and around the site suggest a fort.

DK 121: QABRESTAN-E QADAMGAH
Geographic position: 52° 52' 20" N, 29° 51' 00" E

Elevation: 1600 m
Size: 225 x 76 x 2.40 m
Periods attested: Kaftari, Sasanian, Islamic
Observations: Most of the site is buried under a modern cemetery.

DK 122: TALL-E GASHK
Geographic position: 52° 55' 20" N, 29° 53' 55" E
Elevation: 1585 m
Size: 43 x 33 x 2.90 m
Periods attested: Achaemenid?, Sasanian, Islamic

DK 123: TALL-E MAMALIS (GAP)
Geographic position: 52° 56' 10" N, 29° 50' 50" E
Elevation: 1590 m
Size: 238 x 223 x 6.20 m
Periods attested: Bakun B1/2, Bakun A, Lapui, Kaftari, Shogha/Teimuran, Achaemenid, Sasanian, Islamic

DK 124: TALL-E SEYEDI A
Geographic position: 52° 56' 00" N, 29° 50' 40" E
Elevation: 1590 m
Size: 254 x 153 x 2.00 m
Periods attested: Sasanian, Islamic
Observations: This mound presumably was a residential part of DK 125 (see below).

DK 125: TALL-E SEYEDI B
Geographic position: 52° 55' 45" N, 29° 50' 30" E
Elevation: 1590 m
Size: 361 x 330 x 2.20 m
Periods attested: Sasanian, Islamic
Observations: The site consists of a few low to medium mounds covered with brick and pottery wasters as well as traces of kilns. Architectural remains with stone foundations are also visible.

DK 126: TALL-E GASHKI
Geographic position: 52° 56' 25" N, 29° 49' 50" E
Elevation: 1585 m
Size: 186 x 67 x 2.90 m
Periods attested: Bakun A, Lapui

DK 127: TALL-E TAJABAD
Geographic position: 52° 56' 32" N, 29° 49' 57" E
Elevation: 1600 m
Size: 119 x 99 x 5.40 m
Periods attested: Lapui, Islamic
Observations: A large Islamic industrial

kiln is visible on the western slope of the mound.

DK 128: TALL-E DAM QALE/TALL-E BOZORG
Geographic position: 52° 57' 15" N, 29° 47' 10" E
Elevation: 1578 m
Size: 168 x 150 x 1.50 m
Periods attested: Sasanian, Islamic
Observations: This is the only prehistoric mound in this part of the plain. The water here is brackish, the soil salty and even modern villages are rare sights. The only evidence of a prehistoric occupation were the small, retouched flint blades identical to those found at Tall-e Bakun.

DK 129: TALL-E QALEH
Geographic position: 52° 58' 05" N, 29° 58' 20" E
Elevation: 1646 m
Size: 238 x 196 x 11.00 m
Periods attested: Lapui, Kaftari, Shogha/Teimuran, Achaemenid, Islamic

DK 130: QABRESTAN-E SIVAND
Geographic position: 52° 55' 15" N, 30° 04' 50" E
Elevation: 1650 m
Size: ?
Periods attested: Islamic
Observations: The modern cemetery of the town of Sivand completely covers the site so that it is impossible without excavation to determine its size.

DK 131: TALL-E QASR-E DASHT
Geographical position: n/a
Elevation: 1560 m
Size: 153 x 116 x 15.30 m
Periods attested: Lapui, Kaftari,Shogha/Teimuran, Iron III, Achaemenid, Islamic
Observations: Remains of a castle or fortification are still visible on the mound. According to the local people, the site was the seat of a local chief.

DK 132: TALL-E RAHMATABAD
Geographic position: n/a
Elevation: 1587 m
Size: 198 x 100 x 7.70 m
Periods attested: Lapui, Kaftari,Shogha/Teimuran, Iron III, Achaemenid, Islamic
Observations: Large ashalars were visible on and around the mound.

DK 133: TALL-E QALEH KUHNEH
Geographic position: 52° 57' 00" N, 30° 36' 20" E

Elevation: 2333 m
Size: 124 x 104 x 4.90 m
Periods attested: Iron III, Achaemenid, Islamic
Observations: The site has a huge depression in the middle and what appears as a large opening to the west, suggesting that the whole site might have been a fortification.

DK 134: CHAR-TAQ-E MUSHKAN
Geographic position: n/a
Elevation: 2340 m
Size: —
Periods attested: Sasanian, Islamic
Observations: This is a Sasanian fire temple with perhaps a number of subsidiary buildings around it.

DK 135: TAPPEH DEH BERAL
Geographic position: 52° 38' 25" N, 30° 40' 05" E
Elevation: 2315 m
Size: 380 x 370 x 3.50 m
Periods attested: Sasanian, Islamic
Observations: The topography of this mound is the same as DK 133.

DK 136: TALL-E AB-E BARIK A
Geographic position: 52° 28' 00" N, 30° 42' 05" E
Elevation: 2326 m
Size: 104 x 73 x 3.00 m
Periods attested: Sasanian, Islamic
Observations: Traces of stone foundations are still visible.

DK 137: TALL-E AB-E BARIK B
Geographic position: 52° 28' 50" N, 30° 42' 05" E
Elevation: 2326 m
Size: 62 x 60 x 3.40 m
Periods attested: Shogha/Teimuran, Iron III
Observations: This mound is located only 200 m from DK 136.

DK 138: AQ QALEH
Geographic position: 52° 39' 00" N, 30° 01' 00" E
Elevation: 1600 m
Size: 223 x 220 x 36.30 m
Periods attested: Lapui, Banesh, Kaftari, Shogha/Teimuran, Iron III
Observations: This mound is located on a high natural outcrop overlooking the entire Ramjerd plain.

DK 139: TALL-E KOSHKAK
Geographic position: 52° 36' N, 30° 04' E
Elevation: 1610 m

Size: 85 x 84 x 1.40 m
Periods attested: Achaemenid

DK 140: TALL-E GAP NAZARABAD
Geographic position: 52° 36' 30" N, 30° 04' E
Elevation: 1605 m
Size: 170 x 160 x 6.10 m
Periods attested: Bakun B1/2

DK 141: TALL-E NAZRABAD (QALEH KUHNEH)
Geographic position: 52° 36' N, 30° 05' 40" E
Elevation: 1609 m
Size: 180 x 73 x 3.80 m
Periods attested: Islamic
Observations: Traces of a mudbrick fortification wall still visible on the site.

DK 142: TALL-E MAZARI (BAGYIAN)
Geographic position: 52° 16' N, 30° 20' E
Elevation: 1700 m
Size: 183 x 168 x 7.20 m
Periods attested: Bakun B1/2, Islamic

DK 143: TALL-E MASHHADI BEILU
Geographic position: 52° 11' 55" N, 30° 19' 40" E
Elevation: 1710 m
Size: 199 x 186 x 7.50 m
Periods attested: Islamic

DK 144: TALL-E QALE CHOGHA
Geographic position: n/a
Elevation: 1750 m
Size: 183 x 170 x 18.60 m
Periods attested: Iron III, Achaemenid, Islamic
Observations: A large part of this mound is now submerged in the waters of the Dorudzan reservoir. Substantial remains of a presumably Islamic fortification are still visible on the summit of the mound.

DK 145: TALL-E SHANGOOLI (LAPUII)
Geographic position: 52° 39' 10" N, 29° 43' 05" E
Elevation: 1650 m
Size: 128 x 94 x 1.50 m
Periods attested: Lapui

DK 146: TALL-E ZARI
Geographic position: 51° 75' 00" N, 30° 32' 20" E
Elevation: 2100 m
Size: 76 x 46 x 7.00 m

Periods attested: Jari/Bakun B1, Achaemenid, Islamic

DK 147: TALL-E GAMLI
Geographic position: 51° 56' 50" N, 30° 32' 20" E
Elevation: 2100 m
Size: 95 x 92 x 13.00 m
Periods attested: Bakun A, Lapui, Achaemenid
Observations: Large piles of stones, some hewn, at the base of the mound are mixed with Achaemenid pottery and may have belonged to a fortification.

DK 148: TALL-E ASFYIAN
Geographic position: 51° 56' 48" N, 30° 31' 15" E
Elevation: 2110 m
Size: n/a
Periods attested: Achaemenid?, Islamic
Observations: The mound is buried under the modern village of Asfian.

DK 149: TALL-E KHARESTAN SOFLA
Geographic position: 52° 21' N, 29° 33' E
Elevation: 1580 m
Size: 134 x 55 x 11.80 m
Periods attested: Bakun A, Lapui, Islamic

DK 150: TALL-E DEH-E SUKHTEH
Geographic position: 52° 01' 00" N, 30° 50' 20" E
Elevation: 2270 m
Size: 205 x 183 x 8.80 m
Periods attested: Achaemenid, Islamic
Observations: The summit of the mound has been leveled by bulldozer to accommodate an Islamic cemetery.

DK 151: TALL-E KOOREH
Geographic position: 51° 40' 30" N, 30° 55' 50" E
Elevation: 2200 m
Size: 477 x 140 x 10.30 m
Periods attested: Achaemenid, Islamic
Observations: An Islamic cemetery sits on top of the mound.

DK 152: TALL-E ASPAS
Geographic position: 52° 24' 00" N, 30° 38' 30" E
Elevation: 2155 m
Size: 111 x 33 x 9.30 m
Periods attested: Bakun B1/2, Achaemenid, Islamic
Observations: The name of the village is probably a derivation of the Old Persian *Aspa*, horse. A gendarme post on top of the mound covers a mudbrick platform.

DK 153: TALL-E BABAII

Geographic position: 52° 26' 20" N, 30° 35' 40" E

Elevation: 2147 m

Size: 170 x 168 x 10.80 m

Periods attested: Iron III, Islamic

DK 154: QALEH SHAHR ASHUB

Geographic position: n/a

Elevation: 2160 m

Size: 119 x 91 x 8 m

Periods attested: Lapui, Achaemenid, Kaftari? Iron III, Islamic

Observations: This mound is confined within the fortification walls of a now abandoned village. A large building, presumably the residence of a local chief, sits on the summit of the mound.

DK 155: KOOSHK-E ZAR A

Geographic position: 52° 21' N, 30° 49' E

Elevation: 2314 m

Size: 60 x 40 x 2.50 m

Periods attested: Achaemenid?, Sasanian, Islamic

Observations: The mound is much damaged to accommodate a local shrine. Like many other ancient sites and modern villages in the intermontane valleys, DK 155 is located on the slope of the mountains surrounding the plain of Shadkam.

DK 156: KOOSHK-E ZAR B

Geographic position: 52° 21' N, 30° 49' E

Elevation: 2314 m

Size: 220 x 214 x 5.60 m

Periods attested: Bakun B1/2, Lapui, Achaemenid, Islamic

Observations: This site, located near DK 155, consists of three mounds with varying heights of 7.00, 5.60, and 3.60 m.

DK 157: TALL-E SHAHROYAN

Geographic position: 52° 22' 30" N, 30° 50' 20" E

Elevation: 2311 m

Size: 229 x 183 x 6.30 m

Periods attested: Achaemenid, Sasanian, Islamic

DK 158: QASR-E GOLANDAM

Geographic position: 52° 19' 00" N, 30° 56' 50" E

Elevation: 2336 m

Size: 183 x 168 x 5.30 m

Periods attested: Iron III, Achaemenid

Observations: The square shape of the mound and the stumps of stone architec-ture in the huge depression in the center suggest the existence of a fortification.

DK 159: TALL-E HAJIABAD

Geographic position: 52° 17' 15" N, 30° 39' 50" E

Elevation: 2155 m

Size: 88 x 42 x 2.20 m

Periods attested: Sasanian/Islamic

DK 160: TALL-E BIZJAN

Geographic position: 52° 27' 05" N, 30° 11' 45" E

Elevation: 1610 m

Size: 299 x 296 x 2 m

Periods attested: Islamic

Observations: The mound is cut by the Marvdasht-Sedeh highway. A modern cemetery and morgue are located on the western part of the mound.

DK 161: TALL-E SHOOL

Geographic position: 52° 52' 00" N, 30° 31' 10" E

Elevation: 1645 m

Size: ?

Periods attested: Achaemenid, Islamic

DK 162: TALL-E SAROOII

Geographic position: 52° 50' 00" N, 30° 33' 20" E

Elevation: 1750 m

Size: 183 x 92 x 2.00 m

Periods attested: Islamic

Observations: A large mansion, now abandoned, was built on the southern part of the mound. The mud used for the construction is full of pottery.

DK 163: TALL-E KAMIN

Geographic position: 52° 49' 50" N, 30° 31' 10" E

Elevation: 1650 m

Size: 287 x 192 x 5.40 m

Periods attested: Bakun A, Lapui, Kaftari, Shogha/Teimuran, Achaemenid, Islamic

Observations: Bakun A pottery is primarily found on the northern, much damaged part of the mound.

DK 164: TALL-E EZZABAD

Geographic position: 52° 57' 35" N, 29° 52' 15" E

Elevation: 1650 m

Size: 183 x 153 x 2.30 m

Periods attested: Iron III, Achaemenid, Sasanian, Islamic

Observations: Remains of stone architecture are still visible on the summit of the mound.

DK 165: TALL-E EMAMZADEH SEYYED HAJ GHARIB

Geographic position: 52° 57' 20" N, 29° 50' 50" E

Elevation: 1670 m

Size: 214 x 91 x 1.50 m

Periods attested: Islamic

Observations: A modern cemetery and a lo-cal shrine are located on the southern part of the mound.

DK 166: TALL-E MAQSUDABAD (TALL-E HADI A)

Geographic position: 52° 58' 50" N, 29° 50' 20" E

Elevation: 1670 m

Size: 107 x 97 x 2.50 m

Periods attested: Bakun B1/2, Kaftari

DK 167: TALL-E HADI B

Geographic position: 52° 58' 50" N, 29° 50' 20" E

Elevation: 1670 m

Size: n/a

Periods attested: Bakun B1/2, Bakun A

DK 168: TALL-E DARVAZEH

Geographic position: 53° 10' N, 29° 47' E

Elevation: 1660 m

Size: 137 x 122 x 3.00 m

Periods attested: Bakun A, Achaemenid

Observations: Cut by the paved road from Persepolis to Esmaiilabad, the northern part is almost completely destroyed. The mound is situated at the point where Marvdasht joins the plain of Esmaiilabad to the east, hence, perhaps, the name of the mound, which means gate.

DK 169: TALL-E JAFARABAD

Geographic position: 53° 14' N, 29° 46' E

Elevation: 1700 m

Size: 152 x 137 x 7.5 m

Periods attested: Achaemenid, Islamic

Observations: A large fortification wall of Islamic period surrounds the site.

DK 170: TALL-E EMAMZADEH BIBI SULTAN

Geographic position: 52° 49' 10" N, 29° 50' 20" E

Elevation: 1560 m

Size: 125 x 97 x 1.10 m

Periods attested: Lapui, Islamic

Observations: The mound is currently used as the nearby village cemetery.

DK 171: TALL-E SOOZ A (DOLATABAD A)

Geographic position: 52° 49' 08" N, 29° 50' 10" E

Elevation: 1560 m
Size: 83 x 82 x 2.40 m
Periods attested: Kaftari?, Iron III, Achaemenid

DK 172: TALL-E SOOZ B (DOLATABAD B)
Geographic position: 52° 49' 10" N, 29° 50' 05" E
Elevation: 1560 m
Size: 290 x 244 x 1.00 m
Periods attested: Lapui, Kaftari, Shogha/ Teimuran, Islamic?

DK 173: TALL-E MALEKABAD
Geographic position: 52° 58' 05" N, 29° 43' 05" E
Elevation: 1580 m
Size: 449 x 186 x 3.10 m
Periods attested: Iron III, Sasanian, Islamic

Observations: The site consists of a large central mound and 6 small satellites.

DK 174: NAME UNKNOWN
Geographic position: 52° 50' 02" N, 29° 53' 18" E
Elevation: 1580 m
Size: Height = 1.60 m
Periods attested: Islamic
Observations: The site is located north of the town of Marvdasht, west of the Azmayesh factory. It consists of a number of low mounds.

DK 175: TALL-E QABRESTAN KOOSHK
Geographic position: 52° 50' 40" N, 29° 53' 40" E
Elevation: 1580 m
Size: Height = 0.90 m
Periods attested: Islamic

Observations: The mound is almost completely covered by a local cemetery.

DK 176: TALL-E GAP-E KENAREH
Geographic position: 52° 52' 00" N, 29° 54' 15" E
Elevation: 1600 m
Size: 137 x 88 x 7.70 m
Periods attested: Shogha/Teimuran, Iron III, Achaemenid, Sasanian, Islamic

DK 177: TALL-E KENAREH
Geographic position: 52° 51' 55" N, 29° 54' 10" E
Elevation: 1600 m
Size: 229 x 183 x 2.90 m
Periods attested: Sasanian, Islamic
Observations: A complex of small mounds with traces of brick architecture and brick kiln wasters.

CHAPTER 8

THE EPIPALEOLITHIC IN THE MARVDASHT

MICHAEL ROSENBERG

WILLIAM SUMNER'S 1967–1969 systematic survey of the Kur river basin (Sumner 1972), among many other things, firmly established the fact that there was widespread and persistent occupation of that area during the Paleolithic. It was my good fortune to join the Malyan Project in 1976 and to be actively encouraged and helped by Bill to follow up on his Paleolithic discoveries.

Following a brief reconnaissance survey of the entire Marvdasht in 1976, a systematic survey of Paleolithic sites in the western half of the plain was begun in 1978. It was planned for completion in 1979, but as was also the fate of other projects, the survey was interrupted by the Iranian Revolution. Consequently, the work was never completed as planned and the data derived from the 1978 season suffer accordingly. Their shortcomings notwithstanding, the 1978 survey data do shed some light on the Epipaleolithic cultures of the region. Specifically, they suggest that the lithic industries in the Marvdasht, and by extension in the southern Zagros, do not differ significantly from what is generally considered to be typical of the Zarzian, the industry commonly found at Epipaleolithic sites in the more northerly parts of the Zagros. They also suggest that there is a change in settlement patterns in the western Marvdasht during the Epipaleolithic, with a single large cave site becoming the center of activity in this area.

THE SURVEY

The survey, as originally planned, was to involve a vehicular-based 'cave' survey of all visible potential sites (including caves, rock shelters, and collapsed rock shelters) in the western half of the Marvdasht, coupled with a stratified random sample walking survey of that area. The latter was designed to both control for possible deficiencies in the cave survey and to generate data concerning the range of surface scatters and open air site types occurring within the survey area. The 1978 field season ended with the vehicular survey nearing completion, and only a small handful of potential sites remaining to be visited. However, the associated stratified random sample walking survey had covered only a small fraction of the planned area and no portion of the sampling stratum that was to control for possible deficiencies in the vehicular survey was included in that area. Beyond this last fact, the walking survey results do not pertain to what follows and so will not be discussed further.

The cave survey located and sampled twenty-nine sheltered sites of various sizes in the western Marvdasht. Included in this number are several caves that had been discovered by Sumner during his 1967–1969 survey of the Kur river basin and another that had been discovered by Henry T. Wright during his visit to the Marvdasht in 1976. In addition to numerous dubious rockshelters that were found not to be sites of visible human activity, four of the more promising caves visited in 1978 also lacked visible evidence of past human activity. However, one of these four 'vacant' caves (figure 8.1: site 3) is reported to have yielded a small chipped stone assemblage during Sumner's survey. Unfortunately, this collection was also unavailable for study. An additional two promising caves

98

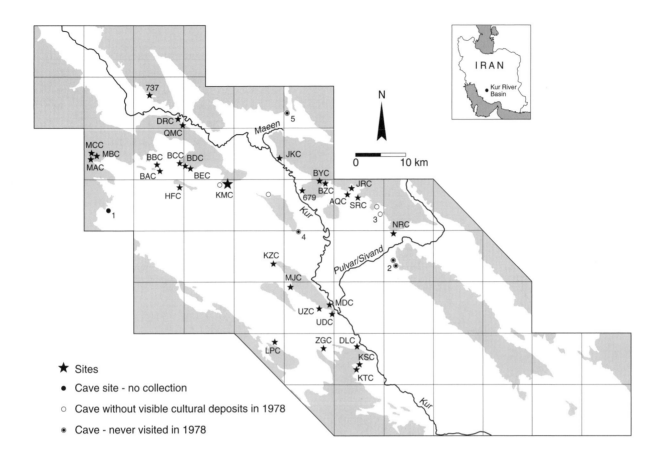

8.1   The Marvdasht (Kur river basin), showing location of caves mentioned in the text. *Original by M. Rosenberg*

(figure 8.1: site 2—the designation refers to the pair of caves) were ignored in 1978 because they had been visited by Wright in 1976 and found not to contain any cultural remains dating to preceramic periods (H.T. Wright, personal communication, 1976).

The discussion that follows concerns those sites that have the remains of human occupation dating to at least one period, and the question of when and how they were used. None of the four promising but never-used caves that were actually visited in 1978 enter into the discussion of settlement patterns that follows. Neither do the two that were never visited in 1978 because Wright had found them to be empty in 1976. These six "vacant" sites presumably exhibit some attribute or attributes that made them unsuitable for any use at any of the times under consideration. The possible implications of the one "vacant" site (figure 8.1: site 3) which yielded a small assemblage during Sumner's survey, but not during the 1978 survey, will be considered later, along with the possible implications of other visible caves that were never visited in 1978.

Aside from the two caves visited by Wright in 1976 and reported to be empty, there are five other clearly visible

caves that were not visited in 1978 for various logistical or timing reasons. Of these, two had been visited by Sumner during his survey. He designated one site no. 679 and the other no. 737 (Sumner, personal communication, 1988). The small collections he made at these sites were available for study in the United States, at the University of Pennsylvania Museum of Archaeology and Anthropology in Philadelphia and are discussed later in this chapter. Another of these five caves (figure 8.1: site 1) is known from observations during the 1976 reconnaissance to have some lithic material on the surface of its talus slope (including a geometric microlith), but no collection was made in 1976 and so none was available for study. The fourth cave is situated just north of the Maeen river (figure 8.1: site 5). Though Sumner records a collection as coming from that cave, the collection was not available for study and nothing further can be said about the site. The fifth and last is a very small cave several hundred meters above the surface of the plain (figure 8.1: site 4). Nothing is known about this site.

All the cave sites surveyed in 1978 (including a number previously visited by Sumner) were given a three-letter field designation, which will be used here. The sites collected by Sumner but not visited in 1978 (for which collections were available) will be referred to by Sumner's numeric field designations.

METHODOLOGICAL CONSIDERATIONS

Aspects of the 1978 survey methodology that pertain to the stratified random sample walking survey are tangential to this discussion and are therefore not reviewed here (see Rosenberg 1988). Of those that pertain to the cave survey, the two key methodological points are: 1) all visible caves and potential rockshelters in the western half of the Marvdasht were to be mapped and sampled and, with the exception of the specific cases listed above, all were; and 2) all visible chipped stone was systematically collected at all sites. This was done by walking repeated one-meter wide transects across the full width of both the sheltered interior area and the full length of the talus slope in front of the site. In the case of sites surveyed in 1978 that Sumner had collected during his survey and for which his collections were available, Sumner's collections were lumped in with the respective 1978 collections for purposes of analysis. The rationale for combining the data in this way is the assumption that, had Sumner not collected the material when he did, it would have remained on the surface of the site to be collected as part of the systematic total pickups made during the 1978 survey.

The overriding methodological consideration pertaining to what follows is the question of how reliable the surface collections are as indicators of the sites' subsurface contents, particularly those dating to the Epipaleolithic. Several points bear on this and will therefore be enumerated.

First, if they are present, Epipaleolithic deposits, being closer to the modern surface than any older and underlying Paleolithic deposits that may also be present at a site, should be more prone to representation in surface samples than remains dating to the older deposits. Therefore, if present, they are the component most likely to be found in surface contexts and the absence of Epipaleolithic surface remains can be considered more (but by no means completely) reliable evidence for the absence of a corresponding subsurface component at a site than would the absence of surface remains attributable to any earlier periods.

Second, by far the vast bulk of lithic material collected at each site visited in 1978 was found eroding out of the talus slope in front of each site, not on its sheltered interior surface. Thus, while material from the uppermost deposits has the highest probability of being represented in all the collections, material from stratigraphically lower

deposits also has a reasonable chance to be represented in all those collections. It also means that the variable nature of the modern overburden within the sheltered area of each site did not seriously distort the comparability of the collections. In addition, it should also be noted that the talus slopes in front of all but one cave (BEC) visited in 1978 were traversed by numerous goat tracks. Thus, for better or worse, surface conditions in the primary collection area at virtually all sites were essentially comparable.

Last, there is one case where excavated material can be compared to surface collections, and so shed light on the general reliability of the surface collections. That case is the site of Eshkaft-e Gavi, also known as MDC under the survey designation system (Rosenberg 1985). The survey collection and the excavated assemblage from that site correspond reasonably well to each other, at least as regards the primary line of evidence to be employed here—index types that can be taken as evidence for the simple presence/absence of Middle, Upper, and Epipaleolithic components at that site.

DATING THE SURVEY SITES

Absolute dates for the Zagros Paleolithic remain scarce and, in most cases, not very useful for determining the precise beginning or end of any specific period. For the Epipaleolithic, the period of central concern to this chapter, the few available dates suggest that it begins sometime prior to 12,000 BP (uncalibrated). For this study, all sites were dated typologically on the basis of index types present in the site collections. Dating sites by more sophisticated means requires assemblages that are both quantitatively representative and attributable to some limited period of time (or reliably divisible into units that are so attributable). Survey data are derived from surface collections. Thus, they are neither representative, nor can the large majority of the artifacts be reliably attributed to a specific period. At this time, the same problems also pose an insurmountable impediment to reliably estimating relative site sizes for the periods in question.

As gleaned from a variety of sources (for example, Coon 1951; Dibble 1984; Hole and Flannery 1967; Olszewski and Dibble 1993; Skinner 1965; Smith 1986), the following types are strongly associated with the following industries present in adjacent parts of the Zagros: single and double side scrapers, convergent pieces, and radially flaked "disc" cores with the Middle Paleolithic Zagros Mousterian; Baradostian points, circular, end, and carinated scrapers, backed and notched blades, and burins with the Upper Paleolithic Baradostian; and thumbnail scrapers, backed bladelets, geometric microliths—particularly scalene triangles—and microburins with the Epipaleolithic Zarzian.

Unfortunately, some of the types do not occur exclusively in assemblages from the periods with which they are said to be most strongly associated. Single side scrapers are a case in point, occurring in Upper Paleolithic as well as Middle Paleolithic assemblages, though they are much more commonly found in the latter. Thumbnail scrapers are another case in point, and one particularly pertinent to the problem at hand, since it focuses largely on the Epipaleolithic.

Traditionally subdivided into an early and late industry, these two variants of the Zarzian are said to be distinguishable by the absence of geometric microliths in the former, versus their presence in the latter (Garrod 1930; Hole 1987c; Smith 1986; Wahida 1981). However, given the association of small tools with both the late Baradostian and early Zarzian (see Hole and Flannery 1967; Olszewski 1993a), distinguishing such an early Zarzian from the late Baradostian on the basis of the simple presence/absence of thumbnail scrapers unaccompanied by geometric microliths is highly problematic. More recent attempts (Olszewski 1993b) to subdivide the Zarzian have focused on the relative frequency of various geometric and non-geometric microlithic types. However, as noted above, survey assemblages cannot be handled in this way.

THE SITE COLLECTIONS

Collections from a total of thirty-one cave sites were available for study. This includes the twenty-nine sites surveyed in 1978, plus Sumner's collections from sites 679 and 737 (figure 8.2, table 8.1). Of these thirty one, more than two-thirds yielded artifacts suggesting that they were utilized during more than one period.

A total of twelve yielded types clearly suggesting they were used during the Middle Paleolithic. Specifically, they yielded convergent pieces (scrapers/points), a type strongly associated with the Zagros Mousterian along with other types (side scrapers, transverse scrapers, and disc cores) typically found in Middle Paleolithic contexts. Another ten yielded one or more examples of only these other types but no convergent pieces, making it less clear whether they contain a Middle Paleolithic component. Of these ten sites, five yielded two or fewer examples of such types. Since the subject at hand is the Epipaleolithic, it is not necessary to dwell on the reliability of evidence for a Middle Paleolithic component in these ten sites. It is, however, important to note that, whether one chooses to focus on just the twelve sites that yielded the full complex of Middle Paleolithic index types or the full set of twenty-two possible Middle Paleolithic sites (12+10), at both levels the sites of that

Table 8.1 Index types in assemblages

	Middle Paleolithic	Upper Paleolithic	Epipaleolithic
KMC assemblage (no)	32	69	91
All assemblages (total no.)	302	413	162
Index types in KMC (% of total)	11%	17%	56%

period are spread over the entire western Marvdasht (see figures 8.1 and 8.2).

A different set of twenty-six sites yielded examples of types suggesting use during the Upper Paleolithic. Of these twenty-six sites, five yielded two or fewer examples of characteristically Upper Paleolithic types. Again, it is sufficient to note that sites of this period are spread over the entire western Marvdasht.

Finally, eleven of these thirty-one sites yielded examples of geometric microliths and microburins, associated in all but one case with thumbnail scrapers, a combination of types strongly associated with the late Epipaleolithic. An additional eight sites yielded examples of only thumbnail scrapers but no geometric microliths. Of these eight sites, only one yielded more than two examples, and all but one also yielded examples of types commonly associated with the Upper Paleolithic. The eighth is an apparent quarry site (designated DRC) that yielded a small number of tools, including two thumbnail scrapers that are very marginal examples of the type. Both are exceptionally thick and approach Upper Paleolithic type steep scrapers in configuration though not in diameter.

Of the thirty-one sites, the site designated "KMC" is the largest in both interior area and size of the collection gathered from its more or less average size talus slope. It is a cavernous single-chambered cave about 400 m² in area that was used to house flocks of sheep in 1978. It is situated about fifteen meters above the plain and overlooks the northern portion of an extensive series of spring-fed marshes that begin only some fifty meters from the cave mouth. With the possible exception of the immediate vicinity of some parts of the Kur river, about 14 km away at the nearest point, this area presently affords the best grazing for well over 20 km in any direction.

A total of 1593 pieces of chipped stone were collected at KMC in 1978. Included in this total are 580 microchips too small to warrant further discussion at this time. Sumner collected another 52 pieces during his survey. Types characteristic of the Middle, Upper and Epipaleolithic periods are all present in appreciable quantities in the KMC collection, suggesting that it was an important site during all these periods (figures 8.3, 8.4). Aside from blades and blade cores, the four most numerous types in the collection made at

<25 km from KMC	BAC	BBC	BCC	BDC	BEC	DRC	HFC	KZC	QMC		TOTAL
Epipaleolithic	-	-	?	-	-	?	?	?	-		0+4?
Upper Paleolithic	+	-	+	+	-	-	+	+	+		6
Middle Paleolithic	+	+	+	+	+	+	+	+	-		8

>25 km from KMC	DLC	KSC	KTC	LPC	MAC	MBC	MCC	MDC	MJC	UDC	UZC	ZGC		TOTAL
Epipaleolithic	-	+	-	+	+	-	?	+	-	-	+	-		5+1?
Upper Paleolithic	+	+	+	+	+	+	+	+	-	+	+	+		11
Middle Paleolithic	-	+	-	+	+	+	-	+	+	+	-	-		7

Across the River	AQC	BYC	BZC	JKC	JRC	NRC	SRC	679	737		TOTAL
Epipaleolithic	+	?	+	+	+	?	+	-	?		5+3?
Upper Paleolithic	+	+	+	+	+	+	-	+	+		8
Middle Paleolithic	+	+	+	+	+	+	-	-	-		6

? = thumbnail scrapers present, but no geometric microliths

8.2   Sites grouped by location relative to KMC, indicating the presence/absence of index types representing specific periods. Note that types characteristic of all periods (Upper and Middle Paleolithic and Epipaleolithic) are represented at KMC. *Original by M. Rosenberg*

KMC in 1978 are: end scrapers (75), thumbnail scrapers (56), geometric microliths (31), and carinated scrapers (28). As used here, however, the end scraper category includes examples of all sizes and the KMC assemblage contains a relatively large number of highly diminutive examples; the thirty-four complete examples of end scrapers in the KMC assemblage average 1.21 g as compared to a 1.62 g mean weight for the 83 intact examples in all the other assemblages combined. Thus, these numbers may in a sense overstate the number of end scrapers and understate the number of thumbnail scrapers.

EPIPALEOLOITHIC INDUSTRIES IN THE MARVDASHT

Olszewski (1993b), in the most detailed analysis of the Zarzian conducted to date, defines four temporal units for the Zarzian levels at Warwasi. The earliest unit (1) is characterized by a predominance of non-geometric microliths (mostly lamelles Dufour) and apparently corresponds to what is otherwise commonly called the early Zarzian. The three later units (2 through 4), characterized by varying frequencies of scalenes, lunates, curved backed bladelets, quadrilaterals, and microgravettes, apparently correspond to what is collectively called the late Zarzian.

The KMC site yielded the single largest group of geometric microliths, totaling thirty-one pieces, and is the only survey site to yield more than a handful of such artifacts. Included in the KMC collection are lunates and curved backed bladelets, at least one scalene, and quadrilateral

pieces, which types are collectively characteristic of the late Zarzian (Olszewski 1993b:222). Attempting to assign survey assemblages to one or another of Olszewski's subdivisions of the late Zarzian is impossible for the methodological reasons mentioned earlier. Nevertheless, one basic point can be made. Based on the index types present in the survey collections, the Epipaleolithic industry in the Marvdasht is apparently in the Zarzian tradition. This suggests that the Zarzian stretched beyond the central Zagros into the southern Zagros, an area in which the presence of Zarzian type industries has until now not been confirmed.

EPIPALEOLITHIC SETTLEMENT PATTERNS IN THE MARVDASHT

Two basic types of hunter-gatherer exploitation systems are often distinguished. They have been labeled in various ways, including circulating versus radiating systems (Mortensen 1972) and foraging versus logistical systems (Binford 1980). The essential difference between the two centers on how sites within a given territory are utilized. A circulating/foraging system entails residential moves between resource locales and protracted seasonal stays at each locale. In contrast, a radiating/logistical system utilizes a "base" camp occupied on a protracted basis from which task groups go out to satellite sites used on a much more intermittent basis. While mobile hunter-gathers are known to utilize both (see Binford 1980), sedentary hunter-gatherers must, of necessity, employ a radiating system and Mortensen (1972) has suggested that such a radiating system is evident in the Zagros by the Zarzian.

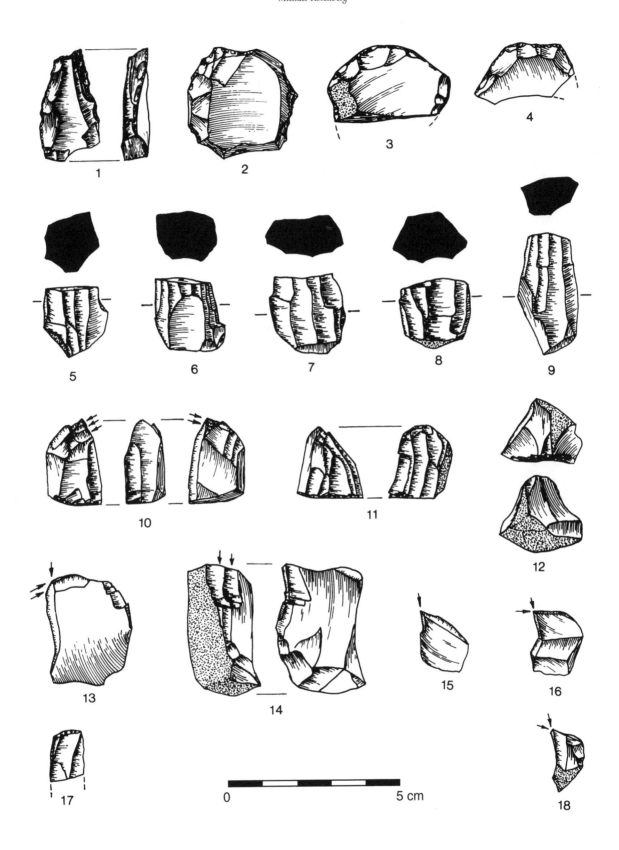

8.3   Chipped stone artifacts from KMC: *1,*convergent scraper; *2–4,* circular scrapers; *5–9,* blade cores; *10–12,* carinated scrapers; *13–16, 18,* burins; *17,* backed blade. *Illustration by M. Rosenberg*

As noted above, eleven of the thirty-one combined survey sites (for which collections were available) yielded reasonably good evidence of use during the Epipaleolithic period, in the form of characteristic geometric microlith types, and another eight yielded some vague evidence of possible use. The distribution of these sites suggests that in the Marvdasht a change to a radiating site utilization pattern (from an earlier circulating one) occurs during the Epipaleolithic. This would be in conformity with what has been suggested to have been the case elsewhere in the Zagros at this time (for example, Mortensen 1972). Specifically, the survey data suggest that during the Epipaleolithic, KMC became by far the single most intensively utilized site in the western Marvdasht, and that this site served as the hub for a radiating exploitation pattern in that area. These data take the form of both artifact frequencies and site distributions.

The number of chipped stone artifacts analyzed from the twenty-nine sites collected in 1978 totaled 4808 (several thousand microflakes and fragments were omitted as being too minute). If we define index types 'broadly' to include types that recur in other industries as minor types (for example, side scrapers for the Middle Paleolithic, thumbnail scrapers for the Epipaleolithic), then of the 4808, 302 are examples of Middle Paleolithic index types; 583 (413 excluding end scrapers) are examples of Upper Paleolithic types; and 162 are examples of Epipaleolithic types.

The 1013 artifacts analyzed from the KMC collection constitute 21% of the 4808 total. Those 1013 pieces include 32 examples of Middle Paleolithic types (11% of the 302 total examples of such types). They also include 69 examples of Upper Paleolithic types, excluding end scrapers (17% of the 413 total examples of such types). Restricting the ratio to just such highly characteristic Upper Paleolithic types as carinated scrapers and polyhedral burins yields essentially the same result (43:268, 16%). While these numbers clearly indicate that KMC was used during both these periods, nothing in these numbers is particularly exceptional when compared to other sites in the survey area.

In contrast to its Middle and Upper Paleolithic components, the KMC collection contains 91 Epipaleolithic types. These 91 artifacts constitute a majority (56%) of the 162 total examples of Epipaleolithic types collected during the 1978 survey from all the sites combined. The 91 artifacts break down to 35 (64%) of the 55 total number of geometric microliths and microburins in the collections and 56 (52%) of the 107 total thumbnail scrapers. There are more Epipaleolithic types at KMC than at the other eighteen sites (that yielded any such types) combined, and the number

of such Epipaleolithic artifacts from KMC is over 600% greater than the number found at the site that yielded the next largest number of such artifacts. Thus, the KMC collection contains a disproportionately high number of all Epipaleolithic tool types compared to other sites utilized during this period (which was not the case for this site in previous periods). This suggests that during the Epipaleolithic, KMC emerged as the single most intensively utilized site in the western half of the Marvdasht.

The apparent increase in the relative utilization of KMC as compared to other sites utilized during the Epipaleolithic also corresponds to a change in the general utilization of sites in the western Marvdasht. Specifically, during the Epipaleolithic, potential sites within 25 km of KMC were no longer being utilized to any significant degree (figure 8.5).

Of the thirty-one total sites under discussion, there are nine sheltered sites to the north of the Kur river. The collections from these nine sites indicate that more than half that number, though not the same combination of sites, were utilized during each of the Middle, Upper, and Epipaleolithic periods. Specifically, six (66%) yielded Middle Paleolithic type artifacts, seven (78%) yielded Upper Paleolithic type artifacts, and five (56%) yielded geometric microliths, indicating use during the Epipaleolithic. An additional three yielded only thumbnail scrapers, but all three of these cases were sites that also yielded Upper Paleolithic types, so their use during the Epipaleolithic is questionable. Only one, site 679, failed to yield artifacts associated to any degree with the Epipaleolithic. In any case, the data for these sites indicate that, as a group, there was no significant increase or decrease in the number of sites used during the Epipaleolithic as compared to previous periods.

Aside from KMC, there are twenty-one sheltered sites situated to the south of the Kur river. Of these twenty-one sites, nine are well within 25 km of KMC, while the remaining twelve are at least 25 km away from that site. Of the twelve sites situated more than 25 km away, five (42%) yielded geometric microliths, seven (58%) yielded Middle Paleolithic artifact types, and Upper Paleolithic types were found at eleven (92%). Thus, as was the case with the nine sites across the river from KMC, a significant number of these sites also were used in all periods.

In contrast, of the nine sites situated within 25 km of KMC, none yielded any geometric microliths whatsoever, though eight (89%) yielded Middle Paleolithic type tools and six (67%) yielded examples of Upper Paleolithic types. Four of the nine did yield thumbnail scrapers unaccompanied by microliths. However, all four of these yielded two or fewer examples, and in three of the four the thumbnail

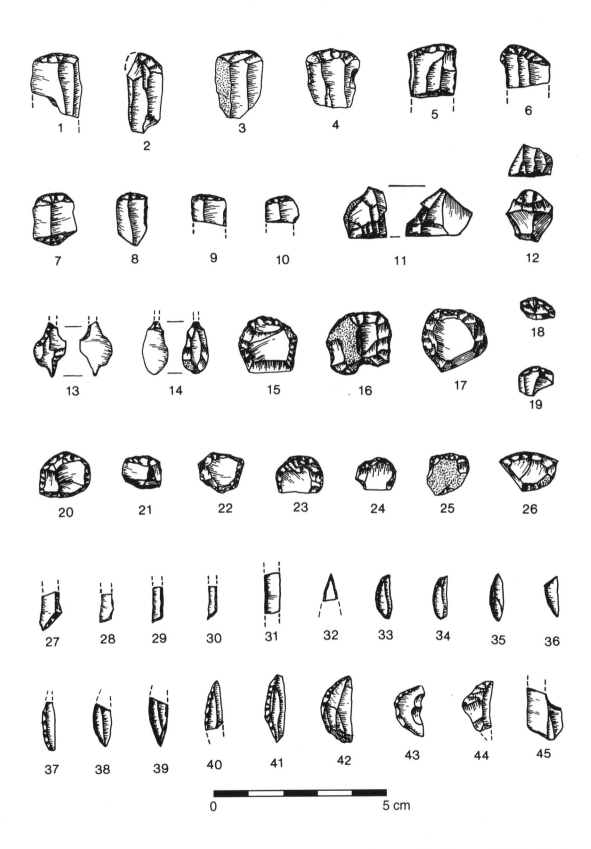

8.4   Chipped stone artifacts from KMC: *1–10*, end scrapers; *11–12*, small carinated scrapers; *13–14*, borers; *15–26*, thumbnail scrapers; *27–44*, microliths; *45*, micro-burin. *Illustration by M. Rosenberg*

scrapers were accompanied by Upper Paleolithic artifact types. The fourth site was DRC, which as noted above yielded two highly debatable examples. As mentioned earlier, the temporal significance of thumbnail scrapers as an index type unaccompanied by microliths is not clear. This is all the more so when they are present (as at these four sites) in very low numbers, because the sole apparent difference between their occurrence in Upper and Epipaleolithic assemblages is their significantly higher frequency in the latter (see Olszewski 1993a, 1993b).

DISCUSSION

Three initial points concerning the Middle and Upper Paleolithic sites are worth noting. First, during both periods, numerous sites on both sides of the Kur river are used and they are distributed in a relatively uniform manner over the landscape. Second, there is no single site that yielded a highly disproportionate number of artifacts attributable to either of these periods, such that the site in question stands out as perhaps more intensively used than any of the other sites also used during that period. Third, there is no indication that potential[1] sites relatively close to the largest site from each of these periods remain unused during the respective period.

It is true that the survey data are particularly unreliable for determining what is actually the largest site from each of these periods (that is, Middle and Upper Paleolithic). That is, these periods, sometimes represented by relatively deep deposits, may be underrepresented in some unknown number of the surface collections such that the largest sites from these respective periods do not appear to be the largest on the basis of surface collections (and vice versa). This fact renders the second point questionable. However, with regard to the third point: given the above-noted relatively uniform distribution of sites from these periods, the existence of sites relatively close to the largest would still be the case no matter which of the various Middle and Upper Paleolithic sites is in reality the largest. Thus, while the survey data do not permit a clear determination of the factors underlying the distribution of Middle and Upper Paleolithic sheltered sites, distance from the most intensively utilized site of either period does not appear to have been one of them.

The Epipaleolithic represents an apparent departure from the Middle and Upper Paleolithic case in two respects. The first is that one site appears to become significantly more important than any other contemporary site in terms of usage, with importance measured by degree of use as reflected in index type frequencies. The second is that sites are less uniformly spread over the landscape than they were in previous periods, in that sites within approximately a half day's walk (that is, 25 km) of the most intensively utilized site stop being used to any meaningful degree. (Note that sites on the other side of the Kur river within 25 km of KMC are likely somewhat more than that in actual walking distance because reaching them requires first traveling to a place suitable for fording the river.) This second observation is based only on the presence/absence of distinctly Epipaleolithic index types (that is, geometric microliths). However, even considering the occurrence of only one or two thumbnail scrapers (typically in association with Upper Paleolithic types) at the aforementioned four sites within 25 km of KMC to be in each case evidence of use during the Epipaleolithic, it is still hard to make the case that the nine caves within 25 km of KMC were used to any significant degree during the Epipaleolithic. Moreover, the original observation would still hold true for activities involving the use of geometrics.

As for the reliability of the survey data for drawing such conclusions, three points should be made. First, in this case we are comparing material eroded from the uppermost strata at all these sites. Thus, what is being compared is the material *most* likely to be present in surface remains at each site where such material exists. That coupled with the fairly uniform surface conditions in the primary collection areas at each site and the uniform collection methods employed means that (if present at the site) such materials are most likely to be present in the collections. Surface collection on early sites is unlikely to miss later material if that material is indeed present.

Second, while quantitative comparisons based on surface collections are generally not valid, in this case the sheer magnitude of the quantitative discrepancy between the Epipaleolithic index types in the KMC collection and to all the others both individually and collectively constitutes a possible exception. The order of the discrepancy suggests that KMC is in reality by far the most important Epipaleolithic site in the western Marvdasht, even if (for obvious methodological reasons) we cannot quantitatively express precisely how much more important it was.

Third, potentially any future data ultimately derived from the six caves for which either no data, noncomparable (that is, only Sumner's) data, or contradictory data are presently available may alter the conclusions suggested by the 1978 survey data. These six caves include the five not visited in 1978 (figure 8.1: sites 1, 4, 5, 676, and 737) and the one that yielded a collection to Sumner but nothing in 1978 (figure 8.1: site 3). The two key variables determining their potential impact are Epipaleolithic index type frequency and proximity to KMC.

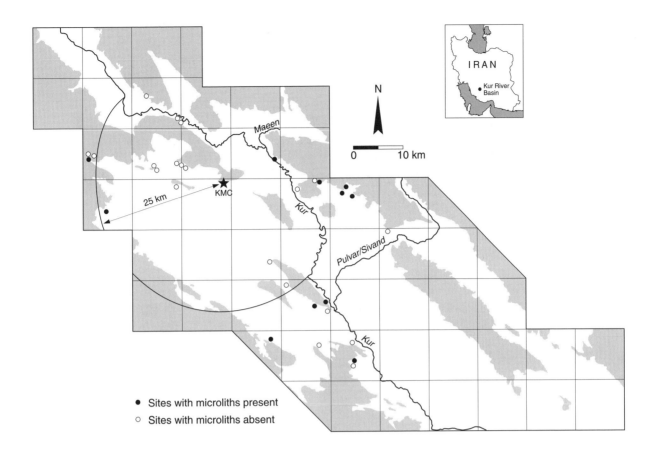

8.5   All potential sites in the western Marvdasht, with the distribution of Epipaleolithic sites indicated. *Original by M. Rosenberg*

With respect to proximity, only two of these caves are relevant (figure 8.1: sites 1 and 4) because only they are situated on the same side of the Kur river as KMC. Of the two, only one is situated within 25 km of KMC (figure 8.1: site 4). The other, which is known from observations made in 1976 to have at least one geometric microlith on its surface but otherwise not a lot of surface material, is at the 25 km line and therefore in conformity with the pattern, even if it proves to contain an Epipaleolithic component. Thus, only one (figure 8.1: site 4) has the potential to contradict the Epipaleolithic site distribution pattern suggested by the 1978 data, indicating that all potential sites within 25 km of KMC appear to have been essentially unused during the Epipaleolithic. This cave, however, is a small, very high cave, seemingly ill-suited to be a site and so is unlikely to actually prove to be a contradiction.

With respect to the issue of KMC being the single most important site in the western Marvdasht, too many caves on the north side of the Kur river remain unknown to say with absolute certainty that nothing of equivalent impor-

tance to KMC exists on that side. Three of the six sites north of the river can be more or less eliminated on the basis of the limited available evidence. They include the one that yielded a small collection to Sumner but nothing in 1978 (indicating that Sumner's *small* collection is a reasonably accurate measure of the site's importance) and nos. 679 and 737 (the collections that contain nothing to indicate that they might rival KMC's degree of use during the Epipaleolithic). In any case, the uniform distribution of sites on the north side of the Kur river implies that a site as important as KMC is not to be expected there. As for the two sites on the south side of the Kur river, the more distant site (figure 8.1: site 1) is known from the 1976 visit not to be particularly productive, despite the presence of geometrics, while, as noted above, the second site is unlikely to prove to have been a site at all.

CONCLUSION
The various survey data suggest that the Epipaleolithic industries of Fars province are in the Zarzian tradition. They

also suggest that KMC emerges as the single largest site by far in the western Marvdasht during the late Epipaleolithic, while alternative sites within a 25-km radius direct access of KMC cease to be used to any comparable degree. Sites more than 25 km away from KMC and sites that require crossing the Kur river (by first traveling to a fording place) continue to be used during the late Epipaleolithic in ratios that are not significantly different from those of previous periods. The demographic and socio-economic changes reflected by this changing Epipaleolithic settlement pattern cannot be determined using survey data alone. However, some centralization of activities is suggested, as might be characteristic of a shift from a circulating to a radiating resource exploitation system. Such a change would be consistent with what is generally thought to have occurred elsewhere in the Zagros at this time.

NOTE

1. In the sense of being presumably suitable for use by virtue of having been used during other periods (thus excluding caves that were never used).

CHAPTER 9

SHERD SIZE AND THE BANESH PHASE OCCUPATION IN THE ABC OPERATION AT MALYAN, IRAN

JOHN R. ALDEN

DURING SEVERAL SEASONS of the excavations at Malyan, a University of Pennsylvania–Ohio State University project carried out under the direction of William Sumner between 1971 and 1978, data on sherd counts and weights were collected from selected excavation units in Banesh phase levels of the ABC sounding. None of us who were involved in the project at that time knew whether such data would be useful; they were collected as an experiment and are frustratingly incomplete.[1] Sumner has recently completed the final report on the ABC excavations, describing the material recovered in that effort and offering an intriguing interpretation of what that material reveals about Banesh phase society at approximately 3000 BCE and the broader Proto-Elamite cultural horizon. This volume, honoring Bill and his contributions to the field of Iranian archeology, seems an appropriate place to examine the Malyan Project's data on average sherd size and see what, if anything, these data reveal about the ABC occupational sequence, about the organization of the Banesh phase city at Malyan, and about the structure of Proto-Elamite society in highland Iran (figure 9.1).

CERAMIC TAPHONOMY AND AVERAGE SHERD SIZE

Ceramics break in systematic ways. Many factors affect the patterns of such breakage; these factors are both technological and cultural, and not all are quantifiable (Bronitsky and Hamer 1986; Chase 1985; Deal 1985; Shott 1996). But when enough data are available to control for the effects of variables such as paste, firing, vessel size, and vessel form,

an examination of the way a corpus of ceramic material has been broken may reveal useful information on the cultural processes behind the formation of the associated archaeological deposits (Sumner 2003). By analogy with archaeological and paleontological studies of how bone fractures, the study and interpretation of patterns in the ways pottery breaks might be called ceramic taphonomy.

There are a number of ways to quantify the degree to which a corpus of archaeological ceramics has been broken up. "Angularity," the ratio of edge length to surface area, and "platiness," the ratio of surface area to sherd thickness, would both provide useful measures of the relative amount of breakage in a collection of sherds. Most archaeologists, however, have better things to do with their time than measuring the edge length, thickness, and surface area of hundreds or thousands of pieces of pottery. The most accessible measure of ceramic fragmentation is average sherd size, which is readily estimated by the ratio of sherd count to total sherd weight. Average sherd weights have been used as an analytical device by archaeologists since at least the 1950s (Solheim 1960). But despite sporadic efforts to encourage the collection and analysis of such data, weighing sherds has never become accepted as standard archeological practice.

The variables affecting average sherd size (or more properly, average sherd weight) can be divided into three broad groups—physical, depositional, and random. Physical variables involve the structure of individual vessels. These variables include technological characteristics like paste, temper, and firing; morphological features like vessel size,

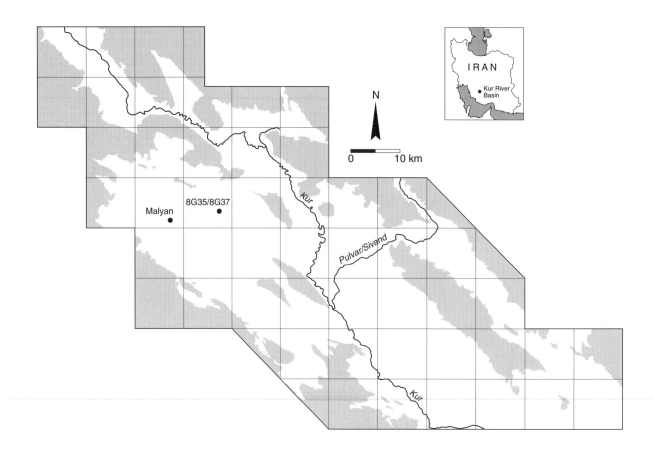

9.1   The Kur river basin, Fars, Iran. *Original by J.R. Alden*

shape, and thickness; and the nature of the force that broke each particular vessel. A sharp blow, for example, would break a pot differently than thermal shock or the pressure of earth on a vessel placed in a burial. Depositional variables involve secondary breakage resulting from the paths or processes by which broken ceramics are incorporated into and removed from archaeological contexts. Random variables—an animal walking across a site, perhaps, or the impact of an excavator's pick—affect individual sherds rather than an entire corpus of ceramics.

Two major factors constrain the utility of average sherd weight as a measure of the degree to which a collection of pottery has been broken up. The first problem involves sampling. When an excavation lot or collection unit contains relatively few sherds, the average sherd weight can be distorted by the presence of one or two unusually large or unusually small sherds. In statistical terms, the sample being examined is a skewed representation of the underlying population. This issue would normally be addressed by weighing each item in a sample individually and using those data to determine the distribution (for example Poisson, normal, multimodal, and so forth) and estimate the vari-

ability (typically measured by standard deviation) of sherd weight in the collection being studied. However, weights of individual sherds were not collected at Malyan. Beyond that, in most field situations the effort required to classify, weigh, and record data on hundreds of individual potsherds would offer little return for the time invested. At this point, it is probably sufficient to suggest that average sherd weights calculated from small collections (fewer than twenty or thirty sherds, perhaps) should be used with caution.

The second problem with average sherd weights involves differential recovery. Simply put, the average sherd weight of an archaeological collection will be higher if more small sherds are discarded and lower if more small sherds are kept. In a few situations, like excavating a burial or recovering pieces of a vessel that was smashed in place, archaeologists will save even tiny pieces of pottery. Normally, they use some arbitrary rule about what to save and what to throw out with the backdirt. "Save anything bigger than a *peso*" was the standard in one excavation I was on; in other cases the rule was "Anything bigger that your thumbnail" and "Anything big enough to write a number on."

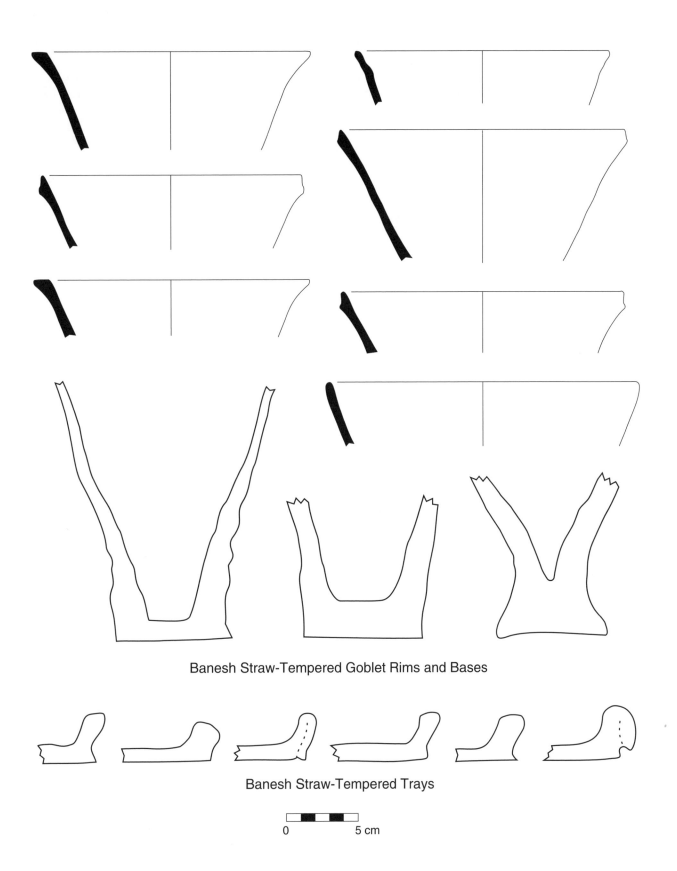

Banesh Straw-Tempered Goblet Rims and Bases

Banesh Straw-Tempered Trays

0   5 cm

9.2   Banesh straw-tempered ware. *Alden 1979:Figs. 31–33*

SHERD SIZE AND THE BANESH PHASE OCCUPATION IN THE ABC OPERATION AT MALYAN, IRAN

If such rules were followed uniformly, they would not cause any analytical problems. But even the most clearly stated standard is likely to be applied differently by different individuals. An excavator's actual behavior may also vary depending on circumstances like how hot it is, how late in the day or the season, and how much material is coming out of each screen or excavation unit. Such collection biases are difficult to identify or correct for, and they add a measure of uncertainty to any analysis using data on average sherd weight.

THE DATA: THE ABC EXCAVATIONS AT MALYAN

The ABC excavations yielded relatively little pottery, and the great majority of this (86%) was the straw-tempered variety (Sumner 2003). Banesh straw-tempered ware, as its name implies, is filled with large quantities of coarsely chopped grass, straw, or chaff. It is a utilitarian ware generally fired at low temperatures (Blackman 1981). Straw-tempered ware is porous with a chalky surface, neither slipped nor burnished, and sherds usually show finger marks from casual forming and smoothing (figure 9.2). Thicker sherds, particularly goblet bases, often have incompletely oxidized cores, and examples of these bases have even dissolved during washing. Charred grains of wheat and barley found in several examples of this pottery from Malyan (Miller 1982:364) indicate that the tempering material was in some cases a by-product of threshing.

In the ABC excavation, straw-tempered ware occurred in two common forms—large goblets with straight-sided ("pedestal") or constricted ("necked") bases (80% of all diagnostic straw-tempered ware sherds) and low-sided trays (17% of the same corpus) (Sumner 2003). The goblets are wheel-made with string-cut bases, while the trays are made by pulling up the edges of a hand-formed sheet of clay. Figure 9.2 illustrates selected examples of these forms from the author's surface survey collections (Alden 1979:Figs. 31–35), while Sumner (2003:Figs. 21–23) and Nicholas (1990:Pl. 13) illustrate straw-tempered vessels from the ABC and TUV excavations at Malyan. A few examples of beveled rim bowls and small jars with flat bases and drooping spouts were also found in ABC, but such forms were atypical.[2]

Count and weight data were collected from thirty-one excavation units in the ABC operation for three categories of straw-tempered ceramics: goblet rims, goblet bases, and low-sided trays. These data are presented in table 9.1. Table 9.1 also summarizes information about the stratigraphic position and kind of deposit from which each set of material was excavated, while figure 9.3 shows simplified architectural plans of the four Banesh phase building levels exposed in the ABC excavation. Stratum 8 deposits come

from building level 2, the latest and most monumental-scale Banesh construction in the ABC area. Stratum 10 and 11 are from building level 3, a structure with a formal, symmetrical floor plan and elaborate frescos decorating the interior walls of its rooms. Stratum 12 deposits come from a layer of fill between the floor of building level 3 and the tops of the walls of building level 4. Strata 13 and 14 are from building level 4, which is distinguished by a curving double wall, perhaps a fortification, along the western edge of the main building. Unfortunately, no data on sherd counts and weights were available from deposits in building level 5, a domestic building, which is the earliest Banesh structure in the ABC area of Malyan. Detailed descriptions and plans of these strata and structures can be found in Sumner (2003).

In the Malyan excavation project, a deposit code (table 9.2) was assigned to each excavation unit. These codes indicate the excavator's judgment of the nature of each particular deposit (Sumner 2003:Table 1). Primary deposits (codes 11–17) were deliberately placed during antiquity and remained in place until they were excavated; they include things like undisturbed floor deposits, caches, and burials. None of the material discussed here comes from primary deposits. Secondary deposits (codes 21–29) include primary deposits that were disturbed during antiquity and trash on floors or in pits. In essence, they result from poor housekeeping or deliberate disposal rather than deliberate placement or sudden abandonment. Tertiary deposits (codes 31 and higher) include surface collections, material from construction debris or from dismantling architectural features, and various sorts of natural or cultural redeposition. Table 9.2 lists the deposit codes assigned to the excavation units examined in this chapter.

THE DATA: SURFACE COLLECTIONS AT OTHER BANESH SITES

In 1976, during a surface survey of Banesh sites in the Kur River basin, the author made several surface collections from two sites, 8G35 and 8G37, with extraordinarily high concentrations of straw-tempered pottery. These sites had been plowed with a large chisel-type plow only a few days before they were visited (a snake with a broken back, still alive, was found trapped amid the sherds on 8G35), and if the area had ever been plowed previously it had certainly never been plowed so deeply.

Sites 8G35 and 8G37 were very similar. Both were small (0.7 and 0.1 ha respectively), both were within a few hundred meters of site 8G38 (a Banesh phase village) and both consisted of a bed of broken straw-tempered pottery a half meter or so in depth. The five collections from 8G35 yielded

Table 9.1 Counts and weights of Banesh straw-tempered ceramics

Op/Site	Lot	F#	STR	DC	R#	RWT	T#	TWT	B#	BWT	Av. RWT	Notes
C	66	71	8B	21	6	51	4	100	2	144	8.5	
B	63	64	13A	21	13	130	8	200	1	62	10.0	
ABCS	77	290	13A	21	2	35	0		0		17.5	heavy?
ABCS	82	307	13A	21	15	•	7	632	3	84	•	
ABCN	148	236	13A	22	9	224	0		2	625	24.9	heavy
ABCN	149	236	13A	22	17	177	3	36	5	622	10.4	
ABCN	152	236	13A	22	5		3	96	1	116	9.4	?
ABCN	153	236	13A	22	23	240	0		2	212	10.4	
ABCN	162	236	13A	22	8	131	8	433	1	296	16.4	heavy
ABCN	139	307	13A	23	450	4249	159	6930	102	10800	9.4	
ABCS	51	130	8C	29	2	13	0		0		6.5	light?
B	49	63	10B	29	7	116	0		0		16.6	heavy
ABCS	65	304	11A	29	28	193	0		0		6.9	light*
ABCS	58	34	11B	29	4	46	0		0		11.5	?
ABCS	59	35	11B	29	2	16	0		0		8.0	?
ABCS	70	267	11B	29	3	35	0		1	7	11.7	?
ABCS	76	269	11B	29	4	84	0		0		21.0	heavy?
ABCN	52	•	12	34	6	75	2	99	0		12.5	
ABCN	54	•	12	34	18	198	1	50	0		11.0	
ABCS	60	•	12	34	42	421	0		3	199	10.0	
ABCN	155	•	12	34	3	39	2	20	0		13.0	?
ABCS	79	307	13A	35	8	63	0		2	218	7.9	
B	43	31	8A	35	16	200	5	186	2	253	12.5	
ABCS	50	155	8C	36	9	86	2	135	2	208	9.6	
ABCN	154	59	14B	36	10	103	0		0		10.3	
ABCN	99	211	10A	37	78	443	5	85	1	38	5.7	light*
B	57	66	13A	37	5	73	0		0		14.6	heavy?
ABCS	73	288	13A	37	1	8	0		0		8.0	?
ABCS	74	241	13A	37	2	15	1	20	1	38	7.5	?
ABCN	146	64	13A	37	14	123	2	55	0		8.8	
ABCN	159	64	13A	37	4	46	5	195	0		11.5	?
8G37	91	16m2	Surf.	31	398	4370	13	610	73	8180	11.0	
8G35	92	9m2	Surf.	31	396	6170	34	2030	291	77120	15.6	heavy
8G35	106	2m2	Surf.	31	109	1450	3	320	51	11650	13.3	heavy
8G35	107	2m2	Surf.	31	87	1470	11	770	60	21380	16.9	heavy
8G35	108	2m2	Surf.	31	89	1300	2	100	38	16630	14.6	heavy
8G35	109	2m2	Surf.	31	120	2200	15	1440	56	27310	18.3	heavy

OP/SITE = Malyan operation or other site; R# = Goblet rim count; LOT = Excavation or collection unit; RWT = Goblet rim weight, g; F# = Feature number or collection area; T# = Tray rim count; STR = Stratum; TWT = Tray rim weight, g; DC = Deposit code; B# = Goblet base count; Av. RWT = Average goblet rim weight; BWT = Goblet base weight, g

an average of more than 300 sherds per m^2 (by weight, over 15 kg per m^2). The single collection from the smaller site 8G37 yielded about 140 sherds, weighing 2.8 kg per m^2—a density less than half that of site 8G35 but still a very large amount (see table 9.1). These collections contained from 96% to 99% straw-tempered ware, and more than 95% of those sherds were from straw-tempered goblets. These two great heaps of broken pottery were interpreted as dumps from a large-scale pottery manufacturing operation producing Banesh straw-tempered goblets (Alden 1979:102–104).

A third site, 7G16, appears to have been a production site for straw-tempered ceramic trays (Alden 1979:102–104 and Table 39). The surface of this site had slightly more than 30 sherds per m^2 (weighing just over 1 kg per m^2); all of this

Table 9.2 Deposit codes used in the ABC excavations

Secondary deposits

21	Trash deposits on a floor or surface
22	Trash in a pit or well
23	Amorphous trashy deposit, with boundaries difficult to establish
29	Removal of a floor (the actual material a floor is made of)

Tertiary deposits

31	Surface pick-up
34	Amorphous bricky fill, with associated wall not identified
35	Bricky fill below tops of identified walls
36	Feature removal (the actual material a feature is made of)
37	Arbitrary floor cleaning lot (fill with no identifiable trash)

material was Banesh and 98% of it was straw-tempered ware. Of 315 rims or bases, 245 (78%) were rims of low-sided Banesh trays, the remainder being goblet rims (66) or bases (4). Unfortunately, the tray and goblet rims from this site were not weighed separately so data comparable to those from the ABC excavation and sites 8G35 and 8G37 are not available; site 7G16 will therefore not be discussed further.

DISCUSSION

Given the large size of the ABC excavation, even the most common sorts of ceramics were rare. Only two depositional features (feature 307, an area of midden debris lying against the west side of the curving double wall in building level 4 and feature 236, a small pit in room 64 of building level 4) yielded more than ten tray rims or pedestal bases, and only a dozen excavation units had more than ten goblet rims. Because tray rims and pedestal bases were so infrequent, the following analysis will focus on goblet rims.

A taphonomic analysis is greatly simplified by examining only a single vessel type (goblet rims) made of a single ceramic ware (Banesh straw-tempered ware) from contexts that, in archaeological terms, are more or less contemporaneous. In such situations, the analysis does not need to consider how average sherd weight would be affected by technological characteristics of the ware (that is, paste, temper, and firing); by vessel morphology (that is, vessel form, size, and thickness); or by chronological changes in production technique or vessel style. Differences in average sherd weight should be due only to how each set of vessels was broken and how each corpus of broken ceramics was incorporated into and removed from its particular archaeological context.

It is not possible to specify how each goblet was broken. However, it can be assumed that the sherds from ABC come from vessels that were broken during use while sherds from the ceramic production sites came from vessels broken during firing or while being prepared for shipping. If there is any systematic difference in the results of these two kinds of breakage, it seems likely that sherds from the production site dumps would, on average, be larger (that is, less thoroughly broken up) than sherds produced by breakage during actual use. Such a difference would be expected because the debris in the production dumps would include vessels that cracked or warped during firing (and thus were hardly broken at all) as well as vessels that were broken by being dropped or knocked together—which experience shows are the kind of accidents responsible for most breakage during use.

Broken vessels from the production sites near 8G38 appear to have been collected and dumped in one of two large surface dumps. Eventually covered by wind-blown soil, these heaps of broken pottery remained more or less undisturbed for five thousand years. They were then plowed up and, within a few days, collected.

The pottery from the ABC excavations was exposed to a wider range of potentially destructive depositional processes. Broken vessels from secondary contexts were left on occupation floors (deposit code 21), thrown into a small pit (deposit code 22, feature 236), or dumped in shallow surface middens (deposit code 23). Deposit code 29 identifies material recovered during the removal of clay floors, and it is not clear whether sherds from these excavation lots were trash that was trodden into the floor (and thus from secondary contexts) or material incorporated into the floor during construction (and thus more properly classified as tertiary deposits). Among these secondary deposits, it seems likely that sherds dumped into pits or surface middens should be less broken up than sherds left on or trodden into occupation floors.

Most of the ABC material from tertiary contexts came from some kind of construction debris. Deposit codes 34 and 35 identify bricky fill; in ABC such material was used to fill in old buildings and to prepare a level surface for a new structure. The sherds from the two deposit code 36 lots come from mud-brick constructions—a wall and a platform—while deposit code 37 material was apparently incorporated into floor fill during the floor's construction.

ANALYSIS

The central assumption of taphonomic analysis is that, for any particular type of vessel, similar patterns of breaking and disposal will produce sherds of similar average size. This does not imply that every different pattern of breaking and disposal will produce sherds of different size. Indeed, there is every reason to believe that many alternate pathways of breaking and disposal could produce sherds of the same average size. But if two collections of sherds from the same kind of archaeological context have different average sizes, then the taphonomic assumption is that they are the product of different pathways of breaking and disposal.

Following that assumption, we would predict that the six collections of sherds from the ceramic production dumps would have similar average weights. In addition, because these sherds were presumably dumped soon after being broken (and were thus exposed to minimal additional breakage before their disposal), they should have higher average weights than collections of the same kinds of pottery from any other class of deposits.

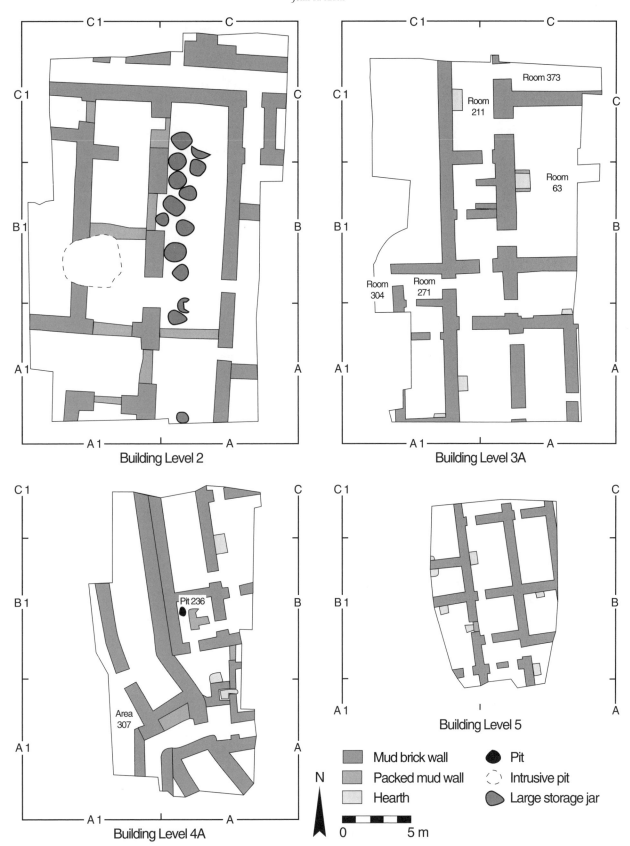

C 1 — C
C 1 — C
C 1 — C

Room 373
Room 211
Room 63
Room 304
Room 271

Building Level 2

Building Level 3A

Pit 236

Area 307

Building Level 4A

Building Level 5

Mud brick wall   ● Pit

Packed mud wall   ⬭ Intrusive pit

Hearth   ● Large storage jar

N

0   5 m

9.3   Banesh phase building levels in the ABC Operation, Malyan, Iran. *Illustration by J.R. Alden, based on Sumner N.D.*

Figure 9.4, a scatter plot of Banesh goblet rim counts and weights for the surface collections from the straw-tempered ceramic production sites, shows that the five collections from site 8G35 do indeed have similar average weights. They all fall close to a straight line, calculated by the least-squares linear regression equation: weight = 15.7 x count, with $r^2 = 0.996$.[3] The sherds from the site 8G37 collection, however, are noticeably smaller. This difference is also evident in the average weight figures for goblet rims listed in table 9.1, which show that every collection from site 8G35 produced heavier goblet rim sherds while the rims from 8G37 fell into the normal range of weights of rims from the ABC excavations.

Four factors might account for this observed difference in average sherd size between the two ceramic production dumps. The two sites could contain straw-tempered goblets that were made or fired differently; the debris in the two dumps could have been broken at different stages of the manufacturing process (for example, during firing, during storage, or during packing for shipping); the two dumps could have been created using different modes of disposal (for example, throwing versus carrying); or the two dumps could have been subject to different postdepositional forces.

I did not notice any visible difference between the collections from these two sites while working with the material, and I collected, washed, counted, and weighed all the pottery myself. I also drew profiles of a large sample of these goblet rims and measured several metric attributes for hundreds of the tray rims and goblet bases. It is possible that the material from one site was slightly harder than material from the other site (as a result, perhaps, of being fired at slightly higher average temperatures), but I was consciously looking for differences between the different collections and did not observe any. In addition, there is no obvious reason to suspect that the patterns of breakage and disposal were different for the material deposited at each site. This would suggest that the lower average weight for the sherds from site 8G37 was a result of different degrees of post-depositional breakage.

This hypothesis can be tested by comparing the average sherd weights of the Banesh tray rims from the two sites. If the goblet rim weights at site 8G37 are lower because of some subtle difference in vessel form (due, perhaps, to chronological variation or minor differences in the products of individual potters or workshops) or if they are smaller because they were broken at different stages of the production process, there is no reason to expect the average weights of the tray rims from the two different dumps to show a similar variation. If the average rim weight at 8G37

is lower because sherds from that location were subjected to greater breakage during disposal or to different levels of postdepositional breakage, we would expect the tray rims from 8G37 to be smaller, too.

Figure 9.5 and table 9.1 show that the average weight of Banesh tray rims from site 8G37 is lower than the average of four of the five collections from site 8G35, and the 8G35 collection with a similarly low average weight consists of only two sherds. The linear regression line for the five collections from 8G35 fits the equation weight = 66.2 x count, with $r^2 = 0.961$. These data thus support the hypothesis that the pottery from site 8G37 suffered more breakage during disposal or due to post-depositional disturbance than the pottery at 8G35.

This difference is most readily explained as a concomitant of site size. Sites 8G35 and 8G37 are both nearly solid pottery, and neither area would be amenable to cultivation or grazing. But because the 8G35 ceramic dump (a roughly triangular area 140 m x 100 m in extent) is much larger than 8G37 (a 30 m x 25 m oval), it is more likely to have been avoided. Over five thousand years, a relatively small difference in the frequency of grazing, plowing, and walking on the two sites could have been enough to cause more breakage at the smaller site than at the larger.

Although there is nothing earth-shattering about these results, the data on average sherd size did indicate, unexpectedly, that these two ceramic production dumps had been altered in different ways through time. But can average sherd weights reveal patterns that would help archaeologists interpret more complex depositional sequences? To answer that question, we will examine the data from the cultural sequence exposed in the ABC excavations at Malyan.

Stratigraphically, the Banesh phase deposits in the ABC excavation are divisible into four superimposed building levels. As described above, the excavation units in this area are each identified as coming from one of a variety of primary, secondary, or tertiary deposits. We will examine the data on average sherd weight from both depositional (deposit code) and chronological (building level) perspectives.

Table 9.1 lists the average weights of straw-tempered goblet rims from the ABC excavation and from surface collections at the ceramic production dump sites. A quick examination of the data indicates that most average weights fall between 7.5 and 13 g per rim sherd. Three of the thirty excavation units, labeled "light" in the notes column, have average weights below this range while six excavation units, labeled "heavy," have weights above 13 g per rim sherd. Twelve of the thirty excavation units contained five or fewer goblet rim sherds; these units are identified with a "?" in

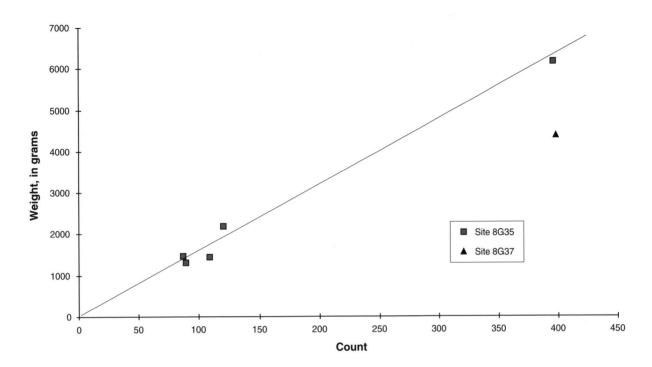

9.4   Goblet rim counts and weights, production site data. *J.R. Alden*

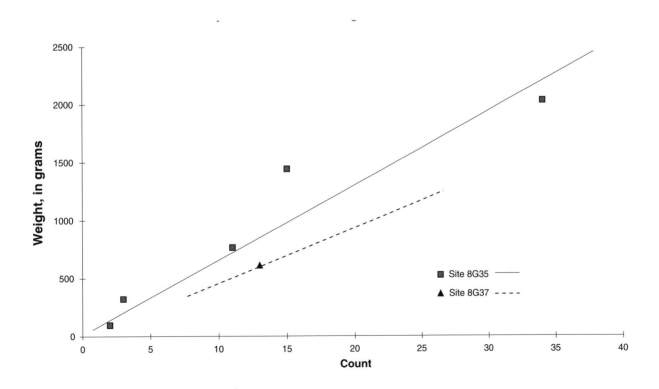

9.5   Tray rim counts and weights, production site data. *J.R. Alden*

Table 9.3 Rim count and weight (in g) data, by deposit code

#/Units	Site/Op	Code	Count	Wt	Avg Wt	Comment
3	ABC	21	21	216	10.29	
5	ABC	22	62	819	13.21	heavy
1	ABC	23	450	4249	9.44	
7	ABC	29	50	503	10.06	
4	ABC	34	69	733	10.62	
2	ABC	35	24	263	10.96	
2	ABC	36	19	189	9.95	
6	ABC	37	104	708	6.81	light
1	8G37	31	398	4370	10.98	
5	8G35	31	801	12590	15.72	heavy

the notes column to emphasize their limited sample sizes. Only two of the excavation units with notably light or heavy rim sherds have sample sizes greater than ten. These units, which both contain sherds that are lighter than normal, are marked with an asterisk.

The data show clearer patterning when the goblet rim counts and weights are combined by deposit code, as shown in table 9.3. Average sherd weights for six of the eight deposit codes cluster neatly between 9.4 and 11.0 g. The goblet rims from the deposit code 22 units, with an average weight of 13.2 g, are notably heavier than goblet rims from other types of deposits, while the deposit code 37 goblet rim sherds (6.8 g) are notably lighter. As for the material from the ceramic production dumps, the rims from 8G37 (average weight 11.0 g) are within the normal range of rim sherd size for the ABC excavations, while the sherds from 8G35, averaging 15.7 g, are notably heavier.

Deposit code 22 identifies trashy material excavated from a pit or well; all five deposit code 22 units in the Banesh portion of the ABC excavations come from pit 236 in room 64 of the building level 4 house. The average sherd weight data indicate that the material from this pit is noticeably less broken up than the material from any other context in the ABC operation. The most likely explanation for this difference is that the material in this pit represents household debris that was collected and dumped very soon after the pottery was broken, without any intervening trampling or reworking. While no archaeologist will be surprised to hear that material from a pit is important, the sherd weight data emphasize that the contents of pit 236 are unlike any other deposit excavated in ABC and confirm the expectation that the material from this feature deserves special attention.

On initial examination, the sherd weight data combined by building level seem uninteresting. Table 9.4 shows that when data from the anomalous deposit code 22 and 37 lots are removed, there is remarkably little difference between the material from the different building levels. But as table 9.5 shows, when the data for the deposit code 37 lots (which,

as shown in table 9.3, had notably lighter goblet rim sherds than any other type of deposit in the ABC excavations) are separated by building level, a sharp difference in average sherd size is evident. The goblet rim sherds from the five deposit code 37 lots in building level 4 have the same average weight as goblet rims from throughout the ABC excavation, but the rims from the single deposit code 37 lot from building level 3 have an average weight of only 5.7 g, roughly half the average weight of goblet rims from every other part of the site.

Deposit code 37 identifies an arbitrary floor cleaning lot of bricky rubble or other fill resting directly on a floor or living surface. Given the imperfect nature of excavations, it would appear that the deposit code 37 lot from building level 3 contains material from a living floor—objects that were trodden into the clay floor during the time the area was being used—and should probably have been labeled as a floor removal lot, deposit code 29. Still, table 9.3 shows that the average goblet rim weight from deposit code 29 units is 10.1 g, very close to the 10.2 gram average weight from the deposit code 37 units in building level 4 and very different from the 5.7 gram average weight of goblet rims from the anomalous building level 3 floor cleaning unit.

Looking at table 9.1, we find that the anomalous deposit code 37 lot came from the floor of room 211 in building level 3. Table 9.1 also reveals that there is one other excavation unit with a reasonably large sample size that had unusually light goblet rim sherds—a deposit code 29 (floor removal) lot from room 304 of building level 3A, where the average weight of the goblet rims is 6.9 g. These two rooms are labeled in the plan of building level 3 (figure 9.3). Once again, a careful examination of average sherd weight data has allowed us to isolate a small number of excavation units that differ from similarly labeled units in the ABC sounding.

Both excavation units that yielded unusually small sherds are floor cleaning or floor removal lots from building level 3. This is the building with the fresco-painted walls, large rooms, and formal floor plan—an elaborate structure that may have been a Banesh temple (Wasilewska 1991) or elite domestic residence (Sumner 2003).

The assumptions underlying ceramic taphonomy imply that the sherds recovered from these rooms were subjected to some cultural process that caused them to be broken up more thoroughly than sherds from elsewhere in the building level 3 structure. The most obvious explanation is that the sherds in rooms 211 and 304 were broken up by trampling from relatively heavy foot traffic (Kirkby and Kirkby 1976:237).

There is good archaeological evidence for such traffic through room 304 (Sumner 2003). During building level 3A, the final occupation of the fresco-decorated building, room 304 was an outside area directly in front of the only known entrance to the main building level 3 structure. In contrast to other doorsills in this building complex, the doorsills in both the east and south walls of room 271 (the small passageway or vestibule directly east of room 304) were badly worn. The plaster on the door jamb in the door between rooms 304 and 271 was also worn away. These features indicate that room 304 was a heavily trafficked passageway during building level 3A times. Stratum 11A in room 304, the excavation unit with unusually small sherds, was a 9 cm-thick layer of clean clay immediately beneath the building level 3A occupation surface. Because this is the floor that people entering the fresco-decorated building would have walked on, it seems likely that the small average sherd size in this excavation unit is a result of extensive trampling.

Unusually small sherds were also found in the floor of room 211 of building level 3, and it is possible that the sherds in the floor of this room were broken up by heavy foot traffic similar to that posited for room 304. Although there is no direct architectural evidence that room 211 served as an entryway to the fresco-decorated building, there is no reason to believe that the door from room 304 was the only, or even the most important, entrance to this large and elaborate structure. The observed pattern of sherd size distribution suggests that room 211 may have been part of a second route into the two large rooms (rooms 63 and 373) in the interior of the fresco-painted building. This would imply the existence of an undiscovered entrance to the western side of the building level 3 structure to the north of the area exposed in the ABC excavation. Alternatively, room 211 could have been heavily traveled because it was the main passageway between rooms 63 and 373. Finally, it is possible that the smaller average sherd size in room 211 is not related to trampling at all but a result of some other pattern of behavior or building function. Further excavation would be needed to resolve these alternative explanations.

One final pattern was revealed in the sherd weight data: goblet rim sherds from the most common sorts of secondary contexts (deposit codes 21 and 29; identifying trash accumulated on a floor and material from the removal of occupation surfaces) are no different in average weight than sherds coming from bricky rubble (deposit codes 34 and 35) or the removal of brick or packed earth constructions (deposit code 36). If Banesh phase mud bricks and bricky rubble contain sherds that are the same size as sherds from common secondary contexts, it would appear that Banesh brickmakers were using older Banesh construction and occupation debris to make new bricks and that the manufacture of mud brick does not cause noticeable addi-

Table 9.4   Rim count and weight (in g) data, by building level

#/Units	Building Level	Stratum	Ct	Wt	Avg Wt	Comment
4	2	8	33	350	10.61	
6	3	10 & 11	48	490	10.21	
4	between 3 & 4	12	69	733	10.62	
5	4	13 & 14	483	4580	9.48	

Note: Data from deposit codes 22 (pit fill) and 37 (arbitrary floor cleaning) units omitted.

Table 9.5   Rim count and weight (g) data from arbitrary floor cleaning lots, by building level

#/Units	Building Level	Dep Code	Ct	Wt	Avg Wt	Comment
	2	37				
1	3	37	78	443	5.68	light
	between 3 & 4	37				
5	4	37	26	265	10.19	

tional breakage of sherds that are incorporated into the brickmaking process.[4]

Is it surprising that ancient brickmakers would rework old mud brick into new? Probably not. Large quantities of backdirt disappeared from the ABC excavation dump between two of the excavation seasons when I worked at Malyan, and when I asked about it one of the workmen at the site told me the dirt had been taken away to make mud bricks. Old brick, he added, was good for making new. I did not ask why this was true, and he did not try to explain it, but he was someone who had worked with mud brick his entire life and I assume his observation was based on extensive practical experience.

Would reprocessing cultural debris into mud brick break up sherds in the reworked material? Again, probably not. Making mud bricks is a simple operation (Wulff 1966:108–112). Clay, water, and chopped straw are dumped in a shallow pit or on a cleared piece of ground and mixed with shovels and by treading around in the muddy mass. The resulting mud, thick and viscous, is either molded into bricks that are dried in the sun or piled directly into packed earth (chineh) constructions. Brickmakers might toss out any large pieces of pottery they noticed in the clay, but typically they seem to make little effort to clean the dirt they use to make mud brick or chineh (Watson 1979:119). In short, there is little in the brickmaking process that would affect the average size of sherds that found their way into the clay-straw mix.

It is important, however, that much of the construction in the ABC area utilized bricks made from older Banesh phase midden or architectural debris. Much of that debris could have come from the upper portions of old mud-brick structures that were leveled in preparation for erecting each new set of buildings. But old structures in a growing, thriving city are not the same as a pile of archaeological backdirt. In addition, from the condition of the wall stubs excavated in the ABC operation, none of the structures in any of the building levels appear to have been noticeably decrepit when they were torn down. Whoever knocked down the old buildings in ABC and built larger structures in their place was in a position to appropriate four valuable resources: existing buildings, urban space, old mud brick, and large quantities of human labor.

As described by Sumner (2003), a fine domestic residence in building level 5 was leveled and replaced with a combination of domestic and communal structures—a residence that was at least as large and well built as the building level 5 residence it replaced, and the gateway/fortification structure of the curving double wall. This building level 4 residence and wall complex was in turn replaced by a large building with a formal floor plan and elaborately painted walls—"part of an elite domestic complex," writes Sumner, that may also "have served an institutional or administrative function." Finally, the palatial building level 3 structure was leveled and a building with even larger walls—a structure full of evidence for activities involving storage, administration, craft production, and long-distance trade—was built above the painted building's remains. In every instance, the bricks and mortar for the new buildings incorporated sherds from earlier Banesh constructions.

The chronological continuity, step-by-step increase in building size, and growing architectural complexity of the ABC building level sequence seems to reflect the activity, over a span of time measured in generations, of an increasingly powerful elite group. The data on average sherd weight examined here reveal virtually nothing about that social elite, about the institution or institutions they may have represented or the nature of the broader society they were members of. But the sherd size data do point to a potentially important difference in the post-depositional conditions affecting two ceramic production site dumps, and they identify three excavation units from the ABC operation that contain atypical material—a pit in building level 4 with unusually large sherds and two rooms in building level 3 with unusually small sherds in their floors. One of those two rooms was clearly subjected to unusually heavy traffic, and it is proposed that this trampling was responsible for the low average weight of sherds from that room.

If trampling caused the low average sherd weight observed in the other room, it would hint that a second entrance to the building level 3 structure may be found to the north of the area exposed in the ABC excavations.

The assumptions of ceramic taphonomy and data on average sherd size are not likely, in and of themselves, to reveal a great deal about the structure and function of ancient societies. They can, however, assist archaeologists in their search for patterns in the data from archaeological excavations and help them interpret the remains they have excavated. These are analytical tools that archaeologists should make a greater effort to systematically employ.

Acknowledgment. John O'Shea, Lynn Rainville, and Henry Wright offered many valuable suggestions on an early draft of this chapter. Comments and questions by Kamyar Abdi and Naomi F. Miller helped me improve the logic and presentation of the revised chapter in ways both large and small. Bill Sumner read an earlier version of the chapter and corrected several errors of fact and interpretation in my presentation. I thank them all for their generous assistance.

NOTES

1. The data collected in the field were not broken down by vessel type and thus were not suitable for the study undertaken here. The counts and weights used in this chapter were either collected by the author during his dissertation research (the data from surface collections at sites 8G35 and 8G37) or taken from study collections from the ABC excavations that were shipped from Iran to Ohio State University. These counts and weights were collected by Bill Sumner during his analysis of that material and I am grateful for his permission to use them in this chapter.

2. A wider range of straw-tempered ware vessel forms was found in the TUV area excavations at Malyan. In particular, beveled rim bowls—rare in the ABC operation—were common in the lower levels of the TUV excavations (Nicholas 1990:56–57, Pl. 13).

3. The linear regression lines shown in figures 9.4 and 9.5 were calculated with SYSTAT 5.2.1 using the general linear model with no constant. This forces the regression line to go through the origin of the graph, fulfilling the expectation that zero sherds should have zero weight. It also tends to inflate the value of r^2, however, so the degree of correlation indicated by the figures reported here should not be considered definitive.

4. Mud bricks could also have been salvaged from buildings that were being torn down and reused directly in later construction. However, because the standard bricks used in each of the four ABC Banesh period building levels are different sizes (Sumner 2003), the reuse of salvaged bricks would not seem to have been common in this part of Proto-Elamite Malyan.

CHAPTER 10

ECONOMY AND ADMINISTRATION AT BANESH MALYAN

Exploring the Potential of Faunal and Chemical Data for Understanding State Process

MELINDA A. ZEDER AND M. JAMES BLACKMAN

THERE CAN BE LITTLE DEBATE that specialized economy, complex hierarchical administration, and stratified social relations form the cornerstones of state level society. While various definitions of the state may highlight one of these fundamental characteristics more than the others, and while disparate explanations of state emergence may feature developments in one of these spheres of social interaction over those in another sphere, all archaeologists concerned with early states rely on the existence of one or more of these characteristics when labeling a particular example of ancient society a state. That the identification of a state rests on isolating the existence of one or more of these features is clear. What is not clear is how to identify and monitor these core attributes with the material remnants that these ancient societies leave behind.

Of the three, stratified social relations and specialized economy seem to leave the most tangible material remains. The trappings of power and prestige are expressed in the personal possessions and furnishings of the elite, those that they amass during their lifetimes and those that accompany them after death. The process of specialized production and the pathways products take from producer to consumer are evidenced in the production debris found in sites of specialized production and in the distribution of goods within and between settlements. The workings of state-level governance is much harder to monitor with archaeological data, however. In the absence of decipherable textual documentation, the existence of complex adminis-

tration may be implied by the presence of purported administrative artifacts whose source and function are often poorly understood, or inferred from the existence of specialized economy or social stratification. Rarely has it been possible to examine all three spheres in a single setting with independent sets of artifactual remains.

In this chapter we present just such an instance at the highland Iranian urban center of Malyan. Furthermore, we use in this examination both more conventional archaeological data—pottery, architecture, and other artifacts—to establish social distinctions within the city, and somewhat unconventional data—animal bones (more commonly used to reconstruct ancient diet and paleoecology) to monitor the development of specialized economic relations in the city and the chemical characterization of artifacts (more frequently employed in tracing long distance exchange relations)—to delineate the nature of administrative regulation of economic activities. The goals of this examination are threefold. The first is to take a close look at economy and administration in two socially distinct sectors at Malyan—an elite/public area and an industrial/domestic sector—during the first phase of urban development in highland Iran in the early third millennium BCE. The broader second goal is to consider the implications of this case example for the study of early states in general. And finally, on a methodological plane, we explore the potential of faunal and chemical data in the study of processes that lie at the core of complex society.

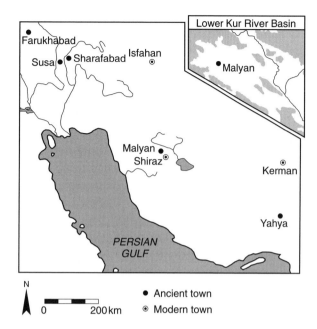

10.1 The Proto-Elamite world and location of Malyan.
Prepared at MASCA based on original by M.J. Blackman

10.2 Malyan, location of Operations ABC and TUV.
After Zeder 1991

LATE FOURTH MILLENNIUM
URBAN DEVELOPMENT IN HIGHLAND IRAN

The setting for this study is the site of Malyan located in the Kur river basin in southwest highland Iran (figures 10.1 and 10.2). The establishment of Malyan as the primary center in the Kur river basin, late in the fourth millennium BCE, followed a long period of increasing economic and,

presumably, political complexity in the region. Alden (1979) has traced the development of specialized economic relations in the valley from the Lapui phase (4000–3600 BCE), with the establishment of specialized pottery production sites on the margins of the valley, to the Early Banesh (3600–3400 BCE), with the founding of spatially segregated distribution centers at more centrally located sites. Probably first emerging as one of several competing centers, Malyan took its position as the dominant center in the Kur river basin in the late fourth millennium BCE, during the Middle Banesh (3400–3000 BCE), at which time it grew to at least 50 ha in size and served as home to a minimum of 4000 people.

Curiously, evidence for increased economic complexity and the ensuing establishment of Malyan as a major center comes at a time of population decline following the collapse of what is thought to be the first chiefly society in the region during the Bakun phase (4500–3900 BCE) (Sumner 1988b, 1990b). By the Middle Banesh the number of settlements fell from its Bakun high of 153 to no more than nineteen, none of which, save Malyan, were more than 1 to 2 ha in size. The growth of Malyan cannot be attributed to a simple aggregation of population from dispersed villages to a single center, however. The Bakun population high is separated from the founding of Malyan as a major center by at least 700 years of steady decline in settled population. Sumner (1986a) attributes the abandonment of Bakun towns and villages to the initial success and ultimate failure of early attempts at irrigation agriculture in the center of the valley. The proliferation of the number of small sites on the spring-watered margins of the valley is seen as part of a process of increasing shift to an emphasis on pastoral economy in the Kur river basin. He places the coordination of economic relations in the hands of prominent nomad "khans" settling in village headquarters that served as hubs for exchange. Banesh Malyan may then have been the site of one of these tribal villages that, due to its access to a large area of arable land and to major passes into the valley, grew to an unprecedented size. In effect, Sumner sees Banesh leaders at Malyan as brokers between pastoral and settled populations, commanding allegiance from nomadic groups because of clan ties and because of their control of agricultural resources and pasture rights, while at the same time offering access to pastoral resources and protection from nomad raiders to the settled population in return for an assured supply of agricultural resources and craft products.

Various studies of Middle Banesh craft activities practiced in the Kur river basin indicate increasing complexity and control over the procurement of rare resources and the production and distribution of goods centered at Malyan

(Blackman 1981, 1982, 1984). The high agricultural potential of the countryside around Malyan and the fact that there are no smaller sites within a 10-km radius of the site suggest to Miller (1982:232–235) that Malyan was essentially self-sufficient in agricultural production during the Middle Banesh. The appearance of traditional markers of Proto-Elamite culture at the site—tablets, seals, chlorite bowls and characteristic Proto-Elamite pottery types, including bevelled rim bowls, goblets, and trays—indicate that Malyan participated in the larger Proto-Elamite sphere of interaction that extended from the Susiana in lowland southwestern Iran across the Iranian Plateau (figure 10.1) as far east as the Helmand valley in extreme eastern Iran (Alden 1982a; Amiet and Tosi 1978; Kohl 1978; Lamberg-Karlovsky 1986).

The case for administrative control of regional economy in the Kur river basin is, however, based inferentially on the apparent complexity of economic relations and not on independent evidence of the nature of economic regulation centered at Malyan. Nor does the picture of Banesh economy just painted tell us much about economic relations and their administration within Malyan itself.

CITY LIFE IN BANESH MALYAN

Excavations at Malyan concentrated on two distinct areas of Banesh occupation that served as home to residents of sharply differentiated social standing in the city (figure 10.2).[1]

OPERATION ABC

Excavation of Banesh deposits in the center of the main western sector of Malyan, at a grid location labeled Operation ABC, encountered four distinct building levels dating to the Middle Banesh (figure 10.3, Sumner 1974, 1976, 1986a, 1988a:308–309; Zeder 1991:120–123). With the exception of the final level of Banesh occupation in this area (building level 2) structures in each building level were cleaned and razed after abandonment to make way for the next stage of construction. Each of these structures was large and well planned, and bore evidence of wall decoration. While the walls were somewhat narrower in the lowest building level 5 than in later Banesh buildings at this site, the plan of this building seen in the relatively small exposure accomplished by excavations seems to echo the regularity and impressive room dimensions of higher levels. Building level 4 followed a somewhat less regular plan than seen in later levels, with large curving walls enclosing long corridor spaces. The density of bone found against the western side of one of these walls suggests that unlike the other building levels encountered in ABC Banesh levels, building level 4 represented the outside margin of a

major building. However like other ABC Banesh building levels, the walls of this building were impressively thick and outlined large spaces. Room contents included some evidence of metal work, bead production, and administrative artifacts, including seals, sealings, and a tablet fragment. Building level 3 at ABC was a particularly impressive complex that extended well beyond the 15 by 25 m boundaries of excavation. The walls of this large structure, some more than 1.3 m thick, followed a highly regular architectural plan. Some walls were brightly decorated with fine polychrome geometric wall paintings (Nickerson 1977). Artifacts recovered here included fragments of painted lime plaster and stone bowls, finely crafted relief ceramic vessels, more than 100 impressed sealing fragments, and seven tablet fragments. The final Banesh building encountered in building level 2 was similarly large and impressive, and contained 13 painted storage jars each over 2 m in height, a number of impressed sealings, inscribed tablets, and small clusters of worked and unworked materials that included specular hematite, shell, and hundreds of small mother-of-pearl geometric inlay pieces.

In sum, each level of Banesh occupation in this sector of Malyan was the site of large carefully planned and constructed buildings with decorated walls and fine ceramic, plaster, and stone wares, indicative of high-status occupancy. Artifacts recovered from these structures also point to a range of specialized activities including bulk storage and distribution, manufacture of luxury craft goods from rare raw materials, and, from the tablets and sealings, administration. While some of these four structures may have housed different ranges of activities, it is safe to say that all Banesh occupation levels at Operation ABC were occupied by high status individuals involved in the administration of economic activities.

OPERATION TUV

Excavations at the small isolated TUV mound, approximately 900 m from Operation ABC in the eastern sector of the site, encountered three levels of Banesh construction that bear witness to a very different stratum of city life in Banesh Malyan (figure 10.4). Nicholas' (1980, 1990) study of Banesh deposits at Operation TUV provide a detailed picture of the evolution of specialized activities in this sector of the city. In her fine-scale analysis of artifact distributions and site depositional history, Nicholas was able to isolate three major activities that are represented in each of the levels of occupation at TUV. First, preparation and serving of food stuffs is documented by hearths, ovens and bins, high densities of faunal remains, and a large number of mass-produced chaff ware serving vessels.

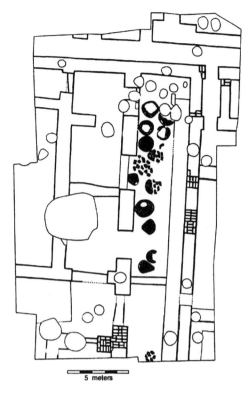

ABC Building Level 2

ABC Building Level 3

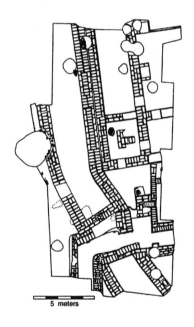

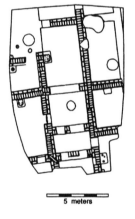

ABC Building Level 4

ABC Building Level 5

10.3   Banesh building levels at Operation ABC. *Redrawn from Sumner 1976*

Second, storage, controlled disbursement of goods, and accounting are indicated by segmented storage areas and large storage vessels, broken door and jar sealings, bullae, and Proto-Elamite tablets. Third, specialized production of small ornamental objects is evidenced by the presence of rare raw materials and production debris resulting from both metallurgical and lapidary activities.

The distribution of artifacts associated with these activities in each successive building level along with changes in the layout and design of different rebuildings, suggest a growing degree of complexity and specialization of activities in this area of the site over time. The earliest excavated building level at TUV, building level 3a-b, was a structure comprised of a series of slightly less than rectilinear rooms reflecting neither the level of planning nor care in construction seen in the buildings in the elite ABC sector of the site. Larger rooms encountered in the eastern section of the excavations, interpreted as some kind of formal living and "entertainment" area (Nicholas 1990), bore traces of wall plaster and paint which suggest that TUV residents, though not of the same stratum as ABC residents, were far from impoverished city dwellers. All of the major activities discussed above are well evidenced in this building level. Craft activities seem centered more in the northeastern portion of the TUV excavations. Food preparation and serving were more frequently evidenced in the western sector of the building, along with artifacts tied to storage, disbursement, and accounting.

Building level 2 sees the growth of the TUV facility with larger, more carefully constructed areas dedicated to food preparation and storage. At least four distinct activity areas have been distinguished including:

- A large courtyard in the southeastern sector of the building associated with short-term storage and mass-produced serving vessels;
- A series of small rectilinear rooms in the southwest portion of the building that contained storage vessels, jar stoppers, and sealings, associated with longer term storage;
- A block of rooms in the northern portion of the limits of excavation that served a similar function to the painted rooms of building level 3; and
- A large kitchen installation consisting of a number of rooms in the northernmost end of the excavated portion of TUV that contained a large quantity of built-in hearths ovens, storage bins, and an extremely high frequency of animal bones.

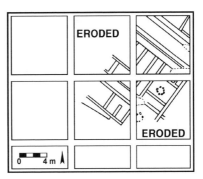

TUV Building Level 1

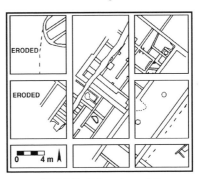

TUV Building Level 2

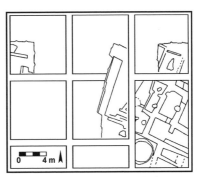

TUV Building Level 3b

10.4 Banesh building levels at Operation TUV. *Redrawn from Nicholas 1990*

In sum, architecture and artifact distribution within the building indicates increasing segregation of activities associated with food preparation, storage, disbursement, and accounting. Evidence of craft activities decreases in this level compared to the earlier smaller building level 3 structure.

Building level 1 seems an enlargement of the narrow storage rooms located in the southwestern portion of building level 2 into a well planned and executed series of small partitioned rooms which now occupy the balance of the excavated area of the site. This final level of occupation had a much lower density of artifacts than earlier levels, due perhaps to ancient house cleaning and post-abandonment site erosion. Artifacts found in two contemporary wells and a pit indicate that food preparation, use of mass-produced ceramics, and limited craft activity occurred also here.

Elsewhere Zeder (1985:247–256, 1991:127–129) has argued that the structures encountered in the southwestern end of the TUV mound served as a kind of institutional kitchen responsible for preparing food and feeding at least a portion of TUV residents, some of whom were involved in the production of nonutilitarian objects of personal ornamentation. Beginning as a relatively small and compact operation, the facility grew in time with an expansion and increasing delineation of areas given over to discrete activities involved in food preparation and serving, storage, accounting, and craft. Each successive TUV building level is like time-lapse photography of a growing, evolving facility. In each level we see the expansion of functionally discrete sectors of the building in which increasingly segregated activities were performed. And in each we capture a smaller portion of this expanding facility—a portion dedicated more exclusively to a narrower range of the total complement of craft, administrative, and so-called "domestic" food related activities evidenced here. Thus the decrease in indications of craft activity in each subsequent rebuilding of the TUV facility may be attributable to the growth of the facility and an increasing segregation of the various functions performed there. While the exposure of the more modest, less formalized structure in building level 3 captured the full range of craft, administrative, and "domestic activities" practiced at the facility, with each rebuilding these functions expanded in scope and became more spatially discrete so that by building level 1 the entire excavation exposure was devoted solely to storage and other functions, like craft production and food preparation, were conducted in more spatially segregated parts of the facility outside the boundaries of excavation on the southwestern lobe of the TUV mound. Certainly the amount of metal slag found on the surface of the mound and the strong magnetometer readings recorded here would indicate the persistence and perhaps expansion of metallurgical craft activities in the more northerly unexcavated areas of the mound.

We see then two different segments of Banesh society at Malyan—elites living in elaborate and richly appointed buildings, and a prosperous community of craftsmen and support personnel situated almost 1 km to the east of the elite sector of the city. Though differing in the size and quality of their domiciles, residents in both sectors of this early city seem concerned with the production of ornaments from rare raw materials, and both sectors bear evidence of the regulation of economic activities through the presence of sealings, seals, administrative artifacts (tokens and bullae), and tablets. And though we are reasonably certain that at least the later levels of

the ABC elite structures are contemporary with the earliest levels at the TUV facility (Stolper 1985:11; Sumner 1988a), we know little of the connection between these two sectors of site. Are there indications of differential access to basic resources at these two sectors of the site other than the evident disparities in housing and ceramics? Is there evidence of any domination or control over the craft and food preparation activities conducted at TUV by the elite occupants of ABC? Or did these two sectors exist as autonomous quarters of this emergent urban center?

MEAT PROVISIONING AT BANESH MALYAN

There are two basic requirements that must be met by a state-level specialized economy. First, certain groups of individuals produce more of a commodity than they consume. And second, some central coordinating mechanism assures that, in exchange for this surplus, producers receive another commodity they themselves do not produce, but that is, in turn, the surplus of some other group of specialized producers (Zeder 1988:3, 1991:12–17). A possible measure of the effectiveness of the economy in meeting the latter of these two requirements might be the degree to which producers abandon involvement in other life-sustaining productive activities because they can rely on the ability of the economy to direct these essential goods their way. Thus the degree to which the production and distribution of basic foodstuffs become specialized activities, the degree to which nonfood producing specialists rely on the economy to supply them with food in return for their full-time devotion to their craft can prove a powerful gauge of the degree to which these kinds of specialized relations have pervaded the workings of the economy as a whole.

In this context, the study of the plant and animal remains from urban contexts becomes one of the most effective tools archaeologists have at their disposal for monitoring the workings of complex economy in urban contexts. While specialization and control over at least certain aspects of the production of food resources is one of the possible outcomes of the emergence of specialized economy in early urban contexts in the Near East, it is the distribution of food to urban dwellers that is the most likely aspect of subsistence economy to come under central control (Zeder 1991:85–86). Distribution of food is also the subsistence activity most readily monitored with archaeological evidence from urban sites (Zeder 1991:245–254). In particular, decreasing involvement in food production and increasing reliance on indirect systems of food distribution (either market or state controlled) is a hallmark of urban life.

Increasingly, archaeobiological studies in the Near East have attempted to approach fundamental questions about origin and organization of complex urban economies through the study of plant and animal remains from urban contexts (for example, McCorriston 1997; Miller 1982, 1997b; Mudar 1982; Stein 1987; Wattenmaker 1997; Zeder 1991, 1996, 1998). In the study of the Malyan assemblage, Zeder developed several measures of the degree of participation in direct versus indirect modes of meat distribution in urban contexts (Zeder 1985, 1988, 1991:33–42, 85–97). Specifically, greater diversity in the species, ages, and sexes of animals consumed may signal direct receipt of meat resources. Body parts representing whole carcasses are expected in the domestic trash of households either raising animals or receiving meat resources directly from producers, and there should be little standardization in butchery practices. In contrast, a restricted range of species, ages, and sexes of animals might signal receipt of meat through indirect, regulated distribution channels either controlled by the state or through market mechanisms. Uneven part distributions with different quality of cuts following social and economic distinctions should be evident. Greater standardization in butchery practices might also be expected with consumers receiving animals from specialized butchers as part of a regulated, indirect system of meat distribution.

Applying these measures to the two sectors of Banesh Malyan contrasted above should, then, allow us to assess the degree to which each of these sectors participated in broader urban economic relations. It should also highlight any differences in provisioning in these sectors that might be linked to the different social standing of the residents of these two areas.[2]

MEAT DISTRIBUTION AT OPERATION ABC

By all of the measures examined here, it would seem that elite residents of Banesh ABC received meat through indirect provisioning channels. Diversity of species is very low, suggesting restricted access to the full range of domestic and wild resources available at the time. Sheep and goats contributed 99% of all meat consumed (table 10.1). Age distribution of ABC caprines shows a strong, essentially exclusive, emphasis on two to three year old animals (figure 10.5a), an emphasis suggests a culling strategy that maximized for meat return rather than for production of secondary products (Payne 1973) or for the overall security and perpetuation of the herd (Redding 1981). The distribution of "medium mammal" elements from ABC indicates that at least some whole animals were butchered here, arriving here either on-the-hoof or as complete carcasses (figure 10.6). However, the relative representation of both meatier axial and limb bones, and

Table 10.1 Banesh identifiable mammal bones

Species	ABC	TUV	TUV III	TUV II	TUV I
Number of bones (in %)					
Bos	+	2	3	1	+
Equid	+	1	1	-	-
Ovis/Capra	99	97	96	99	99
Sus	-	+	+	-	-
Gazella	+	+	-	+	-
Total Number	781	3,591	1,693	1,469	429
Weight of bones in grams (in %)					
Bos	2	14	23	5	+
Equid	1	2	4	1	-
Ovis/Capra	96	83	72	94	99
Sus	-	+	1	-	-
Gazella	+	+	-	+	-
Total Weight	4,506	24,525	12,700	8,879	2,673

- = No bones in this category; + = Less than 1%

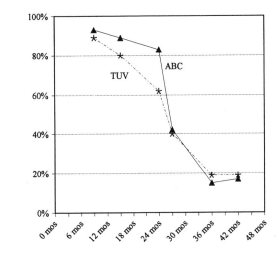

a

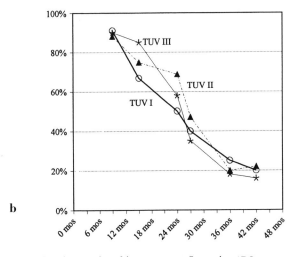

b

10.5 Caprine survivorship curves: *a*, Operation ABC compared to Operation TUV; *b*, TUV building levels *Prepared at MASCA based on original by M.A. Zeder*

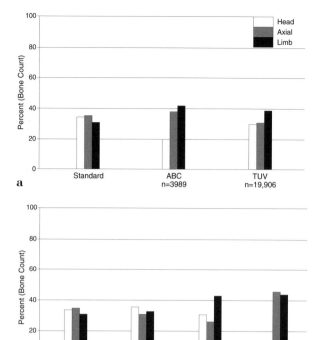

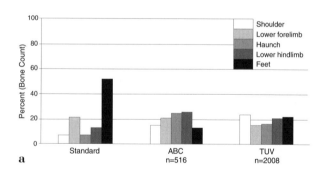

10.6 Medium mammal part distributions: *a*, Operation ABC compared to Operation TUV; *b*, TUV building levels
Prepared at MASCA based on original by M.A. Zeder

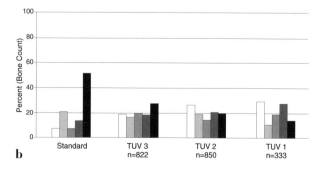

10.7 Caprine limb bone distributions: *a*, Operation ABC compared to Operation TUV; *b*, TUV building levels
Prepared at MASCA based on original by M.A. Zeder

the depressed number of head elements when compared to a standard representing the number of bones in a complete carcass (and, importantly, to the distribution of parts from Operation TUV) also suggest preferential access to meatier cuts. Cuts from the upper and lower portions of the hind limb of sheep and goats seem especially preferred here (figure 10.7a), and nonmeaty limb bones are poorly represented compared to their representation at TUV (figure 10.8a). Finally, the highly focused placement of butchery scars on ABC caprine bones suggests some standardization in butchery practices (Zeder 1991:Fig. 14). The bulk of the ABC sample (67%) is derived from the trashy midden associated with the large, outside wall of the building level 4 structure. However, even the smaller assemblages from the other ABC building levels show the same restrictions in species diversity, similar part distributions, as well as a restricted focus on animals in the two to three year age range. It is safe to assume, then, that like the architecture and artifact contents of these five buildings, the faunal distributions also signal a similarity in function and status over the occupation of ABC during the Banesh phase.

MEAT DISTRIBUTION AT OPERATION TUV

Contrasted to the ABC sample, the combined TUV faunal sample suggests that TUV residents obtained their meat more directly from the source, even if they did not own herds. Species distribution, though heavily focused on caprines, shows a greater utilization of cattle (table 10.1). Both gazelle and wild pig were eaten here in small quantities, and the bird sample from TUV indicates the consumption of at least two species of duck as well as partridge (Zeder 1991:139). Caprine survivorship patterns indicate access to a broader range of ages of animals with an emphasis on slightly younger animals—a culling strategy that may have been more accommodating to herders' goals of perpetuating herd security than to the maximization of possible return (figure 10.5a). Part distributions suggest whole animal carcasses were used and less meaty cuts were more common than at ABC (figures. 10.6a, 10.7a, and 10.8a). Finally butchery scar placement is much more widely dispersed than in the ABC caprine bones indicative of much broader range of butchery practices (Zeder 1991:Fig. 14).

This picture changes, however, when the large assemblages from each of the three building levels are examined separately. Like the architecture and the distribution of activity areas in the building, the faunal data point to increasing specialization and complexity in the mechanism through which this evolving facility obtained animal resources. First, the diversity of animals shows a steady decrease through time at the TUV facility (table 10.1). Though sheep and goat dominate in all levels, large mammals, especially cattle are better represented in building level 3 than in any other Banesh context. In weight of bone, a rough measure of meat contribution (Uerpmann 1973; Zeder 1991:88), cattle bones contribute 23% to the total weight of bones from this level. By building level 1, sheep and goat bones comprise 99% of the both total and the total weight of bones. Wild pig and gazelle, present in low numbers in building levels 3 and 2 are absent in building level 1, as are birds, present in both earlier levels at TUV (Zeder 1991:139).

Caprine long-bone age distributions for the individual building levels exhibit similar change over time, particularly an increasing focus on a narrower range of animals (figure 10.5b). Though survivorship curves for building levels 3 and 2 are similar, the curve for the earliest excavated level at TUV indicates a very generalized focus on animals in the one to three year old categories. In building level 2 there is more of an emphasis on two to three year olds, though there is also some emphasis on animals between 10 to 16 months of age. By building level 1 there is a shift toward a relatively pronounced emphasis on animals in the one to two year and a much weaker emphasis on animals in the two to three year age category. These changes indicate an increasing restriction in access to the complete range of ages available in a herd and an exclusionary focus on a single age class—patterns expected when meat is received through indirect channels.

Similarly, part distributions shift toward patterns consistent with indirect provisioning of meat. Medium mammal part distributions in building level 3 are almost identical to the standard, suggesting butchery and disposal of complete carcasses (figure 10.6b). By building level 2 times there is some emphasis on limb cuts, and by building level 1 head elements are sharply depressed relative to meatier axial and limb elements. Representation of specific limb elements indicate an increasing focus on cuts from the shoulder and lower hind limb, and a drop in the proportion of meat-bearing compared to nonmeat bearing limb bones from building level 3 to building level 1 times (figures 10.7b, 10.8b). Placement of butchery scars which are quite generalized in the caprine assemblages from the first two levels of occupation at TUV, becomes restricted to specific locations in the assemblage from building level 1, indicating increasing standardization of caprine butchery (Zeder 1991:Fig. 15).

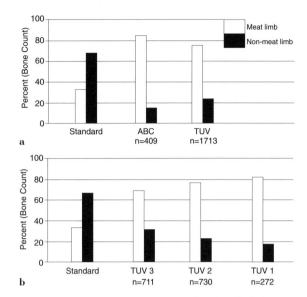

10.8 Caprine meat and non-meat bearing limb bones: *a*, Operation ABC compared to Operation TUV; *b*, TUV building levels. *Prepared at MASCA based on original by M.A. Zeder*

These data give us a window through which we can watch the evolution of urban provisioning at Malyan. While elite residents at ABC received meat through highly controlled channels, at least the initial residents of TUV (contemporaries of the ABC elite) either produced the animal resources consumed there themselves, or procured them directly from herders. Through time access to herds became increasingly more remote, so that by the time of the latest level of occupation during the Late Banesh (3000–2800 BCE), provisioning of meat to the TUV facility was conducted along indirect channels similar to those which once provisioned the elites of the now abandoned ABC public structures.

Thus, the faunal data augment the picture of specialization and complexity of activities conducted at both the elite buildings at ABC and at the institution housed at TUV. At ABC and, at least for the later levels, at TUV, patterns in the faunal data point to the existence of a distribution mechanism through which residents received meat (if not all food) that would seem to require higher level coordination and integration into an extra-local economy. Yet while these data imply a good degree of administrative complexity at the ABC elite sector of Malyan and increasing complexity in administration through time at the TUV facility, they still only do so by inference. We do not, as yet, have a good understanding of the administrative structure that regulated these activities. Moreover, we still have no idea whether contemporary levels at ABC and TUV had

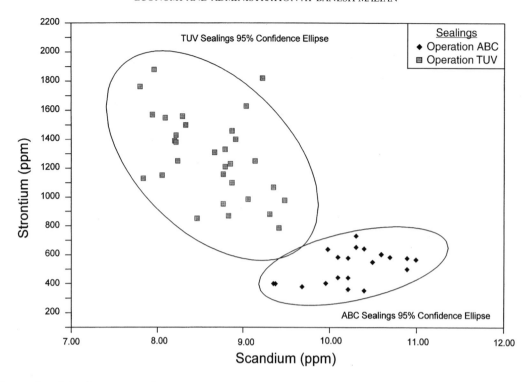

10.9   Binary plot of the elements scandium and strontium in ABC and TUV sealings. Gray squares are TUV sealings and solid diamonds are ABC sealings. Outliers are not shown. Ellipses are 95% confidence intervals. *M.J. Blackman*

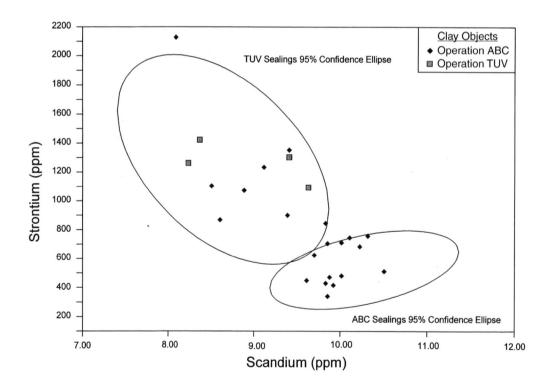

10.10   Binary plot of the elements scandium and strontium in ABC and TUV clay objects. Gray squares are TUV clay objects and solid diamonds are ABC clay objects. Outliers are not shown. Ellipses are 95% confidence intervals. *M.J. Blackman*

Table 10.2 Mean element concentrations for clay sealings from Banesh deposits at Operation ABC (N = 21)

	Ca %	Sc ppm	Cr ppm	Fe %	Co ppm	Rb ppm	Sr ppm	Cs ppm	La ppm	Ce ppm	Sm ppm	Eu ppm	Yb ppm	Lu ppm	Hf ppm	Ta ppm	Th ppm
Mean	14.2	10.3	254.	3.00	16.5	55.3	524.	3.30	20.8	38.3	3.60	0.723	1.78	0.274	2.99	0.635	5.57
c.v.	14.6	4.4	16.7	4.6	10.8	12.1	21.4	10.0	2.7	3.1	4.8	11.0	10.4	6.4	5.9	10.9	3.1
Upper 95%	18.5	11.2	343.	3.28	20.2	69.3	757.	3.99	21.9	40.8	3.97	0.888	2.17	0.311	3.36	0.779	5.94
Lower 95%	9.86	9.34	166.	2.71	12.8	41.3	290.	2.61	19.6	35.9	3.24	0.557	1.39	0.238	2.62	0.491	5.21

Concentrations in tablet excavated at ABC matching TUV compositional group

	Ca %	Sc ppm	Cr ppm	Fe %	Co ppm	Rb ppm	Sr ppm	Cs ppm	La ppm	Ce ppm	Sm ppm	Eu ppm	Yb ppm	Lu ppm	Hf ppm	Ta ppm	Th ppm
MAS110	17.6	8.63	289.	2.52	19.7	40.2	944.	2.49	15.9	30.6	3.05	0.568	1.53	0.217	2.53	0.630	4.51

Table 10.3 Mean element concentrations for clay sealings from Banesh deposits at Operation TUV (N = 31)

	Ca %	Sc ppm	Cr ppm	Fe %	Co ppm	Rb ppm	Sr ppm	Cs ppm	La ppm	Ce ppm	Sm ppm	Eu ppm	Yb ppm	Lu ppm	Hf ppm	Ta ppm	Th ppm
Mean	15.0	8.64	221	2.48	14.5	47.3	1284	3.01	18.0	33.4	3.28	0.648	1.60	0.243	2.64	0.520	4.82
c.v.	12.4	5.8	14.5	6.6	9.3	11.6	22.8	12.0	6.1	5.4	8.1	6.7	8.7	7.0	7.6	14.0	5.6
Upper 95%	18.8	9.66	286	2.82	17.2	58.5	1881	3.75	20.2	37.0	3.83	0.736	1.86	0.278	3.05	0.669	5.37
Lower 95%	11.2	7.62	156	2.15	11.7	36.1	688	2.28	15.8	29.7	2.73	0.560	1.32	0.208	2.23	0.372	4.28

any administrative connection that would have a bearing on the nature of urban integration at Malyan in general.

REGULATION OF ECONOMIC ACTIVITIES AT BANESH MALYAN

The advent of writing gives archaeologists a tremendous advantage in monitoring administrative process in urban contexts in the Near East. This is especially true for the study of administration of economic relations since the earliest texts record not the legends and literary history of ancient states, or even the laws and legislation of their kings, but the totals and tabulations of things bought and sold, manufactured and traded. Reaching back before the appearance of decipherable texts, the counters, the seals, and the sealings that accompanied the movement, storage, and disbursement of goods give us some picture of the degree of oversight and higher level concern with the regulation of commerce in early urban contexts.

All of these artifacts mark administrative control over economy. Yet even texts inscribed with languages well known to epigraphers, do not say how far or from where the goods they accompany and record have moved. Rarely do these objects tell us which individuals or institutions actually controlled the movement and disbursement of these items. Stylistic variables and the geographic patterning of iconographic motifs have helped trace the connections between ancient urban centers, but they cannot tell us if the goods moved or if it is the seal itself that has been traded from the center responsible for that stylistic tradition to the center where the impressed sealing was found. We can only know how far and from where these markers of administrative control have come if we can identify the actual source of the clay that bears the sealing impressions and that forms the counters, the clay on which the numbers and types of objects moved are inscribed. And this end can only be accomplished through the characterization of these clays by chemical analysis. While there are several analytical methods that can be used to measure chemical composition of clay, the most promising results, to date, have been provided by instrumental neutron activation analysis (INAA) (see Rothman and Blackman 1990).

CHEMICAL CHARACTERIZATION OF CLAY SEALINGS IN WESTERN IRAN

In the early 1980s Blackman began a regional study of the chemical composition of impressed clay sealings from five sites in lowland and highland Iran (Malyan, Tepe Yahya, Susa, Farukhabad, and Sharafabad). The initial aim of this study was to use chemical data to identify the movement of

sealed objects between centers linked together in proposed lowland-highland interaction spheres. In all, 212 clay objects and sealings were analyzed using instrumental neutron activation analysis for 25 elements according to the analytical protocol outlined by Blackman (1984). Unfired clay objects (for example, spindle whorls, "sling balls," clay blobs, and squeezes) unlikely to have been traded from outside the settlement were used to characterize the composition of clays local to each site. The chemical signatures of these objects were then contrasted with those of the clay sealings to distinguish sealings applied locally from those arriving from elsewhere (Blackman 1985). While a possible non-local origin of some sealed objects was detected in this study, the vast majority of sealing clays proved to have originated at the same site from which they had been recovered.[3] Chemical data from sealing clays cluster into five distinct site specific compositional groups whose integrity is validated at the 95% confidence interval using Hotelling's T^2 statistic.

Although these findings do not support some long held assumptions based on sealing iconography about the long distance movement of sealed goods, it is actually not surprising that the clay sealings are better indicators of the administration of local rather than long distance economic relations. Economic activities related to local production and distribution were undoubtedly more common and more widespread in these early centers than were those related to the long distance exchange of commodities. Correspondingly it seems likely that the administration of local economic interactions would leave a proportionately greater volume of material remains in the archaeological record than that of long distance exchange relations.

BANESH SEALINGS AT MALYAN

What we did not expect, however, was the extremely localized nature of sealing activities within the site of Malyan. Examination of 58 seal impressed objects from Banesh levels at Malyan assigned 52 of them into two distinct compositional groups that separate ABC sealing clays (table 10.2) from TUV sealings (table 10.3) at the 95% confidence level (figure 10.9). Most (94%) of the seal impressed clays analyzed from TUV, including both portable and non-portable types, were assigned to a distinct TUV chemical composition group (table 10.4). Similarly 91% of the 23 analyzed ABC sealings were assigned to a chemical composition group specific to ABC. Neither of the two TUV sealings that fell outside the TUV compositional group (MAS112 and MAS116) were similar to the ABC compositional group. Nor could the outlying ABC sealings (MAS132, and MAS150) be attributed to the TUV compositional group.

Table 10.4 List of analyzed clay sealings and objects excavated from Banesh levels at Operation TUV. All samples belong to the TUV compositional group except where noted.

A. CLAY SEALINGS

Sample #	Object # (mf)	Bldg Level	Sealing Type	Seal Motif
MAS102	1966	2	jar	geometric
MAS103	1959	?	unknown	geometric
MAS104	1947c	3B	door	random linear
MAS107	1885	3B	jar	geometric
MAS112*	1825o	3B	unknown	geometric
MAS114	1825c	3B	jar	brocade
MAS115	1825d	3B	jar	brocade
MAS116*	1803	3B	jar	no sealing
MAS117	1879c	2	jar	unknown
MAS118	1879j	2	jar	flying bird
MAS119	1879b	2	unknown	brocade
MAS120	1879f	2	stamp	flying bird
MAS121	1965b	2	unknown	figurative
MAS122	1965a	2	unknown	figurative
MAS123	1883a	3B	jar stopper	no sealing
MAS124	1883a	3B	jar stopper	no sealing
MAS125	1951b	?	unknown	unknown
MAS126	1825i	3B	unknown	brocade
MAS127	1825f	3B	unknown	brocade
MAS128	1884b	3B	unknown	figurative
MAS129	1884d	3B	unknown	geometric
MAS130	1885a	3B	jar	brocade
MAS131	1886d	3B	unknown	brocade
MAS137	1958	2	jar	geometric
MAS154	1542	3A	bulla	unknown
MAS155	1567	3A	unknown	figurative
MAS158	1789	3A	jar	figurative
MAS159	1806	3B	unknown	figurative
MAS170	6180	2	bulla	geometric
MAS172	5452	2	bulla	brocade
MAS174	1817	3B	unknown	brocade
MAS176	1886b	3B	stamp	unknown
MAS177	1393	2	bulla	geometric

B. CLAY OBJECTS

Sample No.	Object No. (mf)	Phase	Description
MAC020	7138	Banesh	"clay object"
MAC021	"lot 2"	Banesh	"clay object"
MAC023	"lot 31"	Banesh	"oblong clay object"
MAC024	1522	Banesh	spindle whorl

✻ = Sealings excavated at TUV, not belonging to ABC or TUV chemical composition groups

As ABC and TUV are located only about 900 m from each other, the distinctive chemical profiles of the seal impressed clays from these areas is remarkable and at first suggested the strong possibility of post-depositional alteration. Post-depositional effects, either leaching or precipitation, should affect all objects of similar composition equally. Thus, if such alteration was responsible for the patterning in the Banesh sealing clays, one would expect all clay artifacts, including ceramics, from these two areas to be subject to the same post-depositional contaminants and to show similar locally distinct chemical profiles. As seen in figure 10.10 the four unfired clay objects recovered from TUV that were analyzed (table 10.4) all fall squarely within the TUV sealing compositional group. However, while the majority of clay objects recovered from ABC (table 10.5) clustered together within the ABC sealing compositional group, eight of these objects (33%) fall within the TUV sealing compositional group. The presence of TUV composition clay artifacts in the objects recovered from ABC rules out post-depositional effects as the source of this variability between ABC and TUV sealing clays.

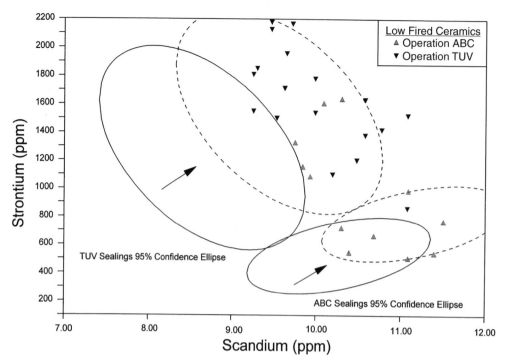

10.11   Binary plot of the elements scandium and strontium in ABC and TUV low fired, chaff tempered ceramics. Black triangles are ceramics excavated at TUV, gray triangles are ceramics excavated at ABC. Solid line ellipses are the 95% confidence intervals for the ABC and TUV sealing groups and the dashed ellipses are extrapolated to account for weight loss due to firing. *M.J. Blackman*

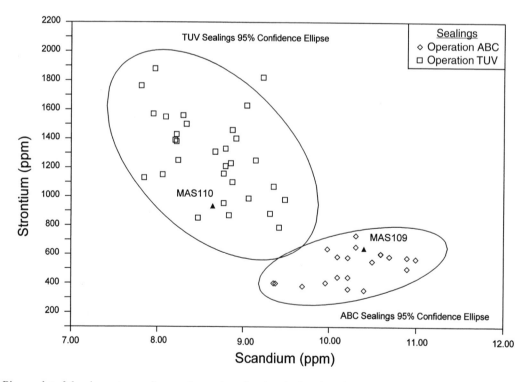

10.12   Binary plot of the elements scandium and strontium showing the location of the two tablets excavated at ABC (solid triangles). *M.J. Blackman*

Table 10.5 List of analyzed clay sealings and objects excavated from Banesh levels at Operation ABC. All samples belong to the ABC compositional group except where noted.

A. CLAY SEALINGS EXCAVATED FROM BANESH LEVELS AT ABC

Sample #	Object # (mf)	Bldg Level	Sealing Type	Seal Motif
MAS101	1970.1	2	jar	"hedgehog"
MAS105	2028	3A	jar	unknown
MAS106	1979.1	4A	unknown	bovine
MAS108	0637	2	bulla	unknown
MAS132*	1978	4A	jar stopper	no sealing
MAS133	1971	4A	unknown	unknown
MAS134	1979.3	4A	unknown	"barber pole"
MAS135	1973	3B	unknown	unknown
MAS136	1639	3	unknown	unknown
MAS150*	2614	3	unknown	unknown
MAS152	1642	3	jar	figurative
MAS153	1569	3	jar	figurative
MAS156	1714	3	jar	figurative
MAS157	1657	3	jar	figurative
MAS160	1571	3	jar	figurative
MAS162	1629	3	jar	figurative
MAS164	1563	3	jar	figurative
MAS165	1637	3	jar	figurative
MAS166	1566	3	jar	figurative
MAS169	1970.2	2	unknown	figurative
MAS173	1575	3	jar	figurative
MAS175	1932.1	4A	jar	figurative
MAS178	1614	3	jar	figurative

B. CLAY TABLETS EXCAVATED FROM BANESH LEVELS AT ABC

Sample #	Object # (mf)	Bldg Level	Sealing Type	Seal Motif
MAS109	2015	3A	tablet	unknown
MAS110**	?	2	tablet	unknown

C. CLAY OBJECTS EXCAVATED AT ABC

Sample #	Object #	Phase	Description
MAC001**	lot 69	Kaftari	"sealing clay"
MAC002	mf 2064	Kaftari	"sealing clay"
MAC004	mf 2394	Kaftari	clay squeeze
MAC008	lot 111	Kaftari	tablet form ?
MAC009	mf 2014	Banesh	clay ball
MAC010	mf 2012	Banesh	clay ball
MAC011	lot 63	Kaftari	tablet form ?
MAC013**	mf 9959	Kaftari	clay squeeze
MAC025	lot 29	Banesh	"clay object"
MAC029**	mf 2013	Banesh	clay ball
MAC030**	mf 1155	Kaftari	clay squeeze
MAC031**	mf 1745	Kaftari	tablet blank ?
MAC033	lot 108	Kaftari	loaf shaped tablet ?
MAC034	lot 42	Kaftari	clay "blob"
MAC035**	mf 1178	Kaftari	figurine fragment
MAC037	lot 20	Kaftari	clay cylinder
MAC038**	M 0059	Kaftari	spindle whirl
MAC039	M 0062	Kaftari	clay ball
MAC040**	mf 2036	Kaftari	clay rod
MAC041	lot 29	Banesh	"sealing clay"
MAC042	lot 66	Banesh	"sealing clay"

* = Sealings excavated at ABC, not belonging to ABC or TUV chemical composition group

** = Objects excavated at ABC, belonging to TUV chemical composition group

Further, low-fired chaff tempered ceramics from ABC and TUV were also subjected to chemical analysis (Blackman 1981). Like the sealing clays, these ceramics displayed a dual compositional pattern with ceramics recovered from TUV forming the majority of samples in one group and samples from ABC the majority of members in the second compositional group (figure 10.11).[4] Like the unfired clay objects, however, a number of chaff tempered ceramics recovered from the elite structures at ABC (42% of the sample) fall within the cluster composed primarily of ceramics recovered from the TUV facility. Moreover, one of the samples recovered from TUV falls within the group consisting primarily of chaff tempered ceramics recovered from ABC. These data make it clear that the site specific compositional pattern of the sealing clays can not be explained by post-depositional alteration. Instead, the specificity of sealing clays to the area of excavation is a pre-depositional phenomenon.[5]

It would seem an inescapable conclusion, then, that the sealing and unsealing of the vast majority of all objects at the elite ABC structures and the facility at TUV was local to each site. This might appear a somewhat trivial finding for the sealings affixed to non-portable objects. It is obvious that the sealings from doors and large storage jars were applied, broken, and discarded in the same location. But this conclusion also applies to the sealings from smaller more portable jars. If imported from different areas, either within the city or from more distant areas, these jars and their contents arrived at either ABC or TUV in an unsealed condition, and were subsequently sealed, impressed, and opened all within the immediate vicinity of these two different sectors of Banesh Malyan. Moreover, all of the bullae, presumably used as accounting devices, were also made and discarded locally. Thus rather than controlling the movement of goods, sealing and unsealing activities at Banesh Malyan seem to have concentrated on local storage, security, and disbursement with a high value placed on controlling and accounting for extremely localized allotments of goods.

Variations in the iconography of ABC and TUV sealings noted by Pittman (personal communication; Pittman 1980) strengthens the argument for the localized nature of sealing and unsealing activities. Of the 26 impressed sealings analyzed that were recovered from the facility at TUV, 18 bear geometric, non-figurative motifs, while 8 bear figurative motifs. All 13 impressed sealings analyzed from ABC carry figurative motifs. While some of the differences in representational motifs displayed in the seal impressions from these two sectors of Banesh Malyan may reflect stylistic change through time, Pittman believes that the presence of both geometric and figurative motifs at the same levels at TUV suggests that at least some of the difference between these seal impressions from ABC and TUV are functionally derived. Different individuals, possibly of different rank and affiliation, were using stylistically distinct seals to impress sealed objects at these two facilities.

In light of our earlier discussion of the status of elite residents of ABC and the nature of the economic activities at the TUV facility, these results may not be as surprising as at first they might seem. The size of the elaborately decorated structures at ABC, the quality of ceramics recovered, the evidence of storage and working of rare and exotic materials would all seem indicative of a major public facility housing highly regulated activities. Moreover, the faunal data from ABC structures suggest a degree of specialization and control over provisioning that would certainly seem to buttress an argument for close accounting and control of economic activities there. If indeed the structures encountered at Operation TUV housed a kitchen/serving facility responsible for the support of craftsmen and othe residents of this sector of the site, we can also understand the need for highly localized control over stores and disbursements at this facility. Management of an institutional kitchen is a complex undertaking. Procurement of foodstuffs, bulk storage, daily allotments to the kitchen and directives to kitchen workers must all be carefully integrated to assure efficient provisioning of nonfood producing specialists. Thus the level of coordination required to run such an operation would seem more than sufficient to account for all the evidence of administrative record keeping and control over disbursement recovered at TUV.

This interpretation does not necessarily mean, however, that economic administration at Banesh Malyan was essentially a decentralized affair—that these two sectors of the site functioned as independent autonomous economic units. Even given the apparent complexity of economic activities in these two areas, it is hard to imagine that such care would have been taken to control the flow of goods within these areas and to record the detailed information inscribed on Proto-Elamite texts found here if ultimate responsibility for these activities stopped at this extraordinarily localized level. After all implicit in the act of accounting is accountability to a higher level authority.

PROTO-ELAMITE TABLETS AT MALYAN

Some clues about the nature of higher level administrative connections are provided by the Proto-Elamite tablets from Banesh Malyan. Tablets recovered from Operations ABC and TUV are made from different colored clays and apparently vary in inscriptional content (Stolper 1985). In addition, the quantities listed are often greater on the tablets from ABC than those listed on tablets from TUV. Moreover, there is one group of tablets from ABC building level 2 which Stolper suggests may be summary memoranda of transactions listed in a fuller form on a tablet from TUV building level 3, causing him to postulate "contemporaneity and even functional connection between ABC II and TUV III" (Stolper 1985:11).

Given the rarity and important informational content of Proto-Elamite tablets, there was some understandable reluctance to allow destructive sampling of these artifacts for chemical analysis. The sample of tablet clay analyzed for this study was, therefore, restricted to two sealed tablet fragments. Both of these tablet fragments were recovered from Operation ABC (table 10.5). One tablet fragment (MAS109) is clearly of ABC chemical composition (figure 10.12). The other (MAS110)—found in the same ABC building level that yielded the possible summary tablets—is made of clay that falls squarely within the TUV sealing group (figure 10.12). It seems quite possible that this tablet was made and inscribed at TUV, recording a summary of economic activities conducted there, and then transferred to the elite public structures at ABC.

It may be further possible to link this finding to the chemical data provided by the analysis of unfired clay objects and ceramics from ABC and TUV. Essentially all the ceramics and unfired clay objects recovered from the facility at TUV clustered together in a distinct group with values similar to those found for the TUV sealing clays. While distinct ABC clusters of ceramics and objects were also identified and chemically linked to the ABC sealing clays, a number of chaff tempered sherds and clay objects recovered at ABC were chemically more similar to the TUV clays than to the ABC clays. It is possible, then, that not only information about economic activities moved from the TUV facility to the ABC public structures. Perhaps there was also movement of ceramics and other objects made from clays local to the TUV area to the ABC public buildings. Moreover, the virtual absence of evidence of a reciprocal flow of goods or information from ABC to TUV may indicate that TUV residents occupied an economically and administratively subordinate status to the elites at ABC.

The differences between motifs of the seals used to impress clays at ABC and TUV may also have some bearing on the relationship between these two sectors of the site. As noted above, while impressed sealings analyzed from ABC all bore figurative motifs, at TUV sealings were impressed with both geometric and representational motifs—possibly signifying multiple lines of administrative authority at TUV. If the figurative seal motifs found at TUV can be linked to motifs found on seals and sealings recovered from ABC it might be further possible to posit that ABC affiliated administrators oversaw at least some of the activities conducted at the TUV facility.

CONCLUSIONS

In summary, our examination of the architecture of buildings in these two sectors of Banesh Malyan and of the contents of these buildings has allowed us to distinguish two socially distinct sectors of this early city, both of which seem to have supported an array of specialized economic and administrative activities. The faunal remains from these two sectors of the site suggest that elite residents of the ABC public structure were not involved in the production of meat resources, if not removed from all food production, and that they received basic subsistence resources through a system of indirect provisioning. In the TUV sector of the city we have been able to trace the evolution of provisioning from a more direct meat procurement system to one at least as specialized and indirect as that evidenced in the elite sector of the city. And we have been able to link these developments to the growth in size and complexity of the kitchen/serving facility encountered on the southernmost end of the small TUV mound.

The chemical analysis of the seal impressed clays has revealed a tightly focused control over economic activities in these two sectors of the city that required strict accounting of the disbursement of goods from local stores to local residents. And yet, from the admittedly limited but provocative chemical analysis of tablet clays, we now also see indications of the transfer of summary information about these activities from this localized level of administration to a possible higher level of control. Thus it would seem that while there was a significant degree of immediate administrative control over the flow of commodities within each of these separate sectors of the site, there was also linkage, on perhaps a higher plane of administrative control, between economic activities on a city-wide basis.

At the beginning of this chapter, we agreed with Sumner (1986a) that Banesh Malyan is probably best interpreted as a conduit through which the products of specialized pastoralists were exchanged for craft and agricultural resources produced by settled populations. In effect, one might say that the *raison d'être* of Banesh Malyan was to serve as an administrative focal point for the integration of disparate economic specializations in the region. With our newly gained perspective on economy and administration within the city, we begin to see how the administrative mechanisms that linked economic activities conducted at different sectors of the city might also have served, on a larger scale, to tie together disparate economic activities of settled and pastoral populations in the region as a whole. The day-to-day management and oversight of diverse productive activities may, then, have been an extremely localized affair. Higher level regulation of the economy focused instead on the articulation of these activities through monitoring the flow of raw materials and coordinating the disbursement of the products of these activities, with little direct intervention from centrally based administrators into the actual production process itself.

Alden (1979) has remarked that the absence of evidence of large scale craft production at Malyan is puzzling in a site purported to have served as a major primate center of a regional urban system. In part this lack of evidence may be a function of the depth of later deposits that cover Banesh levels on the main, higher portion of the mound, and the small portion of the Banesh settlement that was excavated. However, the lack of large-scale craft activity centered at Banesh Malyan may also have more to do with the fact that Malyan commanded its primary position in the region through this integrative role, rather than through an industrial one. It is interesting to note that the only specialized productive activities evidenced at Banesh Malyan are related to the manufacture of small ornamental objects made of rare nonlocal materials. It is possible to see such an enterprise as part of Malyan's integrative function in Banesh regional economy. These exotic rare materials may have been brought to the site by far-ranging mobile populations, who then relied upon the technical and artistic abilities of Malyan based craftsmen to transform these raw materials into small compact symbols of prestige and wealth. Capitalizing on the technological know-how of urban based craftsmen to transform raw materials into portable symbols of wealth may be one of the more tangible markers of Malyan's role in tying together disparate specialized activities of settled and nomadic populations into a coherent state-level regional economy. Other such integrative mechanisms that did not leave physical markers in the archaeological record may, then, have been the primary product offered by Malyan urban dwellers to the regional economy.

The case example of economy and administration at Banesh Malyan has broader implications for understanding early states in general. First the picture we have drawn of intrasite administration of economy corresponds closely to models of state-level decision making that highlight the development of multiple levels of administrative hierarchy, each responsible for processing information increasingly more removed from the activities of the people and institutions they control (Wright 1977). Many studies have identified this kind of administrative hierarchy on an intersite level, seeing a one-to-one correspondence between levels of administrative hierarchy and different site sizes in a regional settlement system (Crumley 1976; Johnson 1973, 1980). And while this is certainly one way in which this kind of administrative structure might manifest itself, our example suggests that a multitiered administrative system may not always find expression on such a large stage. The presence of a three- or four-tiered settlement pattern is not a necessary prerequisite for nomination to the Early State Hall of Fame. Instead, discrete levels of administrative decision making may also be manifest, and be detectable, within settlements as well—especially in primate systems such as that dominated by Banesh Malyan.

This example also highlights our need to reexamine assumptions about the economic role of early cities. Traditional models see agriculture and pastoral enterprises as rural pursuits and crafts as the province of urban centers. In the case of the Kur river basin in the late fourth/early third millennium, agricultural activities may well have focused on urban Malyan, located in the center of one of the largest tracts of arable land in the valley, ceramic production took place at small sites on the valley margins near sources of clays and fuels (see chapter 9), and pastoral pursuits were likely practiced by a mobile, essentially nonresident population that held greater allegiances to the rulers of Banesh Malyan than to settled rural villagers. And yet while traditional notions of urban and rural interactions in early states may not apply here, it is the integrative role that Malyan served in tying together a complex regional political and economic system in the Kur river basin that lead us to believe that it served as the urban focus of an early state.

Finally, we derive some satisfaction from the fact that much of this information about economy and administration at Banesh Malyan has been garnered from two fields sometimes viewed by the archaeological community as technical specialties, marginal to the central avenues that lead to an understanding of complex culture process. What we hope this study demonstrates is that such 'specialties' as zooarchaeology and archaeometry are only limited in the eyes of those with limited vision. In reality the archaeological sciences stand at the forefront of making discoveries of great significance to understanding the forces that shape the development of complex societies in the ancient world.

NOTES

1. Excavation of Malyan was conducted in the early to mid-1970s by the University of Pennsylvania's Malyan Expedition under the direction of William Sumner. Zeder served as zooarchaeologist for the expedition and Blackman was the expedition's geologist.

2. The faunal sample from Malyan, the analytical techniques employed in their analysis, and the patterns of animal exploitation extrapolated from the faunal data are discussed in detail by Zeder (1985, 1988, 1991).

3. Similar findings are reported in a study of sealings from Tepe Gawra in northwestern Iran (Rothman and Blackman 1990) and Arslantepe in central Anatolia (Blackman N.D.)

4. The lack of coincidence between the 95% confidence ellipses generated from the unfired sealing clay data and the clusters of ceramic data are solely due to the effect of firing on the ceramics.

5. Blackman believes the distinction between clays local to ABC and those local to TUV is attributable to different sources of sedimentation at the site. The major drainage in the valley flows in a southeasterly direction with sediments first encountering the site at its northwestern margin (figure 10.2). A natural rise in elevation of the plain in the western half of Malyan, in which ABC is located, serves as drainage breakpoint causing a relatively rapid accumulation of sediments in this portion of the site. The southeastern half of the site, where TUV is located, sits in what might be termed a sedimentary shadow, with sediments from the primary drainage vector in the valley effectively deflected from this area by the natural rise of elevation to the west. Sediments in this lower area of the mound, accumulate at a much slower rate and are derived from such sources as the small stream that flows near the southeast end of the TUV mound. This phenomenon accounts for the fact that Banesh deposits identified in collapsed *qanat*s (underground water conduits) to the northwest of the Malyan city wall are found more than 3 m below the surface, while Banesh deposits in the southeastern portion of the site are found only a few centimeters from current ground level. It also explains the different chemical composition of clays deposited on the higher northwestern portion of the mound as opposed to those deposited in the lower southeastern portion of the mound.

CHAPTER 11

FROM *ÉCRITURE* TO CIVILIZATION

Changing Paradigms of Proto-Elamite Archaeology

KAMYAR ABDI

THE PROTO-ELAMITE PERIOD is the latest phase of Iranian prehistory, characterized by the appearance and use of tablets bearing Proto-Elamite script and seal impressions. In most parts of Iran, the Proto-Elamite period follows periods distinguished by local cultures. In the Kur river basin, evidently the heartland of the Proto-Elamite civilization, the Proto-Elamite period corresponds with the Banesh phase, while at Susa and the surrounding plain the Proto-Elamite period is known as Susa III, following the Late Uruk phase. On the basis of comparative criteria, as well as a few radiocarbon dates, it is safe to date the Proto-Elamite period to 3300 to 2700 BCE (Dyson 1987; Voigt and Dyson 1992; Wright and Rupley 2001), roughly contemporary with the Late Uruk, Jemdet Nasr, and Early Dynastic I periods in Mesopotamian chronological sequence.

The Proto-Elamite period witnessed the emergence of what arguably was the first indigenous civilization on the Iranian Plateau. The wide distribution of Proto-Elamite material culture on the Iranian Plateau through mechanisms not yet entirely clear to us is a phenomenon not definitely surpassed until the Achaemenid period, nearly twenty-five centuries later. These characteristics have made the Proto-Elamite period one of the most fascinating, albeit elusive, eras in Iranian archaeology, attracting several generations of archaeologists to explore and explicate different aspects of this civilization. Among the archaeologists studying the Proto-Elamite civilization, Bill Sumner's contribution has been one of the more profound. Not only is his already classic "Proto-Elamite Civilization in Fars"

(Sumner 1986) now the most widely used outline, periodization, and reconstruction of the rise and demise of the Proto-Elamite civilization, his recent monograph on excavations at operation ABC at Malyan (Sumner 2003) is a landmark in Proto-Elamite studies. In both publications, Sumner's use of the term "civilization" indicates that, after a century of research and debate, the Proto-Elamite entity has met the qualifications required by modern scholarship to be described as a civilization. But what do we mean by "Proto-Elamite civilization"?

DEFINING "CIVILIZATION"

To quote another eminent archaeologist, "like other fields, archeology is cursed with terms so vague and ambiguous that they tend to obscure than they clarify … 'civilization' is one such term" (Flannery 1972:400). In fact, a rather cursory survey of the abundant literature shows that historians, anthropologists —including archaeologists—and other students of social sciences and humanities have different perceptions and definitions of the term "civilization."

Various uses of the term "civilization" can be divided into three broad yet distinct categories. Sometimes this term refers to state of being civilized, that is, possessing or demonstrating noble manners and behaviors such as a high degree of self-control. This meaning is perhaps closer to the original meaning of the term when it was introduced by Enlightenment thinkers such as Voltaire into the French vocabulary (Mortier 1990). From this original meaning, nineteenth-century thinkers, including the first generation of anthropologists, derived a cultural connotation and broadened the meaning of the term to refer to the gradual expansion of human knowledge, dexterity, and behavior that allowed mankind a progress from savagery to civilization. The first generation of anthropologists envisioned progress toward civilization as the ultimate destiny of every human society. To Herbert Spencer, the course of the human career was dictated by a universal law of development. Through a progressive mechanism of adaptation, Spencer argued, mankind will achieve higher degree of fitness. In this process mankind increases its struggle for existence as it goes through stages of savagery and barbarism to finally arrive at civilization (Spencer 1851). Needless to say, Spencer's deep commitment to the doctrine of *laissez-faire* and his sympathy toward Victorian imperialism, sustained many biased stereotypes of natives and preindustrial people.

Following on Spencer's views, Lewis Henry Morgan further envisioned the human career as consisting of three major stages: Savagery, Barbarism, and Civilization. While Morgan's primary interest was kinship systems and terminology, what in his scheme distinguishes Civilization from the preceding stage of "Upper Barbarism" was the innovation of a phonetic alphabet and writing (Morgan 1877:31). While there is little benefit in belaboring the shortcomings of Morgan's evolutionary outline, pointing out the contradicting archaeological evidence (Trigger 1998), we should nonetheless admit that Morgan's scheme was far more advanced than its antecedents who envisioned civilization as the culmination of a unilinear progression leading to the British gentleman (Harris 1968).

As these concerns with the meaning and nature of civilization marked anthropological debates of the late nineteenth century, a new meaning for the term entered the English language from German. Stimulated by nation building in Germany by Bismarck, German writers such as Johann Gottfried von Herder labored to salvage and reform the German language and thought from its borrowed French finery. These scholars tried to emphasize the uniqueness of the German nation and its culture (Eley 1991). From this notion emerged a new meaning of the term referring to distinct entities encompassing every trait that characterized a nation and distinguished it from other nations. By generalization, in literature there appeared debates on German, French, and also newly discovered Sumerian and Semitic civilizations.

The term "civilization" in twentieth-century anthropology and archaeology was a blend of the three definitions mentioned above. Robert Redfield (1955), for example, described civilization as the learned behavior of men who belonged to complex societies and made a contrast between civilization and "culture" of simpler societies. The archaeological indicators of civilization, however, remained unclear. By the late nineteenth and early twentieth century, following Morgan's scheme, archaeologists commonly equated the emergence of civilization with the appearance of metallurgy. Archaeologists working in the Near East, however, preferred the origins of writing as the marker of civilization. Still others argued that a combination of monumental architecture, metallurgy, and writing was the hallmark of civilization.

The credit for a coherent conceptualization of civilization in archaeology should perhaps go to V. Gordon Childe. From the 1920s, Childe developed a model to define and describe civilization. While his attempts to equate civilization with urbanism have been questioned (Kohl and Wright 1977; Zeder 1991:Ch. 1), his principle criteria (outlined in Childe 1950), are still widely adhered to by archaeologists:

1. Increase in settlement size toward "urban" proportions
2. The emergence of class-stratified society
3. Formation of political organizations based on kin ties
4. Central accumulation of capital by imposition of tribute or taxation
5. Monumental public works
6. The invention of writing to keep records of economic transactions
7. Advance toward exact and predictive sciences
8. The emergence and growth of long-distance trade in luxury items
9. Craft specialization
10. The emergence of portrait art

I do not feel it necessary to determine in this present chapter whether or not the Proto-Elamite civilization meets the above criteria. Instead, I will trace the ways scholars have developed their understanding of the Proto-Elamite phenomenon, and their increasing realization that it should be considered a civilization. In the past one hundred years, the term "Proto-Elamite" has itself gone through several stages of metamorphosis. "Proto-Elamite" was originally coined as a purely epigraphic term to describe the script used on Proto-Elamite tablets. Later the term acquired an archaeological connotation and was applied to the archaeological period in which Proto-Elamite tablets were in use. The term "Proto-Elamite" was then used to refer to other material culture found in archaeological layers yielding Proto-Elamite tablets and thus dating to the Proto-Elamite period. From there, the cultural entity that produced Proto-Elamite tablets and associated material culture was labeled Proto-Elamite. Finally, with the discovery of evidence for elite and supra-local activities in Fars and elsewhere on the Iranian Plateau, it became clear that scholars could justifiably speak of a "Proto-Elamite civilization."

However, this cumbersome use of the term "Proto-Elamite" has led to much confusion in the literature. The use of the Proto-Elamite script has prompted a large number of archaeologists, including myself, to call this period Proto-Elamite, a prelude to the Elamite civilization. Some scholars, however, reserve the term Proto-Elamite for the script, the glyptic style, and perhaps the language—when we learn more about it.

Thus it seems appropriate that shortly after the centennial of the discovery of the first Proto-Elamite tablets at Susa, in a volume honoring an eminent scholar of the Proto-Elamite civilization, to pause briefly and examine the origins and the development of the term "Proto-Elamite." Then we return to the question of terminology and ambiguities involved in using the term Proto-Elamite. The essay will conclude with some suggestions to perhaps bring some explicitness to our use of the term and avoid further confusion. Standardization of both terms and concepts should naturally be the first step towards any rigorous scientific endeavor.

EARLY WORKS AND THE COINAGE OF THE TERM "PROTO-ELAMITE"

In the excavation season of 1898-1899, only a year after the beginning of work at the Acropole of Susa by the French delegation under Jacques de Morgan, two small clay tablets with previously unknown signs came to light. The French epigrapher, Vincent Scheil, who studied these tablets, considered them to be cuneiform and stated:

> ...il semble nous ayons sous les yeux un autre système d'écriture cunéiforme, ou du moins résultat d'une évolution très indépendante, très différente de celle qui nous a donné les signes dits babyloniens. (Scheil 1900:130-131)[1]
> [...it seems that we have another system of cuneiform writing, or at least the result of a very independent evolution, very different from that which has given us the signs called Babylonian.]

During further work at the Acropole in 1901, nearly two hundred tablets of the same type were discovered. After detailed study of these tablets, in addition to three stone inscriptions with similar signs also bearing inscriptions in Akkadian of Puzur-Inshushinak, Scheil considered all of them to be contemporary, and labeled them *proto-élamite*, that is, the first texts coming from Elam:[2]

> Quoi qu'il en soit de l'aspect plus ou moins archaïque des signes dans l'une et l'autre partie des doubles légendes, il saute aux yeux, par le simple examen des monuments A et C, que le texte en écriture babylonienne a été gravé le premier, et qu'ensuite, dans l'espace disponible au-dessous, on ajouta le texte en caractères que j'appelle proto-élamite. (Scheil 1905:60)
> [Whatever the more or less archaic aspect of the signs in one or the other part of double legends, the fact jumps out at us that the Babylonian text on monuments A and C was engraved first, and that later, in the available space below, they added the text in characters I call Proto-Elamite.]

Scheil used the term "Proto-Elamite" only to refer to the writing system. However, in order to date these texts, he attributed them to the time of the Second Style pottery of Susa (roughly equivalent to what archaeologists now call Susa IV). Excavation reports (for example, Morgan 1900b) suggest that the French excavators did not define a "Proto-Elamite" level until much later, and the whole sequence of Proto-Elamite material from the Acropole was included—without further phase-by-phase division—in de Morgan's Period II (Morgan 1900b:82). Later, de Morgan refined his periodization to include later discoveries (Morgan 1912). This time, the layer containing Proto-Elamite tablets was lumped with "niveau IV" dated to the time of Naram-Sin, containing cylinder seals and pottery of the Second Style (Morgan 1912:23). Therefore, in a later publication, following de Morgan's chronology, Scheil dated the Proto-Elamite script to the time of the dynasty of Akkad (Scheil 1923).[3] Of particular interest to the origins of the term "Proto-Elamite" was Scheil's surmise of an ethnic duality in Elam and the difference between *susiennes*, with their inscriptions primarily in a Mesopotamian language, and *anzanites*, who wrote in Elamite (see endnote 2). Scheil propounded this dichotomy in the form of a number of questions:

> De l'époque ancienne, on peut dire que nous ignorions tout, jusqu'aux faits les plus généraux. A quel groupe ethnique se rattachent Élamites? Quel rapport y a-t-il entre Élam et Anzan? Existait-il réellement, dans cette contrée, un ensemble d'institutions politiques et religieuses à caractère propre et indépendant, homogène ou mixte, qui fût digne du nom de civilisation? Quelles langues et quelles races se disputaient la prépondérance dans ces pays limitrophes de deux mondes? Quel était le rôle de Suse dans cette histoire? (Scheil 1905:vii)

[Of ancient times, one can say that we knew nothing, not even the most general facts. To which ethnic group did the Elamites belong? What is the relationship between Elam and Anshan? In this region, did there really exist a group of political and religious institutions with their own independent characteristics, homogenous or diverse, which were worthy of the name civilization? What languages and races were fighting for supremacy over the borderlands of those two regions? What was the role of Susa in this history?]

Scheil's foresight in recognizing an ethnic duality in Elam, however, met with little recognition during his lifetime (see Langdon 1925),[4] and it was only fairly recently that some scholars have reconsidered this important aspect of the Elamite history (Amiet 1979a, 1979b; chapter 3).

THE TERM "PROTO-ELAMITE" ACQUIRES ARCHAEOLOGICAL OVERTONES

The first attempt to use the epigraphic term "Proto-Elamite" to refer to an archaeological periodization is in a catalogue of Susian objects in the Louvre Museum (Pézard and Pottier 1913, 1926). In an outline of the history of Elam in these publications, the authors begin the Elamite history with "Période proto-élamite," which, according to them, was "époque ou se manifeste la civilisation la plus antique de l'Elam, caractérisée par la céramique peinte du Ier style" ["the epoch in which the most ancient civilization of Elam manifested itself, characterized by painted ceramics of the First Style"] (Pézard and Pottier 1913:26). In this periodization the Proto-Elamite period was followed by two other periods that were labeled as "élamite, chaldéenne ou chaldéo-élamite," the first of which extended from the end of the Proto-Elamite period to the time of Sargon of Akkad, and the second one from Sargon to Hammurabi. Based on this periodization, Pézard and Pottier (1913:77–78) dated two stone cones discovered in the cemetery at Susa in association with Susa First Style ceramics, and a number of alabaster vases, to the Proto-Elamite period, and two figurines to the time of the "civilisation proto-élamite" (Pézard and Pottier 1913:128–129).[5]

Going over Pézard and Pottier's discussion of their periodization and attributions, one is left with the impression that the period they call "proto-élamite" is in fact what is known today as the Susa I period. The majority of ceramics discussed in Pottier's section on Proto-Elamite pottery come from the Susa cemetery, now dated to Susa I. Two cones and metal tools and arms dated to the Proto-Elamite period are also from the Susa I cem-

etery. Only the figurines and alabaster vessels came from elsewhere, but similar objects are also recorded from the cemetery (see Morgan 1912). It seems that Pézard and Pottier used the term 'Proto-Elamite' to refer to a portion of the period now known as Susa I, and I suspect that is why their periodization did not find many followers among the rest of the French team.

PROTO-ELAMITE PERIOD AND MESOPOTAMIAN CHRONOLOGICAL SEQUENCE

Surprising as it may sound, in the 1920s the periodization of Susa was commonly used to correlate the material from southern and central Mesopotamia with those from Susa. Shortly after the first season of excavations at Jemdet Nasr during the winter of 1925–1926, pottery from that site was compared to Susa Second Style (Anonymous 1926:23). Two years later, following his excavations at Jemdet Nasr, Langdon (1928:v), providing a preliminary description of the pictographic tablets discovered at the site, pointed out that "the painted pottery found with these tablets indicates an intimate relation with the same type of painted pottery (Susa II) found with the Proto-Elamite tablets published by Professor Scheil." In his speech before the 17th International Congress of Orientalists at Oxford (August 28–29, 1928), Langdon placed emphasis on "the great antiquity of Sumerian civilization and the discovery of Sumerian painted ware and pictographic inscriptions, proving their proto-Elamite origin" (Anonymous 1929:51). Furthermore, in the abstract of his paper "The Excavation of Jemdet Nasr by Oxford-Field Museum Expedition" delivered by Langdon before the same Congress, he expanded on this theory:

> The author [Langdon] studied the proto-Elamitic connexions of the antiquities and the language of the inscriptions (which is Sumerian), and introduced the term proto-Sumerian for this earliest stage in the evolution of the Sumerian civilization. (Anonymous 1929:54)

Application of the Susa sequence to southern Mesopotamian sites continued into the 1930s, when the results of excavations at sites such as Kish, Adab, Ur, and Uruk allowed archaeologists working in southern Mesopotamia to devise their own local chronology. The first attempt to banish the use of the Susa sequence for southern Mesopotamia was taken by Watelin (1931), immediately followed by Frankfort (1932) and others. Having now eliminated the Susa periodization from southern and central Mesopotamia and established a local periodization, what then became a subject of inquiry for archaeologists working in both Mesopotamia and southwestern Iran was early relations between these two regions and more distant lands, some obviously adhering to diffusionist perspectives of that era. In his classic *Archaeology and the Sumerian Problem*, Henri Frankfort addressed the problem of Susa I and II (Frankfort 1932:65–72) and by comparing Susa I and II pottery with the pottery traditions of the Iranian Plateau as far as Baluchestan, he did not reject the possibility that "a homogenous civilization prevailed over all the intervening territory" (Frankfort 1932:71). In the meantime, excavations in the Indus Valley brought to light material that pointed to a possibility of connections with the west. In his description of objects discovered at Mohenjo-daro, John Marshall (1931:104) referred to a bone cylinder seal of the "bull and manger" type, which is usually associated with Proto-Elamite tablets, and probably engraved for an Indian settler by an Elamite craftsman. In the same volume, he stated:

> I have assumed that the Proto-Elamitic civilization was older than that of pre-dynastic Egypt....Indeed, further investigations will probably show that the former civilization had greater influence than has hitherto been supposed. That it also influenced the Indus Valley Civilization can hardly, I think, be questioned. (Marshall 1931:581)

Unfortunately, Marshall did not elaborate on his proposition, nor did he explain his notion of a "Proto-Elamitic civilization," a concept utterly forgotten for the next two generations.

In his first season of excavations at Sialk, Kashan in 1931, Roman Ghirshman discovered a group of objects, including ceramics of Susa Second Style, one Proto-Elamite tablet and six cylinder seals similar to those from the corresponding period at Susa (Ghirshman 1934). These finds came from a small structure situated on the highest point of the southern mound. Below this structure, in association with level IV1, were also discovered two adult graves, perhaps female, with rich burial gifts, and four infant jar burials (Ghirshman 1938:59–61). Apparently Ghirshman was initially hesitant to refer to his Period IV as Proto-Elamite. Nonetheless, in the plan of the Period IV structure in the final publication (Ghirshman 1938:Pl. LXXXVII) he used the term "Proto-Elamite"—in parentheses—to distinguish this building. Later, in his general survey of Iranian archaeology and history from prehistory to the Islamic conquest, he elaborated on his terminology and called Period IV "*époque des tablettes proto-élamite*" (Ghirshman 1951:46). According to Ghirshman:

> *À Suse toujours, et peu après, vers les derniers siècles précédant 3000 avant J.-C., se forme une civilisation qui, tout en restant sous une forte influence mésopotamienne, deviendra à son tour la créatrice de sa propre écriture, appelée proto-élamite, et qui est contemporaine de la période de Jemdat Nasr de la grande plaine voisine.* (Ghirshman 1951:41)
>
> [Gradually, towards the last centuries before 3000 BC, a civilization was formed at Susa that, while remaining under a strong Mesopotamian influence, would become in its turn the creator of its own writing, called Proto-Elamite, and which was contemporary with the Jemdet Nasr period of the neighboring great plain.]

Ghirshman's reconstruction did not provide any explanation for the emergence of the Proto-Elamite civilization. He tried, however, to explain the discovery of Proto-Elamite material culture at Sialk in terms of a military conquest by Proto-Elamites coming from Susa. But even this simple reconstruction was ignored by contemporary scholarship; soon those who studied the Proto-Elamite phenomenon came under the spell of the Jemdet Nasr culture of Mesopotamia.

PROTO-ELAMITE VERSUS JEMDET NASR

While chronological contemporanity and similarities in material culture indicate some contact between the Proto-Elamite and Jemdet Nasr cultures, studies that emphasized the study of the former in a framework based on the latter are arguably a creation of the modern scholarship's obsession with comparative studies and negligence of indigenous developments left over from the enduring culture history approach in Near Eastern archaeology. Therefore, it comes as no surprise that for several decades the study of the Proto-Elamite phenomenon was dominated by a Mesopotamia-centered emphasis on its connections with the Jemdet Nasr period in Mesopotamia.[6]

For instance, the synthesis and periodization of Susa material by Donald McCown (1942) is rather ambiguous as the author simultaneously speaks of "the level of the proto-Elamite tablets" and ascribes these tablets to the Jemdet Nasr period (McCown 1942:44). However, it was McCown himself, who, following his excavations at Tal-i Ghazir in the Ram Hormuz plain, adopted the term "Proto-Elamite" to distinguish a layer yielding a fragmentary Proto-Elamite tablet (McCown 1949:54). McCown did not elaborate on his reasons for using this term and in a later paper (McCown 1954:59) abandoned the term "Proto-Elamite period" and called the Tal-i Ghazir layer containing the Proto-Elamite tablet "late Protoliterate" with "essentially Jemdet Nasr" ceramics. Unfortunately, McCown never published a report on his excavations at Tal-i Ghazir. Joseph Caldwell, a member of the original Oriental Institute expedition, published a short overview of the site about twenty years later (Caldwell 1968a). Caldwell referred to McCown's Proto-Elamite layer in quotation marks (Caldwell 1968a:348) but in the rest of his account avoided this term and used instead the term "Jemdet Nasr." Apparently both McCown and Caldwell were so overwhelmed by the abundance of Jemdet Nasr-type polychrome pottery in that particular layer that they did not find a single Proto-Elamite tablet convincing enough to name a period after it.

A few years earlier, in a posthumous article, Louis LeBreton (1957) summarized and for the first time analyzed the results of nearly sixty years of French excavations at Susa and its satellite sites. LeBreton never defined a Proto-Elamite period and, following Mesopotamian chronology, labeled his Susa Cb and Cc periods as "Jemdet Nasr" or "Protoliterate d." To him, the only Proto-Elamite items in the material culture of these phases were the tablets. However, he did not ignore the fact that in the glyptics, beside what he called the Jemdet Nasr-style, there is a distinctive local style that cannot be anything but "Proto-Elamite"(LeBreton 1957:107). This "original" style, which, according to LeBreton (1957:108), developed from Mesopotamian styles, can best be distinguished in animal themes of period Cc characterized by

> sculptural modeling, linear engraving...combined with skillful drill-work...schematic and exaggerated natural forms...heavy proportions...asymmetrical and over-crowding composition...and expressive and vital motion. (LeBreton 1957:108)

Despite his rudimentary treatment of Proto-Elamite material, LeBreton (1957:112) was convinced that Susa had become a Proto-Elamite center after a period of Mesopotamian influence. He did not believe in Mesopotamian colonization of Susa, and found a Mesopotamian-type "temple-city" a more fitting explanation for the presence of Mesopotamian-style material culture at Susa.

In a much neglected study of the Jemdet Nasr period, Nagel (1964:77–82) using the periodization introduced by LeBreton, divided the Proto-Elamite period into four *"Kulturs"*: "frühprotoelamische Kultur" encompassing material from Susa Ba to Bd, "hochprotoelamische Kultur" from Susa Ca to the end of Susa Cb, "spätprotoelamische Kultur" from Susa Cc to Susa Db, and finally "endprotoelamische Kultur" embracing Susa Dc and Dd. Nagel's periodization is rather broad and following LeBreton's sequence encompassed levels dating from the Late Uruk to the Old Elamite periods. Therefore the time Nagel attributed to the Proto-Elamite period is longer than what the present archaeological evidence suggests. Regarding the Proto-Elamite/Jemdet Nasr relationship that concerns us here, Nagel distinguished four pottery styles in this period that deserve a closer look: 1) "Susianische-Gamdat-Nasr-Keramik" (Nagel 1964:Taf. 26:2a–b) is a bichrome ceramic type dated by LeBreton (1957:101) to Susa Cc (late Proto-Elamite) phase; 2) "Frühe-Aliabad-Keramik" (Nagel 1964:Taf. 27:1–2), although Nagel accepts dating of this ceramic type to Susa Da phase, it actually continues throughout the Proto-Elamite period; 3) "Klassische-Aliabad-Keramik" (Nagel 1964:Taf. 27:4–11) dating to the late Proto-Elamite period; and 4) "Susianische-Sub-Gamdat-Nasr-Keramik"(Nagel 1964:Taf. 26:6–11): dated by Nagel to the Susa Dd phase, and indeed later than what is today considered to be the Proto-Elamite period, perhaps as late as Early Dynastic III or early Akkadian. Further, there is "Proto-Susa-II-Keramik"(Nagel 1964:Taf. 28:1–7): this type, known as "Scarlet ware" is definitely later than the Proto-Elamite period. I do not know why Nagel used the prefix "Proto" to refer to this pottery because it is clearly a subtype of Susa Second Style.

Although the general scheme of Nagel's periodization is complicated, he has done a painstaking job extracting information from cumbersome French excavation reports. Moreover, he was the first one to distinguish local styles within painted pottery of the Proto-Elamite period and to propose a parallel development of pottery traditions of Mesopotamia and Susiana rather than a unilinear one.

In 1965 Marie-Joseph Steve and Hermann Gasche of the French mission opened a 10 x 20-m sondage on the high terrace at the Acropole of Susa in order to control the stratigraphic sequence of this section (Steve and Gasche 1971). Their excavations revealed material from Early Uruk phase on, including two Proto-Elamite tablets (Steve and Gasche 1971:126–127). Nevertheless, throughout the report they avoided any reference to a Proto-Elamite level or period, and used terms such as "Phase finale de Djemdet-Nasr" or "Époque proto-dynastic" (Steve and Gasche 1971:133–135).

Later correlations of Proto-Elamite civilization with Jemdet Nasr took a more refined form, trying to emphasize the Elamite aspects of this civilization while concurrently attempting to interpret Proto-Elamite civilization in a Mesopotamian framework. Some approaches even utilized anthropological concepts to reach more synthetic interpretations.

After his short account on Tal-i Ghazir, Joseph Caldwell (1968b) introduced the concept of *oikoumenê*[7] to explain the spread of 'Ubaid and Jemdet Nasr pottery on the Iranian Plateau. Caldwell's *oikoumenê* thesis completely ignored the Proto-Elamite character of this cultural dynamism and ascribed western connections to Mesopotamian influence, a Jemdet Nasr *oikoumenê*, which carried Jemdet Nasr material culture, including "Protoliterate tablets to distant corners of the Iranian plateau" (Caldwell 1968b:182). For the next few years, the *oikoumenê* thesis played a major role in studies of the Proto-Elamite civilization. For example, Donald Whitcomb, who completed his Master's thesis under Caldwell's supervision (Whitcomb 1971), elaborated on his mentor's proposal but took a step ahead and replaced the Jemdet Nasr *oikoumenê* with a Proto-Elamite one, centered in southwestern Iran. However, Whitcomb believed that the Proto-Elamite *oikoumenê* should be considered a "subtype" of the Jemdet Nasr *oikoumenê* and a "phenomenon" that resulted from the extension of the struggle between Mesopotamian city-states into Khuzestan (Whitcomb 1971:69). Following the Character Displacement theory of the biological sciences, Whitcomb (1971:71) attempted to explain the regional variation of Proto-Elamite material culture, especially the Jemdet Nasr-style polychrome ceramics. This analysis led him to envision two parallel, yet concurrent, developments in southern Mesopotamia and Khuzestan which eventually blossomed in the form of two separate political, linguistic, and ethnic entities, those of Mesopotamia and Elam.

FRESH DATA AND NEW INTERPRETATIONS

Like other scientists, archaeologists tend to reevaluate old ideas and devise new models whenever new work provides fresh data. Such was the case with Proto-Elamite studies in the late 1960s and the 1970s when new data prompted some scholars to step out of the Jemdet Nasr shadow and take a more indigenous view of the Proto-Elamite civilization. By the late 1960s the French delegation had resumed work at Susa with a more rigorous problem-oriented research strategy and a more sophisticated field methodology. Furthermore, fresh fieldwork brought more evidence of Proto-Elamite presence and activities on the Iranian Plateau. At Susa controlled stratigraphy allowed archaeologists to abandon older periodizations and ground their analysis on a more refined chronology. Excavations at Acropole I (Le Brun 1971, 1978) demonstrated that:

- There is a layer of ash and leveling debris between layer 17A (the end of the Uruk period) and 16C (beginning of the Proto-Elamite period) which may suggest a chronological gap.

- Proto-Elamite tablets, seals, and seal impressions begin in layer 16C and continue up to layer 14B.
- Some pottery of Uruk type, especially beveled rim bowls, continue through the Proto-Elamite period, but in smaller quantities.
- Monochrome Jemdet Nasr-type pottery occurs from level 16 to 15B, whereas bichrome ware of Jemdet Nasr-type is reported from layer 15A to 14B.
- Besides pottery, Mesopotamian-related material occurs throughout the period.
- The latest Proto-Elamite tablet from Acropole I comes from layer 14A to 13.

Excavations elsewhere at Susa, at Ville Royale II, layers 18–16, produced material comparable to Acropole I, layers 15A–14A (Carter 1980):

- An uninscribed tablet bearing a characteristic Proto-Elamite lion motif seal impression comes from level 18B.
- Seals and seal impressions of Jemdet Nasr-type (Sin IV/V) occur in layers 18A to 17.
- A small number of bichrome Jemdet Nasr-type sherds come from layers 18B to 17. No Jemdet Nasr-type monochrome ware has been reported from these levels, however.

Furthermore, on the basis of the results of excavations in the Acropole I sounding at Susa, Le Brun and Vallat (1978) following an earlier attempt by Amiet (1966b), elaborated on stratigraphic and spatial contexts of the emergence of writing at Susa. This process involved several stages that can be summarized as follows:

- Simple clay tokens (calculi) of various shapes including cone, disc, rod, and sphere that had been in use since the Neolithic period.
- Complex clay tokens in the above-mentioned forms, but with incisions on their surface.

From Acropole I, layer 18 some innovations occur:

- Simple and complex tokens were enveloped in clay balls that bear cylinder seal impressions on their surface.
- Clay balls impressed with cylinder seals were impressed or incised with signs corresponding to the tokens enclosed in them.
- Finally, oblong and rounded clay tablets appear with cylinder seal impressions and impressed or incised numerical signs on their surface.

The fact that examples of all three of these devices (impressed clay balls with tokens inside them, impressed *and* incised clay balls with tokens inside them, and irregular clay tablets) are discovered in the same layer (18) suggests that this development took place in a relatively short span of time which may have not exceeded a few generations. More progress was in hand by Acropole I, layer 17:

- More rectangular clay tablets with cylinder seal impressions and numerical signs appear.

And finally in Acropole I, layer 16C:

- Proto-Elamite tablets appear. These tablets are considerably better made and proportioned than the earlier tablets. Proto-Elamite tablets range in size from 1.2 x 2.5 cm to a maximum of 17.3 x 22.7 cm. They are inscribed with Proto-Elamite signs and impressed with Proto-Elamite cylinder seals.

While the French and American archaeologists were engaged in refining the stratigraphy of the Proto-Elamite period at Susa, fieldwork on the Iranian Plateau broadened our knowledge of the Proto-Elamite presence beyond Susiana. The work on the Proto-Elamite period was informed by a broader archaeological interest in trade during the 1970s (see Lamberg-Karlovsky 1971a, 1972, 1978; Whitcomb 1971).

In 1969, Carl Lamberg-Karlovsky's excavation at level IVC[8] at Tepe Yahya in the Soghun valley of Kerman province, approximately 900 km to the east of Susiana, revealed an architectural complex with a group of Proto-Elamite administrative devices including tablets, cylinder seals and seal impressions (Lamberg-Karlovsky 1970, 1971a, 1971b). To explain the presence of Proto-Elamite remains in this remote corner of the Plateau and similarities between material culture, especially ceramics from Shahr-i Sokhta III, Bampur I to IV, Shahdad, Iblis 5–6, and the Proto-Elamite level at Tepe Yahya, he identified southeastern Iran as the heartland of a Proto-Elamite *oikoumenê* (Lamberg-Karlovsky 1971a:90, 94). In a later article (Lamberg-Karlovsky 1972), he emphasized the requirements of long-range trade as the integrating force on the Plateau, citing a pivotal role for Tepe Yahya, a center for the production of steatite objects in the Proto-Elamite *oikoumenê*. With ongoing fieldwork, however, it became clear that level IVB, which had most of the evidence for steatite-working activity, postdated the Proto-Elamite period, and so production and trade in steatite objects could not explain the nature of Proto-Elamite contact between the resource-rich highlands of Iran and resource-poor plains of Mesopotamia. In an article published a year later, the Proto-Elamite *oikoumenê* is left out of the discussion. Instead, the Diyala region, Persian Gulf, and southeastern Plateau are lumped together as a single interaction sphere based on religious and economic con-

nections, that of Jemdet Nasr culture (Lamberg-Karlovsky and Tosi 1973:52). Thus the primary evidence for Plateau contact with southern Mesopotamia—chlorite and steatite vessels and other objects found in Mesopotamia—became just one of the defining characteristics of Jemdet Nasr culture. But this construct begged the question of the influence of the role of Mesopotamia on the Plateau. Sites on the Plateau, however, were given credit for an internal and interdependent process of urban development resulting from population growth and exploitation of resources (Lamberg-Karlovsky and Tosi 1973:51).[9]

Lamberg-Karlovsky returned to the question of the mechanisms underlying the development of Proto-Elamite civilization in a synthesis published in 1978, in which he suggested that after the fall of the Uruk polity, a strong Proto-Elamite state developed in Susiana. This state was capable of administering several regions and began to expand its political control to distant corners of the Plateau to ensure its access to resources, population, and production potentials of foreign areas. According to Lamberg-Karlovsky this was the time when population fluctuations on the Plateau weakened the productive strength of the indigenous communities such as Tepe Yahya and allowed centrally organized overpopulated areas such as Khuzestan to fill the vacuum. This movement was accompanied not only by the diffusion of a new economic and political formation but also by a migration of people, including scribes, to the new areas. Therefore, by establishing colonies at centers such as Sialk and Tepe Yahya, the Proto-Elamites brought these areas under their control. These colonies served as mercantile centers to export resources in demand back to the Proto-Elamite homeland in Susiana and as sources of inspiration to acculturate indigenous population. However, increasing administrative requirements to control this vast area put an excessive burden on the Proto-Elamite homeland in Susiana in terms of resource costs, production and personnel, and forced the Proto-Elamites to withdraw from remote areas and leave them to independent polities copied from the emergent state system of Susiana. The model continued to depend on identification of "Proto-Elamite" sites as those with Proto-Elamite writing and glyptic.

The argument for the rise and decline of a centralized Proto-Elamite state, however, is not well supported by the conceptual model or the archaeological remains. The proposed driving forces for the establishment of the Proto-Elamite state are population growth in Khuzestan and the requirements of long-distance trade; the proposed evidence is the distribution of Proto-Elamite tablets and glyptic attributable to the Plateau (material and style).

Yet by the end of the Uruk period the population of Susiana itself dwindled sharply, and in any case was not so great later on (Wright and Johnson 1975; see chapters 3 and 6). Neither is there evidence for massive population movement to new areas; the whole settled area of Yahya IVC is about 10 ha, accommodating roughly 500 people (Lamberg-Karlovsky 1978). There may have been Susiana influence on the Plateau as early as Susa I (Caldwell 1976), but long-distance Susiana influence is attested by the Uruk period (=Susa II) at Godin, which appears to have a Susiana-related outpost amid an otherwise local Zagros settlement. The artifactual evidence linking the Proto-Elamite Plateau sites (for example, Sialk, Godin, Malyan, and Tepe Yahya) to each other and to Susa in Khuzestan is not that different from these earlier examples.[10] Thus, Lamberg-Karlovsky's (1978) model leaves unexplained how this state emerged from a declining Uruk polity and achieved administrative capability to control a vast region.

In his Master's thesis, John Alden explains the dynamics of the Proto-Elamite civilization in terms of wholesale-retail trade mechanisms integrating the settlements of southern and western Iran during the late fourth and early third millennia BCE (Alden 1973:1). This theory, adopted from Vance (1970), involves a complex hierarchical organization in which goods are collected and distributed by direct exchange but are transferred between collector and distributor by a specialized mechanism called "wholesale trade." This mode of exchange does not require the producer and consumer to meet, as exchange takes place between middlemen—wholesalers (those who buy from producers and sell in bulk) and retailers (those who buy in bulk and sell to consumers). In this scenario, Proto-Elamites served as middlemen (wholesalers) who collected goods and raw material from the Iranian Plateau and shipped it in bulk to Susa. In turn, Susians acted as middlemen (retailers) in the flow of material from Khuzestan to Mesopotamia (Alden 1973:93).

While the presence of Proto-Elamite tablets is taken as a sufficient criterion to define this period, Alden (1973:2) correctly pointed out that other distinctive artifacts associated with Proto-Elamite tablets can also be used to include other sites and archaeological levels that have not yielded tablets. Alden's reconstruction of this trade mechanism in the Proto-Elamite period seemed to fit the available evidence at the time. In addition, based on pottery comparisons, Alden included Shahdad, Iblis, and Shahr-i Sokhta in the Proto-Elamite world, a thoughtful deduction that proved to be correct at least in the case of Shahr-i Sokhta with the discovery of a Proto-Elamite tablet and associated material there two years later.[11] Nonetheless,

Alden's reconstruction posed more questions than it could answer. Alden accepts Ghirshman's thesis of a Proto-Elamite conquest of Sialk (Alden 1973:27), whereas the appearance of Proto-Elamite material in Marvdasht is said to best fit a peaceful migration of people from Susiana to this area (Alden 1973:31). Believing that Proto-Elamite tablets "represent a numbering and recording system and probably not a language," Alden (1973:2) deliberately set aside the ethnolinguistic aspects of the Proto-Elamite civilization on the grounds of insufficient evidence (Alden 1973:3–4), an approach that eventually left the Proto-Elamite civilization simply as a trade network without making any attempt to elaborate on this civilization's ethnic, cultural, or political foundations.

PROTO-ELAMITE STUDIES REVOLUTIONIZED

While the debate on the Proto-Elamite trade was in its heyday, Bill Sumner's survey of the Kur river basin in the highlands of Fars provided the breakthrough in our perspective on the Proto-Elamite civilization. Sumner (1972:42–44) identified a new phase in the archaeological sequence of the Kur river basin that included the Proto-Elamite period. This phase, named after the village of Banesh on the western edge of the Marvdasht plain, had not been identified in previous surveys of the region. According to Alden (1979:32–33) there are three reasons for earlier surveys' failure to find Banesh material: 1) the so-called "Persepolis magnet" or concentration of most previous surveys on the area around Persepolis, while most Banesh sites are located on the central and northern parts of the plain some 30 km away; 2) the typically small size of Banesh sites, which makes them invisible to cursory or driving surveys; 3) the unspectacular nature of the diagnostic pottery of the Banesh phase, which may easily be missed, or dismissed as aberrant. In addition, a number of Banesh sites were apparently small short-lived nomadic camps, largely destroyed after their abandonment or covered by later occupations. Sumner (1972) identified twenty-six sites with Banesh pottery in the Kur river basin. The notable characteristic feature of these settlements is their small number and unusual location, as many of them are either located near the high hills in the valley or scattered around the edges of the valley.

Shortly afterward, Sumner began a program of investigations at Malyan. His excavations not only established Malyan as the ancient Elamite capital of Anshan but also revealed spectacular Proto-Elamite remains never attested before (Sumner 1974, 1976, 2003). Excavations at operation ABC exposed four Banesh building levels, the third one (building level 3, see figure 10.3) being the most elaborate. This structure consists of at least seventeen rooms—some extending beyond the limits of excavation—with walls and floors finished in white, red, gray, black, and yellow plaster paintings of flowers, swirl, and step motifs (Nickerson 1977). Also discovered in these superimposed buildings were numerous objects indicating elite activities, among them fragments of elaborate pottery with relief decoration, a small gold foil leopard, and Proto-Elamite tablets, seals and seal impressions (Stolper 1985). Further, excavations at operation TUV in the northeast corner of Malyan brought to light evidence of production and consumption and more domestic activities compared with operation ABC (Nicholas 1980, 1990), again associated with Proto-Elamite administrative devices (see also Zeder and Blackman, chapter 10). Furthermore, small test trenches confirmed the observation based on aerial photographs and topographic evidence, that a massive wall was constructed around Malyan in the late Proto-Elamite period (Sumner 1985).

The work by Sumner provided a body of new evidence that revolutionized Proto-Elamite studies. The Malyan project provided ample evidence pertaining to both elite and domestic areas in Proto-Elamite society, while regional surveys in the Kur river basin revealed an elaborate settlement system as well as evidence for craft activities and distribution (Alden 1979, 1982b). The increasing evidence prompted a new series of synthetic reviews all emphasizing the distinctiveness of the Proto-Elamite civilization (Alden 1982a; Amiet 1979a, 1979b, 1986a, 1992; Lamberg-Karlovsky 1985, 1996; Sumner 1986a).

Pierre Amiet was perhaps the first scholar to synthesize the new evidence (1979a, 1979b). He emphatically distinguished the Proto-Elamite culture from Jemdet Nasr using a number of criteria such as different types of pottery and style of cylinder seals. Amiet (1979b:197) argued that "the most prominent aspects of the Proto-Elamite culture appear to be definitely not Mesopotamian." Furthermore, he correctly pointed out that the Proto-Elamite culture has been misleadingly identified with Jemdet Nasr "owing to the survival of some kind of internationalism as revealed by rather diversified polychrome potteries and numerous series of 'schematic' cylinder seals" (Amiet 1979b:196). According to Amiet (1979b:198) the Proto-Elamites were heir to a political formation that began in the Susa I period but was interrupted by the Uruk interlude. After the demise of this Uruk polity, the Proto-Elamite ethnic element present in Lurestan established its hegemony. This ethnic-political entity soon incorporated the Susiana plain and the highlands of Fars. By the founding of Anshan it had spread to the rest of the Plateau, taking control of isolated sites like Yahya and Sialk and transforming them into provincial

capitals. Furthermore, merchants carried Proto-Elamite material culture beyond the Lut Desert and introduced it to Shahr-i Sokhta, where the Proto-Elamite culture may have served as a catalyst and inspired the local population to take initial steps toward urbanism. The presence of Proto-Elamites at Shahr-i Sokhta also brought them into contact with Bactrians. But this Proto-Elamite "empire" was short-lived and collapsed shortly afterwards, not as a consequence of an inner crisis but as a result of a military defeat by the Mesopotamians, such as one ascribed to Enmebaragesi, king of Kish, who claims to have "smitten Elam" (Amiet 1979b:200).

Amiet's scenario of the rise and fall of the Proto-Elamite polity was much more comprehensive than previous argumentations centered around trade. However, his construct also raises further questions. Amiet proposes, without giving supporting evidence or argumentation, that Proto-Elamite culture originated in Lurestan. Another controversial statement in Amiet's work is his thesis that the fall of the Proto-Elamite polity can be attributed to an alleged military defeat by Mesopotamians. It is hard to imagine how even a powerful Sumerian city-state could pose a threat to such a polity as distant as that of the Proto-Elamites in Fars. Nonetheless, Amiet must be credited for reinvigorating the thesis of ethnic duality in the Elamite world—largely ignored since Scheil—and attempting to evaluate it with archaeological evidence.

Perhaps the culmination of the new era in Proto-Elamite studies was the publication of seminal papers by Alden (1982a) and Sumner (1986a). While Alden returned to the question of regional and interregional exchange and its influence on the course of the Proto-Elamite civilization, Sumner took a bolder step and tackled the elusive questions of the formation and structure of the Proto-Elamite civilization. Sumner argued that the rise of Proto-Elamite civilization should be sought in changing subsistence patterns in the Kur river basin. According to Sumner, the shift from sedentary to nomadic life in Fars that may have begun by the end of the Bakun phase continued through the succeeding Lapui and Early Banesh phases. In Sumner's proposal, when the failure of the agricultural system and the success of the new herding strategy became apparent, more and more people turned to nomadic pastoralism as their primary means of subsistence. Perhaps in the absence of a system of centralized political control in the Lapui phase, economic and military advantages of the new system were soon realized, as nomads moved from one patch to another before settled villagers could prevent them from grazing flocks on their fields or muster force to obtain compensation. Eventually, villagers resolved this problem by accepting the sovereignty of tribal leaders and acquiring their protection. Nomadic leaders settled in villages while their subjects continued to migrate. These leaders, already in control of the economic and military resources of their nomadic unit, established their control over their resident villages and embarked on a power struggle with other leaders. From this tribal competition, the leader residing at Malyan emerged as the dominant power of central Fars. This event, although evidence for it is limited, should perhaps mark the beginning of the Proto-Elamite civilization.

AMBIGUOUS TERMINOLOGY, EQUIVOCAL PERCEPTIONS

Even a cursory review of the literature, as outlined above, shows how many different adjectives have been used in association with the term "Proto-Elamite." It was originally coined to describe a distinct script (Scheil) but was soon adopted to refer to the archaeological period in which this script and the later Linear Elamite were in use (Pézard and Pottier). The term "Proto-Elamite" was also used to refer to the culture that produced the Proto-Elamite script (Ghirshman) as well as material culture associated with Proto-Elamite tablets (Alden), whether as a forerunner of later Elamite cultures (Ghirshman) or simply the Iranian manifestation of the Jemdet Nasr culture of Mesopotamia (LeBreton, Nagel, Caldwell, early Lamberg-Karlovsky). Finally, the term "Proto-Elamite" is used to describe a civilization associated with the archaeological evidence including material culture, settlement pattern, and social and political organization (late Lamberg-Karlovsky, Sumner).

Uncertainties overwhelm us when we turn to the nature of the Proto-Elamite civilization. Although some attempts have been made to present a model of Proto-Elamite sociopolitical structure (Sumner 1986a), economic organization (Alden 1982a), and mechanisms of expansion (Lamberg-Karlovsky 1978, 1985), we must admit that we know far too little about these aspects of the Proto-Elamite civilization. Needless to say, future archaeological research should be aimed at finding evidence pertaining to these questions.

I suggest we begin by abandoning the term "period" and call this era "the Proto-Elamite horizon." What I, following standard archaeological terminology (Willey and Phillips 1958:31–34), call horizon is *a distinct archaeological trait that crosscuts and ties together regional sequences*. In the case of the Proto-Elamite horizon, the distinguishing archaeological trait is the assemblage of Proto-Elamite administrative devices, for example, tablets, seals, and seal impressions. In different parts of Iran, this assemblage occurs in archaeological layers characterized by different local cultures. In the Kur river basin, evidently the heartland of the Proto-Elamite civilization, Proto-Elamite administrative devices are discovered in Middle and Late Banesh deposits, while at Susa Proto-Elamite administrative devices are found in Susa III contexts. Likewise, at Sialk (IV2), Yahya (IVC), Shahr-i Sokhta (phase 10), and probably Hissar (phase 8), Proto-Elamite administrative devices occur in local contexts. As argued by Willey and Phillips (1958:32) a horizon is characterized by rapid and widespread distribution of a complex of typical archaeological traits over a wide geographical area. In the New World, the extensively studied Wari and Teotihuacan horizons best illustrate this process. In the case of the Proto-Elamite horizon, characteristic Proto-Elamite traits reach distant corners of the Iranian Plateau in an archaeological instant and disappear shortly afterwards. While how and why this material reached these sites has been and will be the topic of a prolonged scholarly debate, this rapid conjecture further supports the argument that based our present state of knowledge "horizon" is perhaps the best term to describe the period of the Proto-Elamite civilization. Standardization of both terms and concepts should logically be the first step towards any rigorous scientific inquiry.

Acknowledgment. I am grateful to John Alden, Matthew Stolper, and Henry Wright for reading and commenting on earlier drafts of this chapter.

NOTES

1. Already, Gustav Jéquier (1900:138) in his short report of excavation at level III of Acropole refers to "petite tablette portant des signes très archaïque" ["a small tablet bearing very archaic signs"]. Whether this was a Proto-Elamite tablet or not is unclear.

2. Like other scholars of the early twentieth century, Scheil assumed that Susiana and its capital Susa were in Elam. Throughout his work at Susa, Scheil was consistent in his terminology. For him, "Élam" was the name of the country, and "élamite" an adjective to describe the people and things from Elam. Therefore, texts from Susa (which according to him was in Élam) were élamite, hence the earliest texts would be called "proto-élamite." According to Scheil (1900:vii), however, "élamite" texts were written in several languages: "Anzanite" which is now generally called Elamite, and "Sémitique" which included Mesopotamian languages, especially Akkadian, and occasionally Sumerian. Therefore, he divided his publications of texts from Susa into two broad categories of "Textes élamite-anzanites," and "Textes élamites-sémitiques."

3. Later works by the original French delegation on the Proto-Elamite tablets were mostly from an epigraphic point of view (see Mecquenem 1949; Scheil 1923, 1935), and are not considered in the present chapter.

4. Earlier, in the first study of seals and seal impressions discovered at Susa, Legrain (1921:10) suggests that the Proto-Elamite

script was used to write the "Anzanite" language, not the language of the Susiana plain.

5. In the second edition of this catalogue, Pézard and Pottier, more or less following their initial periodization, attributed more objects, including a group of tools and arms, to the Proto-Elamite period (Pézard and Pottier 1926:111–112). Furthermore, Pottier devoted an entire section to painted pottery of the Proto-Elamite period (Pézard and Pottier 1926:212–227). In a conclusion to this section, Pottier made some remarks on the historical role of the Proto-Elamite culture as one of the contributors to the early stages of painted pottery in the Near East. Nevertheless, he rejected the possibility of the diffusion of painted pottery from Elam to the rest of the Near East (Pézard and Pottier 1926:225–227). Although not mentioned, this appears to have been a reply to earlier "Pan-Élamisme" theory of de Morgan (1907).

6. This approach still persists, as indicated by the 1983 symposium in Tübingen where papers on the Proto-Elamite period were included in a meeting on the Jemdet Nasr period (Finkbeiner and Röllig 1986). Even as late as 1994, T. F. Potts takes a Sumer-centered stand in studying Proto-Elamite civilization; for my critique of the latter see Abdi (2000).

7. *Oikoumenê* is a complex of a number of societies which are in communication but need not be culturally very much alike. This term was first used by Kroeber (1945) in the context of Islamic, Oriental, and Classical civilizations, and later by Braidwood and Howe (1962) to explain the spread of 'Ubaid ceramic in the Near East.

8. In earlier reports, Lamberg-Karlovsky (1970, 1971a, 1971b) referred to both phases IVB and IVC as Proto-Elamite, but later, with the progress of excavation and exposure of more area he only defined phase C of level IV as Proto-Elamite.

9. The same approach is apparent in the published text of a lecture given before the British Academy by Lamberg-Karlovsky (1975). Although Lamberg-Karlovsky (1975:283) mentions that he should have called his lecture "Proto-Elamite Problems," throughout the paper he uses the term "Proto-Elamite" only to refer to tablets discovered at level IVC of Tepe Yahya, and the rest of the materials recovered from that level are "unequivocally tied to Jemdet Nasr Mesopotamia" (Lamberg-Karlovsky 1975:296).

10. Lamberg-Karlovsky (1978:114) also mentions Chogha Mish as having Proto-Elamite material, but without a citation. As excavation reports (Delougaz and Kantor 1996) show, however, the occupation at Chogha Mish ceased by the Late Uruk phase and did not resume until the Old Elamite period, and the only tablets we have from Chogha Mish are numerical ones of the Late Uruk phase.

11. In 1975, the discovery at Shahr-i Sokhta on the Afghan border of a single Proto-Elamite tablet with associated seals and seal impressions pushed the frontiers of the Proto-Elamite civilization farther east (Biscione et al. 1977:105; Tosi 1976a). This assemblage came from a deep sounding that penetrated the earliest levels of the site (Amiet and Tosi 1978). Unfortunately excavations at Shahr-i Sokhta were discontinued shortly afterward, and therefore the archaeological context of this discovery is not entirely clear.

a

c

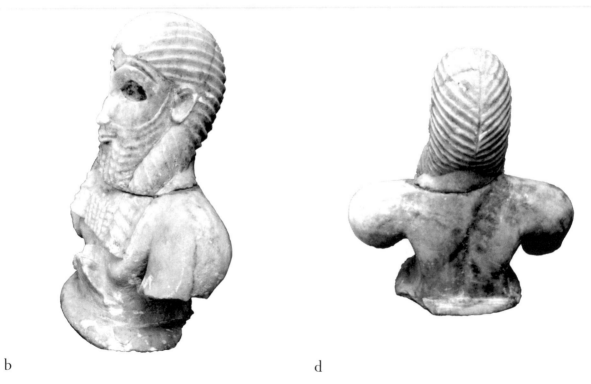

b

d

12.1   Statue found on Khark Island (ht. 27 cm): *a*, front; *b*, side; *c*, bottom; *d*, back. *Photographs by Y. Majïdzadeh*

CHAPTER 12

A SUMERIAN STATUE FROM KHARK ISLAND ON THE PERSIAN GULF

YOUSEF MAJIDZADEH

I N THE LATE 1980s—toward the end of the Iran-Iraq war—a fragmentary marble statue (figure 12.1) was accidentally discovered on Khark Island in the Persian Gulf. This statue was subsequently delivered to the Iranian Cultural Heritage Organization of Tehran province where it is kept today. As is the case with such discoveries, no reliable information on the provenance of the object is available, and thus we will have to rely on iconographic analysis to place this object in its historical context.

The lower part of the statue is broken from the waist, two-thirds of the arms are missing, and the nose is chipped off. The remaining part reaches 27 cm in height; the shoulders are 23.5 cm wide and the distance between the forehead and the nape measures 9.68 cm. The head of the statue was apparently separated from the body before it was transferred to Tehran and subsequently restored. As a result, portions of the hair and the beard are also chipped off. Judging by the well-proportioned statues of similar form from Mesopotamia and Syria, the Khark statue originally must have reached up to 80 cm in height, excluding the height of a base with which these statues are usually furnished. At the point where the lower part of the body is missing, there are clear signs of sawing. Apparently it had already been broken and flattened so it would stand upright.

The Khark statue displays all the major characteristics of similar statues found in Mesopotamia and Syria. It has a long beard and long hair flowing smoothly over the shoulders. The hair is parted in the middle with a fairly narrow groove that continues in the back down to just above the shoulders where the hair is split into two locks that rest on

the chest. None of the precious metal or stone, perhaps lapis lazuli, that once adorned the pupils and eyebrows remains. As with many examples of this type of statue, the torso is sculpted in a rather rigid geometric style. Whereas the head, the chest, and the waist are well-proportioned, the shoulders and arms are relatively wide and bulky. The arms are so sharply set off from the body that they appear as though they had been carved separately and attached to the statue later. The arms are broken off, but traces of breakage just below the chest indicate that originally the hands were typically clasped below the chest, perhaps holding an object. The cheeks are high and bony, and the nose, despite the breakage, is well harmonized with the rest of the face. In profile, the lower lip seems slightly protruding; it is elegantly modeled and the delicate curvature of the upper lip with raised corners suggests a gentle smile.

These characteristics suggest a Mesopotamian origin for the statue and thus it may be attributed to the well-known Sumerian school of sculpture of the Early Dynastic (ED) period. The following discussion will focus on the possible origin of the Khark statue and the contributions it could provide to the ongoing debate on the origin of this type of sculpture in Sumer.

CHARACTERISTICS OF THE EARLY DYNASTIC STATUES

The majority of the ED II free-standing stone statues are male, usually with bare torso. The lower body is usually covered with a kilt that often reaches below the knees. The ED II statues of this type are predominantly geometric in shape, with an overall cylindrical form. They usually exhibit a trapezoidal-shaped torso, from the upper corners of which disproportionately large arms are carved out with pointed elbows and disproportionately small hands. Eyebrows consist of two deeply incised joining crescents, usually with lapis lazuli filling, and eyeballs are made of shell with lapis lazuli or obsidian used for pupils.

Judging mainly by the statues excavated from sites in the Diyala river region (Tell Asmar, Khafaje, and Tell Aqrab), this rigid geometric convention was applied not only to the anatomical and facial features but also to the hair (Frankfort 1970:24). Statues typically have both hands clasped on or just below the chest. They occasionally hold a beaker, a tree branch, or flowers. In some cases, a sharp incision on the back represents the spine. Often such statues have a long rectangular beard and long hair. The hair is usually parted in the middle and hangs freely on the shoulders either in braids or loose bundles resting on the chest. Infrequently, the hair is shoulder-length and grazes the tops of the shoulders (Frankfort 1939:Pl. 5A). Frequently, the hair covers the ears, but sometimes, as on the Khark statue, the ears are exposed (Frankfort 1939:Pl. 11A). Generally, both the hair and the beard are stylized and shaped with horizontal ridges, zigzag lines, or vertical chevrons.

Although the style of the ED III statues largely resembles that of the ED II, it seems that sculptors of the later period tended to render their work more naturally and realistically than their predecessors, resulting, for example, in the common appearance of plump faces (Andrae 1922:Pl. 30a–b; Moortgat 1969:Pl. 77). An important change in ED III was narrowing of the gap between the arms and sides. During the ED III period, the sharply contrasting articulated masses that represented various parts of the torso gave way to smooth, modulated surfaces. In contrast to the rigid shapes of the ED II statues, the ED III examples have a softer and more naturalistic style. In the ED II period, the neck was so short that in most cases the head seems to sit directly on the torso, whereas in the ED III period the neck is elongated and clearly visible. The representational style of some facial features also changes. For example, the bony forehead and temples of the ED II statues become smooth and plump and the cartoonish lips become more naturalistic and better modeled, often giving the impression of a smile (Moortgat 1969:Pls. 78–79; Parrot 1953:Pls. 13–15, 28).

COMPARATIVE ANALYSIS

With the above description, we can now turn our attention to stylistic analysis of the Khark statue. Close observation reveals a number of differences between the Khark statues and those from the Diyala region. The Diyala stat-

ues have a flattish cranium; for that reason, the distance between the eyebrows and the highest point of the central parting line and that of the eyebrows and the tip of the nose is about proportionally 1 to 2 (Frankfort 1939:Pl. 5A); in the case of the statue of the god Abu from the Square Temple at Tell Asmar (Frankfort 1939: Pl. 3), it is 1 to 3.5. In contrast, the cranium of the Khark statue is considerably more rounded, and the proportion is about 1 to 1. In all cases foreheads are very short.

The Khark statue differs from the majority of known specimens in that although from the side view the ridges on its locks appear horizontal, they are diagonal in the back and angular at the parting line. The angles are very sharp at the top but gradually widen toward the nape to almost horizontal ridges (figure 12.1b). At this point the parting line come to an end and the lowest three ridges, unlike the successive horizontal ridges in almost all ED II statues, changes into three loose loops that begin from behind one ear and disappear behind the other. A seated statue from the Nintu Temple V at Khafaje also suggests the same characteristic (Frankfort 1943:Pl. 8).

With a few exceptions including examples from the Nintu Temples V (Frankfort 1943:Pl. 6) and VI (Frankfort 1943:Pl. 21B) at Khafaje, Shara Temple at Tell Agrab (Frankfort 1943:Pls. 32A–B, 40A), and Tell Chuera (Moortgat 1969:Pls. 72–75), all the ED II type male statues have their ears completely hidden under the heavy curly hair, while the ears of the Khark statue are exposed and thus stylistically closer to the Tell Chuera statues. In rare cases such as the statue from Uruk (Moortgat 1969:Pl. 82) or the one in the Vorderasiatisches Museum in Berlin (Moortgat 1969:Pl. 83), the hair does not cover the ears, but in both cases the hair is styled so that the locks neither rest on the shoulders nor in front on the chest but hang down the back. The outward direction of the spirals in the braid of the Khark statue also differs from that of the Diyala. In Mesopotamian examples, with only one exception from Tell Chuera (Moortgat 1969:Pls. 72–73), slopes begin from outside and slide down toward the beard.

Another characteristic of the Khark statue is the way in which the beard is fashioned. Except for a few cases in which the hair is either shorter and rests on the shoulders (Frankfort 1939:Pls. 1, 5A) or the beard is trimmed round at the end (Frankfort 1939:Pl. 43A–B), on the Diyala statues the hair and the beard are predominantly aligned in a horizontal line. This rectangular beard, rarely plain (Frankfort 1939:Pl. 43C–D; 1943:Pl. 11A), is fashioned in various styles:

- Horizontal ridges covering the entire beard from top to bottom (Frankfort 1939:Pls. 1, 5A, 9, 10, 11A, 14)

- Decorated by vertical engraved or scratched zigzag lines horizontal ridges (Frankfort 1939:Pl. 20)
- Horizontal ridges replaced with horizontal rows of chevrons (Frankfort 1943:Pl. 25D)
- more often scratched or sometimes engraved vertical rows of zigzags or chevrons replace the horizontal ridges (Frankfort 1939:Pls. 31, 34, 39A, 42C;1943, Pl. 40A)

To indicate locks in the ED II status, vertical deep (Frankfort 1939:Pl. 45D, 1943, Pl. 35) or shallow (Frankfort 1943:Pls. 8A, 30B) lines divide the beard into two to five strips, and hatched lines inside each strip suggest a spiral. This technique is more effective when the vertical dividing lines as well as hatched lines are deeply cut.

The direction of hatched lines in each lock is also opposite to that of the adjacent ones, so that the spirals appear alternately clockwise and counterclockwise. Although during the ED II period the zigzags and chevrons appear to have been a convention to suggest the curls of the beard, careful observation indicates that from the beginning an attempt had consciously been made to render two different types of beard: curly beard by using vertical zigzag lines (an excellent example is an ED III statue from Mari [Moortgat 1969:Pls. 78–79; Parrot 1953:Pls. 13–15, 28]) and spiral locks by using horizontal chevrons or zigzag lines (the best example is the famous Akkadian bronze head from Nineveh [Mallowan 1936:Pls. 5–7; Thompson and Hamilton 1932: Pl. 50]). The beard style of the Tell Chuera statues is plain (Moortgat 1969:Pl. 70) or a series of plain horizontal ridges (Moortgat 1969:Pls. 72, 74). In the Khark statue the carefully incised vertical and hatched lines suggest spiral locks. They turn alternately clockwise and counterclockwise, and contrary to any other statue of that period where the number of locks is at the most five, the Khark statue has six locks.

A stylistic comparison between the Khark statue and those from the Diyala region and Syria indicates that they share some general features. The Khark statue not only exhibits stylistic elements that seem more akin to the Sumerian school of sculpture than those of Semitic-speaking areas but also appears to belong to a school that produced considerably higher quality work than that of Diyala. Southern Mesopotamia has yielded very few examples of this type of statue, so we do not have sufficient knowledge to attribute any stylistic characteristics exclusively to Sumer; nevertheless, with the help of the Khark statue, we still can glean some general characteristics that may be attributed to these schools.

Despite general similarities of a number of features of the Khark statue to those from the Diyala region, Mari, and Tell Chuera, the comparative mastery in the execution of anatomical and facial features of the Khark statue sets it apart from known examples found outside Sumer proper and, considering the exquisite Sumerian school of sculpture of the earlier periods, it is warranted to assume that the Khark statue may belong to a true Sumerian rather than a Semitic or provincial school of sculpture. We should bear in mind that the original height of the Khark statue was at least 80 cm. In comparison, the tallest ED II statue, namely, that of the god Abu, is only 75 cm tall. We should therefore allow for the possibility of statues still more monumental in size in important Sumerian cultural centers at this period, buried underneath later deposits awaiting discovery.

CONCLUSION

We now face the question of the presence on Khark Island of this Mesopotamian object of monumental nature. A statue of this quality and size must have belonged to a monumental building, most probably a temple. We know that the Sumerians dispatched long-distance land and sea expeditions to obtain raw materials and exchange their products with a number of their neighbors including the Iranian highlands and the Persian Gulf region; therefore their presence on Khark Island, an important way station along the Iranian shores of the Persian Gulf, is not surprising. To date, however, not a shred of evidence has been found of any Mesopotamian occupation of the island nor of any monumental building of corresponding date. This may be an accident of discovery, considering that the Island has never been extensively explored; it is possible that future archaeological investigations will reveal the context from which this statue came. It is also possible that during a later period a passerby simply found this statue in the ruins of a Sumerian temple site in southern Iraq and brought it to Khark Island as a valuable piece of art. Either way, the question will have to remain open until further archaeological investigations are conducted on Khark Island.

Acknowledgment. I thank Abbas Alizadeh for reading and commenting on an earlier draft of this chapter.

Editors' note. This chapter originally appeared as "A Sumerian Fragmentary Statue from Khark Island," *Iranian Journal of Archaeology and History* 21–22 (August 1998):2–14 (in Persian). Translation printed with permission.

CHAPTER 13

ANSHAN, LIYAN, AND MAGAN CIRCA 2000 BCE

D.T. POTTS

BILL SUMNER'S CONTRIBUTIONS to the archaeology of Fars province in general and Malyan in particular have been fundamental. The present essay is offered to Bill in the hope that he will find the intellectual journey from Anshan to Liyan and across the Persian Gulf to Magan a pleasurable one.

OMAN AND IRAN:
THE SOUTHEASTERN CONNECTION

The relationship between the Bronze Age cultures of the Oman peninsula and those of southeastern Iran has been investigated now for nearly forty years (Thorvildsen 1963:219). It is no exaggeration to say that the topic was integral to the earliest intellectual development of southeast Arabian archaeology, which commenced on Umm an-Nar island (Emirate of Abu Dhabi) and at Sohar, Oman in 1958 (figure 13.1). Nor is it difficult to see why this should have been the case. Striking parallels between the painted black-on-gray pottery of the graves excavated by the Danish expedition on Umm an-Nar and that recovered by Sir Aurel Stein in Iranian Baluchestan (Stein 1937:104–125) were noted almost immediately by Knud Thorvildsen (1963:219). Several years later Geoffrey Bibby elaborated on the same parallels in his popular *Looking for Dilmun* (Bibby 1969:278–280), but it was Beatrice de Cardi who, in a series of reports on her 1966 excavations at Bampur, first provided detailed documentation of the parallels between the Umm an-Nar material and both the black-on-gray and incised grayware of Bampur, Damin, Khurab, and other sites throughout the Indo-Iranian borderlands (de Cardi 1967:40, 1968:148–149, 1970:268–276). This was further elaborated by E.C.L. During Caspers (1970), C.C. Lamberg-Karlovsky (1970:80), and Maurizio Tosi (1974, 1976b) and has been commented on by numerous other writers as well (for example, Cleuziou and Tosi 1989; Frifelt 1975; Potts 1981; R. Wright 1989). These parallels, of course, pertain exclusively to the southeasternmost portion of modern Iran, the region that today forms the western part of Baluchestan. In contrast, the evidence of parallels between southwestern Iran and the Oman peninsula circa 2000 BCE is much less abundant.

OMAN AND IRAN:
THE SOUTHWESTERN CONNECTION

To date, the evidence of ties between southwestern Iran and the Oman peninsula has consisted almost exclusively of soft-stone vessels. Parallels between chlorite or steatite vessels discovered in the early excavations at Susa and Liyan, near Bandar Bushehr, and material found at Hili and Umm an-Nar were highlighted over a quarter of a century ago (Miroschedji 1973a:Fig. 13) and have been discussed subsequently on several occasions (for example, Cleuziou 1981:290; Häser 1988; Potts 1990:110, 1999:120, 180). As for ceramic or other ties, until recently the only links detected between the Oman peninsula and southwestern Iran were of Middle Elamite date, as indicated by a faience cylinder seal and assorted sherds from Tell Abraq (Potts 1993b:434–435, Fig. 4, Table 2).

During the final, 1997/1998 season of excavation at Tell Abraq, however, two complete Kaftari jars were recovered

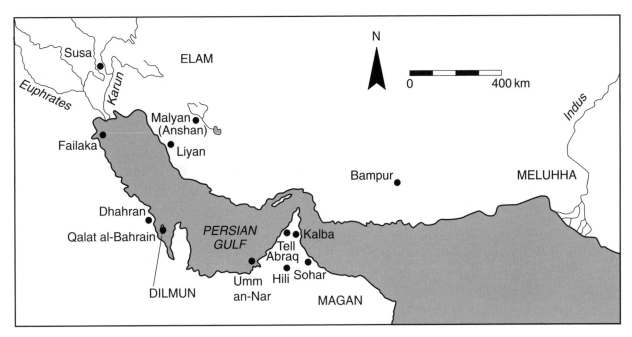

13.1 Sites mentioned in text. *Prepared at MASCA*

in the eastern half of a typical Umm an-Nar-type tomb (figures 13.2, 13.3). With a diameter of circa 6 m, the Tell Abraq tomb (figure. 13.4) is on the small side as Umm an-Nar tombs go, since these are known to vary in size from circa 4 to 14.5 m in diameter. The archaeological assemblage recovered in the Tell Abraq tomb suggested that it dated to the very end of the Umm an-Nar period (2500 to 2000 BCE) and could even be considered transitional to the following, so-called "Wadi Suq" period (2000 to 1300 BCE) based on the presence of artifacts more typically associated with the early second millennium than with the third (for example, a complete Dilmun-type sac-shaped burial jar with crudely scored rim, Bampur V-VI-type black-on-gray ware, almost two dozen socketed spearheads, and so forth). Indeed, this presumption is supported by a series of five AMS radiocarbon dates run on charcoal taken from the tomb (table 13.1).

Both vessels from Tell Abraq are what could be described as small jars or beakers. TA 1804 has an offset band-rim with painted decoration consisting of simple bands, solid triangles, and loose cross-hatching, while TA 2596 shows simple bands, wavy lines and tight cross-hatching. All of these elements can be found on published Kaftari pottery (Sumner 1974:Figs. 6–7, 1991:Fig. 25), albeit never in the same precise configuration. The design elements, however, are diagnostic and were already recognized by the late Louis Vanden Berghe when he first coined the term "Kaftari culture" in 1954 (Vanden Berghe 1953–54:402).

I shall not presume to comment upon the veracity of claims that have been made over the years for the presence of Kaftari pottery elsewhere on the Arabian side of the Gulf, for example, on Failaka island off the coast of Kuwait (Højlund 1987:100), in the Dhahran tombs of eastern Saudi Arabia (Zarins 1989:82; see my remarks in Potts 1990:216) or at Qalat al-Bahrain (Højlund 1994:119). Given the very obvious general similarities between black/brown-painted, chaff-tempered buff ware with horizontal bands and wavy lines in the early Wadi Suq period in the Oman peninsula (or for that matter in period IVA at Tepe Yahya) and the decoration commonly found on Kaftari-period pottery in Fars, none of these claims should be accepted unless verified by compositional analysis of the pottery in question or a clear set of unambiguous parallels to Kaftari pottery.

LIYAN AND MAGAN

Bill Sumner once suggested, "Although we do not know the geographical limits of Anshan [in the Kaftari period] it is not unreasonable to suggest a governor of the southern districts, including Kaftari settlements reported in Fasa, and perhaps a governor at Liyan" (Sumner 1989a:148). It is unfortunate that Liyan, a site located circa 4 km southeast of Sabzabad on the Bushehr peninsula (Matheson 1972:243; Whitcomb 1987:316, Fig. A), is not better known but there are indications that it must have been an extremely important site and that Sumner's suggestion was well-founded (for Elamite texts mentioning Liyan, see Vallat 1993:157). In 1913 Pézard found part of an alabaster socle in his excavations at Liyan bearing the name of Simut-wartash (Malbran-Labat 1995:19, 217, n. 23). If this is the same Simut-wartash known to have been the son of

13.2   TA 1804—E 74.60, N 115.20, elev. 7.25 (layer 1); brown-on-buff, fine chaff; 8.1 cm rim diameter, 5.4 cm base diameter, 15.00 cm tall; excavated 24 December 1997. *Photograph by D.T. Potts; Illustration by Hildreth B. Potts*

13.3   TA 2596—E 74.96, N 115.50, elev. 7.61–7.70 (layer 4); fine brown-on-buff, no visible inclusions or voids; 6.6 cm rim diameter, 4.5 cm base diameter, 12.7 tall; excavated 26 January 1998. *Photograph by D.T. Potts; Illustration by Hildreth B. Potts*

Shiruktuh, then it is indeed likely that Liyan was under the control of the *sukkalmah*s (Vallat 1984b:258; Carter and Stolper 1984:31; Potts 1999:180). Much later, during the Middle Elamite II period (ca. 1400 to 1200 BCE) Humban-numena I (ca. 1350 to 1340 BCE) constructed a high temple or *kukunnum* for Kiririsha at Liyan (Walker 1981:130, no. 192; Vallat 1984b), a building restored during the Middle Elamite III period (ca. 1200–1100 BCE) by both Kutir-Nahhunte (König 1965:§31) and Shilhak-Inshushinak (König 1965:§57–59; Grillot and Vallat 1984; Potts 1999:237–238). Furthermore, Pézard's excavations at Liyan recovered painted pottery (Pézard 1914:Pl. 6) which is widely identified as Kaftari ware (Sumner 1974:173; Cleuziou 1981:290; Carter and Stolper 1984:154; Nickerson 1991:5).

We do not know what sort of a relationship existed between Magan circa 2000 BCE and Elam in general or Anshan in particular. There is, however, plenty of evidence of close links between Magan and Dilmun. In Magan this is demonstrated by the more than six hundred sherds of Barbar red-ridged pottery found at Tell Abraq (Grave et al. 1996); by the presence of sac-shaped Dilmun burial jars at Tell Abraq, Kalba, Shimal, and other sites in the Emirates; and by the recovery of an ivory Persian Gulf seal at Tell Abraq and a stone Dilmun stamp seal at Mazyad near Jabal Hafit (Cleuziou 1981:Fig. 8; Potts 1990:254). In Dilmun, links with Magan are illustrated by the recovery of diagnostic soft-stone in both the major settlements, such as Qalat al-Bahrain (Højlund 1994:386–390) and Saar (Killick et al. 1991:Fig. 16), and tombs (for example, Ibrahim 1982:Pl. 53; Mughal 1983:Pls. L–LI). Further, we know something about Dilmun's relations with Susa in this period from cuneiform sources (Potts 1990:226–228).

If we are to understand Magan's relations with Anshan, I suggest that we look not to Malyan and the highlands of Fars. Rather, in view of Liyan's importance and location, we ought to begin by considering the Bushehr area in general and Liyan in particular as the Gulf coast "hub" for contacts between the *sukkalmah*s and their southern neighbors. This, too, may produce unexpected insights into Elam's relationship with Dilmun which go beyond the data available from Susa. We can only hope that excavations will one day allow scholars to test the hypothesis that Liyan functioned as an important node for interaction between Anshan and such polities of the Lower Sea as Dilmun, Magan, and perhaps even Meluhha.

Acknowledgement. I thank Lloyd R. Weeks for calibrating the latest radiocarbon dates from Tell Abraq and Russell Workman (both University of Sidney) for printing the photographs published here. Finally, many thanks to my wife Hildreth B. Potts for her drawings of TA 1804 and TA 2596.

13.4 Umm an-Nar-type tomb at Tell Abraq, viewed from the south. *Photograph by D.T. Potts*

Table 13.1. Radiocarbon determinations from the tomb at Tell Abraq

Sample	Level (elevation)	¹⁴C age BP	Cal. age	
			range BCE (1σ)	range BCE (2σ)
OZD686	3 (7.40-7.50 m)	3677 ± 58	2140-2070 (0.41) 2070-1970 (0.59)	2200-1890 (1.00)
OZD687	4 (7.60-7.70 m)	3826 ± 57	2400-2390 (0.05) 2340-2190 (0.87) 2160-2140 (0.08)	2460-2130 (0.98) 2070-2050 (0.02)
OZD688	6 (7.80-7.90 m)	3742 ± 50	2200-2100 (0.64) 2090-2040 (0.36)	2290-2010 (0.95) 2010-1980 (0.05)
OZD689	6 (7.80-7.90 m)	3650 ± 70	2130-2080 (0.25) 2050-1920 (0.75)	2190-1870 (0.96) 1840-1780 (0.4)
OZD690	6 (7.87 m)	3779 ± 61	2290-2130 (0.86) 2080-2050 (0.14)	2450-2440 (0.01) 2400-2370 (0.03) 2370-2030 (0.95) 2000-1980 (0.01)

Note: Calibrated by L.R. Weeks; numbers in parentheses represent the probability that the date falls in the range indicated. The dates were run at the Australian Nuclear Science and Technology Organisation's (ANSTO) AMS facility at Lucas Heights, NSW, Australia, and were funded under grant 98/152R from the Australian Institute of Nuclear Science and Engineering (AINSE).

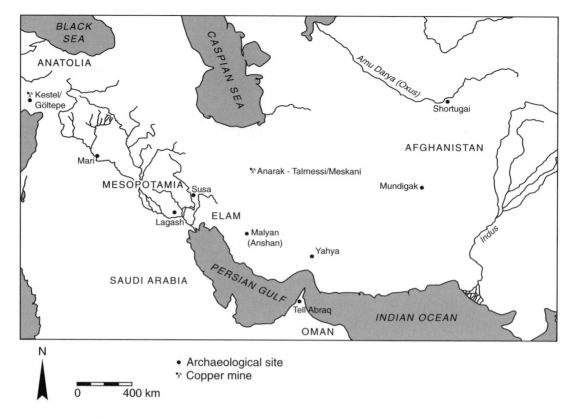

14.1   Malyan and other significant Bronze Age sites on the Iranian plateau. *Prepared at MASCA*

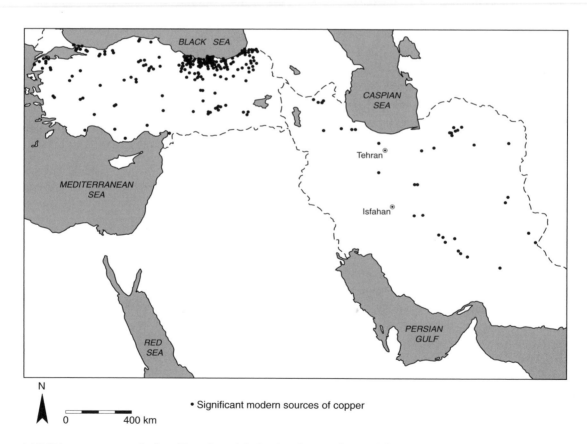

14.2 Primary copper ore bodies of Anatolia and the Iranian plateau. *Sources: Min. Res. and Explor. Inst. of Turkey, No. 133, 1972 and Geo. Survey of Iran, 1976; prepared at MASCA*

CHAPTER 14

ARCHAEOMETALLURGICAL INVESTIGATIONS AT MALYAN

The Evidence for Tin-Bronze in the Kaftari Phase

VINCENT C. PIGOTT, HARRY C. ROGERS, AND SAMUEL K. NASH

THE SITE OF MALYAN is located on the Marvdasht plain in Fars province not far from the famed ruins of Persepolis (figure 14.1). The metal artifacts that are the focus of this archaeometallurgical study come from the Malyan excavations directed by William Sumner. This study was conducted at the University of Pennsylvania Museum Applied Science Center for Archaeology (MASCA) under the direction of the senior author who had the good fortune to excavate at Malyan during its first and second seasons in 1971 and 1972.

Malyan was first inhabited in the later fourth millennium BCE. Several hundred years, however, separate its primary occupation phases, the Banesh (circa 3400 to 2800 BCE) and Kaftari (circa 2400 to 1600 BCE). Little distinguishes them, however, in terms of metalworking techniques. Rather, it is the alloys used that distinguish these phases metallurgically. While the Banesh phase assemblage was exclusively the product of arsenical copper metallurgy (Pigott et al. 2003), the larger fraction of the Kaftari phase assemblage is characterized by artifacts made from tin-bronze alloys (see table 14.1).[1] This dates the early appearance of this alloy to the later third to early second millennium on the Iranian Plateau. Tin-bronze, as we shall see, appears at Susa, off the plateau, at about the same time if not somewhat earlier. The appearance of this alloy is of particular interest, in part due to the question of the sources of the tin and how it might have been acquired by ancient Iranian metalworkers, particularly those in Elam.

At Malyan a total of thirty-six shaped metal artifacts classified as tools, personal ornaments and some miscellaneous items were excavated from Kaftari contexts along with small quantities of debris from metal production and processing (Nickerson 1991:16, 22). The artifacts analyzed for this study fall under the latter category, metal processing remains: casting debris, fragments of sheet metal, barstock, rods. All these artifacts are small and most are not identifiable as to purpose (see appendix at the end of chapter). It is doubtful that they are representative of the use and occurrence of bronze at Malyan, for the collection includes only those permitted by the Iranian government to be sent abroad for analysis. Nevertheless, they comprise what was made available to MASCA for study, and they do allow exploration of larger issues concerning the trade and metallurgy of bronze on the Iranian Plateau, particularly with respect to Elam.

SOURCES OF COPPER

There are abundant sources of copper on the Iranian Plateau (figure 14.2). Most of these deposits are not arsenic-bearing. Nevertheless, the analysis of the Kaftari metal suggests that an arsenical copper source or sources continued to be exploited as late as the early second millennium BCE. Discussions concerning the nature and location of Iranian copper ore sources have been reviewed from a geological perspective by Bazin and Hübner (1969), and from an archaeometallurgical one by Wertime (1968), Berthoud (1979), Berthoud et al. (1982), Stech and Pigott (1986), Moorey (1994), and Pigott (1999a, 1999b). Given current levels of understanding of several sources, no clues exist that might allow us to directly link the Malyan bronzes to any particular source of copper, although we have

Table 14.1 Composition of Kaftari phase copper-base artifacts from Malyan, Operation ABC as determined by PIXE analysis (Elemental composition, %, by weight)

mf #	Cu	As	Sn	Pb	Fe	Ni	Sb	Ag	Cl	S
0762	95.5	0.99	0.82	0.41	0.17	1.02	≤ 0.033	0.035	0.089	0.20
0804.1	97.4	1.0	≤ 0.015	≤ 0.039	0.26	0.50	≤ 0.023	≤ 0.011	≤ 0.003	0.058
0852.2	95.7	0.59	1.9	0.17	0.20	0.26	≤ 0.042	0.13	0.018	0.14
0954.1	93.2	4.5	≤ 0.014	≤ 0.056	0.68	0.52	≤ 0.025	≤ 0.014	≤ 0.004	0.092
1505	80.5	0.36	16.8	0.14	0.26	0.59	≤ 0.048	≤ 0.023	0.18	0.21
3936	85.6	0.84	11.8	0.14	0.25	0.29	≤ 0.046	0.098	≤ 0.004	0.023
6746	97.3	0.93	0.36	≤ 0.043	0.22	0.45	≤ 0.024	0.032	≤ 0.003	0.029
6750.1	88.3	0.87	8.8	≤ 0.059	0.08	0.48	≤ 0.053	≤ 0.027	0.32	0.030
9927	88.5	0.33	9.0	0.30	0.15	0.47	≤ 0.061	0.051	0.076	0.088
9969	94.8	0.45	2.9	0.53	0.08	0.27	≤ 0.055	0.064	0.036	0.11

* Zinc was sought, but not found at a level above its detection limit (typically ≤ 0.57 in this study).

argued elsewhere that the copper-nickel arsenide-bearing deposits of Talmessi and Meskani in the Anarak mining district of Iran constitute one possible source (Pigott et al. 2003).

The only technique that may permit linking the Malyan bronzes with Plateau-based copper sources is lead isotope analysis. Lead isotope analyses of Iranian artifacts, however, have yet to be published, and no Iranian sources of lead and lead-bearing copper have been analyzed that would provide a comparative sample. Given the geographically circumscribed nature of the Iranian Plateau and its well-surveyed, abundant ore sources, future research in this direction should prove to be particularly informative.

THE SECOND MILLENNIUM BCE EVIDENCE FROM SUSA

Malyan—ancient Anshan, the highland capital of the Elamite kingdom—lay at the southeast end of Elam, while Susa, the lowland capital lay hundreds of kilometers to the northwest—at the other end of Elam (see chapter 3). A one-to-one comparison between metalworking and the metals trade at Susa and the relatively meager evidence that Malyan has yielded is tenuous at best. The weight of textual and metallurgical evidence from Susa is such, however, that it merits some discussion in the context of Malyan as a contemporaneous Elamite capital. A major study of Susian metals in archaeological context from their initial occurrence at that site in the fourth millennium into the second millennium, conducted by Françoise Tallon (1987) with the laboratory assistance of Jean-Michel Malfoy and Michel Menu, offers much detailed comparative evidence for the Malyan study.

Malfoy and Menu (1987) describe the beginning of the Isin-Larsa phase (ca. 2000–1750 BCE; Susa VB) as a "decisive point of departure for tin-bronze metallurgy." This is, of course, when we see tin-bronzes appearing at Malyan as

well. At this time Susian metalworkers began to experiment with complex alloys (Malfoy and Menu 1987:371). Malfoy and Menu (following Berthoud 1979; Berthoud et al. 1982) argue that copper from sources in Oman (probably ancient Magan), which are characterized by the elemental trio of arsenic (As), nickel (Ni), and cobalt (Co), was used in the later third millennium at Susa. The presence of the trace elements nickel, cobalt, and iron in copper-base artifacts from the preceding Susa IVA2 phase remains constant throughout Susa VB, the phase under discussion. This consistency fostered the assumption that Omani ores continued to be used into the early second millennium at Susa; the same could hold true for Malyan. Further analysis is necessary, however, because the steps necessary to analyze for cobalt were not taken in the present proton-induced X-ray emission (PIXE) study of Malyan metal.[2] Analyses of Kaftari metal artifacts in table 14.1 show relatively constant amounts of nickel (0.46% nickel on average); three artifacts from the same phase exhibit concentrations of arsenic near 1% with only small traces of tin. Only one artifact (mf 0954) contained a relatively high arsenic content and almost no tin (table 14.1).

While Susa VB is characterized by a preponderance of tin-bronze metallurgy, the use of arsenical copper also continues there (Malfoy and Menu 1987:360). Malfoy and Menu (1987:373) go on to suggest that in this phase in certain classes of artifacts, such as axes, arsenic was intentionally added to ores low in cobalt and nickel, whereas tin was added to ores rich in these two trace elements. Here one must ask how ancient metalworkers could discriminate between ores on the basis of their nickel and cobalt contents. Malfoy and Menu (1987:372) suggest that the ore low in nickel (and cobalt?) may come from a different source, that is, not Oman. As for the ores high in nickel and cobalt but low in arsenic, and to which they argue tin was added, the following suggestion can be made. If the tin oxide ore, cassiterite, was being smelted with an Omani ore rich in arsenic, nickel, and cobalt, then there is every possibility that much of the arsenic was being lost during smelting of the metal (see Hauptmann et al. 1988:40; Moorey 1994:244) and/or hot-working it into an axe. Furthermore, if cassiterite or metallic tin was being added to a crucible of molten copper rich in arsenic, nickel, and cobalt, then the likelihood of volatilizing the arsenic is even greater than in the previous smelting scenario.

Although the trace element analyses show some promise in the context of fingerprinting ore sources, confusion remains. The similarities of the trace element profiles (that is, less than 1% arsenic, nickel, and cobalt) of the Omani and of the Iranian ores (Talmessi and Meskani deposits) may hinder attempts to discriminate between these two potential sources (Pigott 1999a, 1999b). Furthermore, this trace element correspondence makes the argument for the importation of Omani copper difficult to support. Why would Malyan, which, it has been argued, may have used the relatively nearby Anarak deposits during the Banesh phase, turn to a source and trade in copper presumably under the control of middlemen? If Omani copper was exploited at Susa, then issues of commerce and the politics of empire may have dictated that the same sources supply metalworkers at Malyan. At this stage, however, there is little need to speculate any further; we simply will not know what sources were used until an enhanced view of ore procurement patterns and metal exchange routes can be achieved.

SOURCES OF TIN

Determination of the ancient source(s) of tin is one of the critical problems concerning the origins of Bronze Age metallurgy across southwest Asia. This question arises in discussing the appearance and gradual acceptance on the Iranian Plateau of a new metallurgical tradition based on the use of tin-bronze. It is a complex subject which cannot be reviewed here (see Moorey 1994; Pigott 1999a; Stech and Pigott 1986). It is necessary, however, to reiterate the strong case for a substantial eastern tin source in light of repeated textual reference to sources of tin east of Mesopotamia (summarized in Moorey 1994:298–299). The current view sees Afghanistan as the most likely eastern source for Iranian Plateau metallurgy (figure 14.3). While evidence is compelling for tin mining and production from the Bolkardag mining district in the Taurus Mountains of south-central Anatolia, with its Kestel mine, and metalworking quarter in the large settlement at nearby Göltepe (see Adriaens et al. 1999; Earl and Özbal 1996; Vandiver et al. 1993; Yener and Vandiver 1993), it is difficult to argue that this district was supplying metalworkers to the Iranian Plateau. Not only is the distance considerable but also there are no strong cultural connections between the two regions that might suggest any sort of interaction, technological or otherwise. The arguments for Afghanistan (as well as Central Asia [see Alimov et al. 1998]) as a tin source for the ancient Near East are so strong that they should not be placed in the same category with sources as far afield as Cornwall, the Erzgebirge, southeast Asia, or Africa (for example, Yener and Vandiver 1993:213). Yener and Vandiver acknowledge that Afghanistan has tin, but they see little or no other substantive evidence to suggest it as a source for ancient Near Eastern bronze production. While there are no valid arguments for the non-southwest Asian

regions having supplied the ancient Near East with tin, the sources in Afghanistan and Central Asia are still under consideration.

Archaeological evidence supports a substantially earlier beginning of regular copper working on the Iranian Plateau than in the Mesopotamian lowlands. Subsequently, the earliest examples of tin-bronze artifacts occur simultaneously in the later fourth millennium, for example, in the lowlands at Susa and in Afghanistan at Mundigak (Stech and Pigott 1986:43, 47). These initial random occurrences of bronze may be the result of interaction with source(s) from farther east rather than those of Anatolia. Had Anatolian metals been employed, it seems likely that they would have been routed through the centers of southern Mesopotamia; therefore, one would expect to see early bronze by the end of the fourth millennium, in the Mesopotamian heartland as well; yet, at this time, there is none.

Afghanistan, with its juxtaposition of abundant copper and tin deposits, clearly constitutes one very likely source of ancient tin—the enormous amount of geological evidence (Shareq et al. 1977; Stech and Pigott 1986) almost stands on its own. In addition, such factors as the proximity of ore sources, including placer gold as well as tin, contemporaneous Bronze Age occupation (Cleuziou and Berthoud 1982), and the Bronze Age trade in lapis lazuli from Afghan sources (see summary discussion of lapis in Moorey 1994:85–92) all demonstrate that Afghanistan was a very rich source of raw materials including tin, gold, and lapis lazuli and could have easily supplied the needs of both Mesopotamian and Indus Valley civilizations.

MALYAN, ELAM, THE GULF, AND THE INDUS VALLEY

Evidence suggestive of Malyan's involvement in Gulf-based east-west commerce can be found in the distribution of Kaftari phase ceramics as suggested by Sumner:

> Marvdasht is the center of the Kaftari world and Kaftari ceramics are found at few sites elsewhere in Fars; Zohak at Fasa (de Miroschedji 1973[b]) and Nokhodi near Pasargadae (Goff 1963, 1964) have Kaftari pottery. There are several possible Kaftari sherds in Aurel Stein's survey collection and a probable Kaftari phase site near Kazerun on the road to Bushehr. However, typical Kaftari pottery is found in abundance at Liyan (Bushehr). In addition, there are two typical Kaftari 'gin and tonic glasses,' one with birds and rosette on the base, from Failaka/Dilmun (Højlund 1987:100, Figs. 432–434). Oddly, there is also a Harappan sherd (Fig. 435) illustrated on the same page. Perhaps the Liyan and Dilmun Kaftari ceramics were imported from

14.3 Tin occurrences in Afghanistan. *Prepared at MASCA based on Shareq et al. 1977*

Malyan or one of the other Kaftari sites in the Marvdasht. The connection between Malyan and the Gulf is also indicated by the ubiquity of Gulf shell at Malyan. (Sumner, personal communication)

Finally, given Malyan's links to the Gulf, the possible role the Harappans of the Indus valley played as middle-men in trade from the east is in need of a detailed review by the scholarly community (see, for example, summary discussions under Indus valley by Moorey [1994]; also Weeks [1999:61]). In his recent discussion of archaeometallurgy at the third-millennium site of Tell Abraq, UAE, Weeks has reviewed several key points:

> Lapis lazuli and carnelian are frequently referred to in cuneiform sources as coming from the land of Meluhha, now known to be the region of the Indus Valley, and would have reached Mesopotamia via the Persian/Arabian Gulf (Muhly 1973:307). From the reign of Gudea of Lagash (c. 2150–2100 B.C.) we have one text which mentions that, in addition to lapis lazuli and carne-

lian, tin was also traded to Mesopotamia from the land of Meluhha (ibid.). Further evidence of the trade in tin through the Gulf may be indicated by references to 'Dilmun tin' in Mesopotamian texts, particularly in the Old Babylonian Phase (Moorey 1994:298). Dilmun is the Sumerian/Akkadian toponym for the eastern Saudi Arabian coast and Bahrain, and was a region that prospered through its involvement in the mercantile activity linking Mesopotamia to the Indus. (Weeks 1999:51)

Moreover, the presence of a Harappan outpost settlement at Shortugai (Francfort 1989) in northeastern Afghanistan, well within reach of the resources of particular interest to both Harappan and Mesopotamian elites, gives pause for thought. At least we know that the Harappans were well positioned to exploit desirable natural resources in Afghanistan (and perhaps Central Asia as well) and that they had a presence in the Persian Gulf. Weisgerber (1984) has suggested that some of the prodigious production of copper in Oman from the third millennium onward, not earmarked for Mesopotamia and Elam, may have gone east to the Indus valley in return for tin and other commodities. Weeks (1999:53) had made it clear from this work on the metal finds from Tell Abraq that, not only was tin-bronze an important material at this major coastal site but that we should not underestimate the role of the Persian Gulf polities in the movement of tin, copper and bronze into west Asia (see also chapter 13).

Textual evidence offering an additional possible link between Malyan and the Gulf is found in a reference to tin from Anshan (Davidovic 1984, cited in Moorey 1994:298). The larger question is therefore: did Elam, with its capitals at Susa and Anshan, play a role in an eastern-based tin trade, perhaps more significant than has previously been suggested; that is, were the Elamites prominent southwest Asian middlemen once tin (and other eastern resources like lapis) reached the Iranian coast? P. Villard (cited in Moorey 1994:90) comments, "Texts of the eighteenth century BCE from Mari associate the acquisition of lapis lazuli with the procurement of tin indirectly through Elamites or more directly in Elam itself." Thus, given this reference and various others to tin and Elam (see Moorey 1994), one is left with the feeling that there is much more to Elamite, and hence Anshan, involvement with tin and its movements than is currently understood.

THE PRODUCTION OF TIN-BRONZE

Bronze need not have been made at Malyan; it could easily have been imported from elsewhere. Analyses conducted at MASCA by Carriveau (1978) on several pieces of slag from the site suggest, however, they are remnants of bronze processing. Their presence, and that of the tin-bronze artifacts, deserves a fuller technological discussion.

Considering the intense fascination that the issue of the origins of bronze has engendered over the last century, it is remarkable how little research has focused on determining how it was actually produced. Far more effort (much of it speculative) has been expended trying to find the sources of tin than understanding the process of making a tin-bronze artifact. Only a handful of substantive laboratory-based studies, some involving replication experiments, have been conducted (for example, Charles 1980; Cooke and Nielsen 1978; Rostoker et al. 1983; Unglik N.D.; Zwicker et al. 1985). Michael Wayman and colleagues (1988:131–132) reviewed these studies and conducted their own investigations. These suggest at least three ways in which tin-bronze might be produced using either ceramic crucibles or bowl furnaces in the presence or absence of charcoal in the charge.

The first is the remelting of scrap bronze most probably manufactured at another location. While this is always a possibility, it is difficult to imagine that there was enough of the metal around at Malyan to make recycling commonplace in the early second millennium BCE, when bronze first made its appearance. The relative paucity of bronze artifacts at Malyan and the diminutive size of those found do not argue for sufficient metal to support recycling. Furthermore, other than some dross produced by the erosion of the crucible or furnace wall, remelting of scrap would not yield any slag. This method can be conducted with or without charcoal as part of the crucible charge.

The second method is making bronze from the "cofusion," or melting together, of ingots of copper and tin imported from elsewhere. A high-quality bronze can be obtained this way. Such a method would permit the production of recipe bronzes, for example, bronzes of variations on the ratio of one part tin to nine parts copper. Ratios are easily controlled if ingots of comparable size or weight are available. The addition of tin not only acts as a deoxidant but also improves the liquidity of the metal for pouring and casting. Moreover, as Lucas (cited in Moorey 1994:252) indicates, the addition of 5% tin lowers the melting point of copper from 1083°C to 1050°C, 10% lowers it to 1005°C, and 15% tin lowers it to 960°C. Again, no appreciable amount of slag would be produced. The co-fusion method will produce bronze with or without charcoal.

The third method discussed by Wayman et al. (1988) involves reducing cassiterite (SnO_2) in molten copper at about 1200°C. This process proceeds successfully only when charcoal is present in the crucible charge. The charcoal cover over the metal helps to maintain reducing conditions. Moreover, the process will produce ingots of up to 10% tin only when the tin ore is added to the molten copper in a crucible under conditions in which no slag forms to cover the molten pool of metal. If an oxidizing slag cover forms over the molten metal, it promotes oxidizing conditions and, as a result, the tin content of the copper alloy drops dramatically to less than 1%. Cassiterite is 80% tin by weight, which means that, whether it comes in the form of river bed nodules or as a concentrate from panning, it is so rich in tin that there will be very little in the way of gangue (siliceous impurities) that would form a slag. Only mined "hard rock" cassiterite bound up within its host rock would form any appreciable slag. The best-known ancient southwest Asian example of such tin mining is found at the Bronze Age Kestel/Göltepe complex in south central Anatolia (Yener and Vandiver 1993). In the industrial quarter at Göltepe, kilograms of tin concentrate were found along with crucibles that were used for tin smelting. The mined tin ore was apparently crushed to concentrate the ore in powdered form (that is, it was "beneficiated") which,

Table 14.2 ABC Kaftari artifacts

Tin*	mf #	Description	Condition
Very low	0804.1	Bar stock—quadrangular cross section	Annealed
	0954.1	rod—nearly circular cross-section	Annealed
Low (< 1%)	6746	Bar stock—mildly tapered, very roughly Rectangular cross section	Annealed
	0762	Shaped artifact	Annealed
Intermediate	0852.2	Rod—approx. circular cross section	Annealed
	9969	Lump—casting debris	as cast microstructure
High	6750.1	Bar stock—quadrangular cross section	Annealed
	9927	Deformed head (scrap)	Heavily deformed locally
	3936	Bar stock—quadrangular cross section	Annealed
	1505	Bar stock—quadrangular cross section	Annealed, then lightly deformed

* content

by first mechanically reducing the impurities in the material to be smelted, would have lessened the amount of slag formed during final smelting (Adriaens 1999; Earl and Özbal 1996; Vandiver et al. 1993).

In further support of this third method, Charles (1980:175) has shown that when adding cassiterite to the copper melt, "recovery of tin to the melt…can be extremely easy and efficient." The addition of the tin ore can lower the temperature of the operation as much as 200°C from 1250°C. Lowering the reaction temperature facilitates a shorter heating time. This, in addition to reducing the effort involved, also lessens the extent of erosion of the ceramic lining of the crucible that otherwise causes the undesirable surface slag to form on the melt. Such slag inhibits the amount of tin that will dissolve in the copper. Although this method could have been practiced at sites on the Plateau including Malyan, little slag would have been produced, contrary to the finding of sizable lumps of bronze slag at Malyan.

A fourth method, not discussed by Wayman et al. (1988), involves the smelting together of copper and tin ores in the same crucible or furnace (co-smelting). There are many points that cannot be discussed here in the absence of laboratory replication experiments as in the above examples. What can be said about this process, however, is that an ample amount of slag would normally form as a result of the presence of gangue in the copper ore (unless the ore were remarkably rich and/or thoroughly dressed). The slag documented by Carriveau (1978) could be explained in such terms. Also, though purely speculative given the inefficient nature of ancient copper smelting, copper prills often remain trapped in the slag as is seen in the Kaftari slags. Carriveau (1978:66) reports finding 50 to 100-mg prills in

the slag. Emission spectroscopy revealed tin in both prills and associated slag but in rather modest amounts (Carriveau 1978:63, Table 2). Moreover, the variations in tin content seen in the Kaftari artifacts could also be explained in terms of the metalworkers' inability to control the tin content when smelting copper and tin ores together.

A final point: regardless of the choice of process by which tin is alloyed with copper to form bronze, the question remains whether the tin-bronze artifacts with low arsenic have low arsenic primarily as a result of the particular oxidizing characteristics of the process used with resultant volatilization of arsenic. Thus, the slag-producing nature of this fourth process could easily explain the bronze slags from Malyan. Analysis of these slags at some point in the future will help to identify which process was responsible for their production at Anshan, and thereby the processes that produced these Kaftari phase tin-bronzes, which are among ancient Iran's earliest. The MASCA-based metallographic and elemental analyses of the recovered Kaftari phase copper-base artifacts follows (figure 14.4).

METALWORKING DURING THE KAFTARI PHASE: THE EVIDENCE FROM OPERATION ABC

An earlier study metallographically examined Banesh phase artifacts uncovered in operations ABC and TUV at Malyan and determined their compositions (Pigott et al. 2003). All were made out of virtually tin-free copper alloys with varying arsenic contents. From the size and shape of the recovered artifacts from that phase, it is probable that there was a metal workshop at or near operations ABC and TUV where items were made, leaving only trimmings, excess lengths, the remains of unsuccessful attempts to produce the desired item as well as the debris of casting and perhaps smelting. The limited number of artifacts available from the Banesh phase deposits precludes estimation of the frequency of use of various processing techniques during this time. It is likely that if simple stone tools were used in metalworking and for primary shaping into sheet or plate, they were not recognized by archaeologists or else they were removed from the site when it was abandoned.

Based on the artifacts analyzed to date, we infer that by the end of the Banesh phase, metalworkers at Malyan understood the following:

- The strength of metals decreases with increasing temperature of working, while the ductility (that is, the ability to shape metal without cracking) increases with increasing temperatures. This permits the use of cold tools to shape hot metal having the same or greater strength when at the same temperature as the tool alloy. Metal tools, being of copper-base alloys, could have been recycled as scrap and re-melted when they became so deformed that they were no longer useful (and as a result were removed from the archaeological record and are not available for archaeometallurgical study).

- Deformation at ambient temperatures causes a metal to become harder and stronger but more prone to cracking if deformed excessively. For example, by differentially deforming a sharp-edged implement, the edge region can be made harder for improved cutting ability while the bulk of the implement remains softer and tougher (that is, less likely to break) than the edge.
- The softness and toughness can be recovered in a metal hardened by deformation by reheating it at a high temperature but below its melting point for an extended time (annealing).
- The metalworkers' knowledge of the relationship between the alloy content and strengthening of the alloy thereby must have been empirical at best. The limited number of artifacts available for study here precludes any significant analysis that might shed further light on the metalworkers' understanding of alloy technology. With no definitive way to determine alloy content, they may have selected alloys for desired properties based on the difference in behavior of copper alloys from different sources of ore as well as alloy color in tin bronzes.[3]

The appendix lists the Kaftari artifacts analyzed and provides information about shape, composition, and metallurgical state (for example, annealed, deformed, cast)(figures 14.5 to 14.15). The most pertinent information is summarized in table 14.2. Eight of the ten artifacts are classified as either rods or barstock, another (mf 9969, figure 14.4) is in the shape of a lump with a cast microstructure, and one (mf 9927, figure 14.14) is the discarded head of an attempt to hot forge a preform. There is unfortunately no way to tell what the intended shape was in this case. All but the cast lumps are in the "annealed" condition. They in fact may not be annealed in the true sense metallurgically but have been hot-worked and allowed to cool at some unknown rate. This may or may not have been followed by a purely thermal treatment. Table 14.1 summarizes their compositions as determined by PIXE analysis. Six of the ten artifacts are from alloys with tin contents greater than 1%. They range from 1.87% to 16.8% tin. Two others have moderate tin content (0.36% and 0.82%). The other two are essentially free of tin; one (mf 0954), however, has an arsenic content of 4.54%.

Because the shape and metallurgical condition of most of the artifacts are similar, there is no way to deduce the end use of each artifact, and therefore no way to associate the "composition effects" as relating to end use. Thus, the wide variation in tin content appears to be only a poorly controlled composition variable rather than a composition variation by the metalsmith designed to produce the optimum properties for intended use. If these artifacts are indeed the residuum of a metal workshop, then they may be the result of processing trial and error carried out in a strictly empirical manner. Artifacts exhibiting different metalsmithing techniques are:

- mf 9927, by virtue of its flow pattern, exemplifies the attempt to achieve a specific shape in an artifact by pounding a preform into a die of some sort (figure 14.13).
- Similarly, mf 0852.2, which appears to be an attempt at "closed die" forging of a rod originally with an approximately square crosssection into one with a round cross section. It was obviously only partially successful (figure 14.15a, b). Figure 14.15a shows the preexisting fiber in the artifact remaining parallel to the "die" surface during deformation. Conversely, in figure 14.15b, the fiber direction is outward from the center of the artifact in the thick "flash" region.

All of these processes and their variations were also known during the preceding Banesh phase, indicating a centuries-long fundamental conservatism of metalworking technology. Given that artifact mf 3936 (figure 14.4) was moderately tapered, however, the possibility exists that the taper was produced by incremental forging. In an attempt to determine whether this technique was employed, the artifact was immersed in warm 30% formic acid to remove the corrosion crust. Unfortunately, the corrosion penetration and removal of the metal by corrosion was extensive and so variable that the method of forming could not be determined from the current condition of the metal surface after removal of the corrosion crust.

In summary, based on the artifacts recovered from Kaftari deposits in operation ABC, there is no evidence that any new metalworking techniques were developed beyond those already known during the earlier Banesh phase. It is, however, apparent that tin-bronze had now become the alloy of choice, with tin superseding arsenic both as a principal alloy hardening agent and as an element added to copper to produce color changes in the alloy. Composition control and/or optimization were not part of the metalworkers' repertoire. Either they lacked the knowledge, chose not to use it, or were obtaining premixed tin-bronze ingots from elsewhere, and so had no control over the composition.

CONCLUSIONS

The conclusions from the laboratory study are in general agreement with the comments of Nickerson who, in his insightful study of the contexts of Kaftari metal tool finds from a variety of excavation loci at Malyan, states:

> In summary, the data on Group C, metal tools, indicates metal tool use was restricted and not common in the contexts of the analytical units. The tools recovered are types not normally associated with primary manufacturing processes and seem more related to secondary finishing activities. It is evident from the production debris data [that] metalworking/smelting was widespread but not necessarily associated with craft specialized areas. The data suggests the production activities taking place in the analytical units were carried on by part-time consuming producers who directed their activities toward metal production alone and were not involved in producing tools or other finished products. (1991:23; see also Nickerson 1983)

Perhaps the only point of difference is that the MASCA study indicates that metal was being shaped into small tools and implements, the remains of such working having been identified metallographically from ABC. Until an investigation of the "smelting" debris can be undertaken, the nature of metal production at the site remains uncertain.

Regardless of the outcome of a study of production debris, there is little to suggest from either the present study or Nickerson's that Malyan was a major metalworking center. Metal production and metalworking, for which there is remarkably little evidence, appear to have been opportunistic enterprises suiting the immediate needs of people located in a variety of quarters in the settlement. It is, of course, possible that excavation simply did not encounter locations where metal was being produced or worked on the scale one might deem appropriate to a settlement of the size of Kaftari Malyan—130 ha. Surface survey at Malyan did not, however, yield significant concentrations of copper slag and other production debris as is known from other sites on the plateau such as, Tepe Hissar (Bulgarelli 1979; Pigott 1989a) and Shahdad (Hakemi 1992; Salvatori and Vidale 1982).

This apparent lack of major metal processing evidence of any kind at this large site is also interesting in light of suggestions we have made of Elamite involvement in the metals trade. Was metal in ingot form simply passing through on its way elsewhere on the plateau, or perhaps to Khuzestan and Mesopotamia proper? The foregoing study of copper-base metal finds from Malyan has contributed a new body of evidence to our gradually improving understanding of Bronze Age metallurgy in ancient Iran during the late third/early second millennium BCE. It has also shed light on the continually intriguing issue of the trade in metals, especially tin.

Acknowledgments. This study, and its sister study on the Banesh material, have been a long time in reaching print. Bill Sumner in typical fashion exercised inordinate amounts of patience in awaiting the results. The opening seasons at Malyan in 1971 and 1972 were among the very best days Vincent Pigott spent in the field in Iran, and he continues to value Bill's learned counsel and true friendship.

A number of individuals have assisted over time in the laboratory preparation of the Malyan materials in the lab at MASCA. In particular we would like to thank Stephen M. Epstein, Katherine A. Moreau, and Philip M. Nord. Julie Pearce provided invaluable assistance in the preparation of the manuscript and its maps. Stuart J. Fleming (Scientific Director, MASCA) and Charles P. Swann have contributed their considerable expertise in undertaking the PIXE analysis of the copper-base artifacts.

NOTES

1. Malyan's metalworking assemblages fit the time-honored sequence of an arsenical copper use followed by the advent of tin-bronze. In contrast, see the more complex, contemporaneous picture reflected in the metalworking sequences of use from Susa (discussed herein) and Tepe Yahya, where Heskel and Lamberg-Karlovsky (1980) challenge the idea of the traditional linear developmental sequence of native copper, arsenical copper, and tin-bronze (for example, Wertime 1973).

2. At the time PIXE analyses were performed on the Malyan material, we had no reason to undertake the rather difficult detection of cobalt. As Stuart Fleming explains, "Co sits right next to Ni, and usually the Co-level is at least an order of magnitude lower than the Ni-level, so it can be hard to resolve things in the x-ray spectrum. At the same time, to get the best results for the other higher Z elements we look for, we use a selective filter which includes a Co-foil, as a result of which the Co peak usually gets buried. We can use another kind of filter just to search for Co, but that's rather difficult and time-consuming" (personal communication).

3. In ore prospecting, the fact that arsenical copper ores emit a garlicky odor when hammered may well have been used to identify such ores.

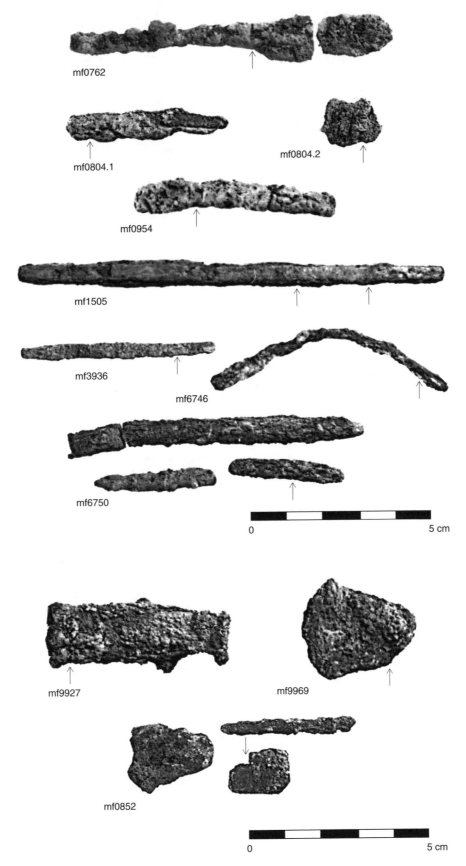

14.4 Kaftari copper-base artifacts: mf 0762, shaped artifact—"hook"; mf 0804.1, barstock, quadrangular in section, pointed at one end; mf 0804.2, slag sample; mf 0954.1.1 and 0954.1.2, rod (mended); mf 1505, barstock, quadrangular section; mf 3936, barstock, quadrangular section; mf 6746, barstock; mf 6750, barstock, quadrangular section; mf 9927, shaped artifact—"blade?"; mf 9969, casting debris—"lump"; mf 0852.2. Arrows show sampled location. *Photographs by Francine Sarin, figure prepared at MASCA*

APPENDIX

MASCA Archaeometallurgical Characterization of Kaftari Phase Copper-base Artifacts from Operation ABC

Small Cu-base Artifacts

Barstock

Rod

Shaped artifacts (including 1 awl, 1 knife, 9 nails, 17 personal ornaments, 6 miscellaneous items—see Nickerson 1991:16, 22)

Cu-base Production Debris in Small Quantities

Prills

Prills in slag

Slag nodules (see Carriveau 1978)

Casting debris

Note: Etchant for all samples was ammonium hydroxide, water, and hydrogen peroxide in the ratio of 5:5:2 unless otherwise noted.

mf 0762

Provenience: Op. C, Lot 21(3), 75, 102

Phase: Kaftari

Form: Shaped artifact—"hook"

Dimensions: L=9.0 cm, W=1.0 cm (flat end), Th=0.5 cm

Sampling location: Longitudinal section taken from shoulder of spatulate end

Metallography (figure 14.5): This artifact is shaped with one end flattened and the other end bent into a "hook." Extensive peripheral corrosion is present. The microstructure is annealed with a very fine grain size (ASTM Grain Size [hereafter GS] no. 9). No significant porosity was seen. Grains are equiaxed with limited evidence of annealing twins, perhaps because of the very small grain size. The artifact was probably worked and reheated several times during shaping.

mf 0804.1

Provenience: Op. A, Lot 13(4)

Phase: Kaftari

Form: Bar stock—quadrangular in section—pointed at one end

Dimensions: L=3.5 cm (thick end), W=0.5 cm, Th=0.4 cm

Sampling location: 2 longitudinal sections were taken from bar—one from each end

Metallography (figure 14.6): Metal was left in the annealed state. Grains are coarse, equiaxed, and contain numerous annealing twins. Moderate number of inclusions elongated and strung out in the lengthwise direction of the strip indicate considerable hot deformation of original material. Extensive coarse porosity flattened and elongated in the lengthwise direction from working was also observed.

The section of the bar at its pointed end shows a large bay extending into the metal. The fiber pattern shows that when sheet was formed, either a trapped piece of mold lining from casting or dirt on the anvil on which the sheet was flattened was hammered into the sheet surface. The trapped piece is not there at present as a result of its removal by corrosion or mechanical means.

Comments: The elemental profile of this sample resembles closely that of the Banesh phase artifacts. This is an arsenical copper artifact bearing no tin in a Kaftari context. Note how similar in composition it is to the other arsenical copper Kaftari artifact mf 0954.

mf 0804.2

Provenience: Op. A, Lot 13(4)

Phase: Kaftari

Form: Prill in slag

Dimensions: L=1.1 cm, W=0.90 cm, Th=0.75 cm

Sampling location: Cross section

Metallography (figure 14.7): Sample shows a dendritic pattern with extensive fine porosity in the interdendritic region.

mf 0954.1.1, mf 0954.1.2

Provenience: Op. B, Lot 7(2), S-17

Phase: Kaftari

Form: Rod

Dimensions: L=5.0 cm, W=0.5 cm, Th=0.4 cm

Sampling location: Cross section and longitudinal section of a roughly circular rod

Metallography (figure 14.8): Two samples of this rod were studied. The cross section of the rod is nearly circular (slightly oval) with two moderately large voids in the center. These may be the remains of a pipe or central porosity from casting. Porosity elsewhere is minimal. There is a high density of fairly small inclusions, slightly coarser in the central region. The aspect ratio of inclusion shape approximates 2 or 3 to 1. No distinct fiber texture is evident. The longitudinal section shows the inclusions to be elongated with an aspect ratio somewhere near 8 to 1 or 10 to 1. There is a strong fiber texture in the axial direction of the rod. This indicates that the original metal was hot deformed, possibly by "open die" forging, reducing the diameter by roughly half and elongating the rod by about four times.

The microstructure is annealed with a moderate grain size (ASTM GS no. 5) and with numerous annealing twins evident. Grains are approximately equiaxed. This sample contains a fine precipitate. This is uniformly distributed throughout the body of the grains; there are, however, some grain boundaries where a precipitate-free zone exists adjacent to that boundary. Precipitate-free zones are also observed near some incoherent annealing twin boundaries.

Comments: The elemental profile of this sample resembles closely that of the Banesh-phase artifacts. The arsenic in particular is unusually high. This is an arsenical copper artifact bearing no tin in a Kaftari context. Note how similar in composition it is to the other arsenical copper Kaftari artifact mf 0804.1.

mf 1505

Provenience: Op. ABC-N, Lot 103(3)/81/200

Phase: Kaftari

Form: Bar stock—quadrangular section

Dimensions: L=12.0 cm, W=0.7 cm, Th=0.4 cm

Sampling location: Cross section

Metallography (figure 14.9): Microstructure appears to be slightly deformed after a prior full annealing treatment. Grains and inclusions are equiaxed; no fibering is seen. The outer periphery is corroded and has extensive corrosion product penetrating inward along strain markings. This sample is different from the others in that a silver-colored, filagreed second phase has formed at many grain corners. These second phase particles tend to be large, comparable to the grain size (ASTM GS no. 3/4). Corrosion along the length of the bar varied widely. At one location the original square cross section remained essentially intact. At two other cross sections the corrosion was so extensive that only a small, nearly circular section of metal remained with a very heavy corrosion crust.

mf 3936

Provenience: N.A., Lot 46 ( )/75/86

Phase: Kaftari

Form: Bar stock—quadrangular section

Dimensions: L=4.6 cm, W=0.4 cm, Th=0.2 cm

Sampling location: Longitudinal section through thickness

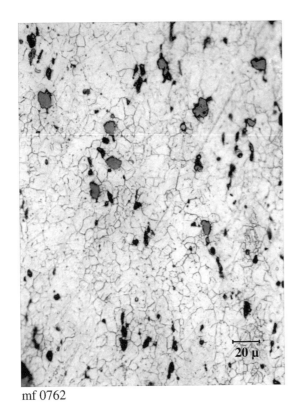

mf 0762

14.5   mf 0762, fine grained, equiaxed, annealed
       microstructure; etched. *Micrograph by S.K. Nash*

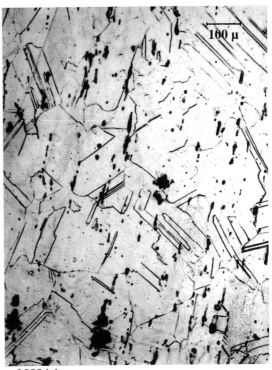

mf 0804.1

14.6 mf 0804.1, coarse grained, equiaxed, annealed
      microstructure, etched. *Micrograph by S.K. Nash*

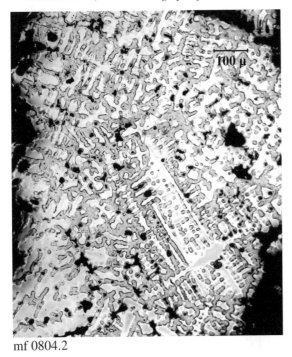

mf 0804.2

14.7   mf 0804.2, prill in slag; as-cast, dendritic
       microstructure; etched. *Micrograph by S.K. Nash*

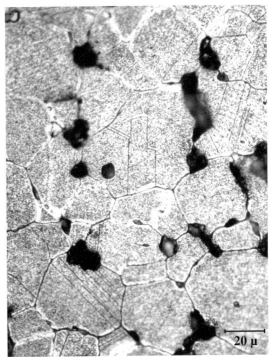

mf 0954

14.8   mf 0954.1, moderate grained, equiaxed, annealed
       microstructure containing a fine precipitate; ammonium
       hydroxide ferric chloride + potassium dichromate etch
       Micrograph by S.K. Nash

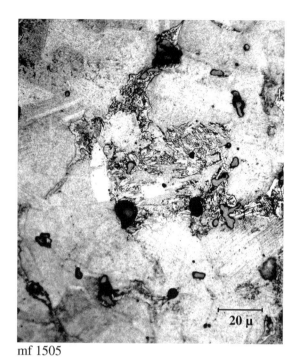

mf 1505

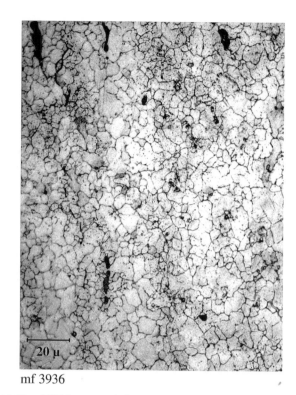

mf 3936

14.9 mf 1505, equiaxed, annealed grains left in light cold-worked condition; ammonium hydroxide ferric chloride + potassium dichromate etch *Micrograph by S.K. Nash*

14.10 mf 3936, extremely fine grained, equiaxed, annealed microstructure; etched. *Micrograph by S.K. Nash*

mf 6746

a

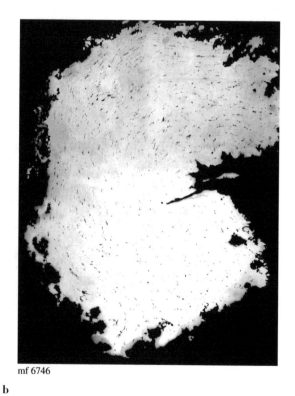

mf 6746

b

14.11 mf 6746: *a*, moderately fine grained, annealed microstructure with matte inclusions; ammonium hydroxide ferric chloride + potassium dichromate etch; *b*, montage of bar cross-section. *Micrograph by S.K. Nash*

Metallography (figure 14.10): This piece of barstock may be a finished artifact as one end is finished: that is, it appears rounded-off. Extensive corrosion is present. Moderate size inclusions are elongated in fiber direction, that is, along the length of the strip. Microstructure appears to be annealed with an extremely fine grain size (ASTM GS no. 10). There appear to be annealing twins present, but the extremely fine grain size makes them difficult to see. Differential etching response reveals the residual trace of a fine cast structure not yet removed by thermal treatment.

mf 6746

Provenience: Op. A, Lot 33(6)/85/
Phase: Kaftari
Form: Bar stock—mildly tapered and irregularly curved
Dimensions: L=6.5 cm, W=0.3 cm, Th=0.3 cm
Sampling location: 2 cross sections, one from each end
Metallography (figure 14.11): Both cross sections have the same periphery, the major portion of which has circular curvature; the remainder is flat with a small notch.

Figure 14.11a shows inclusions that are somewhat elongated, but there is extensive associated porosity that gives a distinctive fiber pattern. The pattern of flow of the metal is parallel to the curved portion of the surface, the curvature increasing as the center of curvature is approached. Microstructure is a moderately fine-grained (ASTM GS no. 5/6) structure with numerous annealing twins. SEM was performed indicating that the nonmetallic inclusions consist of CuFeS, that is, matte. The presence of matte suggests the possibility of the smelting of a copper sulfide ore and/or the practice of co-smelting of a mixture of oxidic and sulfidic ores (Rostoker et al. 1983; Rostoker and Dvorak 1991).

Figure 14.11b is a montage of the bar cross section showing its general shape. Inclusion elongation and fiber pattern indicate that this bar was formed from thick sheet, either bent flat with the flat portion subsequently removed or by removing a small strip from such a sheet and hammering it into a semi-cylindrical "die."

mf 6750.1

Provenience: Op. B1, Lot 6, (3)/3/
Phase: Kaftari
Form: Bar stock—quadrangular section
Dimensions: L=7.5 cm, W=0.6 cm, Th=0.6 cm
Sampling location: Cross section
Metallography (figure 14.12): microstructure shows fine equiaxed grains (ASTM GS approximately no. 7). All grain boundaries are heavily penetrated by corrosion product, but no transcrystalline corrosion is evident. A few relatively large holes are present, but these are probably the result of grain pullout or fallout during polishing. Metal is annealed with a high density of relatively thick annealing twins.

mf 9927

Provenience: Op. C, Lot 44 /72/
Phase: Kaftari
Form: Shaped artifact—"Blade?"
Dimensions: L=3 cm, W=1 cm, Th=0.25 cm
Sampling location: Cross section and longitudinal section (and short transverse)
Metallography (figure 14.13): This appears to be a portion of an originally longer artifact, perhaps a blade. The initial preform was probably a round or square rod, flattened to give a cross section resembling an oval. This low magnification longitudinal section shows the head mushroomed from pounding it into a shaped cavity, a possible "die." This part with the pounded head was then apparently removed from the

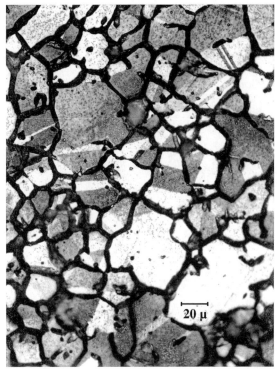

mf 6750

14.12 mf 6750, fine grained, equiaxed, annealed microstructure; ammonium hydroxide ferric chloride + potassium dichromate etch. *Micrograph by S.K. Nash*

remainder of the blade and discarded. This artifact is the discard from this operation.

The artifact is very heavily corroded with a multilayer corrosion crust. In addition, there is extensive intergranular and transgranular corrosion penetration around the periphery.

In terms of the microstructure (figure 14.12b), the bulk of the artifact shows equiaxed grains with numerous annealing twins (ASTM GS no. 6). The mushroomed head area is in a deformed state. There are numerous inclusions and strong fiber texture paralleling the longitudinal direction. Inclusions in longitudinal section have a much larger aspect ratio than in the cross section.

mf 9969

Provenience: Op.C1, Lot 12 (2) /8\ |39|
Phase: Kaftari?
Form: Casting debris (flattish lump)
Dimensions: L=3.2 cm, W=2.8 cm Th=4.0 cm
Sampling location: Cross section near tip, one farther into the artifact itself
Metallography (figure 14.14): This piece of casting debris is highly corroded. Cross section is irregular. The grains are approximately equiaxed, but the grain size is duplex, either ASTM GS no. 0 or 2. This appears to be an as-cast polycrystalline microstructure with no evidence of strain markings or annealing twins. Etching revealed an extensive network of subgrains within each grain. There is also extensive intergranular porosity, particularly in the mid-thickness region. Corrosion has penetrated the grain boundaries of many of the grains in the surface region.

a mf 9927   b mf 9927

14.13 mf 9927, *a*, equiaxed, annealed microstructure possibly "die-formed"; *b*, cross section, length 1.3 cm. *Photograph by Francine Sarin, micrograph by S.K. Nash*

mf 0852.2

Provenience: Op. A, Lot 37

Phase: Banesh/Kaftari

Form: Rod

Dimensions: L=3.0 cm, W=0.25 cm, Th=0.30 cm

Sampling location: Cross section

Metallography (figure 14.15): cross section of a bar having a fully annealed, fine grained (ASTM GS 7/8) microstructure. Bar is roughly circular in cross section but with extensive flow normal to this surface at two locations 180° apart. This flow pattern in figures 14.15a and 14.15b is indicative of an attempt to form a circular bar by a "closed die" forging technique utilizing two hemi-cylindrical dies and using as a preform a square bar cut from a previously formed sheet or plate. The attempt was only partially successful because of insufficient forming pressure and too much material overfilling the die cavity. The material conformed to the cylindrical die cavities showing a pattern of elongated inclusions parallel to the surface. As in any closed die forging operation, the excess material tends to flow laterally out of the "die" cavities to form a flash with fiber and grain flow away from the center of the rod. What would normally be a thin flash formed in the course of a proper execution was very thick in this case because of the excess material present. Figure 14.15b shows extensive corrosion penetration at the "flash" surface caused by the galvanic cells developed by fire alternating metal in fusion couples.

Comments on context and chronology: William Sumner has stated that the three metal artifacts numbered mf 0852.2 come from a mixed lot on the basis of the fact that the lot produced 41 Banesh sherds and 57 Kaftari sherds. We will consider this sample as Kaftari based on its tin content.

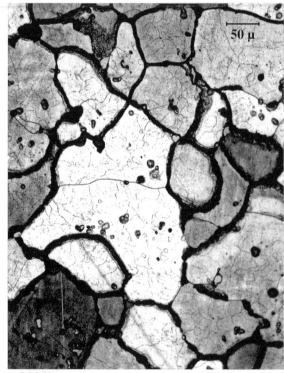

mf 9969

14.14 mf 9969, as-cast, polycrystalline microstructure with extensive network of subgrains; ammonium hydroxide ferric chloride + potassium dichromate etch. *Micrograph by S.K. Nash*

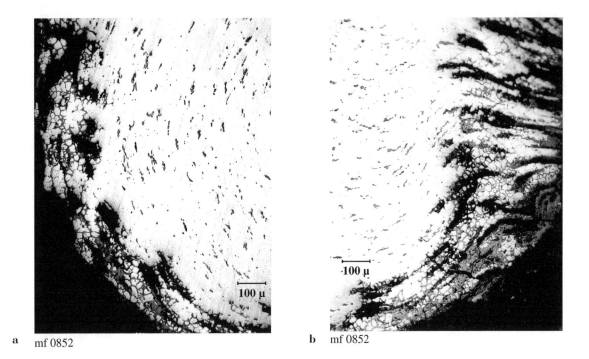

a   mf 0852   b   mf 0852

14.15 *a*, mf 0852.2, fine grained, annealed microstructure possibly "closed-die" formed; as polished/unetched; *b*, mf 0852.2,
Extensive corrosion penetration. *Micrographs by S.K. Nash*

15.1   Bronze statue of Queen Napir-Asu. Susa. *Louvre Museum Sb 2731. After Harper et al. 1992:133, No. 83*

CHAPTER 15

RECONSIDERING
THE *TROUVAILLE DE LA STATUETTE D'OR*

Late Sukkalmah Period at Susa

HOLLY PITTMAN

THE ELAMITES of the second millennium are among the more elusive subjects of modern historical scholarship. We reconstruct their history and culture from fragments of evidence—textual, artifactual—found at sites both in Mesopotamia and Iran. For the most part, these evidentiary bits have only vague archaeological provenance: "the Acropolis at Susa;" "found in Fars;" "said to be from Nippur." As a result of his excavations at Malyan, the Elamite highland capital city of Anshan in the present-day Iranian province of Fars, Bill Sumner has given scholars a rich body of material that we can use to flesh out our collective skeletal efforts to characterize these distant and enigmatic folk. The body of evidence from Malyan is archaeologically well-controlled and well-recorded. Because of its high quality, not only do we learn substantially more about the Elamites from the perspective of their highland capital city but we can also reflect again upon other, weaker evidence and reconsider accumulated and received interpretations with fresh eyes. I owe Bill much, not the least for willingly taking me on as a fledgling and entrusting me with visual treasures through which I have come to know the Elamites. In admiration, gratitude, and friendship, I offer him here a cluster of insights that emerged during my ongoing efforts to illuminate the glyptic art from Malyan. It is a result achieved through art historical analysis, a mode of scholarship that Bill both encourages and appreciates, even though it seems at times like "magic" to him.

THE *TROUVAILLE DE LA STATUETTE D'OR*

Apart from the bronze masterpiece of the queen Napir-Asu (figure 15.1), perhaps the most famous objects of Elamite art are two statuettes of offering bearers, one of gold and the other of silver (figures 15.2, 15.3). In an exceedingly rare situation at Susa, the find spot of these small, powerful sculptures was specifically recorded. They were found along with a number of other objects by Roland de Mecquenem when excavating in Jacques de Morgan's trench 27 close to the base of the ziggurat and in between the temples of Inshushinak and Ninhursag on the Acropolis at Susa (Mecquenem 1905b:131–136). Soon after their discovery, historical and archaeological surveys (Cameron 1936:125–126, 207–209; Carter 1984) placed them chronologically at the height of the Middle Elamite imperial power, during the thirteenth or more likely the twelfth century, when Shutruk-Nahhunte I, king of Anshan and Susa (1150 BCE–1120 BCE), led the Elamites in defeat of the Kassites and carried back to Susa the Codex Hammurabi, the stela of Naram-Sin, and other trophies that were then, as now, paradigmatic monuments of Mesopotamian cultural and political achievement.

What I will argue here is that these two statuettes are not of twelfth-century Middle Elamite date but rather that they and related finds from the vicinity of the temple of Inshushinak on the Acropolis of Susa, were made and used (if not deposited) during an earlier period of Elamite florescence, during the time period of the dynasty of the Sukkalmah. The proposed redating accomplishes two

15.2 Gold figurine from the trouvaille. Susa. *Louvre Museum Sb 2758. After Harper et al. 1992: Front 147, No. 89, Back 148, No. 89*

things. First, these objects have never fit comfortably with securely dated Middle Elamite period visual materials. Second, these objects can now be used to provide stylistic and iconographic detail to a period that we have known up to now primarily through textual evidence. The eighteenth and seventeenth centuries BCE were a time of significant Elamite political achievement when the Sukkalmah dynasty successfully contended with powerful Amorite states for hegemony over the trade routes crisscrossing the resource rich highlands of Iran, northern Mesopotamian and Anatolia and linking them with the sea trade active in the Persian Gulf.

Mecquenem published the group as a coherent find dubbed the *trouvaille de la statuette d'or*. This group, hereafter referred to as the trouvaille, was a cluster of more than eighty small objects found together on top of a small platform constructed of two rows of three glazed bricks set on top of a mass of tightly packed earth. In addition to the two statuettes, there were nine small figurines of faience, a lapis lazuli bird with inlaid gold markings (figure 15.4), a lapis bull's head pendant, a whetstone terminating with the protome of a lion rendered in gold (figure 15.5), an agate pendant carved in high relief as a recumbent lion, an inscribed agate bead, and numerous other beads of agate and carnelian. Mixed together with these objects were bones of a goat or lamb, presumed to be a sacrificial offering.

At first, Mecquenem (1905b) argued that the find was a foundation deposit for a Middle Elamite temple which he surmised stood close to the Middle Elamite ziggurat and temples of Inshushinak and other deities. Later he changed his mind, suggesting that the objects had not been a coherent deposit but that they were from a vaulted tomb that had been looted (Mecquenem 1943–44:141).[1] Tallon (1994:146) accepts neither of these explanations, arguing instead that the objects might be more accurately thought of as votive items that had been deposited in a chapel for the royal funerary cult. Descriptions of such chapels, called *suhters*, tell us that they contained statues of the king, or of members of the royal family and images of protector gods along with other precious objects (Grillot 1983).

It is noteworthy that Mecquenem (1905b:136) does not assign a date of manufacture to any of the objects, preferring instead to speculate only on the time of their interment. He established the *terminus ante quem* for the trouvaille through two independent lines of evidence, neither clearcut. The first is the presence in the deposit of an agate bead inscribed with a dedication to the deity Ishtaran made by one Kurigalzu (Mecquenem 1905b:135). Two kings of that name ruled the Kassite kingdom from Dur Kurigalzu close to Babylon in central Mesopotamia. Kurigalzu II conquered Elam during his reign (1332–1308 BCE). Tallon (1994:153) suggests that the bead might have belonged to

15.3 Silver figurine from the trouvaille. Susa. *Louvre Museum Sb 2759. After Harper et al. 1992: Front 147, No. 90, Back 148, No. 89*

the earlier Kurigalzu I who reigned from 1400–1375 BCE. If that is the case, she reasonably offers that it might have come to Susa along with other Mesopotamian booty brought by Shutruk-Nahhunte I. However, rather than dating the entire contents of the deposit, we must recognize, as Mecquenem did, that this inscribed bead can at best provide a terminal date for the deposit. Even this possibility is thrown in doubt if it was, like other objects in the deposit, an heirloom when buried.

The second independent criterion of date brought to bear on this collection of objects is the fact that it was found slightly below a pavement that is assumed, on the basis of inscribed bricks, to belong to the time of the Middle Elamite kings. However, rather than providing a stratigraphic *terminus ante quem,* all the interpreters of these objects have assumed that the deposit must have been laid down together with or after the pavement was constructed, either as a foundation deposit or as materials from a Middle Elamite tomb or a chapel.

THE STATUETTES

Neither the textual nor the archaeological evidence, then, provides independent criteria of time for the manufacture of the various other objects within the deposit. Their dating can be established best through the scrutiny of individual objects, and by evaluating each through comparison of both

formal and iconographic elements to comparanda securely anchored in the established chronological matrix of Elamite material culture. The iconography of the offering bearer is one that has a long history in greater Mesopotamia and is by itself therefore of little use for dating purposes. This theme, however, combined with features of style, provides evidence for the temporal placement of these objects. Among the highly distinctive stylistic features of these statuettes, their garment and head gear, bodily proportions, and facial features all contribute to this discussion.

The statuettes, just over 7 cm in height including their base, are solid cast, one in silver, the other in gold (Tallon 1994:146–148). Each is secured mechanically by means of an anchoring device to a squarish bronze base that is in poor, and fragmentary, condition. They appear, in fact, to have been cut from a much larger bronze base. Both sculptures represent a bearded male supporting an animal with the left arm while bending the other upward toward the shoulder in a gesture of respect or submission. The images are, for symbolic purposes, virtually identical except for intentional differences in their material and in the species of animal offering they bear. Details of their garment, a skirt covered with dots and their torso covered with stars, and headdress, apparently a net held in place by a twist, have provoked the most extensive discussion in considerations of their date and will continue to be a focus of discussion here.

15.4   Lapis lazuli bird from the trouvaille. Susa.
Louvre Museum Sb 2887.
After Harper et al. 1992:151, No. 96

15.5. Whetstone handle with gold lion protome finial. Susa.
Louvre Museum Sb 2769. After Harper et al. 1992:149,
No. 91

The distinctive garment provides the best way into the discussion of these objects. This stylistic detail was first invoked by Porada (1962:56–58) and most recently remarked by Tallon (1994:148) to justify a late date through comparison to a figure on the second register of the Untash-Napirisha stela (figure 15.6). In fact, the patterned garment compares more closely in the manner of its rendering to one worn by a figure on a stela dated through inscription to the middle of the eighteenth century BCE (figure 15.7). The garment in question is a long skirt, secured at the waist by double belt and trimmed at the bottom by a heavy fringe. Its most striking aspect is the dense pattern of dots distributed evenly over the surface. This dotted garment is unknown in Mesopotamia and the west and seems to be distinctly Elamite. While its precise meaning is uncertain, it is worn by both males (bearded, or bald and clean shaven), and females who engage in acts of offering or homage.

One securely dated comparison made with the dotted garment of the statuettes is found on the Middle Elamite monuments inscribed to Untash-Napirisha (1340–1300

BCE). Both the male figure on the second register of his stela (figure 15.6) and the bronze sculpture of his queen (figure 15.1) wear a skirt similarly covered with an overall pattern of dots. While there is little question that each of these distinctly dotted garments represents the same significantly elaborated textile as that worn by the small figures in bronze, gold, and silver, a close comparison among them reveals a marked stylistic difference that can function as independent criterion of date. The dots on the statuettes are made by a single punch with a pointed graver while the dots on the stela of Untash-Napirisha as well as on the bronze statue of queen Napir-Asu are composite, formed by a circle inscribed around a central point. All of the Middle Elamite examples of this distinctive form of dotted pattern are constructed in this way regardless of medium, including the skirt of a fragmentary large limestone statue inscribed with a dedication to Untash-Napirisha found at Susa (figure 15.8) (Spycket 1981:No. 199).

INSHUSHINAK TEMPLE DEPOSIT

Before pursuing this stylistic detail further, another group of figures, also found at Susa, can be brought into the discussion. This is a series of small statuettes closely related to the precious metal ones under consideration here. Cast in bronze, these also depict male figures in an act of offering an animal sacrifice, in these instances usually a bird (figures 15.9, 15.10). While differing in some details, especially the treatment of the head, they are strikingly similar to the precious metal figurines in iconography, bodily proportions, facial features, and garment. It is likely for that reason that they too are assigned to the Middle Elamite period (Amiet 1966a, 1985; Porada 1962; Tallon 1994). Given their close similarity with the gold and silver statuettes, I include these bronze figures as well in the following argument which seeks to establish their date.

Nine of these bronze figures, reported as part of a large corpus of objects, were discovered just before the trouvaille. This assemblage is far less homogeneous than the trouvaille and was spread over a larger area in de Morgan's trench 23. These objects were found in a layer some 60 cm thick at a depth of 4 m below the surface of the mound and, like the trouvaille, just below the so-called Middle Elamite pavement. Unfortunately no observations were made about the internal association of objects or their relationship to architectural features. Mecquenem presents them in the final report not by provenance or cluster but by material (Mecquenem 1905a:61–130).

It seems that the *terminus ante quem* of this mass of objects was determined by the presence of inscriptions on fragmentary sheets of gold and one of silver. According to

a   b

15.6   *a*, Untash-Napirisha stela; *b*, drawing of Untash-Napirisha stela. Susa. *Louvre Museum Sb 12, after Miroschedji 1980*

Scheil, who never formally published them, they are in the Elamite language and they seem to make allusions to the god Shushinak and to women, either queens or priestesses. Reportedly, he related them to Untash-Napirisha, Shutruk-Nahunte, or Shilhak-Inshushinak (Mecquenem 1905a:69, 71 n. 1, Pl. 12, Figs. 17–30). Subsequent examination by assyriologists M.W. Stolper, E. Leichty, and J. Polonsky (personal communications) suggests that nothing in the sign forms requires they be late rather than early second millennium. Unlike the smaller and more coherent trouvaille, Mecquenem realized that some of the objects in the Inshushinak deposit were much older than Middle Elamite. Subsequently Amiet (for example, 1966a:310–311, 407) assigned a number of objects from this deposit to the Sukkalmah period on the basis of style and iconography.

STELA OF SHIRUKTUH

There is to my knowledge only one securely dated example of this distinctive garment rendered as it is on the small bronze, gold, and silver statuettes by means of individually gouged marks made with a pointed tool. It appears on the fragment of a stela carved of limestone, without known provenance, first published by Peter Calmeyer (1973). Farber (1975) assigns the stela to the king Shiruktuh on the basis of its fragmentary but extensive inscription (figure 15.7). Shiruktuh was an Elamite ruler of the Sukkalmah dynasty known from Mesopotamian records to have been a contemporary of Shamshi-Adad of Assyria (1812 BCE–1781 BCE). The stela carries a relief representation of a skirted figure at the top. Below the figure and continuing on the side and back of the stela, a list, written in Elamite

15.7 Stela of Shiruktuh. Provenance unknown. *After Farber 1975:Abb. 1*

cuneiform, enumerates the places "taken" by the Shiruktuh as sukkalmah.

The fragmentary representation preserves the bottom half of a human figure, probably male, standing facing left on a distinctively shaped niched, two-tiered platform. Significant for this discussion is his skirt which is covered with a dense pattern of dots each made through a single strike of an engraving tool. The skirt is a textile wrapped around the waist of the figure. A heavy fringe borders one edge and surrounds his feet before continuing up his side probably to be tucked in at the waist. This garment can either be a long tube or it can be a wrapped length of fabric with fringed border. It is on the basis of the close stylistic similarity of garment that I conclude that the statuettes of gold, silver, and bronze were made at a time not too distant from that of the stela, that is to say during the latter part of the long period of the dynasty of the Sukkalmah. With that established, we can make other iconographic and stylistic observations that reinforce this conclusion and that throw light on this obscure but significant period of the Late Sukkalmah. Before turning to those individual details, a summary of historical context is useful.

HISTORICAL BACKGROUND

I draw here on a variety of secondary sources to summarize very briefly what is relevant from the little we know of the Sukkalmah period (Cameron 1936; Charpin 1986; Durand 1986; Edzard 1957; Farber 1975; Grillot and Glassner 1991; M. Lambert 1971; W. Lambert 1979; Limet 1985; Stolper 1982, 1984a; Vallat 1989a, 1989b, 1989c, 1990a; Van Dijk 1970, 1978; see also chapter 3). The Sukkalmah was the longest-lived stable political system in the history of ancient Elam. Its duration is measured through the use of a triad of titles: the sukkal of Susa, the sukkal of Elam and Shimashki, and the paramount ruler, or the sukkalmah. These titles are originally Mesopotamian, carried by the Ur III officials who governed late third millennium Elam. After this Mesopotamian hegemony was broken, the Elamites retained the titles, transforming their meaning to denote levels in the hierarchy of what has been reconstructed as a sovereign tripartite confederacy which joined together in one larger political system people from much of southwestern Iran. The triad of titles first appears associated with a ruler who comes to power in the twentieth century and continues in essentially unbroken use for a long time. Stolper associates this titulary with as many as five sovereigns who reigned after Ammisaduqa, the late Old Babylonian king (1646 BCE–1626 BCE) suggesting that the

15.8 Untash-Napirisha statue. *Louvre Sb 61. After Spycket 1981:Pl. 199*

2   1   3

15.9 Bronze statuette from the Inshushinak deposit. *Louvre Museum Sb 2889. After Mecquenem 1905a:Pl. 15, nos. 2, 1, 3*

5   4   6

15.10 Bronze statuette from the Inshushinak deposit. *Louvre Museum Sb 2747. After Mecquenem 1905a:Pl. 15, Nos. 5, 4, 6*

confederate form of political organization may have continued in existence "into the sixteenth and possibly as late as the early fifteenth century BC"(1984a:32).

Given the paucity of evidence, we can characterize little more than an earlier and a later phase of this long Elamite political and cultural entity. The early phase begins with the founding of the dynasty by a certain Ebarat, the second king of that name and the ninth king of the Shimashki king list. Although Ebarat II's dates are not certain, Vallat (1989a, 1990a) argues that he held power as early as the first half of the twentieth century some time around 1970 BCE. During this time, southern Mesopotamia had reorganized into a series of kingdoms following the collapse of the Ur III empire. It was dominated by the Dynasty of Isin (2017 BCE–1794 BCE) and the contemporaneous Dynasty of Larsa (2025 BCE–1763 BCE), especially under Gungunum (1932 BCE–1906 BCE).

Early in the twentieth century, Bilalama held sway over an independent Eshnunna controlling access into central Mesopotamia from the east. Merchants at Assur were active in northern Mesopotamia until it was unified almost a hundred years later under the Amorite king Shamshi-Adad (1813 BCE–1781 BCE). This combination of powerful western kingdoms seems to have kept the core of Elamite power at a safe distance to the east. During this early part of the Sukkalmah period, the capital of the confederacy was Malyan (ancient Anshan), an enormous city with a densely populated agricultural hinterland in an upland valley of Fars (Sumner 1988a, 1989a).

While we know next to nothing of the politics of this dynamic phase, we do have artifactual residue in the archaeological record that suggests that there was intense interaction between the Elamites, both at Anshan and at Susa, and their neighbors to the east, northeast, and southeast. This is obvious in particular through materials found along the southern route to the east at Tepe Yahya and at Shahdad as well as in the Persian Gulf (Amiet 1986a).

The transition to the later Sukkalmah phase occurred in the power vacuum created by the death of Shamshi-Adad in the early eighteenth century. The center and the focus of Sukkalmah political power shifted; we know through both Elamite and Mesopotamian documents that the Elamites extended their western border, probably beginning under Shiruktuh, whose victories are recorded on his stela. Under his leadership and that of his subordinate relatives and successors, the sukkals Simut-wartash, Siweparaluk, and Kudulush, the Elamites took control of Eshnunna in the Diyala river valley, the pivotal point on the trade route to the northeast. Eshnunna had been a powerful independent kingdom before the time of Shamshi-Adad, who in turn used it as a buffer between Assyria and Elam. With Shamshi-Adad gone, the Elamites felt little resistance on their western border.

Apparently it is during this time of great Elamite power that the titulary of the Sukkalmah confederacy changed to a sukkal of Elam and Shimashki. From this point on Anshan does not appear in the titulary of the Sukkalmah. Perhaps this new emphasis on Shimashki in the titulary reflects a new balance of power among the geographic centers of the confederacy (Börker-Klähn 1970:187). This Elamite hegemony, which at its greatest extended all the way to Mari on the Khabur, was brief, lasting no more than fifty years. During the thirtieth year of Hammurabi (1792 BCE–1750 BCE), the Elamites were driven back, first expelled from Mari, and later from Eshnunna. Although kept at bay until the end of the reign of Ammisaduqa, the Elamites were a constant source of irritation for the Old Babylonian monarchs.

After this brief moment as a global player, Elam was reduced and kept in check by its neighbors the Kassites, who took control of Babylon following the collapse of the Old Babylonian dynasty before the Hittites in 1595 BCE. The Kassites held stewardship over the Tigris and Euphrates region until they were eclipsed in the twelfth century by another phase of Elamite interregional dominance. Following the reestablishment of a powerful Elamite political entity under Untash-Napirisha, Shilhak-Inshushinak projected Elam once again onto the global stage for a second brief moment of glory, known to us as the Middle Elamite period.

PRE- AND EARLY SUKKALMAH ART

Coinciding with the roughly defined historical phases of the Sukkalmah confederacy, two corresponding phases can be discerned in the glyptic art defined through features of carving, materials, size, and iconography (Pittman N.D.). Given the historical record, it is not surprising that connections to the east are apparent in the early phase while during the later phase these seem to recede, allowing the connections to Mesopotamia to predominate.

Our knowledge of the visual arts is even more spotty than the history for the early phase of the Elamite record. For the period preceding the Sukkalmah, we have several major Elamite sculptural and relief monuments identified through bilingual inscriptions naming Puzur-Inshushinak the last king of the Dynasty of Awan (ca. 2100 BCE). The statue of the goddess Narunde, her lion,[2] and fragments of a door socket all exhibit Elamite imagery rendered in a style strongly influenced by Mesopotamian prototypes.

a   b

15.11   Silver vase. *Tehran, Iran Bastan Museum. After Hinz 1969: Tf. 4, 5*

Another notable contemporary visual monument is the silver vase (figure 15.11) reported to have been found in Fars not far from Persepolis (Hinz 1969). The vase carries representations of two female figures and a linear Elamite inscription certainly to be associated with the time of Puzur-Inshushinak.

Apart from the distinctive bituminous limestone tripods and vessels carved with animal and divine figures (Amiet 1966a:278–282), only the glyptic art is well-known for the Sukkalmah period. Beginning late in the Dynasty of Shimashki and continuing through the entire span of the Sukkalmah, it is possible to chart the development of Elamite glyptic iconography and style through inscribed seals or their ancient impressions (Amiet 1972, 1973a, 1980a; Börker-Klähn 1970; W. Lambert 1979; Porada 1988, 1990; Seidl 1990). There are two categories in the Sukkalmah glyptic—official seals that are usually inscribed and more crudely cut seals that never carry extensive in-scriptions. Both types are well represented at Susa and at Anshan, suggesting that we do not have a reflection of sharp regional differences (contra Amiet 1986a:153). Among the inscribed seals, the theme of the offering bearer approaching a divine figure is attested in the official glyptic associated with the reign of Attahushu (figure 15.12). It is also used on official seals of two earlier Shimashkian kings.

The theme of the offering bearer has its origin in mid-third millennium Mesopotamia. Its earliest attestation at Susa, dating to the dynasty of Awan (Amiet 1966a:190–191), is a three-dimensional sculpture which is hardly distinguishable from its Mesopotamian prototype. The offering bearer is a theme in the glyptic of the Old Akkadian period (Boehmer 1965:Abb. 387) and may enter the Elamite repertory at that time. The theme is found only on seals of the Sukkalmah having strong Mesopotamian connections; indeed, a good number of them are recut Mesopotamian seals (see, for example, Amiet 1972:No. 1756). More often

15.12 Offering bearer sealing. *Louvre Museum Sb 1445. After Amiet 1972:No. 1684*

a

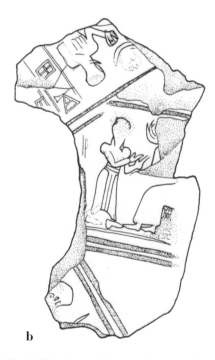

b

15.13 *a*, Typical Elamite worshipper seal. *Louvre Museum Sb 5398. After Amiet 1972:No. 1682; b,* Drawing of ancient impression of seal showing typical Elamite worshipper. Malyan (M1318/mf 5552, H5 lot 100, building level 4a). *H. Pittman*

the Elamite worshiper is not shown carrying an offering but rather with both hands extended forward, palm up, either in a gesture of anticipated receipt or in a gesture of adoration as on a seal from Susa (figure 15.13a) and on an unpublished seal impression from Malyan (figure 15.13b). Although perhaps an accident of preservation, the theme of the king as offering bearer is not recorded from Malyan. Alternatively, it is possible that it denoted an office or a ritual that was not relevant to highland Iranian cultural life but rather was more meaningful to Elamites who were closer to the Mesopotamian sphere.

The theme of offering bearer is also attested among the terracotta figures dated typologically to the Sukkalmah period (Spycket 1992:No. 838). It is interesting that some of these terracotta figurines wear skirts having dotted garments identical to those of the bronze, gold, and silver figures considered here.

The dedication of a golden statue of the king is found among the year names from the reigns of the Old Babylonian kings Ammiditana (1684 BCE–1647 BCE) and Samsuditana (1625 BCE–1595 BCE) (Finkelstein 1959; Porada 1965:233; Tallon 1994:148). Further, we know that Samsuiluna named a year marking the creation of two royal images, one of silver and one of gold. With our present evidence we can only speculate that the general purpose of making the statuettes of the trouvaille was adapted from a Mesopotamian practice just as the theme itself.

In addition to the Mesopotamian theme of the offering bearer, three details of iconography elaborated in the seals are relevant to our statuettes: the dotted garment, the stepped and niched platform with pointed sides, and the unusual headgear. Interestingly, each of them raises connections to the Iranian plateau to the east. I have found the dotted garment only once on seals, represented on one of five known early Sukkalmah royal seals.[3] This type was first identified by W. Lambert in the collection of the Gulbenkian Museum (figure 15.14). While these royal seals are not recorded at Susa, several examples can be reconstructed among the materials excavated from Anshan (for example, figure 15.15). In addition, three unprovenanced examples are published, all carved from extremely hard, semiprecious, stones including amethyst, and rock crystal in a refined style closely comparable to the impressions from Malyan. One of these seals (Porada 1990:Pl. 1a), carved in amethyst, carries a seated royal figure who wears a dotted garment and offers plant-sprouting water to a female who squats before him on a low platform (figure 15.16). While the basic scheme of this royal iconography is ultimately Mesopotamian, this composition is distinctly Elamite with features that strongly associate it with highland tradition

(Porada 1990; Steve 1989). I suggest that the dotted garment might have had its earliest royal associations from a highland rather than a lowland symbolic source.

A second iconographic detail associated with the figure wearing the dotted skirt may also reflect eastern ties. This is the architectural feature of a stepped niched platform whose ends are shaped as right triangles. While not directly related to the statuettes, this platform is clearly associated with the dotted skirted figure on the Shiruktuh stela (figure 15.7). The earliest appearance of this platform known to me is, like the dotted garment, found on seals. But this time, it is documented on a seal that can be dated to a period equivalent to Yahya IVA, that is to say sometime around 1900 BCE (figure 15.17) (Amiet 1986a:300, No. 137). This platform is first documented in the iconography of the Sukkalmah in the Shiruktuh stela, and it remains important in the royal iconography of the Elamites through the later part of the Sukkalmah, appearing on seals from the reigns of Kuk-Nashur and Tan-Uli (figure 15.18a, b, c). On these official seals of the Sukkalmah, as on the earlier seal from the east, the platform supports divine figures who receive homage from a mortal, probably royal, figure. Further, it probably serves as a support for the enthroned diety carved on the rock relief at Kurangun (figure 15.19).

A final detail of imagery that links the statuettes to the Elamite east is their unique headgear. Porada (1965) and Tallon (1994) have both compared the netting to that worn by the copper head now in the Metropolitan Museum of Art (Muscarella 1988). While this is certainly a valid comparison, another feature of the headgear may also be relevant. This is the twist of fabric or hair that crosses the crown. This same twist adorns the head of the female figure who squats opposite her standing counterpart on the silver vase in Tehran (figure 15.11). Although the metaphysical status (royal or divine) and the identity of this figure is unknown, she is certainly related to sculptural examples such as one found in regular excavations (Hiebert 1994:150, Fig. 9:12) and many others reportedly from northern Afghanistan (Pottier 1984:136–140); she is also related to the squatting woman on the royal seals of the early Sukkalmah who receive the abundance of the king. Indeed, the twist crossing the crown of the head of the squatting female on the vase is formally identical to the band worn by the precious metal kings of the trouvaille. Further, the overflowing length of the skirt of the statuettes in each case, generously covering the shoes whose toes peek out, uses the same convention as the bare feet of the skirted figures on the silver vase.

OTHER OBJECTS IN THE TROUVAILLE AND THE INSHUSHINAK DEPOSIT

While I do not propose to examine the entire contents of the two deposits here, there are several other categories of objects that can be profitably brought into this discussion as likely to also belong to the Sukkalmah period. The first is the approximately forty cylinder seals that were found in the Inshushinak deposit (Mecquenem 1905a:Pls. 20–23). It is striking that among them none of the seals from the deposit are later than the Sukkalmah period. While it is not impossible that all of these seals were heirlooms when taken out of circulation and added to this deposit, we see a very different practice in the Middle Elamite chapels at Chogha Zanbil. There in the chapels close to the ziggurat seals were frequently deposited as votives. Only a very few among the seal votives were heirlooms (Porada 1970). Assuming commonality of cultural practice, the homogeneity of the Inshushinak seals may also have been offered to the deity when they were still administratively current.

THE LAPIS LAZULI BIRD

Another remarkable object found in the trouvaille deserves mention in this consideration of the date of the statuettes. This is a stunning and large sculpture of a bird at rest, carved from a single large piece of solid lapis lazuli, with separate pieces used only for the beak and tail (see figure 15.4). Its plump body is inlaid with large spots of gold (Amiet 1966a:435–436; Tallon 1994:151–154). While the gold and silver statuettes of the trouvaille carry a quadruped as offering, the bronze figures in the Inshushinak deposit carry a bird, usually identified as a dove, as do several of the faience figures found in the trouvaille.

Unlike the goat as offering, the dove seems to be a central Mesopotamian and Elamite theme that is not found commonly in southern Mesopotamia (Börker-Klähn 1970:Tf. 13). Beginning in Sukkalmah, both water fowl and doves are abundantly represented, being especially common on the pottery both from Susa and Anshan (Amiet 1966a:No. 111; Sumner 1974:Figs. 6–7, 1989a). On the seals of the Sukkalmah as well, such birds are often present in scenes of homage, placed between figures, or resting on an offering table (Amiet 1972:Nos. 1893–1899).

Another, more enigmatic, association is established between the figure with the dotted skirt and birds on the Shiruktuh stela. There, two doves serve as the shoes (or feet) of the standing figure. That such a large chunk of lapis would be devoted to the theme of the dove is consistent with the symbolic interests of the Sukkalmah as well as with their long distance relations to the sources of lapis lazuli in the east.

15.14 Modern impression of cylinder seal of Ebarat II. *Gulbenkian Museum of Oriental Art, University of Durham, N2410. After Lambert 1979*

15.15 Ancient impression of cylinder seal. Malyan, reconstructed from mf 9015 and mf 9060, GGX98, lot 170. *Tehran, Iran Bastan Museum. H. Pittman*

15.16 Modern impression of cylinder seal. Provenance unknown. *Rosen Collection No. 05855. After Porada 1990:Pl. I, No. 1*

15.17 Modern impression of cylinder seal. Provenance unknown. *Private collection. After Amiet 1986b: No. 137*

 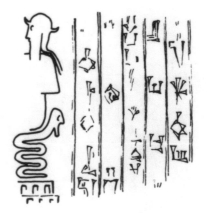

a   b

c

15.18 *a, b,* Ancient impressions of cylinder seals of Kuk-Nashur. Susa. *Tehran, Iran Bastan Museum (a, after Amiet 1972:No. 2015; b, after Miroschedji 1981d); c,* Ancient impression on tablet of the cylinder seal of Tan-Uli. Susa. *Louvre Museum, Sb 8748. After Amiet 1972:No. 2330*

15.19 Drawing of rock relief at Kurangun. Fars. *After Seidl 1986:Abb. 2a*

15.20 Gold objects from the Inshushinak deposit. Susa. *Tehran, Iran Bastan Museum. After Mecquenem 1905a:Pl. 12, Nos. 8, 5, 9, 10, 7, 11, 12, 6, 13, 14, 15*

GOLD OBJECTS

Gold objects comprise a final category of object represented in the trouvaille and the Inshushinak deposit that must be included in this reconsideration of date.

From the trouvaille comes a unique whetstone with a lion protome rendered in gold with granulation and filigree. From the Inshushinak deposit come gold beads, gold rings similiarly elaborated with granulation and gold wire, in addition to pendants with eight-pointed stars and bosses and fragments of inscribed gold sheet (Mecquenem 1905a:Pls. 12, 14) (figure 15.20). As discussed above, the inscriptions of the gold leaf apparently give no clear indication of a date in the second half of the second millennium, but both the protome and the jewelry have been dated, along with the statuettes and the bird, to the Middle Elamite period (Amiet 1966a:Nos. 311–316; Maxwell-Hyslop 1971:186–187). Given the earlier date we have established here for the statuettes, however, much of this material

should be considered as possibly Sukkalmah period. While not as spectacular as those found in the goldsmiths' hoard at Larsa,[4] the Inshushinak personal ornaments are thematically related. The lion head protome is also related to the Larsa ornaments in the extensive use of granulation and filigree around the band. Further, the features of the face of the lion are rendered by stamped dots imitating granulation. This quite specific technique is seen on a bead found in an early second millennium tomb at Susa (Amiet 1966a:No. 195; Tallon 1994:96). Indeed this technique was also found in the Larsa goldsmiths' hoard. The technical comparison will, I believe, be upheld by an analysis of style which shows that the lion's facial features are fundamentally different from those on the axe inscribed to the Middle Elamite king Untash-Napirisha (Amiet 1966a:No. 265).

CONCLUSION

The weight of the evidence, here analyzed through art historical techniques, strongly suggests that at least some of the material from both the trouvaille and the less well-defined deposit of the Inshushinak Temple at Susa belongs to the eighteenth or seventeenth rather than the twelfth century.

I have attempted in this preliminary study to deal only with certain categories of objects, most importantly the gold, silver, and bronze statuettes, but also the bird, the whetstone terminal, and some of the gold ornaments. It is likely that other objects among these finds also belong to those earlier centuries including those like the Central Asian axe which Amiet (1986a:196) has recently suggested might be of early second millennium date. And as pointed out above, the deposit certainly includes numerous cylinder seals. It is of course possible that some of the materials both in the trouvaille and in the Inshushinak deposit are of Middle Elamite date. Indeed the fragmentary condition of the bases of the gold and silver statuettes suggests that they may have been removed from their original context of display before they were buried.[5]

The gold and silver statuettes have never fit easily into our collective characterizations of Middle Elamite figural style. Amiet indirectly addressed this problem in his monograph on Susa in which he asserts that the statuettes "illustrent l'aspect sévère de l'art "élamite" (Amiet 1988:102). While never developing this conclusion, Amiet associates this "severe style" with the "montagnards d'Anzan" while a contemporary style "tantôt amiable avec une pointe d'humour" he associates with the Elamites of the lowland. This construct fits the very interesting and important model that he has set up for understanding the complex and dynamic relationship between the highland

and the lowland peoples of southern Iran (Amiet 1979b). In visual terms he sees that the works of highland origin are more severe, and generally cruder, while those of the lowlands are more naturalistic and refined. However, this dichotomy is not supported by the analysis of the Sukkalmah material from Malyan (Pittman N.D.). It is more consistent with the evidence reviewed here to argue that the statuettes are not representative of a highland regional style of the Middle Elamite period but rather that they are rendered according to conventions shared throughout greater Elam across media during the period of the late Sukkalmah.[6]

Once this complex of objects and images are removed from the Middle Elamite period and established in an earlier period sometime in the seventeenth century, both the Middle Elamite and the Sukkalmah period become more coherent and comprehensible art historically. No longer must we posit the existence of a "severe" style alongside the more "humor-loving" lowland style of Middle Elamite. As important is that we now have nonverbal symbolic witness to what we know from both Mesopotamian and Elamite texts and from the archaeology of both Anshan and Susa was a highpoint in the history of ancient Elam. The long-lived confederacy of the Sukkalmah is one that we know very little about. Before excavations at Malyan, we had scraps of history through juridical and other documents, but little else. Bill Sumner's work at Malyan has given us a view of the Sukkalmah from a highland perspective. From that vantage point it is possible to look again to Susa, to enrich and expand our knowledge through the dialectic process fundamental to recreating our stories of the past.

Thanks to Bill, and building on the achievements of other scholars who have visited this material, a few more pieces fall into our still woefully schematic reconstruction of the glory days of the Sukkalmah. Through the subject matter as well as style we can see through these retrieved bits their connections to the east and west, the skill and the originality of the longest lasting political entity of ancient Elam, the dynasty of the Sukkalmah. It is with eager anticipation that we can all look forward to more information which will appear as the work begun at Malyan by Bill is carried on by the next generation of archaeologists.

NOTES

1. Amiet (1966a:412) reports that this was an idea that Jacques de Morgan had had early on based on the presence of charred bones. This suggested a type of burial practice known from other graves at Susa that was subsequently well-documented at Chogha Zanbil.

2. The lion was, interestingly enough, found as part of the so-called Inshushinak deposit.

3. The official iconography of the Sukkulmah hierarchy will be elaborated in the study of the Malyan glyptic (Pittman N.D.).

4. This is securely dated by inscription to no later than 1736 BCE, the eighth year of the reign of Samsuiluna (Arnaud et al. 1979). From her monumental study of the metalwork from Susa, Tallon (1994:96) observes, "it is characteristic of Susian jewelry-making of that period [the late third and early second millennia] in which precious metals are lavishly employed, but the techniques are less refined than those used in Mesopotamia." This description fits the Inshushinak deposit jewelry perfectly.

5. Perhaps they come from a platform to which a number of such figures were attached, an early version of the remarkable three dimensional diorama, the *sit shamshi* (Amiet 1966a:No. 297).

6. Distinctive of the body are the very long legs, high waist, muscular torso and arms, slight forward lean of the posture, and large head. Compare figures on the official seals of Kuk-Nashur, Tan-Uli (figure 15.18), and others of unknown officials from Anshan (figure 15.13b). As telling are the details of facial characteristics. In all examples of bearded males, the mustache flows abundantly over the beard. Further the eyes of late Sukkalmah figures are closely set, slanting upward, and outlined by heavy lids. These are features that are very similar to terra-cotta funerary heads found in the vaulted tombs of the late Sukkalmah period (Amiet 1966a:No. 350; Spycket 1981:No. 201) (figure 15.19).

16.1   Tall-i Qaleh (1952). *Photograph by L. Vanden Berghe*

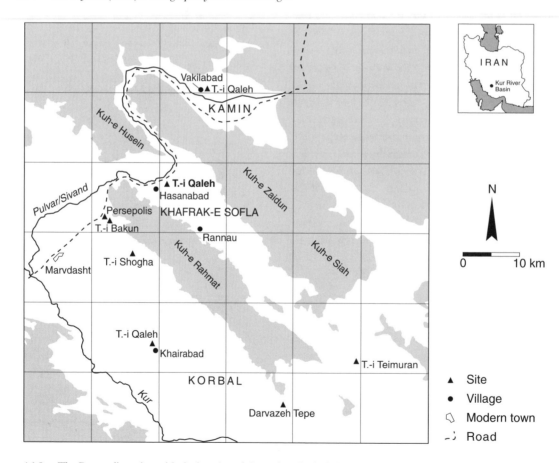

16.2   The Persepolis region with the location of the archaeological sites mentioned in the text. *Prepared at MASCA from authors' original*

CHAPTER 16

SOUNDINGS AT TALL-I QALEH (HASANABAD), FARS PROVINCE, IRAN

ERNIE HAERINCK AND BRUNO OVERLAET

B Y THE TIME WILLIAM SUMNER started his research in Fars in the late 1960s, Louis Vanden Berghe had already shifted his fieldwork to Lurestan, in order to try to document the chronological framework of the Lurestan bronzes. Nonetheless he took a very keen interest in Sumner's work, most of all because he had pleasant memories of his visits to Fars. After Vanden Berghe retired from Ghent University, he intended to review his own field notes on Fars and write a final report. Unfortunately, he passed away before he could take up this project. When we were invited to contribute to this volume honoring William Sumner, an esteemed colleague and scholar, we thought it would be appropriate to present him some of the unpublished material from Fars.

Tall-i Qaleh, northeast of the modern village of Hasanabad, is a large tell in the agricultural district (*buluk*) Khafrak-e Sofla, which is enclosed by the mountains Kuh-e Rahmat, Kuh-e Husain, and Kuh-e Zaidun (figures 16.1, 16.2). The site lies on the left bank of the Pulvar river, close to the modern road from Isfahan to Shiraz. Linda Jacobs, who surveyed the tell in 1976, describes the site as a multipeaked mound that rises 13 m above the present level of the plain and covers an area of about 5 ha. Although the area around the mound is cultivated, the tell itself has not been touched because of the steepness of its slopes which are covered with spiny, xerophytic plants (Jacobs 1980:141, Fig. 43). Sumner estimates the site at 4.5 ha (1972:285). Vanden Berghe numbered the different mounds from 1 to 5, a reference system we will use throughout this report (see figures 16.1, 16.3, 16.4).

Vanden Berghe made two soundings at Tall-i Qaleh, one in 1952 and another in 1955. They were part of his extensive and pioneering field project to establish the prehistoric sequence of the plains in the Persepolis region of Fars province. By making a series of soundings on the main mounds, conducting extensive surveys, and collecting surface sherds, Vanden Berghe produced the first chronological framework for the area. Different ceramic assemblages were considered to represent "cultures," which were named after the first or the major site where they were encountered. Tall-i Qaleh is Vanden Berghe's type site for the "Qaleh ware." The circumstances in which Vanden Berghe had to work were extremely difficult. Without any trained help, he had to direct the soundings, register and photograph the finds, see to their transport, and deal with any other problems that arose. Therefore, it is not surprising that the stratigraphic control and data recording of this early research is not up to modern standards. Nevertheless, the chronological framework he established still largely stands (see also chapter 7).

For a more refined understanding of the changes within the Kur river basin, however, one of the main problems remains the limited stratigraphic and chronological information available. Many years of field research by William Sumner remedied this lacuna to a large extent (Sumner 1972, 1988a). For instance, Sumner was able to show that Qaleh ware first appeared late in the Kaftari phase, circa 1600 BCE (Sumner 1989a:139). Qaleh ware developed from and was partially contemporary with Kaftari, but the transition between both phases is not clear yet and more

16.3   Vanden Berghe's field
        sketch of Tall-i Qaleh
        (1952). English
        translations are
        added to his
        handwritten
        comments, which are
        in Flemish.
        Illustration by
        L. Vanden Berghe

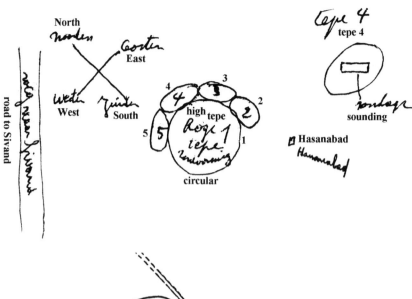

16.4   Plan of Tall-i
        Qaleh. *After Jacobs*
        1980:Fig. 43

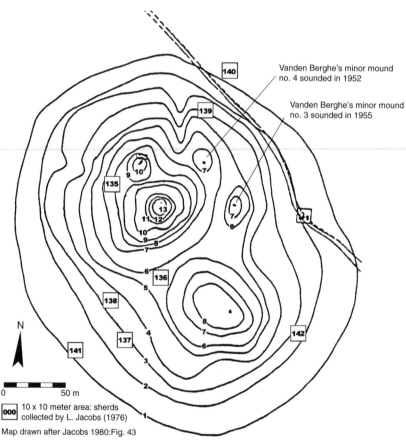

Vanden Berghe's minor mound
no. 4 sounded in 1952

Vanden Berghe's minor mound
no. 3 sounded in 1955

N

0   50 m

000   10 x 10 meter area: sherds
      collected by L. Jacobs (1976)

Map drawn after Jacobs 1980:Fig. 43

fieldwork is needed to clarify the matter. Qaleh ware was produced for many centuries during the second millennium, as is indicated by Sumner's excavations at Malyan (Sumner 1988a; Carter 1996:25–26, 43–44, 50). The ware was still produced at the end of the second millennium and Malyan was probably a major production center. Sumner also suggested that at a given moment Qaleh pottery was mainly used in the western half of the Kur river basin, while the Shogha/Teimuran wares became more characteristic of the eastern part.

It is clear, however, that new, large scale research in the pivotal Kur river basin is needed to elucidate our picture of its cultural changes and to see whether the theoretical explanations are tenable. After all, more than forty years have elapsed since Vanden Berghe's first proposals. Even though the survey and excavations directed by William Sumner have helped clarify the archaeological picture, this work was accomplished more than twenty years ago.

For the moment we can only bring forward some of the unpublished material, realizing that we are unable to solve any of the main problems nor go much beyond what has already been said. To be sure, the notes left by Vanden Berghe are not exhaustive nor always very informative, but they still give us some idea about his soundings and allow us to reconstruct the contents of most burials he excavated. As it is, we can merely provide as much information as is available and thus complete the data he published in his preliminary reports. Eventually, the complete publication of all the type sites from Vanden Berghe's work in Fars will give us a better understanding of the basis of his chronological framework (on Tall-i Teimuran, see Overlaet 1997) and may also help us to define future research objectives.

Apart from the two soundings by Vanden Berghe in 1952 and 1955, the site was sampled in the 1970s, first by Sumner (1972:61–62, site no. 629, location 9KI, Pl. XXIV:L–M = Qaleh ware; XXVII:C–D = Kaftari Red ware; XXXVII:H = Qaleh ware, J–R = unidentified wares; XXXIX:E = Shogha ware; XLII:C–D = Late Plain Ware) and later by Linda Jacobs. Jacobs collected several thousands of surface sherds, as well as other objects including digging-stick weights, grinding stones, lithic tools, and an engraved shell (Jacobs 1980:143–147, Fig. 40:7, 51, 52). Both Sumner and Jacobs concluded that the site had been occupied from the sixth millennium (Bakun and Lapui phases) through to the Islamic era. Sumner and Jacobs both mention that T. Cuyler Young would have made a small sounding at Qaleh in 1961, but he reported "that the site had been turned completely upside down, possibly in Sassanian times" (Jacobs 1980:143; Sumner 1972:61). However, there may have been some confusion with site names since this observation of T. Cuyler Young accords very well with another Tall-i Qaleh, to the east of the village of Vakilabad, in the buluk Kamin. There, Vanden Berghe also made a sounding and found "Sassanian" pottery, in addition to Shogha and Bakun sherds (Vanden Berghe 1953–54:395). Tall-i Qaleh is a common name in the area. Apart from the two Qaleh's already mentioned, Vanden Berghe registered three others in the buluk Khafrak-e Sofla plain. They are situated near the villages of Dalleh, Faruq and Rannau; yet another Tall-i Qaleh is situated near Khairabad in the buluk Korbal (figure 16.2).

THE SOUNDING OF 1952

During the second season of survey in Fars from May 23 to August 3, 1952, Vanden Berghe stayed at Tall-i Qaleh for six days. He investigated one of the low mounds (mound 4, see figures 16.3 and 16.4) and opened an 8.5 by 3.5–m

trench that he excavated to a depth of 3 m (Vanden Berghe 1953-54:395, 403). He mentions finds at two specific depths.

In the top layer very few sherds were encountered (only some Shogha ware), but at a depth of 1 m he reports *numerous* large rounded jars. Unfortunately, there is no further information on these jars, making it impossible to propose a date.

At a depth of 2.5 to 3 m a simple earth burial was found with the body in a flexed position, its face oriented to the northeast. Close to the skull three painted vessels were found. Next to the body was an 11-cm long copper or bronze needle and an 11-cm long copper or bronze blade (figure 16.5d). The skeleton and the vessels were apparently in poor condition. Vanden Berghe gave the following description: 1) A yellowish-gray bowl, some parts reddish, with black-painted decoration both on the exterior and the interior, height 8 cm, diameter 19 cm (figure 16.5a); 2) a yellowish vase with geometric black painted decoration on the shoulder, height 10 cm (figure 16.5b); 3) a very well-fired yellowish vase of fine paste with black-painted decoration on the shoulder, geometric designs and birds, height 21 cm (figure 16.5c); and 4) a copper or bronze needle and blade. Vanden Berghe was of the opinion that the body had been buried below the floor of a building, because of the large storage vessels and several stone querns he had found 1.5 to 2 m above it. He mentions in his notes the importance of this find because a Shogha ware bowl and two Qaleh ware vases were found in the same burial. In view of Sumner's suggestion that both styles were produced in different centers and were at least partially contemporary, this co-occurrence should not be surprising.

Also found in the same sounding, but without more specific references as to their exact location, were sherds of painted Qaleh, Shogha (figures 16.6, 16.7) and Bakun ware (figure 16.8). There were also some sherds from unpainted vessels with incised or ribbed decoration, from pottery sieves or strainers with perforated walls, and as Vanden Berghe writes, from "Giyan IV type vessels with double carinated rims." For this category, however, we do not know what he really means. Jacobs suggested that the unpainted sherds with incised decoration may very well have been Kaftari Buff ware (see Jacobs 1980:142; Sumner 1972:47). Also found were one sherd of Teimuran ware and one red sherd of "final Tall-i Bakun" (Bakun A5), which can now be labelled as Lapui ware (Sumner 1972:41–42; 1988b; 1991:284–285, Fig. 23). Apart from ceramics, a fragment of an incised softstone vessel with a diameter of 4.5 cm was found (figure 16.9). A 10-cm "ram-headed figurine in

16.5 *a–d*, Burial goods from the tomb on mound 4 (1952). *From files of L. Vanden Berghe*

16.6   Selection of the sherds found in 1952. *Photograph by L. Vanden Berghe*

16.7   Selection of Shogha and
        Qaleh ware sherds found in
        1952. *As drawn by
        L.Vanden Berghe (not to
        scale). From files of L.
        Vanden Berghe*

grayish-black stone" was also recorded (figure 16.10). It is the front part of a (broken) stick-like object with a squarish section. A very similar one, 22 cm long, was found on the surface of Darvazeh Tepe (Jacobs 1980:89–90, 291, Fig. 35). Others were excavated at Marlik Tepe (Negahban 1996:299, Pl. 130), Surkh-i Dum (Schmidt et al. 1989:352, 356, Pl. 216f) and Hasanlu (Dyson 1961:535, Fig. 12). Their square section favors an interpretation as a whetstone rather than as a pestle since these are usually round in section. The wear on the fracture of the Tall-i Qaleh specimen does suggest, however, that this fragment may have been reused as a pestle.

THE SOUNDING OF 1955

During his third survey in Fars from December 26, 1954 to January 21, 1955, Vanden Berghe returned to Tall-i Qaleh where he worked from January 16 to 19. He made a sounding on another one of the smaller mounds, notably the one on the "north-east side" (mound 3, see figures 16.3, 16.4) and distinguished four main levels:

In the uppermost level, immediately below the surface, he found the remains of some badly preserved skeletons without any burial gifts. Due to the presence of some sherds of Shogha ware, he suggested that there had originally been a graveyard of the Shogha phase on top of this low mound. This top level had a depth of only about 20 cm.

Below the top level, he found Qaleh ware sherds. At a depth of 2 m, a grave was excavated (figure 16.11). It was a simple earth burial, with an east-west orientation. The face was turned to the northwest. Three copper/bronze pins and one bracelet were found on the body. Near the head stood three painted globular, wide-mouthed jars. One of them held a 10-cm high painted beaker, similar to one Vanden Berghe had excavated only weeks before at Tall-i Teimuran IV (Overlaet 1997:43, Fig. 27:2). At the feet, another jar was excavated. The jars show wavy lines framed by horizontal bands placed on the shoulder. The jars are buff with dark brown painting on the shoulder. Only some rough field sketches of these vessels exist, and the wavy lines may in fact have been much closer to each other than depicted in the drawings. In the same level, Vanden Berghe found sherds painted with swimming birds and unpainted sherds with incised decoration.

In his third level, at 2.50 m, unpainted, well-fired, red sherds were discovered. The surface is usually polished or burnished; some had a red slip. Other sherds are reddish or yellowish-grayish with simple, geometrical black painted decoration. This description would accord with Sumner's Lapui ware (Sumner 1972:41–42, 1988b, 1991:284–285, Fig. 23) as well as with his Kaftari Red ware and Kaftari Painted Buff ware (Sumner 1972:45–46).

Even lower, at 3.25 m, Vanden Berghe found three sherds of painted Bakun ware. At 4 m there were some sherds of Bakun B2 style. Sterile soil was reached at 4.50 m.

CONCLUSION

The results of Sumner's and Jacobs's surface surveys and the soundings of Louis Vanden Berghe are generally in accord. Yet Vanden Berghe's soundings add some important details to the information obtained from surface collections.

The presence of painted Bakun, Lapui, and Kaftari sherds, as well as of Qaleh, Shogha, Teimuran and Late Plain Ware sherds indicates that Tall-i Qaleh has been regularly occupied since at least the sixth millennium BCE. There is, however, no reference to Banesh ware. Vanden Berghe did not register any Kaftari ware either, although it is possible that some of the sherds from his 1952 sounding were in fact Kaftari ware. The incised sherds he mentioned in his 1955 report could have been Kaftari ware, as suggested by Jacobs (1980:142). It is also possible that some of his "Qaleh ware" would now be considered late Kaftari ware.

As on several other sites, Vanden Berghe observed that Shogha ware occurred *above* the Qaleh stratum (Vanden Berghe 1952:218, 1953-54:404, 1959:42–43; see too

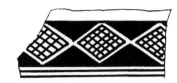

16.8   Selection of Bakun ware sherds found in 1952. *As drawn by L. Vanden Berghe (not to scale). From files of L. Vanden Berghe*

16.9   Fragment of a softstone vessel from the 1952 sounding. *Photograph by L. Vanden Berghe*

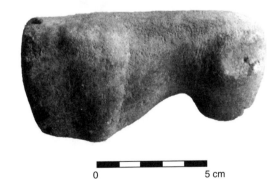

16.10   Stone ram-headed pestle (?) from the 1952 sounding. *Collection of The Royal Museums of Art and History, Brussels, inv. nr. IR 2305. From files of L. Vanden Berghe*

16.11 Burial goods from the tomb on mound 3 (1955). *From files of L. Vanden Berghe*

Overlaet 1997:5, 45, 49). The two graves from Tall-i Qaleh both contained pottery that qualify as Qaleh ware. Differences in shape and decoration may stand for distinct but still undefined phases in the long Qaleh-phase habitation of the site. The grave excavated in 1952 at Tall-i Qaleh contained, apart from the two vessels of Qaleh style, a bowl that can be considered Shogha ware. As already suggested by Sumner and others, both wares were likely to be produced in different centers and were at least partially contemporary. If so, it should not surprise us to have both wares in the same burial.

Tall-i Qaleh is by far the largest and highest tell in the Khafrak-e Sofla plain. Its size and its strategic location near the Pulvar river and on the route from Isfahan to Shiraz, that is, one of the major ancient routes from the Iranian Plateau to the Persian Gulf, highlights the importance of the site. Vanden Berghe's soundings and the surface surveys conducted by Sumner and Jacobs suggest that large scale excavations may provide crucial information on the cultural changes that occurred in the Kur river basin.

CHAPTER 17

THREE STRAY ELAMITE TABLETS
FROM MALYAN

MATTHEW W. STOLPER

IN 1987 three Elamite administrative tablets were offered for sale in the United States. Their contents and seal impressions showed beyond serious doubt that they came from Malyan. In fact, they belonged to the same ancient group as the texts excavated in level IV of the EDD building (Middle Elamite building) and published by Stolper (1984b). They were acquired and donated to the University Museum to be held in trust.

How and when these tablets were taken from Malyan is a matter of concern, but inquiries have produced no useful clues and there are no obvious parallel cases. Other known stray texts from Malyan were exemplars of the "Anshan brick" of Huteluduš-Inšušinak. The intact brick published in 1972 with the remark that it had been acquired very recently in Fars (Lambert 1972:61) must have come from digging at Malyan; it probably did not come from the vicinity of the excavated tablets, since no such intact bricks were found during the University Museum excavations of the 1970s. Other fragments of the "Anshan brick" in various museum collections (F. Vallat, personal communication) had already been collected before the University Museum excavations began, but they might have been surface finds taken from the site at any time.

These tablets are unweathered and almost undamaged, so they were surely not found on the surface but must have come from deliberate digging. Three possibilities come to mind: they may have been taken after excavations were suspended in 1978, at some time when the site was loosely guarded; they may have been taken from excavations of the Middle Elamite building during the 1972 or 1974 seasons, when the comparable tablets were excavated, at a moment when the excavators' attention—our attention—flagged; or they may have been collected during or after the excavations in the area of the EDD building in the early 1960s (Sumner 1974:158 n. 9; see "Addendum").

The resemblance between the strays and the excavated tablets is unmistakable. Each of the three items includes names, words, and/or seal impressions that are otherwise found in the texts published by Stolper (1984b) and only there, assuring that these isolated tablets once belonged to the excavated group. This secure provenience means that the strays are valuable complements to the excavated group, for each also includes elements that are new.

These tablets therefore bring a few new items to the whole body of Elamite words and names, restore a few fragments to the reconstruction of a particular shattered ancient artifact, the original group of texts, and provide an occasion for reconsidering an open question of interpreting the group, the source of the characteristic administrative terminology.

The following is an edition of the three supplementary texts. (Format and style generally follow Stolper 1984b except that the determinative horizontal and vertical wedges are not represented as h. and ^{m}, but as ^{AŠ} and ^{DIŠ}, respectively. Cuneiform texts are cited with conventional abbreviations. PF = texts in Hallock 1969; MDP 9 = texts in Scheil 1907; TTM 1 = texts in Stolper 1984b).

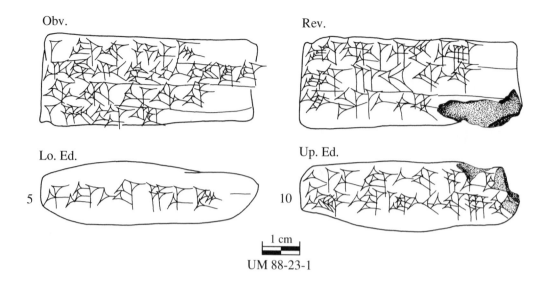

Obv. Rev.

Lo. Ed. Up. Ed.

5 10

1 cm

UM 88-23-1

17.1 UM 88-23-1. *Illustration by M.W. Stolper*

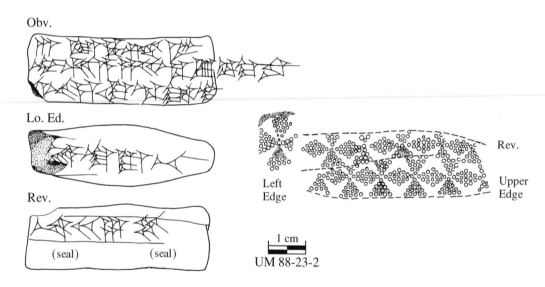

Obv.

Lo. Ed.

Rev.

Left
Edge

Rev.

Upper
Edge

(seal) (seal)

1 cm

UM 88-23-2

17.2 UM 88-23-2. *Illustration by M.W. Stolper*

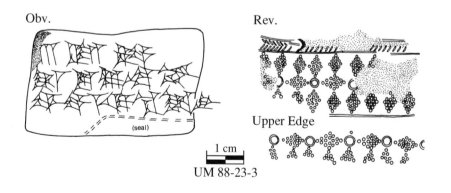

Obv. Rev.

(seal)

Upper Edge

1 cm

UM 88-23-3

17.3 UM 88-23-3. *Illustration by M.W. Stolper*

202

TABLET 1

UM 88-23-1 (figure 17.1)

Obverse

1.	1 MA.NA ZA.BAR.MEŠ	1 mina of copper,
2.	*hu-up-hu-up-pu uk-ku-ma*	that was replaced(?),
3.	*pi-te-ka₄* PI+PÍR	upon(?) a knob:
4.	DIŠ*Ha-ap-ru*	(Accountability) trans-
		ferred to Hapru.

Lower Edge

5.	½ MA.NA ZA.⌜BAR.MEŠ⌝	½ mina of copper

Reverse

6	*ša al-gi-ip*	for ....-s
7.	*ša* 3:20 PI+PÍR	of the King.
8.	*Ak-ka₄-me-en*	(Accountability) trans-
		ferred to Akkamen.

Upper Edge

9.	PAP 1½ MA.NA ZA.⌜BAR.MEŠ⌝	Total 1½ minas of copper.
10.	AŠITI *La-lu-be* AŠUD.8.KÁM	Month Lalube, day 8.

No seal impression.
Burned. All surfaces even dark gray.

2. *huphuppu*: see Stolper 1984b:61 (followed by Hinz and Koch 1987:721) suggesting two ranges of meaning: a finished product, perhaps an ornamental knob or pommel; and a constituent of other products, perhaps an ingot.

2–3. *ukkuma piteka*: the nearest parallels to this phrase are in late Neo-Elamite administrative texts from Susa: *ukkuma zikkak* "deposited on account(?)" MDP 9 93:12, 187 r. 13, and *ukkuma ullaka* "delivered on account(?)" ibid. 143 r.6, 213:2f., *ukkuma ulla[k]* ibid. 110:8, and in the late Neo-Elamite inscription on the bronze plaque found in the Treasury at Persepolis: *ukkuma daka belka* "restored to the proper place(?)" (Schmidt 1957:Pl. 28 cited in Hinz and Koch 1987:178 and 1212). Semantic and functional parallels to these phrases are *ukku* (or: *ukke, ukkap*, but never *ukkuma*) *zikkaka, ukku daka* in Persepolis Fortification Texts of Category C1 recording deposits.

The directional element *ukku* "upon," common in Elamite, is not found in other Malyan texts. The postposition *-ma* is scarce and uncertain in Malyan texts (*hi-ma* TTM 1 44:6, see Stolper 1984b:26). Final *-ma* may instead represent the inanimate classifier ("gender-suffix") *-me* (expressing concord with the preceding inanimate *huhuppu*) + nominalizing or relative *-a*.

One of the meanings attributed by Hallock (1969:767) to *ukku* in Achaemenid Elamite texts from Persepolis, "instead of," is also proposed by Steve (1967:69) for *ukkuma* in the Neo-Elamite administrative texts from Susa.

The word *ukku* and derived forms (*ukke* written *uk-gi*) and *ukkap* in Persepolis texts are also held to mean "on, to (his/their) account" (Hallock 1969:14, 76, 767; Hinz and Koch 1987:1209–1211, with disagreements on formal analysis). Koch (1980) argued that *ukku* in Persepolis texts and in earlier Elamite has the more specific meaning "tax, payment, obligation," a meaning also offered for *ukkuma* in the Neo-Elamite Susa texts by Hinz and Koch (1987:1212).

The word *piteka*, new to Malyan texts, is found as *pitika* in Persepolis texts, where the translation is a matter of disagreement: "(it has been) replaced" and "(it has been) transferred" (Hallock 1969:745); "(has been) lost" (Hinz and Koch 1987:225, also Cameron 1948:53); cf. *piti-* "remove, withdraw, set aside" (Grillot 1978:88). The clearest context is in the pair of letters sent by the chief administrative officer at Persepolis, Parnaka, saying "the seal that was formerly mine has been replaced(?) (or: lost(?), or: set aside(?); *pitika*), now this seal that has been impressed on this tablet is mine" PF 2067, 2068. Other passages describe poultry and livestock as *pitika*, parallel to *katukka* "alive," *halbaka* "slaughtered," and *mazzika* "withdrawn" (references in Hinz and Koch 1987:225).

The parallel phrases in Neo-Elamite and Achaemenid Elamite administrative texts suggest that the meaning of *piteka* should be a contrasting parallel to *zikkaka* "deposited," *ullaka* "delivered," and *daka* "placed." No. 1:1–2 could be interpreted in this administrative sense as recording the replacement of a missing item: "copper that was replaced, instead of a *huphuppu*." If so, might *piteka* (or the phrase *ukkuma piteka*) be the Elamite counterpart to the quasi-Sumerogram LÁL.Ú corresponding to Sumerian la'u, Akkadian *ribbatu* (LÁL.U), "arrears, outstanding item" (Stolper 1984b:45; but cf. x *zabar* LÁL.Ú.MEŠ *huphuppum* TTM 1 68:1f.)?

Nevertheless, phrases in this position in other Malyan texts ordinarily have concrete, not abstract, meanings. They indicate how raw materials are to be used or how objects are to be made. In at least one Middle Elamite dedicatory inscription, the directional element *ukkume* occurs in such a phrase, collocated with verbs that also appear in the Malyan administrative texts: *lansitima sisbah ak ukkume zuzkatah* "(I made a bronze support[?]), I decorated it with gold and set it up on it [= the 'Barrière de Bronze' that bears the inscription]" König 1965:98 No. 45 §4, cf. *zabar ... kassu* GAL *aha zuzkamaka* TTM 1 42:4). It is more straightforward to treat *ukkuma* in No. 1:2 as a parallel to *aha* (Stolper 1984b:26), and *piteka* in a concrete sense: "(bronze) which was replaced on it (=the *huphuppu*)."

4. *Hapru*: otherwise unattested. Cf. the personal names *Hu-un-ha-ab-ri*, *Hu-un-ha-bu-ur* in Ur III texts (Hinz and Koch 1987:719) and the divine name *Hapruh*, an element in personal names (Zadok 1984:10).

6. *algip* (or: *šalgip*): otherwise unattested. Final *-p* indicates an animate plural, hence perhaps people. Animate plurals are exceptional in Malyan texts: *zubarip* TTM 1 97:1, the heading of a column of personal names; and perhaps *zalmu-*, "figurine, statue" (see Stolper 1984b:34 and 35). The word following *ša* in other Malyan texts, however, regularly indicates the object to be made from the metal or to which the metal is to be applied, so this form may refer, like *zalmu-*, to a material representation of something animate.

7. *Akkamen*: fourteen other occurrences in Malyan texts following PI+PÍR "transferred to(?)" or preceding *duš* or *dušda* "(which) he (has) received" (see Stolper 1984b:11, 192 s.v.).

3, 7. PI+PÍR: Vallat (1987) was right to characterize as not entirely satisfactory the reading and graphic etymology proposed in Stolper 1984b:10–12, that PI+PÍR is a local graphic variant of Sumero-Akkadian IGI+PÍR = k u r u m $_7$, with a meaning corresponding to *piqittu*, an Akkadian reading of k u r u m $_7$.

Vallat offered a different proposal: that the sign or ligature read PI+PÍR is a local graphic variant of the sign GIR, used in place of the homophonous GÌR and having the meaning expressed by GÌR in Sumerian and Babylonian texts, that is, indicating the assignment of administrative accountability for disbursements, hence often translated "via." This proposal, like the other, seeks the ultimate source in Neo-Sumerian and Old Babylonian administrative usage and postulates a change in the shape of the sign. It also adds an intermediate step, the replacement of the historically correct Mesopotamian logogram with a sign that has a homophonous syllabic value. Vallat (1987) cites examples of such replacements in texts from Susa, the same examples adduced by Stolper (1984b:20).

Like my proposal, Vallat's is not entirely satisfactory, because the comparanda are inappropriate and because the implications of the proposal are improbable.

First, the proposed substitution of GIR for homophonous GÌR does not parallel the practice in Susa texts. In the plainest example from the late Neo-Elamite administrative texts from Susa, the writing E.GAL (for É.GAL) "palace," the syllabic sign *e*, which is common in those texts,

replaces the logographic sign É, which is not used in those texts. In the postulated substitution at Malyan, these relationships are reversed. The historically "correct" sign GÌR actually does occur at Malyan with the syllabic value *gìr*. The sign GIR does not occur. The Malyan syllabary avoids the use of homophonous signs. The postulated substitution requires both that GIR was known but unattested and that it was read as a homophone of Sumerian GÌR but *not* as a homophone of Elamite *gìr*.

Furthermore, the postulated change in the shape of the sign is also without a persuasive parallel. It is true that Elamite sign forms differ from common Mesopotamian sign forms in the ways indicated by Vallat (1987). Most of these differences appear in two paleographic settings. First, many sign-forms in Middle Elamite royal inscriptions are complex and ornate in ways roughly parallel to the sign-forms of contemporary monumental scripts in Babylonia (as observed by Reiner 1969:68), forms that were not used in contemporary Babylonian administrative texts. Second, many sign-forms in Neo-Elamite texts after about 650 BCE and in Achaemenid Elamite texts are sharply distinct from contemporary Mesopotamian forms of the same signs in systematic ways (that is, signs that have similar shapes in standard Mesopotamian scripts are altered in similar ways). In these late Elamite scripts a few logographic signs were even reinterpreted as ligatures of two signs, sometimes divisible (GEŠTIN as DIN+KAK, ANŠE as PA+x, NUMUN as NU+MUN and even as MAN+NU, for example, PF 455). But sign-forms of the Malyan tablets are neither ornate nor systematically altered. All sign-forms are easily recognizable counterparts of standard Mesopotamian forms. The only characteristically Elamite forms are the signs *hu*, *ri*, and *ar* (with trailing *Winkelhaken*), and the sign *ru*, all with minor changes from common Babylonian forms.

Moreover, the sign GIR is attested in Elamite scripts that are both earlier and later than the Malyan tablets, in Middle Elamite monumental script and in Achaemenid Elamite script (Steve 1992:No. 346). No attested form resembles the sign read PI+PÍR in Malyan texts. All attested forms, like Mesopotamian forms and like the Old Babylonian forms adduced by Vallat (1987) from Fossey (1926), are recognizable as elaborations of contemporary forms of the sign HA (that is, in Assyriological parlance, GIR=ḪA-*gunû*, for example, Labat 1959:12; Borger 1981:397). But the Malyan sign read PI+PÍR bears no recognizable resemblance to the forms of HA used in Malyan texts. In short, the sign is not GIR, and the substitution of GIR for GÌR is unfounded.

The reasons for preferring to see the persons named after the formula PI+PÍR as receiving intermediaries rather than disbursing intermediaries (as implied by GÌR = "via") are enumerated in Stolper (1984b:11–12). But neither Vallat's proposed translations ("sous la responsabilité de," "sous le contrôle de," "par l'entremise de, l'intermédiaire de") nor mine ("transferred to") adequately reflect the syntax of the phrase. With one exception (PI+PÍR PN-*na* TTM 1 36:6), there is no mark of grammatical connection between PI+PÍR and the following name. The relationship between the two elements is not posssessive or attributive but appositive. If so, the Elamite word underlying PI+PÍR is perhaps an agent noun or an active participle, and the emphasis is on the role of the named person who takes responsibility for the material, not on the administrative process of assigning responsibility to him: "the PI+PÍR (person) is PN," or "doing the PI+PÍR is PN."

The source and Elamite reading of these signs remain to be ascertained.

TABLET 2
UM 88-23-2 (figure 17.2)

Obverse

1	3 GÍN KÙ.GI.MEŠ	Three shekels of gold,
2.	*ak-ti a-ha si-ib-ba-ma-ka*$_4$	with which ... is to be
3.	PI+PÍR ^{DIŠ}*Ki-si-ša-ak*	decorated(?):
		(accountability) trans-
		ferred to Kisišak.

Lower Edge

| 4. | [^{AŠ}]ITI *La-lu-be* | Month Lalube, |

Reverse

| 5. | ^{AŠ}UD.25.KÁM | day 25. |

Seal impression No. 1 (= Stolper 1984b:17, Fig. 4; Carter 1996:35 and Fig. 34:6) reverse, upper edge, left edge. Not burned. All surfaces even light brown to buff.

2. *akti*: a material for construction and ornament, attested in Middle Elamite inscriptions, usually with bricks, never with metal, and never otherwise as a bare stem without suffixes (*upat aktinnima, upat aktipna, upat aktippa* all "bricks of *a*.," but also *siyan aktimma* "a temple (made of) *a*." (Hinz and Koch 1987:44–45 with references and literature).
    aha sibbamaka: see Stolper (1984b:31–32) on the same phrase in TTM 1 3:3, also referring to use of gold.

3. *Kisišak*: six other occurrences in Malyan texts (see Stolper 1984b:11 and 196, after PI+PÍR and as the subject of *duš* or *dušda*), and below, tablet 3.

TABLET 3
UM 88-23-3 (figure 17.3)

1.	3 GÍN KÙ.BABBAR	Three shekels of gold
2.	*ša lu-ú-la-am*	for .... :
3.	PI+PÍR ^{DIŠ}*Ki-si-ša-ak*	(Accountability)
		transferred to Kisišak.

Seal impression no. 2 (= Stolper 1984b:17, Fig. 5) reverse, lower edge, upper edge. This impression is more complete than the only other preserved example, on the reverse of TTM 1 45. This impression shows the edges and the double-wire wrapped border of the object—evidently a metal cap for a seal—that made the impression. Burned. Even dark gray.

2. *lulam*: cf. *lu-ú-lu*.MEŠ TTM 1 87:1, 88:1 and, *lu-lu*.MEŠ TTM 1 67:4. At first look, this spelling favors seeing the word as a loan from Akkadian, here borrowed from an accusative singular, against the form *lulu* borrowed from a nominative like most other plausible Akkadian loanwords (Stolper 1984b:22). The other contexts support identifying *lulu* as a metal, hence perhaps Akkadian *lûlu* "antimony" (parallel amounts of *zabar* "copper" and *l*. in ratios of approx. $7\frac{1}{2}$–$8\frac{1}{2}$:1 in TTM 1 87 and 88, an amount of *zabar* and *l*. parallel to smaller amounts of *zabar* and of *anaku* "tin(?)" in TTM 1 67).

But the resulting meaning here, silver "of" or "for" antimony, raises problems. The word following *ša* after amounts of metals regularly indicates objects, not material. If alloying is meant, a verb phrase is expected, corresponding to the phrases indicating the utilization of metals in other texts, for example *aha* with a verb terminating in -*maka*, "to be (alloyed) with it." If, on the other hand, an exchange or purchase is intended, this text is unique.

Hence, it seems preferable to separate *lulu* and *lulam* as two different words, the former a metal, the latter a metal object (cf. *lulmû* "(ear)ring," rare, perhaps foreign in Akkadian).

ADDENDUM: TEXTS FROM MIDDLE ELAMITE BUILDING, ROOM 12

Modern excavations, probably those of the Fars Department of Archaeology carried out in the early 1960s, sounded at least one area where inscribed items were later found, room 12 of the Middle Elamite building (Carter 1996:10, cf. Stolper 1984b:5), so one might hope that items found near this area offer a clue to the source of the stray tablets. Unfortunately, that is not so. None of the texts excavated in room 12 was in

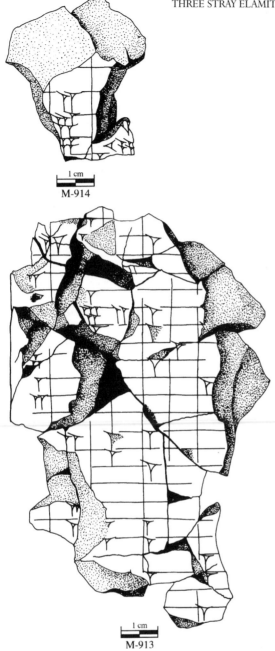

1 cm

M-914

1 cm

M-913

17.4   M-913 and M-914. *Illustration by M.W. Stolper*

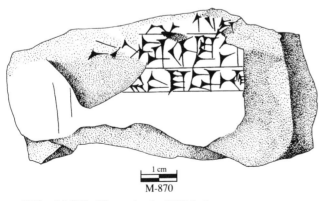

1 cm

M-870

17.5   M-870. *Illustration by M.W. Stolper*

a well-stratified context, and none resembles the strays. Conversely, the earlier excavations did not affect the rooms where the main groups of tablets that are very closely comparable to the stray tablets were found.

The two tablet fragments from room 12, M-914 (=mf 1596) and M-987 (=mf 1672), were both excavated in a mixed lot from "loose dirt at the edge of the modern disturbance" (Carter 1996:10 and 60). M-914 (figure 17.4 top) preserves part of one surface of what was probably a large tablet. The inscribed surface includes parts of three columns of numbers between 1 and 15, but no words. M-987 (not copied) is a smaller fragment (2.2 x 2.4 x 1.8 cm) from a similar tablet, with parts of three columns. Successive entries 5 and 4 are preserved in the middle column, but no words. The preserved part of the reverse is not inscribed. The most nearly comparable item from Malyan is M-913 (=mf 1595) (figure 17.4 bottom), found isolated from other tablets in doorway 89 near the north corner of the excavated courtyard (Stolper 1984b:5). It is a fragment from a very large tablet with parts of seven columns of numbers between one and five on the obverse and at least three columns on the illegible reverse, but no preserved words.

Of more intrinsic interest is M-870 (=mf 1503) (figure 17.5), excavated in the fill of the area disturbed by the earlier excavation of room 12 (Carter 1996:60). It is a fragment of creaM-colored sandstone from an object whose original shape is indeterminate. It has one dressed face, with fragments of three lines of writing, the lower left corner of an inscription. The opposite face is not preserved. The object—perhaps a stela—was at least 16.5 cm thick.

The lapidary sign forms are not distinctive enough to allow a clear choice between a Middle Elamite or early Neo-Elamite date, but the form of the sign *na* suggests the older date. The text seems to be part of a dedicatory inscription. I am not able to restore or identify it.

No complete signs are preserved in the first line. The second line has the sign *ù* (not used in the Malyan administrative texts), probably for the pronoun "I." The third line has the sequence (-)*in ku-ba-na*(-), probably a resumptive pronoun and a form of the verb *kuba-*. Forms of same verb, construed with a preceding resumptive pronoun, occur in an inscription of the Middle Elamite king Šilhak-Inšušinak I and in inscriptions of the Neo-Elamite Šutruk-Nahhunte II (Hinz and Koch 1987:496 s.v. *ku-ba-h, ku-ba-hu-na, ku-bak*, and 517 s.v. *ku-pu-h*, proposing *kuba-*, variant *kupu-* = "set up," said of images and votive objects).

CHAPTER 18

STYLE ZONES AND ADAPTATIONS ALONG THE TURKISH-IRANIAN BORDERLAND

MITCHELL S. ROTHMAN

THE POTENTIAL of stylistic variation in artifacts to define sociocultural phenomena—these might include ethnic groups, cultures, trading networks, migration routes, and so forth—have both enticed and frustrated archaeologists since the beginning of our discipline. For example, Childe (1929:v–vi) wrote, "We find certain types of remains—pots, implements, burial rites, house forms—consistently recurring together. Such a complex of regularly associated traits we shall term a 'cultural group' or 'culture'. We assume that such a complex is the material expression of what today would be called a people." This axiom of Childe's has proven too simplistic and often simply untrue. It places primary emphasis on artifact style as the defining variable for cultures. Further, this formula presumes that stylistic change automatically means cultural change. In 1977, Kramer critiqued the assumption dating to the earlier days of our field, that pots equal peoples. As Emberling (1999) points out, the same core of cultural symbols can remain for a long period, and yet change in their cultural meaning while the organization of society is altering. What is worse, by making style the dependent variable instead of an independent one, the possibility of studying how cultures use a repertoire of stylistic information for a variety of messages is foreclosed.

An alternative view to Childe's trait-listing definition of culture and style may be that of Kroeber and Steward. Kroeber (1939) and later Steward (1977) developed theories of commonalities in cultures that occupy contiguous space. These ideas emphasized the adaptations of the peoples living in these areas to the peculiarities of their

climate and natural resources. That is to say, they both emphasized the way the people living in a common area or environment used available technology to carve out a sustainable way of life. For Kroeber, this pattern represented the overlapping of cultural and natural areas, for example, the Great Plains of the United States and the Indian societies that developed there with the advent of the horse. Beyond the practicalities of living, however, these ever-changing adaptations to the natural environment in a common environmental zone had implications for the content of cultures, including the styles of artifacts shared among groups. For Steward this was the cultural core. As Voget (1975:676) writes of Kroeber:

> In the development of uniformities, culture areas were implicated in a common culture-historical growth. For Kroeber, it was a point of great interest to delineate the efflorescence or cultural climax within an area and to relate it to culture growth and decline. The essence of any culture climax was the strain toward integration—toward an "organization, in part into a conscious system of ideas, but especially into an integrated nexus of styles, standards, and values. (Kroeber 1939:225)

This essay began as I was preparing the publication of the results of an archaeological survey I conducted in 1991 and 1993 in the mountain highlands of eastern Turkey, particularly the Muş plain west of Lake Van. In an article on the Early Bronze I to III periods Gülriz Kozbe and I noticed an interesting pattern in style distribution (Rothman and

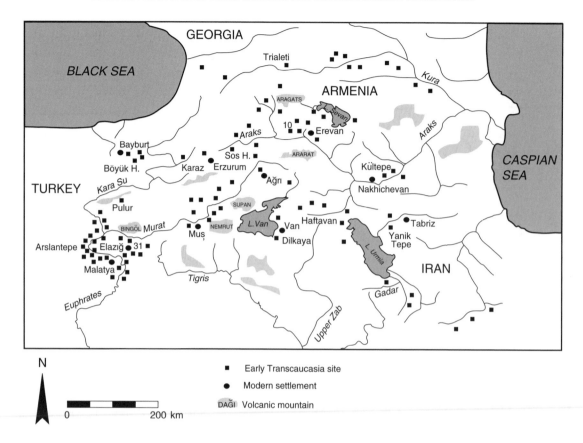

18.1 Kura-Araks sites, after Rothman (1993), Sagona (1984), Russell (1980), Whallon (1979), Burney and Lang (1971). *Original by M.S. Rothman*

Kozbe 1997). Within the larger Early Transcaucasian (ETC) style zone of modern eastern Turkey, western Iran, Armenia, and Georgia, there was an area defined by one subset of incised design: the "groove and circular groove" or "dimple and groove." While mapping out the Urartian period sites of roughly a millennium and a half later, I noticed that the two overlapped almost precisely. Further, while researchers described the ETC cultures as largely pastoral nomad and small farmers (Sagona 1984; Yakar 1985), the Urartians were categorized as founders of a great, though short-lived empire. One would not expect these two organizationally disparate cultures to occupy the same exact territory.

The questions raised by Kroeber, Steward, and others regarding the culture area and stylistic variation came immediately to mind. In this chapter I will ask whether such a direct correlation existed between the ETC and Urartian cultures and if so why. Clearly, this analysis will not answer all outstanding questions about the meaning of stylistic similarities. It should add another variable to investigate formally.

The area I am investigating consists of lands at higher elevations north of the Mesopotamian steppe within the Taurus and Zagros mountain ranges. It includes the small

plains and hilly country from around Lake Van in eastern Turkey west toward Malatya, east toward Lake Urmia in Iran, north toward Lake Sevan in Armenia, and northwest toward the Black Sea in Georgia (figure 18.1).

This geographical area has been of particular interest to archaeologists, historians, and modern political scientists for some time. As political changes have redefined the borders of nation states and of the distribution of ethnic groups, the permeability and delineation of boundaries in this area have changed. For example, the Shah of Iran attempted to forge a purely Persian national identity for the modern nation of Iran through symbols of a fictitiously long tradition of rule and the teaching of *farsi* (the modern Persian language). Despite his efforts, the use of the Turkish language continued to expand into the area under discussion here. This occurred although most residents in the area were of Kurdish ethnic background, whose native tongue is a cognate language of Persian. In an earlier time the spread of the Seljuk Turks and before them the Hittites, Hurrians, and Persians have obscured or altered political and linguistic boundaries. Please note that I make a distinction here between borders and boundaries. Borders are distinct political dividing lines between polities. Boundaries are more

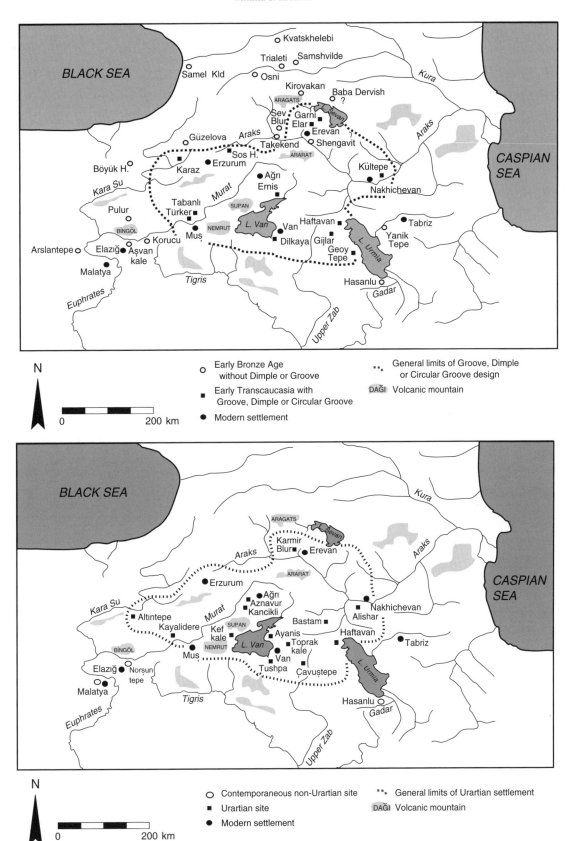

18.2 *a*, Kura-Araks sites with groove and circular groove, dimple and groove motifs; *b*, Urartian and non-Urartian sites. *Originals by M.S. Rothman*

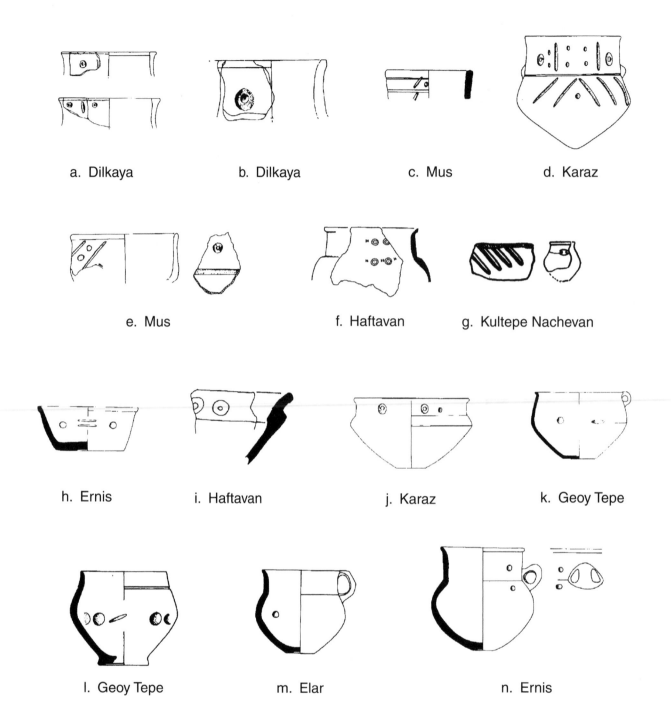

a. Dilkaya   b. Dilkaya   c. Mus   d. Karaz

e. Mus   f. Haftavan   g. Kultepe Nachevan

h. Ernis   i. Haftavan   j. Karaz   k. Geoy Tepe

l. Geoy Tepe   m. Elar   n. Ernis

18.3   Grove and circular groove (a, h), dimple and groove (k, n) designs. *Sources: a, Kozbe 1990, Resim 17; b, Kozbe 1990, Resim 3b; c, Rothman and Kozbe 1997, Fig. 10; d, Sagona 1984, Vol. üi: Fig. 14; e, Rothman and Kozbe 1997, Fig. 9; f, Summers 1982, Fig. 33; g, Bahşaliyev 1997, Levha/Plate V; h, Sagona 1984, Vol. üi: Fig. 55; i, Summers 1982, Fig. 26; j, Sagona 1984, Vol. üi: Fig. 39; k, Sagona 1984, Vol. üi: Fig. 37; l, Sagona 1984, Vol. üi: Fig. 26; m, Sagona 1984, Vol. üi: Fig. 19; n, Sagona 1984, Vol. üi: Fig. 20). Illustration by M.S. Rothman*

amorphous and often cannot be drawn precisely on a map but demarcate some cultural or natural difference, whether linguistic, ethnic, religious, or ecological.

EARLY TRANSCAUCASIAN CULTURES

The ETC artifact styles are first evident in the fourth millennium BCE in the Transcaucasian area. The earliest signs of the ETC outside that area appear at Arslantepe and Sos Höyük VB (figure 18.2a). The Early Bronze Age as defined by the prevalence of these styles has been thought to end no later than about 2000 BCE. This range of dates is currently being debated, because Sagona (2000) has shown through careful excavation and radiocarbon dating at Sos Höyük, as Burney had speculated (Burney and Lang 1971:46–47), that the burnished pottery from Transcaucasia began in the late fourth millennium and lasted well into the second millennium. Considerable confusion occurs in the relative dating of sites in the larger region because of different criteria for assigning Early Bronze dates. Often what is assigned to an Early Bronze I date in Georgia, Armenia, and Azerbaijan is still termed Late Chalcolithic in northern Mesopotamia and eastern Turkey. This confusion is clear, for example, in the dating of Arslantepe level VIA as being either in the Late Chalcolithic or Early Bronze I (see Conti and Persiani 1993). In the following discussion, I accept Sagona's division of time into Kura-Araks 1 to 3. Kura-Araks 1 is contemporaneous with the end of the Late Chalcolithic or Uruk in Mesopotamia, Turkey, and Iran (3500 BCE–3000 BCE). Kura-Araks 2 (beginning at roughly 3000 BCE) is synonymous with the Early Bronze Age I in Mesopotamia, Turkey, and Iran. Kura-Araks III (very roughly 2600 BCE–2000 BCE) is the equivalent of the Early Bronze Age II and III (Sagona 1984, see also Voigt and Dyson 1992). These three phases are cultural benchmarks from the point of view of the eastern Turkish-Iranian zone.

The spread of ETC artifact styles is extremely broad (figure 18.1). It stretched from the basins of the Kura and Araks rivers south into northwestern Iran (Azerbaijan province) and Turkey (the Erzurum, Bayburt, Ağrı, Van and Muş provinces of eastern Turkey). It then moved west along the Murat river to the Euphrates (Elâzığ and Malatya provinces), and southwest, according to some, into Syria-Palestine, the last represented by Khirbet Kerak ware. Amiran (1952) was first to propose the connection of Levantine Khirbet Kerak wares and Early Transcaucasian ware. Todd (1973) sees no such connection.

A number of theories have been proposed that attempt to account for the spread of these cultural artifact styles. The most cited of these theories is that a large out-migration of people from Transcaucasia accounts for the wide geographical distribution of these wares as well as for an architectural style represented by round buildings and light wattle and daub rectangular structures (Burney and Lang 1971; Yakar 1985). Recent research suggests that there had been some movement of people, but not a continuous and gradual wave of migration. Rather, the data indicate a series of smaller ripples of quite different peoples followed by an admixture of new immigrants with preexisting populations (Burney 1996; Rothman 1998; Rothman and Kozbe 1997; Sagona 1994). These ripples of population represented farmers, traders, pastoral nomads, and probably itinerant craftsmen (Rothman N.D.). The manufacture of and trade in metals clearly played some role in the exposure of peoples to new manufacturing techniques, in both metals and pottery. Increased exchange of goods over a large geographical area was made possible in part by the domestication of the donkey and horse in this broad region at the end of the fourth millennium (Bökönyi 1987).

Increasing information about the distribution of ETC artifact styles indicates that there was great variability within the Transcaucasian assemblage. Part of this variability can be explained by the long temporal span of the Kura-Araks phases. Part of it, however, must reflect variability in the populations that produce variations in style within the larger ware category. Even within the Kura and Araks basins, Sagona (1984) notes variations in the Transcaucasian tradition. Sub-traditions include the Kvemo Kartli, Shida Kartli, Tsalka, Armenian, Upper Euphrates, Trialeti, and others. As Yakar writes, " when the Early Transcaucasian culture is examined in different geographical areas of its distribution, it becomes clear...that the reasons for its expansion must have been rather varied at different periods" (1985:279–80). Sagona notes as well the probable mixing of Transcaucasian and local traditions when he writes that "it has become increasingly apparent that cultural developments in the Late Chalcolithic and Early Bronze Age owe much to both local and foreign influences.(1994:15) .

THE PATTERN: THE DISTRIBUTION OF THE "GROOVE AND CIRCULAR GROOVE" AND "DIMPLE AND GROOVE" DESIGNS AND THE EARLY TRANSCAUCASIAN STYLE

When Gülriz Kozbe and I (1997) studied the Transcaucasian pottery of Muş, we noticed that the pottery on the open plain was almost all decorated with what is called the groove and circular groove (figure 18.3:a–g, i, j) or "dimple and groove" incised design (figure 18.3:h, k–n). These designs vary only because dimples are made by pressing a finger or object creating a deeper even concavity or hole while the circular groove is made by carving out a circle as a round line. The texture of the circular groove and dimple are different. The appliqué of grooves on ETC pottery was apparently done later in time than the incised groove, the latter dating to the late Kura-Araks III period (Sagona, personal communication).

Pottery from the hills of Muş, north along the Murat river route toward Transcaucasia, is typical of what Summers (1982) would classify as Kura-Araks IIA. These wares typically have rail rims (with square, flat profile, for example Rothman and Kozbe 1997:Fig. 12c), incised designs and grit temper. Pottery from the plain is best dated to Kura-Araks IIB and III, based on the groove and circular groove and dimple and groove incised designs (Summers 1982:116). These design elements are also on vessels with Nakhichevan lug handles in parts of their geographic range. In our analysis and subsequently (Rothman 1998), I began to catalogue the occurrences of this particular design element and plot the boundaries beyond which it does not occur or occurs so infrequently that it must represent the odd trade ware.

The distribution of the groove and circular groove and dimple and groove incised wares appears to represent a cultural boundary. Whereas these design elements exist on the western side of Lake Urmia at Haftavan (Summers 1982) and Geoy Tepe K2, K3 (Voigt and Dyson 1992:178), they do not exist on the eastern side of Urmia at Yanik Tepe (Sagona 1984; Summers 1982:116). The white-filled incised designs of Yanik Tepe are not found to the west of Lake Urmia, although they are typical of the mountain valleys of the central Zagros, including Godin IV (Voigt and Dyson 1992:176; Young 1969:Fig. 11). Contemporary with this Yanik Tepe EB I or Kura-Araks II-III design element is the orange ware of Hasanlu VII. This ware, according to Voigt and Dyson (1992:175), indicates that "a boundary between the northern and southern portions of the Urmia basin developed after the Pisdeli period" (the last pre-Bronze Age level). A single dimple sherd was found with orange ware at Hasanlu. To the west, the boundary of the groove and circular groove and dimple and groove incised designs appears to be east of the Altınova plain. Arslantepe is outside this boundary as well.

As the groove and circular groove and dimple and groove incised designs were becoming most common in the eastern areas, a red and black painted pottery tradition developed in the Altınova and at Arslantepe (Conti and Persiani 1993; Ertem 1982; Marro 1997; Sagona 2000; Whallon 1979:31). Patterns similar to the groove and circular groove and dimple and groove but in relief are found in the Altınova (Sagona 1994) and Georgia (Sagona 1984), but they are appliqué, not grooved. This is particularly

important, as the heaviest concentration of settled population in the Early Bronze Age with significant amounts of Transcaucasian pottery is in the area of the Altınova and Malatya (figure 18.1). Within Transcaucasia itself, defining any clear cultural boundaries is difficult at best. Groove and circular groove and dimple and groove incised designs do appear in the Nakhichevan region at the Transcaucasian site of Kültepe and in Armenia at Elar and Garni (figure 18.2), and perhaps in Azerbaijan at Baba Dervish. Italian surveyors also collected this ware type at Gijlar, in period B, north of Lake Urmia (Pecorella and Salvini 1984:Figs. 72–74). Within the boundaries thus defined, the groove and circular groove and dimple and groove incised designs are a major component of Transcaucasian wares.

Between the Bronze Age ETC and the Iron Age Urartians, this area is very poorly understood. Burney and Lang describe the situation this way:

> Most of eastern Anatolia remains in obscurity [from 2000 BC] until the ninth century BC, [...]. The old cultural uniformity of the third millennium continued to disintegrate, yet its traditions survived to mingle with and thus to influence the succeeding cultures. The decline in settled life, alluded to in the preceding chapter, had begun by the Early Transcaucasian II period and continued through the second millennium BC. This decline was particularly marked in the bleaker highlands, such as the regions of Erzurum and Van, where the Early Transcaucasian culture lingered on, to be followed by a long dark age when nomadism may have predominated. (Burney and Lang 1971:86)

Despite the new discoveries at Sos mentioned above and the attempts of others to find markers of the second millennium (French and Summers 1994), scholars really have little idea what happened after the end of the ETC and the beginning of Urartu.

URARTU

The heartland of the Urartian empire coincides almost exactly with the distribution of groove and circular groove and dimple and groove wares, yet Urartu rose to prominence almost two millennia later (figure 18.2b). Urartians conducted military operations and constructed some hill forts outside of this area (Kleiss and Hauptmann 1976; Sevin 1994). Using the history of the Urartian dynasties and placement of rock inscriptions, however, Burney (1994) argues that in defining the heartland of Urartu, one must distinguish between the core area and the area into which they conducted military campaigns:

Of course, campaigns were conducted beyond the limits of Urartian rule, for example, against Malatya in the west....Few suggest that Malatya ever came under direct Urartian control; likewise, Parsua, to the southeast of Lake Urmia... (Burney 1994:31)

It was the Urartians who sacked Hasanlu (Dyson and Muscarella 1989) in what had earlier been the area typified by the Early Bronze orange ware, and although they occupied a fortress there (Dyson 1989b), the area south of Lake Urmia was a military frontier zone, not part of the Urartian cultural core area.

For an "empire," Urartu seems to have been carved out of a fairly mobile and small-scale society. Although the Urartian fortresses and the associated temples are very impressive, there are no indications of large cities or deep political or cultural coherence:

What we really see in the Urartian assemblage is a set of styles, artifacts, and features that pertain to a military elite, rather than to a broad spectrum of the population. The best known Urartian sites are fortresses, and the most characteristic artifacts are bronzes, particularly pieces of royally dedicated equipment. (Zimansky 1995b)

The historical record of Urartu begins with royal Assyrian inscriptions of the thirteenth century BCE, which refer to the sixty clans of Urartu (Ararat) (Luckenbill 1926:236). The empire was founded in the ninth century, and was gone by the late seventh or early sixth centuries. Its interactions with the kingdom of Assyria from earlier times gave the leaders of Urartu a model for presenting the image of a state society, but in substance they may not have created the permanent institutions that typify such a society. When the leadership or elite administrative and military structures collapsed, the society quickly reverted to a simpler form. (Burney 1996; Zimansky 1985).

Based on the third and first millennium distribution of artifact style and the historic evidence of later documents, this area of Anatolia, Iran, and Armenia was occupied by groups with some underlying cultural similarities (see also chapter 21). These groups interacted with, yet were distinct from their neighbors to the northeast, west, south, and east. The question I have asked, and to which I will offer a possible answer, is why did two seemingly different cultures almost two thousand years apart occupy an almost identical geographical area? I will argue below that the answer is related to the way these two cultures adapted to a similar environment, but at the same time lived in very different political and economic circumstances.

ENVIRONMENT AND HUMAN ADAPTATION IN TRANSCAUCASIA

As scholars of many disciplines have argued, the natural environment affects the ways human beings and human groups construct their society from subsistence to governance to religion to cultural traditions (Rothman 2000). For those who lived in and moved through eastern Turkey, Transcaucasia, and western Iran in antiquity, what did its landscape and geology have to offer? Was there a subsistence strategy that was common to members of ETC and Urartian cultures?

Geologically, eastern Turkey, Armenia and northwestern Iran are best defined by the two great east–west upthrust massifs of the eastern Taurus mountains, the northwest–southeast running Zagros front, and the five large bodies of water, Lake Van, Lake Urmia, Lake Sevan, and the Black and Caspian seas. In the area of Lake Van the lowest elevation is 1300 m (4300 feet) above sea level, the highest is about 2950 m (9700 feet). A million years ago Lake Van covered a much wider area than it does today. Before the explosion of the Nemrut Dağı volcano, the Muş plain was part of the bed of Lake Van (Dewdney 1971). To the east of Elâzığ the open plains rest on a large plate of sandstone conglomerate not well suited to drainage and soil accumulation (MTA 1988). A similar situation appears to exist in the area west of Lake Urmia, and north toward Lake Sevan.

Was the ancient environment like the modern one in the Early Bronze Age? Based on paleoenvironmental pollen corings (Degens and Kurtman 1978; van Zeist and Bottema 1982:279–280), prior to the fifth millennium desert steppe conditions prevailed throughout the region. By the fifth millennium oak-juniper forest—presumably indicative of a warmer and wetter climate—developed in the area, certainly around Lake Van. By the second millennium BCE, forests were common in the region.

Snowfall strongly affects the cultural environment with regard to routes of communication and subsistence in Transcaucasia, northwestern Iran and eastern Turkey. In the Van area maximum precipitation falls as snow in the winter, and deep snow typically covers the ground for up to seven months a year. The Altınova and Malatya, outside the zone of groove and circular groove, dimple and groove design, are outside the zone of maximal snow. The winters are shorter (approximately three months) and almost twice as much of the winter-spring precipitation is rain rather than snow (Whallon 1979:7). There is no reason to believe that it was considerably different in earlier times. In general, extremes of weather are common during any given year, as the region's weather is influenced by the mountain climate of the Taurus and the drier, hotter northern Mesopotamian regime. The area is habitable, but movement during the winter months is difficult either along the edge of the northern massif or along the Murat river, which empties into the Euphrates. As Burney and Lang (1971:128) point out, a truly centralized state could not develop among the Urartians, in part because they had no means of controlling distant population in winter. The multi-capital structure of Urartu (Burney 1994; Zimansky 1985) is partially explained by this factor.

In terms of subsistence, the area encompassing the groove and circular groove, dimple and groove wares of the ETC is among the more marginal agriculturally in the highland zone. The best agricultural zones are, in fact, in the areas with painted pottery and with orange ware. Located in the dry-farming zone, the area south of Lake Urmia near Hasanlu "is one of the most productive agricultural regions in Iran" (Voigt 1983:271). Similarly, the Altınova and Malatya are agriculturally very productive. The alluvium of the Altınova

> is covered with a thick and fertile soil, and the plain...is well watered by many small, spring-fed streams. Villages were numerous here, and crops were varied and abundant. (Whallon 1979:5)

As mentioned above, the climatic problems of snow are not felt as badly in the Altınova as in the more easterly areas. In the third millennium large settlements such as Korucutepe and Norşuntepe enjoyed agricultural abundance. The distribution of ancient sites reflects their agricultural potential (figure 18.1). The Elâzığ and Malatya areas, especially the Altınova plain, supported a high concentration of people. The Georgian part of the Transcaucasian area is much more agriculturally productive than the area of the southern Armenian Plateau.

The same cannot be said for the area of Van, Muş, Ağrı, or immediately west of Lake Urmia. The area of the northern Murat river is agriculturally marginal. The spring thaw provides farmers with a strong flow from run-off streams and rivers, but also with extensive swampy areas and frequent flooding. Near modern Ağrı, for example, the environment is typified by gravelly, poor soils. That area would be largely useless for farming communities. Various locations in the hills north of the plains have a more propitious geology for agriculture, but there is not enough open land for large fields. Agriculture remains small-scale on plots

difficult to plow. Similarly, agriculture is limited for most of the area of small parallel valleys running northeast to southwest north of the northern Taurus massif, and for the hilly area across the Turkish frontier toward Lake Urmia. Sagona (1984:26) describes the open basin between Mount Aragats and Mount Ararat as semi-arid, needing irrigation for agriculture and prone to salinization.

Transport of bulk commodities is difficult, especially in winter. Farmers would most likely depend on the yields from their spring and summer crops to survive the winter. They would not be likely to engage in much exchange of agricultural products and would adopt subsistence farming techniques with low risk.

Throughout the region, however, good pasture is and has been available. For example, the area north of the northern massif of the Bingöl mountains is among the largest and finest pasture lands in the whole region (figure 18.1) (Altınlı 1963:56). In earlier times irrigation works may have been used to improve pasture, not arable fields. The Assyrian king Sargon II describes an area most probably near Haftavan saying, "The ground of his uncultivated areas he made like a meadow, flooding it abundantly in summertime, and grass and pasture did not fail, winter and summer" (Luckenbill 1926:160). As Burney (1977:4) states, "The lands of the Urmia Basin and its neighboring districts depended, however, primarily on their flocks and herds, sheep and cattle."

In short, the probability is fairly high that the area encompassing the groove and circular groove and dimple and groove designs, as well as the Urartians, is one where pastoralism was at least as important for subsistence as agriculture. This is not to say that people did not farm. However, small-scale subsistence farming was probably the primary form of agriculture, and some significant percent of the population was likely engaged in pastoral nomadism. There is a close correspondence between modern day migration routes of nomadic pastoralists in the greater Van region and areas where the core of groove and circular groove and dimple and groove are found.

Cribb (1991:220) argues that the Early Transcaucasian culture was one with a large number of pastoral nomads, although in the end, not a pastoral nomad society. In his analysis of ETC, he includes material from Elâzığ and Malatya provinces as part of the core area of these cultures. He points to elements of mobility in the artifacts of the excavated Early Transcaucasian sites. These include portable hearths or andirons, whose modern nomadic equivalent is a metal version of the same functional object. The architecture of much of the Transcaucasian area is also reminiscent of modern nomadic encampments. The architecture of Kvatskhelebi in

Georgia (Sagona 1984:fig. 125) is very similar to Bakhtiari encampments (Digard 1975:fig. 5) and to similar structures in eastern Turkey (Cribb 1991:fig. 11.4; see also Hole 1974). The squatter settlement of wattle and daub houses at Arslantepe (Frangipane 1997:fig. 13) immediately after the abandonment of the VIA palace/temple complex certainly fits this profile as well. In Muş province, on the Bulanık road toward the high pasture (*yayla*), I have seen pastoral nomads return to circular or square stone structures into which they put upright log structures, covered with thatch. With their herds on the flat pasture around these structures, they stay perhaps a month before moving on to the higher pasture. Cribb (1991:75–76) also argues that nomadic groups today, and probably in the past, use pottery vessel types similar to those of settled villagers. The difference tends to be in the amount of pottery.

In addition, changes in subsistence practices and reliance on lighter wattle and daub housing appear to coincide with the spread of the groove and circular groove and dimple and groove design in Kura-Araks IIB and III periods. In the Nakhichevan area,

> In the first phase of the Kura-Araks culture cattle took priority in animal husbandry...However, by the third phase (that is, approximately in the mid-3rd millennium BC) these animals had gained greater importance and usurped first place from cattle. (Bahşaliyev 1997:99)

The increased use of sheep and goat made a pastoral nomad strategy both more practical and necessary, as these animals are more easily moved over long distances and are more sensitive to changes in temperature.

CONCLUSION

For at least this one case, the ideas of Kroeber and Steward make theoretical sense. The distribution of groove and circular groove and dimple and groove design on black burnished pottery of the Kura-Araks IIB and III appears to cover approximately the same geographical range as the heartland of Urartu. Although we still lack the density and variety of data to do more than make suggestions at this time, this area seems to be defined by the distinct adaptation of its residents. That adaptation includes small-scale farming, herding, and pastoral nomadism. Although the range of climate, topography, and subsistence resources

defines the general boundaries of this zone, both Early Transcaucasians and Urartians crossed those boundaries to the east, west and southwest. The core area represented by groove and circular groove and dimple and groove design is distinct from areas using black burnished wares with a different repertoire of designs. Whether for the Urartians south of Lake Urmia or for Early Transcaucasians at Arslantepe, members of the core culture did not stay outside of their boundary for long. Cribb argues that the general Early Transcaucasian culture cannot be identified as a pastoral nomad society or one with a dominance of transhumant pastoralism only because he includes settlement in the Malatya and Elâziğ area as part of regional adaptation. As I have argued above, these provinces lie outside the boundaries of the groove and circular groove, dimple and groove variations in ETC pottery decoration.

Having argued for a distinct "culture area," I must admit that the boundaries are fuzzy at best, and that there are areas where several contemporary pottery traditions overlap across their range. Even for the Urartians, therefore, these were not real political borders as we think of the borders of modern states. They demonstrate the fluidity or permeability of boundaries in much of this area over time. Part of that fluidity is probably related to trade relations, especially in metals. Pastoral nomads in the present day often serve as agents of exchange (Ferdinand 1962), and the early appearance of Early Transcaucasian wares at Arslantepe may signal a role for pastoral nomads in this role. This case should in the end encourage further thought and fieldwork about the eastern Turkish and western Iranian highland border zone in its relation to its neighbors, and to the ecological basis of style distribution.

Acknowledgments. My own relation to Bill Sumner was built during my time as an excavator at Tal-i Malyan in 1978. At the time I sometimes felt that Bill gave us square supervisors too much freedom; that is to say, I was always worried that I was messing up. I realized when I faced my own first season as a field director how hard the job was and how amazingly well Bill did it. With all due respect to anyone else with whom I worked (even myself), I now realize how perfectly Bill combined subtle control, confidence building, independence, encouragement, even temper, occasional outbursts, personal concern and nightly games of Hearts as a formula for directorial success. Thanks.

The research for this project was supported by the Research Council of the National Geographic Society.

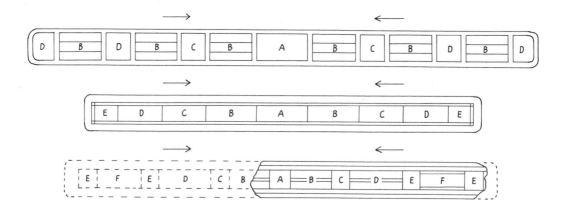

19.1　Urartian bronze belts with different fields of pictures. *Illustration by W. Kleiss*

19.2　*Upper*, Bronze belt from Çavuş Tepe, castle; *lower*, reconstructed. *Illustration by W. Kleiss*

19.3　Pictures of castles from non-Urartian cultural assemblages of the first millennium BCE. *Illustration by W. Kleiss*

CHAPTER 19

OBSERVATIONS ON
URARTIAN BRONZE BELTS

WOLFRAM KLEISS

AMONG THE URARTIAN BRONZE BELTS known to date, only a few are preserved well enough to discern the representations rendered on them. It is striking, however, that on some, but not others, the middle of the belt is emphasized through the arrangement of the figural decoration. Here, I shall discuss these differences, although there are only a few available examples of belts preserved in their entirety or even in great part to which we can refer. The provenance of most of these belts is unknown. Further, we do not know whether they belonged to men or women.

There are examples of Urartian bronze belts with two friezes composed of animals or plants that converge or move out from the center of the belt.[1] In addition to these pieces, there are also bronze belts that carry friezes composed of pairs of opposing animals.[2] Finally, there are bronze belts that are subdivided into individual fields.[3] This type will be considered here.

Among the bronze belts divided into individual fields, panels with designs of essentially similar size are symmetrically arranged on either side of a unique central panel. Three such belts that exhibit different arrangements of long field sequences are presented here:

On a belt in the Liebighaus Collection (Lands of the Bible Archaeology Foundation 1981) (figure 19.1, upper), elaborated by thirteen fields,[4] the central scene (designated A) carries human, primarily female, images. These figures in profile face out from the center toward the ends of the belt. This group is flanked on each side by a scene composed of three animals aligned horizon-

tally through the middle of a panel (B). In turn, these panels are flanked symmetrically by an architectural image—a fortress with an accentuated gate (C). Following the same pattern are the representation of three animals (B), a group of two human figures (D), and three animals (B). The terminal panel on each end contains a two-figure group (D). Thus, the pattern of the design motifs can be formulated as: D-B-D-B-C-B-A-B-C-B-D-B-D.

Another belt (from Çavuş Tepe in eastern Anatolia) is decorated with nine fields (figure 19.1, middle; Ahrens 1979:58). The central field shows a group of human figures (A). As in the above example, these figures move out from the middle of the belt. This group is flanked on each side by the image of a fish aligned horizontally (B). The fish are followed by a representation of a fortress with an accentuated tower (C) followed by a representation of mixed creatures (D). The sequence ends on both sides with a fish-tailed bird (E). The resulting design can be formulated as: E-D-C-B-A-B-C-D-E.

A third, and fragmentary, belt is reconstructed to have thirteen fields (figure 19.1, lower).[5] Its central scene is the representation of a sacrificial ceremony (A). This scene is followed by two rows of fish-tailed birds that are aligned in the middle of the panel (B), followed by a fortress with an emphasized gate (C), two rows of fish (D), a fabulous creature (E), and a row of striding animals (F). Each end of the belt ends with the image of a fabulous creature (E). The reconstructed pattern of design motifs can be formulated as E-F-E-D-C-B-A-B-C-D-E-F-E.

The central scene in these segments of divided belts always has a representation of humans or human activity (that is, a sacrifice). The fields with animal representations may have a cultic meaning or they may refer to cult figures. This may also be the case with the human figures. The architectural representations are to be understood as symbols, similar to the little pictures of cities woven into the garments of the guardsmen in Susa from the Achaemenid period (Calmeyer 1992).

When a fortress is represented (Kleiss 1982), it is usually placed in the middle of the composition and shown with an open gate. The architecture is unique, however, in the upper walls, the framing of the gate, the opening of the walls, and the form of the battlement towers. These differences can probably be attributed to the various craftsmen who engraved the images.

The damaged and incomplete bronze belt from Çavuş Tepe (figure 19.1, middle) is elaborated with two accentuated citadels. The gate of this fortress is half open and placed on the right side, consistent with other Urartian representations of military architecture. The structure has three towers emerging out of the façade (figure 19.2; Ertmann 1994:71, Pls. 2, 3, 7, and Fig. 1a) and three-tiered battlements between the towers. The gate is closed on the left side, in contrast to other Urartian representations of gates in bronze which have the right side of the gate closed (Kleiss 1982:53, 1b).

The Urartian representations on bronze belts (as well as on other bronze plaques) are considerably different from non-Urartian, Mesopotamian representations of fortresses or cities. To cite only one example, consider the representation of Imgur-Enlil on the bronze gates of Balawat (Oates 1974) in Assyria dated to the reign of Shalmaneser III in the ninth century BCE (figure 19.3, upper). Here the artist neglected to fill in basic architectural detail. In contrast, the illustration of a city, probably Assyrian, on an Assyrian bronze helmet (figure 19.3, second from top; Born and Seidl 1995:Fig. 22) shows a fortified city in considerable

detail, with the citadel exhibiting numerous details, palms, and two types of architectural elaboration on the towers.

The representation of a city or great fortress from Arjan near Behbehan in the western Zagros in Khuzestan (figure 19.3, third from top) (Vatandust 1988) shows a unique gate form, prominently placed in the middle of a highly detailed rendering of a façade. Two-tiered battlements are shown on the gate tower next to the three-tiered battlements on the top of the fortress wall.

The images of Urartian fortress and city, with exaggerated height of the towers and oversized gates, would seem to more acccurately describe an actual building than do the images from Assyria or from Arjan. The latter exhibit many details that could not have been actually observed and thus have a higher symbolic content than the Urartian examples.

Such symbol-bearing images appear up to the European Middle Ages, as shown by the example of a silver beaker in the Leipzig City Museum (Altes Rathaus) from the twelfth century CE. There, symbols of tower and basilica alternate around the beaker joined by a stylized rendering of a wall (figure 19.3, bottom). While it is, of course, not possible to show a direct influence from the Near Eastern examples of the first millennium BCE on medieval objects from Europe, such symbols may have been transmitted to Europe during the time of the Roman and later Byzantine empires.

Editors' Note. Translated from German by Naomi F. Miller with assistance from Holly Pittman.

NOTES
1. Vanden Berghe and de Meyer 1983:Cat. no. 97; Kellner 1976:Cat. nos. 156, 158, 160–164, 180, and 185.
2. Van Loon 1966:Fig. 15; Kellner 1976:Cat. nos. 157, 179, and 181.
3. Kroll 1980:Figs. 46, 49; Van Loon 1966:Fig. 14; Vanden Berghe and de Meyer 1983:Fig. 43; Kellner 1976:Cat. nos. 152–155, 159, 165, 177, 195, and 196.
4. Lands of the Bible Archaeology Foundation 1981:192f.
5. Vanden Berghe and De Meyer 1983:95, Fig. 43, Cat. no. 104.

CHAPTER 20

A TEMPLE AT HASANLU

ROBERT H. DYSON, JR. AND MARY M. VOIGT

N 1968 BILL SUMNER AND HIS FAMILY traveled from their home in Shiraz to Azerbaijan, to participate in fieldwork conducted as part of the Hasanlu Project. Bill excavated at Hajji Firuz Tepe and then at Dinkha Tepe while Frances kept the crews at each site well fed and generally happy. Bill returned to the Solduz valley in 1970 to continue the Hasanlu regional survey. We dedicate this article to both Bill and Frances as a small repayment for friendship and for work well done, with fond memories of the Sumners and everyone else who danced in the ruins of Hasanlu IV one night in early August more than thirty years ago.

HASANLU TEPE

The village of Hasanlu is located in a relatively well-watered zone within the Solduz valley of northwest Iran, just to the south of Lake Urmia (Harris 1989; Voigt 1983:268–272, Fig. 120). From 1956 through 1977 archaeological remains within the valley were investigated by members of the Hasanlu Project of the University of Pennsylvania Museum of Archaeology and Anthropology under the direction of Robert H. Dyson, Jr. (Dyson 1983). Excavations on the ancient mound at Hasanlu revealed a large complex of relatively elaborate buildings that burned around 800 BCE (Dyson and Muscarella 1989; Dyson and Voigt 1989). Designated as Period IVB within the archaeological sequence for the Solduz valley, the burned settlement has provided a rich and detailed picture of life in Iron Age Iran. The cause of the fire is clear: weapons scattered throughout the excavated area as well as the bodies of armed warriors and their

victims indicate military action. By the ninth century BCE Hasanlu lay near the borders of three competing polities: Urartu to the north, Assyria to the west, and Mannai to the east. The adoption of Assyrian styles and iconography and the presence of Assyrian imports within its ruins suggest that the rulers of Hasanlu IVB at this time were strongly influenced by the Assyrians if not their allies (Marcus 1989; Winter 1977), and that their city probably fell to an Urartian army (Dyson 1989a:109–110).

Of all the structures within ninth-century Hasanlu, Burned Building II (figure 20.1) is the largest and most impressive, both as a standing ruin and as a reconstruction (see Dyson 1989a:Fig. 17; Dyson and Voigt 1989:cover). That Burned Building II was the most important structure within ancient Hasanlu during the late second and early first millennium (Hasanlu Period IV) is clear, not only from its grand scale and from the more than 1500 artifacts of many materials and types found within its ruins but also from specialized features of its construction and plan. In seeking to understand the role of this structure within the life of the settlement we previously suggested that Burned Building II may have been a temple (Dyson 1989a:118). In this chapter we compare Burned Building II to Mesopotamian buildings that have been well-documented as cult buildings or temples (often by texts or inscriptions), delineating formal similarities between Burned Building II and the organizational plan of straight-axis temples (Baqir 1946:23; Jacobsen 1987:463–464; Margueron 1997; Oppenheim 1977:172; Roaf 1995:426–427). This architectural comparison is fol-

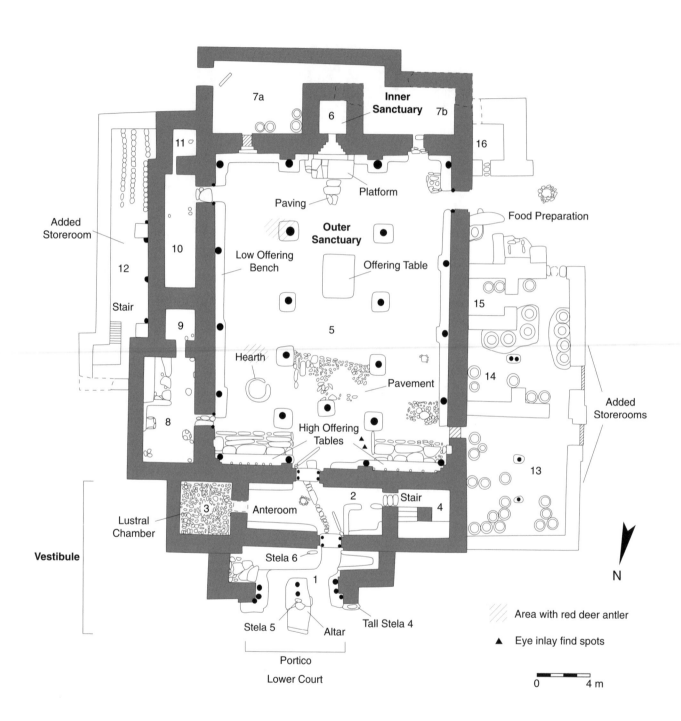

20.1   Plan of Burned Building II at Hasanlu. Functional temple features and the location of two clusters of red deer skulls and antlers and two eye inlays on the first floor of the columned hall are shown. Walls of Period IVB are shaded; those of IVC are open. *Redrawn by T. Hemmaplardh after original by R.H. Dyson, Jr., courtesy of Hasanlu project*

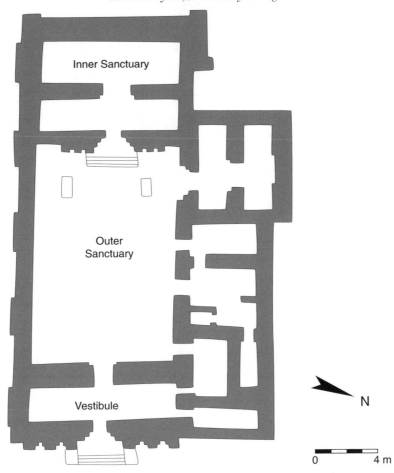

20.2   Example of a Mesopotamian straight-axis temple. Tell Harmal, Temple of Nisaba and Haya. Note that this latter plan has been corrected from Baqir's (1946) photographic Plate 3: the buttresses to the left of the front door were incorrectly drawn. They should match those of the right, and the solid pilasters flanking the door to the inner sanctuary are not in fact single blocks, but made of three units each. *Redrawn by T. Hemmaplardh and R.H. Dyson, Jr., after Amiet 1980c:963*

lowed by a second step that Margueron (1997:165) considers essential in identifying temples: a description of selected artifacts found within Burned Building II that support its interpretation as a structure dedicated to the maintenance of a deity and the deity's household (see also Robertson 1995). The third step is isolation of a specific iconographic element that may have been used to represent Hasanlu, the larger political context in which it functioned during the ninth century, and perhaps the deity that resided in Burned Building II. Finally we pose a series of unanswered questions related to this structure.

MESOPOTAMIAN TEMPLE FORM
Buildings dated to the second millennium are the most appropriate for comparison with Hasanlu Burned Building II since the latter was originally constructed around 1250 BCE (see below and Dyson 1989b:Fig. 5; Dyson and Muscarella

1989:l, 10, Fig. 15). In the absence of any relatively complete second-millennium temple plans from nearby areas on the Iranian Plateau, we must of necessity turn to the west, to Mesopotamian temples of the Middle Assyrian and Middle Babylonian periods. The predominantly straight-axis or *langraum* temple plan (figure 20.2) is exemplified by excavated structures at sites such as Tell Harmal (Baqir 1946:23, Fig. 54) and Ishchali (Frankfort 1936:63, Fig. 60) in southern Mesopotamia and Tell al-Rimah (Oates 1968:Pl. XXVII), Tell Leilan (Weiss 1985:Fig. 14), and Tell Mardik (Buccellati and Kelly-Buccellati 1985:215, Fig. 47) from northern Mesopotamia and Syria. Jean-Claude Margueron (1997:165) in a recent summary article on Mesopotamian temples states that while details of form vary, "...the same three elements and an identical organizing principle unify all the temples that can be recognized as such: inner sanctuary, outer sanctuary, and vestibule, to which a court or annexes may be added as accessories."

If we look at the temple holistically, as an ordered space through which a human servant or visitor might move, he or she would first enter the court, an open air space where blood sacrifices could be made. The temple proper would be entered through the vestibule, which marks a transition from the ordinary world of humans into the sacred world of the god; from the vestibule one then entered the outer sanctuary where daily rituals such as the offering and serving of food were carried out. The inner sanctuary or actual residence of the god might be simply a special area within the outer sanctuary (perhaps a podium) or a separate room "at the end of the progression that orders the temple" (Margueron 1997:165). In our examination of Hasanlu Burned Building II we will proceed from court to inner sanctuary, describing each room and its architectural fitting in some detail.

BURNED BUILDING II

Before considering the ninth-century construction stage of Burned Building II, two important issues for interpretation of its form and contents must be discussed: evidence for the long and complex history of the building, and evidence for a second story. Three distinct construction stages can be recognized for Hasanlu Period IV and, more specifically, for Burned Building II. At construction and during its initial period of use (Hasanlu Period IVC), the basic plan of the building appears to have been in position (figure 20.1, walls marked in gray; note that this plan supersedes a preliminary drawing published by Dyson [1989b:Fig. 6a], where the portico was not included as part of the IVC structure). Burned Building II was dominated by a large central hall with columns supporting the roof (room 5). Entrance into the columned hall was through a broad open-fronted porch or portico (room 1), and then through a second long and narrow room (room 2). Doorways at either end of this second room led to square chambers, the entrance to the west containing a stairway (room 4). At the south end of the columned hall, opposite its entrance, was a very small approximately square room (room 6) with an elaborate entrance. Doors to either side of this small room led to a relatively large roofed space (room 7a-b) which had an exit out of the building to the east. Inside the columned hall, doorways led through the east wall at both ends of the room; each door led into a long narrow room (rooms 8, 10); at the south end of each long room was a narrow door into a much smaller square chamber (rooms 9, 11).

Rereading of the original field notes and examination of computer-enhanced photographs indicate that the end of Period IVC is marked by a major fire (dated around 1100 BCE by radiocarbon), after which Burned Building II

was reconstructed. The fire and rebuilding are visible archaeologically as a layer of pebbles and small pieces of charcoal enclosed in a double layer of mortar that runs between the first and second courses of brickwork above the free-standing stone foundation of the first construction phase. The storerooms on the east (room 12) and west (rooms 13–15) lack this feature and were therefore added after the IVC fire and date to Period IVB (figure 20.1). The walls of room 16 are too poorly preserved to determine its date of construction, but since the foundations abut the west wall of the IVC building in a manner similar to that found in rooms 13–15 there is a good possibility that room 16 is also a VIB addition. Other changes made within Burned Building II included the blocking of two doorways, one in the south wall and one in the west wall of the columned hall, and construction of a small kitchen in the northwest corner of the anteroom (room 2). Period IVB again ends with a fire, and it is this event that preserved the structure that we know best archaeologically.

Stratified above the Period IVB ruins of Burned Building II were sparse traces of occupation including pits and flimsy architectural remains that have been referred to as a "squatter" occupation, otherwise known as Hasanlu Period IVA (Dyson 1965:203). While most of the Period IVB building remained sealed beneath a thick and heavy layer of collapsed brick, Period IVA activities did disturb some parts of Burned Building II, especially the southern end (rooms 6-7, see below).

Given this brief history, it should be clear that we know little about the Period IVC Burned Building II beyond its plan as documented by stone foundations. For Period IVB, however, our information on architecture (as well as building contents) is unusually complete, allowing us to look at architectural details preserved on the first floor as well as aspects of the wood and brick superstructure of the building. When Burned Building II collapsed as a result of the fire that ended Period IVB a section of wall fell into the columned hall (room 5); this intact brickwork indicates that in this room the walls rose to a height of at least 7 m, providing a minimum estimate for the total height of the building. The stratigraphy of deposits within the building allows us to determine that it had a second story, reached by the stairway in room 4. Throughout Burned Building II (as well as other Period IVB structures), objects as well as people were found lying on the floor at ground level, sealed beneath a layer of burned debris. Well above this first floor deposit, resting in collapsed brick, and sometimes clearly stratified above ceiling beam and matting fragments, were a great many objects, most of which must have come from second floor rooms.

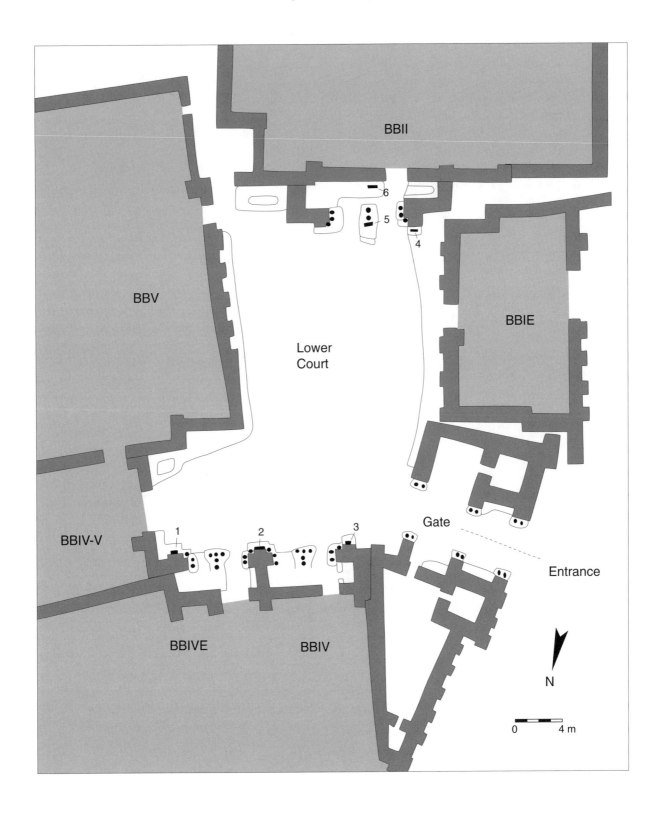

20.3 Plan of the Lower Court at Hasanlu showing the approach to Burned Building II. Arabic numerals refer to stelae.
Redrawn by T. Hemmaplardh after original by R.H. Dyson, Jr., courtesy of Hasanlu project

The stratigraphic evidence is compelling for anyone who has excavated a Hasanlu building with this double layer of artifacts, including both authors. We find no satisfactory explanation for the wood and matting fragments and second layer of (often very valuable) artifacts except the presence of a second floor. Thus the statement by Roaf (1998:77) that it is merely a "supposition that many of the objects derive from a possible upper storey" must be disregarded. This does not preclude the possibility that some items fell from the roofs of the buildings. An isolated cluster of iron spear and pike heads was found in the brick collapse above the first floor near the center of the columned hall of Burned Building II (Dyson 1989a:Fig 23b). It is possible that in this case, we have recovered a cache of weapons stored on the roof.

A preliminary study of both stratigraphy and the distribution of artifacts within this upper layer indicates that the second story did not extend above the entire first floor but was probably restricted to the areas above the surrounding rooms to the north, south and west. We can say nothing about the layout of this second floor but can make some inferences about function based on room size and contents. The second-floor rooms must have been relatively small, since they are located above long and narrow first-floor spaces. Because of the large quantities of artifacts that spilled out of these rooms it seems most likely that the second story contained storage areas rather than living space, and served as a "treasury" for the building.

THE LAYOUT OF BURNED BUILDING II

FORECOURT

In Margueron's model, a court or open space is not an essential part of the temple but is often present (1997:166). In front of the entrance to Burned Building II was a stone-paved courtyard (the lower court) that could be entered at its northwestern corner (figure 20.3; Dyson 1989a:Figs. 6b, 10; see also Amiet 1980c:Fig. 992 for an isometric drawing). To approach Burned Building II, one moved through an impressive gate with brick buttresses on its exterior. Once in the court, one was surrounded by buildings two stories high with ornamented façades; thus although the lower court was a relatively large unroofed space, it was dominated by architecture. It should be emphasized that the buildings bordering the lower court to the north, east, and west functioned during Period IVB as service buildings, containing kitchens, stables, and storage areas for food, weapons and horse gear (de Schauensee 1989). The fact that the utilitarian function of these buildings is at odds with their elaborate exteriors indicates that it is the lower

court itself that is important during Period IVB, as would be expected for the forecourt of a temple.

Two forms of ornamentation were used on the lower court façades. Walls to the east and west carried brick buttresses that must have symbolized the presence of religious and/or royal power (Dyson 1989a:126–127; Roaf 1995:426, Fig. 5). This inference is supported by the extensive use of buttresses on the ziggurat and associated thirteenth-century temples at Chogha Zanbil (Ghirshman 1966); David Oates (1970:2) notes that in northern Mesopotamia during the Middle Assyrian period "...buttressed façades...were a conventional feature of even the most provincial public temple." Because buttressed façades are not confined to the lower court and its gate but occur in other areas of Hasanlu IVB (Dyson 1989b:Fig. 11), that architectural element by itself does not allow us to distinguish structures dedicated to religion from those serving a secular elite, that is, "royal" structures. A second element in the decoration of the lower court may be more diagnostic: along the northern side of the court, a series of tall limestone stelae had been placed in a symmetrical fashion adjacent to porticoed entrances as part of the Period IVB rebuilding (compare Dyson 1989a:Figs 6a, 6b). The three stelae in front of Burned Buildings IV and IVE reached a maximum height of 4.5 m (figure 20.3, stelae 1, 2, and 3; Dyson 1989a:Fig. 12); they were set at the eastern and western ends of the pair of small porticos that led into Burned Buildings IV and IVE as well as in the center between the porticos.

On the south side of the court, three stelae were associated with the entrance to Burned Building II: a 1.74 m tall slab with a pointed top stood to the right or west of the portico (figure 20.1, room 1; figure 20.3, stela 4; Dyson 1989a:Fig. 14); a smaller rectangular stone sat on an altar (see below) at the center of the portico; and a nearly square slab (figures 20.1, 20.3, stela 6) had been placed to the left (east) of the doorway leading from the portico into room 2 of Burned Building II. When one is actually standing in the lower court the stelae have a mirror effect, clearly linking the northern and southern façades, and providing a unifying element in a space that has irregular boundaries. Since the stelae bore neither decoration nor inscriptions, they would appear to be aniconic markers similar to those known from religious contexts at Mari, Byblos, Altıntepe and elsewhere (Muscarella 1971:264).

VESTIBULE

This first space within a temple proper is characterized by Margueron as the transition point between the exterior world and the outer sanctuary of the temple, the place where a relationship between profane and sacred is estab-

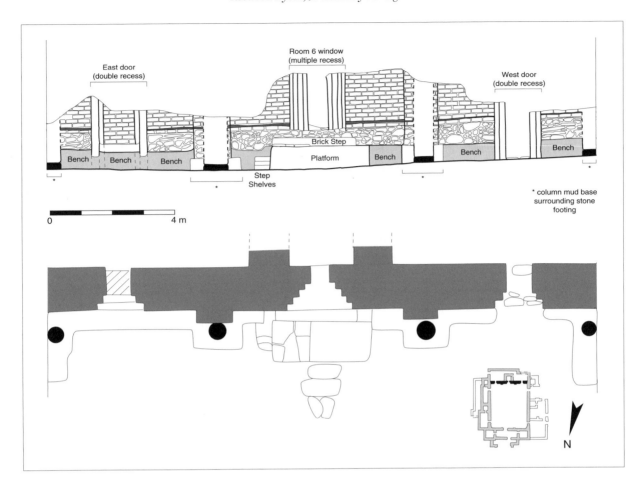

20.4   Diagrammatic elevation (top) and plan (bottom) of Burned Building II, south wall of room 5, period IVB.
Redrawn by T. Hemmaplardh from original by E.J. Keall, courtesy of Hasanlu project.

lished. Such transitional zones are potentially dangerous, requiring those who enter to undergo "...a transformation of being, most often generated by one or several transition rituals" (Margueron 1997:166). Within Burned Building II, the space equivalent in function to the Mesopotamian temple's vestibule is divided into two long narrow rooms with offset doorways (rooms 1 and 2), an accessory chamber to the east (room 3), and a stairway to the west (room 4).

Room 1 is a portico, a porch with a broad opening stretching across most of its width to the north; three pairs of wooden columns within the opening supported a second-story room, which could have been an open space (that is, a balcony) or closed. In the center of the portico opening, directly in front of its two central columns, was a large flat stone set on a low foundation made of smaller stones. Resting on the large flat stone was stela 5 (figure 20.3), and in front of stela 5, set against its base, was a highly distinctive "smooth, waterworn slab of bluish-grey stone"(figure 20.1; Dyson 1989a:116, Fig. 14; Van Loon 1962:16). This raised stone structure with stela and slab can be interpreted

as an altar (Haak 1997), visible to those allowed into the court, some of whom could not enter the temple itself. Across the front of the altar was a narrow shelf, too high above the floor to have functioned as a step (Dyson and Voigt 1989:cover); this feature is duplicated on altars in various Mesopotamian temples and served no doubt for the outdoor display of offerings or items connected to ritual activities (for examples of such "two-step" altars see Delougaz and Lloyd 1942:Pl. 20a-b, Figs. 152, 157; Deshayes 1969:Fig. 110; Roux 1964:176; Woolley 1954:169 ff).

Most of the area within the portico (room 1) was filled with raised benches and platforms built of brick and stone. To the east or left of the door into room 2, a wide brick platform (with remnants of stone paving) ran along the back of the portico; small stela 6 is set on this platform next to the door (Dyson 1989a:Fig. 14; Dyson and Voigt 1989:cover). In the narrow space at the western end of the portico the entire floor was raised; resting on this low platform was a narrow bench running along the walls of this alcove.

From the portico, one moved into the second part of the vestibule, another long, narrow space (room 2) that provided access to the columned hall (room 5) as well as to a small stone-paved room to the east (room 3) and a stairway to the west (room 4). A paved drain ran across this "anteroom" between the doorways that link it to the portico and the columned hall. The presence of a stone doorsocket in the northern and southern doorways of room 2, and their similarity in form indicates that this room had wooden doors. Room 2 had a hearth edged with stones in an enclosed "kitchen" area at its western end, leaving only a narrow passage to a western doorway and a stair that provided access to the second floor (room 4). The stairway was built around a central brick pier, with the lower stairs of brick and the upper part of wood, exactly the same kind of construction still used by the villagers of Malyan in southern Iran. In the eastern half of room 2 low benches flanked the northern and southern walls. A door in the anteroom's eastern wall led into a square room with a fully stone-paved floor and a pottery jar drain beneath the floor (room 3). The room is suitable for bathing, and a small hearth set against the wall for warmth could have provided hot water.

Taken together, the portico, anteroom and paved chamber at the entrance to Burned Building II fulfill the requirements for a temple vestibule, and form a suitable space for "transition rituals" (Margueron 1997:166). At the portico entrance, the altar provided a place for blood sacrifice in the open air, but also at the edge of sacred space. The benches and platforms in both portico and anteroom could have been used to display offerings or perhaps even the image of the deity on certain feast days. The transitional nature of the Burned Building II vestibule is also clear if we consider its dual role as an arena for display as well as a means of blocking or obscuring vision; while objects set on the altar or platform at the back of the portico could be viewed by anyone allowed into the lower court, the doorways through the vestibule into the main room of Burned Building II (room 5) were offset so that activities within the outer sanctuary as well as the image of the deity within the inner sanctuary, its normal residence, could not be seen from the lower court or even from the portico entrance, whether or not the anteroom doors were closed. In this respect the layout of Burned Building II differs from many Mesopotamian temples, which were arranged so that the cult figure could be seen from the street when all the doors were open (for example, Tell Harmal; figure 20.2). On the other hand, the reconstruction of the Ishtar temple of twelfth-century Assur shows offset doorway alignments (Andrae 1977:Fig. 169) as does the Temple of Nabu at

Khorsabad in the eighth century (Amiet 1980c:Fig. 911). Apparently, a long tradition for this offset arrangement also seems to have existed in northeast Mesopotamia. Initiates or supplicants who passed through the vestibule could have purified themselves by bathing in the paved room or lustral chamber (room 3) before entering the sanctuary proper (see Moorey 1982:84).

OUTER SANCTUARY

The outer sanctuary of a Mesopotamian temple was "the room where the daily rituals, especially the food offerings were carried out" (Margueron 1997:165) and where the cult image's dress and ornaments were changed (Winter 2000:139). The cult image may reside in this main room, or in an adjacent closed space (the inner sanctuary). Within Burned Building II, the large columned hall (room 5) served as the outer sanctuary.

Room 5 is rectangular, measuring 18 x 23.5 m. It is entered from the vestibule through an off-center door in the north wall. A row of wooden columns was arranged along the eastern and western (side) walls of the room. Two central rows of free-standing columns divided the hall into three long spaces. Each of these two central rows ended against a pilaster on the north and south walls of the hall. All of the columns were of poplar wood about 50 cm in diameter; each column stood on a stone floor slab and was surrounded by a mud base (figure 20.1). Architectural details and features built within the room are numerous and varied.

At the northern end of the columned hall, flanking the doorway from the vestibule, were two high benches built of brick and mud plaster standing 1.20 m above the floor and measuring 80 cm from front to back. The front edge of both benches was reinforced by a small square wooden beam, suggesting that the upper surfaces were meant to be used with some frequency. In front of the benches were slightly sloping rectangular stone-pavements, the front edge of which ended in stone-paved catchment drains. Anything placed on these high benches would have been visually framed by architectural elements. At either end of the benches were the northernmost of the four rows of columns in the hall. The space between the columns on the north wall was emphasized by mudbrick pilasters set behind the two central columns and by triple recesses or rabbets[1] set on each bench in the room corners (figure 20.1). In the area between rabbet and mudbrick pilaster at the back of each bench was a row of six small postholes 15 cm in diameter to support some higher paneling or other wooden structure standing in front of a white-plastered wall face. Thus when looking at the north wall the viewer would see two small unified stages composed of high benches, the wall behind them and the paving in front. We interpret the benches as high offering tables; the paving and drains were presumably to catch liquids such as wine, beer or milk lost during ritual libations carried out on the tables by someone standing in front of the tables (see Winter 2000).

On the east and west walls of the columned hall, facing the ends of the stone pavements were fully preserved shallow niches about 80 cm above the pavement. Although there was no direct evidence (since the original plastered face of the wall was not preserved), these niches may have been used for lamps, as was the case at Ziwiye where we excavated seven shallow triangular niches about the same height above floor level that showed localized areas of smoke-blackened plaster where small lamps must have burned (Dyson 1964b:4). Along the wall faces in the rest of the room ran a low bench built of mud with its surface 60 cm above floor level. Evenly spaced burned-out holes that once held the wooden side columns were found embedded in the bench. The bench along the east wall (like the high offering tables to the north) had been reinforced along the front edge with a small square beam of wood. In front of some columns on the west wall the bench had been built out or reinforced, suggesting that one of the functions of the low benches was to protect and support the column base. A line of small pots found in first floor debris in front of the bench along the west wall suggests that these benches also served to display objects within the outer sanctuary (Dyson 1989a:Fig. 19a). Roux points out that "low brick benches around the cella and the antecella [outer and inner sanctuaries] supported the statues of other gods and of worshipers, together with royal steles and various *ex votos*" (1964:176). The use of such "benches" in temples goes back at least to the end of the Early Dynastic period at Assur (Amiet 1980c:898, Temple of Ishtar, level G).

At the northern end of the columned hall in front of the eastern high bench and pavement lay a round hearth bordered by a raised edging or curb. A second less obvious "hearth" is represented by a shallow ash pit surrounded by paving stones in front of the high bench and pavement on the west. A structurally similar arrangement was found in Burned Building I West, where benches on the east wall of the columned hall flanked the door leading to the anteroom. Centered above each bench was a triple-rabbeted niche. A round curbed hearth lay in front of the south niche, while a square curbed hearth lay in front of the north niche (Dyson 1989a:Fig. 10). This repetition of arrangement and shape suggests that the hearths carried a gendered meaning, perhaps in a similar manner to the presence of round

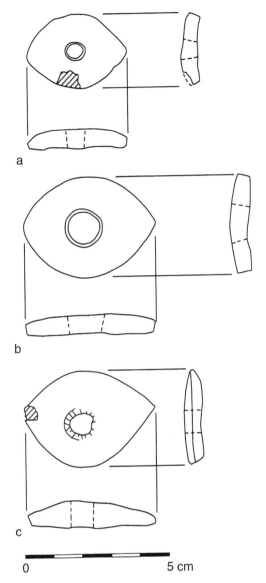

a

b

c

0   5 cm

20.5 Ivory eye inlays: *a*, One of a pair, not identical, suitable for a life-size figure, recovered from the northwest corner of the columned hall of Burned Building II (found near body 4 according to Maurits Van Loon, the excavator [HAS 60-899a, UPM 61-5-205; ivory? 3.4 cm l, 2.5 cm w, 0.5 cm th; published in Muscarella 1980:102, 103, 189, No. 205]. The second inlay [HAS 60-899b, Tehran] described as "similar" was not drawn but is recorded in a field photograph]); *b*, found in the second floor collapse in the southeast room of Burned Building II ([HAS 64-515a, UPM 65-31-339; bone; 4.5 cm l, 3.4 cm w; 0.5 cm th; published in Muscarella 1980:102, 103, 189, No. 206]. A second eye inlay recovered from the same location was not drawn and is now in Tehran [HAS 64-515b: 4.0 cm l, 3.1 cm w, 0.5 cm th]); *c*, found between the entrance and the paved area in the columned hall of Burned Building I West (most probably found on the floor as the upper part of the deposit had been stripped away in the following period leaving only a shallow layer of burned debris [HAS 58-430, Tehran: 4.5 cm l, 4.2 cm w, 0.7 cm th]). *Hasanlu project*

hearths in female burials, and square hearths in male burials in Late Bronze Age Central Asia (Gupta 1979:192; Mallory 1989:53).

To the south of the benches and hearths in room 5 on the floor in the center of the room lay a sub-rectangular paved area measuring about 3 x 6 m, underlain by a large sunken pithos. This pavement and drain (framed by columns on three sides but open to the south) could have been used for pouring offerings, providing a visually restricted indoor location for such activity. The purification of the cult figure and other paraphernalia was an important part of daily ritual in ancient Mesopotamian (Winter 2000), and this centrally located pavement would have been an obvious place for such activity within the outer sanctuary of Burned Building II. On the other hand, the isolated central column could need additional roof support, perhaps near an opening in the roof. Such an opening would have admitted light as well as rain and snow, precipitation that would have landed on the paving rather than the room's mud floor.

From this central paving, one looked south between the two central rows of wooden columns toward a rectangular mudbrick platform and beyond that to another platform in front of an elaborately decorated opening into a small room (room 6). We argue below that this small room served as the inner sanctuary of the temple; the position of the central brick platform suggests that it had an important function in relationship to the inner sanctuary, and that it was used as an offering table, repeating a relationship commonly seen in Mesopotamian temples (for example, at Ur; Moorey 1982:Fig. 32). Although the surface of the table was burned, this is true of most brick surfaces in the room; moreover, there was no accumulated ash or other debris to suggest the regular burning of items or substances in this location.

The focal point in the columned hall was its south wall (figure 20.4). Symmetrically arranged on this wall were a raised central opening 60 cm wide and two flanking doorways with widths of 80 cm (east) and 100 cm (west) framed by receding brick elements referred to as "stepped recesses," or "niched doorways" (Dyson 1989a:118) or "triple recessed entrances" (Mallowan 1966:Fig. 270), or "doorways with multiple rabbets" (Roaf 1998:57, 63–65). The central opening in the south wall, like the outer corners of the high offering tables at the opposite end of the room, was multi-rabbeted. It had a high sill at its base that lay 1.3 m above the floor level of the outer sanctuary. Access to the opening was by means of the stone-paved platform that lay in front of it with a single mudbrick "step" 20 cm high on it. The sill itself was 20 cm above the step. This arrangement allowed access to room 6, and recalls the stepped

approach to the similarly raised sanctuary at Tell Harmal (Amiet 1980c:986; Baqir 1946:Pl. 3), but the brick floor inside the room was a full 40 cm below the sill, making access even more difficult. Clearly the opening was more functional as a means of viewing the interior of the room than it was for ease of entry; in other words, it was not a doorway in the usual sense.

The platform rises 90 cm above the floor of the columned hall; note that this was not a "wider raised part" of the low benches that run along the south wall (as stated by Roaf 1998:65) but was built as an independent and separate structure (Dyson 1989a:Fig. 15). On the east (left) side of the platform, backed by the south wall and facing into the room, were three mud shelves stepped above floor level, each rising 15 cm above the others. These surfaces must have served for display of offerings, as their soft surface, small size, and orientation preclude their use as real steps; similar stepped offering shelves have also been found in Mesopotamian temples (for example, Moorey 1982:Fig. 32, cella). A small area of stone paving extended into the room along the axial line from the front of the platform, visually linking the platform and multi-rabbeted opening to the raised-brick offering table. Multiple rabbets have a very restricted occurrence and their study should not be confused with that of single and double rabbets (pace Roaf 1998). Double rabbets are often linked to ordinary doorway construction: for example, some double rabbets retain the remains of door framing beams or door pivot stones set in the recess. The opening with multiple rabbets at the south end of Burned Building II is unique within the excavated architectural sample from Hasanlu. In general, multiple rabbets appear to have been somehow symbolic so they occur almost exclusively in association with cult buildings (Dyson 1989a:118; Roaf 1995:426; 1998:58–62; see also Barnett 1975:99, 145). In Mesopotamia the association of triple-rabbeted doorway and temple cella or sanctuary occurs as early as the Early Dynastic III period as illustrated on a plaque from Ur (Moorey 1982:185). This form was later used on all of the doorways of the ziggurat at Chogha Zanbil, built in the late second millennium (Ghirshman 1966:68); triple rabbets occur as late as the Hellenistic period in Central Asia where they form external wall features on the "temple à niches indentées" at Ai Khanum (Shkoda 1998:Fig. 1). In early Iron Age Iran the best examples of multiple rabbets used with doorways in religious structures occur in the so-called Fort and the Painted Chamber at Babajan, and in the shrine at Surkh Dum (Roaf 1998:67–68, 70, Figs. 10–11).

To the east and west of the central door and platform were double-rabbeted doorways that had stone sills at floor level. These doors led into rooms 7a and 7b which were joined by a narrow corridor behind the inner sanctuary (figure 20.1); access to the outside of the building was from the southeastern room 7a. The double rabbets on these doorways rose from floor level to the full 2.5-m height of the preserved wall (unlike the doorway to room AB6 at Nimrud where the rabbets turn to form basal ledges at floor level; Mallowan 1966:Fig. 270). At the time of the Period IVB destruction, only the doorway on the right side was still in use; the eastern doorway had been filled with brick and then blocked in front by a low offering bench, indicating that some if not all of the existing low benches were installed late in Period IVB.

INNER SANCTUARY

At the end of the progression of rooms in a temple is the inner sanctuary, the place where the deity lives (Margueron 1997:165). Room 6 in Burned Building II is a nearly square chamber a little over two meters on a side that could be entered through a rabbeted opening from the columned hall as described above. The walls of room 6, standing to a height of over two meters on all sides, had lost much of their mud-plaster facing, and contained no windows or niches. The floor, 40 cm lower than the high sill (but still 90 cm above the floor of the columned hall) was paved with mudbrick. The form of the multi-rabbeted opening is significant; because of the high sill, this opening is more properly a "window" than a "doorway." While it is not difficult to step over a 40-cm high barrier to gain access to room 6, the sill still restricts rather than facilitates movement. An intriguing parallel for the opening into the inner sanctuary is found on an ivory panel from Nimrud (Mallowan 1966:Cat. no. 429), where the barrier across the base of a triple-rabbeted opening takes the form of a balustrade; a female face peers out from the opening, identified as a window by Barnett (1975:145, 147). While Mallowan considers the ivory figure a representation of a courtesan, he notes that the architectural forms are typical of Assyrian temples and palaces (1966:522).

Room 6, the focal point of Burned Building II, meets the criteria for an inner sanctuary or cella not only by virtue of its location within Burned Building II and its elaborate entrance, but also because of its elevated floor level. Oppenheim states that in Mesopotamian temples, "the image was lifted above the level of human activities by means of a pedestal, enclosed in the recessed niche [or small room] of the cella" (Oppenheim 1977:186). If a cult statue were placed in room 6 it would stand on a surface 90 cm above the floor of the columned hall; this height would be increased to 1.3 m if the image were placed on a stool or

chair so that its base would stand at the level of the sill. With or without a basal podium, an image standing in the inner sanctuary would have been at a height *above* people carrying out activities in the outer sanctuary.

SUBSIDIARY ROOMS

In addition to the three primary spaces within a temple, additional rooms are often found, usually associated with the outer sanctuary. Margueron states that such rooms "were designed for storage or for the daily life of the priest who lived in the temple" (1997:166; see also Leemans 1952); among other activities, food preparation would take place in such rooms (Oppenheim 1977:187). Undecorated (single-rabbeted) doorways in the eastern and western walls of the columned hall lead into small rooms with varying functions based on their contents.

Subsidiary rooms flanked the temple sanctuary to the east, west and south. The four smaller rooms on the east side of the columned hall (rooms 8–11) formed pairs consisting of a long narrow room with a small square room leading off to the south. Room 8 had a special but unknown function, as shown by features set against its east wall. A hearth set on the floor and backed by four pottery tubes with a square section may have served to warm the room; a collapsed shelf-like structure that stood against the southeast wall may once have been a table. The outermost room to the east (added during Period IVB) had no doors, and was presumably entered from above via the stairway at its northern end. Rows of bricks could have supported large storage jars. Small rooms are found in the Kititum temple at Ishchali where Frankfort referred to them as "a row of single storerooms" (1936:83, Fig. 60), but within Burned Building II, room 8 (and perhaps others) had some other function. Other examples of small auxiliary rooms are found in the Temple of Shu-Sin at Tell Asmar (Frankfort 1940:Pl.1; Oates 1986, Fig. 29), the Ningal temple at Ur (Moorey 1982:Fig. 32), and the temple of Building Level II at Tell Leilan (Weiss 1985:Fig. 14).

To the west of the columned hall was a complex of larger rooms (added sometime after the IVC fire) that contained giant pithoi for food storage and other smaller vessels as well as weapons and other equipment (Dyson 1989a:Fig. 23a–b). The unroofed area to the south of the western storerooms (figure 20.1) was apparently for food preparation. Room 7a to the south of the columned hall was also used for cooking based on the presence of pots, jars (some bridge-spouted), pithoi and close to thirty pottery funnels on the floor. While some of the auxiliary rooms around the columned hall were used for domestic activities such as food storage and preparation, they do

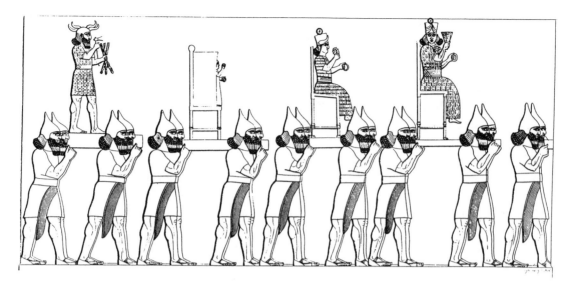

20.6   Palace relief of Tiglath-Pileser III (745-727 BCE). According to Mesopotamian custom, the gods of a defeated city were
taken captive by victors, as shown on this relief from Nimrud where Assyrian troops are carrying four cult statues. The two
seated female figures and the small figure in the box have not been identified, but the standing male figure is the storm god
Teshub identified by his horned headpiece and the trident and axe that he carries. *Barnett and Falkner 1962*

not appear suitable as apartments and we must assume that the temple attendants and priests lived elsewhere in the lower court complex.

To summarize, the architectural features and general plan of Hasanlu Burned Building II fulfill the primary functional requirements for a "temple" as set out by Margueron. This is, however, only half of the case that must be made. Margueron points out, "Only a cluster of convergent indices can signify a sanctuary within a given edifice. In the absence of texts, the criteria for identification usually applied include the form of the building *and the nature of its installations and furnishings* [our italics]" (1997:165). The second section of this paper examines a small sample of the artifacts found within Burned Building II.

SOME TEMPLE FURNISHINGS
Margueron emphasizes the fact that in the Near East, a temple was the residence of a god, serving as a shelter or "house"; temples were places where "...the tasks of daily life were carried out, no different from those of humans, except that they concerned a god" (1997:165; see also Robertson 1995). Thus the contents of a temple may, and in fact should, include elements expected in an elite residence, as well as elements that are *not* found in "palaces." Burned Building II meets this expectation.

EYE INLAYS
At the north end of the outer sanctuary, near the western high offering table and associated with a group of six

skeletons, were two flat, lenticular pieces of bone or ivory each pierced through the center for the insertion of an inlay disc (figure 20.5a). Based on size and form these pieces may be identified as eye inlays. Although the inlays differ slightly in size, they are a rare artifact type that by virtue of archaeological association could be considered a pair. If so they may well come from a cult statue made in Mesopotamian style.

In Mesopotamia, statues of deities or cult figures took human form and were life size (figure 20.6). Not one of these images has been recovered archaeologically, but texts, representations on seals and reliefs, fragments (especially eye inlays), and small replicas provide information on their form and use. They were made of wood, and had large staring eyes made of precious material (Oppenheim 1977:184). The texts tell us that statues of deities were dressed in splendid garments, adorned with jewelry and sheathed in metal to cover exposed wood. The deity was "considered present in its image" (Oppenheim 1977:84) and normally resided on a pedestal in the cella or inner sanctuary of its temple where it was served by priests and received visits from other gods and supplicants. Irene Winter (2000) provides a detailed description of similar practices in a modern Hindu temple.

When a Mesopotamian cult image or statue was moved in antiquity, for example, in processions or when captured in warfare, the deity moved with it. Given the strong Assyrian influence generally seen at Hasanlu in late Period IVB (Winter 1980:22–32), and the presence of imported

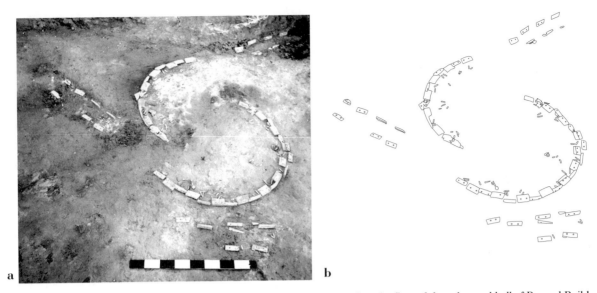

a   b

20.7   *a*, Ivory plaques and pins from a circular object with three legs. Found on the floor of the columned hall of Burned Building II; charcoal fragments were associated with the circle of plaques when they were found. Diameter: 57.5 cm. *Photograph from Hasanlu project archive*; *b*, Schematic plan of circular object. *Drawing by T. Hemmaplardh*

Mesopotamian and Syrian goods stored in Burned Building II (for example, ivories [Muscarella 1980], seals [Marcus 1996], lion censers [Muscarella 1974; Van Loon 1962]) it is not unreasonable to postulate some similarity in religious practice between Hasanlu and nearby Mesopotamia. If the eye inlays do represent a cult image it must have resided in the inner sanctuary with its raised floor (room 6). The floor of this chamber was clean when excavated, presumably cleared out before the building collapsed in flames. Assuming that the eyes represent a near life-size cult image, we may hypothesize that several of the temple attendants were trying to carry the deity to safety. No other elements that might be part of such a statue were found, but given the amount of carbonized material found within room 5, carbonized and crushed fragments of a wooden image would have been virtually indistinguishable in the general debris if they survived at all. Harder to explain is the absence of metal sheeting, since Mesopotamian deities seem to have had gold or silver "skins" covering unadorned parts of their body (Oppenheim 1977:184).

A second pair of eye inlays was found in the second-story debris of room 7a at the southeast corner of the building (figure 20.5b); a single lenticular bone inlay was recovered in Burned Building I West. Again, looking at Mesopotamian practices, these might have been part of another cult figure stored upstairs in a "treasury" or they could have been separate gifts to the temple—material for the manufacture of a new cult figure at some future date (Ellis 1986 and personal communication 1990). At Chogha

Zanbil five pairs of eye inlays were found in the antechamber to the Temple of Ishnikarah and two other pairs in chamber 38 of the Kiririsha temple (Ghirshman 1966:125, 130; Pls. LI, 3, LXIII, 56).

Fragments of a few small human statuettes made of ivory and wood (Dyson 1964a:33, 1965:Fig. 6A, wrongly labeled ivory; Muscarella 1980:Cat. nos. 58–71) were also recovered from Burned Building II, fallen from second-story storerooms. Muscarella (1980:179–180) has raised the possibility that some of these may represent divine rather than human figures. If any of these statuettes actually was a depiction of a deity, it would necessarily have been a small-scale version of a much larger cult statue in which the deity resided (see Voigt 1983 for a general discussion of small figures and replicas).

DRUM?

A second group of artifacts from the floor of the outer sanctuary, potentially linked to Mesopotamian religious ritual, consists of a series of rectangular bone plaques and dowels. Alternating plaques (one flat and the next downward at a right angle) once fixed in position by dowels make up two segments of a circle with three double lines of plaques splayed outward from the central arcs (figure 20.7). These fragments are tentatively interpreted as the remains of a round drum, the bone pieces outlining the top of a circular frame with three supporting legs. Four or five types of drums are documented by texts as well as by images from ancient Mesopotamia, ranging in size from

20.8 Relief of Sargon II
(721–705 BCE).
Showing his conquest
of the city of Kishesim.
Stag horns set into the
topmost row of towers
presumably served as
symbols identifying the
city or its region to
those viewing the relief
in the Assyrian capital
of Khorsabad.
*Botta and Flandin
1849–50, vol. 1:Pl. 68.
Photograph by
Francine Sarin*

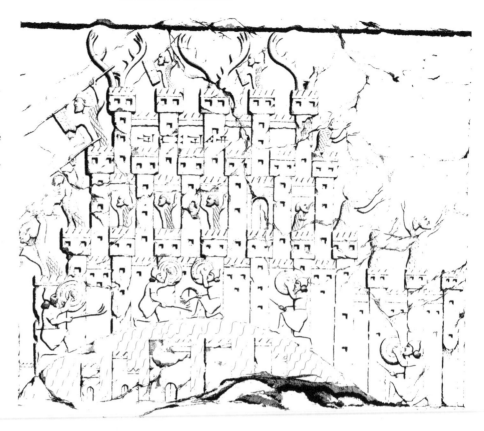

small and easily portable instruments to drums as tall as the men who strike them (C. Sachs 1940:73–78). In texts, drums are frequently associated with temples and rituals; more specifically, kettle drums covered with the skin of a bull were used in exorcism ceremonies by temple priests (Oppenheim 1977:179; A. Sachs 1955:334–338; C. Sachs 1940:77–78). The Hasanlu circular frame recalls drums depicted on the Mesopotamian reliefs from Ur and Lagash that date to the end of the third millennium (Moortgat 1969:Fig. 199–200). An alternative interpretation of this artifact cluster is as a table (Maude de Schauensee, personal communication).

RED DEER ANTLERS

A third group of finds within Burned Building II, particularly intriguing within the historical context of Hasanlu IVB, is the presence of two groups of red deer skulls and antlers on the eastern side of the columned hall. A cluster composed of a complete deer skull and two or three antlers, associated with one or two pairs of ram's horns, was found fallen to the floor near the circular hearth at the northeastern end of the hall (Muscarella 1989:Fig. 20). A second cluster with at least two complete skulls with antlers was found toward the southeastern corner of the hall, and field records indicate a significantly greater number of antlers were

evidenced from this general area. The stratigraphic record indicates that the animal heads lay beneath (rather than in) brick collapse; apparently they had fallen from the interior of the columned hall rather than from the rooms above. Presumably groups of two or more deer heads were attached to the east wall of the hall, or perhaps to the columns. Deer heads were not found anywhere else *in situ* within the Period IV settlement. The custom of attaching animal horns to the walls of special buildings (not necessarily temples) has a long history, going back in Iran at least to the fourth millennium at Susa (Pittman 1992:Fig. 28). We will return to the possible significance of the red deer antlers in Burned Building II at the end of this chapter.

FURNITURE

Mesopotamian records indicate that thrones and podia of precious materials for various deities were presented as votive offerings by a variety of rulers, and in the Hindu temple studied by Winter (2000:139) such furniture was also used to support cult images. Evidence for such furniture may have been found badly burned and fragmented at the right front corner of the platform that stands in front of the entrance into the inner sanctuary (Dyson 1989a:Fig. 18a). These wooden furniture remains are currently under study by Maude de Schauensee who reports that two backless chairs or thrones were present, as documented by two sets of four legs that are too tall to have been used as foot-stools. In addition, the remains of a tall iron tripod lamp were found lying against the eastern corner of the platform (Dyson 1989a:120).

WALL TILES

Stratified above the furniture fragments at the south end of the columned hall were two wall ornaments of copper or bronze. One had a complete central knob attached to a flat base while the other had only a round central hole; both had short studs around the edge for attachment to some other backing. On the platform itself lay fragments of two square glazed wall tiles with "Assyrianizing designs" (Heim N.D.) that may have decorated the adjacent walls. Another mass of tiles was found at the south end of the columned hall (Dyson 1989a:Fig.18b), but these artifacts are clustered in fill well above the floor and appear to have been stored together on the second floor rather than attached to the walls. Wall tiles are found in both temples and palaces in Mesopotamia. An exact parallel for the knobbed copper/bronze piece from Hasanlu was found at Nuzi, "in close association with objects of votive intent" (Starr 1937:Cat. No. 482, Pl. 127E).

HEIRLOOMS

Leonard Woolley (as quoted in Moorey 1982:189) has pointed out that "a Sumerian temple, like a modern cathedral, was a veritable museum of antiquities; for centuries pious kings and others had been offering their treasures for the service of the gods, and the temple storerooms would contain objects of all ages." Some of the 1500 objects stored in Burned Building II certainly document that statement. A fragment of a stone vessel (Pigott 1989b:Fig. 16) once inlaid with alternating figures of goats and trees bears a partially preserved inscription that refers to "Kadashmin-Enlil," either the First (early fourteenth century BCE) or, more probably, the Second (ca. 1275 BCE). This vessel was clearly an heirloom from the early years of Burned Building II, which we believe to have been founded late in the second millennium. A macehead inscribed with the same name found its way to the Ishtar temple at Nineveh (Brinkman 1976:134; Thompson and Hamilton 1932:107, Pl. LXXXIII). Among other important items dating to the later second millennium and found in Burned Building II are the remains of mosaic glass Kassite beakers (Marcus 1992), and a group of stone maceheads. Twenty maceheads made of limestone, and three of black stone or hematite inlaid with circular patterns, fell in a cluster into room 7a, stratified in the second floor debris at a height of one to

two meters above the floor. Three of these maceheads bore cuneiform inscriptions, two of them referring to the Elamite ruler of Susa, Tan Ruhuriter (probably the Second), who lived not long before Kadashmin-Enlil II (Carter and Stolper 1984:21, 148, Table 4). In the small shrine of the thirteenth-century East Temple of Kiririsha at Chogha Zanbil a deposit of over a hundred similar plain and inlaid maceheads was found (Ghirshman 1966:100, 161, Pls. VIII, 4, LIX). Five of the plain ones duplicate shapes at Hasanlu and bear inscriptions, including three of Untash-Napirisha (1260 BCE–1235 BCE).

In the second-story fill of the vestibule (room 2) was found a very beautiful Neo-Assyrian lion-bowl censer made of Egyptian blue, covered with gold foil (Dyson 1989a:Fig. 22). Such vessels were traditionally used for offering incense to the gods in Syria and Egypt (Van Loon 1962). A fragment of a similar censer made of ivory was found in the fill of the southeast room 7a of Burned Building II, fallen from above (Muscarella 1974:Fig. 5).

BEADS

One small, square auxiliary room on the west (room 15) housed hundreds of beads or necklaces of paste, glass, carnelian, lapis, copper, Baltic amber, and other materials. A second similar deposit occurred in the second floor fill of room 7a where beads filled two buckets when collected. A deposit of necklaces composed of beads was found in the Ninkavrak temple at Terqa (Buccellati and Kelly-Buccellati 1985: 220, Fig. 50). Large quantities of beads were also associated with the Ishtar temple at Assur (Andrae 1935:96–100, Pls. 39–40; Moorey 1994:178), Temple A at Nuzi (Starr 1937:87–115, 445–446) and the sanctuary at Surkh Dum (Curvers 1989:381–411, Pls. 230–232).

ATTENDANTS

Within the outer sanctuary (room 5) of the Burned Building at its northern end were found the bodies of fifty-five adults and children who perished in the fire. The "children" are aged eight years or younger on the evidence of the eruption of their molars. A number of these children lay around the central column just south of the north door. While jewelry suggests that many of the bodies may have been those of women, the crushed and burned nature of many of them makes gender identification impossible. Most of the bodies lay between the column base and the front of the door as well as to either side of the door (Marcus 1993:159; Muscarella 1989:32, Figs. 14, 20). Scattered military gear, including helmets and weapons possibly associated with some skeletons, suggests that one or two of these victims may have been soldiers (Dyson 1989a:124), but many others were

20.9 *a*, Ivory fragment decorated in Hasanlu *local style,* showing a man holding an object that appears to be the base of an antler (Muscarella 1980:Cat. no. 97) found in the second floor collapsed material in the southeast room of Burned Building II. The fragment is not flat (that is, a plaque), but comes from a cylindrical object [HAS 64-900, UPM 65-31-352: 7.1 cm h, 3.1 cm w, 0.5 cm th]. *Photograph courtesy of University of Pennsylvania Museum, neg. #S4-142985; b,* Reconstruction. Working from photos, Mary Voigt and Ruth Stern interpreted the head ornament as a feathered crown similar to those worn by other figures on Hasanlu ivories (for example, Muscarella 1980:Cat. nos. 98, 102). Maude de Schauensee, who examined the artifact, agrees with Muscarella that the man wears a fillet binding his curly hair. *Drawing by Ruth Stern*

young women and children. In general, the bodies were associated with valuable metal personal ornaments, and about half of the victims wore distinctive jewelry referred to as "lion pins" (Pigott 1989b:Fig. 13 a–c). Michelle Marcus argues that these pins indicate not only high rank for the individuals wearing them, but also military power for the institution that they served (Marcus 1993, 1995:2503).

To summarize, a relatively diverse group of artifacts found within Burned Building II have counterparts in temple deposits in Mesopotamia and Elam. In some cases, artifact types are found in both temples and palaces (for example, wall tiles), but one can argue that any royal residence might be ornamented with objects that invoke supernatural power to supplement or complement the secular power of the ruler. Thus while we cannot say that all of the objects reviewed are restricted in their distribution to temples, at least some of them appear to be diagnostic of sacred spaces

(for example, the eye inlays). Even at this preliminary stage of analysis, the artifacts found within Burned Building II strengthen the argument that this structure was a temple.

ANTLERS AS EMBLEMS

During the Iron Age, stags are a relatively common motif within Greater Mesopotamia, used in both religious/mythological and secular contexts along with lions, bulls, composite animals, and caprines (for example, the orthostat from the Herald's Wall at Carchemish illustrated in Winter 1980:Fig. 33). At Hasanlu during Period IVB, deer appear in hunting scenes depicted on locally made items including seals (Marcus 1989:Figs. 7, 19; 1996:Fig. 20), an iron quiver (Pigott 1989b:Fig. 14), and ivories (Muscarella 1980:Cat. no. 156). The location and distribution of the deer skulls and antlers within a cult building suggests that in this case the red deer heads were more than sporting trophies, or symbols of conquest over animals and by extension humans. This conclusion based on archaeological evidence is supported by a historical source: the use of stag horns as an iconic element on a relief from the palace of the Assyrian king Sargon II at Khorsabad (Dur-Sharukhin) dated to the eighth century BCE (Gunter 1982:105, Pl. IIIb). In a scene depicting an Assyrian victory, the besieged citadel has huge pairs of deer antlers rising from its innermost and highest towers (figure 20.8). An inscription identifies the citadel as being Kishesim, generally placed in western Iran, but placed by Louis Levine well to the south of the Lake Urmia basin, perhaps near the border between Parsua and Elam (Levine 1974a:110). The stag heads in Burned Building II certainly suggest that Hasanlu and Kishesim shared an emblem, but does this emblem refer to a deity, to political affiliation or to both?

Religion and politics were closely entwined in most premodern polities, but another artifact from Hasanlu may indicate an association of red deer antlers with human rather than mythological actors. An ivory fragment carved in low relief in the Hasanlu local style shows a striding male with an elaborate long-skirted costume holding aloft an object that is best interpreted as the base of an antler: the object curves upwards away from the man, with a knob projecting from the outer edge of the curve adjacent to the figure's face (figure 20.9). This figure, recovered from the second-story collapse in the southeast corner (room 7a) of Burned Building II, appears to be a member of the local elite, based on his elaborate long-skirted costume. While long garments are rare in the corpus of local ivories from Hasanlu they are worn by the deities in chariots on the gold bowl and the silver beaker found in Burned Building I West (Porada 1967; Winter 1989). The fillet that binds the figure's long curly hair appears in the all too real world of warfare (for example, Muscarella 1980:169–170, Cat. nos. 53, 63) and in procession and drinking scenes (for example, Muscarella 1980:Cat. nos. 73, 75, 79, 98).

The object held aloft by the Hasanlu figure is particularly significant, presumably an icon that specifies his identity. Muscarella (1980:50) sees this object as either an antler or a branch, and to us the form is clearly that of an antler. An alternative interpretation—that the icon is a lightning bolt, a symbol associated with the storm god Teshub—can be rejected on several grounds. First, the Hasanlu figure wears a long-skirted garment rather than Teshub's kilt, and a simple fillet rather than the tall crown of the deity (for example, figure 20.6 from Assyria, and examples from ninth- and eighth-century north Syria illustrated in Amiet 1980c:Pls. 550–551, 553–554). Second, the item that the Hasanlu figure holds in his left hand has

a single outward curving spike with a knob rather than the distinctive two- or three-pronged staff of Teshub. Finally, Teshub generally holds an axe aloft in his right hand, but the right hand of the Hasanlu figure, though damaged, is held at waist level.

But we need not rely on individual readings of the image on the ivory plaque to make an association between powerful human figures and antler bearing beasts. Within the corpus of Hasanlu local style glyptic, one well-documented seal impression clearly juxtaposes stags with an elite person, identifiable as male by his activities (Marcus 1996:86–91, Fig. 20, Pls. 3–6, Cat. no. 5). The cylinder seal used to make the ten preserved impressions (seven recovered from the second-story collapse of Burned Building II) had two registers: in the upper register a mounted horseman throws a spear at an animal with clearly depicted antlers; in the lower register, an attendant offers a goblet to a seated person holding a lenticular object that Marcus interprets as a bow. Significantly, the seated figure on the seal shares distinctive elements of costume with the standing figure on the ivory plaque. Not only does the seated figure wear an ankle-length garment, but he has "an extra prominent cluster of vertical striations of hair or a cap on top of his head" (Marcus 1996:90). It matters little whether the man with the long-skirted garment depicted at Hasanlu is priest or king or priest-king, or whether the item grasped is an icon denoting his specific role or the institution that he serves; the symbolic association between a powerful west Iranian personage and deer antlers is established.

Whether the emblem is specific to Hasanlu or to a larger political and/or religious entity can only be known when our knowledge of the archaeology and history of Iron Age Iran is broadened by new research. What we can say now is that if Burned Building II was a temple, the cult housed within it almost certainly was associated with the well-being of Hasanlu's rulers. Pushing the interpretation a little bit further, the presence of antlers on city walls links these items to protection and specifically to protection against military attack. The presence of antlers in Burned Building II thus reinforces the proposed military significance of the lion pins worn by people with access to the temple sanctuary. It is entirely plausible that Burned Building II was dedicated to a deity that represented the settlement and was responsible for its defense.

ARCHITECTURAL LAYOUT + ARTIFACTS = TEMPLE?
Our analysis brings together the architectural plan and selected contents of Burned Building II in the context of a test to see how the available evidence fits a model derived from the traditional Mesopotamian temple. The layout of

the building follows the tripartite logic of the straight-axis temple model quite well, but does not reflect the kind of organization with interlocking living quarters, reception halls and service areas seen in most Mesopotamian palaces (Margueron 1982). Various features, such as altars, offering tables, offering benches, and the cult-figure chamber have their counterparts in known Mesopotamian temples and allow a reasonable interpretation of religious function. Finally, the limited corpus of artifacts reviewed supports the appropriateness of the temple model since similar finds elsewhere are associated with religious contexts.

There remains a series of caveats and questions. First of all, it must be remembered that we have described only a few of the 1500 objects found in the building. Until these have all been analyzed in their archaeological context, with place and date of manufacture determined, we do not have anything like a final statement of the evidence and its implications. Second, there is the question of how the whole complex of buildings around the lower court functioned, both as a formal setting for religious activities and as places where the domestic needs of people associated with the temple were satisfied, for example, food preparation, bathing, storage for belongings, and storage for accumulated wealth in various forms. Burned Buildings IW, IVE and V share features with Burned Building II to which we have assigned a religious function (such as low offering benches along walls and high offering tables with frontal pavements), so that the identification of purely residential units is difficult. A particularly vexing problem is our lack of information on the back walls and rooms of Buildings IW (where a Period IIIB fortification wall truncated the building) and IVE (not completely excavated). The possibility remains that one or both of these buildings had a small chamber at the far end of the columned hall. It may be that Burned Buildings I–V are *all* religious structures and that true residences lie in unexcavated areas of the site. A third (and related) task is the elucidation of the exact order of construction within the lower court complex and possible changes in the function of buildings between Hasanlu Periods IVC and IVB (see Dyson 1989a:113–119).

Finally, we have the enormously difficult problem of understanding how, why, and exactly when the Mesopotamian temple model was introduced to Hasanlu. We know that the burial customs and the ceramic assemblage that appear at the beginning of Hasanlu Period V originate on the Iranian Plateau. We also know that remains of this period underlie Period IVC remains in most areas where we have excavated, and that at least one large structure with a buttressed façade and low benches existed in Hasanlu Period V (Dyson 1977), but we do not know what the full architectural layout of a large building was like at that time. Since we also lack information on monumental structures for Period VI, we have no way to measure any conceptual changes in the architectural planning of secular and religious structure that may have occurred between Periods VI, V and IVC. We currently believe that there is a cultural disconformity between Period VI (ending ca. 1450 BCE), which is characterized by Mesopotamian Khabur ware (Frane 1996; Hamlin 1974), and Period V (?1450 BCE–?1250 BCE), characterized by completely different burial customs and pottery (burnished red, brown, and gray ware in different shapes) that are of uncertain origin, but are certainly not Mesopotamian. The degree to which changes in material culture reflect changes in political control and/or affiliation of the people at Hasanlu remains to be examined in the light of further analysis and, eventually, new evidence. Speculations on ethnicity in the absence of texts are even less fruitful at this point and are to be avoided. Whatever the mechanism by which Mesopotamian temple and ritual forms came to be adopted in northwest Iran, our argument that Burned Building II functioned as a temple deserves careful consideration in the ongoing study of Hasanlu IV.

NOTE

1. According to Roaf, "rabbet" is a technical term used by architectural historians for "a rectangular recess made along a projecting edge"(1998:57).

CHAPTER 21

THE HASANLU GOLD "BOWL"

A View from Transcaucasia

KAREN S. RUBINSON

IN THE COURSE OF EXCAVATION, precious objects are occasionally found that stimulate extensive discussion and study by virtue of their special, even unique, nature. Such is the so-called Gold Bowl excavated at Hasanlu, Iran in 1958 (Barrelet 1984; Winter 1989).[1] William Sumner's career in Iranian archaeology, as well as my own, began at Hasanlu. This discussion is offered in recollection of those days.

When the Gold Bowl was first published by Edith Porada, she noted a few comparisons between the piece from Iran and the silver goblet from the excavations at Trialeti, in what is today the Republic of Georgia (figures 21.1–21.4). Porada (1959:22) remarked, "While certain details of costume and furniture such as the tail-like tassels of the garments and the bull's feet of the throne suggest some relationship with Hasanlu customs as reflected in the bowl, and while even the chinless short-bearded men seem like caricatures of the ethnic type found on the bowl, the style of the Caucasus vessel is stiffer, cruder, less accomplished." She further suggested that the artists who produced the Trialeti goblet may "have been influenced by Hasanlu" (Porada 1959:22).

We now know that the Trialeti goblet is earlier than the Hasanlu "bowl," since the goblet was found in a burial dating to the first few centuries of the second millennium BCE. (Miron and Orthmann 1995:238; Rubinson 1977:243) and the Gold Bowl is later, made either toward the end of the second millennium or the beginning of the first (Winter 1989:90–92). Since these earlier discoveries, a further

silver piece belonging to the Trialeti culture that sheds light on this problem has become available. It is a goblet excavated from the Grand North Kurgan at Karashamb in Armenia (Oganesian 1992; Pilipossian and Santrot 1996:65–67). Like the other two vessels, the goblet from Karashamb has human figures with tails attached to their garments and offering stands (in this case with objects on them) with hoofed animal feet, as well as figures with a similar kind of stylized face, although beardless. In addition, the Karashamb goblet has, in the third register, a group of daggers or swords suspended in space, an image also found on the Hasanlu bowl (Pilipossian and Santrot 1996:66; Shahnazarian and Mkrtchian N.D.:16; Tiratsian 1992:39 [where the image is reversed]).

Since the Transcaucasian silver vessels and the Hasanlu Gold Bowl are separated by at least five hundred years, what might explain the occurrence of this shared imagery in both areas? The imagery does not seem to be native to Transcaucasia but rather borrowed from Anatolia, imagery recorded particularly in the Anatolian-style seals of the Assyrian colony period (Rubinson 1977:243, N.D.). It is likely that the transfer of this imagery to the Trialeti cultural sphere is a reflection of an economic exchange, a phenomenon known in other times and places, as, for example, the West Asian imagery, particularly Sasanian, found in Tang China (Vollmer et al. 1983:46–47, 65, 70–73). But given the lack of contemporaneity of the Trialeti culture and the Gold Bowl, regardless of its date of manufacture, economic interchange cannot be the

21.1   Detail of Hasanlu Gold "Bowl" showing offering table/altar. *Photograph courtesy of the University of Pennsylvania Museum (neg. #S35-78114:31)*

21.2   Detail of Trialeti silver goblet showing offering table/altar. *Photograph by K.S. Rubinson, with permission of the National Museum of Georgia*

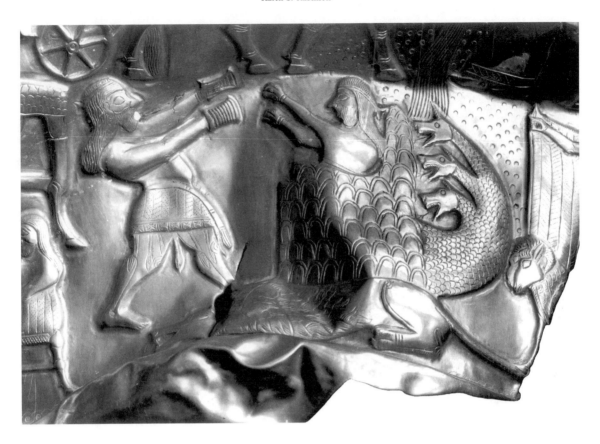

21.3   Detail of Hasanlu Gold "Bowl" showing "hero" with animal tails suspended from his garment.
Photograph courtesy of the University of Pennsylvania Museum (neg. #S35-78113:0)

explanation in this case. Is it possible to suggest another plausible explanation for how, as Burney (Burney and Lang 1972:95) puts it, the Trialeti culture imagery is "echoed" in the Gold Bowl?

The ethnolinguistic and cultural context of the silver vessels of the Trialeti culture is not certain, since we have no written documents from the area (Dzhaparidze 1995:87). The excavator made the case that the Karashamb goblet displays tales of an Indo-European tradition, with the boar hunt as the essential element, also found in myths of the Greeks, Germans, Scandinavians, Celts and others (Oganesian 1992:97–99). The boar hunt, however, is a subsidiary motif on this piece, much smaller than the two central registers, and seems to me not visually significant enough to support Oganesian's argument for the centrality of the boar hunt to the myth depicted on the vessel. Additionally, the imagery on the Trialeti goblet has often been compared to that found in Hittite art, from the original publication by Kuftin (1941:89–92), where he compared the standing human figures to those at Yazılıkaya who wear similar garments, to recent exhibition catalogues where general comparisons of gift-bearing processionals are made (Miron and Orthmann 1995:238), sometimes with efforts

to draw ethnolinguistic interpretations (Kuftin 1941:90–91, 163). These visual parallels are indeed quite striking, but imagery in Hittite art has Hurrian influence and is not strictly Indo-European (Archi 1995:2373–2374; Kohlmeyer 1995:2649; Wilhelm 1995:1250).

The Hasanlu Gold Bowl is also found in an archaeological milieu without texts, and the ethnolinguistic context of its manufacture has also been long-discussed (Barrelet 1984:57). Even with some images corresponding closely to known Hurrian myth, Winter (1989:104) concludes only that "the identification of Hurrian components on the bowl... has been strengthened" by the investigation of herself and others. How much more difficult the situation is for the identification of the ethnolinguistic/cultural origin of the Trialeti culture goblets, where no known story can be clearly seen in the silver images. Nevertheless, there are arguments to be made for a Hurrian-related population in Transcaucasia in the early second millennium, based on the relationship between the Hurrian and Urartian languages (Wilhelm 1989:4–6, 1995:1244), and even earlier if one accepts that the Early Transcaucasian culture was Hurrian-speaking. Both arguments rely on the evidence for the late third-millennium appearance of Hurrian names and words

21.4   Detail of the Trialeti silver goblet showing walking figures with animal tails suspended from their garments.
Photograph by K.S. Rubinson, with permission of the National Museum of Georgia

at the northeastern borders of Mesopotamia, and assume an east Anatolian-Transcaucasian origin for the Hurrian-speaking population (Burney and Lang 1972:49).

In looking at the silver vessels, there is nothing in the overall narrative that links the imagery to the Gold Bowl. Rather, it is the small details noted by Porada, as well as the weapons placed in the field on the more recently found Karashamb goblet, also seen on the bowl. Of those, only one image, the weapons in the field, may possibly suggest a tie to known Hurrian myth. The Hurrian connection is summarized by Winter (1989:95) and need not be repeated here. It is true that on the Karashamb goblet the weapons are grouped with shields and bounded by scenes of men fighting (Pilipossian and Santrot 1996:66; Tiratsian 1992:39). But it might be possible to read the images on more than one level, both literally and as reference to a symbolic figure or concept. On the other hand, perhaps the weapons in the field of the Gold Bowl are a shorthand reference to the expanded battle seen on the Karashamb goblet. It may prove to be instructive to collect the Anatolian-style seals bearing weapons in the field of the Assyrian trading colony period for comparison. For example, Özgüç (1965:Pl. V:15a) illustrates a seal in which a

dagger "floats" in the field behind an offering scene centered on a hoofed table, recalling the daggers behind the kneeling figure before the hoofed table on the Gold Bowl.

The hoofed table on the Hasanlu bowl recalls the offering tables/altars seen on both the Trialeti and Karashamb goblets. Like that on the bowl, the Trialeti table has nothing placed on the surface, unlike the two different hoofed tables on the Karashamb goblet, both of which support vessels and other objects on the surface (Shahnazarian and Mkrtchian N.D.:16; Tiratsian 1992:39). The forms and scale of the offering tables are not the same, although one of the Karashamb tables is very similar to that depicted on the Trialeti goblet. Again, other examples of the hoofed table are found on several Anatolian-style seals from Kültepe Kanesh (Özgüç 1965:Pl. IV:11a, Pl. XXIV:73, Pl. XXV:75b). Also from the early centuries of the second millennium, hoofed offering tables/altars are shown on the cult basins from Ebla (Amiet 1980c:388, Figs. 448, 450). Amiet (1980c:164) has noted the affinity of the Anatolian-style seals with the Ebla basins in style; perhaps there is also some affinity of meaning. It is interesting to note that in all four areas—Ebla, Kültepe Kanesh, the Trialeti culture, and Hasanlu—the hoofed table is associated with figures of human form holding goblets or cups. In her analysis, Winter (1989:95) stresses the empty top of the piece of furniture as part of its meaning, so perhaps it is not related to the early second millennium examples, of which only the Trialeti goblet table is unburdened. But it is worth considering that the hoofed feet of the altar/table/stool may themselves have meaning, a motif seen also on a clay tripod stand from Kültepe Kanesh II (Özgüç 1965:86, Pl. XXXII:100), as well as on the feet of many Urartian bronzes, including a candelabrum and cauldron stand (Azarpay 1968:56–58, Pls. 30, 41, 47–48) and other pieces of furniture (Merhav 1991:252–253). It is a stretch to take the use of this image in Urartu and connect it to its earlier use in a possible Hurrian-related area in Transcaucasia simply because of the relationship of the languages (Zimansky 1995a:1135–1136), much less extend it to the probably Hurrian context of the Hasanlu Gold Bowl. However, given the lack of texts in the latter two areas, such circumstantial evidence is worth noting.

An equally tenuous tie is the appearance of animal tails on human-form figures on the three precious-metal objects. However, this image is rare in the ancient Near East. The tails illustrated on all three objects are quite different in appearance; those on the Hasanlu Gold Bowl look like lions' tails, with tufts on the ends, those on the Trialeti goblet look like wolves' tails, with bushy long hair along their whole length, and the tails on the Karashamb goblet, extending from the figure's waist to the ground in most cases, consist of a stylized herring-bone pattern that is harder to identify with a specific animal. The stylization of the Karashamb tails is close to that on an Anatolian-style seal from Kültepe Kanesh, where it appears on a bull-man (Özgüç 1965:82,

Pl. XX:61). Whether this type of well-known Near Eastern image was the inspiration for the Transcaucasian metalwork cannot be proven, but is a tantalizing thought. Perhaps on the Trialeti-culture metalwork, a Near Eastern pictoral image was conflated with a native cultural tradition to yield human-form figures with attached tails. Again, could this Transcaucasian image be inspired by stories related to some of those illustrated on the Gold Bowl?

Of course, imagery traditions had a long life in the ancient Near East, and were used in many cultures and geographical areas, transformed in style and even meaning (see, for example, Winter 1980:11–12). This conservative tendency in artistic vocabulary may be the explanation for what could be an accidental similarity between the Trialeti culture and Hasanlu precious vessels. But given the probable Hurrian relationships of the Gold Bowl and the possible Hurrian-related context of Transcaucasia in the Bronze Age, perhaps we can say of the Trialeti and Karashamb goblets what Stein (1989:84) said of the Hasanlu Gold Bowl, which she wrote "...ultimately derived from the same cultural milieu in which the Hurrians also participated prior to their entry on the northern plain of Syria and Mesopotamia, where the process of acculturation can be traced from the third millennium." Only further excavation and study of the Late Bronze and early Iron Age remains in Transcaucasia and Iran will be able to help solve this question. Surely William Sumner's students and colleagues will contribute to this research.

Acknowledgment. Trialeti photographs taken through a grant from the American Philosophical Society.

NOTE

1.   In her important study of this object, Winter (1989) identified it as a vessel taller than a bowl.

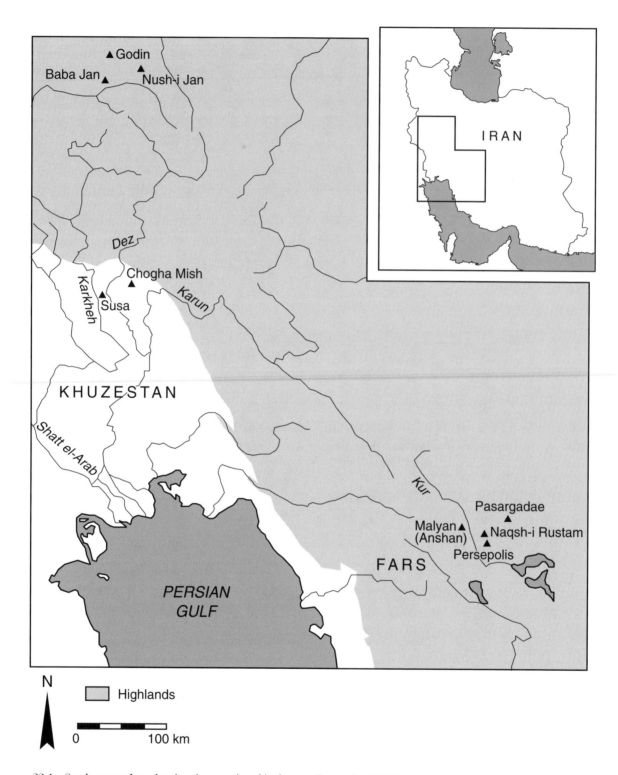

22.1 Southwestern Iran showing sites mentioned in the text. *Prepared at MASCA*

CHAPTER 22

PARSUA, PARSA, AND POTSHERDS

T. CUYLER YOUNG, JR.

OME TWENTY-FIVE YEARS AGO Bill Sumner wrote, "The small number and diminutive size of the Achaemenid settlements [in Fars], aside from Persepolis itself, is a final puzzle which awaits the further attention of historians and archaeologists" (Sumner 1974:158). Over a decade later Sumner himself gave this issue further attention in his splendid article, "Achaemenid Settlement in the Persepolis Plain" (Sumner 1986b). This chapter represents another effort to examine aspects of Achaemenid settlement in Fars, offered in the spirit of the title of this book, *Yeki bud, yeki nabud* ("Once upon a time..."; Sumner 1986b:28, n. 124).

Our critical problem in dealing with the archaeology of Late Iron Age Fars is the apparent gap in occupation between roughly 900 BCE and our earliest evidence for the presence of the Achaemenid Persians in the area (see chapters 23, 24). In addressing this puzzle I focus on three main issues: first, the possible relationship between the Parsua[1] of the Assyrian sources and Parsa, the homeland of the Achaemenid Persians in modern Fars; second, the date of our earliest firm evidence for settled peoples in Parsa following the end of the Shogha/Teimuran phase (late second or early first millennium: Sumner 1974:156–157 and 1994a:101); and third, the question of ceramic parallels among the sites of Pasargadae, Godin II and Achaemenid Khuzestan and the Achaemenid sherds from the survey published by Sumner (1986b) (figures 22.1, 22.2). Using those parallels I will suggest that in fact we have some evidence for a Late Iron Age/pre-Achaemenid dynasty occupation in Fars.

PARSUA/PARSA

It is widely held that King Kurash of Parsua, who became tributary to Assurbanipal (668 BCE–627 BCE) following the Assyrian conquest of Elam circa 646 and destruction of Susa circa 642 BCE, might well be the Achaemenid Cyrus I, king of Parsa (Briant 1984:92–93; Carter and Stolper 1984:52 and n. 408; Hansman 1994:32; Levine 1974a:111; Stronach 1978:284). If this is so, then the Neo-Assyrian Parsua of the mid-seventh century is Parsa, already settled by the Persians. Stolper, in fact, has gone so far as to suggest that the Parsua of the time of Sennacherib (704 BCE–681 BCE) might already have been the Parsa of the Achaemenids (Carter and Stolper 1984:48 and n. 408), possibly because the Parsua of the inscription reporting Sennacherib's eighth campaign is listed in conjunction with Anshan.

The argument that the Kurash of the Assurbanipal text is Cyrus I is thought by some to be confirmed, in part, by the appearance on a Persepolis Fortification Text of a seal impression of one Kurash, who is understood to be Cyrus I, ancestor of Cyrus the Great. Both Miroschedji (1985:277–287) and Young (1988:15–16) have argued against these interpretations, however, and I see at this time no reason to change my mind.

All of the evidence on the Neo-Assyrian geography of western Iran in Sennacherib's time indicates that the Parsua mentioned in that king's texts must still refer to a place in the west-central Zagros, where it had been since its first appearance in the Neo-Assyrian sources in the mid-ninth century BCE (Levine 1974a:106–112; Young 1967:17–19). It is generally recognized now that the Parsua of the central

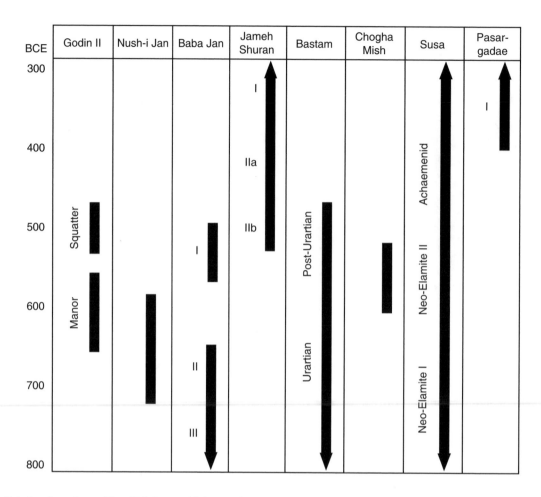

22.2   Relative chronology of Iron III/Achaemenid sites. *Redrawn at MASCA from Gopnick 2000:Fig. 5.13*

western Zagros cannot have any direct connections with the Parsa of Fars. We are left with the conclusion that there were two separate territories with a similar name (see Young 1988:15).

Though the Parsua of Sennacherib's time cannot have been the Parsa of Fars, might not the Parsua of Assurbanipal's time have been the Parsa of the Achaemenids? Miroschedji argues persuasively against this proposition. He rejects the genealogy of the earliest Achaemenids as it occurs on the Bisitun inscription of Darius I and argues that the only certain history of the Achaemenid royal house is that which we have in the Cyrus Cylinder (Miroschedji 1985:282–283). With others (for example, Briant 1984:76–78), I have long been bothered by the assertions of Darius regarding his ancestry (Young 1988:27–28), and after careful consideration again of Miroschedji's arguments, I am now convinced that the Cyrus Cylinder is the only historically acceptable genealogy of the early Achaemenids.[2] If this is so, then it is chronologically highly improbable, if not impossible, for

Cyrus I as we know him from the cylinder of his namesake, Cyrus II, to have been Kurash, king of Parsua in 646 BCE (Miroschedji 1985:283–284).

Furthermore, a central Zagros location for the Parsua of Assurbanipal remains quite reasonable. On the one hand, it can be argued that Assurbanipal exaggerates considerably in telling the story of the defeat and destruction of Elam in 646 BCE. (He would not be the first Neo-Assyrian king to indulge in hyperbole.) The archaeological evidence from Susa and from survey in Khuzestan shows little in the way of a major disruption in the middle of the seventh century. There is clear cultural continuity between Neo-Elamite Periods I and II (Miroschedji 1981b:148–150, but note reservations by Carter 1994a:73), and there is good evidence for continued occupation of the Khuzestan plain through both of these periods (Miroschedji 1981c:171–172). Elamite kingship also continues well past 646 BCE (Carter and Stolper 1984:52–56; Miroschedji 1985:267). Thus, while a general decline in the wealth, power and significance of Elam after the mid-seventh century can be seen in the historical record, there is no evidence for a complete and thorough destruction of Elam as claimed by Assurbanipal (see also Boucharlat 1994:220).

On the other hand, Parsa is a long way from lowland Elam and is traditionally one of the distant plateau areas to which Elamites are known often to have fled for safety from their Mesopotamian enemies. It seems unlikely that a Persian king ruling in distant Anshan would feel so threatened by Assurbanipal's successful invasion of Khuzestan, however complete the destruction by the Assyrians, as to send his son hostage to Nineveh. A king ruling in a Parsua in the central western Zagros, however, might well be very concerned by Assurbanipal's campaign in lowland Elam. Mountain kingdoms in this area of the Zagros were traditional allies of the Elamites and Babylonians against the Assyrians, and were close enough to the center of Assyria to be frightened by that power's successes.

Finally, mention must be made of two Fortification Texts (PF 692-5 and 2033), which are impressed by a seal with an inscription reading, "Cyrus, the Anshanite, son of Teispes." It has been argued that this is clear evidence for an Achaemenid Persian occupation in Parsa well before the time of Cyrus II. Arguments on stylistic grounds, however, date this seal to the time of Darius I (or slightly earlier), and suggest that the Cyrus of the seal is not a royal person but simply a Persian using a royal name.[3] Therefore this Kurash cannot be taken as corroboration of the presence of a king Kurash in Parsa in the mid-seventh century BCE (Miroschedji 1985:285–287; Young 1988:27).

In sum, I would argue on both negative and positive grounds that the Parsua of the Assurbanipal records is still located in the central western Zagros, as it always had been under that king's predecessors.[4] My final conclusion, therefore, is that we have no evidence from the Neo-Assyrian sources for any occupation of Parsa.

THE EARLIEST FIRM EVIDENCE FOR OCCUPATION IN PARSA

The textual evidence for the earliest occupation of Parsa has already been remarked upon effectively by Sumner (1986b:28f.). I summarize here only to refresh memories.

The identification of the city (town?) of Mattezzish of the Persepolis Fortification Texts with the sites that compose Persepolis West is convincing (Sumner 1986b:23). Furthermore, it now seems clear that Mattezzish must be the location of the recording of several Babylonian legal texts dating to the reign of Cambyses (Stolper 1984c; Zadok 1976). There is also fairly good, non-ceramic,

archaeological evidence for a significant, even monumental, occupation of Persepolis West as early as the reign of Cambyses, if not perhaps slightly earlier (Tilia 1974). Babylonians and Babylonian scribes were clearly not living amongst a group of tenting nomads, and the construction that can be associated with Persepolis West or Mattezzish is not peasant village architecture. Therefore, we have clear textual and architectural evidence for a settled population in the Persepolis plain by at least the third quarter of the sixth century BCE.

An Elamite rock relief at Naqsh-i Rustam, albeit difficult to interpret, is perhaps further evidence for an occupation of the Persepolis area prior to Darius I. Miroschedji (1985:279–280) would tentatively date this relief to the middle of the seventh century, and it could be argued that the presence of such a relief suggests some settled population in the region at the time of its carving. It is true, however, that an Elamite relief in that location might have been so positioned for purely traditional religious reasons, not because there was a settled village population in the vicinity (Root 1979:195–196).

Finally, we should note the bronze plaque found at Persepolis engraved with a long Elamite text mentioning Gisat (or Kesat), a geographic name also found in the Fortification Texts. On the basis of script this text can be compared with administrative documents from Susa that have been dated to the very end of the seventh and the first half of the sixth centuries BCE (Carter and Stolper 1984:54–55, n. 484).[5]

In sum, therefore, we have solid textual and architectural evidence for settled occupation in the Persepolis plain at least as early as the reign of Cambyses, and we have some perhaps less satisfactory art historical evidence that there may have been settlement in the area even earlier in times prior to the rise of Cyrus II to kingship.

In the continuing spirit of *yeki bud, yeki nabud,* however, let us speculate beyond the fixed limits of the local textual and material evidence for a pre-Achaemenid occupation in the Persepolis region and the Marvdasht.

Cyrus II comes to the throne of Parsa in 559 BCE. He clearly rules a people and a territory that the Medes wish to conquer, as we are told they set out to do in the Babylonian sources (Sancisi-Weerdenburg 1994:53; Young 1988:31). I have doubts that Astyages, last king of the Medes, though not portrayed by Herodotus as a particularly wise ruler, was so dim as to wish to invade and conquer a people who were purely nomadic pastoralists and a land containing only sheep and goats (with accompanying dogs). Herodotus, in fact, specifically tells us that the early Persians were a people who combined settled agriculture with pastoralism (H.I.125), as

Sumner has correctly suggested they continued to do in Achaemenid times, for it is a logical way to maximize the output of the landscape (Sumner 1986b:29). It also seems reasonable to assume that, even though Cyrus II built his capital at Pasargadae, the Marvdasht and the Persepolis area would have been part of his kingdom at the time of Astyages' attack. On these admittedly speculative grounds, therefore, I think we may assume a settled occupation of Parsa well before the time of Cyrus II's ascension to the Achaemenid throne and possibly even as early as the eighth century BCE.

If all this is so, then it is entirely reasonable to suppose that we might already have found, or be able to find, pottery on settlements that would date after the end of the Shogha-Teimuran phase and before Achaemenid times. Miroschedji was first to point out this possibility but resigns himself to saying nothing found could be earlier than the sixth century BCE (Miroschedji 1985:293, n. 118).

CERAMIC PARALLELS

In wrestling with this sad conclusion—that we have no archaeological evidence for a Persian occupation of the Marvdasht between circa 900 BCE and the sixth century BCE— Sumner offers two suggestions: one pessimistic, one optimistic.

His pessimistic suggestion is that the early Persians were primarily pastoralists whose camp sites would be almost impossible to identify archaeologically except perhaps through highly intensive survey (Sumner 1986b:4–7). While he tentatively admits that some of the pottery found in his surveys might date to before Darius I and the late sixth century BCE, Sumner errs, I think, on the side of even greater caution than that expressed by Miroschedji when he hesitates to assign any of his pottery a pre-Achaemenid date because "... no excavated corpus of Achaemenid pottery in Fars can be assigned a date earlier than the late fifth century. Very few sherds found in surface collections are without parallels in the assemblages from Persepolis and Pasargadae" (Sumner 1986b:4).

Sumner's (1994a) optimistic suggestion is that there was already a strong tendency to pastoralism in the Shogha-Teimuran phase, and that there is a considerable overlap in settlement patterns between Shogha-Teimuran sites and sites with Achaemenid pottery. This leads him to conclude that "...the evidence for settlement continuity from the end of the Kaftari phase (circa 1600 BCE) to the establishment of the Achaemenid settlement system...implies an earlier arrival of the Persian population than previously contemplated" (Sumner 1994a:105).

What I will now argue is that indeed there is such evidence, regardless of which of Sumner's suggestions one prefers.[6] First, a good deal of Sumner's survey material has no parallels at Pasargadae and thus probably predates that site. Second, some of his material is paralleled only in Iron III contexts, many of which are pre-Achaemenid. Therefore, we have ceramic evidence for a settled occupation of Parsa at least as early as, and probably earlier than, our firm textual, art historical, and architectural evidence allows.

Table 22.1 presents ceramic parallels as I see them, almost exclusively for bowls, between Sumner's survey data and those from the sites of Pasargadae, Godin II, Achaemenid Susa (Ville Royale II, levels 5 and 4), and other contemporary sites in Khuzestan.[7] These data may be summarized as follows:

- Eleven of Sumner's sherds have no parallels at any of the other sites under consideration. Thus about 38% of Sumner's material is unique. Does this fact suggest that the survey material contains a pre-Achaemenid component found only in Fars? Twenty-three survey sherds are not paralleled at Pasargadae, which is 59% of Sumner's corpus. This absence of parallels with Pasargadae is particularly noteworthy and could perhaps be explained by the vagaries of excavation and survey. On the other hand, I strongly suggest that this fact indicates that the survey material contains a considerable number of ceramic types which date to a time earlier than anything found at Pasargadae.[8]

- Eight survey types have parallels only at Pasargadae: two Achaemenid, two Late Achaemenid, and four Post-Achaemenid. We may assume that all of these shapes are post-Iron III in date.

- Six of the survey types have parallels at both Pasargadae and Godin II. At Pasargadae, five date to Post-Achaemenid times and one to the Late Achaemenid period. Nevertheless, two of these parallels (1O and 2B) involve sherds from Godin II which with certainty can be associated stratigraphically with the primary occupation of the fortified Manor House. On several grounds, the Godin II Manor House can be dated to the Iron III phase and is therefore definitely pre-Achaemenid.[9] Thus at least the two Godin II parallels suggest the survey material includes a pre-Achaemenid component. The data as a whole demonstrate something many have long known: that a number of Iron III ceramic shapes, some of which can be traced back to at least the mid-eighth century BCE, are very long-lived indeed.

- Six of the survey types have parallels at Godin II only, one of which (1M) dates at Godin II to the final primary occupation of the fortified Manor House. This again suggests a definite Iron III or pre-Achaemenid component in the survey material.

- Two survey types have parallels only in Khuzestan (one from survey, one from Ville Royale II). This fact is perhaps somewhat odd. As one might expect, a number of the parallels between the highland Plateau assemblages and lowland Khuzestan are weak, but there are clear connections. Why two would appear exclusively in only one highland assemblage must reflect the chance of discovery.

- Four of the survey types are found at Godin II and in Khuzestan only. This could be more evidence for a pre-Achaemenid date for some of the survey material, and/or more evidence for the continuation of Iron III shapes into Achaemenid times.

- Two survey types are found in Khuzestan and at Pasargadae only, and two are found at all three excavated sites. This fact again may, in part, suggest that a number of Iron III shapes continued well into Achaemenid times. On the other hand, it may mean nothing more than that certain Achaemenid types were widespread.

- Finally, two general observations may be made. First, horizontal handles on bowls occur in Khuzestan and at Godin II but are entirely missing in the material from Fars. Horizontal handles are characteristic of the Iron III phase. Why did this feature survive into Achaemenid times only in lowland Khuzestan? Second, a considerable number of the ceramic shapes characteristic of Susa and Khuzestan survey pottery have parallels only at sites in lowland Mesopotamia and, in the main, the wares in Khuzestan are quite different from those in Fars and at Godin II. This fact is not surprising given the geography of western Iran and indicates that the Achaemenid ceramic tradition of the plateau definitely follows that of the Iron III tradition, while that of the lowlands is more influenced by earlier and contemporary Mesopotamian ceramic types. Sherds of Iron III/Achaemenid plateau wares are found, however, in Khuzestan in either Iron III or Achaemenid contexts as a separate entity (personal observation of pottery excavated at Chogha Mish. See also parallels drawn by Miroschedji [1987:Figs. 7–11] between Ville Royale II levels 5 and 4 and Chogha Mish).[10]

CONCLUSIONS

It is true that, in limiting the argument to published material only, our sample for ceramic comparisons is painfully small. Nevertheless, in that "once upon a time" spirit, it can be suggested that these data clearly allow for the possibility of ceramic evidence for a pre-Achaemenid settled population in Fars at least as early as, and quite possibly

Table 22.1 Ceramic shape parallels among assemblages from the Marvdasht, Pasargadae, Godin II, and Khuzestan

Marvdasht* (Ill. #)	Pasargadae (Fig. #)	Godin (Fig. #)	Khuzestan (Fig. #)
1.A	108:4 (PA)	47:1	-
1.B	108:6 (PA)	48:20	-
1.C	108:4 (PA)	46:11	-
1.D	-	45:12	-
1.E	-	45:13	-
1.F	-	-	-
1.G	-	-	-
1.H	-	-	-
1.I	-	45:16	-
1.J	-	-	-
1.K	107:19 (PA)	-	-
1.L	-	46:2	VR, 7:12
1.M	-	46:4	-
1.N	108:9 (PA)	-	DK, 63:2
1.O	108:8 (LA)	46:5	VR, 9:6
1.P	106:16 (PA)	-	-
1.Q	-	46:12	VR, 9:2 and 7:7
1.R	121:5	-	-
1.S	-	-	-
1.T	119:9 (PA)	-	-
1.U	117:9 (A)	-	-
1.V	113:2 (LA)	-	-
2.A	-	-	-
2.B	106:17 (PA)	45:17	-
2.C	-	-	-
2.D	-	-	DK, 63:4
2.E	-	46:10	VR, 10:3
2.F	-	-	-
2.G	-	45:21	-
2.H	-	-	-
2.I	106:1 (LA)	-	-
2.J	106:13 (A)	-	-
2.K	-	-	-
2.L	-	-	-
2.M	-	45:25	VR, 8:12
2.N	-	46:19	-
2.O	-	-	VR, 7:11
2.P	109:8 (PA)	45:29	VR, 7:16
2.Q	111:19 (LA)	-	VR, 9:3

Source: Marvdasht (Sumner 1986b); Pasargadae (Stronach 1978: A=Achaemenid, LA= Late Achaemenid, PA= Post-Achaemenid); Godin II (Young and Levine 1974); Khuzestan: Ville Royale II (VR, Miroschedji 1987) and DK (Miroschedji 1981c)
* These parallels reflect a high degree of similarity in rim shape, carination, and the combination of stance and rim shape. Exceptions are noted below. I have completely ignored paste, surface color, and surface finish, for I believe these are less important traits for comparisons of Iron III (Late Western Buff Ware) and Achaemenid sherds than they are in certain other periods in Iranian archaeology.

1.A	Neither parallel strong	1.R	Pasargadae example unstratified; jar not pot
1.B	Pasargadae parallel better		
1.C	Problem with stance. Pasargadae example comparatively deep	1.U	This rim type is long-lived and deserves special study
1.D	Strong parallel	1.V	Or Post-Achaemenid
1.E	Strong parallel	2.B	See comment on 1.M
1.I	Bowls with vertical rims rare at Pasargadae	2.E	Godin parallel strong. VR stance wrong
1.K	General concept common, but details differ site to site	2.M	VR parallel weak
1.L	Slightly different stance	2.O	VR parallel in carination only
1.M	Strong parallel. Godin example from a level just prior to the abandonment of the primary occupation of the fortified Manor House	2.P	VR parallel not strong. A long-lived rim type worthy of independent study. Note well that Pasargadae examples mostly late and have dish bases not found at Godin and VR
1.O	See comment on 1.M		
1.Q	Godin example more sharply carinated. VR example more rounded	2.Q	Pasargadae parallel not strong; VR parallel weak

earlier than, that documented by other sources. If this proposition is accepted, then Sumner was too modest about the import of his ceramic survey data, and his more optimistic solution to our problem may carry the day. Modesty and optimism are characteristic of first-class scholarship.

NOTES

1. Parsua is used here for all of the variant spellings in the Neo-Assyrian texts such as Parsumash or Parsuash.

2. On problems with such genealogies as that of Darius I, see Sancisi-Weerdenburg (1994:53, n. 6).

3. Many males born in Canada some fifty years ago are named Charles. I wonder how many wish they were not?

4. I have even argued elsewhere that a Parsua located in the central western Zagros, lasting as late as the middle of the seventh century BCE, could well have been absorbed, along with so many other groups in the area, by the Median kingdom as it rose to power in the second half of that century and therefore might represent the Persians whom Herodotus (H.I.127–129) understood to be vassals of the Medes (Young 1988:32, n. 93).

5. Kesat (mentioned eight times in the Fortification Texts) would appear to be a fairly important site located probably not too far from Persepolis, yet it does not appear in Sumner's schematic presentation of the settlements in the environs of Parsa (Sumner 1986b:22).

6. A detailed critique of Sumner's second (optimistic) suggestion for solving our problem would require another article. While I am not entirely convinced that there is quite as good a fit between Shogha/Teimuran and Achaemenid settlement patterns as Sumner argues for (what about the twenty-one Achaemenid sites built on entirely new foundations?), nevertheless there is much food for productive thought in his suggestion. It would be most interesting to see more of Sumner's survey pottery and to see it related to specific sites in the Marvdasht corpus. One could then compare the distribution of these materials, sorted into pre-Achaemenid, Achaemenid and Post-Achaemenid, to Shogha/Teimuran settlement patterns. For example: does Achaemenid and Post-Achaemenid pottery concentrate on the sites which are new Achaemenid foundations? But maybe this would ask too much of the data, which, if tortured long enough, will of course confess to anything.

7. Ceramic shape comparisons are of necessity idiosyncratic. Individual archaeologists require different levels of exactitude in order to accept or reject a parallel. Stance is a particular problem: some think it vital, others do not. Getting stance right is also one of the hardest aspects of drawing pottery. This article was written and submitted for publication in 1999. I therefore confined my discussion of parallels from Godin II to examples published and widely available in the preliminary excavation reports. Hillary Gopnik subsequently (June, 2000) defended with distinction her Ph.D. dissertation for the University of Toronto in which she presents a detailed analysis of the stratification of Godin II and of all the ceramics from Early and Late Manor House and Squatter levels. Since her dissertation is available only in the Library of the University of Toronto and the National Library of Canada, Ottawa, it seems reasonable to leave further comparisons which are now possible between Sumner's survey materials and Godin II to another article. I can only hope that such future research does not prove that what you are now reading is, in fact, "a fairy tale"!

8. A total of 146 bowls and bowl sherds are illustrated in the Pasargadae excavation report. Twenty-six are Achaemenid, seventeen late Achaemenid, twenty-three late or Post-Achaemenid, and eighty Post-Achaemenid or unstratified. Given the occupational history of the site this is only to be expected. Thus, sadly, only 29% of the bowls from Pasargadae can be dated to the Achaemenid period.

9. Material from the Squatter occupation of the Manor House at Godin II very probably dates to a time following the firm establishment of the Achaemenid dynasty under Cyrus II. Thus the Godin II ceramic corpus, as presently understood, in the main involves a mixture of Iron III and what I call Iron IV pottery.

10. A bowl, unique in shape and ware, found in the Ville Royale II excavations in a Neo-Elamite context could well have been imported from the Plateau in Iron III times (Miroschedji 1981a: Fig. 33, no. 9).

CHAPTER 23

THE TOMB AT ARJAN AND THE HISTORY OF SOUTHWESTERN IRAN IN THE EARLY SIXTH CENTURY BCE

DAVID STRONACH

AS THOSE WHO ARE ACQUAINTED with the works of the late Roman Ghirshman will recall, this notable contributor to the study of ancient Iran took a decidedly individual approach to the reconstruction of early Persian history between the late eighth and the mid-sixth centuries BCE (Girshman 1964). His was an interpretation which depended, to a very great extent, on a series of idiosyncratic datings for the period of his own excavations in Khuzestan (with special reference to Achaemenid Village I at Susa as well to other supposedly late eighth- or seventh-century occupations at Masjid-i Sulaiman and Bard-i Nishandeh), not to mention the witness of a number of more easterly, uninscribed monuments (namely, Da-u Dukhtar, Gur-i Dukhtar, and the Tall-i Takht at Pasargadae) which he tended to associate with correspondingly high dates between 650 and 550 BCE (figure 23.1).[1] The findings of this pioneer reconstruction were not long in being questioned (Stronach 1974), but in the absence of sustained fieldwork during the past two decades it has nonetheless remained unclear whether any more apt selection of archaeological "signposts" could be said to be available.

In the present paper, in which it is the greatest pleasure to acknowledge Bill Sumner's stellar contributions to the archaeology of Iran, it may be useful, especially in the context of the recently discovered tomb at Arjan (figure 23.1), to take a fresh look at what now seem to be a number of more pertinent lines of archaeological and historical inquiry. Any exploration of the subject necessarily begins, chronologically, with Bill Sumner's own recent claim that

the Persians possibly reached the Kur river basin—the effective heartland of Fars—as early as 1600 BCE (Sumner 1994a).

It is clear that a number of cogent factors combine to lend weight to this specific date. In keeping with a sudden decline in the size and number of sites throughout the Kur river basin, Malyan, the ancient city of Anshan (figure 23.1), shrank from accommodating a population of 30,000 to 20,000 in the Kaftari period (ca. 2000 BCE–1600 BCE) to no more than 8000 to 4000 persons in the subsequent Qaleh/Middle Elamite period (ca. 1600 BCE–1000 BCE) (Sumner 1988a:318; Carter 1994a:65). While the Kaftari pottery that had once been ubiquitous in the region was soon replaced by related Qaleh buffwares in the northwestern part of the valley (in the vicinity of Malyan) the opposite southeastern portion of the valley exhibited handmade (Shogha) and wheelmade (Teimuran) orange wares over a still longer period of time (perhaps extending down to 800 BCE; see Sumner 1994a:101). Not surprisingly, these distributions were seen to point to coexisting, possibly competing groups (Sumner 1988a) or to the arrival, with reference to the seemingly intrusive Shogha and Teimuran traditions, of "new peoples...from other regions of Iran" (Carter 1994a:67). Indeed, with a very frank acknowledgment of the speculative nature of his latest reconstruction, Bill has suggested that such mid-second-millennium intruders, his "hypothetical early Persians," entered the valley from the southeast and forced the Qaleh people "to retreat gradually to the north-west...where the remnant of Elamite power was still present" (Sumner 1994a:104).

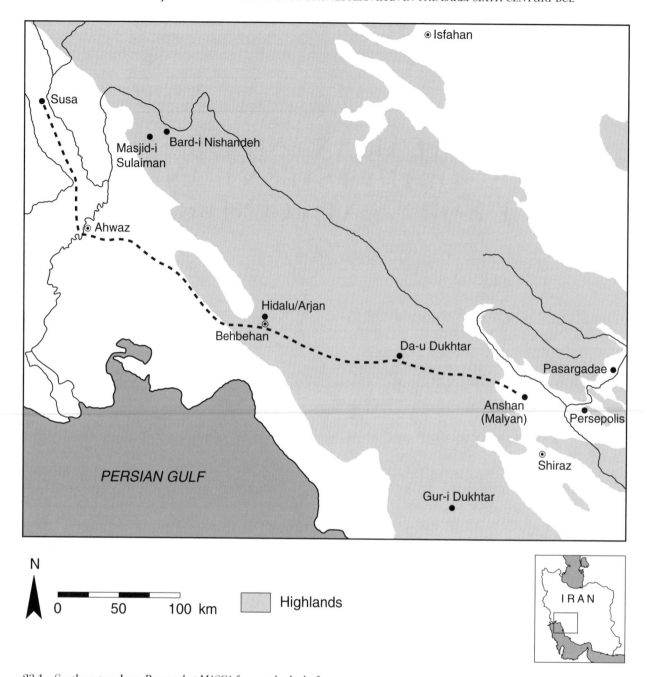

23.1   Southwestern Iran. *Prepared at MASCA from author's draft*

Evidence for a surprising degree of subsequent "settlement continuity" (possibly extending all the way down to the late sixth century BCE when fully evolved Achaemenid sites suddenly dot the valley), is reported to be "quite strong" (Sumner 1994a:102 ff); and, if nothing else, there is of course no indication on the ground of any late second or early first millennium intrusion of newcomers akin to that which seems to have taken place near 1600 BCE.

Nonetheless an alternative and perhaps preferable view of the mechanics of the Persian migration is one

that takes a round date of 1000 BCE (Miroschedji 1985; Stronach 1997a) as a more likely moment for the beginnings of a gradual process of infiltration into the eventual homeland. Such a process is one that is admittedly unsupported by the recovery of any kind of separate ceramic corpus (at any rate within the broad Marvdasht or "grassy plain," the closely surveyed core area of the Kur river basin), but it could well find an indirect echo, induced by nomadic pressures, in the disappearance of the last Marvdasht settlements of any consequence in the interval that extends from just before 1000 BCE down to, at the latest, 850 BCE (for which date see Carter 1994a:66).

Apart from the conceivable significance of the desertion of Malyan and the more southeasterly site of Darvazeh (Sumner 1986b:4) within the early years of the first millennium BCE, one external consideration may be said to fortify the case for the less remote time-frame espoused here. This is the fact that the first Assyrian encounter with any Persians whatsoever took place in the western central Zagros in 844 BCE (Grayson 1996:40; Waters 1999:100), while the Persians' close cousins, the Medes, received their earliest mention in the annals of Assyria (again in the same general region) in 836 BCE. It also has to be stressed that, while the existence of this Persian entity, "Parsua," in the interval between 844 BCE and the closing years of the eighth century BCE used to be seen as a "proof" that the main body of the Persians could only have migrated southwards from the central Zagros at some date immediately prior to 700 BCE[2] this is now recognized as a spurious claim. Instead, one relatively small group of Persians is now understood to have almost certainly broken away from the mainstream of the Persian migration and to have moved westwards to the northern Mahidasht (Levine 1974b:112; Frye 1984:66) where circumstances did not for long favor their separate existence. Furthermore, Parsua's brief moment of notoriety should be seen at this point to have nothing more than a strictly general bearing on the chronological context within which the bulk of the Persians duly made their way southwards in what led, as far as can be detected, to a very positive fusion of indigenous and incoming peoples within the bounds of the ever-inviting region of Fars.

HISTORICAL NOTES-I

As far as relevant historical considerations in the interval between 700 BCE and the accession of Cyrus II (the Great) in 559 BCE are concerned, the first clear reference to a Persian entity in southwestern Iran comes from the annals of Sennacherib. There, most intriguingly, the lands of "Parsuash" (a variant reading for "Parsumash," discussed below) and "Anzan" (that is, Anshan) head a long list of local states that are said to have contributed contingents to the "vassal host" of the Elamite king, Humban-nimena (692 BCE–689 BCE), who met the Assyrians at the battle of Halule in 691 BCE (Luckenbill 1924:43; Carter and Stolper 1984:48). This was a time when Assyrian pressure on Elam was beginning to exact a heavy toll. Sennacherib's annals locate the capital of the previous Elamite ruler, Kudur-Nahunte (who ruled for only ten months before being deposed and killed), as be-

ing not at Susa but rather at the more remote, northerly city of Madaktu (Cameron 1936:165). When even Madaktu came under Assyrian pressure, Humban-nimena apparently withdrew still deeper into the mountains to Hidalu on the road to Fars.[3] From this time onwards, in fact, as the political authority of the unstable Elamite monarchy steadily eroded, these last two upland strongholds figure with increasing prominence in Mesopotamian records, and Susa itself is not mentioned again by the Assyrians until the moment of its terrible destruction in 646 BCE (Carter and Stolper 1984:47).

The year 691 BCE also takes on the shape of a watershed juncture for the early Persians. That is to say that, even if the Elamite royal house no longer exerted any real degree of suzerainty in the heartland of Fars, it is clear that, up to that point, the Elamite king was in a position to call upon highland contingents from Fars to help to confront any threat as substantial as that posed by an Assyrian advance. This was not the case in subsequent years, however. Not only is there no direct evidence to suggest that Persian auxiliaries ever had to answer any such a call again but the presence of a contingent from Anshan in the vassal host at the battle of Halule is enough in itself to show that the time-honored Elamite royal title "King of Anshan and Susa" no longer meant what it said. Indeed, whether or not Anshan at this time was in indigenous hands or in Persian hands, Sennacherib's mention of "Anzan" duly signals the emergence of a new kingdom in the Kur river basin that was effectively independent of Madaktu/Susa (see Briant 1984:82; Potts 1999:262). The associated mention of Parsuash (in second place in the listing of vassal forces) may also be seen to suggest that the once spacious land of Anshan already stood divided at this time into at least two separate kingdoms, each occupying separate parts of Fars (see Carter and Stolper 1984:48).

Almost half a century later Assurbanipal records, with not a little satisfaction as it would seem, that the example of the havoc inflicted on Elam had sufficed to induce Kurash, the king of Parsumash, to send his son, Arukku, to Nineveh as a hostage. If nothing else, this statement indicates (Carter and Stolper 1984:52) that, by 646 BCE, at least parts of Fars were under autonomous Persian control (as they perhaps had been since the 690s) and that Parsuash (now known as Parsumash) already constituted one of southwestern Iran's principal political entities. It is vital to emphasize, however, that Assurbanipal's mention of Kurash does not permit us to assume that this same ruler exercised paramount rule over the whole of Fars; for various reasons Persian rule of this magnitude—and unified Persian rule at that—is not likely to have come so early.

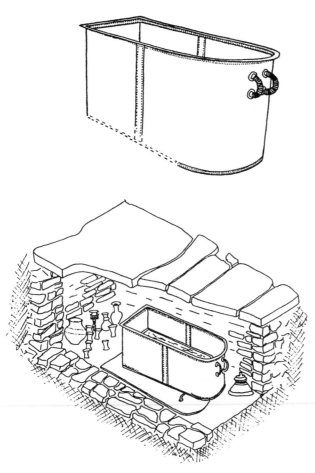

23.2 Drawing of the tomb found at Arjan. *After Alizadeh 1985:Fig. 2*

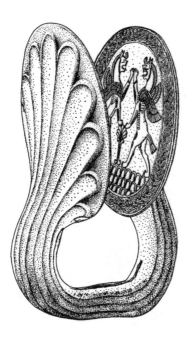

23.3 The gold "ring" from Arjan. *After Alizadeh 1985:Fig. 3*

THE ARJAN TOMB

Although Hans Nissen's survey of the Behbehan region, which stands midway between Susa and the city of Anshan, did not succeed in identifying any Middle Elamite or Neo-Elamite settlements (1976:279), the desirability of new surveys in this fertile, intermontane enclave is fast becoming clear. This is indicated not only by the innate interest of the major Sasanian and early Islamic town of Arjan, situated 10 km north of Behbehan (Stein 1940:78 ff; Gaube 1987:519–520), but also—most particularly—by the chance discovery in 1982 of an important Neo-Elamite tomb near the northern limit of Arjan on the left bank of the Marun river.

Fortunately, two of the more striking objects from the tomb are inscribed, in Elamite, with the legend "Kidin-Hutran, son of Kurlush." On palaeographic grounds F. Vallat (1984a) has determined that the script can be dated between 646 BCE and 525 BCE, that is, between the time of Assurbanipal's assault on Susa and, in essence, the last possible moment at which a script lacking the characteristics of subsequent Achaemenid Elamite could still have been current.

From various perspectives there is much about the character of the tomb at Arjan (figure 23.2) that is less than strictly Elamite. The construction of the chamber documents an interesting compromise. Built of stone as opposed to baked brick (a no doubt logical concession to its stone-rich highland setting), it nonetheless boasts a typical interior coat of gypsum plaster (Tohidi and Khalilian 1982; Alizadeh 1985:51). Also unusual is the method of interment. In contrast to prior Middle Elamite traditions of elite burial in which the remains of the deceased were usually placed on some kind of raised brick platform (see Ghirshman 1968:Pl. 43), the body in this case was placed in a bronze coffin, and in contrast to the oft-noted scarcity of burial goods of any kind (see Ghirshman 1968:Pl. 40), the Arjan burial was accompanied by funerary objects of high worth.

The coffin is of a well-known variety with straight sides, rounded at one end and squared off at the other. That form begins to be found in Assyria in the second half of the eighth century BCE (Curtis 1983; Damerji 1999:Fig. 38) and, as John Curtis (1995:22) has noted, the example from Arjan documents a decidedly late use of the type. Since no prior bronze coffins are known from Elam, it is possible to see in this mode of burial a new awareness of outside factors that were beginning to break down the once rigid conventions of Elamite burial practice.

The character of the grave goods only reinforces this observation. While a group of bronze vessels from Arjan (Alizadeh 1985:Fig. 5) can be closely compared to a second group of bronze vessels from tomb 693 at Susa (Miroschedji

1981a:Fig. 40) which D.T. Potts (1999:303) would ascribe, together with the Arjan vessels, to a Neo-Elamite IIIB phase falling between the years 605 BCE and 539 BCE, relatively few of the other objects from Arjan are incontrovertibly "Elamite" in appearance.

A unique gold "ring" weighing 237 g (Alizadeh 1985:53) with flaring disc-shaped finials (figure 23.3) is one outstanding object that underlines the latter point. This apparent symbol of office, found resting on the chest of the deceased, close to his left hand, shows precisely the same repoussé and chased design on its two opposed circular plaques: a palmette tree flanked by rampant winged monsters of principally leonine appearance. Each element stands on the same scaled (that is, mountainous) ground line and the design as a whole is framed by a prominent guilloche band. While the pose of the Arjan monsters has been understandably compared (Carter 1994a:73; Potts 1999:303) to that of various rearing, sometimes distinctly muscular, creatures in late Neo-Elamite seal designs (Amiet 1973b:Nos. 11–12), the question has to be raised whether such comparisons are compelling enough to justify a Neo-Elamite cultural label (see Muscarella 1994:63, n. 8), even when this same ring happens to be one of two objects from Arjan that carry Kidin-Hutran's inscription.

I find myself in some sympathy with Abbas Alizadeh's (1985:63 ff) finding that many of the eighth-century and earlier parallels to details in the gold ring's exquisite disc-like finials are to be found in contexts that appear to stem from north or northwestern Iran. Without wishing to add too much to what has already been said in this respect, I might only note that the quiff of hair that emerges from the forehead of each Arjan monster and the visible curve that distinguishes the neck of each of these creatures does much to recall similar elements in the appearance of—to name just one parallel—the "unicorns" that occur on one of the better known vessels from Marlik Tepe (Negahban 1983:16). Where the sheer bulk of the hand-held hollow portion of the gold ring is concerned, it is difficult not to think of the similarly fluted, solid hoops of the heavy gold bracelets of perhaps late seventh century date that were at one time ascribed to Ziwiye (see Porada 1965:134 and Pl. 39) and which still deserve to be associated, in all likelihood, with western or northwestern Iran.

On the other hand, most discussions so far have done relatively little to explore still closer connections between the Arjan ring and the conventions of somewhat later, fully evolved Achaemenid art. In this regard the elaborate, complementary images on the ring's two closely juxtaposed discs could perhaps be thought to anticipate the late sixth-century and later Persian interest so often

taken in extensively repeated so-called mirror-images. If we think of the Arjan ring being in some way based on the concept of a bracelet, it is of interest to observe, as Alizadeh (1985:66) indeed has, that the base of the hoop shows a slight inward bend—a diagnostic feature that is widely present in Achaemenid bracelets of late sixth century BCE and later date (see Stronach 1999:182). More arresting still, however, are the close parallels that can be drawn between the pose and style of the rampant monsters in the opposed Arjan discs and the rampant, regardant lion-griffins that adorn the justly celebrated sword-scabbard from Persepolis (figure 23.4)—an object which was almost certainly carved at some point during the first quarter of the fifth century BCE.

While the paired Persepolis griffins stand back to back in a felicitous stratagem that served to fill the entire field of the shield-shaped scabbard top, there is much in the stance of the two beasts that is otherwise familiar from the Arjan design. Notably, the near foreleg of each beast extends downwards to touch the top of a palmette, while the far foreleg rises to touch (in this case) a ribbed border pattern. Each creature stands on an imaginary ground line that is close in its relative position to the mountainous ground line in the Arjan composition and each has a tripartite brush-like tail that is not so very different in appearance from the very distinctive tails sported by the Arjan monsters. Finally, the fact that the wings and tails are each relatively straight in the Arjan emblem and curved in the similar design from Persepolis is no more, needless to say, than a function of the passage of time. It is the difference between one emblem that was very possibly formulated somewhere between 575 BCE and 550 BCE (if a preliminary guess may be hazarded) and another that was most probably carved soon after the accession of Xerxes (485 BCE–465 BCE).

A second singular object from the Arjan tomb—the tall bronze stand which is illustrated in figure 23.5—presents a curious mixture of chronological clues. On the one hand, the lower part of the stand includes Atlas figures of markedly Assyrian appearance, such as occur on a table depicted in a bas-relief of Sargon (721 BCE–705 BCE) (see Curtis 1996:176 and Pl. 51c), and, in an obvious contrast, both the adjacent bull protomes and the various representations of lions with outwardly turned heads possess qualities that point, as Curtis (1995:21) has observed, to "a rather later date." Indeed, any such lower date is not likely to be far from that just ventured for the production of the "ring."

This brief review of certain of the more significant objects found in the Arjan tomb cannot conclude without reference to the truly remarkable Arjan bowl (figure 23.6).

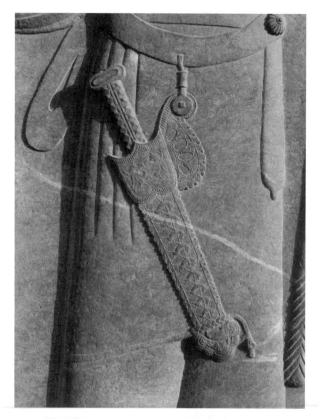

23.4 Persepolis. Detail of the scabbard displayed by the king's weapon-bearer in the southern Treasury relief. *Courtesy of the Oriental Institute of the University of Chicago*

Following its careful conservation and the consequent detection of its lively, incised decoration, not to mention the presence of a second inscription reading "Kidin-Hutran, son of Kurlush," its signal attributes have been discussed by several authors, including R. Vatandust (1988), M.R. Sarraf (1990), and Y. Majidzadeh (1992). Majidzadeh (1992:142) uses the iconography on the bowl to lower the original estimate of the date of the tomb from "the first half of the eighth century BC" (Alizadeh 1985:68) to "the mid-seventh century BC."

It is not one of the purposes of this paper to comment on all aspects of the Arjan bowl. Nonetheless, as I have tried to indicate with reference to the ring and the stand, not to mention certain of the bronze vessels from the tomb, most of the Arjan objects could be said to fit within the chronological limits of the Elamite IIIb period, that is, between 605 and 539. In this context the gold "ring of kingship" is likely to be one of the latest objects from the corpus and the bronze bowl (allowing for the fact that it could have been inscribed well after its date of manufacture) could well be one of the earliest—that is to say it could have been manufactured in or near the first quarter of the sixth century. On close inspection the vessel does not look like the product of an Assyrian workshop; even if the presence of five concentric registers can be compared to one of the characteristics of the widely distributed "Phoenician bowls" of the Mediterranean and the Near East (Markoe 1986), the bowl does not have to be attributed to some hypothetical center of design and production in either north Syria or the Levant.[4] Instead, a host of visibly local, Elamite elements (see Majidzadeh 1992:136ff) would seem to suggest that a metalsmith, skilled in the design of this kind of richly decorated vessel, was employed somewhere in the vicinity of the southwestern Zagros, to produce the composition in question; and that this composition was expected to accord with many of the specifics of the region—and of local court life.

In the third register of the bowl (reading inwards from the rim) we see a ruler seated in state, with his crown prince and three attendants standing behind him and a procession of animals, birds, and other commodities about to pass before him in formal review. It is a time-honored, loosely Assyrianizing scene that appears to accord at first sight with the dictum, with reference to Persepolis, that "every scene" shown on the Achaemenid reliefs (with the obvious exception of the king worshipping in front of a fire altar) can also be found "in an almost identical form on the Assyrian palace reliefs" (Roaf 1989:39). The Arjan bowl, which includes a typically Assyrian raised open-handed salute (see Parrot 1961:Fig. 112) by the fourth figure in front of the enthroned king (figure 23.6), also bears witness, however, to the birth of a new, local artistic device.

Here the crown prince (if it is in fact he) is shown standing directly behind the seated monarch, and a dignitary who would seem to be the parade-marshal (and not the crown prince as would be the case in Assyria) heads the procession.[5] The official in front of the king leans forwards from the waist, with his leading knee sharply bent and his hand held in front of his mouth, presumably in a gesture of reverence or respectful speech. The parallel with the pose of the parade-marshal at Persepolis (figure 23.7) is almost complete except that the forward inclination of the Arjan figure is clearly greater.[6] Also, while the pine-cone feet of the standard Assyrian throne (Curtis 1996:Fig. 1) find a confused echo in the upright cone behind the king's head, it is noticeable that the ruler in the Arjan bowl is seated on an armless throne—a distinctly rare item of furniture for an Assyrian king but a standard one for Darius I (522 BCE–486 BCE) and his successors.

HISTORICAL NOTES-II

From the foregoing overview of relevant evidence from Arjan several deductions may be drawn. It is possible to infer, for example, that a separate Elamite political entity continued to flourish in the vicinity of Hidalu into at least the early years of Cyrus's reign; that local audience scenes at Hidalu (if not in the adjacent region of Fars in general) already included innovative court procedures that stand affirmed by later evidence from Persepolis; and that, in a period of intense external contacts (see Carter 1994a:73), and perhaps also at a time of concomitant self-doubt, traditional Elamite material culture had started to give way, in the late seventh to early sixth centuries, to a complex mix of Elamite, Persian, and Assyro-Babylonian elements.

In historical terms alone the survival of a local Elamite principality at Hidalu, at a date possibly within the first years of the reign of Cyrus the Great (559 BCE–530 BCE), is a telling indication of the probably fragmented nature of political power in southwestern Iran before the accession of the founder of the Achaemenid empire—and it may even document an indulgent "hands off" policy towards what was left of independent Elam prior to the approximate moment of Cyrus's attack on Babylon in 539 BCE. Above all, it may now be appropriate to question most reconstructions that suggest that no more than one dynastic line exercised control over Fars for most of the period between, say, the fall of Susa and the accession of Cyrus.

Such magnified perceptions of the extent of earlier local rule may indeed find one reflection in the cylinder of Cyrus (Pritchard 1969:316), where he refers to himself as

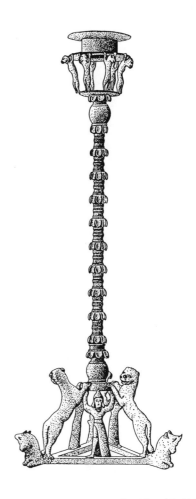

23.5   The bronze stand from Arjan. *After Alizadeh 1985:Fig. 4*

"son of Cambyses, great king, king of Anshan, grandson of Cyrus, great king, king of Anshan, great-grandson of Teispes, great king, king of Anshan."[7] In view, in short, of the newly documented longevity of Hidalu's seemingly independent status and the presence of numerous other petty kings in the twilight years of independent Elam near Malamir (Potts 1999:301), not to mention Susiana as well (Vallat 1996a), the whole region of southwestern Iran, east and west of Hidalu, should probably be regarded as having been occupied by "kingdoms" whose strength was in reality quite circumscribed. In addition, as Potts (1999:307) has recently stressed—and as the "Elamo-Persian" contents of the Arjan tomb would only seem to underscore—the Elamites and the Persians may have been "much more closely" bound to each other than was formerly supposed—and we should not think of them as being inevitably in opposition.

In keeping with this interpretation, D.T. Potts (1999:307), following Pierre de Miroschedji's earlier observations along the same lines, has noted that "the arrival of Cyrus the Great in Susiana, which must have occurred by 540, considering that Babylon was taken by 539 BCE,

23.6   The Arjan bowl. *Drawing by R. Vatandust; after Majidzadeh 1992:Fig. 1*

may have appeared to a lowland Elamite as nothing more than a restoration of the old kingdom of Anshan and Susa"(1985:305). It is a persepective that calls for close consideration.

Of at least equal interest is Darius I's claim to have been ultimately descended from Achaemenes, for which reason he and his line had the privilege of being known as "Achaemenids" (Kent 1953:119). As long as many of us believed that we had to choose between the verity of Cyrus's claim to a long-enduring royal line and Darius's claim to a similar distinction, the case for doubting Darius's veracity appeared to be strong. Now, however, if the limits of the territorial authority of Cyrus' forebears can be presumed to have been relatively circumscribed (that is, latter-day "Anshan" may not have comprised the greater part of Fars, before say, 570 BCE, but may have been more closely iden-

tified with the Kur river basin), a case can be made for the legitimacy of Darius's assertion that he was from a family that "from long ago... had been kings" (Kent 1953:119). To take this reconstruction one stage further, Darius's distant ancestors could well have ruled in some other part of Fars (in the south or the east perhaps?) until their lands were absorbed by the line of Cyrus; by this same token Achaemenes could have been—and very possibly was— just as real a "founder figure" as Teispes.

In Darius's own account of his origins he reports, in part, that:

> My father was Hystaspes; Hystaspes' father was Arsames; Arsames' father was Ariaramnes; Ariaramnes' father was Teispes; Teispes' father was Achaemenes. (Kent 1953)

23.7   Persepolis: Tentative reconstruction of the eastern bas-relief from the Treasury. *Tilia 1972:Fig. 3; photograph by Francine Sarin*

23.8   Persepolis: Composite drawing of the seal of "Kurash, the Anshanite, son of Teispes." *After Garrison and Root 1996:Fig. 2a*

The stratagem of placing his own ancestor, Achaemenes, before Cyrus's first known forebear was brilliant. At one stroke a new seamless Achaemenid Persian past was called into being (Stronach 1997a:39) and each regnant member of Cyrus's line was redefined, effectively, as a member of Darius's still older family. This inclusive dynastic vision may also have sanctioned the prominent use that was made within the Persepolis chancellory of the once personal cylinder seal of Kurash, the grandfather of Cyrus the Great (figure 23.8), from at least the late sixth century onwards. Equally, however, the use of this seal may serve to illuminate another interesting perspective: namely, the degree to which

a certain "continuity" in personnel and administrative practice still obtained at a time of dynastic change.[8]

At all events, we have to be unusually grateful for this use of a far from contemporary artifact. Thanks to the excavations at Persepolis, where numerous sealings from this object chanced to be recovered, we now know (or can very strongly presume) that Cyrus I traced his own royal line to Teispes, not Achaemenes, and since the mounted figure of Cyrus's ancestor (figure 23.8) is carved in the style of Neo-Elamite IIIB glyptic (see Potts 1999:306), we can also be sure that he ruled *late* in the seventh century BCE at the earliest and that, hence, he is not to be confused with the

"Kurash of Parsumash" who was obliged to treat with Assurbanipal in the mid-640s BCE(see especially, Miroschedji 1985:286).

CONCLUSIONS

We may never know exactly when the first Persians began to reach the region of Fars (see chapters 24 and 22). But from perspectives provided, at least in part, by the new-found tomb at Arjan this excursus allows a number of concluding points to be made, especially with respect to local circumstances after 646 BCE. First and foremost, a clearer picture now exists of many different petty kings jostling for power throughout southwestern Iran in the aftermath of the fall of Susa to the Assyrians. Among such rulers, we may now count *both* Achaemenes and Teispes, each of whom possibly came to power at much the same time, that is, near 635 BCE.[9] For this reason, if we accept that the Teispids—the ancestors of Cyrus the Great—were not necessarily paramount in Fars until well into the sixth century there also seems to be no insuperable objection, not least in art historical terms, to dating the Achaemenid period (with various subdivisions that will no doubt go on being refined for many years) from, say, 635 BCE onward.

For those who are interested in the formation of the Achaemenid Persian empire it also remains not a little mysterious that Cyrus I, Cyrus II, and even Cambyses II (530 BCE–522 BCE) can each be shown to have insisted on the "Anshanite" identity of their ancestors.[10] With reference to this insistence, Potts (1999:306–307) takes the late sixth-century uses of the title king of Anshan as "an intriguing indication that the Achaemenid empire, however 'Persian' it may have been, in one sense evolved from the Neo-Elamite social, cultural, linguistic and perhaps even political milieu, or at least made the claim of Anshanite ancestry." At the same time, it is not at all certain that the contents of the Arjan tomb provide a totally ringing endorsement of Elam's latter-day political and cultural clout. The presence of the superb gold ring (an object of Persian design and manufacture to my mind) bespeaks a powerful new Persian sensibility in the region: one that very much heralds the wave of the future even at the same time as it visibly draws on various broadly Iranian and conceivably also Neo-Elamite sources of inspiration.

For this reason among others it may be appropriate to return to the question of why Teispes chose to invoke the name of Anshan. Were he and his descendants Elamites (or at all events local Anshanites) who became Persian by a process of acculturation (see Amiet 1992:93)? Or were they—especially if the Persians had in fact been present in Fars for far longer periods than currently available onomastic evidence suggests—already quite Persian in their identity by 635 BCE and thus took the age-old Anshanite title only in order to upstage certain local rivals? Of this we may never be sure (see also Stronach 1997b:356 ff); and even further exploration of the not necessarily Persian names of Cyrus II's predecessors (Stronach 1997a:38) is not likely to reveal new certitudes.

In an area of southwestern Iran long accustomed to institutions of kingship and statehood, Pierre Briant has characterized the rise of the Achaemenids as a change in political leadership via an *"ethno-classe dominante"* in contrast, in other words, to the ascendancy of a "new" tribal group over an "exhausted" civilization (Briant 1990:53; see also Potts 1999:307). This definition of the political changes that took place in literate southwestern Iran in the period under review offers one more reminder, in fact, of the dangers inherent in accepting what Potts has called "Herodotus' simplistic division of [the] Persians into nomads and agriculturalists" (1999:307). Finally, with respect to such ambitions of overarching dominion as the Median royal house may well have entertained in southern Iran as well as elsewhere, especially following the fall of the Assyrian empire in 612, the difficulties inherent in recognizing a Median presence remain as intractable as ever. In this context I may well stand accused, *inter alia,* of stressing the Persian as opposed to the conceivable Median artistic connections of the handsome scabbard (figure 23.4) that has loomed so large in the foregoing discussions. To this I can only respond that these two strands of Iranian taste may not have been so very different. Furthermore, I believe it only appropriate to label the Persepolis scabbard as "Persian." It is some time since scholarly opinion endorsed the literal view that every figure in so-called Median dress in the reliefs at Persepolis had to be considered a Mede[11] and, even if this object was conceivably meant to identify an especially loyal individual (of Persian *or* Median identity) any knowledgeable bystander would have known that this exquisite example of the armorer's art was either a gift from the king or a possession of the king which was "on display" on the monarch's behalf.[12]

NOTES

1. For the details of Ghirshman's reconstruction, which first brought the Persians to Khuzestan from northwestern Iran just before 700 BCE, then to the western borders of Fars in the course of the seventh century, and finally to the vicinity of Pasargadae at some date after 600 BCE, see especially Ghirshman (1964:129–131).

2. See note 1.

3. Based on information contained in the Persepolis Fortification Texts, Hidalu lay approximately seven days' journey (Vallat 1993:96) to the southeast of Susa.

4. On the lack of hard evidence for centers of production for Phoenician bowls in either of these regions, see most recently Moorey (1988:29) and Muhly (1988:337).

5. For the Assyrian evidence, see conveniently, Parrot (1961:Figs. 112, 113).

6. At the same time the Ayan pose is not to be confused with the extremes of full prostration, for which see Frankfort (1970:Pl. 88) and Parrot (1961:Fig. 113).

7. For the reading "great-grandson of Teispes," see Waters (1996:13). Pritchard prefers "descendant of Teispes" (1969:316).

8. I am indebted to Antigoni Zournatzi for this latter suggestion.

9. If Teispes is removed from the genealogy of Darius, the generations do move very comfortably in concert, with Teispes preceding Cyrus I and Achaemenes preceding Ariaramnes. A date of circa 635 BCE also serves to accommodate the passing from power of "Kurash of Parsumash" who, for a time at least, could have been an obstacle to the rise of others.

10. Especially when, as P. Briant has observed, "sans exception aucune, les satrapes de Cyrus et de Cambyse soient issus de familles perses" [without any exception, the satraps of Cyrus and Cambyses came from Persian families](1996:93).

11. Especially when the named dignitary, Aspathines, one of Darius I's original Persian adherents, is represented, in "Median" dress, in one of three superposed panels on the left side of Darius's tomb at Naqsh-i Rustam (Schmidt 1953:169) and when alternating patterns of dress lent needed variety to otherwise potentially monotonous scenes.

12. Compare, for example, DNd where the text that identifies Aspathines also relates that this trusted individual "holds the battle-ax of Darius the king"(Kent 1953:140).

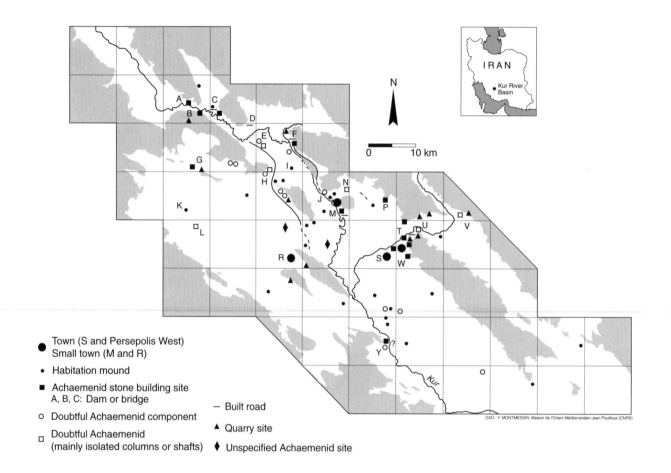

Town (S and Persepolis West)
Small town (M and R)

• Habitation mound

■ Achaemenid stone building site
A, B, C: Dam or bridge

○ Doubtful Achaemenid component

□ Doubtful Achaemenid
(mainly isolated columns or shafts)

— Built road

▲ Quarry site

♦ Unspecified Achaemenid site

24.1   Surface traces of Achaemenid activity in the Kur river basin. Widespread remains mask low settlement density (adapted from Sumner [1986b, 1994a], with some other sites added from Kleiss [1993b] and Tilia [1978]). *Prepared at MASCA from original by DAO: Y. Montmessin, Maison de l'Orient Méditerranéen and Jean Pouilloux, CNRS; base map Sumner 1986b*

CHAPTER 24

THE PERSEPOLIS AREA IN THE ACHAEMENID PERIOD

Some Reconsiderations

RÉMY BOUCHARLAT

FOR NEARLY ONE HUNDRED YEARS, the terrace of Persepolis and its associated remains have been intensely studied, but the Achaemenid occupation of the region itself has attracted comparatively little interest. Ernst Herzfeld's architect, Karl Bergner (1937), Erich F. Schmidt (1957), and Louis Vanden Berghe (1953) all took an interest in varying degrees. Ann Britt Tilia (1978) surveyed the architectural remains in the Kur river basin (known in antiquity as Anshan), and the German archaeologist, Wolfram Kleiss, explored the mountain slopes of the region (figures 24.1, 24.2). In the late 1960s, William Sumner was the first to survey the plain systematically. Of the seven phases distinguished in Sumner's original survey of the Kur river basin, six are protohistoric. The last one, Phase VII (Achaemenid period), is one of the most difficult to deal with for two reasons (Sumner 1972:267–270). First, it is historical and, unlike the preceding phases, rich in textual data; yet, the chronology is far from precise. Second, Phase VII is represented by mounds with potsherds as well as by vestiges of other types of activities.

It is greatly to his credit that Sumner returned to this problem with new observations, stimulating questions, and hypotheses always presented as such (Sumner 1986b). His attempt to interpret the settlement pattern and administrative system on the basis of archaeological and historical evidence remains unequalled. Never satisfied, and stimulated by more recent articles, Sumner (1994a) set to work once more, refining his hypotheses, with clarity and great honesty as always, paying particular attention to the question of the arrival of the Iranian populations in the region.

To go beyond the reconstruction proposed by Sumner is difficult at the present time (see also Briant 1984, 1996; Miroschedji 1985, 1990a). Therefore, this essay does not offer new information but rather emphasizes some of the problems identified by Sumner as of 1972, problems whose consequences are perhaps more important than he imagined for identifying the sites and plotting their distribution in the region of Persepolis in the second half of the first millennium BCE.[1]

CHRONOLOGY: THE END OF PHASE VI AND THE BEGINNING OF PHASE VII

Both the model and the chronology proposed by Sumner for the Achaemenid period depend upon the definition and the dating of the preceding Phase VI, the end of the second and the beginning of the first millennia BCE. Sumner hypothesized that Phase VI corresponds to a growing pastoral economy and to the penetration of new populations, probably Iranian-speakers, who mixed progressively with the local populations of Anshan. They later formed the Persians, who gave rise to the Achaemenids. Phase VI is characterized by categories of ceramics that are different but contemporary, often painted (Qaleh pottery, mainly in the northwestern part of the basin, Shogha pottery and Teimuran pottery mainly in the southeastern part). The Iranians, presumably nomad tribes, used the latter two types of pottery which gradually spread towards the northwest (Miroschedji 1985; Sumner 1972:265–266).[2] The pottery of Shogha-Teimuran disappears at about 800 BCE, or even as early as 900 BCE, according to radiocarbon dates from

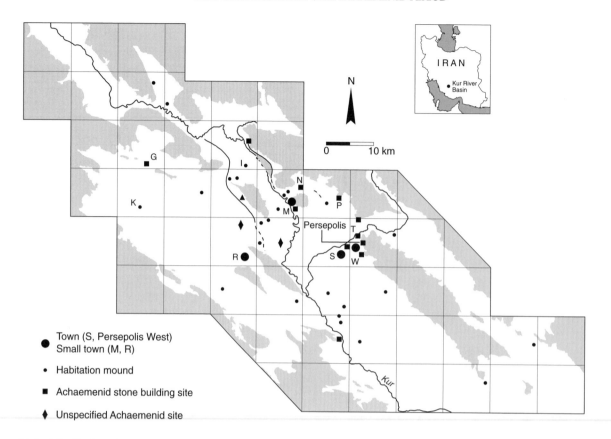

24.2　Distribution of the archaeological remains in the Kur river basin restricted to the inhabited sites and excluding the stone-working areas (quarries, roads, abandoned pieces of stones and "doubtful sites"). Overall settlement density is low. *Prepared at MASCA from original by DAO: Y. Montmessin, Maison de l'Orient Méditerranéen and Jean Pouilloux, CNRS; base map Sumner 1986b*

Darvazeh Tepe (Jacobs 1980:115–119; Sumner 1972:62–63, 1986b:4, 1994a:101).

Phase VII thus marks a break: the total disappearance of painted pottery and its replacement by Late Plain Ware which may have continued into the Seleucid and Parthian periods (Sumner 1972:51). Thus, the first problem is that the transition from the Persians of Phase VI to the Achaemenids of Phase VII is marked by a complete change in pottery tradition. As Sumner (1972:267) notes, "certain phenomena, such as the sudden and complete change in the style of pottery between Phase VI and VII, are not explained by speculations."

The beginning of Phase VII was first assigned to the Late Achaemenid period, that is fourth and third centuries BCE, based on dates proposed by Schmidt (1957:96) at Persepolis and Stronach (1978:183–185) at Pasargadae. Sumner (1972:64, 1986:4) dates this phase to the beginning of the Achaemenid period in the sixth century BCE. At the same time, he is willing to advance the end of Phase VI to 700 BCE, because it reduces the chronological gap. Miroschedji (1987:32–35, 1990:53) puts the break at the

end of Phase VI and the beginning of Phase VII, that is, the end of the sixth century BCE, because the forms of Late Plain Ware had been present since Iron III elsewhere in the central Zagros, as well as in certain parts of Susiana (for example, at Chogha Mish but not at Neo-Elamite Susa).

Even if Sumner's earlier date of the sixth century BCE is accepted for the beginning of Phase VII, there still remains a gap of two to three centuries with the end of Phase VI, which is crucial for understanding the occupation of the region (Sumner 1994a:103). Moreover, within the sixth century BCE, we need to determine a more precise date for Late Plain Ware: Does it represent the principal marker of the period of Cyrus II (ca. 550 BCE), who did not establish himself in the Kur river basin, or rather that of Darius and his successors who were to transform the economy and the settlement of the region by the construction of Persepolis after about 520 BCE? The end of Phase VII is apparently not marked (Sumner 1972:51) by Alexander's conquest, which, while inaugurating a new period in the region, apparently did not affect pottery styles for several centuries.

It is hard to believe that a single type of pottery would last six or seven centuries over three or four occupation phases, each characterized by historically different activities, but no other solution presents itself at this time. It is rather unlikely that the Late Plain Ware of Fars, which is also found in the royal palaces of Pasargadae and Persepolis, predates Cyrus II. Rather, it more likely starts with him or with Darius, the builder of Persepolis. In fact, a similar process has been noticed at Susa; well before the Achaemenids, Persians certainly were present in the region, and even in Susa itself, as evidenced by changes in glyptic and the occurrence of Persian anthroponyms in the economic tablets of the first half of the sixth century BCE found there (Amiet 1973b; Steve 1986:17–18; Vallat 1984a:6 and n. 44). Yet there was no change in the traditional neo-Elamite pottery until the city was chosen as a capital by Darius around 520 BCE. We may assume that before the advent of Darius, the pre-Achaemenid Persians of Fars used the Shogha-Teimuran ware they had known for centuries. These "tent-dwelling nomads" (Sumner 1972:268) did not leave observable traces after 900 BCE. We may thus question the identity of the users of Shogha-Teimuran pottery. As for Late Plain Ware, its appearance should correspond to the beginnings of the empire when the movements of individuals and groups brought central Fars into direct contact with that the central Zagros and Khuzestan.

DISTRIBUTION AND TYPOLOGY OF SITES

Prior to the first millennium, settlement phases are characterized almost entirely by mounds. The Achaemenid period, however, is represented by evidence quite different from that of the earlier phases; the sites are also more difficult to date; lacking ceramic material, attribution to the Achaemenid period is based on other criteria.

In his survey, Sumner identified twenty-four sites of Phase VII (Sumner 1972:50–51). Later, he included the irrigation works and a paved road for a total of thirty-nine sites (Sumner 1986b:3), and then, with the discovery of rock cut remains (quarries) and architectural elements, bases and shafts of stone columns, tallied forty-two (Sumner 1994a:Fig. 1 and Table 1).

Half of these forty-two sites with Achaemenid components dating to Period VII cover an earlier occupation; in only ten cases is that occupation dated to Period VI. The other twenty-one consist of new sites on the level plain (Sumner 1994a:102 and Table 1). To assess the continuity or discontinuity of settlement, consider whether the habitation site was, for example, established on new location or on a previously occupied or archaeological site.

Achaemenid mounds are usually less than 1 ha in area

and under 2 m in height, with six exceptions (a similar situation is seen in Khuzestan, where only one site is larger than 5 ha [Miroschedji 1982:171–172]). Of the six prominent sites, the two largest lie very near Persepolis: site W, less than 1 km away, covers 25 ha; Firuzi, situated 4 km away, covers a total of 600 ha as a cluster of twelve mounds, several of which lack potsherds. The Firuzi mound group is probably ancient Matezzish (Sumner 1986b:20–21), referred to in the Persepolis Fortification Tablets as a major center near Persepolis. It was very likely an administrative center, but also the town where the builders, scribes and servants were to live.[3]

Several mounds on the plain and other sites in the foothills lack any Late Plain Ware sherds; indeed, some are totally devoid of any sherds. They are dated to the Achaemenid period because of the presence of architectural elements characteristic of this period or by traces of stone quarrying. The chronological and cultural significance of these "architectural" sites may be questioned on several grounds. Some blocks may have been displaced in later times as, for example, at the Islamic city Qasr-i Abu Nasr, near Shiraz, where the blocks of the monumental doorway were certainly taken from the Tachara of Darius at Persepolis (they have since been returned). In other cases, especially at points close to the mountain, fragments of shafts and bases of columns, usually unfinished, could be evidence of a stage in the stone work, between the quarry and the palaces of Persepolis or other sites. Sites E, F, G, J, P, T, U, and V (figure 24.1) are perhaps such "sites" (Sumner 1986b:9–11). Finally, it remains to be shown that all these architectural remains are definitely of the Achaemenid period and not later imitations. This taste for imitation may be seen in rock cut monuments that are Achaemenid in appearance, but postdate this period (for example, Akhur-i Rustam, 5 km south of Persepolis, or Qadamgah 50 km farther south).

If all the questionable sites were removed from the list, Sumner's map of Achaemenid period sites would be profoundly different. If Late Plain Ware is a pertinent marker, its absence would eliminate practically all the sites above the plain level. If one were willing to include other sites of uncertain date, the map could be enriched by more points, such as the settlements with stone architecture at Kuh-e Ayyub (Kleiss 1993c) as well as others.

DIVERSITY OF ACTIVITIES IN THE REGION DURING THE ACHAEMENID PERIOD

Keeping in mind the uncertain chronology of many sites and remains, we can regroup the sites by including not only habitation sites but also any non-settlement activity areas. Single-function sites of this type are much more prominent in the Achaemenid period than in previous times. In this category I also include places with stone blocks that are not *in situ*.

SITES WHERE REMAINS ARE CLEARLY IN SITU

Sites with the most straightforward interpretation are mounds with an Achaemenid occupation represented by Late Plain Ware. In addition, there are a variety of sites, generally without pottery, that are identifiable "points" on the landscape. These sites include:

Quarries. Recorded by Bergner (1937), Kleiss (1992b, 1993b), Sumner (1986b), Calmeyer (1990), stone quarries are not datable, but they are most probably Achaemenid, as that is the main period of stone architecture before the Sasanian period (at Istakhr for example) and Islamic work and reuse.

Rock inscriptions. Some grafitti near Persepolis are Greek, dated to 500 BCE.

The other "sites" are listed in decreasing order of probable Achaemenid date.

Dams, bridges, canals, paved roads. Only some of these landscape features (Kleiss 1994; Nicol 1970; Sumner 1986b), such as Dorudzan and Bard Burideh II, can be confidently dated to the Achaemenid period (Sumner 1986b; Tilia 1978). For some of the others, it is the massive working of the rock that points to an Achaemenid date, but for the rest, later reuse of "noble" materials, in general worked blocks, is also possible. If this reuse was carried out on the spot, it is legitimate to consider such sites as Achaemenid.

Traces of construction, terraces, fortified walls, buildings. Many of the possible Achaemenid sites are located above the cliff of Naqsh-i Rustam (Kleiss 1994), others along the west flank of Kuh-e Husein (Kleiss 1981:45–46; Sumner 1986b:11 and Ill. Sites F and P), and on the west flank of Kuh-e Ayyub (Kleiss 1993c).

Rock-cut niches. No rock-cut niches are of certain Achaemenid date. Those which exhibit an Achaemenid style, such as Akhur-i Rustam and Kuh-e Ayyub, probably date to later centuries.

Rock cut (funeral) troughs. These are not datable, but usually are attributed to the Sasanian period.

Rock-cut "fire altars." In fact, these are either column bases or ossuaries to be dated most probably to post-Achaemenid periods (see Huff 1998).

Traces of rock-cutting with unknown significance. The most striking example is the enormous monument of Qadamgah at the southern tip of Kuh-e Rahmat. With a series of rectangular niches cut into the cliff, it appears to be a sanctuary or a series of funerary niches; more likely in my opinion, it could be a large unfinished tomb of the royal Achaemenid-type, postdating that period.

ARCHITECTURAL ELEMENTS, DISPLACED AND REUSED, OR ABANDONED DURING TRANSPORT

Blocks of worked stone and Achaemenid architectural elements. Many of these items were reused at Istakhr as well as in the temple of the Fratadara at the foot of the Persepolis terrace. This could also be the case at Firuzi and elsewhere, except where excavation has revealed them to be associated with their original Achaemenid structures or foundations (for example, sites B, E, G; Tilia 1978:80–84).

Baked and enamelled bricks. At the site Firuzi 10, (Tilia 1978:83–85, Sumner 1986b:9), these items were found on the surface. Only if there are relatively large numbers of bricks can we consider a place to be Achaemenid; our confidence in the dating of these elements is even greater if they are found in an Achaemenid architectural context.

THREE DISTINCT ZONES OF ACTIVITY AROUND PERSEPOLIS

Several maps of site distribution could be constructed, according to the degree of reliability of the sites selected. They would demonstrate the existence of two principal types of remains, quite distinct from each other: on the plain, concentrations of potsherds or zones with fragments of architecture; in the foothills, traces of cut-rock work, evidence of stonework, quarries, or remains of stone walls.

The sites on these maps cannot be simply added up to reflect Achaemenid occupation. For example, how should we assess a small mound with potsherds, located near a quarry, with an architectural element nearby that had been in the process of being transported? The abandoned stone marks just a single moment in time, where the site and quarry were places where people lived and worked.

Sumner (1986b) has pointed out the relative lack of settlement in the region during the Achaemenid period, and estimates a maximum of forty-two sites (all inclusive). The reservations expressed here would clearly lower the number of "sites" in the sense of inhabited places by excluding from the count the quarries, elements in the process of being transported, or graves. Under these conditions, the calculation that 43,600 people lived in the region (including Firuzi/Matezzish) is an overestimate (see Sumner 1986b:12, Table 1) and must be dramatically reduced.

These maps are certainly, however, a reflection, if not of settlement, at least of activities in the region during the Achaemenid period. We can therefore distinguish three zones around Persepolis.

First, the royal area, which includes both the palaces built on the terrace and at its foot as well as the town of Matezzish to the west (Persepolis West and Firuzi), is surrounded by an empty zone. Although site W is only 1 km from Persepolis, there is no proof that it was occupied concurrently with the palaces—fragments of column shafts at this site do resemble those of Dasht-e Gohar predating Darius (Tilia 1978:80), but there are no potsherds.

Beyond the royal area, the first notable Achaemenid sites lie at a distance of 15 or 20 km. They comprise a second zone of several towns (sites M, P, R, Y; Sumner 1986b:Ill. 3) and scattered small sites, large farms and/or aristocrat residences. This second zone follows the banks of the Kur river which flows south across the plain. It extends as far north as the dams built across the Kur, in the Dorudzan sector. In this zone, site density dwindles as one approaches Band-e Amir at the southern end of the zone (Sumner 1986b:16–17). The low density of sites, in comparison with that of the fourth and especially the third millennium (compare with Sumner 1972:Figs. 11–15), would indicate a landscape organized into large farms, perhaps with "paradises" (from *paradeisos*, a royal hunting park and garden), as suggested by Herzfeld (site R, Sumner 1986b:10). A similar interpretation could also apply to other zones where pieces of finished columns have been found. This zone appears to have been important for agricultural and pastoral production, with farming activities in open areas or in paradises, and in the foothills outside the cultivable zones, some settlements probably concentrated on animal breeding. The remains of construction do not seem to correspond to fortifications but rather to settlements or agricultural terraces. The outer third zone was also devoted to the exploitation of raw materials for construction, mainly stone but probably also clay for bricks.

The outer zone was presumably devoted to herding and is probably the one that changed the least between the second millennium and the Achaemenid period. As was the case for Phase VI, however, herding would not have left visible archaeological traces.[4]

CONCLUSIONS

The site distribution proposed here is quite comparable to that prevailing in the area around Susa. There too, the Achaemenid occupation is very limited around the city, particularly in the immediate environs (Wenke 1975–76:Fig. 16) in comparison with the later occupations from the Seleucid through Sasanian periods when Susa is no longer a royal capital (Wenke 1975–76:Figs. 17–21).[5] The establishment of the two Achaemenid capitals, Persepolis and Susa, had a similar impact in the immediate neighborhoods (see Miroschedji 1981c:171 for Susiana east of Susa). We may thus ask whether the king intentionally emptied the zone immediately around the capital to suppport his court, especially its military and agricultural activities. In Fars, the region hardly seems affected by the new political and economic situation beyond a radius of about 20 to 25 km apart from the sites along the Kur river, yet in the region beyond a radius of about 25 to 30 km, the pastoral way of life remained undisturbed.

After the fall of the Achaemenid empire, perhaps the central zone reverted to the nomadic pastoral way of life. If we agree that Late Plain Ware is indeed chronologically restricted to the Achaemenid period, we can argue that the collapse of Achaemenid administration changed the settlement pattern of the area, practically bringing sedentary life to a halt until many centuries later. In fact, the way of life in the Kur river basin was largely nomadic and pastoralist from the second millennium BCE to the early first millennium CE; the Achaemenid interlude transformed this way of life for only a brief period of time in a relatively small area.

Acknowledgment. I thank Elizabeth Willcox, who translated the text of this chapter.

NOTES

1. This chapter is limited to the settlement pattern and does not deal with the administrative geography as Sumner did excellently (Sumner 1986b).
2. Overlaet (1997:48–49) seems to be skeptical about Sumner's reconstruction regarding the relative chronology of the three groups of pottery and the respective users of them. He recognizes, however, that Vanden Berghe's excavations do not provide clear stratigraphic information. See also chapter 16.
3. This was not clearly recognized in my recent paper on the Achaemenid capitals (Boucharlat 1997:222–223); locating Matezzish here makes the palace complex less isolated than I suggested.
4. It must be stressed that this concerns only the Kur river basin and not the Pulvar valley in the Pasargadae area, where several irrigation works, bridges, and dams, some of possible Achaemenid date, have been noted (Kleiss 1992a).
5. It is difficult to demonstrate this precisely because Wenke's chronology is too late for his first two periods. Pottery that he calls "Achaemenid" is mainly Late Neo-Elamite in date and what he calls "Seleuco-Parthian" includes some Achaemenid sherds. I fully agree with Miroschedji's (1987:43 and n. 85) critique.

CHAPTER 25

CONTEXT AND CONTENT OF THE PERSEPOLIS INSCRIPTIONS

The Interchange of XPb and XPd

MICHAEL KOZUH

THE FIRST RELIABLE COPIES of cuneiform inscriptions appeared in Carsten Niebuhr's *Reisebeschreibung nach Arabien und andern umliegenden Ländern* II (1778), which contained copies of two sets of three inscriptions from Persepolis. The first steps towards the decipherment of cuneiform proceeded from these copies. Niebuhr himself recognized that three different scripts were used for the three inscriptions of each set. In 1802 F. Münter correctly concluded that the three scripts represent three different languages, which he thought to be Zend, Pehlevi and Farsi. We now know that the languages are Old Persian, Elamite, and Babylonian. More importantly, he also postulated that when the three different languages are displayed together as a set, each should say the same thing (Münter 1802:86ff.). Therefore, deciphering one of the three inscriptions would provide the key to the other two. Later, Grotefend assumed that of the three languages, the one displayed in the most prominent position was that of the Achaemenid kings; the decipherment process continued from these observations.

After completion of the decipherments there were clear examples of trilingual inscription sets at Persepolis where one version of the three displayed together makes a significant rhetorical departure from the other two. Here we consider departures in XPb and XPd. In each case the Babylonian version departs from its companion Old Persian and Elamite versions. A close examination reveals that the two Babylonian versions were interchanged. This interchange, I suggest, reflects a greater concern for the physical and decorative context of the inscriptions than for their having matching rhetorical content.

XPb and XPd are two of four trilingual inscriptions written on the major stairways of Persepolis.[1] Each neatly divides into three sections, the first two of which are identical in both inscriptions and nearly identical in the three versions.[2] The first section begins with a dedication to Ahuramazda:

> A great god is Ahuramazda, who created this earth, who created yonder sky, who created man, who created happiness for man, who made Xerxes king, one king among many, one lord among many.

The second section names Xerxes and gives his titles:

> I am Xerxes the great king, king of kings, king of countries containing all kinds of men, king in this great earth far and wide, son of King Darius, an Achaemenian.

The third and final section of each inscription begins with the words "thus says Xerxes the king"; what comes after this statement differs between XPb and XPd. Therefore, we shall consider only section three, the final section, of these inscriptions.

XPb

An Old Persian exemplar (XPb 1) is in a panel on the western end of the inner north stairway façade of the Apadana (without a Babylonian or Elamite counterpart; see Schmidt 1953:Pls.60, 61; Shahbazi 1985:Pls. 19–21). Another Old Persian exemplar (XPb 2) is in a panel at the southern end

266

25.1 Design schema of XPb. *Prepared at MASCA from author's draft*

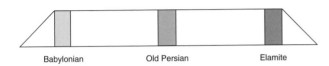

25.2 Design schema of XPd. *Prepared at MASCA from author's draft*

of the inner east stairway façade of the Apadana (Schmidt 1953:21A; Shahbazi 1985:22–25). An Elamite (XPb 02) and a Babylonian (XPb 002)[3] counterpart are stacked in one panel at the northern end of the same inner eastern stairway façade, the Elamite above the Babylonian (see Schmidt 1953:Pl. 21B). The inscription frames are arrayed symmetrically on the stairway façade (for a full view of the stairway see Schmidt 1953:Pl. 19).

The arrangement of XPb has troubled some scholars (for example, Schmidt 1953:82), as the "normal" arrangement has the Old Persian in the center, the Elamite to the left and the Babylonian to the right. However, Ann Tilia (1972:191–208) has shown that the two so-called "Treasury" reliefs originally belonged to the center of the east and north outer stairway façades of the Apadana, and that the center of the stairway, as it is preserved today, is a later carving made after the Treasury reliefs were removed in antiquity.[4] Therefore, at the time of the engraving of the inscriptions, the center of the stairways was completely filled with a relief, thus explaining the layout. Schematically, the arrangement of the inscriptions and Treasury relief on the eastern Apadana stairway façade is represented in figure 25.1. Usually where versions of an inscription are displayed one above another, the longest version is uppermost and the shortest version lowest, and the usual order of the inscriptions is Old Persian uppermost, Elamite in the middle and Babylonian lowest. In XPb the Elamite and Babylonian are displayed in the usual order, but the Elamite above is slightly shorter than the Babylonian below, both in actual size and in number of lines (18 vs. 19). The final section (§3) of each of the inscriptions reads as follows:

XPb OP §3 : *θ-a-t-i-y : x-š-y-a-r-š-a : x-š-a-y-θ-i-y : v-z-r-k : t-y : m-n-a : k-r-t-m : i-d-a : u-t-a : t-y-m-i-y : a-p-t-r-m : k-r-t-m : a-v : vi-i-s-m : v-š-n-a : a-u-r-m-z-d-a-h : a-ku-u-n-v-m : m-a-m : a-u-r-m-z-d-a : p-a-tu-u-v : h-d-a : b-g-i-b-i-š : u-t-a-m-i-y : x-š-ç-m : u-t-a : t-y-m-i-y : k-r-t-m* (21–30)

Thus declares Xerxes the great king: What has been built by me here, and what has been built by me at a distance, all that by the favor of Ahuramazda I built. Me may Ahuramazda, together with the (other) gods, protect, and my kingdom, and what has been built by me.

XPb El §3 : *na-an-ri* [DIŠ]*ik-še-ir-šá* [DIŠ]ESŠANA *ir-šá-ir-ra ap-pa* [DIŠ]*ú hu-ut-tá-ra* [AŠ]*ma-at-tá ku-ut-tá ap-pa* [AŠ]*me-šá-me-ra-ka₄-tá hu-ut-tá-ra hu-pè mar-ri-tá za-u-mi-in* [d]*u-ra-mas-da-na hu-ut-tá* [DIŠ] [d]*u-ra-mas-da un nu-iš-kí-iš-ni* [d]*na-ap-pi-pè hi-tá-ka₄ ku-ut-tá* [AŠ]*su-un-mu-me ku-ut-tá ap-pa hu-ut-tá-ra* (12–18)

Says Xerxes the great king: What I built here, and what in addition (to other things) I built, all that I built by the favor of Ahuramazda. Me may Ahuramazda, together with the other gods, protect, and my kingship and what I built.

XPb Bab §3 [m]*ḫi-ši-ʾ-ar-ši* LUGAL GAL-*ú i-qab-bi ina* GIŠ.MI *šá* [d]*a-ḫu-ru-ma-az-da-ʾ* É *a-ga-a a-na-ku e-te-pu-ús-su* [d]*a-ḫu-ru-ma-az-da-ʾ a-na-ku li-iṣ-ṣur-an-ni it-ti* DINGIR.MEŠ *a-na* LUGAL *-ú-ti-ia u a-na šá e-pu-uš-šu* (14–19)

Xerxes the great king declares: In the shadow of Ahuramazda I built this house. Me may Ahuramazda, along with the (other) gods, protect, and my kingship and what I built.

XP d

XPd is a trilingual inscription with four exemplars: XPd 1 (01, 001) and 2 (02, 002) are located in the Palace of Xerxes (Hadish), the western and eastern antae of the portico respectively (Schmidt 1953:Pls. 175A, B; Shahbazi 1985:Pls. 27, 28), and XPd 3 (03, 003) and 4 (04, 004) are located on the west and east stairway façades respectively of the same palace (Schmidt 1953:Pls. 162A, B, C, 167A, B; Shahbazi 1985:Pls. 29–31, 32–35). XPd 1 and 2 are written in three vertical panels, with the Old Persian on top, Elamite in the center and Babylonian at the bottom, corresponding to the decreasing height and amount of lines (19, 12, and 11 respectively). XPd 3 and 4 are inscribed exactly alike on both staircases (for a full view of the western staircase, see Schmidt 1953:Pl. 159; for the eastern staircase see Plate 166), with the Babylonian at the left, the Old Persian in the center, and Elamite to the right. Each version is exactly the same height and nearly identical in width, schematically represented in figure 25.2. The final section of each inscription reads:

XPd OP §3 *θ-a-t-i-y : x-š-y-a-r-š-a : x-š-a-y-θ-i-y : v-z-r-k : v-š-n-a : a-u-r-m-z-d-a-h : i-m : h-d-i-š : a-d-m : a-ku-u-n-v-m : m-a-m : a-u-r-m-z-d-a : p-a-tu-u-v : h-d-a : b-g-i-b-i-š : u-t-m-i-y : x-š-ç-m : u-t-a : t-y-m-i-y : k-r-t-m :*
(Composite text. In XPdOP 1 and 2 = lines 15–19, 3 and 4 = lines 21–28)

Thus declares Xerxes the great king: By the favor of Ahuramazda I built this palace. Me may Ahuramazda, together with the (other) gods, protect, and my kingdom, and what has been built by me.

XPd El §3 *na-an-ri* ᴰᴵˢ*ik-še-ir-šá* ᴰᴵˢ*EŠŠANA ir-šá-ir-ra za-u-mi-in* ᵈ*u-ra-mas-da-na hi* ᴬˢ*ul-hi.*MEŠ ᴰᴵˢ*ú hu-ut-tá* ᴰᴵˢ*ú* ᵈ*u-ra-mas-da un nu-iš-kí-iš-ni* ᵈ*na-ap-pi-pè i-tá-ka₄ ku-ut-tá* ᴬˢ*su-un-mu-me ku-ut-tá ap-pa hu-ut-tá-ra*
(Composite text. In XPdEL 01 and 02 = 9–12, 03 and 04 = 17–23)

Says Xerxes the great king: By the favor of Ahuramazda I made this house. Me may Ahuramazda, together with the other gods, protect, and my kingship, and what I built.

XPd Bab §3 *µḫi-ši-ʾ-ar-ši* LUGAL GAL-*ú i-qab-bi šá a-na-ku a-kan-na e-pu-uš-šu u ina qaq-qa-ru šá-nam-ma e-pu-uš-šu gab-bi ma-la e-pu-uš-šu i-na* GIŠ.MIS *šá ðᵃ-ḫu-ru-ma-az-da-ʾ e-te-pu-uš a-na-ku ðᵃ-ḫu-ru-ma-az-da-ʾ li-ṣur-an-ni it-ti* DINGIR.MEŠ *u a-na* LUGAL-*ú-ti-ia u a-na šá e-pu-uš-šu*
(Composite text. In XPd Bab 001 and 002 = 7–11, 003 and 004 = 15–22)

Xerxes the great king declares: What I built here and build at another place, everything I built, I have built in the shadow of Ahuramazda. Me may Ahuramazda, along with the (other) gods, protect, and my kingship and what I built.

The Old Persian and Elamite versions of XPb §3 correspond closely to each other but not to the Babylonian version, and the Old Persian and Elamite versions of XPd §3 also correspond closely to each other but not to the Babylonian. The Babylonian versions of the two inscriptions appear to have been interchanged. That is, XPb Babylonian §3 corresponds to XPd Old Persian and Elamite §3, while XPd Babylonian §3 corresponds to XPb Old Persian and Elamite §3.

In fact, XPb Babylonian §3 corresponds word for word with XPd Old Persian and Elamite §3. There is no need to document the Babylonian translation *ina ṣilli sa Ahuramazda* for OP *vašnā Auranmazdmāha* or Elamite *zaumin Uramazdana*, nor the translation of OP *akunavam* and Elamite *hutta* with Babylonian *epēsu*, as these are common throughout the trilingual Achaemenid inscriptions. The word order of each version follows in lockstep. Moreover, we find OP *hadiš*, Elamite ᴬˢ*ul-hi.*MEŠ and Bab *bītu* equated in the following sources: DSj (OP broken, El 4 = *ul.hi.*MEŠ, Bab 5 = *bi-it*); XPc (OP 11, El 10, Bab 9),[5] and XSa (OP 2, El 1, Bab 2); note also DSf (OP 22 = ha[diš], Bab 16 = ⌜É⌝.GAL, 1 = [ᴬˢ*ul*].*hi.*MEŠ). Thus, it is clear that XPb Babylonian is an exact translation of XPd Old Persian and Elamite.

On the other hand, the correspondences between XPd Babylonian §3 and XPb Old Persian and Elamite §3 are more complicated. The idea is clear: Xerxes built both here and elsewhere, and he built everything by the favor of Ahuramazda. Each version, however, differs in the way it expresses this idea. In the first two clauses, the Old Persian uses the passive participle *kartam*, agreeing with the pronoun *taya*,[6] whereas the Babylonian uses an active verb in a subordinate clause. The syntax of the Elamite phrase is still debated (Paper 1955:47; Hallock 1959:7; Grillot-Susini 1987:35). In the first clause the Elamite word *ma-at-tá* renders Old Persian *idā* and Babylonian *akanna*, the latter two words clearly meaning "here." In the second clause Old Persian *apararam* renders Babylonian *ina qaqqaru šanamma* and the Elamite hapax *me-šá-me-ra-ka₄-tá*. The Old Persian adverb *apararam* has the clear meaning of "farther off," and this is its only known usage outside of the phrase *apararam hacā Pārsā*[7] "far off from Persia." Thus, although the equation of *apataram* to *ina qaqqaru šanamma* is not word for word, both mean "at another place." In the final clause, Old Persian *ava visam* "all that" is embellished in the Babylonian *gabbi mala ēpušu* "everything I built." The Elamite follows the Old Persian.

Clearly, then, the Babylonian version of XPb translates XPd Old Persian and Elamite, and the Babylonian version of XPd translates XPb Old Persian and Elamite. But what was the reason behind this interchange? Clarisse Herrenschmidt (1983:69) postulates two stages in the making of the inscription: in the first, a scribe composed

Michael Kozuh

the Babylonian version on a disposable object—perhaps a clay or wax tablet—from which it was to be copied; in stage two, an illiterate copyist made the actual engraving. In her view the scribe and the copyist mistakenly interchanged the two versions in the transition. She is undoubtedly correct in separating the process into two stages, hints of which can be seen in an unfinished exemplar of XPh (see Kent 1953:Pl. III). The copyist abandoned the inscription in the middle of a line, but he was copying the line from right to left, opposite the way it was to be read. This, it seems to me, can only indicate that the display copy was made from another exemplar, by a copyist not concerned with (or perhaps unaware of) the actual sequence of the script.

However, I do not agree that the interchange of the Babylonian version of XPb and XPd was the result of some sort of error in transition. On the contrary, a close look at the physical setting of each inscription reveals that the interchange was deliberate. The scribes and copyists at Persepolis made a conscious effort to present the trilingual inscriptions in a symmetric way; monumental writing at Persepolis was not only a means to convey a message but also an element of architectural design, in much the same vein as, for example, monumental Arabic calligraphy (for example, see Ettinghausen 1974). In presenting the inscriptions, however, the scribes and copyists had to deal with the idiosyncrasies of each language and script. Old Persian is written in a quasi-alphabetic script and very few logograms were used, whereas Elamite and Babylonian are written in a syllabic script with many logograms. When the three versions correspond closely, that is, when the Elamite and Babylonian are exact translations of the Old Persian, the Babylonian uses much less space than the Old Persian, and the Elamite uses less space than the Old Persian but more than the Babylonian. Therefore, when attempting to display the same thought in the three languages, the amount of space used per language varied.

To maintain symmetry, the scribes and copyists dealt with the spatial characteristics of each language and script by controlling either the height or the width of each version. When the three inscriptions were arranged side by side each version had equal height but varying width, and the Old Persian version always took pride of place.[8] When the inscriptions were arranged vertically the Old Persian was always on top (again in the most prominent position), the Elamite in the middle, and the Babylonian at the bottom, each version having varying height but equal width.[9]

The arrangement of the panels on the stairway façade of the Palace of Xerxes gave the scribes a fixed amount of space with which to work. With each version in a panel of exactly the same size, the ability to compensate for the disparity of length among the versions by manipulating the width or height was lost.

How could the scribes keep the symmetry of the inscriptions and yet compensate for the fact that a Babylonian translation of XPd §3 was shorter than the other versions, in fact, too short to fill the space prepared for it? They solved the problem with the interchange of §3 of the Babylonian version of XPb and XPd. For the Palace of Xerxes inscriptions, the Old Persian and Elamite versions of XPd say simply, "I built this palace" whereas the Babylonian says "What I built here, and what I built in another place, everything I built, I built in the shadow of Ahuramazda"; that is, the Babylonian version not only differs, it is also longer. The expected Babylonian version "I built this house" was placed on the Apadana stairway along with the longer Old Persian and Elamite versions—because the Babylonian shares a panel with the Elamite version there was no need to lengthen the Babylonian inscription.

That the scribes and copyists sacrificed matching content in favor of physical context can be seen in one other example. XPc, like XPd, is written on three panels of the same size on the southern stairway façade of the Palace of Darius; the Old Persian is in the center, the Elamite to the right and the Babylonian to the left (see Schmidt 1953:Pl. 130; Shahbazi 1985:Pls. 16–18). It is inscribed in the usual order on vertical panels of the east and west antae of the portico of the palace of Darius (see Schmidt 1953:Pls. 131B, C; Shahbazi 1985:Pls. 13–15). In this case, the lines following "thus says Xerxes the king" are similar in all three versions: Xerxes claims that he completed the work that Darius had begun. However, a close reading of the royal appellatives reveals a curious embellishment in the Babylonian. The Old Persian[10] and Elamite[11] passages read:

one king among many, one lord among many

whereas the Babylonian reads:

king of many kings, who alone rules over all the lands

The Babylonian embellishment is curious because an exact Babylonian translation exists of "one king among many, one prince among many," which is used every other time at Persepolis (XPa, b, d, f, and h):

iš-ten i-na LUGAL.MEŠ ma-du-ú-tu iš-ten mu-te-ʾ-e-ʾ ma-du-ú-tu

However, we see that the XPc version is considerably longer:

LUGAL šá LUGAL.LUGAL.MEŠ ma-du-ú-tu₄ šá e-diš-ši-šú a-na nap-ḫa-ar KUR.KUR.MEŠ ga-ab-bi ú-ta-ʾ-a-ma
(XPc 001 and 002 = lines 4–5, 003 = 6–8)

269

Thus, we see that the scribes and copyists of XPc realized that the common word for word Babylonian counterpart of the Old Persian and Elamite phrases would not fill the space intended for it. As a result, they composed a somewhat different—but most importantly longer—Babylonian text to fill that space.

Taken at face value, these interchanges and enlargements may seem trivial; indeed, they concern only a few lines among hundreds. Yet they have important implications. First, they reveal that the content of royal inscriptions developed from conditions other than royal ideology. If these inscriptions were dictated by the king, they were edited and arrayed by the scribes and copyists. Second, when need be, the scribes at Persepolis were willing to sacrifice matching content in order to preserve physical symmetry, thus subordinating the message to its exhibition. This subordination implies something significant: writing as an *objet d'art*—that is, writing to be viewed, not read—conveyed a message irrespective of what the actual words said; a tacit message the scribes at Persepolis took great care to present aesthetically. However, both the explicit and tacit messages were lost over time. How the former was rediscovered has been described many times; perhaps a glimpse of this tacit message can be caught in the writings of the early pioneers of assyriology. Once scholars of the late eighteenth and early nineteenth centuries agreed that the site of Takht-i Jamshid was indeed Persepolis and that the inscriptions from there must be attributed to the famous Achaemenid kings, they used this tacit message to guide them in their initial steps toward translations. In other words, their original assumptions—that the inscriptions were boastful; that the native language of the Achaemenids must have pride of place; that the inscriptions must have the king's name, the words "great king" and give royal genealogy; that three scripts displayed together must say the same thing in three different languages—should coalesce at some level with the intended tacit message of the Persepolis inscriptions. Indeed, their observations may provide a hint as to the message of these inscriptions to their illiterate viewers of antiquity.

Bibliographic note. Synoptic versions and translations of the Persepolis inscriptions are online at www-oi.uchicago.edu/OI/PROJ/ARI/ARI.html. Older, sometimes incomplete, synoptic versions are also found in Herzfeld (1938) and Weissbach (1911). Lecoq (1997) provides useful translations of Achaemenid inscriptions, including variants.

Acknowledgment. A version of this chapter was presented at the 208th meeting of the American Oriental Society on 5 April 1998. I would especially like to thank Professor Matthew Stolper for his many insightful comments and criticisms; also thanks to Professor Martha Roth, David Testen, and Jennifer Joos for additional comments and to Professor Fred Donner for bibliographic information. Inscriptions are identified with the sigla of Kent 1953:4 and 107–115. Versions are identified as OP (= Old Persian), Bab (= Babylonian), and El (= Elamite). Following Steve 1987:54, Old Persian exemplars are labeled 1, 2, 3,...; Elamite exemplars 01, 02, 03...; and Babylonian exemplars by 001, 002, 003, and so on.

NOTES

1. The other two trilingual inscriptions are: XPc on the south stairway of the Palace of Darius (Tachara; see p. 269) and A¹Pa on the northwest stairway of Palace H, which is fragmentary (see Schmidt 1953:280f.).
2. See Lecoq (1997:252ff.) for the slight variants in the Babylonian versions.
3. There is no XPbEl 01 or XPbBab 001.
4. Root (1979:Fig. 11) is an illustrated reconstruction of the north stairway with the central relief in its original position. Tilia (1978) dates the removal of the "Treasury" reliefs to the reign of Artaxerxes III. However, on stylistic grounds, Roaf (1983:144f.) dates the re-carving of the Apadana reliefs, and therefore the removal of the "Treasury" reliefs, to the reign of Artaxerxes I.
5. Line numbers follow XPc 1, 01, and 001 respectively.
6. That is, the Old Persian uses the periphrastic perfect, which commonly is used with the sense of an active perfect.
7. As in DNa 17f., DSe 15f., and XPh 14f.
8. For example, DPa, a short, four-line trilingual inscription (see Kent 1953:135; Lecoq 1997:226f.), the three versions of which are inscribed side by side exactly alike twice in the main hall of the Palace of Darius, both on door jambs connecting the portico to the main hall. On the east doorway, the Old Persian is on the right, the Elamite in the center, and Babylonian on the left (see Schmidt 1953:138A); on the west doorway, the Old Persian and Babylonian are reversed (see Schmidt 1953:139A). Each inscription is above a relief depicting the king and two attendants. In each case, the Old Persian is above the figure of the king, as he leads the procession either into (east jamb) or out of (west jamb) the main hall, and the Elamite and Babylonian follow respectively, each version having equal height but varying in width.
9. For example, XPd 1 and 2 (see above p. 4f.)
10. *a-i-v-m : p-ru-u-n-a-m :* XŠ*-m : a-i-v-m : p-ru-u-n-a-m : f-r-m-a-t-a-r-m* (XPc OP 1 and 2 = lines 4–5, 3 = 7– 9)
11. DIŠ.*ki-ir* DIŠ.*ir-še-ik-ki-ip-in-na* DIŠ.EŠŠANA DIŠ.*ki-ir* DIŠ.*ir-še-ik-ki-ip-in-na pír-ra-ma-tá-ra-um* (XPc El 01 and 02 = lines 4–5, 03 = 6–9)

CHAPTER 26

THE CONCEPT OF *ZEITGEIST* IN MIDDLE ISLAMIC ARCHAEOLOGY

DONALD WHITCOMB

THE IDEA OF BROAD SUPRAREGIONAL TRENDS in the archaeology of the ancient Near East is a respected and usually well-utilized concept. The application to Islamic archaeology is not common, because of a strong tendency to limit studies to single regions and their particular historical contexts. Some recent ceramic studies in Syria for the tenth–eleventh centuries CE have incorporated data from Sirjan in southern Iran (figure 26.1). This chapter will explore this practice of broad comparanda and the significance of Iranian evidence in Islamic archaeology.

The concept of archaeological horizons originated in New World archaeology to describe a widespread, contemporary uniformity of style (a sort of *Zeitgeist*). The implication is a shared cultural inventory, shapes and symbols, whether or not there was actually mass distribution of ceramic products. When dealing with more fully historical periods, often with fields of inquiry of less than a hundred years duration, the horizon may be redefined as a time of cosmopolitan interaction (similar to Caldwell's [1965] concept of an "interaction sphere"). The alternative is a relative absence of cultural integration, usually described as a reversion to regionalism. Often, there is an assumption that finer products, in this case more elaborate decorated glazed ceramics, would travel farther as a result of greater intrinsic value. There is correspondingly less likelihood for broad distribution of common wares, other than incidental transfer as containers for other products.

Morony (1995:n. 46) uses the concept of archaeological horizon based on ceramics to posit a general movement from regionalism to a cosmopolitan integration, especially in light of patterns of Islamic urbanism (see below). As an example, Morony sees the urban identity of Aqaba as alternating cultural phases: the broadly eclectic importations of a cosmopolitan Byzantine world (fifth and sixth centuries) are followed by reorientations into a regional identification (seventh and eighth centuries), while a third phase is the growth of a strong cosmopolitan identity as a reflection of eastern Islamic cities (ninth and tenth centuries). Happily, he avoids using dynastic identifications (that is, Umayyad and Abbasid) commonly applied by historians. At issue is the differential utilization of ceramic evidence by archaeologists and by historians; quite naturally, there is some confusion about the limits of inference appropriate to the evidential corpora. Three examples are adduced in this chapter, each depending on interpretations of ceramic changes in the eleventh century CE. This century functions as a fulcrum separating Early Islamic and Middle Islamic assemblages (see figure 26.2). The focus of each example is archaeological research in Iran, either directly or indirectly resulting from the Marvdasht survey.

William Sumner (1972:51) discussed the Late Period in the Marvdasht (or Kur river basin) as comprising, in its Islamic part, three periods: 1 (ca. 800 CE–1150 CE), 2 (1150 CE–1550 CE), 3 (1550 CE–1900 CE). Although he did not elaborate on this time range, his methodology presumably reflects the practice of drawing ceramic parallels for prehistoric periods from a broad Iranian region: Susa and Deh Luran on the southwest; Godin, Giyan and Sialk on the west; and Bampur, Iblis, and Shahr-i Sokhta on the east. This resulted in prehistoric periods that are broadly sketched in 500- to 1000-year blocks (1972:55, Table V). Clearly such

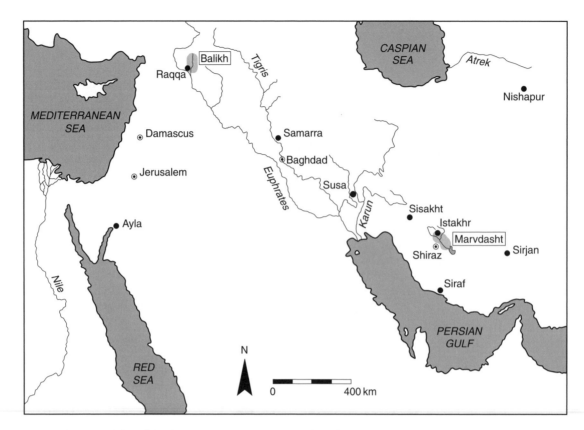

26.1   Archaeological sites of the eleventh century with survey regions of the Marvdasht and the Balikh valley.
Prepared at MASCA from author's draft

broad comparanda are intended to confirm sequencing or relative chronology without discussing the nature of the implied interactions; observed commonalities in material culture are described as an archaeological horizon and their causality as an ephemeral *Zeitgeist* phenomenon.

SIRJAN AND THE BALIKH VALLEY

An archaeological appreciation of Islamic artifacts has been slow to develop due principally to the predominance of art historical and museological interests, as Jean Sauvaget described more than fifty years ago (Cahen 1965:57). The weight of evidence from excavations and intensive surveys has begun a revision of the stylistic structures that have organized artifact analysis. This was evident when Williamson tackled the Islamic periods in the Marvdasht, materials that William Sumner entrusted to him in 1969 (Whitcomb 1979; Sumner and Whitcomb 1999). Williamson (1969, 1988) based his analysis on extensive surveys in southern and eastern Iran, which led him to divide the Islamic history of this region into 350-year periods. Thus, his Period I encompassed the Abbasid, Buyid, and Seljuq periods (ca. 800–1150 CE; see figure 26.2). The ceramic criteria used by Williamson were

splashed ware (cf. Sirjan kiln ware), thin yellow glaze, spinach green (cf. Nishapur). Istakhr [the type site in the Marvdasht] has a wide range of polychrome glazed ware and practically no 'Seljuc' frit ware, which became very common after ca. 1150 AD This is probably the most discrete period since its beginning and end are determined by important technological innovations. It is also best represented at Siraf. (Williamson 1969)

The technological innovations, readily recognized during field survey by diagnostic potsherds, were glazing introduced circa 800 CE in this region and the production of frit ware (stonepaste body) datable to 1150 CE (see Mason 1996 for definition and discussion).

The ceramic repertoire of the Marvdasht reveals an eastern orientation in parallels with Nishapur and Sirjan. Reference to Sirjan (the site of Tepe Dasht-i Deh) (Williamson 1971) must be taken as preliminary impressions in these unpublished notes. Shortly after his preliminary study of the Marvdasht materials, Williamson began excavations at this site but they remained unpublished until the study undertaken by Morgan and Leatherby (1987). The site of Sirjan was a pre-Islamic and important early Islamic urban center, perhaps reaching its apogee in

Donald Whitcomb

Political Periodization

450 550 650 750 850 950 1050 1150 1250 1350 1450 1550 1650 1750 1850

| Byz./Sasan. | Um. | Abbasid | Buyid | Seljuq | | Ilkhanid | | Safavid | | |
| | | | Fatimid | | Ayy. | Mamluk | | Ottoman | | |

Marvdasht	S		1		2		3	
Siraf	1	2	3	4		5		
Arrajan	A		B		C		D	
Qasr-i Abu Nasr	2a	2b		West		West		
Susa	IV	III	II		I			
Jazira survey	Sasan.-Early Islam.		Early Islam.	Middle Islamic		Late Islamic		
Amman	VII VI	Vb Va	IVb	III	IIa	IIb		
Ayla		A	B	C	D	E		

| Sasan. | Early Islamic 1 | Early Islamic 2 | Middle Islamic 1 | Middle Islamic 2 | Late Islamic 1 | Late Islamic 2 | Modern |

600 800 1000 1200 1400 1600 1800

Archaeological Periodization

26.2 Periodization of key archaeological sites in Iran and Syria during Islamic times. *Prepared at MASCA from author's original*

the ninth and tenth centuries. As Williamson (1988:22) notes, there were extensive kilns less than 500 m away from the palace of Adud al-Dawla. However, no kilns were actually excavated and the most conscientious efforts of the recent redactors have failed to extract convincing stratigraphic information from the old trenches. They have produced a remarkable ceramic corpus, both of glazed and unglazed wares, which seems a consistent assemblage of one period. This period is described as 950 CE–1050 CE based on historical deductions and the absence of frit wares (Morgan and Leatherby 1987:52). While this dating may be slightly early, the corpus has become a type site for the eleventh century in southern Iran.

Perhaps more surprising is the adoption of the Sirjan corpus as relevant to ceramic evidence from surveys and excavations in northern Syria and, more importantly, as chronological indicators for eleventh-century occupation. A convenient focus for this research tendency is the survey of Karin Bartl (1994) in the Balikh valley, an important tributary meeting the Euphrates at Raqqa, and other, less thoroughly published research in northern Mesopotamia (Bartl and Hauser 1996). Thus, Madinat al-Far has a number of parallels with Sirjan, mainly in unglazed forms (Bartl 1994:134–135, 161–163; she casts a wide net for many other

Iranian sites as well). These archaeological field surveys have a virtue in their careful consideration of the various phases of the Islamic periods, and yet they are limited by the research traditions within which ceramic diagnostics are polarized into the early Islamic achievements under the Umayyads and Abbasids versus the resurgences under the Ayyubids until the Mongol disruptions. In this light, archaeologists will grasp at evidence to fill this post-Abbasid/pre-Ayyubid lacuna, a period of manifest material change.

A specific example is the analysis of the ceramic types found at Tell Shahin in the middle of the Balikh valley. Tonghini (1995) has posited a "new ceramic type" from this site, a glazed ceramic on clay body that appears to anticipate the great frit ware traditions of the Raqqa kilns. The ware suggests a developmental relationship with the evidence from Sirjan and is therefore accorded an eleventh-century date. It follows that any comparanda in ceramic forms and decorative elements should tend to confirm this developmental stage. Tonghini has pursued a logic that is also utilized by Bartl, Guérin (1996), and other archaeologists in this area; the resulting pattern is reciprocally accepted for Syria by Morgan (1995:122). The assumption of simultaneous stylistic change implies a causative relationship between developments in southern Iran and northern Syria.

MADABAD WARE AND HANDMADE GEOMETRICAL PAINTED WARE (HMGPW)

One of the striking anomalies in the Islamic corpus of the Marvdasht was a handmade geometric painted pottery which has been called Madabad ware (Sumner and Whitcomb 1999:Fig. 3). The ware has immediate analogies with ceramics found in surveys both north and south of Behbehan (Sisakht) and from Khuzestan (Susa) to the Gulf shores at Siraf and datable from the eleventh to fourteenth centuries (Whitcomb 1991).

This ceramic type has a broader referent known as "Arab geometric" or "pseudo-prehistoric" painted wares; it is well-known on Middle Islamic sites in the Levant and Syria. Johns (1998) labels the phenomenon HMGPW (handmade geometrical painted ware). He traces this ceramic throughout Syria and surrounding regions and dates its beginning to the late twelfth century. He refers, however, to an elaborately designed product and is reluctant to associate a simple line painting as an earlier phase. The simple line geometric is found at Ayla (Aqaba), where it must date to the eleventh century at the latest (Whitcomb 1988). Both products have parallels in southern Iran, the simpler being more typical of Madabad and the more complex (and better made) being found at Sisakht (Behbehan) and Siraf.

These very designations suggest the confusions introduced into art historical trajectories; the ceramic is seen as a serious example of recidivism which can only point to cultural disruption and decline. It is instructive to note that a periodic reliance on local production of handmade ceramics has been documented in the Negev during the Chalcolithic, Iron Age, Early Islamic and Middle Islamic periods (Haiman and Goren 1992). Rautman (1998:96) discusses similar ceramics in seventh-century Cyprus and sees this phenomenon as "a broad, decentralized response to the collapse of established economic and social systems." He makes a strong case that adoption of such ceramics may be interpreted as a local response of communities to varied disruptions. In the case of the Levant in the eleventh century, one may suggest a transition beginning with the Seljuq occupation and subsequently intensified by the Crusader conquests. Though the stimulus need not always have been the same, the pattern seems recurrent and tends to cover broad encompassing regions. In the case of the eleventh century, there seem to be variations from Iran to the Mediterranean.

NISHAPUR IN THE ELEVENTH CENTURY

Madabad ware may be viewed from another perspective, one element in a constellation of changes in Iranian material culture which signal reorientation toward the eastward

regions in the first part of Williamson's period 3 (eleventh to fourteenth centuries). Thus, Kerman province, represented by Sirjan, Jiroft, and other sites noted by Stein (see Morgan and Leatherby 1987) was connected to Khorasan, a north-south axis that affected the contemporary Gulf (for example, Oman) as well. The port of Siraf was part of this interaction sphere, which characterizes Siraf's Middle Islamic period (Siraf 4, 1000–1300 CE [Tampoe 1989]). One might characterize the assemblages from these sites as representing an east Iranian culture sphere or *oikoumenê;* this may be considered a Persian periphery to western Islamic realms (Bulliet 1992, see below).

The search for ceramic comparanda often disregards distance, with references for sites in Egypt sought in Susa and Nishapur. The publication of Susa ceramics by Rosen-Ayalon (1974) provides a large corpus of well-illustrated types, unfortunately with minimal chronological controls for most of the contexts. Publication of another very influential corpus of Islamic ceramics appeared that same year, as the results of The Metropolitan Museum of Art excavations at Nishapur (C. Wilkinson 1974). One continues to find scattered references to isolated parallels in this beautiful volume, a continuing tribute to the artistry of its author. Wilkinson may be credited with a caution in placing the Nishapur results within the prevailing chronological interpretation of Samarra and Susa; while he hazarded dates for each ceramic type, he added limited data from Afrasiab (Samarkand) as having potential for further chronological refinement.

Wilkinson was convinced that the ceramics presented in his volume had little potential for further chronological or ethnic identification; the types were thoroughly mixed. Nevertheless, an innovative study by Bulliet (1992) sees indications of social and socioreligious change in these ceramic types, not unlike those advanced for handmade ceramics above. While this particular analysis may be shown to have statistical and conceptual fallacies (Whitcomb 1995:58–60), such ethnohistorical conclusions are precisely what historians and many archaeologists would like to see come out of ceramic studies. Bulliet's study, a putative influence of the *Annales* school, results in a facetious use of archaeological evidence by historians against which James Russell (1986) has cautioned.

SPECULATIONS

The utilization of the Sirjan corpus to determine the date of Syrian sites assumes synchronous adoption of attributes and implies parallel sequential changes. This assumed connection would seem to result from long-distance interaction without specifying the mechanisms involved. Recent discussions of handmade, and in this case geometric painted, ceramics have posited various historical mechanisms (Johns 1998) and have ventured economic and social causes as common stimuli. The case of Nishapur seeks to situate "technological change within social conceptions of ethnicity and ideology" (Sherratt 1992:140) and Bulliet (1994:138) offers another hypothesis that might hold an explanation for these ceramic phenomena, namely, that Iranian culture came to dominate the Islamic world, metaphorically the edge shifting into a central influence. In this analysis, an imbalance between urban and rural population ratios in Iran, a widespread case of overurbanization, began to be felt in the eleventh century. This resulted in a cultural and physical diaspora in which "thousands of Iranians...emigrated to the Arab lands or to the recently conquered territories of Anatolia and India" (Bulliet 1994:166). Bulliet is primarily concerned with the migration of intelligentsia (*ulema*), but this historical agency might have indirectly induced more material manifestations, detectable as an archaeological horizon.

As discussed above, Morony has moved ceramic research into the realm of urban identity, where the social organization of the city reflects more than regional or cosmopolitan concerns. Similarly, the urban structure of Nishapur witnessed the transfer of its urban center from the traditional *shahrestan* (or *madina*) to the *rabad,* a walled suburban center (in this case, Shadyakh). This happened in many cities of Khorasan in the eleventh and twelfth centuries (Wheatley 2001) and indeed may be a common response to dramatic change. Further analysis of ceramic production should see it situated within an urban context and study how rural production is affected by urban relationships (as in HMGPW). The Islamic city becomes the locus of patterned evidence amenable to archaeological comparison and the paradigm for understanding Braudelian *conjonctures* in Middle Eastern history.

CHAPTER 27

MOHAMMADABAD KHARREH CARAVANSERAI

Field Institute of Archaeology, Tehran University

EZAT O. NEGAHBAN

I FIRST MET BILL SUMNER IN 1961, when he was a young U.S. Navy officer taking my course on Iranian archaeology at Tehran University. I recall that he took a leave of absence for a few days from his duties to pay a visit to our excavations at Marlik. As Bill's interest in ancient Iran grew and he resigned his commision to pursue a career in Iranian archaeology, we had other opportunities to meet and talk while he was en route to Hasanlu or Godin. When he arrived in Iran in 1967 to begin his dissertation research in Marvdasht, he visited excavations at Haft Tepe and, back in Tehran, we had a sociable evening at my house in Tajrish with a group of archaeologists associated with the University of Pennsylvania. In 1970, while still working in Marvdasht, Bill visited Zaghe and Sagzabad and Mohammedabad Kharreh caravanserai when it was still under renovation. I remember Bill was particularly impressed with the architecture and the renovation work being done there. We had the pleasure of hosting him on another occasion a few years later, when the caravanserai, then fully restored and renovated, served as the Field Institute of Archaeology of Tehran University. It gives me great pleasure to present parts of my memoirs (Negahban 1997) on the early developments of the Department of Archaeology of the Tehran University and the foundation of its field school to Bill in appreciation of nearly forty years of friendship.

When Tehran University was founded in 1934, it consisted of six faculties, one of which, the Faculty of Literature, included the departments of Persian literature, philosophy, history and geography, psychology, foreign languages (French, English, German and Russian) and archaeology (Hejazi 1959). The establishment of the university, an expression of pride in the highly developed culture of ancient Iran, had been part of a tremendous modernizing drive in Iran under Reza Shah.

With the foundation of the Iran Bastan Museum in 1937 and the formation of the Archaeological Service of Iran, the study of archaeology was professionalized. The Department of Archaeology of Tehran University began to attract some students who were eager to study and learn, rather than registering only to obtain a degree for its privileges of government employment, which had been the pattern.

When I enrolled in the Department of Archaeology in 1946, most classes were held jointly with the other departments of the Faculty of Literature. The only courses specific to the Department of Archaeology were those on the history of art and aesthetics. Students of the department who received a B.A. degree would have some general knowledge of Iranian culture and civilization but receive no courses on archaeological method and theory, or field techniques. Obviously this superficial program could not meet the needs of a country such as Iran with its rich cultural heritage and thousands of archaeological and historical sites.

The only experience outside of the classroom that students of the Department of Archaeology received during their three years of study for a B.A. degree was a two-week bus tour of monuments and archaeological remains in the cities of Isfahan and Shiraz; since there were no sleeping facilities near the archaeological sites, we could manage only side trips to Persepolis and Pasargadae. This trip was not compulsory and, since it was scheduled at the *No-Ruz* (New Year's) holiday, most students skipped it, preferring to participate in family activities at that time. During my three years of study in the Department of Archaeology this tour was carried out only once, with a joint group of students from the other departments of the faculty joining the archaeological students.

At this time when the study of archaeology in Iran was in its earliest stages of development, foreign archaeological expeditions were carrying out extensive archaeological research there, including surveys and excavations, and publishing scientific reports of their investigation of the ancient culture and civilization of Iran. In contrast, the Archaeological Service of Iran, due both to a lack of national experts and a lack of funds, carried out almost no scientific research.

This was the situation at the time I went for graduate studies in the United States. When I returned to Iran to be hired as an associate professor in the Department of Archaeology of the University of Tehran, I was eager to develop the study of archaeology on a more professional basis and to increase the amount and variety of field work training for our students. Initially, I arranged for my students to join archaeologial expeditions in unplanned casual ways, but this obviously was not enough.

I wanted to establish an institute of archaeology at the Faculty of Literature that would offer graduate studies in archaeology and provide compulsory fieldwork for its students. My written proposal for the Institute was certified by Ali Naqi Vazieri, the chairman of the Department of Archaeology, and sent to the Dean of the Faculty of Literature, Ali Akbar Siasi, who approved it and forwarded it to the High Council of the university. Only with constant pressure was it finally accepted. As I was a recently hired associate professor, my opportunities to put pressure on the bureaucracy of the university were limited. My best chance came at the monthly dinners for the academic staff at the Faculty Club and at other such extracurricular gatherings. On these occasions it was rather difficult to pursue long conversations, but nevertheless I kept the subject alive.

Finally, I met with the chancellor of the university, Ahmad Farhad, who agreed to give me an appointment to discuss the matter. In our meeting I described the condition of the department and explained the absolute necessity of fieldwork in archaeological training. Although the chancellor approved my reasoning, he explained that the university budget was very tight. He said, however, that he would consider the establishment of the Institute of Archaeology for the next fiscal year. Throughout the next few months, I continued to inquire about the measure whenever I saw

him. Eventually my persistence began to pay off and finally, one time when I saw the chancellor, before I even had a chance to say anything, he said that probably I wanted to talk about the Institute, and if this was so, I should come to his office. On the appointed day I entered the chancellor's office with a feeling of excitement. He arose from behind his desk and, after replying to my salute, said, "Supposing the Institute was established, where would you dig for antiquities? Do you have a special place in mind?"

I replied, "In a country like Iran, which for thousands of years has been inhabited by rich ancient cultures, anywhere I dug would bring good results. If I excavated deeply enough right here in your office, I would find something." Chancellor Farhad said, with a surprised gesture, "In my office?" and then proceeded to process the proposal for the establishment of the Institute of Archaeology. Thus, after two years of constant pressure and persistence, the Institute of Archaeology was approved by the High Council of the University.

In 1959, the Institute of Archaeology was established in a few rooms on the second floor of the old office of the dean of the Faculty of Literature, in *Daneshsara-ye 'Ali*. Until the Institute received its own budget, the faculty approved payment for current projects and expenses which, of course, had to be kept to a minimum.

In its first years the Institute participated in foreign and national archaeological expeditions as a way of providing field experience for our students, but this did not satisfy our goal of developing an organized program of field training that would meet the need for scientifically trained archaeologists. In the fall of 1961 the Institute joined the Archaeological Service in excavations at Marlik in northern Iran that provided field training for some of our students. This excavation, however, could not provide our students with continuous, year after year opportunities for field training.

A more far-reaching opportunity arose with the opening, under my direction, of the excavation of Haft Tepe in Susiana in the winter of 1965, funded and staffed by the Archaeological Service of Iran and the Institute of Archaeology. At Haft Tepe our students participated in excavation under the supervision of professional staff. Since the Sugar Cane Project of Haft Tepe provided residential facilities for the staff and students during the first few seasons, many students were able to join the excavation for varying periods and receive some field training. With the excavation continuing season after season, year after year, the Institute and Department of Archaeology were able to revise and improve their curriculum, including many technical aspects of fieldwork in the program. At Haft Tepe,

27.1 Main entrance on southern side of caravanserai. *Photograph by E.O. Negahban*

27.2 Outer view of eastern wall before restoration. *Photograph by E.O. Negahban*

graduate students studying for an M.A. degree would participate in the excavation as a compulsory course during their last semester of study before graduation. With this compulsory fieldwork the quality of archaeological teaching at the university definitely improved. Students working for a B.A. degree could also volunteer to participate in the excavation, particularly during the *No-Ruz* holiday, with the sightseeing—mentioned above—replaced by a working session. This program was followed for fourteen continuous seasons of work on the Haft Tepe project.

Despite this and other field projects, we still lacked a permanent fieldwork program for all of our students. By

the late 1960s, as the chairman of the Department of Archaeology and director of the Institute of Archaeology of the Tehran University, I decided to make a radical improvement in our archaeological curriculum by introducing many courses on technical and field training in both the B.A. and M.A. programs. For this purpose I needed an independent, reliable, and permanent excavation run by the university. I described my ideas to the chancellor, at that time Ali Naqi Alikhani, and explained how it would provide more qualified graduates to meet the needs of our country. Dr. Alikhani showed much interest in my views and suggested that I make a proposal to this effect within a few days.

At the beginning of winter 1969, I made a proposal that the Institute and the Department of Archaeology of the university begin survey and excavation in the Qazvin plain. This was approved by Dr. Seyyedd Hossein Nasr, dean of the Faculty of Literature, and sent to the office of the chancellor who, without any delay, forwarded the proposal to the Ministry of Culture and Arts where it was approved by the minister, Mehrdad Pahlbod. With a permit for survey and excavation in the Qazvin plain issued to Tehran University, a permanent and reliable site close to Tehran had been established for the field training of our students.

In the summer of 1970, I proposed that the Department of Archaeology revise the curriculum of the B.A. degree by adding twenty required credit hours or a full semester of field training. My colleagues who were all anxious for such changes, approved my proposal. With this essential step we moved closer to our goal of producing trained graduates (Shahmirzadi 1986).

HISTORY AND BACKGROUND

By the winter of 1970, our archaeological students were participating in the excavation at Sagzabad in the Qazvin plain. The public school officials of Sagzabad village agreed to let us use the elementary school as our headquarters for the three months of summer vacation, but we would have to move out when school started in the fall. Throughout the summer I searched for another place for our headquarters for the fall season. At first I looked in the vicinity of Sagzabad, but after several weeks I realized that there were no buildings there large enough to house our team since it was a rural area of small houses containing at most two or three little rooms.

Finally, I decided to go to the governor general of Qazvin, about 60 km away, and ask for his help. After looking into the matter for several days, he informed me that he also could not find any suitable place in the vicinity of the excavation. The only possible site available was the village of

Esmatabad at the side of the road to Boin Zahra, which had been rebuilt by Armenian Christians after an earthquake. The houses had been abandoned by the local people because of religious conflict and prejudice. I drove to Esmatabad and found only some single room units which, having been derelict for nearly a year, were not even livable. I returned to the governor general, described the condition of the houses of Esmatabad, and asked him to keep us in mind if anything came up in the future.

After buying supplies in the Qazvin bazaar, I set out to return to our excavation. On the way back we passed a ruined caravanserai next to the village of Mohammadabad. A gendarmerie station occupied one corner of the structure. I asked the gendarmes if they knew of any suitable building for our expedition headquarters. After some discussion with the head of the gendarmerie, I inquired about the abandoned caravanserai. I was told that those parts of the caravanserai where the roof was still in place were used during the winter months by shepherds to house their flocks. The only permanent occupation was by the gendarme post which had a temporary holding cell for detainees before they were transferred to Qazvin prison. I was becoming more and more interested in the caravanserai and decided to investigate it more thoroughly.

As I entered the caravanserai, it was obvious that it had been deserted for years without any upkeep. It had been exposed to extremes of weather and much of the roof had fallen in, while the floors were packed with dirt and debris mixed with sheep droppings (figures 27.1–27.3). The villagers living next to the caravanserai had used the better preserved parts of the structure to store hay, straw and other dry farm supplies and the more ruined parts to dump trash and garbage. Overall a very pronounced unpleasant odor permeated the entire structure. There was a stairway leading from the entrance hall to the roof, most of which was still in place, so I decided to climb up. When I walked out onto the roof, I saw a large baked brick construction built around an inner courtyard, apparently a rather large caravanserai of the type constructed by Shah Abbas the Great, the famous Safavid king, in the late sixteenth to seventeenth centuries CE.

The main gate was located on the southern side of the building. On both sides of the gate were two rows of open porticoes about one meter high, providing a place for visitors to sit and rest while waiting to enter the caravanserai. Inside the large entrance hall, in addition to the stairway to the roof, there was a large door at each side leading to the main halls on the southern side of the building. In the center of each side of the structure was a large iwan that opened to the central courtyard. Small doors on each side

of these iwans led to the main halls on each side. Open porticoes surrounded the inner courtyard and at the four outer corners of the structure were round watch towers.

I could see that this large and solid structure would provide enough space not only for our expedition headquarters but also for a permanent Field Institute of Archaeology. Restoring this caravanserai would also save a Safavid building, in itself a great step toward preservation of our national monuments. I knew it would be difficult to convince the university authorities to agree to such an extensive project, but since it would combine our archaeological work with restoration of an ancient monument at a relatively modest cost, I decided to try. I was lost in daydreams as I descended from the roof, climbed over the piles of debris, and returned to the gendarme post where I inquired about ownership of the monument; I was told it was under the care of the government's Office of Religious Endowments.

It was near sunset when I said goodbye to the gendarmes and drove back to Sagzabad village, our current headquarters. With plans forming in my mind, I determined to find temporary housing near the excavation, no matter how uncomfortable, for the remainder of the working season. Fortunately, in the village of Ebrahimabad, there was a deserted school building, without doors or windows, that we could use temporarily. I decided to cover the windows and doors with plastics sheets to prepare it for use when we had to evacuate our present headquarters.

To advance my plans for establishing the Field Institute, I decided to invite Ali Naqi Alikhani, the chancellor of the university, who was active both in the expansion of the university and the advancement of archaeological and other cultural activities, to visit the excavation site to show him our work and present him with my plans for the caravanserai. During my weekly trip to Tehran, I extended the invitation, which he immediately accepted. He set the date for the following Friday (the weekend in Islamic countries) so he could bring along his family and a few interested friends.

On the appointed day, the team went to work at 6 a.m., our normal time. It was a clear bright sunny day with a blue autumn sky. At about 11 o'clock the chancellor and his family arrived at the excavation, along with Dr. Ziai, the vice chancellor for Administration and Finance, and his family, two well-known Iranian architects Nader Ardalan and Jamshid Kouros, and a few university colleagues. First, they went to each of the three separate digs of Tepe Zaghe, Tepe Qabrestan and Tepe Sagzabad. At each the professor in charge reported on the remains while the students and workers carried on with their normal activity. After this programmed visit, there was an hour for the guests to stroll

27.3   Inner courtyard before restoration. *Photograph by E.O. Negahban*

around the excavations, talking with the workers, students, and professors. At about 2 p.m., as we did every day, we left the site to return to our camp in the village school of Sagzabad, about 3 km away. On the way back, the team stopped at the *qanat*-fed stream as always to wash before returning to headquarters for lunch. We all washed away the accumulated dust in the crystal clear water of the qanat and returned to our camp. In the course of visiting the digs, roaming around the excavation site, and stopping at the qanat, an atmosphere of ease without formality had developed among us and we had a very pleasant lunch. Some of the group then visited Sagzabad village while others stayed to rest in the schoolhouse until it was time to assemble for the return to Tehran.

Dr. Alikhani was thinking of returning by way of Eshtehard, the shorter route, but I asked him to take the road to Qazvin where there was a very interesting place I wanted to show him. He agreed and we drove toward Qazvin together. After a half hour we arrived at the Mohammadabad Kharreh caravanserai. I explained that this was the spot I wanted to show him. Everyone left their cars and walked toward the caravanserai, climbing over the heaps of trash and animal droppings on the way. I led the group along with the chancellor, while some of the others hesitated to follow and dropped behind.

We reached the central entrance hall and climbed by the spiral staircase to the roof. Some did not want to venture up the broken staircase and remained below in the entrance hall. As we reached the open roof and viewed the surrounding prospect, I described my proposal to restore the caravanserai and use it as the Field Institute of Archaeology of Tehran University. At this time, while part of the group were on the roof and others were still on the ground

floor in the entrance hall, my colleagues there, who had heard my proposal, were talking among themselves without realizing that we could clearly hear their conversation rising through the stairwell. Someone said, "He is getting crazy. We would never come to this dirty place to work."

Dr. Alikhani, who had heard their words, looked at me and asked,"Did you hear what your colleagues said?" and then, smiling pleasantly, he added, "I am crazy, too," at which everyone started laughing. Then the chancellor asked Dr. Ardalan, the architect who was also a professor at the university, "What would be the cost of restoring this caravanserai?" After a pause, Ardalan said, "To build such a large construction would probably cost several million tomans, but to restore this already existing structure would probably not take more than one million tomans. However, since Dr. Negahban is experienced in the restoration of archaeological monuments, his estimate might be more reliable."

The chancellor looked at me and said, "Although I like your proposal, still, as you know yourself, the university cannot financially meet such an expense." I turned to him and said, "I only need 50,000 toman for the first year." The chancellor asked, "How about the following years?" and I replied that I would need the same amount each year. He turned to Dr. Ziai and asked, "Can we provide that amount by the time Dr. Negahban comes to Tehran on Tuesday so that there will be no delay in starting the project?" Dr. Ziai replied affirmatively. I was overjoyed and thanked the chancellor as we proceeded to view other parts of the building from the roof. By this time it was late and so the guests said goodbye and proceeded toward Tehran while my colleagues and I returned to Sagzabad.

The next day I drove to Qazvin to look further into the status of the caravanserai. I paid a visit to the Director of the Endowments Office and, after expressing my respects, told him of the university's interest in restoring the caravanserai and using it to house the Field Institute of Archaeology. He received me warmly and called for the file on the caravanserai which showed that as recently as two years before the shepherds who were using the building to house their herds in the wintertime had made rent payments, but for the last two years their contract had not been renewed and they had paid no rent. He said it would be preferable for the university to contact their central office in Tehran directly and arrange an agreement for the caravanserai.

Back in Tehran I met with Dr. Ziai who took me to the office of the chancellor, who received us warmly and expressed his appreciation for his pleasant visit to the excavation. I thanked him for the check for restoration, described my trip to the Endowments Office in Qazvin, and explained about the need for a letter to the central Office of Religious Endowments requesting approval for renting the caravanserai to the university. The chancellor immediately called the central Office of Religious Endowments and spoke to Dr. Nassir Assar, the director. After cordial greetings the chancellor explained the situation and Dr. Assar, who was a friend of his, approved the proposal, saying that, in order to follow proper procedures, he would need a letter from the university concerning the plan. He also mentioned that General Ardalan, who was in charge of the Qazvin Endowments Office, happened to be in his office and would wait there until I arrived with the letter from the university.

I arrived at the Office of Religious Endowments as soon as possible and, after the usual greetings, Dr. Assar introduced me to General Ardalan, who was awaiting me. I handed the university letter to Dr. Assar who indicated his approval on the margin, referring it to the Endowments Office of Qazvin. Then he handed the letter to General Ardalan who said that he was aware of my work, including the restoration of the caravanserai at Bisitun, near the famous inscription of Darius the Great and had heard of me even earlier in connection with the survey for the restoration of the monument of Taq-i Bostan near Kermanshah. He asked me to come to his office in Qazvin the next Saturday (the first working day of the Iranian week) by which time the routine work would be finished and we could make the rent contract.

When I appeared at General Ardalan's office, he explained that the Endowments Office of Qazvin had approved the university's proposal and expressed their appreciation to the university for its plan to restore such an important monument. The rent contract was made out for ten years, with a rent of 700 toman per year, which Tehran University was authorized to spend on restoration of the caravanserai. We signed the contract and the caravanserai came under the control of the university. With this act we underook the difficult but satisfying task of restoring the caravanserai of Mohammadabad Kharreh under the auspices of the Institute of Archaeology of Tehran University.

RESTORATION AND PRESERVATION

I left Qazvin and headed back toward Sagzabad village. As I drove I was completely absorbed in planning the restoration project in the best and most economic way. With winter approaching, I decided that we would work first in those parts of the building where the roof was still in place and we could work through the cold weather. The next morning I returned to the caravanserai with one of my

27.4 *(top)*, 27.5 *(above)* Restoration of foundation wall.
Photographs by E.O. Negahban

27.6 Rebuilding fallen wall according to original plan.
Photograph by E.O. Negahban

27.7 Restoration of fallen towers. *Photograph by E.O. Negahban*

27.8 Restoring mortar on roof. *Photograph by E.O. Negahban*

experienced senior students, Mansur Seyyed Sajjidi, whom I made responsible for removing trash and debris and cleaning the building with the help of several hired workers from the adjacent village of Mohammadabad Kharreh.

While cleaning the building we followed routine excavation procedures to avoid damaging any remains found. This slowed our cleaning process but was essential to our work. The caravanserai was built of baked brick and the lower part of the building still standing was covered by the upper fallen part. Working carefully, we were able to reconstruct the plan of the original building. We started at the main entrance where, after removing piles of trash and animal droppings, we saved and cleaned the fallen brick to be used in reconstruction (figures 27.4–27.8). Soon almost the whole area of the central courtyard was cleared and the original foundation plan of the main entrance emerged.

During the process of cleaning the caravanserai, Dr. Mansour Seyyed Sajjidi, then a student and now my learned colleague and fellow archaeologist, found a copper coin bearing the words "bandeh-i Shah-Velayet Ismail" (figure 27.18), indicating that the building was in use during the time of Shah Ismail III, the Safavid king, in the mid-eighteenth century CE. It is clear that the caravanserai of Mohammadabad Kharreh conforms to the general plan of construction of caravanserais built by Shah Abbas the Great in the seventeenth century CE. Later, during the reign of Shah Ismail III, some traveller lost the small copper coin, thereby allowing us to corroborate our original dating of the building.

While we were carrying out the cleaning, we were faced with two additional problems. First, we had to empty the roofed parts of the structure where the villagers had stored hay and dried straw. To solve this problem we arranged a meeting with the *kadkhoda* (village headman) and other village elders along with the head of the gendarme post. After prolonged discussion, the villagers agreed to gradually evacuate the halls by the end of the winter season and bring no new supplies of hay or other materials into the building for storage. Although they were not really pleased to do this, they were happy that we were hiring many workers from the village and they also recognized that the gendarmes had to enforce the rent contract with the university. The elders, the gendarmerie head, and I all signed the order of the meeting and we had no further difficulty with the villagers.

Our second problem was to vacate the gendarme post at the southwestern corner of the building. This was more complicated and had to be negotiated with either the provincial office in Qazvin or the central office in Tehran, since the local gendarmes were not authorized to act in this

27.9 Planting garden in
  inner courtyard.
  Photograph by E.O.
  Negahban

27.10 Planting garden in
  inner courtyard.
  Photograph by E.O.
  Negahban

27.11 Outer garden view.
  Photograph by E.O.
  Negahban

27.12 Student exhibitions in inner alcoves. *Photograph by E.O. Negahban*

matter, although they were agreeable to leaving this dirty, smelly place and promised to help us in any way they could. I went to Qazvin to discuss the matter with the director of gendarmes who had already been informed that the university had rented the caravanserai and was planning to establish a Field Institute of Archaeology there. The director received me warmly and I briefly described the intentions of the university in evacuating the whole building including the gendarmerie station and preparing it for restoration. He said he would be glad to cooperate if he could find a structure of at least three or four rooms nearby to use for a gendarme post.

Since I had already investigated the whole region in my search for a place to house our excavation headquarters, I was almost sure that no such building was available in the vicinity of the caravanserai and accepting this condition was almost useless. After further discussion the director said that, since the final decision would be made by the central office in Tehran, it might be better for me to contact them directly. During my weekly visit to Tehran, I discussed the matter with Dr. Alikhani who agreed to contact the gendarmerie. The following week Dr. Alikhani told me that it would be best for us to build a small new post according to the standard plan of the gendarmerie, which would not cost more than sixty to seventy thousand toman. Since it was now at the end of the fiscal year, he would budget this expense for the coming year. I told the chancellor that building a new post was feasible, but it would take a long time to get it through the government bureaucracy and I was sure that the cost of construction for such a small building would not be as high as estimated. He agreed and we decided to obtain the general plan for a small gendarme post and estimate the cost ourselves. I discussed the matter with the mason in charge of our restoration team, Ostad Ahmad Banna, who made a detailed estimate and determined that the total expenses of labor and material could not be more than 15,000 toman.

27.13 Student presentations of exhibitions. *Photograph by E.O. Negahban*

27.14, 27.15 Student presentations of exhibitions. *Photographs by E.O. Negahban*

27.16 Photographing discovered objects. *Photograph in possession of author*

27.17 Dining hall. *Photograph by E.O. Negahban*

27.18 Coin of Shah Ismail III: *left*, front view; *right*, back view. *Photographs by E.O. Negahban*

I reported back to the chancellor who discussed the matter with the Director of the Gendarmerie. The university agreed to build a new post near the old one. Since it was almost winter I decided to start building the new post the following spring. In cooperation with the local gendarmerie head we selected a piece of land near a deep well and, since it was not easy under university regulations to buy land, I paid a few hundred tomans for the land myself so that there would be no delay in construction. At the beginning of the spring season we started to build the new post; when it was completed the gendarmes evacuated the caravanserai and moved into their new quarters.

As the weather became colder, we stopped work in the open areas and confined ourselves to areas inside the building where the roof was still in place and the structure could be warmed by burning straw and desert thorn in stoves. I regularly visited the caravanserai twice a week, to oversee the progress of the work and to bring construction materials from Qazvin, sometimes driving through the severe snowfalls of the winter on roads which at that time were not well asphalted. All continued to go well and the difficulties diminished as I came closer to my ultimate goal.

Another problem arose when, with the coming of cold weather at the end of the fall season, the shepherds who had been accustomed to house their herds in the caravanserai returned to the Qazvin plain, expecting to occupy the building for the winter season. When they arrived they tried to move into the caravanserai, but Ostad Ahmad, the mason in charge of restoration, who had gradually built up prestige and respect in the area as the representative of the university, stopped them with the help of the gendarmes and asked them to wait until I arrived to decide what to do. The shepherds set up their tents on vacant land around the caravanserai and waited for my arrival.

Thus, one day I arrived to find many black tents set up around the caravanserai with one large one in front of the main gate. Within a few minutes several elderly men came to introduce themselves as the owners of the herds of sheep and goats. They asked to be allowed to bring their herds inside the caravanserai and keep them there for the winter as they had always done. I took the men on a tour of the sections of the building that were already cleaned and partly restored and asked them what would be their answer if they were the representative of the university. They were impressed by the work we had done and made no reply, requesting only that they keep their black tents as they were around the caravanserai until they could find another shelter for their herds, to which I agreed. They soon found other places to stay and left after a couple of weeks.

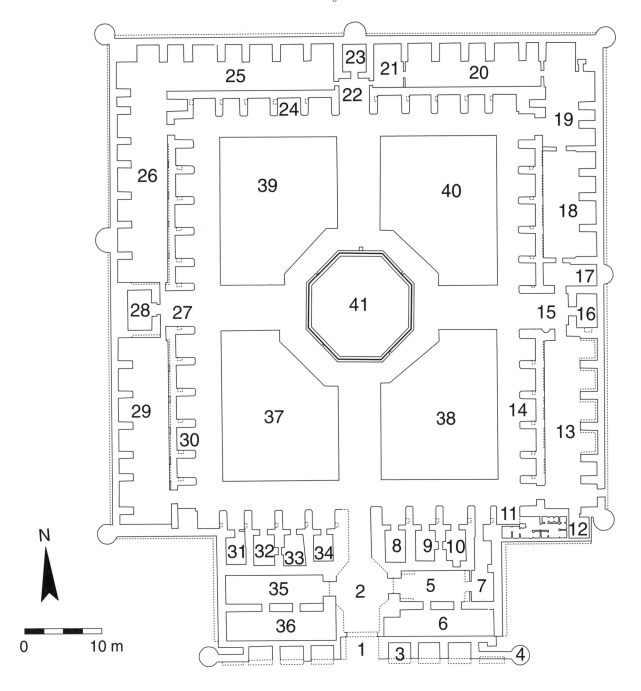

27.19 Plan of the various areas of the restored caravanserai that were assigned for use in the Field Institute of Archaeology: *1*,
Main entrance with large wooden door; *2*, Entrance hall; *3*, Row of terraces with porticoes in front of building; *4*, Outer
corner towers; *5, 6*, Library; *7*, Photography studio; *8, 9, 10*, Single staff rooms; *11*, Toilets and washing facilities; *12*,
Kitchen; *13*, Dining hall; *14*, Rows of terraced alcoves in inner court; *15*, Large portico on eastern side; *16*, Single room for
professor; *17*, Guest room (female); *18*, Rooms for female students; *19*, General lounge; *20*, Rooms for male students; *21*,
Guest room (male); *22*, Large northen portico; *23*, Room of Director; *24*, Row of interior terraced porticoes; *25, 26*,
Museum for antiquities discovered in Qazvin plain; *27*, Large western portico; *28*, Single room for professor; *29*,
Classroom, lecture hall, restoration room, seminar room; *30*, Row of inner terraced alcoves; *31-34*, Single rooms for
instructors; *35, 36*, Storage halls; *37-40*, Garden areas; *41*, Courtyard pool. *Prepared at MASCA from author's original*

Winter, spring and summer were spent cleaning the structure, removing construction debris, and restoring and rebuilding the fallen roofs and domes according to the original plan. By the end of summer, a year after I had first seen the abandoned caravanserai, the whole interior of the building had been cleaned and a section was ready for the expedition teams to move in. With its large spacious halls and corridors, the caravanserai gave us enough space so that we could improve and expand our technical field courses. After we began living in the caravanserai we found more time for organization and restoration and were generally more efficient in all arrangements. In addition, the new facilities allowed us to offer twenty credit hours of courses of field techniques: excavation, survey, technical drawing, techincal mapping, archaeological photography, a seminar and an exhibition, and archaeological report (figures 27.12–27.16).

We continued to work on the restoration of the caravanserai including reconstruction of the inner central courtyard and its central pool, whose original oulines were determined through excavation (figures 27.9, 27.10). I also bought and donated to the university some land around the caravanserai to make an outside garden and enhance the atmosphere of the Institute (figure 27.11). By the time our work was finished we had facilities for fifty persons, including professors, staff, students, and visitors—including my colleague William Sumner. We had established a library, a museum, classrooms, a seminar room, a staff room, separate dormitories for male and female students, a dining hall, a kitchen, guest rooms, and exercise area and volleyball ground and garages (figures 27.17, 27.19).

Completing the renovation took nearly two and a half years, with our total expenses for all the work, including cleaning, construction material, renovation, installation of electricity and power unit, new doors and windows, furniture including beds, tables, benches, chairs, and other equipment, adding up to 268,000 toman altogether (back then almost $45,000). With this small cost a very important national monument of the Safavid period covering about 3600 m^2 was restored according to its original plan and adapted for a Field Institute of Archaeology of Tehran University, becoming an essential aid in producing scientifically trained archaeologists to study and research the cultural heritage of ancient Iran.

As I review all the difficulties that we had to overcome in our pursuit of the goal of establishing this Field Institute of Archaeology, I am satisfied that after all the project was carried through successfully and I would like to express my sincere thanks to all who supported this work. My special appreciation goes to Dr. Ali Naqi Alikhani, then chancellor of Tehran University, who, with open hands worked to solve any problem we faced.

Acknowledgment. For their valuable support in making the Institute possible, I would like to express my heartiest thanks to Colonel Ali Naqi Vaziri, the former chairman of the department of archaeology and history of art, H.E. Dr. Ali-Akbar Siasi, the former dean of the Faculty of Literature and Human Sciences, and H.E. Dr. Ahmad Farhad, the former chancellor of Tehran University.

Editors' note. Dr. Ezat Negahban's description of the early stages of the establishment of archaeology as an academic discipline in Iran and the establishment of an archaeology field school at Tehran University is so informative about the ethnography of bureaucracy that we felt it particularly appropriate for honoring someone interested in early state-level societies; Dr. Negahban provided his own translation of an essay that appeared first in Persian.

CHAPTER 28

QASHQA'I NOMADIC PASTORALISTS AND THEIR USE OF LAND

LOIS BECK

IN THIS CHAPTER I examine how some nomadic pastoralists in Iran changed their use of the physical environment over the past thirty-three years and how these changes related to their economic practices. This account is based on my cultural anthropological research among Qashqa'i nomadic pastoralists in southwestern Iran in the 1970s, 1990s, and early 2000s, including eleven visits since the revolution in 1978–1979 and the Islamic Republic of Iran's formation. I draw on my observations of the varying ecological adaptations and diversifying economic strategies of these tribal people as they exploited a vast section of the southern Zagros mountains. Their practices included use and protection of natural pastureland in different ecological zones, investment in arable land, adoption of agricultural techniques, construction of water-control systems, hunting, gathering, construction of shelters for people and animals, increased reliance on roads and motorized transportation, and closer ties with the national government and the market economy. Although much of the land these nomadic pastoralists used was not suitable for productive activities other than seasonal pastoralism, hunting, and gathering, the people were increasingly forced to compete with settled agrarian communities for the available cultivable land and for access to water and rights of passage. They did enjoy, however, the competitive advantage of a continuing reliance on mobility and migration, which allowed them to exploit a succession of seasonal resources, and the primary products of pastoralism (meat, dairy goods, wool, weavings) were in market demand.

This chapter is directed to the interests of archaeologists who draw data and insights from accounts of contemporary peoples in order to gain a better understanding of the ways physical evidence relates to actual human behavior and practices. I focus therefore on the physical environment and on changes in the ways these nomadic pastoralists interacted with it. The study adds new observations to the ethnoarchaeological literature of Iran, some of which concerns nomadic pastoralism (see Hole 1978; authors in Kramer 1979; Watson 1979).[1]

This discussion may inspire scholars and others to take fuller consideration of the people actually making use of a specific territory. However land is used, it obviously consists of more than just physical features. Environmental studies too often ignore or neglect the people who make a livelihood there and whose use of land plays a part in their political, social, and cultural systems. People develop strategies of land use through processes of trial and error over long periods—decades, centuries, and even millennia (see chapter 7). Such strategies and the people who devise them deserve our respect, support, and protection.

Mobile residents of the plateaus and valleys of the Zagros mountains of southwestern Iran, the Qashqa'i are members of a tribal confederacy of approximately 800,000 individuals (as of 2002). They speak a Central Asian-derived Turkish language and constitute one of Iran's many ethnic and national minorities. Until the 1960s most Qashqa'i people were nomadic pastoralists who migrated semiannually hundreds of kilometers between winter pastures at low

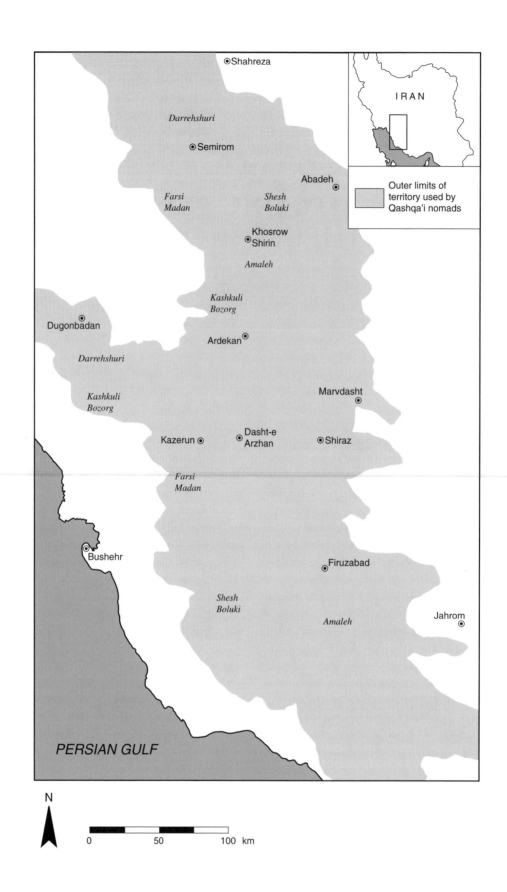

28.1   Qashqa'i territory. *Prepared at MASCA from Beck 1991:6*

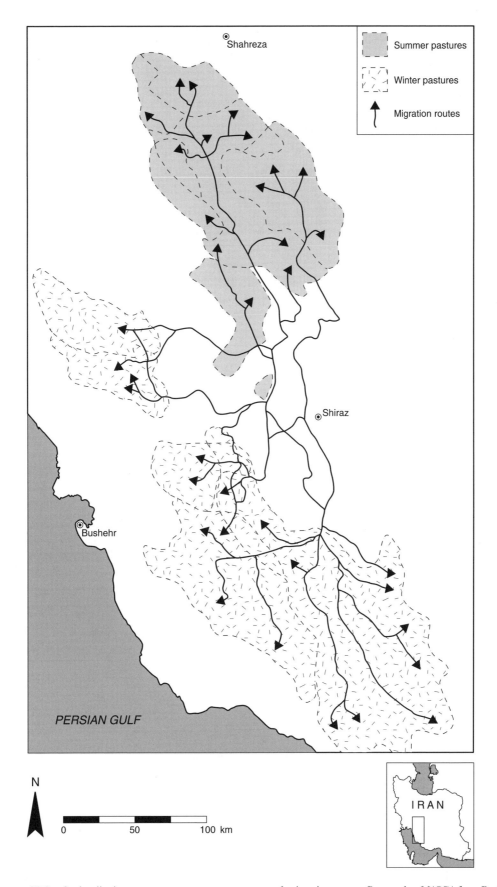

Summer pastures

Winter pastures

Migration routes

Shahreza

Shiraz

Bushehr

PERSIAN GULF

N

0   50   100 km

IRAN

28.2   Qashqa'i winter pastures, summer pastures, and migration routes. *Prepared at MASCA from Beck 1991:13*

altitudes near the Persian Gulf and summer pastures high in the mountains to the north and east (figures 28.1 and 28.2). Since the 1960s many Qashqa'i have moved to villages and towns, although often retaining pastoralism as one of several means of livelihood. Despite the new places and patterns of residence for many of these people, most remained socially and even emotionally attached to their customary seasonal pastures, regularly visited their kin there, and continued to exploit the natural resources, often in cooperation with these kin. For most, their tribal ties remained strong if not enhanced, and their sense of themselves as forming part of a unique sociocultural entity in Iran was heightened.

This chapter focuses on the contemporary ecological, economic, and social conditions in southwestern Iran as I have directly observed them—most recently in 2002—during eleven periods since the revolution in 1978–1979 and the Islamic Republic of Iran's formation. Because of anthropological research I also conducted there in the 1970s, I am able to follow precisely the changes that individuals, families, and tribal groups have made over the past thirty-three years. Publications drawing on this earlier research (for example, Beck 1980, 1981a, 1981b, 1984, 1991) provide comparative information about previous periods.[2] I discuss post-revolutionary conditions in published and forthcoming work (Beck 1992, 2000, 2003, N.D.). The past tense used in this chapter reflects the continuous nature of change.

I ask these key questions. How have the Qashqa'i people made the best of the inherent environmental constraints of these rugged, mountainous, and semiarid lands? How and why do many of them continue pastoralism and nomadism, despite pressures to change their livelihoods and lifestyles? How and why have these pressures changed over the years? And why does the current Islamic government, unlike previous Iranian governments in this century, support nomads and their livelihoods? Despite the profound changes that all Qashqa'i people have undergone in the past thirty-three years, I am still impressed by the remarkable continuities in their society and culture. In examining my photographs to find details to add to this chapter, I was struck by how many of them could have been taken at any time during the past three decades, as long ago as 1969 or as recently as 2002. I also recognize how much seasonal and annual variation in patterns occurs and how difficult it is to document and date the emergence of major trends.[3]

A TYPICAL CAMP: 1970 AND 1998

Several brief descriptions will help to demonstrate the kinds of changes experienced by Qashqa'i nomadic pastoralists

and to establish a context for this discussion. Their winter and summer pastures were located in the valleys and on the slopes and plateaus of the southern Zagros mountains. Mountain peaks rise above the nomads' camps, each of which was usually secluded by the rugged terrain. The ecological differences between their widely separated winter and summer pastures will be apparent here and in the rest of the chapter.

WINTER PASTURES, 1970

A typical campsite in winter pastures in 1970 contained three woven goat-hair tents with slanted roofs to deflect rain and snow. Each dwelling held an extended family of seven or more people. The black tents were pitched on flat areas on the slopes of gullies to protect the occupants and their possessions from flash floods while also still providing some shelter from wind. Several nearby huts built of stones, tree branches, and bundled reeds were used for cooking, storage, and refuge in inclement weather. Simple, roughly circular, open-air enclosures made of rocks heaped with dried thorny bushes protected the animals at night and helped to discourage predators. Each household owned and managed its own sheep and goats, which were tended together in herds from one hundred to three hundred animals. Small trees and shrubs and low-lying plants grew in the terrain surrounding the camp. Green leafy shoots appeared as the weather warmed during and after the winter's rains. Several nearby shallow depressions, fortified along the sides with rocks and dried mud, held rainfall and run-off for the animals to drink. Accompanied by donkeys to carry the filled goat-skin bags, the camp's women and children spent many hours a day traveling to and from a well in the valley below, the nearest source of clean drinking water. Newborn lambs and kids were sheltered in reed pens inside the tents and released two to four times a day to be reunited with their mothers for nursing. Before dawn shepherds took the sheep and goats to graze different parts of the surrounding hills and mountainsides, while a camel herder tended his animals closer to camp and collected firewood for the camp's use. Men and boys kept periodic watch over several small fields of sown barley protected by rock walls, the crop to be used as supplemental animal feed if sufficient rain germinated the seeds and grew the plants to maturity. Birds seemed to eat as much grain as was eventually harvested.

SUMMER PASTURES, 1998

By contrast, in terms of both space and time, a typical residential site in summer pastures in 1998 contained several rudimentary one-room houses constructed from stones gathered nearby and mortared with cement, fine gravel, and dirt. They stood on the very spots where the people had erected their flat-roofed summer tents only a few years previously. A small kitchen area enclosed by cement blocks and roofed with old tent fabric stood to the side of each house, and just beyond that lay heaps of firewood, wooden and woven-reed racks for drying dairy products and wild plants, and miscellaneous equipment that had not found a place in these new dwellings. Gunnysacks filled with barley, dried alfalfa, and straw leaned against the houses' outer walls. A black goat-hair tent was pitched by one house, where a newly married son and his bride resided and where guests were entertained, as if to celebrate the past nostalgically. Holding the sheep and goats at noon and at night when the shepherds returned to camp to eat and rest, pens made of metal mesh supported by wooden stakes stood behind the houses at the edge of the mountain slope. Men had cemented a small pool at the mouth of the nearest natural spring where people drew clean water for drinking and household use, and a cement channel led water to another pool where the animals drank. A decrepit Land Rover was parked beside one of the houses. The dirt track used by the vehicle's owner to reach the camp was also traveled by the Persians and Lurs who cultivated fields and orchards in the valley below. The dust-raising traffic annoyed everyone, especially mothers trying to watch young children. These trespassers demonstrated no concern for the campsite's borders; they did not care that the camp was a defined territory to be used exclusively by its inhabitants. Downhill near a small stream stood a toilet, a small, open-air, cement-block structure containing a ground-level ceramic platform precariously balanced over a pit. The stumps of shade trees, planted along a water course but cut down by irate Persian and Lur cultivators who resented the nomads' presence, stood as stark evidence of the conflict. Stripped of branches, their trunks lay on the ground. The surrounding terrain was bare compared with winter pastures. No trees or large shrubs grew here naturally, only small bushes and low-lying vegetation. The valley below, its streams blocked against the pastoralists' animals since the early 1980s, was green with walled cultivated fields and fruit orchards. Hostile encounters between the Persian and Lur cultivators there and the pastoralists occurred almost daily.

Various topics mentioned or alluded to in these two passages are discussed in the following eight sections: land, nomadism and pastoralism, agriculture, management of water, construction of shelters, hunting and gathering, the government, and the market economy. I focus on the postrevolutionary period (1979–2002) with comparative information provided for earlier periods. The wider con-

text, in which many individuals and groups other than the Qashqa'i competed for the same natural resources, cannot be discussed in detail here.

LAND

Both before and after the revolution, problems over land caused great uncertainty among Qashqa'i nomadic pastoralists and significantly affected the ongoing decisions they made about their livelihoods and lifestyles. No single government agency held all the information on land use and deeds for any given territory, and some offices possessed conflicting information. Such bureaucratic chaos offered the potential for great abuse. Settled non-Qashqa'i people with influential government connections and sufficient wealth to bribe officials could determine their own land use in areas where Qashqa'i people held long-standing claims. The nomads were especially vulnerable to these incursions because they did not reside in any territory year-round and hence could not easily protect the lands on which they relied. They lived only seasonally in winter and in summer pastures, were mobile within these locales, and spent many months on the migrations. To support their own interests, Qashqa'i individuals held onto any documents pertaining to land. Even papers concerning disputes on other issues contained a record of people's location at the time, necessary for proof of residence. School records also provided evidence for the presence of certain families in specific places.

The status of nationalized pastureland, a broad policy introduced for all of Iran by Mohammad Reza Shah in 1962 as part of his "bloodless" revolution, was unclear after his ouster in 1979 and still remained so in 2002. His programs, even exemplary ones, were tainted by their association with him. Since 1962, natural water courses following the pull of gravity and the contours of the often hilly if not mountainous terrain were generally recognized by government officials as the legal division between pasture and cultivable land. Land uphill from the channels was nationalized to be used as pastures and was potentially available to pastoralists through short-term and long-term leases. Land downhill from the channels was subject to land reform, opened up for cultivation if not already cultivated, and available for distribution or purchase. Most nomads were not eligible then for either distribution or purchase of this cultivable land, partly for political reasons but also because they lacked the requirements met by many others permanently settled in the area year-round. By the 1990s the dividing line between these two types of land was increasingly unclear because of the expansion of irrigation systems and the new land brought under cultivation in both pastoral and agricultural areas. Some legal changes did occur in the mid-1990s, such as newly introduced rights to rent, transfer, and sell pasture leases to others. Rights over collectively used land were locally negotiated but not always formalized by legal documentation. (Lambton [1953, 1969] discusses land reform; Abrahamian [1982] offers the wider historical context.)

The issue of land considered as privately owned with or without supporting legal documents was still under discussion in Iran's national parliament in 2002, in part because of problems created by the many thousands of often-wealthy landowners who had fled into exile during or after the revolution and who later attempted to return and/or claim their (former) land. Some influential officials, including some Muslim clergymen, supported a land reform that would give legal title to the cultivators who actually worked the land. Other officials, also including some clergymen, were themselves large landholders relying on paid laborers and resisting any new comprehensive reform that would jeopardize their own interests and those of their political and economic backers.

NOMADISM AND PASTORALISM

Qashqa'i nomadic pastoralists had herded their sheep and goats seasonally between lowlands and highlands, distances of 200 to 600 km each way, and exploited the pastoral resources along the routes. They spent approximately four months in lowland winter pastures, two months migrating in the spring to highland summer pastures, three to four months residing there, and two to three months migrating in the autumn back to lowland winter pastures. These migrations were not merely passages between two regions, for the vegetation along the way, especially in spring, was a vital part of the animals' sustenance. Also, seasonal pastures did not provide sufficient natural grazing and water to support the nomads and their animals for periods beyond a specific season. Once arriving in winter or summer pastures, the nomads did not stay in one location for the season. Rather, they moved periodically from place to place within these areas and the periphery to seek fresh grazing, better access to water and other natural resources, and clean campsites and to change campmates and neighbors.

Most Qashqa'i people had spent the year traveling in these ways and residing in goat-hair tents wherever they set up camp. Diverse and flexible patterns had always emerged, however, as people made ongoing individual and group decisions to continue, adjust, or change their current modes of livelihood, residence, and lifestyle. For example, even by the 1970s some Qashqa'i lived in huts or small rudimentary houses in winter or summer pastures

and migrated in the spring and autumn. Some resided in tents and did not migrate at all. Others inhabited villages in the winter and tents at higher altitudes in the summer. Some Qashqa'i lived in tents and practiced only agriculture, while others occupied houses and practiced only pastoralism. Some families divided their labor between pastoral and agricultural ventures and their residences between nomads' camps and fixed settlements. And some Qashqa'i migrated without having any sheep and goats. All these patterns and the more standard ones described above could change on a yearly and even a seasonal basis. For any single local group, the specific patterns its members created during a year were never to be exactly replicated. It is sometimes difficult, therefore, to document and date the emergence of any particular change or trend, because activities occurring one year might not recur the next. Of course some developments, such as increased use of motorized vehicles, are possible to document. Even using this example, however, few changes are irreversible, for a man buying a pickup truck one year might sell it the next for income to purchase more sheep.

By the late 1970s many nomads had found the autumn's trek lasting two to three months to be too strenuous and troublesome for their sheep and goats. The routes they had taken that season usually followed the valley bottoms where grazing and water were most likely to be located. Pastoral resources along the route that time of the year had become increasingly scarce, and expanding human settlements and agrarian activity as well as heavy traffic on newly asphalted roads forced the nomads to take strenuous and time-consuming detours. In response, many nomads began to hire trucks to transport their animals in a single day. This change put new stress on the pastoral resources of their summer and winter territories on which they now depended for longer periods than before. Remaining in summer pastures longer than in the past, beyond the time when natural vegetation was nearly depleted, they increasingly relied on cultivating, purchasing, storing, and transporting supplemental animal feed. They also entered winter pastures well before they had gone there in the past, exploited natural growth that they had formerly conserved until later in the season, and cultivated, bought, and stored quantities of fodder there as well. Those nomads who could not afford the high cost of truck rentals, who wanted to avoid the expense, or who had other reasons (such as insufficient grazing in winter areas) accompanied their animals on the customary overland autumn migration.

The newly growing natural vegetation along the migratory route in the spring was too lush and beneficial to bypass, especially because it usually cost nothing, and so almost all pastoralists continued to send their animals by hoof during that season. Their routes then took them along the lower mountain slopes, and usually not the valleys, and they avoided the settlements, agrarian areas, and vehicular traffic that troubled them during the autumn trek. As they traveled from one point on the route to the next, each new one usually at a slightly higher altitude, they found fresh growth. On a slightly accelerated schedule, they entered summer pastures several weeks sooner than in the past, but the natural vegetation there was usually adequate for their herds then. Their early use of these plants decrease the pasturage available later in the season, when they also needed it. They enhanced methods they had previously employed to conserve and protect vegetation, by means of careful scheduling and rotation, removing rocks to encourage plant growth, creating physical barriers, and guarding against encroachers in protected and other areas.

Until the late 1970s most nomads had relied on camels and other pack animals (mules, donkeys, horses) to carry their goat-hair tents and other household possessions semiannually between winter and summer pastures. Since then, many people have sold their camels and many of their other pack animals because of their new reliance on motorized transportation. Although increasingly expensive because of rapid national inflation, the use of such vehicles (pickup trucks, larger trucks, jeeps, Land Rovers, motorcycles) did offer many obvious benefits. Also, tending the camels during winter and summer, when the animals' services were not in much demand, had become burdensome and expensive even for those able to hire specialized herders.

Twice a year many families now contracted with truck owners in nearby towns to carry their possessions to the other seasonal pastures. Formerly the herds, pack animals, possessions, and people of individual households had followed the same schedules and routes together for the semiannual treks, but now the sheep, goats, and remaining pack animals usually traveled separately from most people for part of the spring. Accompanied by shepherds and donkeys carrying only the supplies the men would need during the one-month-or-so trek, the herds followed their customary meandering routes through the mountains and valleys. Most herders' families stayed behind in seasonal pastures, then traveled directly by newly asphalted roads in trucks carrying all their household goods. Changes in dairy production were one result of these new activities, for the women and girls previously present to milk the ewes and nanny goats and process the products did not accompany the herds. To the detriment of people's diets and needs for income, dairy production was delayed until people and animals were reunited in summer pastures. Care of the

lambs and kids during the spring migration was another problem, for they could not accompany the adult animals without special supervision. Now committed to formal education and restricted by school schedules, the children who had formerly tended the young animals rarely migrated with the herds. The solution most pastoralists devised was to postpone mating and hence births or to keep the young animals and their mothers behind in winter pastures and then transport them by truck to summer pastures when the herds migrating overland arrived there.

The increasing availability of rapid transportation facilitated the nomads' further economic diversification. A family could engage in a variety of activities simultaneously as long as at least one person could travel from one location to another quickly. For example, a man could irrigate his newly planted apple orchard for the twelve-hour period stipulated by those with whom he shared water rights, and then he could return to camp by motorcycle in time to accompany the sheep he had selected to be driven to market by a hired truck. Another man could transport freshly harvested alfalfa from summer pastures to winter ones in anticipation of the herds' early arrival there while his son managed the animals during his brief absence. Trips to town for errands, health care, and government business were no longer as onerous and time-consuming.

The absence of camels and the decrease of other pack animals freed up some kinds of natural pasturage for sheep and goats, although camels had usually consumed plants that were too thorny, tough, or tall for the other animals, especially sheep. One type of single-stemmed thorny plant in particular was no longer grazed by any animals, and it grew to apparently unprecedented heights, two or more meters, and appeared to be taking over some areas of summer pastures to the detriment of other vegetation. With no camels to graze them, thorny bushes also proliferated, but in this case, by providing shade, erosion control, and protection for young plants, they supported the opportunistic growth of the surrounding low-lying vegetation that the sheep and goats preferred. Their populations expanding, small animals such as birds, rodents, rabbits, weasels, lizards, toads, and snakes found shelter in and around these bushes.

Slow-burning dried camel dung used to provide an important fuel for all pastoralists but was no longer available when they sold these animals. They eventually bought propane-gas burners and lanterns and kerosene heaters when they saw that natural fuels (wood, charcoal, brush) were not nearly sufficient for their many needs (cooking, bread baking, milk processing, wool dyeing, lighting, heating).

In the 1960s and 1970s the shah's government had tried by various means to impede or prevent the nomads' migrations. After 1979, by contrast, the new Islamic government adopted supportive policies. Its agencies, especially the new Ministry of Rural Reconstruction, seeded many areas along major migratory routes and posted durable signs explaining their intentions. Officials chose locations where many pastoralists camped overnight during the migration, especially in the spring, so that the herd and pack animals could fortify themselves for the next day's journey without trespassing on anyone's personal or group grazing lands. According to local reports, the apparently successful program resulted in decreased pressure on other pastoral resources and fewer conflicts along the routes.

Also offered by the new government at low or no cost to the nomads, modern veterinary medicine played a major role in the pastoralists' ability to keep their animals alive and healthy and less subject to the catastrophic diseases that used to wipe out entire herds. The Ministry of Rural Reconstruction created regional veterinary clinics where the pastoralists could bring their animals for treatment and preventive care, and government-paid specialists also frequently toured seasonal pastures to inoculate animals and dispense drugs and services.

One apparent result of the increasingly widespread use of modern veterinary care was the pastoralists' decreased use of ritual and symbolic acts to achieve these same ends. Until the 1980s most people had conducted rituals, offered prayers, and employed amulets to protect and care for their animals. Of course they had also relied on many practical methods, but they still faced constantly the diseases and accidents that routine care did not necessarily prevent. In the 1990s many rituals were not observed at all or only by those individuals who still believed in their efficacy. Many prized rams in 2002 were still outfitted with carved wooden talismans decorated by multicolored braided tassels, but some nomads stated that these charms simply added beauty to the animals, reminded people of customary Qashqa'i practices, and did not offer any real protection. Almost all pastoralists did continue to abide by their notions of auspicious and inauspicious days of the week in order to avoid jeopardizing acts central to their livelihood such as branding, shearing wool, transporting sheep to market, and dividing herds between fathers and newly independent sons. People still talked about the rain ceremonies they used to perform and the other rituals that marked the critical stages of the seasonal round and safeguarded the animals, but by the mid-1990s most people did not actually engage in them, and children rarely knew anything about them (see Beck 1991).

A low-cost life insurance program for sheep and goats was introduced by state-run banks in 1996. Its immediate drawbacks were the complicated requirements for physical proof of an animal's accidental or unplanned death and for impartial witnesses to the circumstances. These requirements were especially difficult, even impossible, to meet during the migrations when many of the unexpected deaths occurred.

Since 1979 the new government paid special attention to building new roads and improving existing ones in Qashqa'i territory—especially in remote places—and in surrounding areas. A mixed blessing for the pastoralists, these roads assisted them in their new or increased reliance on motorized transportation and their efforts to carry products to and from markets (including supplies for construction—see below). But the roads also allowed outsiders to enter their territories more frequently, thereby increasing the competition over pastoral and agricultural land, water, and other resources. New and improved roads opened previously unexploited areas to outsiders wanting to tap water resources, plant orchards, engage in mechanized agriculture, and hunt game animals. Urban, middle-class, Persian tourists also took advantage of the new roads—and the territories' greater military security—to invade seasonal pastures for picnics and outings on Fridays and other holidays. Anxious to flee the city's heat, dirt, crowds, and costly entertainments, these unwelcome visitors presumed upon the customarily offered hospitality of their reluctant Qashqa'i hosts (Beck 1982, 1991).

Commercial stock-breeding and commercial animal contracts involving non-Qashqa'i people had been a significant feature of pastoralism in southwestern Iran in the 1960s and 1970s. By the early 1980s commercial stock owned by non-Qashqa'i urban entrepreneurs and tended by hired and often non-tribal herders had virtually disappeared from Qashqa'i territory. Causing this change were newly enforced government regulations about the illegal use of nationalized pastures and difficulties with the economics of this kind of animal husbandry. Also, the Qashqa'i, disarmed by the shah since the early 1960s but immediately rearmed during the revolution, were now better able to guard and defend their own pastoral resources. Commercial animal contracts, under which non-Qashqa'i urban merchants and moneylenders became part owners of the nomads' herds because of the nomads' unpaid and deepening debts, had also decreased in number and by the 1990s were rare. This change resulted in part because new government regulations covering moneylending and interest-taking forced at least a temporary refiguring of debts according to what were said to be Islamic principles. The government's revolutionary guards publicly flogged the most abusive moneylenders.[4] Many pastoralists were able to renegotiate their existing debts, and they undertook new loans under revised terms. (They were now also eligible for low-interest loans for specific projects from state-run banks.) Interest rates declined, and debts did not escalate in the way they had done before the revolution. Because of meat and dairy shortages in regional and national markets, prices rose for the pastoralists' commodities, and their needs for loans and credit thereby decreased.

The absence of or significant decrease in sheep and goats belonging to outsiders significantly improved the quantity and quality of pastoral resources for the Qashqa'i users. The numbers of herd animals owned by the Qashqa'i as a whole did not increase and, in fact, may have decreased as part of the process of settlement and the adoption of new livelihoods.

AGRICULTURE

The legal status of land classified as "cultivable" was not yet resolved in many areas of Qashqa'i territory and the periphery in 2002. Disputes were common, and many pastoralists were insecure about their own and others' rights and claims.

Agricultural production in Qashqa'i territory had rapidly increased since the 1960s, both by outsiders able to appropriate land in the area and by the Qashqa'i themselves. Sections of winter and summer pastures and many areas along the migratory routes became cultivated. In the uplands above water channels, crops depended on moisture from seasonal rain and snow. Downhill, below water channels, crops were often irrigated. Much pastoral land, never plowed before, was now transformed into agricultural land and became off-limits during the growing and harvest seasons to the pastoralists' herd and pack animals. Even where the pastoralists themselves added or enlarged their own areas of cultivation, the land became lost or diminished as a viable pastoral resource, at least until after the harvests. Natural pasture was permanently destroyed, and the stubble of harvested crops provided only temporary grazing. Villagers and landowners who expanded the land they cultivated in and near seasonal pastures and along migratory routes were often aided by mechanized equipment, such as tractors and harvesting and threshing machines, and they improved their own supply of water by excavating underground water channels (qanats), digging wells, installing motorized pumps, and constructing irrigation systems. As villages expanded in population size and land use, their inhabitants denuded the surrounding terrain of viable pastoral and other natural resources. The nomads found that they were increasingly forced to travel circuitous or indirect routes in order to avoid these growing settlements and locate adequate grazing and water.[5]

The creation and expansion of fruit orchards throughout these regions of southwestern Iran was a major part of these changes. The trees planted in summer pastures were mostly apple, apricot, cherry, mulberry, walnut, almond, and pistachio, while in winter pastures, an area of high summer heat and dryness, they were primarily date, lime, lemon, orange, and pomegranate. Many villagers also grew grapes and figs, especially in areas between winter and summer pastures. People with claims to land and access to sufficient water planted saplings and vines, constructed irrigation works, erected protective walls, and committed themselves—knowingly or not—to a dependence on chemical fertilizers and pesticides. The sources of water they enclosed included natural springs, wells, and the mouths of qanat channels, which were thereby now off-limits to the pastoralists both traveling through the area and resident in nearby seasonal pastures. When I asked pastoralists in the 1990s to tell me the single most troubling difficulty threatening their main livelihood, many answered, "orchards."

To handle these and other problems, most pastoralists tried to increase the production of fodder crops for their animals and wheat for household use. (Unleavened flat bread made from wheat flour remained the people's staple food.) During times of inadequate rain and snow, naturally growing vegetation was insufficient for the herd and pack animals, for which quantities of supplemental feed were required. This feed included barley, straw, and fresh and dried alfalfa, clover, and hay. The prices of these commodities rose rapidly during times of poor moisture because of scarcity; crops grew poorly under such conditions, and the regional demand for them increased, especially from settled people who also owned animals but who lacked much if any access to natural pasturage. Hence, the pastoralists fortunate enough to have available land, water, seed, labor, draft animals, machinery (in some cases), and time tried to produce as much fodder as possible, to avoid high and often escalating market prices, without jeopardizing other aspects of their livelihood. In recording household budgets, I noted that barley and alfalfa comprised the single largest annual expense for many pastoralists. Dried sugar-beet pulp, a by-product of the region's sugar factories and used widely in the 1970s as fodder, was no longer much used in the 1980s and 1990s, even though still available, because of its apparent lack of adequate nutrients. Many pastoralists in winter pastures in the early 2000s added corn and acorns as important sources of food for their hungry animals. They purchased corn from cultivators and collected acorns from distant wild-oak forests.

Increased cultivation in and near Qashqa'i territory did offer several other important advantages to Qashqa'i pastoralists. Overall, however, these benefits did not replace those of the natural pasturage permanently lost because of expanding agriculture and related factors.

The main advantage for the pastoralists in the expansion of their own and others' cultivation was their ability to graze animals on the stubble and other crop residues after the harvests were completed. Because of the mountainous terrain and the different altitudes where cultivation was practiced, the pastoralists herded their animals from one elevation to another in order to exploit sequential harvests. Remaining in their summer territories beyond the point when natural pasturage was depleted, the pastoralists came to rely heavily on the remnants in these fields. Sometimes they could exploit this resource without cost, but increasingly they were forced to pay rent to the cultivators, even arranging for the transaction months ahead when the demand and competition were likely to be great. Mechanized harvesters and combines, increasingly used in wide flat areas relatively free of large stones and other obstructions, left the stalks of harvested crops standing as high as fifteen centimeters, which the pastoralists used for grazing. Hired by large-scale cultivators and often-absentee landowners, the drivers and laborers using mechanized methods of harvesting often did not bother about the quantities of grain either left unharvested (such as along field edges and around rocky outcroppings) or spilled on the ground, and the pastoralists' animals gleaned the remains. By contrast, the cultivators who harvested grain by hand sickles cut the stalks close to the ground in order to maximize their own supply of fodder and hence left little for ruminants. Harvesting by hand was still a widespread practice in southwestern Iran in 2002 , especially in mountainous and other physically restricted areas and by those unable to afford the machine owners' escalating rental fees.

Another new advantageous factor—this one related to expanded irrigation—was the lush, wild, and opportunistic vegetation growing along the verges of cultivated fields, between trees in orchards, and beside water channels and catchment basins. The pastoralists grazed their animals on the live plants, cut armfuls and filled gunnysacks to take to the animals, and dried and stored quantities for use later on. The spaces between the plants of some crops, such as irrigated pulses and dry-farmed barley, allowed the pastoralists to collect other vegetation growing wild there. They competed for these resources with the cultivators, who also needed animal fodder or who wanted to sell it for a profit. The pastoralists and cultivators contested the ownership and control of these resources just as they contested the ownership and control of the land and water. The pastoralists claimed, often correctly, that the cultivators had illegally usurped the land, and hence the pastoralists were entitled, at the very least, to any wild vegetation growing there. The cultivators asserted that their own labor had created this wild vegetation, and hence it belonged to them.

In the 1970s and 1980s, some far-sighted pastoralists had planted poplar trees in summer pastures in order to use the trunks as roof beams and other supportive structures for the houses they expected they would ultimately build there. During mid-autumn and mid-spring, unhampered by the heavy snows of winter, trespassers sometimes cut down these unguarded trees for their own use or just out of spite, especially when tension between cultivators and pastoralists was high.

MANAGEMENT OF WATER

Changes also occurred in the management of water. Until the early 1970s most pastoralists in this large stretch of the southern Zagros mountains had relied, without much human intervention, on the natural sources of water available. In winter pastures they sometimes deepened or fortified naturally occurring shallow basins to collect seasonal rainfall and runoff for the animals, while in summer pastures they dug shallow trenches to direct the flow of water from natural springs to the small pools they excavated. The areas the pastoralists improved in these ways did not need much maintenance from year to year. They always tried to find clean spring or well water for drinking, food preparing, milk processing, and wool dyeing. Women and children aided by pack animals loaded down with goat-skin bags spent time and effort traveling to and from the nearest sources. An area of seasonal and unpredictable water, winter pastures were more troublesome than summer pastures, an area of many natural springs.

Since the early 1980s the managing of water became more labor intensive and expensive, and the new government offered assistance. Officials of the Organization for Nomads' Affairs (part of the new Ministry of Rural Reconstruction) were instrumental in transforming water use for Qashqa'i pastoralists. With aid also from the Ministry of Agriculture, these officials helped some people to secure low-interest bank loans and low-cost or subsidized construction supplies (such as cement and gravel) and assisted them in acquiring land-use permits from the agency responsible for Iran's natural resources. In many areas, pastoralists together with hired specialists and workers dug wells, built or repaired *qanats,* and constructed cement channels and catchment basins, all of which they hoped would deliver a reliable supply of clean water. In winter pastures where springs are not common, government agencies dug many wells in convenient locations. They also constructed covered reservoirs and delivered large metal tanks and periodically filled them with clean water from tankers, at low or no cost to the pastoralists. Overgrazing in these areas was not much of a problem because shepherds led their animals to drink and then immediately returned to their own grazing lands.

Some of these recent efforts to manage water caused at least a temporary and possibly a longer-term or even a permanent decrease in water in the vicinity. In some areas of summer pastures, many natural springs dried up in 1997 after the previous winter's sparse snow and rain. The following winter's snow and rain replenished the ground water and restored the flow of some of these springs, although at decreased levels. Pessimistic, many residents blamed the nearby non-Qashqa'i cultivators and their overexploitation of ground water for the death or decline of the springs. Where large-scale orchard owners and cultivators, mostly non-Qashqa'i outsiders, dug deep wells and installed motorized pumps, a lowered water table resulted. According to residents and observers, once the pumps began to operate, water in the vicinity never returned to its previous levels and quantities. In 1997 many orchards held dead, dying, stunted, or fruitless trees due to insufficient irrigation water, although whether this condition came about primarily because of the year's low levels of precipitation or because of a longer term lowering of the water table was not clear. Many authors, including English (1998), note that deep wells in arid and semiarid areas, which extract water beyond replacement levels, fail to increase agricultural production and are in fact an ecological threat.

CONSTRUCTION OF SHELTERS
Human dwellings, accompanying structures, and animal pens and shelters also altered the landscape of areas formerly inhabited only by the seasonal, mobile tents of nomads. These changes are explained by the processes of development and modernization and by the nomads' insecurity about their claims to land.

The building of dwellings accompanied a general rise in the standard of living for most Qashqa'i people, who also wanted to protect and shelter the new kinds of possessions they now owned (such as propane-gas burners and metal looms). Many pastoralists, even those who were fully nomadic year-round, chose to construct huts and houses for themselves and pens and shelters for their animals in winter and/or summer pastures. While some invested equally in construction in winter and in summer pastures, others favored one locale over the other, a decision influenced by the choices made by other members of the social and tribal groups of which they were a part. They all focused their efforts on the locations where they expected they might live more permanently. Each area had major and often debilitating climatic drawbacks, however, mainly severe heat and aridity in winter pastures during the summer and oppressive cold and snow in summer pastures during the winter.

When the pastoralists saw that their new or improved dwellings were likely to be vandalized during the seasons when they were absent, they cut back on some of their efforts and investments. For example, they decided to buy previously used, inexpensive wooden and metal doors and window frames when the new ones they had purchased and installed were roughly pried away from the walls and stolen by trespassers. Even though they always stored miscellaneous, often bulky, equipment and supplies in these dwellings when they departed for their other seasonal pastures, they learned not to lock the doors. The cost to repair the damage that thieves and vandals caused by breaking locks, doors, and windows was sometimes greater than the cost or effort of replacing any stolen items. They did find that these dwellings were periodically lived in during their absence, and they resented the unwelcome intrusions.

Using locally available rocks for the foundations and tree branches, long bundled reeds, and woven-reed mats for the walls and roofs, many men built simple one-room huts for their families in winter pastures to help protect them from the winter's rain, snow, mud, wind, and cold. (The pastoralists who remained part or all of the summer in winter pastures also used such huts then, rather than their goat-hair tents whose fabric would be destroyed by prolonged exposure to the heat and intense sunlight at this low altitude.) Some men built more substantial huts by also using cement mixed with gravel, sand, or dirt for mortar and flooring; rocks, cement, and plaster for the walls; and wooden beams for the roofs. They often talked about how miserable life had been in past winters when only airy goat-hair tents sheltered them. Their perception of the nomadic life's rigors seemed to have changed, especially when they compared their limited physical comfort in the winter with the higher degree of comfort enjoyed by their protected, house-dwelling relatives.

Many nomads also built more substantial one-room or two-room houses in summer pastures. They did not need physical shelter as much in the summer, when the weather is dry and usually mild, but because they have recently chosen to arrive there earlier in the spring and to stay later in the summer, they did desire more protective shelter during these two, often cold and windy, periods. People with increased agricultural activities, more prevalent in most summer pastures than in most winter ones, had to be present there for a longer duration than in the past. Those owning trees or vines bearing fruit needed to collect or oversee the autumn's harvests, whose schedules varied from year to year depending on climatic conditions.

People who improved their access to water also wanted to live nearby on a more permanent basis. Until the late 1970s the nomads had moved periodically from place to place within seasonal pastures to find fresh grazing and clean campsites, but more recently they have remained in specific locations, often to exploit the water over which they now claimed greater rights. Needing to travel farther and farther away from camp every day to locate adequate grazing, shepherds and herd animals were burdened by these more stationary residential practices.

The pastoralists' decreased reliance on hired shepherds, due largely to their scarcity and expense, figured in their decisions to construct pens and shelters where they could temporarily leave their animals unsupervised. At night and periodically during the day, sheep and goats in summer pastures and sometimes in winter ones had rested and slept in the open, often on patches of unprotected terrain, and hence were subject to predators' attacks and stampeding if the owners and shepherds were not vigilant enough. Since the late 1970s, many households were forced to devise new ways of handling the actual herding and daily animal care, largely because of the scarcity of hired shepherds in the region. Reflecting the shortage, shepherds' salaries rapidly escalated, making the hiring of herders even more problematic and forcing the nomads to rely on more protective pens and shelters. In the 1990s many families were again hiring shepherds because their increasingly diversifying economies meant shortages in household labor, a situation exacerbated by more of their children attending school, continuing beyond the primary level, and seeking employment in the larger society. Willing to work for low wages, many of the new shepherds were non-Qashqa'i men and boys from the surrounding regions and even Afghan refugees. In 2000 I was astonished to see that some pastoralists in winter pastures left their sheep and goats unattended for long periods during the day while they handled other matters. Free to graze surrounding pastures, the animals—the slow-witted sheep led by the more attentive goats—responded to people whistling for them to return to camp for supplemental feed. Their owners outfitted many of them, and not just the lead ones, with bells so that they would be alerted if stampeding, straying, or other mishaps occurred. Hired shepherds were once again scarce and expensive.

Greater use of animal pens also aided the pastoralists by concentrating the accumulation of dung, which they all periodically collected to use as fertilizer in their orchards and fields or to sell to others. Mounds of dung stood beside the pens to await transport.

Many pastoralists also built huts, houses, and animal shelters in their seasonal pastures because of their insecurity about land rights. By 2002 the government had still not passed the land-reform legislation that was promised soon after the revolution in 1979, and the pastoralists asserted that the existence of permanent structures would help them to fortify their claims to the land in any eventuality. Dwellings offered "hard facts" to touring government agents assigned to handle disputes over land.

HUNTING AND GATHERING

Patterns of hunting and gathering, which also affect the environment, continued in the 1990s and early 2000s in many of the same ways as in the 1960s and before. The major changes include the use of firearms and the decreased exploitation of natural resources along the migratory routes.

The shah had forcibly disarmed the Qashqa'i in the 1960s because of his fear about their military and political threat to him. With his ouster in 1979, many Qashqa'i men immediately rearmed themselves and resumed game hunting in their territories. The climate of freedom also excited other Iranians who enjoyed hunting. Within a year or two of the revolution, these hunters and the local residents complained that the most prized game animals in southwestern Iran had been exterminated. The game included wild sheep and goats, ibex, gazelles and other antelopes, and deer—in fact, any animals with horns to be valued or displayed as trophies. Several wildlife preserves created by the shah in the southern Zagros mountains were decimated after his removal, the few game wardens still coming to work profiting from bribes and even partaking in the slaughter themselves. Many Qashqa'i men claimed to have practiced wildlife conservation in the past, but their efforts after the revolution were pointless, given the many outsiders eager to shoot any and all wildlife. Qashqa'i men had grown up learning the mountaineering skills necessary to hunt in this rugged terrain and to retrieve the game after they had pursued and shot it, skills many urbanites and other outsiders lacked. These outsiders often shot animals that they left dead, dying, or wounded where they fell, and hence the activity was simply sport and not, as in the Qashqa'i case, also an important source of food. Qashqa'i hunters continued to track wild boars, bears, mountain lions, wolves, foxes, hyenas, and other predators preying on their flocks, and, as before, they avidly sought wild game birds (partridges, quail) to consume as food. Those living near lakes and rivers hunted water fowl and fished. At least a few men found the use of dynamite to be an effective way to capture quantities of fish with little effort.

The gathering of many natural resources was still a major part of the subsistence and economy of the Qashqa'i in 2002. In fact, reliance on these items allowed some families to continue with migratory pastoralism when they would otherwise have lacked adequate food or income. Their herds might have been too small to sustain them, and they might have lacked land and water rights for cultivation and other means of producing supplementary income. Dairy products for home consumption were available only in the spring and part of the summer (except for limited quantities of dried milk solids saved for the winter), and hence all pastoralists enjoyed, if not depended on, the many foods they gathered throughout the year. The seasonal residents of winter and summer pastures, and their settled kin and other tribal affiliates who came to visit, continued to exploit their own and surrounding territories for many kinds of foods for people (wild fruits, nuts, vegetables, herbs, mushrooms, truffles, bird eggs), animal fodder, medicines, salt, dyes, fuels, and raw materials (wood, reeds) for tools and other constructed objects. Most of these items were seasonal in nature, and the pastoralists sought them according to their fine-tuned skills and their expertise about schedules and techniques.

Because most people not responsible for daily herding now traveled by truck between winter and summer pastures, they were no longer able to gather the many natural resources along the migratory routes. The often newly paved roads they followed bypassed the remote valleys and mountainsides where most resources were now located. Those having acquaintances in villages along the migratory routes were eventually able to barter for some items, and itinerant peddlers traded others. People who visited these areas always collected, acquired, and bartered for the resources that were unique or special there and later shared them with others. The men who led the sheep and goats on the migrations gathered what they could, but their time was occupied by herding and safeguarding the animals, and they lacked the means to process or to transport quantities of gathered resources.[6]

The non-Qashqa'i people who used to gather natural resources before the 1980s in Qashqa'i territory, primarily for sale but also for their own consumption, came less frequently or not at all in the 1990s and early 2000s because of government sanctions against them. These resources included wood (for fuel, making charcoal, and construction), wild fruits and nuts, herbs and many other plants includ-

ing wild artichokes, mushrooms, truffles, garlic, dyes, and tree and shrub saps including the gum tragacanth exported abroad. Guided by western-inspired notions of environmental protection, the agency responsible for Iran's natural resources was supposed to control or eliminate these activities on what was usually nationalized pastureland, but it had not been successful under the shah's regime. Under the Islamic government, the agency was more effective in preventing outsiders from exploiting Qashqa'i pastures in these ways or in limiting their numbers. Collectors of gum tragacanth, for example, could buy government permits enabling them to exploit certain territories if they also obtained the approval of the resident pastoralists. Qashqa'i people, many of whom relied on selling and consuming these same resources, collected them on their own lands and were not harassed by government agents if they could demonstrate land titles or usufructuary deeds.

Because of the increasingly widespread use of electricity and propane and natural gas by many people in southwestern Iran, including some rural areas, the regional demand for firewood and charcoal significantly decreased. The agency responsible for natural resources tried to protect the environment from further deforestation and depletion of other natural resources. Until the revolution, the agency's forest rangers had patrolled sections of Qashqa'i territory but were susceptible to bribery and did not appear to have restricted the ways people exploited the land. Since the early 1980s their activities have focused instead on pursuing the claims that local residents brought against trespassers engaged in destructive acts.

Aided now by motorized vehicles, many Qashqa'i pastoralists transported quantities of firewood from winter pastures to summer ones, where wood was scarce or unavailable and where camel dung, formerly used as the primary fuel there, was no longer found. Although most of them now used propane gas for some cooking and other tasks, its cost was expensive and the transport and refilling of canisters sometimes problematic. People still favored firewood and charcoal for many practical purposes (grilling meat, milk processing, dyeing wool, branding young animals, and other chores requiring a long-term continuous source of heat) and for cultural and aesthetic reasons (keeping a ceramic teapot hot and sitting around an open fire at night).

THE GOVERNMENT

The government continued to play a major role in the 1990s and early 2000s in determining who resided on and worked which parcels of land, but in some ways different from the government in the 1960s and 1970s. The Islamic government supported people it classified as "nomads" (*ashayer*) and offered them services that the previous two shahs (1925–1979) had refused to provide (Tapper [1994] and Beck [N.D.] discuss the activities of the Organization for Nomads' Affairs). Short-term and long-term leases for land still classified as "pastures," as well as leases and ownership deeds for land still considered as "cultivable," were obtained by many people through various state ministries and agencies. People who chose to reside in villages and especially in towns found it difficult to hold onto pastoral and agricultural land in their customary seasonal territories. Some families divided their labor force in order to retain rights to land. As an example of an increasingly prevalent pattern found within extended families, one man migrated between winter and summer pastures with the sheep and goats and maintained the family's pasture-use deeds, while his brother lived in a village to cultivate grain and fodder crops on land he rented or purchased, and a third brother resided in a town to work for wages in a factory or a government office.

Government ministries and agencies also aided the pastoralists by building roads and bathhouses in remote areas and by offering veterinary care, animal life insurance, pasture seeding, water management, bank loans, commodity pricing, economic cooperatives, and formal education. Many state agents, especially in ministries having special interests in nomads and pastoralists, were of ethnic, tribal, nomadic, and pastoral backgrounds and had often been born and raised as nomadic pastoralists themselves. They had benefited from the government's expansion of formal education into tribal areas and had continued their education in towns and cities. Now employed as state agents, they tended to be supportive of and sympathetic to the needs of people who perpetuated nomadic and pastoral lifestyles despite difficulties, and they were effective in delivering services throughout the 1980s, 1990s, and early 2000s. When I asked Qashqa'i people about the changes in their relationship with the government after the revolution, many responded by noting that people with backgrounds and identities similar to their own were now state officials and agents who supported rather than hindered or oppressed them.

Some officials of the Islamic government were fascinated by people in Iran whom they considered to be exotic or picturesque. While the last two shahs had feared many of these same groups of people for the military and political threat they were believed to have posed, the current government appeared to be less concerned. The Ayatollah Khomeini had even declared that nomads were the "treasures of the revolution," a statement often quoted by state agents (despite these nomads having played virtually no role in revolutionary activities). While providing such people with many beneficial services, the Islamic government also developed programs to use them for its own purposes. For example, in the 1980s and 1990s a national, annual Day of the Nomad, organized by the officials responsible for delivering state services to the nomads, was officially celebrated in different regions by provincial dignitaries and spectators to mark the many contributions of nomads to Iran's history, economy, and cultural diversity. Recorded on videotape and later broadcast on national television, these elaborate events included poetry, music, and demonstrations of indigenous lifestyles and technologies (such as weaving). These and other government-sponsored or -supported projects about nomads, including publications, films, and conferences, were designed to provide appealing images for a national and sometimes an international audience. For example, the film *Gabbeh,* which focuses on a story relating to Qashqa'i weaving, has been especially popular among western viewers (see Makhmalbaf and Ahmadi 1996). Among other reasons, these publicized images were aimed to moderate the harsh views that many foreigners had developed about Iranians in general.

Apparently unintentionally, and perhaps ironically, such official attention helped the Qashqa'i (and other similar groups) to pursue their chosen lifestyles, which for many remained a combination of pastoralism and nomadism, and to engage in customary practices that these officials now considered meaningful, authentic, colorful, or quaint (depending on their outlook). For example, many Qashqa'i women maintained—and were allowed to maintain—their customary dress and head gear, despite the attire's violating the requirements of modest "Islamic" dress imposed on almost all other Iranian women, especially in urban areas.

THE MARKET ECONOMY
The impact of the market economy is another important factor in understanding the ways the Qashqa'i people used land. They had always directed their productive activities toward market demands and not just toward household consumption. When the price of sheep and goats was considered favorable, they focused more attention on animal husbandry. When regional needs for agricultural products were great, they tried to produce their own and relied on the market for the purchase of more. Market demands for the pastoralists' dairy products, other pastoral produce (woven goods, sheep wool, goat hair, skins), and gathered resources also played a role in determining the economic decisions that households made on a daily, seasonal, and yearly basis.

Since the revolution, especially during and since the Iraq-Iran war (1980–1988), national inflation was high and rising, and all Iranians, not just Qashqa'i pastoralists, were forced to change their patterns of production and consumption. In the middle and late 1990s and early 2000s most Qashqa'i people were financially unable to change in any significant way the methods by which they exploited the land, such as adopting new mechanized agricultural equipment and installing irrigation systems. Even commonplace construction materials such as bricks and cement were sometimes scarce and prohibitively expensive. Qashqa'i and other producers of essential market commodities were especially affected by volatile and unpredictable economic trends. The election of a new, moderate president of Iran in 1997 brought hopes that the national economy would be brought under greater control, but these hopes were largely unrealized by 2002, even after his re-election in 2001.

The pastoralists complained that the prices they received for live sheep and goats did not rise as rapidly as the costs of the goods they needed to buy, especially those essential to the pursuit of a viable livelihood. They were especially disturbed by meat prices and the high mark-up from the amount they received per kilogram at government slaughterhouses to the amount customers paid in urban butcher shops. The government and a series of middlemen, and not the actual producers, apparently derived the most profit from the pastoralists' enterprise. (Although not legally required to sell their animals at government slaughterhouses or through other government programs, the pastoralists had few other means by which they could quickly sell many animals at a time and at a dependable, fixed price.) In some years the pastoralists incurred more expenses for tending the animals than they received for their sale. Those fortunate to have other sources of income, especially fruit orchards, found that these activities were sometimes necessary to finance or subsidize the herd animals' care. In the mid-1990s the rates of return from fruit orchards were much higher than those from animal husbandry. Often unpredictable fluctuations in prices, however, meant that any and all economic ventures were risky. For example, a regional abundance of apples in 1995 caused a sharp decline in their prices, while a sparse crop in the same area in 1998 resulted in elevated prices.

Why pastoralists would continue with migratory animal husbandry when the venture was sometimes a losing proposition is also explained by other factors: their dislike and distrust of potential alternative occupations (such as wage labor among the rural and urban proletariat), their pride in their tribal and ethnic identities (which their physical and social separation from non-Qashqa'i society

enhanced), and the cultural values they have historically placed on their livelihood and lifestyle. Even in the 1980s, 1990s, and early 2000s most Qashqa'i pastoralists were still more self-sufficient economically than many other rural and especially urban people of the middle and lower classes. They consumed their own products, relied on gathering and hunting, and constructed many necessary items from locally available resources, and hence they were much less reliant on the market economy and could often avoid its inflationary prices. Residing in relatively secluded locations in the mountains, away from the costly temptations offered by towns and cities, they lived cheaply compared with many rural and urban people (including their permanently settled relatives). They were quick to list the expenses they avoided by continuing their cherished livelihoods and lifestyles.

CONCLUSION

In this chapter I outline a variety of factors that have influenced the ways that many Qashqa'i nomadic pastoralists used land during the past thirty-three years, from the late 1960s to the early 2000s, and explain how and why these patterns have or have not changed.

Certain new patterns of local social organization are largely explained by changes in people's productive activities during this thirty-three-year period. Groups of families could better exploit a larger territory in both winter and summer pastures and the periphery, use many spatially separate locations, engage in diversifying economic activities, and interact with the market economy more successfully if they devised new ways to cooperate with one another.

At a time when we understand that locally managed and controlled subsistence strategies in many parts of the world appear to be more viable, sustainable, and protective of the environment than, for example, the practices of large-scale agropastoral corporations, the case provided by the Qashqa'i people may be informative. The Qashqa'i make the best of the inherent environmental constraints of their rugged, mountainous, and semiarid lands, in ways that have served them, their ancestors, and those who preceded them for hundreds, even thousands, of years. They have also frequently adjusted the ways they related to the land, as the information in this article about the past thirty-three years demonstrates. They obviously do not blindly follow patterns simply because they practiced them in the past, nor do they ignore the consequences of the actions they take in the present. Outsiders can at least try not to impede them as they continue to find solutions to the many obstacles that confront them. One prevalent theme in the recent literature on the natural environment is concern about depletion and destruction, and the solution often proposed is the removal of people. But when we compare, for example, Qashqa'i land-use strategies with the whole-scale destruction wreaked upon the environment by warfare, multinational corporations, and nation-states eager for development, it seems nonsensical to prevent people such as the Qashqa'i from living in the ways they have found rewarding for themselves and their society.

I hope that scholars and others interested in archaeology, especially ethnoarchaeology, will draw insights from the Qashqa'i case. Offering material gathered over a thirty-three-year period, a span certainly considered short by most archaeologists, I demonstrate how much change is actually possible in this interval and analyze some of the complex explanatory factors.

Author's note and acknowledgment. I met Bill Sumner in 1969 when I first began cultural anthropological research in Iran. As director of the American Institute for Iranian Studies in Tehran, he assisted me in many ways, and his interest in the peoples of rural Fars province, whom he had encountered during his archaeological surveys and projects, coincided with mine.

I thank Yale University's Center for International and Area Studies and the Council on Middle East Studies for a stimulating conference in 1997 on Middle Eastern environments. An earlier version of this chapter appeared in the conference proceedings, *Bulletin Series, Yale School of Forestry and Environmental Studies* (Beck 1998). Linda Schilcher offered helpful comments on an early draft as did David Browman and Patty Jo Watson on a later one.

NOTES

1. For historical studies of tribal groups in Iran, see Beck (1986), Garthwaite (1983), and Tapper (1983, 1997). For comparative material on other groups of nomadic pastoralists in Iran in the pre-revolutionary period, see Barth (1961), Black-Michaud (1986), Bradburd (1990, 1998), Mortensen (1993), Salzman (1972, 1992, 1999, 2000), and Tapper (1979). Useful studies on nomadic pastoralists and tribal groups in other parts of the Middle East include Barfield (1993), Bates (1973), Chang and Koster (1994:Chs. 2, 8, 9), Chatty (1986, 1996), Cole and Altorki (1998), Dresch (1989), Eickelman (1998:Chs. 4, 6), Khazanov (1994), Khoury and Kostiner (1990), Lancaster (1997), and Layne (1994). Salzman (1980, 1996a, 1996b) and Spooner (1975) offer general studies of nomadic pastoralists and the process of settling. For studies of village life in southwestern Iran, see Friedl (1989, 1997) and E. Hooglund (1982, 1997). For an account of Qashqa'i women in postrevolutionary Iran, see Beck (2003).

2. I conducted anthropological research among Qashqa'i nomadic pastoralists in Iran in 1970–1971, 1977 (two visits), 1979, 1991, 1992, 1995 (two visits), 1996, 1997, 1998, 1999, 2000–2001, and 2001–2002. Research in the 1990s and 2000s was supported in part by grants from the National Endowment for the Humanities (1990–1993, 1998), the Social Science Research Council, the American Philosophical Society, and Washington University in St. Louis.

3. The conclusions I draw in this chapter about transformations for the Qashqa'i can be compared with those illustrated in *Atlas d'Iran* (Hourcade et al. 1998) for Iran as a whole. In several recent publications (Beck 2000, N.D.), I discuss the impact of long-term longitudinal research, as compared with short-term research, on understanding these issues.

4. Linda Schilcher (personal communication, December 1997) notes that government interventions to rescue rural people from urban entrepreneurial greed were also found elsewhere, such as in Syria under the Ottoman Empire in the 1880s and 1890s.

5. Kouchoukos et al. (1998) note certain major trends in southwestern Asia: the extension of cultivation into marginal steppe lands, the expansion of irrigation, and the degradation of the vegetation of the steppe. Unsustainable production systems, such as many forms of agriculture in arid and semiarid lands, cause the rapid depletion of resources and the destruction of the natural environment (Christensen 1998).

6. For a discussion of gathering by pastoralists in Morocco, see Steinmann (1998).

BIBLIOGRAPHY

Abdi, Kamyar

2000 Review of T.F. Potts 1994. *Journal of Near Eastern Studies* 59:277–284.

Abrahamian, Ervand

1982 *Iran Between Two Revolutions*. Princeton: Princeton University Press.

Adams, Robert McC.

1962 Agriculture and Urban Life in Early Southwestern Iran. *Science* 136:109–122.

1965 *Land behind Baghdad*. Chicago: University of Chicago Press.

1981 *Heartland of Cities*. Chicago: University of Chicago Press.

Adriaens, A., P. Veny, F. Adams, R. Sporken, P. Louette, Bryan Earl, Hadi Özbal, and K. Aslihan Yener

1999 Analytical Investigation of Archaeological Powders from Göltepe, Turkey. *Archaeometry* 41:81–89.

Ahrens, C.

1979 *Urartu, das Reich am Ararat*. Katalog Helms-Museum. Hamburg: Hamburgisches Museum für Vor- und Frühgeschichte.

Alden, John R.

1973 The Question of Trade in Proto-Elamite Iran. M.A. Thesis, Department of Anthropology, University of Pennsylvania, Philadelphia.

1979 Regional Economic Organization in Banesh Period Iran. Ph.D. Dissertation, Department of Anthropology, University of Michigan, Ann Arbor.

1982a Trade and Politics in Proto-Elamite Iran. *Current Anthropology* 23:613–640.

1982b Marketplace Exchange as Indirect Distribution: An Iranian Example. In *Contexts for Prehistoric Exchange*, edited by T. Earle and J. Ericson, 83–101. San Diego: Academic Press.

1987 The Susa III Period. In *The Archaeology of Western Iran*, edited by F. Hole, 157–170. Washington DC: Smithsonian Institution Press.

Algaze, Guillermo

1989 The Uruk Expansion, Cross-cultural Exchange in Early Mesopotamian Civilization. *Current Anthropology* 30:571–608.

1993a *The Uruk World System: The Dynamics of Expansion of Early Mesopotamian Civilization*. Chicago: University of Chicago Press.

1993b Expansionary Dynamics of Some Early Pristine States. *American Anthropologist* 95:304–333.

Algaze, Guillermo, R. Breuninger, and James Knutstad

1994 The Tigris-Euphrates Archaeological Reconnaissance Project: Final Report of the Birecik and Carchemish Dam Survey Areas. *Anatolica* 20:1–96.

Algaze, Guillermo, R. Breuninger, Christopher Lightfoot, and Michael Rosenberg

1991 The Tigris-Euphrates Archaeological Reconnaissance Project: A Preliminary Report of the 1989–1990 Seasons. *Anatolica* 17:175–240.

Algaze, Guillermo, Adnan Mısır, and T.J. Wilkinson

1992 Şanlıurfa Museum/University of California Excavations and Surveys at Titriş Höyük, 1991: A Preliminary Report. *Anatolica* 18:33–60.

Alimov, K., N. Boroffka, M. Bubnova, J. Burjakov, J. Cierny, J. Jakubov, J. Lutz, H. Parzinger, E. Pernicka, V. Ruzanov, and G. Weisgerber

1998 Vorislamische Zinngewinnung in Mittelasien. Vorbericht der Kampagne 1997. *Eurasia Antiqua* 4:137–199.

Alizadeh, Abbas

1985 A Tomb of the Neo-Elamite Period at Arjân, near Behbahan. *Archäologische Mitteilungen aus Iran* N.F. 18:49–73.

1987 A Review of *Eine Randebene des Zagros in der Frühzeit*. *Bibliotheca Orientalis* 5/6:800–806.

1988a Socio-Economic Complexity in Southwestern Iran during the Vth and IVth Millennia B.C.: The Evidence from Tall-i Bakun A. *Iran* 26:17–34.

1988b Mobile Pastoralism and the Development of Complex

Societies in Highland Iran: The Evidence from Tall-e Bakun A. Ph.D. Dissertation, Department of Near Eastern Languages and Civilizations, University of Chicago, Chicago.

1992 *Prehistoric Settlement Patterns and Cultures in Susiana, Southwestern Iran. The Analysis of the F.G.L. Gremliza Survey Collection.* Technical Reports 24. Ann Arbor: University of Michigan Museum of Anthropology.

N.D. *The Origins of State Organizations in Prehistoric Fars, Southern Iran.* Chicago: Oriental Institute of the University of Chicago. In press.

Altınlı, İ. Enver

1963 Türkiye Jeoloji Haritası, Erzurum. Ankara: Maden Tetkik Arama Enstitüsü.

Amiet, Pierre

1966a *Élam.* Auvers-sur-Oise: Archée.

1966b Il y a 5000 ans les élamites inventaient l'écriture. *Archaeologia* 12:16–23.

1972 *Glyptique susienne, des origines à l'époque des Perses achéménides.* Mémoires de la Délégation Archéologique en Iran 43. Paris: P. Geuthner.

1973a Glyptique élamite, à propos de documents nouveaux. *Arts Asiatiques* 26:3–45.

1973b La glyptique de la fin de l'Élam. *Arts Asiatiques* 28:3–32.

1976a Disjecta Membra Aelamica. *Arts Asiatiques* 32:13–28.

1976b *L'art d'Agadé au Musée du Louvre.* Paris: Éditions de la Réunion des Musées Nationaux.

1977 Appliques iraniennes. *Revue du Louvre* 27:63–69.

1979a Alternance et dualité, essai d'interprétation de l'histoire élamite. *Akkadica* 15:2–22.

1979b Archaeological Discontinuity and Ethnic Duality in Elam. *Antiquity* 53:195–204.

1980a La glyptique du second millénaire en provenance des chantiers A et B de la Ville Royale de Suse. *Iranica Antiqua* 15:133–147.

1980b Trois colliers iraniens. *Revue du Louvre,* Avril 1980, No. 2:88–90.

1980c *Art of the Ancient Near East.* New York: Harry N. Abrams.

1985 Quelques témoins des contacts de Suse avec les pays du Levant aux IIIe et IIe millénaires. In *Miscellanea Babylonica,* edited by J.-M. Durand and J.-R. Kupper, 9–12 Paris: Éditions Recherche sur les Civilisations.

1986a *L'âge des échanges inter-iraniens, 3500–1700 avant J.-C.* Notes et documents des Musées de France 11. Paris: Éditions de la Réunion des Musées Nationaux.

1986b Kassites ou Élamites? In *Insight through Images, Studies in Honor of Edith Porada,* edited by M. Kelly-Buccellati, P. Matthiae, and M. Van Loon, 1–6. Bibliotheca Mesopotamica 21. Malibu: Undena.

1988 *Suse, 6000 ans d'histoire.* Paris: Éditions de la Réunion des Musées Nationaux.

1989 Autour de Marlik. In *Archaeologia Iranica et Orientalis, Miscellanea in Honorem Louis Vanden Berghe,* edited by L. De Meyer and E. Haerinck, 311–322. Gent: Peeters Press.

1990 Marlik et Tchogha Zanbil. *Revue d'Assyriologie* 84:44–47.

1992 Sur l'histoire élamite. *Iranica Antiqua* 27:75–94.

1996 Observations sur le sceaux de Haft Tépé (Kabnak). *Revue d'Assyriologie* 90:135–143.

Amiet, Pierre, and Maurizio Tosi

1978 Phase 10 at Shahr-i Sokhta: Excavations in Square XDV and the Late 4th Millennium B.C. Assemblage of Sistan. *East and West* 28(4):9–31.

Amiran, Ruth

1952 Connections between Anatolia and Palestine in the Early Bronze Age. *Israel Exploration Journal.* 2:89–103.

Andrae, Walter

1922 *Die archäischen Ischtar-Tempel in Assur.* Wissenschaftliche Veröffentlichung der Deutschen Orient-Gesellschaft 39. Leipzig: J.C. Hinrichs.

1935 *Die jüngeren Ischtar-Tempel in Assur.* Wissenschaftliche Veröffentlichung der Deutschen Orient-Gesellschaft 58. Leipzig: J.C. Hinrichs.

1977 *Das wiedererstandene Assur.* Munich: Beck.

André, Béatrice, and Mirjo Salvini

1989 Reflexions sur Puzur-Inšušinak. *Iranica Antiqua* 24:53–72.

Anonymous

1926 Kish. *Archiv für Orientforschung* 3(1):23.

1929 *Proceedings of the Seventeenth International Congress of Orientalists, Oxford, 1928.* Wiesbaden.

Archäologie zur Bibel

1981 *Archäologie zur Bibel.* Frankfurt-am-Main: Katalog Liebighaus.

Archi, Alfonso

1995 Hittite and Hurrian Literatures: An Overview. In *Civilizations of the Ancient Near East,* vol. IV, edited by J.M. Sasson, J. Baines, G. Beckman, and K.S. Rubinson, 2367–2387. New York: Charles Scribners' Sons.

Arnaud, Daniel, Yves Calvet, and Jean-Louis Huot

1979 Ilšu-Ibnišu, orfèvre de l'E.babbar de Larsa, La jarre L. 76.77 et son contenu. *Syria* 56:1–64.

Arrian

1933 *Indica.* Translated by E.I. Robson. Cambridge: Cambridge University Press.

Arsebük, G.

1979 Altınova'da (Elâzığ), Yüzlü, Açkıltı ve Karaz Türü, Çanak Çömlek Arasındaki İlikleri, *VIII. Türk Tarih Kongresi Kongreye Sunulan Bildirileri* (1976), 81–92. Ankara.

Azarpay, Guitty

1968 *Urartian Art and Artifacts: A Chronological Study.* Berkeley and Los Angeles: University of California Press.

Badler, Virginia, Patrick E. McGovern, and Rudolph H. Michel

1990 Drink and Be Merry!: Infrared Spectroscopy and Ancient Near Eastern Wine. In *Organic Contents of Ancient Vessels: Materials Analysis and Archaeological Investigation,* edited by W.R. Biers and P.E. McGovern, 26–36. MASCA Research Papers in Science and Archaeology 7. Philadelphia: University of Pennsylvania Museum of Archaeology and Anthropology.

Bahşaliyev, Veli

1997 *The Archaeology of Nakhichevan.* Istanbul: Arkeoloji ve Sanat Yayınları.

Balikci, Asen

1981   Pastoralism and Class Differentiation Among the Labenkhel. In *Change and Development in Nomadic and Pastoral Societies,* edited by J.G. Galaty and P.C. Salzman, 150–157. Leiden: E.J. Brill.

Banning, Edward B.

1996   Highlands and Lowlands: Problems and Survey Frameworks for Rural Archaeology in the Near East. *Bulletin of the American Schools for Oriental Research* 301:25–45.

Baqir, Taha

1946   Tell Harmal: A Preliminary Report. *Sumer* 2(2):22–30.

Barfield, Thomas

1993   *The Nomadic Alternative.* Englewood Cliffs, NJ: Prentice Hall.

Barnett, Richard D.

1975   *A Catalogue of the Nimrud Ivories.* 2nd ed. London: British Museum.

Barnett, Richard D., and M. Falkner

1962   *The Sculptures of Assur-Nasir-Apli II (883–859 B.C.) Tiglath-Pileser III (745–727 B.C.) Esarhaddon (681–669 B.C.) from the Central and South-west Palaces at Nimrud.* London: The British Museum.

Barrelet, Marie-Thérèse

1984   *Problèmes concernant les Hurrites II.* Mémoire 49. Paris: Éditions Recherche sur les Civilisations.

Barth, Fredrik

1959   The Land Use Pattern of Migratory Tribes of South Persia. *Norsk Geografisk Tidsskrift* 17:1–11.

1961   *Nomads of South Persia.* London: Allen and Unwin.

Bartl, Karin

1994   *Frühislamische Besiedlung im Balikh-Tal/Nord Syrien.* Berlin: D. Reimer.

Bartl, Karin, and Stefan R. Hauser (editors)

1996   *Continuity and Change in Northern Mesopotamia from the Hellenistic to the Early Islamic Period.* Berliner Beiträge zum Vorderen Orient 17. Berlin: D. Reimer.

Bar-Yosef, Ofer

1998   The Natufian Culture in the Levant, Threshold to the Origins of Agriculture. *Evolutionary Anthropology* 6(5):159–177.

Bates, Daniel

1973   *Nomads and Farmers: A Study of the Yoruk of Southeastern Turkey.* Anthropological Papers 52. Ann Arbor: University of Michigan Museum of Anthropology.

Bazin, D., and H. Hübner

1969   *Copper Deposits in Iran.* Report 13. Tehran: Geological Survey of Iran.

Beck, Lois

1980   Herd Owners and Hired Shepherds: The Qashqa'i of Iran. *Ethnology* 19:327–351.

1981a   Economic Transformations among Qashqa'i Nomads, 1962–1978. In *Modern Iran: The Dialectics of Continuity and Change,* edited by M. Bonine and N. Keddie, 99–122, 404–407. Albany: State University of New York Press.

1981b   Government Policy and Pastoral Land Use in Southwest Iran. *Journal of Arid Environments* 4:253–267.

1982   Nomads and Urbanites, Involuntary Hosts and Uninvited Guests. *Journal of Middle Eastern Studies* 18:426–444.

1984   The Qashqa'i of Iran. *Cultural Survival Quarterly* 8(1):19–22.

1986   *The Qashqa'i of Iran.* New Haven: Yale University Press.

1991   *Nomad: A Year in the Life of a Qashqa'i Tribesman in Iran.* Berkeley: University of California Press.

1992   Qashqa'i Nomads and the Islamic Republic. *Middle East Report* 22(4):36–41.

1998   Use of Land by Nomadic Pastoralists in Iran, 1970–1998. *Yale School of Forestry and Environmental Studies Bulletin Series* 103:58–80.

2000   Local Histories: A Longitudinal Study of a Qashqa'i Subtribe in Iran. In *Iran and Beyond: Essays in Middle Eastern History in Honor of Nikki R. Keddie,* edited by R. Matthee and B. Baron, 262–288. Costa Mesa, CA: Mazda Publishers.

2003   Qashqa'i Women in Post-Revolutionary Iran. In *Women in Iran from 1800 to the Islamic Republic,* edited by G. Nashat and L. Beck. Champaign: University of Illinois Press.

N.D.   *Nomads Move On: Qashqa'i Tribespeople in Post-Revolutionary Iran.* Manuscript.

Bergner, Karl

1937   Bericht über unbekannte achämenidische Ruinen in der Ebene von Persepolis. *Archäologisches Mitteilungen aus Iran* 8:1–4.

Berman, Judith

1994   The Ceramic Evidence for Sociopolitical Organization in 'Ubaid Southwestern Iran. In *Chiefdoms and Early States in the Near East,* edited by G.J. Stein and M.S. Rothman, 23–33. Madison: Prehistory Press.

Bernbeck, Reinhard

1993   *Steppe als Kulturlandschaft.* Berlin: D. Reimer.

1995   Don't Pick up These Sherds! *Orient Express* 1995(3):89–91.

Berthoud, Thierry

1979   Étude par l'analyse de traces et la modelisation de la filiation entre minérai de cuivre et objets archéologiques du Moyen-Orient (IVème et IIIème millénaires avant notre ère). Doctoral Thesis, Université Pierre et Marie Curie, Paris.

Berthoud, Thierry, Serge Cleuziou, L. P. Hurtel, Michel Menu, M., and C. Volfovsky

1982   Cuivres et alliages en Iran, Afghanistan, Oman au cours des IVe et IIIe millénaires. *Paléorient* 8(2):39–54.

Beyer, Dominique

1989   Un nouveau témoin des relations entre Mari et le monde iranien au IIIème millénaire. *Iranica Antiqua* 24:109–120.

Bibby, T. Geoffrey

1969   *Looking for Dilmun.* New York: Alfred A. Knopf.

Binford, Lewis R.

1980   Willow Smoke and Dogs' Tails: Hunter-Gatherer Settlement Systems and Archaeological Site Formation. *American Antiquity* 45:4–20.

Biscione, Raffaele, Sandro Salvatori, and Maurizio Tosi
1977 Shahr-i Sokhta: The Protohistoric Settlement and the Chronological Sequence. In *La città bruciata del deserto salato,* edited by G. Tucci, 77–112. Venice: Erizzo.

Bishop, Isabella
1891 *Journeys in Persia and Kurdistan, Including a Summer in the Upper Karun Region and Visit to the Nestorian Rayahs.* London: J. Murray.

Blackman, M. James
1981 The Mineralogical and Chemical Analysis of Banesh Period Ceramics from Tal-i Malyan, Iran. In *Scientific Studies in Ancient Ceramics,* edited by M.J. Hughes, 7–20. British Museum Occasional Studies 19. London: British Museum.
1982 The Manufacture and Use of Burned Lime Plaster at Proto Elamite Anshan (Iran). In *Early Pyrotechnology,* edited by T. Wertime and S. Wertime, 107–115. Washington DC: Smithsonian Institution Press.
1984 Provenience Studies of Middle Eastern Obsidian from Sites in Highland Iran. In *Archaeological Chemistry III,* edited by J. Lambert, 19–50. Washington DC: American Chemical Society.
1985 Chemical Characterization of Sealing Clays from Fourth Millennium B.C. Sites in Iran. *The Transactions of the American Nuclear Society* 49:168–169. La Grange, IL.
N.D. Chemical Characterization of Arslantepe Sealings. Manuscript in possession of author.

Black-Michaud, Jacob
1986 *Sheep and Land: The Economics of Power in a Tribal Society.* Cambridge: Cambridge University Press.

Boehmer, Michael Rainer
1965 *Die Entwicklung der Glyptik während der Akkad-Zeit.* Berlin: de Gruyter.

Bökönyi, Sandor
1987 Horses and Sheep in East Europe in the Copper and Bronze Ages. In *Proto-Indo-European: The Archaeology of a Linguistic Problem,* edited by S. Skomal and E. Polomè, 136–44. Washington: Institute for the Study of Man.

Bollweg, Jutta
1988 Protoachämenidische Siegelbilder. *Archäologische Mitteilungen aus Iran* 21:53–61.

Boonzajer Flaes, Robert. M.
1982 Surplus Creation and Surplus Circulation in Pastoral Nomadism. In *Contemporary Nomadic and Pastoral Peoples of Asia and the North,* edited by P.C. Salzman, 87–95. Williamsburg: College of William and Mary.

Borger, Rykele
1981 *Assyrisch-babylonische Zeichenliste,* 2nd ed. Alter Orient und Altes Testament 33/33a. Kevelaer and Neukirchen-Vluyn: Butzon & Bercker and Neukirchener Verlag.

Börker-Klähn, Jutta
1970 Untersuchungen zur altelamischen Archäologie. Dissertation. Berlin.
1982 *Altvorderasiatische Bildstelen und vergleichbare Felsreliefs.* Baghdader Forschungen 4. Mainz.

Born, Hermann, and Ursula Seidl
1995 *Schutzwaffen aus Assyrien und Urartu, Sammlung Axel Guttman.* Berlin.

Boserup, Esther
1965 *The Conditions of Agricultural Growth.* Chicago: Aldine.
1981 *Population and Technological Changes: A Study of Long-Term Trends.* Chicago: University of Chicago Press.

Botta, Paul E., and M.E. Flandin
1849-50 *Monument de Ninive découvert et décrit.* Paris: Imprimerie Nationale.

Botte, Roger
1979 Agriculteurs/éleveurs et domination du groupe pastoral. In *Pastoral Production and Society/Production pastorale et société, Actes du colloque international sur le pastoralisme nomade.* Paris, 1–3 Déc. 1976, L'Equipe écologie et anthropologie des société pastorales, Paris, 399–418. Cambridge: Cambridge University Press.

Boucharlat, Rémy
1994 Continuités à Suse au Ier millénaire av. J.-C. In *Achaemenid History 8: Continuity and Change,* edited by H. Sancisi-Weerdenburg, A. Kuhrt and M.C. Root, 217–228. Leiden: Nederlands Instituut voor Het Nabije Oosten.
1997 Camp royal et résidences achéménides. In *Recherches récentes sur l'Empire achéménide. Topoi,* Supplément 1: 217–228. Lyon: Diffusion de Boccard.

Bourgeot, André
1981 Nomadic Pastoral Society and the Market. In *Change and Development in Nomadic and Pastoral Societies,* edited by J.G. Galaty and P.C. Salzman, 116–27. Leiden: Brill.

Bradburd, Daniel
1990 *Ambiguous Relations: Kin, Class, and Conflict Among Komachi Pastoralists.* Washington DC: Smithsonian Institution Press.
1998 *Being There: The Necessity of Fieldwork.* Washington DC: Smithsonian Institution Press.

Braidwood, Robert J., and Bruce Howe
1962 Southwestern Asia Beyond the Lands of the Mediterranean Littoral. In *Courses toward Urban Life,* edited by R.J. Braidwood and G.R. Willey, 132–146. Viking Fund Publications in Anthropology 32. Chicago: Aldine.

Briant, Pierre
1984 La perse avant l'Empire (un état de la question). *Iranica Antiqua* 19:71–118.
1990 The Seleucid Kingdom, the Achaemenid Empire and the History of the Near East in the First Millennium BC. In *Religion and Religious Practice in the Seleucid Kingdom,* edited by P. Bilde, T. Engberg-Pedersen, L. Hannestad, and J. Zahle, 40–65. Studies in Hellenistic Civilization 1. Aarhus: Aarhus University Press.
1996 *Histoire de l'Empire perse: de Cyrus à Alexandre.* Paris: Fayard.

Brinkman, John A.
1976 *Materials and Studies for Kassite History.* Chicago: University of Chicago Press.

Bronitsky, Gordon, and R. Hamer

1986   Experiments in Ceramic Technology: The Effect of Various Tempering Materials on Impact and Thermal-Shock Resistance. *American Antiquity* 51:89–101.

Bronson, Bennet

1975   The Earliest Farming: Demography as cause and consequence. In *Population Ecology and Social Evolution,* edited by S. Polgar, 53–78. Chicago: Aldine.

Brookes, Ian, Louis D. Levine, and Robin W. Dennell

1982   Alluvial Sequences in Central West Iran and Implications for Archaeological Survey. *Journal of Field Archaeology* 9:285–299.

Buccellati, Georgio, and Marilyn Kelly-Buccellati

1985   Terqa and the Kingdom of Khana. In *Ebla to Damascus: Art and Archaeology of Ancient Syria*, edited by H.Weiss, 217–222. Washington DC: Smithsonian Institution Traveling Exhibition Service.

Bulgarelli, Grazia

1979   The Lithic Industry of Tepe Hisar in the Light of Recent Excavation. In *South Asian Archaeology 1977,* vol. 1, edited by M. Taddei, 39–54. Naples: Istituto Universitario Orientale.

Bulliet, Richard W.

1976   Medieval Nishapur: A Topographic and Demographic Reconstruction. *Studia Iranica* 5:67–89.

1992   Pottery Styles and Social Status in Medieval Khurasan. In *Archaeology, Annales, and Ethnohistory,* edited by A.B. Knapp, 75–82. Cambridge: Cambridge University Press.

1994   *Islam: The View from the Edge.* New York: Columbia University.

Burney, Charles

1958   Eastern Anatolia in the Chalcolithic and Early Bronze Age. *Anatolian Studies* 8:157–209.

1977   The Economic Basis of Settled Communities in North-Western Iran. In *Mountains and Lowlands: Essays in the Archaeology of Greater Mesopotamia*, edited by L.D. Levine and T.C. Young, Jr., 1–8. Bibliotheca Mesopotamica 7. Malibu: Undena.

1994   Urartu and Iran: Some Problems and Answers. In *Anatolia Iron Ages 3: Proceedings of the Third Iron Age Colloquium,* edited by A. Çilingiroğlu and D. French, 31–35. Ankara: British Institute of Archaeology.

1996   The Sheep are Sweeter. In *Cultural Interaction in the Ancient Near East,* edited by G. Bunnens, 1–15. *Abr Nahrain,* Supplement series 5. Louven: Peters.

Burney, Charles and David M. Lang

1971   *The Peoples of the Hills: Ancient Ararat and Caucasus.* London: Weidenfeld and Nicolson.

1972   *The Peoples of the Hills: Ancient Ararat and Caucasus.* New York: Praeger Publishers.

Cahen, Claude

1965   *Jean Sauvaget's Introduction to the History of the Muslim East.* Berkeley: University of California.

Caldwell, David H.

1976   The Early Glyptic of Gawra, Giyan and Susa and the Development of Long Distance Trade. *Orientalia* 45:227–250.

Caldwell, Joseph R.

1965   Interaction Spheres in Prehistory. In *Hopewellian Studies,* edited by J.R. Caldwell and R. R. Hall, 133–143. Scientific Papers 12. Springfield, IL: State Museum.

1968a Tall-i Ghazir. *Reallexikon der Assyriologie* 3:348–355.

1968b Pottery and Cultural History on the Iranian Plateau. *Journal of Near Eastern Studies* 27(3):178–183.

Calmeyer, Peter

1973   Zur Genese altiranischer Motive. *Archäologische Mitteilungen aus Iran* NF 6:135–152.

1988   Mâlamir, C. Archäologisch. *Reallexikon der Assyriologie* 7/3-4:281–287.

1990   Madjabad. Zur Datierung von Steinbruch-Arbeiten um Persepolis. *Archäologische Mitteilungen aus Iran* NF 23:185–190.

1992   Zur Genese altiranischer Motive XI. *Archäologische Mitteilungen aus Iran* NF 25:95–124.

Cameron, George

1936   *History of Early Iran.* Chicago: University of Chicago Press.

1948   *Persepolis Treasury Tablets.* Publication 65. Chicago: Oriental Institute of the University of Chicago.

Carriveau, Gary W.

1978   Application of Thermoluminescence Dating Techniques to Prehistoric Metallurgy. In *Application of Science to the Dating of Works of Art,* edited by W.J. Young, 59–67. Boston: Museum of Fine Arts.

Carter, Elizabeth

1971   Elam in the Second Millennium B.C.: The Archaeological Evidence. Ph.D. Dissertation, Oriental Institute, University of Chicago.

1980   Excavations in Ville Royale I at Susa: The Third Millennium B.C. Occupation. *Cahiers de la Délégation Archéologique Française en Iran* 11:11–134.

1984   Archaeology. In *Elam: Surveys of Political History and Archaeology,* by E. Carter and M.W. Stolper, 103–230. University of California Publications, Near Eastern Studies 25. Berkeley: University of California Press.

1986   The Piedmont and the Pusht-i Kuh in the Early Third Millennium B.C. In *Préhistoire de la Mésopotamie: la Mésopotamie préhistorique et l'exploration récente du djebel Hamrin,* edited by J.-L. Huot, 73–83. Paris: CNRS.

1990   Elamite Exports. In *Contribution à l'histoire de l'Iran: mélanges offerts à Jean Perrot,* edited by F. Vallat, 89–100. Paris: Éditions Recherche sur les Civilisations.

1994a Bridging the Gap Berween the Elamites and the Persians in Southwestern Khuzistan. In *Achaemenid History 8: Continuity and Change,* edited by H. Sancisi-Weerdenburg, A. Kuhrt, and M.C. Root, 65–95. Leiden: Nederlands Instituut voor Het Nabije Oosten.

1994b Mittelelamische Kunstperiode (Middle Elamite (ME) Period). *Reallexikon der Assyriologie* 8/3-4:309–316.

1996 *Excavations at Anshan (Tal-e Malyan): The Middle Elamite Period.* Malyan Excavation Reports, vol. 2. University Museum Monograph 82. Philadelphia: University Museum, University of Pennsylvania.

1998 The Archaeology of Elam. In *Encyclopaedia Iranica,* vol. 8, fasc. 3, edited by E. Yarshater, 313–325. Costa Mesa, CA: Mazda Publishers.

1999 Neuelamische Kunstperiode. *Reallexikon der Assyriologie* 9/3-4:279–283.

Carter, Elizabeth, and Matthew W. Stolper

1984 *Elam: Surveys of Political History and Archaeology.* University of California Publications, Near Eastern Studies 25. Berkeley and Los Angeles: University of California Press.

Caubet, Annie

1995 Un vase d'argenterie pré-achéménide. *Revue du Louvre* 4:81.

Chang, Claudia, and Harold Koster, eds.

1994 *Pastoralists at the Periphery: Herders in a Capitalist World.* Tucson: University of Arizona Press.

Charles, James A.

1980 The Coming of Copper and Copper-base Alloys and Iron. In *The Coming of the Age of Iron,* edited by T.A. Wertime and J.D. Muhly, 151–181. New Haven: Yale University Press.

Charpin, Dominique

1986 Les Élamites à Šubat-Enlil. In *Fragmenta historiae aelamicae: mélanges offerts à M.-J. Steve,* edited by L. De Meyer, H. Gasche and F. Vallat, 129–137. Paris: Éditions Recherche sur les Civilisations.

Charpin, Dominique, and Jean-Marie Durand

1991 La suzeraineté de l'empereur (Sukkalmah) d'Élam sur la Mésopotamie et le "nationalisme" amorrite. In *Mésopotamie et Élam, actes de la XXXVIème Rencontre Assyriologique Internationale (Gand, 10–14 juillet 1989),* 59–66. Mesopotamian History and Environment, Occasional Publication 1. Gand: University of Ghent.

Chase, Philip G.

1985 Whole Vessels and Sherds: An Experimental Investigation of their Quantitative Relationships. *Journal of Field Archaeology* 12:213–218.

Chatty, Dawn

1986 *From Camel to Truck: The Bedouin in the Modern World.* New York: Vantage Press.

1996 *Mobile Pastoralists: Development Planning and Social Change in Oman.* New York: Columbia University Press.

Cherry, John F.

1983 Frogs Round the Pond: Perspectives on Current Archaeological Survey Projects in the Mediterranean Region. In *Archaeological Survey in the Mediterranean Area,* edited by D.R. Keller and D. W. Rupp, 375–416. BAR International Series 155. Oxford: British Archaeological Reports.

Childe, V. Gordon

1929 *The Danube in Prehistory.* Oxford: Clarendon.

1950 The Urban Revolution. *Town Planning Review* 21(1):3–17.

Christensen, Peter

1998 Middle East Irrigation: Legacies and Lessons. *Yale School of Forestry and Environmental Studies Bulletin Series* 103:15–30.

Çilingiroğlu, Altan

1987 Van-Dilkaya Höyüğü Kazıları, 1985. In *VIII . Kazı Sonuçları Toplantısı I,* 81–94. Ankara: T.C. Kültür Bakanlığı.

1988 Van-Dilkaya Höyüğü Kazıları, 1987. In *IX. Kazı Sonuçları Toplantısı I,* 229–248. Ankara: T.C. Kültür Bakanlığı.

Clark, N.T.

1984 Some Probable Effects of Drought on the Flock Structure and Production Parameters in Northwestern Afghanistan. *Nomadic People* 15:67–74.

Cleuziou, Serge

1981 Oman Peninsula in the Early Second Millennium B.C. In *South Asian Archaeology 1979,* edited by H. Härtel, 279–293. Berlin: D. Reimer.

Cleuziou, Serge, and Thierry Berthoud

1982 Early Tin in the Near East: A Reassessment in the Light of New Evidence from Afghanistan. *Expedition* 24(3):14–19.

Cleuziou, Serge, and Maurizio Tosi

1989 The Southeastern Frontier of the Ancient Near East. In *South Asian Archaeology 1985,* edited by K. Frifelt and P. Sørensen, 15–47. London: Curzon Press.

Cole, Donald, and Soraya Altorki

1998 *Bedouin, Settlers, and Holiday-Makers: Egypt's Changing Northwest Coast.* Cairo: American University in Cairo Press.

Conan, Jacques, and Odile Deschene

1996 *Le bitume à Suse: collection du Musée du Louvre, Paris.* Réunion des Musées Nationaux; Fondation Elf.

Conti, Anna Maria, and Carlo Persiani

1993 When Worlds Collide: Cultural Developments in Eastern Anatolia in the Early Bronze Age. In *Between the Rivers and Over the Mountains,* edited by M. Frangipane, H. Hauptmann, M. Liverani, P. Matthiae, and M. Mellink, 361–414. Rome: Universitá di Roma.

Cooke, Strathmore R.B., and B.V. Nielsen

1978 Slag and Other Metallurgical Products. In *Excavations at Nichoria in Southwestern Greece,* edited by G. Rapp, Jr. and S.E. Aschenbrenner, 182–224. Minneapolis: University of Minnesota Press.

Coon, Carleton S.

1951 *Cave Explorations in Iran 1949.* University Museum Monographs 5. Philadelphia: University Museum, University of Pennsylvania.

Costantini, Lorenzo

1977 Le Piante. In *La città bruciata del deserto salato,* edited by G. Tucci, 159–228. Venice: Erizzo Editrice.

N.D. Archaeobotany in Iran: A Contribution to the Knowledge of Ancient Agriculture and Environment. In press.

Costantini, Lorenzo, and L. Costantini Biasini

1985   Agriculture in Baluchistan between the 7th and the 3rd Millennium B.C. *Newsletter of Baluchistan Studies* 2:16–30. Naples: Istituto Universitario Orientale.

Costantini, Lorenzo, and Robert H. Dyson, Jr.

1990   The Ancient Agriculture of the Damghan Plain: The Archaeobotanical Evidence from Tepe Hissar. In *Economy and Settlement in the Near East: Analyses of Archaeological Sites and Materials*, edited by N.F. Miller, 46–64. MASCA Research Papers in Science and Archaeology, Supplement to vol. 7. Philadelphia: University of Pennsylvania Museum of Archaeology and Anthropology.

Cribb, Roger

1991   *Nomads in Archaeology.* Cambridge: Cambridge University Press.

Crumley, Carole

1976   Toward a Locational Definition of State Systems of Settlement. *American Anthropologist* 78:59–73.

Curet, L.A.

1997   New Formulae for Estimating Prehistoric Populations for Lowland South America and the Caribbean. *Antiquity* 72:359–375.

Curtis, John

1983   Late Assyrian Bronze Coffins. *Anatolian Studies* 33:85–95.

1995   Introduction. In *Later Mesopotamia and Iran; Tribes and Empires 1600–539 BC,* edited by J. Curtis, 15–24. London: British Museum Press.

1996   Assyrian Furniture: The Archaeological Evidence. In *The Furniture of Western Asia, Ancient and Traditional,* edited by G. Herrmann, 167–180. Mainz: Philipp von Zabern.

Curvers, Hans

1989   Iron Age Beads. In *The Holmes Expeditions to Luristan,* edited by M.N. Van Loon and H.H. Curvers, 381–411. Publication 108. Chicago: Oriental Institute of the University of Chicago.

Damerji, M.S.B.

1999   *Gräber assyrischer Königinnen aus Nimrud.* Mainz: Verlag des Römisch-Germanischen Zentralmuseums.

Davidovic, V.

1984   Testi di Ur III concerneti bottini di guerra? *Annali* 44:177–205. Naples: Istituto Universitario Orientale.

Deal, Michael

1985   Household Pottery Disposal in the Maya Highlands: An Ethnoarchaeological Interpretation. *Journal of Anthropological Archaeology* 4:243–291.

de Cardi, Beatrice

1967   The Bampur Sequence in the 3rd Millennium B.C. *Antiquity* 41:33–41.

1968   Excavations at Bampur, S.E. Iran: A Brief Report. *Iran* 6:135–155.

1970   *Excavations at Bampur, a Third Millennium Settlement in Persian Baluchistan, 1966.* Anthropological Papers of the American Museum of Natural History 51/3. New York: American Museum of Natural History.

Degens, Egon T., and F. Kurtman, eds.

1978   *The Geology of Lake Van.* Ankara: Maden Tetkik Arama Enstitüsü.

Delougaz, Pinhas, and Helene J. Kantor

1996   *Chogha Mish: The First Five Seasons of Excavations, 1961–1971,* edited by A. Alizadeh. Publication 101. Chicago: Oriental Institute of the University of Chicago.

Delougaz, Pinhas, and Seton Lloyd

1942   *Pre-Sargonid Temples in the Diyala Region.* Publication 42. Chicago: Oriental Institute of the University of Chicago.

Demange, F.

1996   Une coupe d'argenterie pré-achéménide. *Revue du Louvre* 3:12–13.

De Roche, C.D.

1983   Population Estimates from Settlement Area and Number of Residences. *Journal of Field Archaeology* 10:187–192.

de Schauensee, Maude

1989   Horse Gear from Hasanlu. *Expedition* 31(2-3):37–52.

Deshayes, Jean

1969   *Les Civilisations de l'Orient ancien.* Paris: Arthaud.

de Waele, Eric

1972   Shutruk-Nahunte II et les reliefs rupestres dits néo-élamites d'Iseh/Malamir. *Revue des Archéologues et Historiens d'Art de Louvain* 5:17–32.

1973   Les reliefs rupestres d'Izeh-Malamir. *Archéologia* 60 (juillet 1973):31–45.

1989   Musicians and Musical Instruments on the Rock Reliefs in the Elamite Santuary of Kul-e Farah (Izeh). *Iran* 27:29–38.

Dewar, Robert E.

1991   Incorporating Variation in Occupation Span into Settlement-Pattern Analysis. *American Antiquity* 56:604–620.

1994a   Changing Population Patterns during the Early Phases of Occupation on the Deh Luran Plain. In *Early Settlement and Irrigation on the Deh Luran Plain, Iran,* by J.A. Neely and H.T. Wright, 200–211. Technical Reports 26. Ann Arbor: University of Michigan Museum of Anthropology.

1994b   Contending with Contemporaneity: A Reply to Kintigh. *American Antiquity* 59:149–152.

Dewdney, J.C.

1971   *Turkey, an Introductory Geography.* New York: Praeger.

Dibble, Harold L.

1984   The Mousterian Industry from Bisitun Cave (Iran). *Paléorient* 10:23–34.

Dieulafoy, M.A.

1893   *L'Acropole de Suse d'après les fouilles exécutées en 1874, 1885, 1886.* Paris: n.p.

Digard, J.P.

1975   Campements Baxtyari. *Studia Iranica* 4:117–129.

Dittmann, Reinhard

1984   *Eine Randebene des Zagros in der Frühzeit: Ergebnisse des Behbehan-Zuhreh Surveys.* Berliner Beiträge zum Vorderen Orient, Band 3. Berlin: D. Reimer.

Dollfus, Geneviève

1971 Les fouilles de Djaffarabad de 1969 à 1971. *Cahiers de la Délégation Archéologique Française en Iran* 1:17–161.

1975 Les fouilles à Djaffarabad de 1972 à 1974. Djaffarabad, periodes I et II. *Cahiers de la Délégation Archéologique Française en Iran* 5:11–220.

1978 Étude de la Susiane (Ve–IVe millénaire). *Paléorient* 4:140–167.

1983a Tépé Djowi: contrôle stratigraphique. *Cahiers de la Délégation Archéologique Française en Iran* 13:17–131.

1983b Tepe Bendebal, travaux 1977, 1978. *Cahiers de la Délégation Archéologique Française en Iran* 13:133–275.

1985 L'occupation de la Susiane au Ve millénaire et au début du IVe millénaire avant J.-C. *Paléorient* 11(2):11–20.

Dresch, Paul

1989 *Tribes, Government and History in Yemen.* Oxford: Oxford University Press.

Duchêne, J.

1986 La localisation de Huhnur. In *Fragmenta historiae aelamicae: mélanges offerts à M.-J. Steve,* edited by L. De Meyer, H. Gasche, and F. Vallat, 65–74. Paris: Éditions Recherche sur les Civilisations.

Durand, Jean-Marie

1986 Fragments rejoints pour une histoire élamite. In *Fragmenta historiae aelamicae: mélanges offerts à M.-J. Steve,* edited by L. De Meyer, H. Gasche and F. Vallat, 111–128. Paris: Éditions Recherche sur les Civilisations.

1994 L'empereur d'Élam et ses vassaux. In *Cinquante-deux reflexions sur le Proche-Orient ancien offertes en hommage à Léon De Meyer,* edited by H. Gasche, M. Tanret, C. Janssen, and A. Degraeve, 15–22. Occasional Publication II, Mesopotamian History and Environment. Leuven: Peeters.

During Caspers, E.C.L.

1970 Trucial Oman in the Third Millennium B.C. *Origini* 4:205–276.

Dyson, Robert H., Jr.

1961 Excavations at the Mannoean Citadel of Hasanlu; and New Light on Several Millennia of Persian Azerbaijan. *Illustrated London News* (30 September 1961):534–537.

1964a A Stranger from the East. *Expedition* 7(1):32–33.

1964b *Hasanlu Newsletter* 2. On file, Hasanlu Project Archives, University of Pennsylvania Museum. Philadelphia.

1965 Problems of Protohistoric Iran as Seen from Hasanlu. *Journal of Near Eastern Studies* 24:193–217.

1977 Architecture of the Iron I Period at Hasanlu in Western Iran and Its Implications for Theories of Migration on the Iranian Plateau. In *Le Plateau iranien,* edited by J. Deshayes, 150–170. Colloque 267. Paris: CNRS.

1983 Introduction: The Genesis of the Hasanlu Project. In *Hajji Firuz Tepe, Iran: The Neolithic Settlement,* by Mary M. Voigt, xxv–xxviii. University Museum Monograph 50. Philadelphia: University Museum, University of Pennsylvania.

1987 The Relative and Absolute Chronology of Hissar II and the Proto-Elamite Horizon of Northern Iran. In *Chronologies in the Near East/Chronologies du Proche Orient,* edited by O. Aurenche, J. Evin, and F. Hours, 647–678. BAR International Series 379(ii). Oxford: British Archaeological Reports.

1989a The Iron Age Architecture at Hasanlu. *Expedition* 31(2/3):107–127.

1989b Rediscovering Hasanlu. *Expedition* 31(2/3):3–11.

Dyson, Robert H., Jr., and Oscar White Muscarella

1989 Constructing the Chronology and Historical Implications of Hasanlu IV. *Iran* 27:1–27

Dyson, Robert H., Jr., and Mary M. Voigt, eds.

1989 East of Assyria: The Highland Settlement of Hasanlu. *Expedition* 31(2-3).

Dzhaparidze, Otar

1995 Die Trialeti-Kultur. In *Unterwegs zum goldenen Vlies,* edited by A. Miron and W. Orthmann, 81–87. Saarbrücken: Museum für Vor- und Frühgeschichte.

Earl, Bryan, and Hadi Özbal

1996 Early Bronze Age Tin Processing at Kestel/Göltepe, Anatolia. *Archaeometry* 38:289–303.

Edens, Christopher

1995 Transcaucasia at the End of the Early Bronze Age. *Bulletin of the American Schools of Oriental Research* 299/300:53–64.

Edzard, Otto Deitz

1957 *Die "Zweite Zwischenzeit" Babyloniens.* Weisbaden: O. Harrassowitz.

Eickelman, Dale

1998 *The Middle East and Central Asia: An Anthropological Approach.* 3rd edition. Upper Saddle River, NJ: Prentice Hall.

Eidem, Jesper, and David Warburton

1996 In the Land of Nagar: A Survey around Tell Brak. *Iraq* 58:51–64.

Eley, Geoff

1991 *Reshaping the German Right: Radical Nationalism and Political Change after Bismarck.* Ann Arbor: University of Michigan Press.

Ellis, Maria deJong

1986 Delivery Records from the Archives of the Kittitum Temple at Ishchali. In *Cuneiform Archives and Libraries,* edited by K.R. Veenhof, 112–120. Istanbul: Nederlands Historisch-Archaeologisch Instituut.

Emberling, Geoffrey

1999 The Value of Tradition: The Development of Social Identities in Early Mesopotamian States. In *Material Symbols: Culture and Economy in Prehistory,* edited by J. Robb, 277–301. Carbondale IL: Center for Archaeological Investigation.

English, Paul

1998 Qanats and Lifeworlds in Iranian Plateau Villages. *Yale School of Forestry and Environmental Studies Bulletin Series* 103:187–205.

Ertem, H.

1982 *Han Ibrahim Şah Excavations 1970-71.* Middle East Technical University Keban Project Publications. Ankara: Türk Tarih Kurumu Basımevi.

Ertmann, E.L.
1994   An Urartian Belt and Other Unpubished Objects from a Private Collection. In *Anatolian Iron Ages 3,* edited by A. Çilingiroğlu and D. French, 63–74. Ankara: British Institute of Archaeology.

Ettinghausen, Richard
1974   Arabic Epigraphy: Communication or Symbolic Affirmation. In *Near Eastern Numismatics, Iconography, Epigraphy, and History: Studies in Honor of George C. Miles,* edited by D.K. Kouymjian, 297–317. Beirut: The American University of Beirut.

Falconer, Steven E., and Stephen H. Savage
1995   Heartlands and Hinterlands: Alternative Trajectories of Early Urbanization in Mesopotamia and the Southern Levant. *American Antiquity* 60:37–58.

Farber, Walter
1975   Eine elamische Inschrift aus der 1. Hälfte des 2. Jahrtausends. *Zeitschrift für Assyriologie* 64:74–86.

Ferdinand, Klaus
1962   Nomadic Expansion and Commerce in Central Afghanistan. *Folk* 4:123–160.

Finkbeiner, Uwe, and Wolfgang Röllig
1986   Gamdat Nasr: Period or Regional Style? *Beihefte zum Tübinger Atlas des Vorden Orients, Reihe B, Nr. 26.* Wiesbaden: Dr. Luding Reichert Verlag.

Finkelstein, Israel
1995   *Living on the Fringe. The Archaeology and History of the Negev, Sinai and Neighbouring Regions in the Bronze and Iron Ages.* Monographs in Mediterranean Archaeology 6. Sheffield: Sheffield Academic Press.

Finkelstein, Jacob Joel
1959   The Year Dates of Samsuditana. *Journal of Cuneiform Studies* 13:39–49.

Flannery, Kent V.
1972   The Cultural Evolution of Civilizations. *Annual Review of Ecology and Systematics* 3:399–426.

Foley, Robert
1981   *Off-site Archaeology and Human Adaptation in Eastern Africa.* BAR International Series 97. Oxford: British Archaeological Reports.

Forest-Foucault, Chantal
1980   Rapport sur les fouilles de Keit Qasim III-Hamrin. *Paléorient* 6:221–24.

Fossey, Charles
1926   *Manuel d'Assyriologie,* II: *Évolution des cunéiformes.* Paris: Louis Conard.

Francfort, Henri-Paul
1989   *Fouilles de Shortughai. Recherches sur l'Asie Central protohistorique.* 2 vols. Mémoires de la Mission Archéologique Française en Asie Centrale. Paris: Diffusion de Boccard.

Frane, Julia Elizabeth
1996   *The Tell Leilan Period I Habur Ware Assemblage.* Ph.D. Dissertation, Department of Classics, University of North Carolina, Chapel Hill.

Frangipane, Marcella
1997   Changes in Upper Mesopotamia/Anatolian Relations at the Beginning of the 3rd Millennium B.C. *Subartu* 4:195–218

Frankfort, Henri
1932   *Archaeology and the Sumerian Problem.* Studies in Ancient Oriental Civilizations 4. Chicago: Oriental Institute of the University of Chicago.
1936   Progress of the Work in Iraq, 1934/35. *Oriental Institute Communications* 20:74–100.
1939   *Sculpture of the Third Millennium B.C. from Tell Asmar and Khafaja.* Publication 44. Chicago: Oriental Institute of the University of Chicago.
1940   *The Gimilsin Temple and the Palace of the Rulers of Tell Asmar.* Publication 43. Chicago: Oriental Institute of the University of Chicago.
1943   *More Sculpture from the Diyala Region.* Publication 60. Chicago: Oriental Institute of the University of Chicago.
1970   *The Art and Architecture of the Ancient Orient.* 4th edition. Baltimore: Penguin Books.

French, David, and Geoffrey Summers
1994   Pre-Urartian and Urartian Pottery from the Muş Region. *Anatolian Studies* 44:77–84.

Friedl, Erika
1989   *Women of Deh Koh: Lives in an Iranian Village.* Washington DC: Smithsonian Institution Press.
1997   *Children of Deh Koh: Young Life in an Iranian Village.* Syracuse: Syracuse University Press.

Frifelt, Karen
1975   On Prehistoric Settlement and Chronology of the Oman Peninsula. *East and West* 25:359–424.

Frye, Richard
1984   *The History of Ancient Iran.* München: C.H. Beck.

Galaty, John G.
1981   Land and Livestock Among Kenyan Masai. In *Change and Development in Nomadic and Pastoral Societies,* edited by J.G. Galaty and P.C. Salzman, 68–88. Leiden: E.J. Brill.

Garrison, Mark B., and M.C. Root
1996   Persepolis Seal Studies: An Introduction with Provisional Concordances of Seal Numbers and Associated Documents on Fortification Tablets 1-2087. *Achaemenid History* 9:1–141.

Garrod, Dorothy A.E.
1930   The Paleolithic of Southern Kurdistan: Excavation in the Caves of Zarzi and Hazar Merd. *Bulletin of the American School of Prehistoric Research* 6:8–43.

Garthwaite, Gene R.
1983   *Khans and Shahs: A Documentary Analysis of the Bakhtiyari in Iran.* Cambridge: Cambridge University Press.

Gasche, Hermann
1973   *La poterie élamite du deuxième millénaire a.C.* Mémoires de la Délégation Archéologique en Iran 47. Leiden: E.J. Brill.

Gasche, Hermann, James A. Armstrong, Steven W. Cole, and V.G. Gurzadyan

1998 *Dating the Fall of Babylon. A Reappraisal of Second-Millennium Chronology.* Memoirs IV, Mesopotamian History and Environment, Series II. Ghent and Chicago: University of Ghent and Oriental Institute of the University of Chicago.

Gaube, H.
1987 Arrajan. *Encyclopaedia Iranica,* vol. 2, fasc. 5, edited by E. Yarshater, 519–520. London: Routledge & Kegan Paul.

Gautier, Joseph E., and Georges Lampre
1905 Fouilles de Moussian. *Mémoires de la Délégation en Perse* 8:59–149.

Gerber, C.
1996 Die Umgebung des Lidar Höyük von hellenistischer bis frühislamischer Zeit. In *Continuity and Change in Northern Mesopotamia from the Hellenistic to the Early Islamic Period,* edited by K. Bartl and S. Hauser, 303–332. Berliner Beiträge zum Vorderen Orient 17. Berlin: D. Reimer.

Ghirshman, Roman
1934 Une tablette proto-élamite du plateau iranien. *Revue d'Assyriologie* 31(1):115–119.
1938 *Fouilles de Sialk, près de Kashan, 1933, 1934, 1937.* Paris: Geuthner.
1951 *L'Iran des origines à l'Islam.* Paris: Payot.
1964 *Persia From the Origins to Alexander the Great.* London: Thames and Hudson.
1966 *Tchoga Zanbil (Dur Untash).* Vol. I: *La ziggurat.* Mémoires de la Délégation Archéologique en Iran 39. Paris: P. Geuthner.
1968 *Tchoga Zanbil (Dur Untash).* Vol. II: *Temenos, temples, palais, tombes.* Mémoires de la Délégation Archéologique en Iran 40. Paris: P. Geuthner.

Gilbert, Allan S.
1983 On the Origins of Specialized Nomadic Pastoralism in Western Iran. *World Archaeology* 15:105–119.

Gilles, J.L., and K. Jamtgaard
1982 Overgrazing in Pastoral Areas: The Commons Reconstructed. *Nomadic People* 10:1–10.

Glassner, Jean-Jacques
1994 Ruhušak - mar ahatim: la transmission du pouvoir en Élam. *Journal asiatique* 282:219–236.
1996 Les dynasties d'Awan et de Simashki. *Nouvelles assyriologiques brèves et utilitaires* 1:25–29.
1998a Les tablettes dites urukéennes de Sialk IV1. *Nouvelles assyriologiques brèves et utilitaires* 4:102–104.
1998b Questions de succession en Élam: mise au point. *Nouvelles assyriologiques brèves et utilitaires* 2:48.

Glassner, Jean-Jacques (and Françoise Grillot)
1991 Les textes de Haft Tépé, la Susiane et l'Élam au 2ème millénaire. In *Mésopotamie et Élam, actes de la XXXVIème Rencontre Assyriologique Internationale (Gand, 10–14 juillet 1989),* 109–126. Mesopotamian History and Environment, Occasional Publication 1. Gand: University of Ghent.

Goff, Clare L.
1963 Excavations at Tall-i-Nokhodi. *Iran* 1:43–70.
1964 Excavations at Tall-i-Nokhodi, 1962. *Iran* 2:41–52.

Gopnick, Hillary
2000 The Ceramics of Godin II: Ceramic Variability in the Archaeological Record. Ph.D. Dissertation, Department of Near and Middle Eastern Studies, University of Toronto. Toronto.

Grave, Peter, D.T. Potts, N. Yassi, W. Reade, and G. Bailey
1996 Elemental Characterisation of Barbar Ceramics from Tell Abraq. *Arabian Archaeology and Epigraphy* 7:177–187.

Grayson, A. Kirk
1996 *Assyrian Rulers of the Early First Millennium BC, II (858–745 BC).* Royal Inscriptions of Mesopotamia, Assyrian Periods 3. Toronto.

Grigg, David
1982 *The Dynamics of Agricultural Change.* London: Hutchinson.

Grillot, Françoise
1978 Notes à propos des bases élamites zukki-zukka. *Cahiers de la Délégation Archéologique Française en Iran* 8:85–88.
1983 Le 'suhter' royal de Suse. *Iranica Antiqua* 18:1–24.

Grillot, Françoise, and Jean-Jacques Glassner
1991 Problèmes de succession et cumuls de pouvoirs: une querelle de famille chez les premiers sukkalmah? *Iranica Antiqua* 26:85–99.
1993 Chronologie susienne. *Nouvelles assyriologiques brèves et utilitaires* 1:12–13

Grillot, Françoise, and François Vallat
1978 Le verbe élamite "pi(š)(š)i." *Cahiers de la Délégation Archéologique Française en Iran* 8:81–85.
1984 Dédicace de Šilhak-Inšušinak à Kiririša. *Iranica Antiqua* 19:21–29.

Grillot-Susini, Françoise
1987 *Elements de grammaire élamite.* Paris: Éditions Recherche sur les Civilisations.

Guérin, Alexandrine
1996 L'occupation Abbaside de Nasibin, typologie et chronologie préliminaires de la céramique prospectée en surface. In *Continuity and Change in Northern Mesopotamia from the Hellenistic to the Early Islamic Period,* edited by K. Bartl and S.R. Hauser, 377–400. Berliner Beiträge zum Vorderen Orient 17. Berlin: D. Reimer.

Gunter, Ann
1982 Representations of Urartian and Western Iranian Fortress Architecture in Assyrian Reliefs. *Iran* 20:103–112.

Gupta, S.P.
1979 *Archaeology of Soviet-Central Asia and the Indus Borderland,* vol. 2. *Protohistory.* Delhi: B.P. Publishing Co.

Haak, Robert D.
1997 Altars. In *The Oxford Encyclopedia of Archaeology in the Near East,* vol. 1, edited by E.M. Meyers, 80–81. New York: Oxford University Press.

Haerinck, Ernie
1986 The Chronology of Luristan, Pusht-i Kuh in the Late

Fourth and First Half of the Third Millennium B.C. In *Préhistoire de la Mésopotamie: la Mésopotamie préhistorique et l'exploration récente du djebel Hamrin,* edited by J.-L. Huot, 55–72. Paris: Éditions du CNRS.

Haiman, Mordechai, and Yuval Goren

1992 "Negbite" Pottery: New Aspects and Interpretations and the Role of Pastoralism in Designating Ceramic Technology. In *Pastoralism in the Levant: Archaeological Materials in Anthropological Perspectives,* edited by O. Bar-Yosef and A. Khazanov, 143-151. Madison: Prehistory Press.

Hakemi, Ali

1992 The Copper Smelting Furnaces of the Bronze Age at Shahdad. In *South Asian Archaeology 1989,* edited by C. Jarrige, 119–132. Madison, WI: Prehistory Press.

Hallock, Richard T.

1959 The Finite Verb in Achaemenid Elamite. *Journal of Near Eastern Studies* 18:1–19.

1969 *Persepolis Fortification Tablets.* Publication 92. Chicago: riental Institute of the University of Chicago Press.

Hamlin, Carol (Kramer)

1974 Early Second Millennium Ceramic Assemblage of Dinkha Tepe. *Iran* 12:125–153.

Hansman, John

1967 Charax and the Karkheh. *Iranica Antiqua* 7:21–58.

1994 Anshan in the Median and Achaemenid Periods. In *The Cambridge History of Iran,* vol. 2, edited by I. Gershevitch, 25–35. Cambridge: Cambridge University Press.

Harper, Prudence O., Joan Aruz, and Françoise Tallon, eds.

1992 *The Royal City of Susa. Ancient Near Eastern Treasures in the Louvre.* New York: The Metropolitan Museum of Art.

Harris, David R., and Chris Gosden

1996 The Beginnings of Agriculture in Western Central Asia. In *The Origins and Spread of Agriculture and Pastoralism in Eurasia,* edited by D.R. Harris, 370–389. London: University College London Press.

Harris, David R., Chris Gosden, and Michael P. Charles

1996 Jeitun: Recent Excavations at an Early Neolithic Site in Southern Turkmenistan. *Proceedings of the Prehistoric Society* 62:423–442

Harris, Marvin

1968 *The Rise of Anthropological Theory: A History of Theories of Culture.* New York: T.Y. Crowell.

Harris, Mary Virginia

1989 Glimpses of an Iron Age Landscape. *Expedition* 31(2-3):12–23.

Häser, Jutta

1988 Steingefäße des 2. vorchristlichen Jahrtausends im Gebiet des Arabischen/Persischen Golfes: Typologie der Gefäße und Deckel aus Serpentinit, Chlorit, Steatit und verwandten Steinarten. M.A. Dissertation, Seminar für Vorderasiatische Archäologie, Freie Universität Berlin.

Hassan, Fekri A.

1981 *Demographic Archaeology.* New York: Academic Press.

Hauptmann, Andreas, Gerd Weisgerber, and Hans-Gert Bachmann

1988 Early Copper Metallurgy in Oman. In *The Beginning of the Use of Metals and Alloys,* edited by R. Maddin, 34–51. Cambridge, MA: MIT Press.

Heim, Suzanne

N.D. *Catalogue of Glazed Architectural Elements from Hasanlu in the Metropolitan Museum of Art.* Ms. on file, Hasanlu Archives, The University of Pennsylvania Museum, Philadelphia.

Hejazi, Mohammad

1959 (1338 a.H.) Mihan-i Ma. Publication of the Ministry of Education, 475–476.

Helbaek, Hans

1969 Plant-Collecting, Dry-Farming, and Irrigation Agriculture in Prehistoric Deh Luran. In *Prehistory and Human Ecology of the Deh Luran Plain,* by F. Hole, K.V. Flannery, and J.A. Neely, 383–426. Memoirs 1. Ann Arbor: University of Michigan Museum of Anthropology.

Henrickson, Elizabeth F.

1985 The Early Development of Pastoralism in the Central Zagros Highlands (Luristan). *Iranica Antiqua* 20:1–42.

1994 The Outer Limits: Settlement and Economic Strategies in the Central Zagros Highlands During the Uruk Era. In *Chiefdoms and Early States in the Near East, the Organizational Dynamics of Complexity,* edited by G.J. Stein and M.S. Rothman, 85–102. Madison: Prehistory Press.

Henrickson, Robert C.

1984 Šimaški and Central Western Iran: The Archaeological Evidence. *Zeitschrift für Assyriologie* 74:98–122.

1986 A Regional Perspective on Godin III: Cultural Development in Central Western Iran. *Iran* 24:1–55.

1987 The Godin III Chronology for Central Western Iran 2600–1400 B.C. *Iranica Antiqua* 22:33–116.

Herrenschmidt, Clarisse

1983 Notes sur les deux textes accadiens de Persépolis. *Revue d'Assyriologie* 77:69.

Herzfeld, Ernst

1938 *Altpersische Inschriften.* Archäologischen Mitteilungen aus Iran, Ergänzungsband 1. Berlin: Reimer.

Heskel, Dennis L., and C.C. Lamberg-Karlovsky

1980 An Alternative Sequence for the Development of Metallurgy: Tepe Yahya, Iran. In *The Coming of the Age of Iron,* edited by T.A. Wertime and J.D. Muhly, 229–265. New Haven: Yale University Press.

Hiebert, Fredrik T.

1994 *Origins of the Bronze Age Oasis Civilization in Central Asia.* American School of Prehistoric Research Bulletin 42. Cambridge, Massachusetts: Peabody Museum Press.

Hiebert, Fredrik T., and C.C. Lamberg-Karlovsky

1992 Central Asia and the Indo-Iranian Borderlands. *Iran* 30:1–15.

Hillman, Gordon C.

1984 Interpretation of Archaeological Plant Remains: The

Application of Ethnographic Models from Turkey. In *Plants and Ancient Man,* edited by W. van Zeist and W.A. Casparie, 1–41. Rotterdam: A.A. Balkema.

Hinz, Walther
1969 *Altiranische Funde und Forschungen.* Berlin: de Gruyter.

Hinz, Walther, and Heidemarie Koch
1987 *Elamisches Wörterbuch.* Archaeologische Mitteilungen aus Iran Ergänzunsband 17. Berlin: D. Reimer.

Hjort, Anders
1981 Ethnic Transformation, Dependency and Change: The Iligira Smburu of Northern Kenya. In *Change and Development in Nomadic and Pastoral Societies,* edited by J.G. Galaty and P.C. Salzman, 50–67. Leiden: E. J. Brill.

Højlund, Flemming
1987 *Failaka/Dilmun: The Second Millennium Settlements.* Vol. 2: *The Bronze Age Pottery.* Jutland Archaeological Society Publications 17(2). Aarhus.

1994 *Qala'at al-Bahrain.* Vol. 1: *The Northern City Wall and the Islamic Fortress.* Jutland Archaeological Society Publications 30(1). Aarhus.

Hole, Frank
1969 Report on the Survey of Upper Xuzestan. Preliminary Reports of the Rice University Project in Iran, 1968/9. Ms. on file, Department of Anthropology, Yale University, New Haven.

1974 Tepe Tula'i: An Early Campsite in Khuzistan, Iran. *Paléorient* 2(2):219–242.

1978 Pastoral Nomadism in Western Iran. In *Explorations in Ethnoarchaeology,* edited by R.A. Gould, 127–167. Albuquerque: University of New Mexico Press.

1983 Symbols of Religion and Social Organization at Susa. In *The Hilly Flanks and Beyond. Essays in the Prehistory of Southwestern Asia presented to Robert J. Braidwood,* edited by T.C. Young, Jr., P.E.L. Smith and P. Mortensen, 315–334. Studies in Ancient Oriental Civilizations 36. Chicago: Oriental Institute of the University of Chicago.

1984 Analysis of Structure and Design in Prehistoric Ceramics. *World Archaeology* 15(3):326–347.

1985 The Organization of Susiana Society: Periodization of Site Distributions. *Paléorient* 11(2):21–24.

1987a Archaeology of the Village Period. In *The Archaeology of Western Iran,* edited by F. Hole, 29–79. Washington DC: Smithsonian

1987b Settlement and Society in the Village Period. In *The Archaeology of Western Iran,* edited by F. Hole, 79–105. Washington DC: Smithsonia.

1987c Chronologies in the Iranian Neolithic. In *Chronologies in the Near East/Chronologies du Proche Orient,* edited by O. Aurenche, J. Evin, and F. Hours, 353–379. BAR. International Series 379(i). Oxford: British Archaeological Reports.

1991 Middle Khabur Settlement and Agriculture in the Ninevite V Period. *Bulletin of the Canadian Society for Mesopotamian Studies* 21:17–30.

1997 Evidence for Mid-Holocene Environmental Change in the Western Khabur Drainage, Northeastern Syria, In *Third Millennium BC Climate Change and Old World Collapse,* edited by H.N. Dalfes, G. Kukla, and H. Weiss, 67–106. NATO ASI Monographs in Global Environmental Change. Berlin: Springer.

1998 Paleoenvironment and Human Society in the Jezireh of Northern Mesopotamia 20,000-6,000 BP. *Paléorient* 23(2):39–49.

Hole, Frank, and Kent V. Flannery
1967 The Prehistory of Southwestern Iran: A Preliminary Report. *Proceedings of the Prehistoric Society* 33:147–206.

Hole, Frank, Kent V. Flannery, and James A. Neely
1969 *Prehistory and Human Ecology of the Deh Luran Plain.* Memoirs 1. Ann Arbor: University of Michigan Museum of Anthropology.

Holland, Thomas A.
1976 Preliminary Report on Excavations at Tell Sweyhat, Syria, 1973/74. *Levant* 8:36–70.

1977 Preliminary Report on Excavations at Tell Sweyhat, Syria 1975. *Levant* 9:36–65.

Hooglund, Eric
1982 *Land and Revolution in Iran, 1960–1980.* Austin: University of Texas Press.

1997 Letter from an Iranian Village. *Journal of Palestine Studies* 27(1):76–84.

Hopf, Maria, and U. Willerding
1989 Pflanzenresten. In *Bastam II, Ausgrabungen in den Urartäischen Anlagen 1977–1978,* W. Kleiss, 263–318. *Teheraner Forschungen* 5. Deutsches Archäologisches Institut.

Hourcade, Bernard, Hubert Mazurek, Mahmoud Taleghani, and Mohammad-Hosseyn Papoli-Yazdi
1998 *Atlas d'Iran.* Paris: La Documentation Française.

Huff, Dietrich
1998 'Fire Altars' and Astodans. In *The Art and Archaeology of Ancient Persia. New Light on the Parthian and Sassanian Empires,* edited by V. Curtis, R. Hillenbrand, and J.M. Rogers, 74–83. London: I.B. Tauris.

Ibrahim, Moawiyah
1982 *Excavations of the Arab Expedition at Sar el-Jisr, Bahrain.* Manama: Ministry of Information.

Jacobs, Linda K.
1980 Darvazeh Tepe and the Iranian Highlands in the Second Millennium B.C. Ph.D. Dissertation, Department of Anthropology, University of Oregon, Eugene.

Jacobsen, Thomas W.
1984 Seasonal Pastoralism in Southern Greece: A Consideration of the Ecology of Neolithic Urfirnis Pottery. In *Pots and Potters,* edited by P. Rice, 27–44. Monograph 24, University of California Institute of Archaeology. Los Angeles: University of California Press.

Jacobsen, Thorkild
1987 Mesopotamian Religions: An Overview. In *The Encyclo-*

pedia of Religion, vol. 9, edited by M. Eliade, 447–469. New York: Macmillan Publishing Company.

Jasim, Sabah A.
1985   *The Ubaid Period in Iraq.* BAR International Series 267. Oxford: British Archaeological Reports.

Jéquier, Gustave
1900   Travaux de l'hiver 1898–1899. *Mémoires de la Délégation en Perse* 1:113–138.

Joannès, Francis
1991   L'étain, de l'Élam à Mari. In *Mésopotamie et Élam, actes de la xxxvième Rencontre Assyriologique Internationale (Gand, 10–14 juillet 1989),* 67–76. Mesopotamian History and Environment, Occasional Publication 1. Gand: University of Ghent.

Johns, Jeremy
1998   The Rise of Middle Islamic Hand-Made Geometrically-Painted Ware in Bilad al-Sham (11th–13th c. A.D.). In *Colloque international d'archéologie islamique,* edited by R.-P. Gayraud, 65–96. Cairo: Institut Français d'Archéologie Orientale.

Johnson, Gregory A.
1973   *Local Exchange and Early State Development in Southwestern Iran.* Anthropological Papers 51. Ann Arbor: University of Michigan Museum of Anthropology.
1980   Rank-Size Convexity and System Integration: A View from Archaeology. *Economic Geography* 56:234–247.
1987   Nine Thousand Years of Social Change in Western Iran. In *The Archaeology of Western Iran,* edited by F. Hole, 283–291. Washington DC: Smithsonian Institution Press.
1987   The Changing Organization of Uruk Administration on the Susiana Plain. In *The Archaeology of the Western Iran,* edited by F. Hole, 107–139. Washington DC: Smithsonian Institution Press.

Kellner, Hans-Jörg, ed.
1976   *Urartu, ein wiederentdeckter Rivale Assyriens.* Munich:Prähistorische Staatssammlung München.

Kent, Roland G.
1953   *Old Persian: Grammar, Texts, Lexicon.* American Oriental Series 33. New Haven: American Oriental Society.

Khazanov, Anatoli M.
1980   The Size of Herds Among Pastoral Nomads. *Nomadic People* 7:8–13
1994   *Nomads and the Outside World.* 2nd edition. Madison: University of Wisconsin Press.

Khoury, Philip S., and Joseph Kostiner
1990   *Tribes and State Formation in the Middle East.* Berkeley: University of California Press.

Killick, R.R., H.E.W. Crawford, K. Flavin, H. Ginger, A. Lupton, C. Maclaughlin, R. Montague, J.A. Moon, and M.A. Woodburn
1991   London-Bahrain Archaeological Expedition: 1990 Excavations at Saar. *Arabian Archaeology and Epigraphy* 2:107–137.

Kirkby, Anne, and Michael J. Kirkby
1976   Geomorphic Processes and the Surface Survey of Archaeological Sites in Semi-Arid Areas. In *Geoarchaeology: Earth Science and the Past,* edited by D.A. Davidson and M.L. Shackley, 229–253. London: Duckworth.

Kirkby, Michael J.
1977   Land and Water Resources of the Deh Luran and Khuzistan Plains. In *Studies in the Archeological History of the Deh Luran Plain,* by F. Hole, 251–288. Memoirs 9. Ann Arbor: University of Michigan Museum of Anthropology.

Kleiss, Wolfram
1981   Ein Abschnitt der achämenidischen Königsstrasse von Pasargadae und Persepolis nach Susa, bei Naqsh-i Rustam. *Archäologische Mitteilungen aus Iran* 14:45–53.
1982   Darstellungen urartäischer Architektur. *Archäologische Mitteilungen aus Iran* 15:53–77.
1992a   Dammbauten aus achämenidischer und sasanidischer Zeit in der Provinz Fars. *Archäologische Mitteilungen aus Iran* 25:131–145.
1992b   Beobachtungen auf dem Burgberg von Persepolis. *Archäologische Mitteilungen aus Iran* 25:155–167.
1993a   Kurangun, die Burganlage am elamischen Felsrelief in Sudwest-Iran. In *Aspects of Art and Iconography: Anatolia and Its Neighbors, Studies in Honor of Nimet Özgüç,* edited by M.J. Mellink, E. Porada, and T. Özgüç, 357–360. Ankara: Türk Tarih Kurumu Basımevi.
1993b   Flächensteinbrüche und Einzelsteinbrüche in der Umgebung von Persepolis und Naqsh-i Rustam. *Archäologische Mitteilungen aus Iran* 26:91–103.
1993c   Achämenidische Befestigungen und Anlagen in der westlichen Umgebung von Persepolis am Kuh-e Ayub. *Istanbuler Mitteilungen* 43: 31–338.
1994   Istakhr und Umgebung archäologische Beobachtungen und Befunde. *Archäologische Mitteilungen aus Iran* 27:165–189.

Kleiss, Wolfram, and Harald Hauptmann
1976   *Topographische Karte von Urartu.* Archaeologische Mitteilungen aus Iran 3. Berlin: D. Reimer.

Koch, Heidemarie
1980   Steuern in der achämenidischen Persis? *Zeitschrift für Assyriologie* 70:105–137.

Kohl, Philip L.
1978   The Balance of Trade in Southwestern Asia in the Mid-Third Millennium B.C. *Current Anthropology* 19:463–492.

Kohl, Philip L., and Rita Wright
1977   Stateless Cities: The Differentiation of Societies in the Near Eastern Neolithic. *Dialectical Anthropology* 2:271–283.

Kohlmeyer, Kay
1995   Anatolian Architectural Decorations, Statuary, and Stelae. In *Civilizations of the Ancient Near East,* vol. IV, edited by J.M. Sasson, J. Baines, G. Beckman, and K.S. Rubinson, 2639–2669. New York: Scribner's.

Komoróczy, György
1982   Die Beziehungen zwischen Mesopotamien und dem

iranischen Hochland in der sumerischen Gedichte. In *Mesopotamien und seine Nachbarn, politische und kulturelle Wechselbeziehungen im alten Vorderasien vom 4. bis 1. Jahrtausend v. Chr.,* edited by H.J. Nissen and J. Renger, 87–96. Berlin: D. Reimer.

König, Friedrich W.

1965   *Die elamischen Königsinschriften.* Archiv für Orientforschung 16. Graz.

Kordevani, Mahmoud

1971   Les fouilles de Tchogha Gavaneh. *Bastan-Chenassi va Honar-e Iran* 7/8:36–51 (in Persian), 30–35 (in French).

Kouchoukos, Nicholas

1998   *Landscape and Social Change in Late Prehistoric Mesopotamia.* Ph.D. Dissertation, Yale University, New Haven.

Kouchoukos, Nicholas Nicholas Kouchoukos, Ronald Smith, Art Gleason, Prasad Thenkabail, Frank Hole, Youssef Barkoudah, Jeff Albert, Paul Gluhosky, and Jane Foster

1998   Monitoring the Distribution, Use, and Regeneration of Natural Resources in Semi-arid Southwest Asia. *Yale School of Forestry and Environmental Studies Bulletin Series* 103:467–491.

Kozbe, Gülriz

1990   Van-Dilkaya Höyüğü Erken Transkafkasya Keramiği. In *VII. Araştırma Sonuçları Toplantısı,* 533–554. Ankara.

Kramer, Carol

1977   Pots and People. In *Mountains and Lowlands: Essays in the Archaeology of Greater Mesopotamia,* eds L.D. Levine and T.C. Young, Jr., 91–112. Bibliotheca Mesopotamica 7. Malibu, California: Undena Publications.

1979   *Ethnoarchaeology: Implications of Ethnography for Archaeology.* New York: Columbia University Press.

1980   Estimating Prehistoric Populations, an Ethnographic Approach. In *L'archéologie de l'Iraq: perspectives et limites de l'interpretation anthropologique des documents,* 315–334. Paris: Colloques internationaux du CNRS 580.

1982   *Village Ethnoarchaeology.* New York: Academic Press.

Kroeber, Alfred L.

1945   *The Ancient Oikoumenê as an Historic Cultural Aggregate.* Huxley Memorial Lecture for 1945. London: Royal Anthropological Institute of Great Britain and Ireland.

Kroll, Helmut

1999 [2000] Vor- und frühgeschichtliche Weinreben—wild oder angebant? Eine abschliessende Bemerkung. *Zeitschrift Trierer* 62: 151–153.

Kroll, Stephan

1980   *Urartu, ein wiederentdeckter Rivale Assyriens.* Munster.

Kuftin, B.A.

1941   *Arkheologicheskiye Raskopki v Trialeti, I.* Tbilisi: Akademii Nauk Gruzinskoi SSR.

Kyllo, M. A., and R.N.L.B. Hubbard

1981   Median and Parthian Plant Remains from Tepe Nush-i Jan. *Iran* 19:91–100.

Labat, René

1959   *Manuel d'épigraphie akkadienne.* Paris: Imprimerie Nationale.

Lamberg-Karlovsky, C.C.

1970   *Excavations at Tepe Yahya, Iran 1967–1969.* Bulletin of American School of Prehistoric Research 27. Cambridge, MA: Peabody Museum of Archaeology and Ethnology.

1971a   The Proto-Elamite Settlement at Tepe Yahya. *Iran* 9:87–96.

1971b   Proto-Elamite Account Tablets from Tepe Yahya, Iran. *Kadmos* 10:97–99.

1972   Trade Mechanisms in Indus-Mesopotamian Inter-relations. *Journal of American Oriental Society* 92:222–229.

1975   Urban Interaction on the Iranian Plateau: Excavations at Tepe Yahya. *Proceedings of the British Academy* 49:283–319.

1978   Proto-Elamites on the Iranian Plateau. *Antiquity* 52:114–120.

1985   The Longue Durée of the Ancient Near East. In *De l'Indus aux Balkans, recueil à la mémoire de Jean Deshayes,* edited by J.-L. Huot, M. Yon, and Y. Calvet, 55–72. Paris: Éditions Recherche sur les Civilisations.

1986   Third Millennium Structure and Process: From the Euphrates to the Indus and the Oxus to the Indian Ocean. *Oriens Antiquus* 25:189–219.

1996   *Beyond the Tigris and Euphrates: Bronze Age Civilizations.* Studies by the Department of Bible and Ancient Near East Vol. IX. Beer-Sheva: Ben-Gurion University of the Negev Press.

Lamberg-Karlovsky, C.C., and Maurizio Tosi

1973   Shahr-i Sokhta and Tepe Yahya: Tracks on the Earliest History of the Iranian Plateau. *East and West* 23(1-2):21–57.

1989   The Proto-Elamite Community at Tepe Yahya: Tools of Administration and Social Order. In *South Asian Archaeology 1985,* edited by K. Frifelt and P. Sørenson, 104–113 (Table 3, data by L. Costantini). London: Curzon Press.

Lambert, Maurice

1971   Investiture de fonctionaires en Élam. *Journal asiatique* 259:217–221.

1972   Hutelutush-Inshushinak et le pays d'Anzan. *Revue d'Assyriologie* 66:61–76.

1976   Tablette de Suse avec cachet du Golfe. *Revue d'Assyriologie* 70:71–72.

Lambert, Wilfred G.

1979   Near Eastern Seals in the Gulbenkian Museum of Oriental Art, University of Durham. *Iraq* 41:1–45.

1992   Further notes on a Seal of Ebarat. *Revue d'Assyriologie* 86:123–124.

Lambton, Ann K.S.

1953   *Landlord and Peasant in Persia: A Study of Land Tenure and Land Revenue Administration.* London: Oxford University Press.

1969   *The Persian Land Reform, 1962–1966.* Oxford: Clarendon Press.

Lancaster, William

1997   *The Rwala Bedouin Today.* 2nd edition. Prospect Heights, IL: Waveland Press.

Langdon, Stephen

1925   Review of Scheil 1923. *Journal of the Royal Asiatic Society* (1925), 169–173.

1928   *Pictographic Inscriptions from Jemdet Nasr Excavated by the*

Oxford and Field Museum Expedition. London: Oxford University Press.

Langsdorf, Alexander, and Donald McCown

1942　*Tall-i Bakun.* Publication 54. Chicago: Oriental Institute of the University of Chicago.

Layard, Austin Henry

1894 [1971] *Early Adventures in Persia, Susiana and Babylonia.* London: John Murrary.

Layne, Linda

1994　*Home and Homeland: The Dialogics of Tribal and National Identities in Jordan.* Princeton: Princeton University Press.

LeBreton, Louis

1947　Notes sur la céramique peinte aux environs de Suse et à Suse. *Mémoires de la Mission Archéologique en Iran* 30:120–219. Paris: Presses Universitaires de France.

1957　The Early Periods at Susa: Mesopotamian Relations. *Iraq* 19:79–124.

Le Brun, Alain

1971　Recherches stratigraphiques à l'acropole de Suse (1969-1971). *Cahiers de la Délégation Archéologique Française en Iran* 1:163–214.

1978　Suse, chantier "Acropole I." *Paléorient* 4:177–192.

Le Brun, Alain, and François Vallat

1978　L'origine de l'écriture à Suse. *Cahiers de la Délégation Archéologique Française en Iran* 8:11–52.

Lecoq, Pierre

1997　*Les inscriptions de la Perse achéménide.* Paris: Gallimard.

Leemans, W.F.

1952　*Ishtar of Lagaba and Her Dress.* Leiden: E.J. Brill.

Legrain, Léon

1921　Empreintes des cachets élamites. *Mémoires de la Délégation en Perse* 16. Paris: Édition Ernest Leroux.

Lemcke, Gerry, and Michael Sturm

1997　^{18}O and Trace Element Measurements as Proxy for the Reconstruction of Climate Changes at Lake Van (Turkey): Preliminary Results. In *Third Millennium BC Climate Change and Old World Collapse,* edited by H.N. Dalfes, G. Kukla, and H. Weiss, 653–678. NATO ASI Monographs in Global Environmental Change. Berlin: Springer.

Levine, Louis D.

1974a *Geographical Studies in the Neo-Assyrian Zagros.* Toronto and London: Royal Ontario Museum and British Institute of Persian Studies.

1974b Geographical Studies in the Neo-Assyrian Zagros II. *Iran* 12:99–124.

Limet, Henri

1985　Les rapports entre Mari et l'Élam à l'époque de Zimri-Lim. *Studi epigrafici e linguistici sul Vicino Oriente antico* 2:43–52.

Loftus, W. K.

1857　*Travels and Researches in Chaldea and Susiana.* London: Nisbet & Co.

Luckenbill, D.

1924　*The Annals of Sennacherib.* Chicago: University of Chicago.

1926　*Ancient Records of Assyria and Babylon.* Chicago: University of Chicago Press.

Lyonnet, Bertille

1996　La prospection archéologique de la partie occidentale du Haut-Khabur (Syrie du nord-est): méthodes, résultats et questions autour de l'occupation aux IIIe et IIe millénaires av. n.é. *Amurru* 1:363–376.

Mahboubian, Houshang

1995　*Treasures of the Mountains. The Art of the Medes.* London: Watmoughs Financial Print Ltd.

Majidzadeh, Yousef

1992　The Arjan Bowl. *Iran* 30:131–144.

1998　A Sumerian Fragmentary Statue from Khark Island (in Persian) *Iranian Journal of Archaeology and History* 21/22:2–14.

Makhmalbaf, Mohsen, and Mohammad Ahmadi

1996　*Gabbeh: Film Script and Photographs* (in Persian). Tehran: Ney Publishing House.

Malbran-Labat, Florence

1995　*Les inscriptions royales de Suse.* Paris: Éditions de la Réunion des Musées Nationaux.

Malfoy, Jean-Michel, and Michel Menu

1987　La métallurgie du cuivre à Suse aux IVe et IIIe millénaires: analyses en laboratoire. In *Métallurgie susienne I,* vol. 1, edited by F. Tallon, 355–373. Paris: Éditions de la Réunion des Musées Nationaux.

Mallory, J.P.

1989　*In Search of the Indo-Europeans.* London: Thames and Hudson.

Mallowan, M.E.L.

1936　The Bronze Head of the Agade Period from Nineveh. *Iraq* 3:104–110.

1966　*Nimrud and Its Remains,* vol. I. New York: Dodd, Mead and Co.

Marcus, Michelle I.

1989　Emblems of Authority: The Seals and Sealings from Hasanlu IVB. *Expedition* 31(2-3): 53–63.

1992　The Mosaic Glass Vessels from Hasanlu: A Study in Large Scale Stylistic Trait Distribution. *Art Bulletin* 73: 536–560.

1993　Incorporating the Body: Adornment, Gender, and Social Identity in Ancient Iran. *Cambridge Archaeological Journal* 3:157–178.

1995　Art and Ideology in Ancient Western Asia. In *Civilizations of the Ancient Near East,* vol. IV, edited by J.M. Sasson, J. Baines, G. Beckwith, and K.S. Rubinson, 2487–2505. New York: Scribner's.

1996　*Emblems of Identity and Prestige: The Seals and Sealings from Hasanlu, Iran.* University Museum Monograph 84. Philadelphia: The University of Pennsylvania Museum.

Marfoe, Leon

1979　The Integrative Transformation: Patterns of Socio-political Organization in Southern Syria. *Bulletin of the American Schools for Oriental Research* 234:1–42.

Margueron, Jean-Claude

1982 *Recherche sur les palais mesopotamiens de l'âge du bronze.* Paris: Paul Geuthner.

1987 Quelques remarques concernant l'architecture monumentale à l'époque d'Obeid. In *Préhistoire de la Mésopotamie: la Mésopotamie préhistorique et l'exploration récente du djebel Hamrin,* edited by J.-L. Huot, 349–378. Paris: CNRS.

1997 Temples. In *The Oxford Encyclopedia of Archaeology in the Near East,* vol. 5, edited by E.M. Meyers, 165–169. New York: Oxford University Press.

Markoe, G.

1986 *Phoenician Bronze and Silver Bowls from Cyprus and the Mediterranean.* Berkeley: University of California Press.

Marro, Catherine

1997 *La culture du Haut-Euphrate au Bronze Ancien: essai d'interpretation à partir de la céramique peinte de Keban (Turquie).* Paris: De Boccard.

Marshall, John

1931 *Mohenjo-Daro and the Indus Civilization.* 3 vols. London: A. Probsthain.

Mason, Robert B.

1996 Petrography and Provenance of Timurid Ceramics. In *Tamerlane's Tableware: A New Approach to the Chinoiserie Ceramics of Fifteenth- and Sixteenth-Century Iran,* edited by L. Golombek, R.B. Mason, and G.A. Bailey, 16–56. Toronto: Royal Ontario Museum.

Matheson, Sylvia

1972 *Persia: An Archaeological Guide.* London: Faber and Faber, Ltd.

Maxwell-Hyslop, Rachael

1971 *Western Asiatic Jewellery c. 3000–612 B.C.* London: Methuen.

McCorriston, Joy

1997 The Fiber Revolution: Textile Extensification, Alienation, and Social Stratification in Ancient Mesopotamia. *Current Anthropology* 38:517–549.

McCown, Donald E.

1942 *The Comparative Stratigraphy of Early Iran.* Studies in Ancient Oriental Civilizations 23. Chicago: Oriental Institute of the University of Chicago.

1949 The Iranian Project. *American Journal of Archaeology* 53:54.

1954 The Relative Stratigraphy and Chronology of Iran. In *Relative Chronologies in Old World Archaeology,* edited by R.W. Ehrich, 56–68. Chicago: University of Chicago Press.

McGovern, Patrick E., Donald L. Glusker, Lawrence J. Exner, and Mary M. Voigt

1996 Neolithic Resinated Wine. *Nature* 381:480–481.

McNeil, Robert C.

1978 The "Messenger Texts" of the Third Ur Dynasty. Ph.D. Dissertation, University of Pennsylvania. Ann Arbor: University Microfilms.

Mecquenem, Roland de

1905a Offrandes de fondation du Temple de Chouchinak. *Mémoires de la Délégation en Perse* 7:61–130.

1905b Trouvaille de la statuette d'or. *Mémoires de la Délégation en Perse* 7:131–136.

1943 Fouilles de Suse, 1933-39. *Mémoires de la Mission Archéologique en Iran* 29:3-161.

1943-44 Note sur les modalities funéraires susiennes et leur chronologie. *Vivre et penser* 52:133–147 (*Revue biblique,* sér. 3).

1949 Épigraphie proto-élamite. *Mémoires de la Délégation en Perse* 31:5–150.

1980 Les fouilleurs de Suse, with forward remarks by Pierre Amiet. *Iranica Antiqua* 15:1–48.

Meijer, Diederik

1986 *A Survey in Northeastern Syria.* Istanbul: Netherlands Historical-Archaeological Institute.

Merhav, Rivka

1991 Secular and Cultic Furniture. In *Urartu: A Metalworking Center in the First Millennium B.C.E,* edited by R. Merhav, 246–271. Jerusalem: The Israel Museum.

Michel, Rudolph H., Patrick E. McGovern, and Virginia R. Badler

1993 The First Wine and Beer. *Analytical Chemistry* 65:408A–413A.

Miller, Naomi F.

1981a The Plant Remains. In *An Early Town on the Deh Luran Plain, Excavations at Tepe Farukhabad,* edited by Henry T. Wright, 227–232; 427–430. Memoirs 13. Ann Arbor: University of Michigan Museum of Anthropology.

1981b Plant Remains from Ville Royale II, Susa. *Cahiers de la Délégation Archéologique Française en Iran* 12:137–142.

1982 Economy and Environment of Malyan, a Third Millennium B.C. Urban Center in Southern Iran. Ph.D. Dissertation, Department of Anthropology, University of Michigan, Ann Arbor.

1983 Paleoethnobotanical Results from Bendebal and Jaffarabad. *Cahiers de la Délégation Archéologique Française en Iran* 13:277–284.

1984 The Use of Dung as Fuel: An Ethnographic Example and an Archaeological Application. *Paléorient* 10(2):71–79.

1985 Paleoethnobotanical Evidence for Deforestation in Ancient Iran: A Case Study of Urban Malyan. *Journal of Ethnobiology* 5:1–19.

1990a Clearing Land for Farmland and Fuel. In *Economy and Settlement in the Near East, Analyses of Ancient Sites and Materials,* edited by N.F. Miller, 71–78. MASCA Research Papers in Science and Archaeology, Supplement to vol. 7. Philadelphia: University of Pennsylvania Museum of Archaeology and Anthropology.

1990b Godin Tepe, Iran: Plant Remains from Period V, the Late Fourth Millennium B.C. MASCA Ethnobotanical Laboratory Report 6. Ms. on file, MASCA, University of Pennsylvania Museum of Archaeology and Anthropology, Philadelphia.

1996a Appendix C. Palaeoethnobotany. In *Excavations at Anshan (Tal-e Malyan): The Middle Elamite Period,* by E. Carter, 99–108. Philadelphia: University of Pennsylvania Museum.

1996b Seed-Eaters of the Ancient Near East: Human or Herbivore? *Current Anthropology* 37:521–528.

1997a The Macrobotanical Evidence for Vegetation in the Near East, c. 18000/16000 BC to 4000 BC. *Paléorient* 23(2):197–207.

1997b Farming and Herding along the Euphrates: Environmental Constraint and Cultural Choice (Fourth to Second Millennia B.C. In *Subsistence and Settlement in a Marginal Environment: Tell es-Sweyhat, 1989–1995 Preliminary Report,* edited by R.L. Zettler, 123–132. MASCA Research Papers in Science and Archaeology 14. Philadelphia: University of Pennsylvania Museum of Archaeology and Anthropology.

1998 Review of *Agricultural Changes at Euphrates and Steppe Sites in the Mid-8th to the 6th Millennium B.C.* by Dominique de Moulins. *Paléorient* 24(1):113–114.

1999 Agricultural Development in Western Central Asia in the Chalcolithic and Bronze Ages. *Vegetation History and Archaeobotany* 8:13–19.

Miron, Andrei, and Winfried Orthmann, eds.

1995 *Unterwegs zum goldenen Vlies.* Saarbrücken: Museum für Vor- und Frühgeschichte.

Miroschedji, Pierre de

1973a Vases et objets en stéatite susiens du Musée du Louvre. *Cahiers de la Délégation Archéologique Française en Iran* 3:9–79.

1973b Prospections archéologique dans les vallées de Fasa et de Darab. In *Proceedings of the First Annual Symposium on Archaeological Research in Iran, 1972,* edited by F. Bagherzadeh, 1–7. Tehran: Iranian Centre for Archaeological Research.

1974 Tépé Jalyan, une nécropole du IIIe millénaire av. J.-C. au Fars oriental (Iran). *Arts Asiatiques* 30:19-64.

1976 Stratigraphie de la période néo-élamite à Suse (c. 1100-c. 540). *Paléorient* 4:213–227.

1980 Le dieu élamite Napirisha. *Revue d'Assyriologie* 74:129–143.

1981a Fouilles du chantier Ville Royale II à Suse (1975–1977). I. Les niveaux élamites. *Cahiers de la Délégation Archéologique Française en Iran* 12:9–136.

1981b Observations dans les couches néo-élamites au nord-ouest du tell de la Ville Royale à Suse. *Cahiers de la Délégation Archéologique Française en Iran* 12:143–167.

1981c Prospections archéologiques au Khuzistan en 1977. *Cahiers de la Délégation Archéologique Française en Iran* 12:169–192.

1981d Le dieu élamite au serpent et aux eaux jaillissantes. *Iranica Antiqua* 16:1–25.

1982 Notes sur la glyptique de la fin de l'Élam. *Revue d'Assyriologie* 76:51–63.

1985 La fin du royaume d'Anšan et de Suse et la naissance de l'empire perse. *Zeitschrift für Assyriologie* 75:265–306.

1986 La localisation de Madaktu et l'organisation politique de l'Élam à l'époque néo-élamite. In *Fragmenta historiae aelamicae: mélanges offerts à M.-J. Steve,* edited by L. De Meyer, H. Gasche and F. Vallat, 209–225 Paris: Éditions Recherche sur les Civilisations.

1987 Fouilles du chantier Ville Royale II à Suse (1975–1977). II. Les niveaux d'époques achéménide, séleucide, parthe et islamique. *Cahiers de la Délégation Archéologique Française en Iran* 15:11–143.

1989 Review of U. Seidl, *Die elamischen Felsreliefs von Kurangun und Naqs-e Rustam,* Iranische Denkmäler 12/2, Berlin, D. Reimer Verlag 1986. *Syria* 66:358–362.

1990a La fin de l'Élam: essai d'analyse et d'interprétation. *Iranica Antiqua* 25:47–95.

1990b Note d'orfèvrerie élamite. In *Contribution à l'histoire de l'Iran: mélanges offerts à Jean Perrot,* edited by F. Vallat, 181–194. Paris: Éditions Recherche sur les Civilisations.

1997 Chogha Zanbil. In *The Oxford Encyclopedia of Archaeology in the Near East,* vol. 1, edited by E.M. Meyers, 487–490. New York: Oxford University Press.

Moorey, P.R.S.

1982 *Ur of the Chaldees.* Ithaca, NY: Cornell University Press.

1988 Problems and Perspectives. In *Bronzeworking Centers of Western Asia, c.1000–539 B.C.,* edited by J. Curtis, 23–32. London: Kegan Paul International in association with the British Museum.

1993 Iran: A Sumerian El-Dorado? In *Early Mesopotamia and Iran: Contact and Conflict 3500–1600 B.C.,* edited by J. Curtis, 31–76. London: British Museum Press.

1994 *Ancient Mesopotamian Materials and Industries: The Archaeological Evidence.* Oxford: Clarendon Press.

Moortgat, Anton

1969 *The Art of Ancient Mesopotamia.* London and New York: Phaidon.

Morgan, Jacques de

1894 *Mission Scientifique en Perse I.* Paris: E. Leroux.

1900a Note sur la basse Mésopotamie. *La géographie* 2:247–262.

1900b Travaux au tell de la Citadelle. *Mémoires de la Délégation en Perse* 1:81–87.

1907 Observation sur les origines des arts céramiques dans le bassin méditerranéen. *Révue de l'École d'Anthropologie de Paris* 17:401–417.

1912 Observations sur les couches profondes de l'Acropole à Suse. *Mémoires de la Délégation en Perse* 13:1–25.

Morgan, Lewis H.

1877 *Ancient Society.* London: MacMillan & Co.

Morgan, Peter

1995 Sgraffiato: Types and distribution. In *Cobalt and Lustre: The Nasser D. Khalili Collection of Islamic Art,* vol. 9, edited by Ernst Grube, 119-123. Oxford: Oxford University Press.

Morgan, Peter, and Janet Leatherby

1987 Excavated Ceramics from Sirjan. In *Syria and Iran: Three Studies in Medieval Ceramics,* edited by J. Allan and C. Roberts, 23–172. Oxford: Oxford University Press.

Morony, Michael G.

1995 Material Culture and Urban Identities: The Evidence of Pottery from the Early Islamic Period. In *Identity and Material Culture in the Early Islamic World,* edited by I.A. Bierman, 2–45. Los Angeles: University of California, Near East Center Colloquium Series.

Morrison, Kathleen D.

1996 Typological Schemes and Agricultural Change: Beyond Boserup in Precolonial South India. *Current Anthropology* 37:583–608.

Mortensen, Inge Demant

1993 *Nomads of Luristan: History, Material Culture, and Pastoralism in Western Iran.* London: Thames and Hudson.

Mortensen, Peder

1972 Seasonal Camps and Early Villages in the Zagros. In *Man, Settlement and Urbanism,* edited by P.J. Ucko, R. Tringham, and G.W. Dimbleby, 293–297. London: Duckworth.

Mortier, Roland

1990 *Le cœur et la raison: recueil d'études sur le dix-huitième siècle.* Oxford: Voltaire Foundation.

Moulins, Dominque

1997 *Agricultural Changes at Euphrates and Steppe Sites in the Mid-8th to the 6th Millennium B.C.* BAR International Series 683. Oxford: British Archaeological Reports.

MTA (Maden Tetkik ve Arama Genel Müdürlüğü).

1988 Türkiye Jeoloji Haritalar Serisi. Muş (H33, G33). Ankara.

Mudar, Karen M.

1982 Early Dynastic III Animal Utilization in Lagash: A Report on the Fauna from Tell al-Hibba. *Journal of Near Eastern Studies* 4:23–34.

Mughal, M. Rafique

1983 *The Dilmun Burial Complex at Sar: The 1980–82 Excavations in Bahrain.* Manama: Ministry of Information.

Muhly, James D.

1973 Copper and Tin. *Transactions of the Connecticut Academy of Arts and Sciences* 43:155–535.

1988 Concluding Remarks. In *Bronzeworking Centers of Western Asia, c. 1000–539 B.C.,* edited by J. Curtis, 329–342. London: Kegan Paul International in association with the British Museum.

Münter, Friederich

1802 *Versuch über die keilförmigen Inschriften zu Persepolis.* Copenhagen: Proft.

Muscarella, Oscar White

1965 Lion Bowls from Hasanlu. *Archaeology* 18(1):41–46.

1971 Hasanlu in the Ninth Century BC and Its Relations with other Cultural Centers of the Near East. *American Journal of Archaeology* 75:263–265.

1974 A Third Lion Bowl from Hasanlu. *Expedition* 16(2):25–30.

1980 *The Catalogue of Ivories from Hasanlu, Iran.* University Museum Monograph 40. Philadelphia: The University of Pennsylvania Museum.

1988 *Bronze and Iron. Ancient Near Eastern Artifacts in the Metropolitan Museum of Art.* New York: Metropolitan Museum of Art.

1989 Warfare at Hasanlu in the Late 9th Century B.C. *Expedition* 31(2-3):24–36.

1994 Miscellaneous Median Matters. *Achaemenid History 8: Continuity and Change,* edited by H. Sancisi-Weerdenburg, H. Kuhrt, and M.C. Root, 57–64. Leiden: Nederlands Instituut voor het Nabije Oosten.

Nagel, Wolfram

1964 *Djamdat Nasr-Kulturen und Frühdynastische Buntkeramiker.* Berlin: Bruno Hessling Verlag.

Neely, James A., and Henry T. Wright

1994 *Early Settlement and Irrigation on the Deh Luran Plain, Iran.* Technical Reports 26. Ann Arbor: University of Michigan Museum of Anthropology.

Negahban, Ezat O.

1983 *Metal Vessels from Marlik.* Prähistorische Bronzefunde, Abteilung II, Band 3. München: C.H. Beck.

1991 *Excavations at Haft Tepe, Iran.* University Museum Monograph 70. Philadelphia: University Museum, University of Pennsylvania.

1996 *Marlik. The Complete Excavation Report.* University Museum Monograph 87. Philadelphia: University Museum, University of Pennsylvania.

1997 *Fifty Years of Iranian Archaeology* (in Persian). Tehran: Iranian Cultural Heritage Organization.

Nesbitt, Mark, and Geoffrey D. Summers

1988 Some Recent Discoveries of Millet (*Panicum miliaceum* L. and *Setaria italica* (L.) P. Beauv.) at Excavations in Turkey and Iran. *Anatolian Studies* 38:85–97.

Nicholas, Ilene M.

1980 A Spatial/Functional Analysis of the Late 4th Millennium Occupation at the TUV Mound, Tal-e Malyan, Iran. Ph.D. Dissertation, Department of Anthropology, University of Pennsylvania, Philadelphia.

1990 *The Proto-Elamite Settlement at TUV.* Malyan Excavation Reports, vol. 1. University Museum Monograph 69. Philadelphia: University Museum, University of Pennsylvania.

Nickerson, Janet W.

1977 Malyan Wall Paintings. *Expedition* 19(3):3–6.

Nickerson, John L.

1983 Intrasite Variability during the Kaftari Period at Tal-e Malyan (Anshan), Iran. Ph.D. Dissertation, Department of Anthropology, The Ohio State University, Columbus

1991 Investigating Intrasite Variability at Tal-e Malyan (Anshan), Iran. *Iranica Antiqua* 26:1–38.

Nicol, Murray B.

1970 Rescue Excavations near Dorudzan. *East and West* 20:245–265.

Niebuhr, Carsten

1778 *Reisebeschreibung nach Arabien und andern umliegenden Ländern,* II. Copenhagen: Möller.

Nissen, Hans J.

1976   The Behbehan Plain in the Fifth Millennium B.C. In *The Memorial Volume of the VIth International Congress of Iranian Art and Archaeology, Oxford, September 11–16, 1972,* edited by M.Y. Kiani, 273–280. Tehran: Iranian Centre for Archaeological Research.

1983   Political Organization and Settled Zone: A Case Study from the Ancient Near East. In *The Hilly Flanks and Beyond. Essays in the Prehistory of Southwestern Asia presented to Robert J. Braidwood,* edited by T.C. Young, Jr., P.E.L. Smith, and P. Mortensen, 335–346. Studies in Ancient Oriental Civilizations 36. Chicago: Oriental Institute of the University of Chicago.

Oates, David

1968   The Excavations at Tell al-Rimah 1967. *Iraq* 30:115–138.

1970   The Excavations at Tell al-Rimah 1966. *Iraq* 32:1–26.

1974   Balawat (Imgur Enlil): The Site and Its Buildings. *Iraq* 36:173–178.

Oates, David, and Joan Oates

1994   Tell Brak: A Stratigraphic Summary. *Iraq* 56:167–176.

Oates, Joan

1986   *Babylon.* London: Thames and Hudson.

Oganesian, V.E.

1992   A Silver Goblet from Karashamb. *Soviet Anthropology and Archaeology* 30(4):84–102.

Olszewski, Deborah

1993a   The Late Baradostian Occupation at Warwasi Rockshelter, Iran. In *The Paleolithic Prehistory of the Zagros-Taurus,* edited by D. Olszewski and H.L. Dibble, 187–206. University Museum Monographs 83. Philadelphia: University of Pennsylvania Museum.

1993b   The Zarzian Occupation at Warwasi Rockshelter, Iran. In *The Paleolithic Prehistory of the Zagros-Taurus,* edited by D.I. Olszewski and H.L. Dibble, 207–236. University Museum Monograph 83: Philadelphia: University of Pennsylvania Museum.

Olszewski, Deborah, and Harold L. Dibble, eds.

1993   *The Paleolithic Prehistory of the Zagros-Taurus.* University Museum Monograph 83: Philadelphia: University of Pennsylvania Museum.

Oppenheim, A. Leo

1977   *Ancient Mesopotamia. Portrait of a Dead Civilization.* 2nd revised edition. Chicago: University of Chicago Press.

Overlaet, Bruno

1997   A Report on the 1952 and 1954/55 Soundings at Tall-i Taimuran (Fars), Iran. A File-Excavation at the Royal Museums of Art and History, Brussels. *Iranica Antiqua* 32:1–51.

Özgüç, Nimet

1965   The Anatolian Group of Cylinder Seal Impressions from Kültepe. *Türk Tarih Kurumu Yayınlarından* V. seri, no. 22. Ankara: Türk Tarih Kurumu Basımevi.

Paine, Richard R., ed.

1997   *Integrating Archaeological Demography: Multidisciplinary Approaches to Prehistoric Populations.* Occasional Papers 24. Carbondale, IL: Southern Illinois University.

Paper, Herbert

1955   *The Phonology and Morphology of Royal Achaemenid Elamite.* Ann Arbor: University of Michigan Press.

Parrot, André

1953   *Mari: documentation photographique de la Mission Archéologique de Mari.* Neuchâtel et Paris: Éditions Ides et Calendes.

1961   *Nineveh and Babylon.* London: Thames and Hudson.

Payne, Sebastian

1973   Kill-Off Patterns in Sheep and Goats: The Mandibles from Aşvan Kale. *Anatolian Studies* 23:281–303.

Pecorella, Paolo E., and Mirjo Salvini

1984   *Tra lo Zagros e l'Urmia.* Rome: Edizioni dell'Ateneo.

Perrot, Jean

1978   Introduction. *Paléorient* 4:133–140.

Pézard, Maurice

1914   *Mission à Bender Bouchir.* Mémoires de la Délégation enPerse 15. Paris.

Pézard, Maurice, and Edmond Pottier

1913   *Antiquités de la Susiane (Mission J. de Morgan).* Paris: Ernest Leroux.

1926   *Catalogue des antiquités de la Susiane (Mission J. de Morgan).* 2nd edition. Paris: Musées Nationaux.

Pigott, Vincent C.

1989a   Archaeo-metallurgical Investigations at Bronze Age Tappeh Hesar, 1976. In *Tappeh Hesar, Reports of the 1976 Restudy Project,* edited by R.H. Dyson, Jr. and S.M. Howard, 25–33. Florence: Casa Editrice La Lettere.

1989b   The Emergence of Iron Use at Hasanlu. *Expedition* 31(2-3):67–79.

1996   Near Eastern Archaeometallurgy: Modern Research and Future Directions. *The Study of the Ancient Near East in the Twenty-first Century,* edited by J. Cooper and G.M. Schwartz, 139–176. Winona Lake, IN: Eisenbrauns.

1999a   The Development of Metal Production on the Iranian Plateau: An Archaeometallurgical Perspective. In *The Archaeometallurgy of the Asian Old World,* edited by V.C. Pigott, 73–106. MASCA Research Papers in Science and Archaeology 16. Philadelphia: University of Pennsylvania Museum of Archaeology and Anthropology.

1999b   A Heartland of Metallurgy. Neolithic/Chalcolithic Metallurgical Origins on the Iranian Plateau. In *The Beginnings of Metallurgy,* edited by A. Hauptmann, E. Pernicka, T. Rehren, and U. Yalcin, 109–122. *Der Anschnitt 9.*

Pigott, Vincent C., Harry C. Rogers, and Samuel K. Nash

2003   Archaeometallurgical Investigations at Tal-e Malyan: The Banesh Period. In *Early Urban Life in the Land of Anshan: Excavations at Tal-e Malyan in the Highlands of Iran,* edited by W.M. Sumner. Philadelphia: University of Pennsylvania Museum.

Pilipossian, Achot P., and Jacques Santrot
1996   34. Goblet à scènes de chasse et de guerre. In *Arménie: trésors de l'Arménie ancienne des origines au IVe siècle,* edited by J. Santrot, 65–67. Paris: Somogy Éditions d'Art.

Piotrovskii, Boris B.
1967   *Urartu: The Kingdom of Van and Its Art.* London: Evelyn Adams and Mackay.

Pittman, Holly
1980   Proto-Elamite Art from Malyan: Work in Progress. Paper presented at 45th Annual Meeting of the Society for American Archaeology, Philadelphia.
1992   The Late Uruk Period. In *The Royal City of Susa,* edited by P.O. Harper, J.Aruz, and F. Tallon, 48–53. New York: The Metropolitan Museum of Art.
1994   *Glazed Steatite Glyptic Style: The Structure amd Function of an Image System in the Adminstration of Protoliterate Mesopotamia.* Berliner Beitrage sum Vorderen Orient. Berlin: D. Reimer.
N.D.   *The Glyptic Art from Tal-i Malyan.* University of Pennsylvania Museum Monograph. Philadelphia: University of Pennsylvania Museum. In preparation.

Pollock, Susan
1983   Style and Information: An Analysis of Susiana Ceramics. *Journal of Anthropological Archaeology* 2:354–390.

Pollock, Susan, and Henry T. Wright
1987   Regional Socio-Economic Organization in Southern Mesopotamia: The Middle and Late Fifth Millennium. In *Préhistoire de la Mésopotamie: la Mésopotamie préhistorique et l'exploration récente du djebel Hamrin,* edited by J.-L. Huot, 317–329. Paris: Éditions CNRS.

Porada, Edith
1959   The Hasanlu Bowl. *Expedition* 1(3):19–22.
1962   *Alt Iran: die Kunst in vorislamischer Zeit.* Baden-Baden: Holle Verlag.
1965   *The Art of Ancient Iran.* New York: Crown Publishers.
1967   Notes on the Gold Bowl and Silver Beaker from Hasanlu. In *A Survey of Persian Art,* vol. 14, edited by A.U. Pope and P. Ackerman, 2971–2978. London: Oxford University Press.
1970   *Tchoga Zanbil (Dur-Untash).* Vol. IV: *La glyptique.* Mémoires de la Mission Archéologique en Iran 42. Paris: P. Geuthner.
1988   Discussion of a Cylinder Seal, Probably from Southeast Iran. *Iranica Antiqua* 23:139–143.
1990   More Seals of the Time of the Sukkulmah. *Revue d'Assyriologie* 84:171–182.

Postgate, Carolyn, David Oates, and Joan Oates
1997   *The Excavations at Tell Rimah: The Pottery.* Iraq Archaeological Reports no. 4, British School of Archaeology in Iraq. Warminster: Aris and Phillips.

Postgate, Nicholas
1994   How Many Sumerians per Hectare? — Probing the Anatomy of an Early City. *Cambridge Archaeological Journal* 4(1):47–65.

Pottier, Marie-Hélène
1984   *Matérial funéraire de la Bactriane méridionale de l'âge du bronze.* Paris: Éditions Recherche sur les Civilisations.

Potts, D.T.
1981   Towards an Integrated History of Culture Change in the Arabian Gulf Area: Notes on Dilmun, Makkan and the Economy of Ancient Sumer. *Journal of Oman Studies* 4: 29–52.
1982   The Zagros Frontier and the Problem of Relations between the Iranian Plateau and Southern Mesopotamia in the Third Millennium B.C. In *Mesopotamien und seine Nachbarn, politische und kulturelle Wechselbeziehungen im alten Vorderasien vom 4. bis 1. Jahrtausend v. Chr.,* edited by H.J. Nissen and J. Renger, 33–55. Berlin: D. Reimer.
1990   *The Arabian Gulf in Antiquity,* vol. 1. Oxford: Clarendon Press.
1993a   Patterns of Trade in Third-Millennium BC Mesopotamia and Iran. *World Archaeology* 24/3:379–402.
1993b   Rethinking Some Aspects of Trade in the Arabian Gulf. *World Archaeology* 24:423–440.
1999   *The Archaeology of Elam: Formation and Transformation of an Ancient Iranian State.* Cambridge: Cambridge University Press.

Potts, Timothy F.
1994   *Mesopotamia and the East. An Archaeological and Historical Study of Foreign Relations ca. 3400–2000 BC.* Oxford University Committee for Archaeology Monograph 37. Oxford: Oxbow Books.

Prickett, Martha
1986   Man, Land and Water: Settlement Distribution and the Development of Irrigation Agriculture in the Upper Rud-i Gushk Drainage, Southeastern Iran. Ph.D. Dissertation, Harvard University, Cambridge MA.

Pritchard, James B.
1969   *Ancient Near Eastern Texts Relating to the Old Testament.* Princeton: Princeton University Press.

Rautman, Marcus
1998   Handmade Pottery and Social Change: The View from Late Roman Cyprus. *Journal of Mediterranean Archaeology* 11:81–104.

Rawlinson, Henry C.
1839   Notes on a March from Zohab…to Khuzistan, and Thence through the Province of Luristan to Kermanshah. *Journal of the Royal Geographical Society* 9:26–116.

Redding, Richard W.
1981   Decision Making in Subsistence Herding of Sheep and Goats in the Middle East. Ph.D. Dissertation, University of Michigan, Ann Arbor.

Redman, Charles L.
1973   Multistage Fieldwork and Analytical Techniques. *American Antiquity* 38:61–79.

Redfield, Robert
1995   *The Little Community: Viewpoints for the Study of a Human Whole.* Chicago: University of Chicago Press.

Reiner, Erica

1969 The Elamite Language. In *Altkleinasiastiche Sprache.* Handbuch der Orientalistik 1. Abteilung, 2. Band, 1.-2. Abschnitt, Lieferung 2, 54–118. Leiden and Köln: E. J. Brill.

1973a The Location of Anshan. *Revue d'Assyriologie* 67:57–62.

1973b Inscription from a Royal Elamite Tomb. *Archiv für Orientforschung* 24:87–102.

Renfrew, Colin

1972 Patterns of Population Growth in the Prehistoric Aegean. In *Man, Settlement and Urbanism,* edited by P.J. Ucko, R. Tringham, and G.W. Dimbleby, 383–399. London: Duckworth.

1978 Trajectory Discontinuity and Morphogenesis: The Implications of Catastrophe Theory for Archaeology. *American Antiquity* 43:203–222.

1979 Systems Collapse as Social Transformation: Catastrophe and Anastrophe in Early State Societies. In *Transformation: Mathematical Approaches to Cultural Change,* edited by C. Renfrew and K.L. Cooke, 481–506. New York: Academic Press.

Roaf, Michael

1982 The Hamrin Sites. In *Fifty Years of Mesopotamian Discoveries,* edited by J. Curtis, 40–47. London: The British School of Archaeology in Iraq.

1983 Sculptures and Sculptors at Persepolis. *Iran* 21.

1987 The 'Ubaid Architecture of Tell Madhhur. In *Préhistoire de la Mésopotamie: la Mésopotamie préhistorique et l'exploration récente du djebel Hamrin,* edited by J.-L. Huot, 425–435. Paris: CNRS.

1989 The Art of the Achaemenians. In *The Arts of Persia,* edited by R.W. Ferrier, 26–47. New Haven: Yale University Press.

1995 Palaces and Temples in Ancient Mesopotamia. In *Civilizations of the Ancient Near East*, vol. I, edited by J.M. Sasson, J. Baines, G. Beckwith, and K.S. Rubinson, 423–441. New York: Scribner's.

1998 Multiple Rabbets on Doors in Iron Age Assyria and Iran. *Iranica Antiqua* 33(1):57–80.

Robertson, John F.

1995 The Social and Economic Organization of Ancient Mesopotamian Temples. In *Civilizations of the Ancient Near East*, vol. I, edited by J.M. Sasson, J. Baines, G. Beckwith, and K.S. Rubinson, 443-454. New York: Scribner's.

Root, Margaret Cool

1979 *The King and Kingship in Achaemenid Art.* Leiden: E.J. Brill.

Rosen-Ayalon, Myriam

1974 *La poterie islamique, Ville Royale de Suse IV.* Mémoire de la Délégation Archéologique en Iran 50. Paris.

Rosenberg, Michael

1985 Report on a Sondage at Eshkaft-e Gavi, Iran. *Iran* 23:51–62.

1988 Paleolithic Settlement Patterns in the Marv Dasht, Fars Province, Iran. Ph.D. Dissertation, Department of Anthropology, University of Pennsylvania, Philadelphia.

Rosenberg, Michael, and H. Togul

1991 The Batman River Archaeological Site Survey, 1990. *Anatolica* 17: 241–254.

Rostoker, William, and James Drorak

1991 Some Experiments with Co-Smelting to Copper Alloys. *Archaeomaterials* 5:5–20.

Rostoker, William, M. McNallan, and Elizabeth R. Gebhard

1983 Melting/Smelting of Bronze at Isthmia. *Journal of the Historical Metallurgy Society* 17:23–27.

Rothman, Mitchell S.

1998 The Second Wave: Transcaucasian-Anatolian Interaction in the Murat/Euphrates Basin at the Beginning of the Third Millennium B.C. Paper presented at the Annual Meeting of the American Institute of Archaeology, Washington DC.

2000 Environmental and Cultural Factors in the Development of a Marginal, Highland Zone. *The Archaeology of Jordan and Beyond: Essays in Honor of James A. Sauer,* edited by L.E. Stager, J.A. Greene and M.D. Coogan, 429–433. Boston: Scholars Press.

2001 *Tepe Gawra: The Evolution of a Small, Prehistoric Center in Northern Iraq.* Philadelphia: University Museum Publications.

2003 Ripples in the Stream. Transcaucasian-Anatolian Interaction in the Murat/Euphrates Basin at the Beginning of the Third Millennium B.C. In *Archaeology in the Borderlands: Investigations in Caucasia and Beyond,* edited by A.T. Smith and K.S. Rubinson. Monograph 47. Los Angeles: Cotsen Institute of Archaeology.

Rothman, Mitchell S., and M. James Blackman

1990 Monitoring Administrative Spheres of Action in Late Prehistoric Northern Mesopotamia with the Aid of Chemical Characterization (INAA) of Sealing Clays. In *Economy and Settlement in the Near East: Analyses of Ancient Sites and Materials,* edited by N.F. Miller. MASCA Research Papers in Science and Archaeology, Supplement to vol. 7. Philadelphia: University of Pennsylvania Museum of Archaeology and Anthropology.

Rothman, Mitchell S., and Gülriz Kozbe

1997 Muş in the Early Bronze Age. *Anatolian Studies* 47:105–126.

Roux, George

1964 *Ancient Iraq.* New York: World Publishing.

Rowton, Michael

1973a Autonomy and Nomadism in Western Asia. *Orientalia* 42:247–258.

1973b Urban Autonomy in a Nomadic Environment. *Journal of Near Eastern Studies* 32:201–215.

1974 Enclosed Nomadism. *Journal of Economic and Social History of the Orient* 17:1–30.

1981 Economic and Political Factors in Ancient Nomadism. In *Nomads and Sedentary Peoples,* edited by J.S. Castillo, 25–36. Mexico: El Colegio de Mexico.

Rubinson, Karen S.

1977 The Chronology of the Middle Bronze Age Kurgans at Trialeti. In *Mountains and Lowlands: Essays in the Archaeology of Greater Mesopotamia,* edited by L.D. Levine and T.C.

Young, Jr., 235–249. Bibliotheca Mesopotamica 7. Malibu: Undena.

2003 Silver Vessels and Cylinder Sealings: Precious Reflections of Economic Exchange in the Early Second Millennium B.C. In *Archaeology in the Borderlands: Investigations in Caucasia and Beyond*, edited by A.T. Smith and K.S. Rubinson. Monograph 47. Los Angeles: Cotsen Institute of Archaeology.

Russell, H.F.

1980 *Pre-Classical Pottery of Eastern Anatolia*. British Institute of Archaeology at Ankara Monograph 2. BAR International Series 85. Oxford: British Archaeological Reports.

Russell, James

1986 Transformations in Early Byzantine Urban Life: The Contribution and Limitations of Archaeological Evidence. In *The 17th International Byzantine Congress, Major Papers*, 137–154. New York: Aristide D. Caratzas.

Rutten, M.

1935 *Encyclopédie photographique de l'art I*. Paris: n.p.

Sachs, A.

1955 Ritual to be Followed by the *Kadur*-Priest when Covering the Temple Kettle-Drum. In *Ancient Near Eastern Texts*, edited by J.B. Pritchard, 334–338. Princeton: Princeton University Press.

Sachs, Curt

1940 *A History of Musical Instruments*. New York: W.W. Norton.

Sagona, Antonio

1984 *The Caucasian Region in the Early Bronze Age*. BAR International Series 214. Oxford: British Archaeological Reports.

1994 *The Aşvan Sites 3. Early Bronze Keban Rescue Excavations, Eastern Anatolia*. British Institute of Archaeology Monographs 18. Ankara.

2000 Sos Höyük and the Erzurum Region in Late Prehistory: A Provisional Chronology for Northeast Anatolia. In *Chronologies des pays du Caucase et l'Euphrate aux IVe-IIIe millénaires*, edited by C. Marro and H. Hauptmann, 329–374. Paris: DeBoccard.

Salvatori, Sandro, and Massimo Vidale

1982 A Brief Surface Survey of the Protohistoric Site of Shahdad (Kerman, Iran): Preliminary Report. *Rivista di Archaeologia* 6:5–10.

Salvini, Mirjo

1998 Linear Elamite. In *Encyclopaedia Iranica*, vol. 8, fasc. 3, edited by E. Yarshater, 330–332. Costa Mesa, CA: Mazda.

Salzman, Philip Carl

1972 Multi-Resource Nomadism in Iranian Baluchistan. In *Perspectives on Nomadism*, edited by W. Irons and N. Dyson-Hudson, 60–68. Leiden: E.J. Brill.

1992 *Kin and Contract in Baluchi Herding Camps*. Baluchistan Monograph Series 2. Naples: Instituto Universitario Orientale, Dipartimento di Studi Asiatici.

1996a Introduction: Varieties of Pastoral Systems. In *The Anthropology of Tribal and Peasant Pastoral Societies*, edited by U. Fabietti and P.C. Salzman, 21–37. Pavia: Collegio Ghislieri.

1996b Peasant Pastoralism. In *The Anthropology of Tribal and Peasant Pastoral Societies*, edited by U. Fabietti and P.C. Salzman, 149–166. Pavia: Collegio Ghislieri.

1999 *The Anthropology of Real Life: Events in Human Experience*. Prospect Heights, IL: Waveland Press.

2000 *Black Tents of Baluchistan*. Washington DC: Smithsonian Institution Press.

Salzman, Philip Carl, ed.

1980 *When Nomads Settle: Processes of Sedentarization as Adaptation and Response*. New York: Praeger.

Sancisi-Weerdenburg, Heleen

1994 The Orality of Herodotus' Medikos Logos or: The Median Empire Revisited. In *Achaemenid History 8: Continuity and Change*, edited by H. Sancisi-Weerdenburg, A. Kuhrt and M.C. Root, 39–55. Leiden: Nederlands Instituut voor Het Nabije Oosten.

Sarraf, M.R.

1990 Kiddin-hutran's Bronze Bowl from Arjan, Behbahan. (in Persian). *Asar (Athar)* 17:4–61.

Sayre, Edward V., K. Aslihan Yener, and Emil C. Joel

1992 Statistical Evaluation of the Presently Accumulated Lead Isotope Data from Anatolia and Surrounding Regions. *Archaeometry* 34:73–105.

Schacht, Robert M.

1976 Some Notes on the Development of Rural Settlement on the Susiana Plain. *Proceedings of the 4th Annual Symposium on Archaeological Research in Iran, 1975* 4:446–462.

1981 Estimating Past Population Trends. *Annual Review of Anthropology* 10:119–140.

1984 The Contemporaneity Problem. *American Antiquity* 49:678-695.

1987 The Early Historic Cultures. In *The Archaeology of Western Iran*, edited by F. Hole, 171–203. Washington DC: Smithsonian Institution Press.

Scheil, Vincent

1900 Petites textes. *Mémoires de la Délégation en Perse* 2:129–133.

1901 *Textes élamites-anzanites. Première série*. Mémoires de la Délégation en Perse 3. Paris: E. Leroux.

1905 Document archaïque en écriture proto-élamite: considérations générales. *Mémoires de la Délégation en Perse* 6:57–128.

1907 *Textes élamites-anzanites. Troisième série*. Mémoires de la Délégation en Perse 9. Paris: E. Leroux.

1923 *Textes de comptabilité proto-élamite. Nouvelle série*. Mémoires de la Délégation en Perse 17. Paris.

1935 *Textes de comptabilité proto-élamite (Troisième série)*. Mémoires de la Délégation en Perse 26. Paris.

Schmidt, Erich F.

1940 *Flights Over the Ancient Cities of Iran*. Chicago: University of Chicago Press.

1953 *Persepolis I. Structures, Reliefs, Inscriptions*. Publication 68. Chicago: Oriental Institute of the University of Chicago.

1957   *Persepolis II. Contents of the Treasury and Other Discoveries.*
       Publication 69. Chicago: Oriental Institute of the Uni-
       versity of Chicago.

Schmidt, Erich F., Maurits N. Van Loon, and Hans Curvers
1989   *The Holmes Expedition to Luristan.* Publication 108. Chi-
       cago: Oriental Institute of the University of Chicago.

Seidl, Ursula
1986   *Die elamischen Felsenreliefs von Kurangun und Naqs-e Rustam.*
       Iranische Denkmäler, Lieferung 12, Reihe 2, Iranische
       Felsreliefs H. Berlin: D. Reimer.
1990   Altelamische Siegel. In *Contribution à l'histoire de l'Iran:
       mélanges offerts à Jean Perrot,* edited by F. Vallat, 129–135.
       Paris: Éditions Recherche sur les Civilisations.

Sevin, Veli
1994   Three Urartian Rock-Cut Tombs from Palu. *Tel Aviv*
       21(1):58–67.

Shahbazi, A. Shapur
1985   *Old Persian Inscriptions of the Persepolis Platform.* Corpus
       Inscriptionum Iranicarum, pt. 1, v. 1. London: Lund
       Humphries.

Shahmirzadi, Sadegh Malek
1986   A Review of the Development of Archaeology in Iran
       (in Persian). *Asar (Athar)* 12–14:133–160.

Shahnazarian, Alfred, and Iveta Mkrtchian
N.D.   *The State History Museum of Armenia.* Watertown, MA and
       Yerevan: ALMA.

Shareq, A., V.M. Chmyriov, K.F. Stazhilo-Alexseev, V.I. Dronov,
       D.J. Gannon, G.K. Lubemov, A.Kh. Kafarshiy, and E.P.
       Malyarov
1977   Mineral Resources of Afghanistan, 2nd ed. Afghan Geo-
       logical and Mines Survey, United Nations Development
       Support Project, AFG/74/012. Kabul: Ministry of Mines
       and Industries.

Sherratt, Andrew
1992   What Can Archaeologists Learn from Annalistes? In *Ar-
       chaeology, Annales, and Ethnohistory,* edited by A.B. Knapp,
       135–142. Cambridge: Cambridge University Press.

Shkoda, Valentine
1998   Iranian Traditions in Sogdian Temple Architecture. In
       The Art and Archaeology of Ancient Persia, edited by V.S.
       Curtis, R. Hillenbrand, and J.M.Rogers, 122–132. New
       York, London: I.B.Taurus.

Shott, Michael J.
1996   Mortal Pots: On Use Life and Vessel Size in the Forma-
       tion of Ceramic Assemblages. *American Antiquity* 61:463–
       482.

Sigrist, Marcel, and K. Butz
1986   Wirtschaftliche Beziehungen zwischen der Susiana und
       Südmesopotamien in der Ur-III-Zeit. *Archäologische
       Mitteilungen aus Iran* 19:27–31.

Skinner, J.H.
1965   The Flake Industries of Southwest Asia: A Typological
       Study. Ph.D. Dissertation, Columbia University, New
       York.

Smith, Philip E.L.
1986   *Paleolithic Archaeology in Iran.* American Institute of
       Iranian Studies Monographs 1. Philadelphia: University
       of Pennsylvania Museum.

Smith, Philip E.L., and T. Cuyler Young Jr.
1972   The Evolution of Early Agriculture and Culture in
       Greater Mesopotamia. In *Population Growth: Anthropological
       Implications,* edited by B. Spooner, 1–59. Cambridge,
       MA: MIT Press.
1983   The Force of Numbers. Population Pressure in the Cen-
       tral Western Zagros, 12,000–4500 B.C. In *The Hilly
       Flanks and Beyond. Essays in the Prehistory of Southwestern
       Asia Presented to Robert J. Braidwood,* edited by T.C. Young,
       Jr., P.E.L. Smith, and P. Mortensen, 141–161. Studies
       in Ancient Oriental Civilizations 36. Chicago: Oriental
       Institute of the University of Chicago.

Solheim, Wilhelm G. II
1960   The Use of Sherd Weights and Counts in the Handling
       of Archaeological Data. *Current Anthropology* 1:325–329.

Sollberger, E., and J.R. Kupper
1971   *Inscriptions royales sumériennes et akkadiennes.* Littératures
       anciennes du Proche-Orient 3. Paris: Éditions du Cerf.

Spencer, Herbert
1851   *Social Statics.* London: John Chapman.

Spooner, Brian
1975   *The Cultural Ecology of Pastoral Nomads.* Addison-Wesley
       Module in Anthropology 45. Reading, MA: Addison-
       Wesley.

Spycket, Agnès
1981   *La statuaire du Proche-Orient ancien.* Leiden and Cologne:
       E.J. Brill.
1992   *Les figurines de Suse, I: les figurines humaines.* Mémoires de
       la Délégation Archéologique en Iran 52. Paris.

Stack, Edward
1882   *Six Months in Persia.* 2 vols. New York: G.P. Putnam's Sons.

Starr, Richard F.S.
1937   *Nuzi: Report on the Excavations at Yorgan Tepe near Kirkuk,
       Iraq.* Harvard-Radcliffe Fine Arts Series. Cambridge:
       Harvard University Press.

Stech, Tamara, and Vincent C. Pigott
1986   The Metals Trade in Southwest Asia in the Third Mil-
       lennium B.C. *Iraq* 48:39–64.

Stein, Diana
1989   Art and Architecture. In *The Hurrians,* by G. Wilhelm,
       80-90. Warminster: Aris and Phillips.

Stein, Gil J.
1987   Regional Economic Integration in Early State Societies:
       Third Millennium B.C. Pastoral Production at Gritille,
       Southeast Turkey. *Paléorient* 13:101–111.

Stein, Gil J., and Patricia A. Wattenmaker
1990   The 1987 Tell Leilan Regional Survey: Preliminary Re-
       port. In *Economy and Settlement in the Near East, Analyses of
       Ancient Sites and Materials,* edited by N.F. Miller, 5–18.
       MASCA Research Papers in Science and Archaeology,
       Supplement to vol. 7. Philadelphia: University of Penn-
       sylvania Museum of Archaeology and Anthropology.

Stein, Marc Aurel
1936 An Archaeological Tour in the Ancient Persis. *Iraq* 3:112–225.
1937 *Archaeological Reconnaissances in North-western India and South-eastern Iran.* London: Macmillan.
1940 *Old Routes of Western Iran.* London: MacMillan.

Steinkeller, Piotr
1982 The Question of Marhaši: A Contribution to the Historical Geography of Iran in the Third Millennium B.C. *Zeitschrift für Assyriologie* 72:237–265.
1987 The Administrative and Economic Organization of the Ur III State: The Core and the Periphery. In *The Organization of Power, Aspects of Bureaucracy in the Ancient Near East,* edited by McG. Gibson and R.D. Biggs, 19–41. Studies in Ancient Oriental Civilization 46. Chicago: Oriental Institute of the University of Chicago.

Steinmann, Susanne
1998 Gender, Pastoralism, and Intensification: Changing Environmental Resource Use in Morocco. *Yale School of Forestry and Environmental Studies Bulletin Series*103:81–107.

Steve, M.-J.
1967 *Tchoga Zanbil (Dur-Untash).* Vol. III: *Textes élamites et accadiens de Tchoga Zanbil.* Mémoires de la Délégation Archéologique en Iran 41. Paris: P. Geuthner.
1968 Fragmenta Elamica. *Orientalia* 37:290–303.
1986 La fin de l'Élam: à propos d'une empreinte de sceau-cylindre. *Studia Iranica* 15:7–21.
1987 *Nouveaux mélanges épigraphiques. Inscriptions royales de Suse et de la Susiane.* Mémoires de la Délégation Archéologique en Iran 53. Nice: Éditions Serre.
1989 Des sceaux-cylindres de Simaški? *Revue d'Assyriologie* 83:13–26.
1991 Elam: histoire continue ou discontinue? In *Mésopotamie et Élam, actes de la XXXVIème Rencontre Assyriologique Internationale (Gand, 10–14 juillet 1989),* 1–9. Mesopotamian History and Environment, Occasional Publication 1. Gand: University of Ghent.
1992 *Syllabaire élamite, histoire et paléographie.* Civilisations du Proche-Orient, Série 2 (Philologie), vol. 1. Neuchâtel and Paris: Recherches et Publications.
1994 La couche XII du chantier 'A' de la 'Ville Royale' et la fin de l'époque des Sukkalmah. In *Cinquante-deux réflexions sur le Proche-Orient ancien offertes en hommage à Léon De Meyer,* edited by H. Gasche, M. Tanret, C. Janssen and A. Degraeve, 23–30. Mesopotamian History and Environment, Occasional Publication II. Leuven: Peeters.

Steve, M.-J., and Hermann Gasche
1971 L'Acropole de Suse. *Mémoires de la Délégation Archéologique en Iran. Mission de Susiane 46.* Paris: Paul Geuthner.

Steve, M.-J., Hermann Gasche, and Leon De Meyer
1980 La Susiane au deuxième millénaire a.C.: à propos d'une interprétation des fouilles de Suse. *Iranica Antiqua* 15:49–154.

Steve, M.-J., and François Vallat
1989 La dynastie des Igihalkides: nouvelles interprétations.

In *Archaeologia Iranica et Orientalis, Miscellanea in Honorem Louis Vanden Berghe,* edited by L. De Meyer and E. Haerinck, 223–237. Gent: Peeters Press.

Steward, Julian
1977 *Evolution and Ecology.* Urbana: University of Illinois Press.

Stolper, Matthew W.
1978 Inscribed Fragments from Khuzistan. *Cahiers de la Délégation Archéologique Française en Iran* 8:89–96.
1982 On the Dynasty of Šimaški and the Early Sukkalmahs. *Zeitschrift für Assyriologie* 72:42–67.
1984a Political History. In *Elam, Surveys of Political History and Archaeology,* by E. Carter and M.W. Stolper, 1–100. University of California Publications, Near Eastern Studies 25. Berkeley and Los Angeles: University of California Press.
1984b *Texts from Tall-i Malyan, I. Elamite Administrative Texts (1972–1974).* Occasional Publications of the Babylonian Fund 6. Philadelphia: University Museum.
1984c The Neo-Babylonian Text from the Persepolis Fortification. *Journal of Near Eastern Studies* 43:299–310.
1985 Proto-Elamite Texts from Tall-i Malyan. *Kadmos* 24/1:1–12.
1988 Mâlamir, B. Philologisch. *Reallexikon der Assyriologie* 7/3-4:276–281.

Stolper, Matthew W., and Henry T. Wright
1990 Elamite Brick Fragments from Chogha Pahn East and Related Fragments. In *Contribution à l'histoire de l'Iran: mélanges offerts à Jean Perrot,* edited by F. Vallat, 151–163. Paris: Éditions Recherche sur les Civilisations.

Storey, Glenn R.
1997 Estimating the Population of Ancient Roman Cities. In *Integrating Archaeological Demography: Multidisciplinary Approaches to Prehistoric Populations,* edited by R.R. Paine, 101–130. Occasional Papers 24. Carbondale, IL: Southern Illinois University.

Stronach, David
1974 Achaemenid Village I at Susa and the Persian Migration to Fars. *Iraq* 36:239–248.
1978 *Pasargadae.* Oxford: Oxford University Press.
1997a Anshan and Parsa: Early Achaemenid History, Art and Architecture on the Iranian Plateau. In *Mesopotamia and Iran in the Persian Period, Conquest and Imperialism, 539–331 BC,* edited by J. Curtis, 35–53. London: British Museum Press.
1997b Darius at Pasargadae: A Neglected Source for the History of Early Persia. In *Recherches récentes sur l'Empire achéménide. Topoi,* Supplément 1:351–363.
1999 The Achaemenid Lobed Bracelet. In *The Iranian World. Essays on Iranian Art and Archaeology presented to Ezat O. Negahban,* edited by A. Alizadeh, Y. Majidzadeh, and S. Malek-Shahmirzadeh, 178–193. Tehran: Iran University Press.

Subramanian, V.S., and M.F. Van Osten
1959 Report of the Semidetailed Soil and Land Classification of the Ram Hormuz Plain, Khuzistan, Iran. Prepared

for the Khuzestan Water and Power Authority by the Food and Agriculture Organization of the United Nations and the Soils Research Organization, Tehran. Unpublished manuscript in the archives of the K.W.P.A., Andimeshk, Khuzestan.

Summers, Geoffrey D.

1982 A Study of the Architecture, Pottery, and Other Material From Yanik Tepe, Haftavan Tepe VIII and Related Sites. Ph.D. Dissertation, Faculty of Arts and Sciences, University of Manchester, Manchester.

Sumner, William M.

1972 Cultural Development in the Kur River Basin, Iran, an Archaeological Analysis of Settlement Patterns. Ph.D. Dissertation, Department of Anthropology, University of Pennsylvania, Philadelphia.

1974 Excavations at Tall-i Malyan, 1971–72. *Iran* 12:155–180.

1976 Excavations at Tall-i Malyan (Anshan) 1974. *Iran* 14:103–115.

1979 Estimating Population by Analogy: An Example. In *Ethnoarchaeology: Implications of Ethnography for Archaeology,* edited by C. Kramer, 164–174. New York: Columbia University Press.

1985 The Proto-Elamite City Wall at Tal-e Malyan. *Iran* 23:153–161.

1986a Proto-Elamite Civilization in Fars. In *Gamdat Nasr: Period or Regional Style?,* edited by U. Finkbeiner and W. Röllig, 199–211. Beiheft zum Tübinger Atlas des Vorderen Orients, Reihe B, Nr. 26. Wiesbaden: Dr. Ludwig Reichert Verlag.

1986b Achaemenid Settlement in the Persepolis Plain. *American Journal of Archaeology* 90:3–31.

1988a Maljân, Tall-e (Anṣan). *Reallexikon der Assyriologie* 7/3–4:306–320.

1988b Prelude to Proto-Elamite Anshan: The Lapui Phase. *Iranica Antiqua* 23:23–43.

1989a Anshan in the Kaftari Phase: Patterns of Settlement and Land Use. In *Archaeologia Iranica et Orientalis: Miscellanea in Honorem Louis Vanden Berghe,* edited by L. De Meyer and E. Haerinck, 135–161. Gent: Peeters Press.

1989b Population and Settlement Area: An Example from Iran. *American Anthropologist* 91:631–641.

1990a An Archaeological Estimate of Population Trends Since 6000 B.C. in the Kur River Basin, Fars Province, Iran. In *South Asian Archaeology 1987,* edited by M. Taddei, 1–16. Rome: Istituto Italiano per il Medio ed Estremo Oriente.

1990b Full-coverage Regional Archaeological Survey in the Near East: An Example from Iran. In *The Archaeology of Regions: A Case for Full-coverage Survey,* edited by S.K. Fish and S.A. Kowalewski, 87–115. Washington DC: Smithsonian Institution Press.

1991 Ceramics vi. Uruk, Proto-Elamite, and Early Bronze Age in Southern Persia. In *Encyclopaedia Iranica,* vol. 5, fasc.

3, edited by E. Yarshater, 284–288. Costa Mesa, CA: Mazda Publishers.

1994a Archaeological Measures of Cultural Continuity and the Arrival of the Persians in Fars. In *Achaemenid History 8: Continuity and Change,* edited by H. Sancisi-Weerdenburg, A. Kuhrt, and M.C. Root, 97–105. Leiden: Instituut voor het Nabije Oosten.

1994b The Evolution of Tribal Society in the Southern Zagros Mountains, Iran. In *Chiefdoms and Early States in the Near East: The Organizational Dynamics of Complexity,* edited by G.J. Stein and M.S. Rothman, 47–56. Madison: Prehistory Press.

2003 *Early Urban Life in the Land of Anshan: Excavations at Tal-e Malyan in the Highlands of Iran.* Malyan Excavation Reports, vol. 3. Philadelphia: University of Pennsylvania Museum.

Sumner, William M., and Donald Whitcomb

1999 Islamic Settlement and Chronology in Fars: An Archaeological Perspective. *Iranica Antiqua* 34:309–324.

Swift, Jeremy

1979 The Development of Livestock in Nomad Pastoral Economy: The Somali Case. In *Production pastorale et société, Actes du colloque international sur le pastoralisme nomade,* Paris, 1–3 Dec. 1976, L'Equipe écologie et anthropologie des sociétés pastorales. Cambridge: Cambridge University Press.

Tainter J.A.

1988 *The Collapse of Complex Societies.* Cambridge: Cambridge University Press.

Tala'i, Hassan

1978 An Archaeological Survey of the Dimceh Region: A Brief Report. Ms. on file, Susiana Archive, Department of Anthropology, Yale University, New Haven.

Tallon, Françoise

1987 *Métallurgie susienne. I. De la fondation de Suse au XVIIIe siècle avant J.-C. (1) et (2), Catalogue et illustrations.* Notes et Documents des Musées de France, 15. Paris: Éditions de la Réunion des Musées Nationaux.

1994 The "Trouvaille de la statuette d'or" from the Inshushinak Temple Precinct. In *The Royal City of Susa. Ancient Near Eastern Treasures in the Louvre,* edited by P.O. Harper, J. Aruz, and F. Tallon, 145–153. New York: Metropolitan Museum of Art.

Tampoe, Moira

1989 *Maritime Trade Between China and the West: An Archaeological Study of the Ceramics from Siraf (Persian Gulf), 8th to 15th Centuries A.D.* BAR International Series 555. Oxford: British Archaeological Reports.

Tapper, Richard

1979 *Pasture and Politics: Economics, Conflict and Ritual Among Shahsevan Nomads of Northwestern Iran.* London: Academic Press.

1994 Change, Cognition and Control: The Reconstruction of Nomadism in Iran. In *When History Accelerates: Essays*

on Rapid Social Change, Complexity and Creativity, edited by
C.M. Hann, 188–211. London: The Athlone Press.

1997   Frontier Nomads of Iran: A Political and Social History of the
        Shahsevan. Cambridge: Cambridge University Press.

Tapper, Richard, ed.

1983   The Conflict of Tribe and State in Iran and Afghanistan. Lon-
        don: Croom Helm.

Thiebault, Stéphanie

1989   A Note on the Ancient Vegetation of Baluchistan Based
        on Charcoal Analysis of the Latest Periods from
        Mehrgarh, Pakistan. In South Asian Archaeology 1985,
        edited by K. Frifelt and P. Sørenson, 186–188. London:
        Curzon Press.

Thomas, Kenneth

1990   Aspects of Soils and Early Agriculture. World Archaeology
        22(1):vi-xiii.

Thompson, R. Campbell, and R.W. Hamilton

1932   The British Museum Excavation on the Temple of Ishtar
        at Nineveh, 1930–31. Liverpool Annals of Archaeology and
        Anthropology 19(3-4):55–116.

Thorvildsen, Knud

1963   Burial Cairns on Umm-en Nar. Kuml 1962:208–219.

Thrane, Henrik

1999a   Pots and People—Once Again. The Goblets from the
        Bronze Age Settlement at Tepe Guran, Luristan. Iranica
        Antiqua 34:21–40.

1999b   Excavations at Tepe Guran. Publications of the Danish Ar-
        chaeological Expedition to Iran 2. The Bronze and Iron
        Age Periods. Aarhus.

Tilia, Ann Britt

1972   Studies and Restorations at Persepolis and Other Sites of Fars.
        Rome: IsMEO.

1974   Discovery of an Achaemenid Palace near Takht-i Rustam to
        the North of the Terrace of Persepolis. Iran 12:200–204.

1978   Studies and Restorations at Persepolis and Other Sites of Fars II.
        Reports and Memoirs 18. Roma: IsMEO.

Tiratsian, Guevork

1992   Découvertes récentes en Arménie. Les dossiers d'archéologie
        177:32–39.

Tobler, Arthur J.

1950   Excavations at Tepe Gawra. Philadelphia: University of Penn-
        sylvania Press.

Todd, Ian

1973   Anatolia and the Khirbet Kerak Ware. In Orient and Oc-
        cident: Cyrus Gordon Festschrift, edited by H. Hoffner, Jr.,
        181–206. Alter Orient und Altes Testament 22.

Tohidi, Faeq, and Ali-Mohammad Khalilian

1982   Report on the Study of Objects from the Ajran Tomb,
        Behbahan (in Persian). Asar (Athar) 7–9:232–286.

Tonghini, Christina

1995   A New Islamic Pottery Phase in Syria: Tell Shahin. Le-
        vant 27:197–207.

Tosi, Maurizio

1974   Some Data for the Study of Prehistorical Cultural Areas

on the Persian Gulf. Proceedings of the Seminar for Arabian
Studies 4:145–171.

1975   Hasanlu Project 1974: Paleobotanical Survey. Iran
        8:185–186.

1976a   Shahr-i Sokhta. Iran 14:167–168.

1976b   The Dating of the Umm an-Nar Culture and a Pro-
        posed Sequence for Oman in the Third Millennium BC.
        Journal of Oman Studies 2:81–92.

Trigger, Bruce G.

1998   Sociocultural Evolution: Calculation and Contingency. Oxford:
        Blackwell.

Tucker, David

1992   A Middle Assyrian Hoard from Khirbet Karhasan. Iraq
        54:157–177.

Tuplin, Christopher

1994   Persians as Medes. In Achaemenid History 8: Continuity and
        Change, edited by H. Sancisi-Werdenburg, A. Kuhrt and
        M.C. Root, 235–256. Leiden: Nederlands Instituut voor
        Het Nabije Oosten.

Uerpmann, Hans-Peter

1973   Animal Bone Finds and Economic Archaeology: A Criti-
        cal Study of Osteo-Archaeological Method. World Archae-
        ology 4:307–322.

Unglik, H.

N.D.   Copper Alloy Objects, Iron Objects and Slag from
        Carthage, Fifth to Seventh Centuries A.D.: A Metallur-
        gical Study. Ottawa: A Report of the National Historic
        Parks and Sites Branch, Parks Canada.

Vallat, François

1980   Suse et l'Élam. Recherche sur les grandes civilisations,
        mémoire 1. Paris: A.D.P.F.

1981a   Un fragment de brique de Tépé Bormi inscrit en élamite.
        Cahiers de la Délégation Archéologique Française en Iran
        12:193–196.

1981b   L'inscription de la stèle d'Untash-Napirisha. Iranica
        Antiqua 16:27–33.

1983   Les briques élamites de Deylam. In Kunst, Kultur und
        Geschichte der Achämenidenzeit und ihr Fortleben, by H. Koch
        und D.N. Mackenzie, 11–18. Archäologische
        Mitteilungen aus Iran 10. Berlin: D. Reimer.

1984a   Kidin-Hutran et l'époque néo-élamite. Akkadica 37:1–
        17.

1984b   Une inscription cunéiforme de Bouchir. Dédalo 23:255–
        260.

1986   The Most Ancient Scripts of Iran: The Current Situa-
        tion. World Archaeology 17(3):335–347.

1987   Le signe PI+PÍR dans les textes élamites de Malyan.
        Notes assyriologiques brèves et utilitaires 1987 No. 8.

1989a   Le scribe Ibni-Adad et les premiers sukkalmah. Nouvelles
        assyriologiques brèves et utilitaires 2, notes brèves 34, 23–24.

1989b   L'expression ADDA LUGAL an-ša-an ù MÙŠ.EREN (ki)
        dans un texte d'Attahušu. Nouvelles assyriologiques brèves et
        utilitaires 4, notes brèves 101, 75–76.

1989c   L'inscription du sceau-cylindre du sukkalmah Tan-Uli.
        Nouvelles assyriologiques brèves et utilitaires 117, 75–76.

1990a Reflexions sur l'époque des Sukkalmah. In *Contribution à l'histoire de l'Iran: mélanges offerts à Jean Perrot,* edited by F. Vallat, 119–127. Paris: Éditions Recherche sur les Civilisations.

1990b Une inscription élamite de Tépé Horreeye. In *Contribution à l'histoire de l'Iran: mélanges offerts à Jean Perrot,* edited by F. Vallat, 147–149. Paris: Éditions Recherche sur les Civilisations.

1993 *Les noms géographiques des sources suso-élamites.* Répertoire géographique des textes cunéiformes 11, edited by W. Röllig. Beihefte zum Tübinger Atlas des Vorderen Orients, Reihe B, Nr. 7. Wiesbaden: Dr. Ludwig Reichert Verlag.

1994 Succession royale en Élam au IIème millénaire. In *Cinquante-deux réflexions sur le Proche-Orient ancien offertes en hommage à Léon De Meyer,* edited by H. Gasche, M. Tanret, C. Janssen, and A. Degraeve, 1–14. Mesopotamian History and Environment, Occasional Publication II. Leuven: Peeters.

1996a Nouvelle analyse des inscriptions néo-élamites. In *Collectanea Orientalia. Histoire, arts de l'espace et industrie de la terre. Études offertes en hommages à Agnès Spycket,* edited by H. Gasche and B. Hrouda, 385–395. Civilisations du Proche-Orient série I, Archéologie et environnement 3. Neuchâtel et Paris: Recherches et publications.

1996b Le royaume néo-élamite de Samati. *Nouvelles assyriologiques brèves et utilitaires* 1:21–22.

1996c Le retour de Hutelutuš-Inšušnak à Suse. *Nouvelles assyriologiques brèves et utilitaires* 3:78–79.

1997 Les trois Kuk-Nashur. *Nouvelles assyriologiques brèves et utilitaires* 3:102–103.

1998 The History of Elam. In *Encyclopaedia Iranica,* vol. 8, fasc. 3, edited by E. Yarshater, 302–313. Costa Mesa, CA: Mazda Publishers.

Vance, James E.
1970 *The Merchant's World: The Geography of Wholesaling.* Englewood Cliffs, NJ: Prentice-Hall.

Vanden Berghe, Louis
1952 Archaeologische Opzoekingen in de Marv Dasht Vlakte (Iran). *Jaarbericht ex Oriente Lux* 12:211–220, Pls. XLVIII-LIV.

1953 Monuments récemment découverts en Iran méridional. *Bibliotheca Orientalis* 10:5–8.

1953-54 Archaeologische Navorsingen in de Omstreken van Persepolis. *Jaarbericht ex Oriente Lux* 13:394–408, Pls. LXXXV-LXXXIX.

1959 *Archéologie de l'Iran ancien.* Leiden: E.J. Brill.

1963 Les reliefs élamites de Mâlamir. *Iranica Antiqua* 3:22–39.

1970 La nécropole de Kalleh Nisar. *Archeologia* 32:64–73.

1973 La nécropole de Hakalan. *Archeologia* 57:49–58.

1986 Données nouvelles concernant le relief rupestre élamite de Kûrangûn. In *Fragmenta historiae aelamicae: mélanges offerts à M.-J. Steve,* edited by L. De Meyer, H. Gasche and F. Vallat, 157–173. Paris: Éditions Recherche sur les Civilisations.

Vanden Berghe, Louis, and Leon de Meyer
1983 *Urartu, een vergeten cultuur mit het bergland Armenië* Ghent:Centrum voor Kunst en Cultuur.

Van Dijk, Jan
1970 Remarques sur l'histoire d'Elam et d'Ešnunna. *Archiv für Orientforschung* 23: 63–71.

1978 Išbi-Erra, Kindattu, l'homme d'Élam, et la chute de la ville d'Ur: fragments d'un hymne d'Išbi'Erra. *Journal of Cuneiform Studies* 30:189–208.

1986 Die dynastischen Heiraten zwischen Kassiten und Elamern: eine verhängnisvolle Politik. *Orientalia* NS 55:159–170.

Vandiver, Pamela. B., K. Aslihan Yener, and L. May
1993 Third Millennium Tin Processing Debris from Göltepe (Anatolia). In *Materials Issues in Art and Archaeology III,* edited by P.B. Vandiver, J. Druzik, and G.S. Wheeler, 545–569. Pittsburgh: Materials Research Society.

Van Loon, Maurits N.
1962 A Lion Bowl from Hasanlu. *Expedition* 4(4):14–19.

1966 *Urartian Art.* Uitgaven van het Nederlands Historisch-Archaeologisch Instituut te Istanbul 20. Istanbul: Nederlands Historisch-Archaeologisch Instituut.

van Zeist, Willem
1986 Some Aspects of Early Neolithic Plant Husbandry in the Near East. *Anatolica* 7:75–89.

van Zeist, Willem, and Sytze Bottema
1977 Palynological Investigations in Western Iran. *Palaeohistoria* 24:19–85.

1982 Vegetational History of the Eastern Mediterranean and the Near East During the Last 20,000 Years. In *Palaeoclimates, Palaeoenvironments, and Human Communities in the Eastern Mediterranean Region in Later Prehistory,* edited by J.L. Bintliff and W. van Zeist, 277–321. BAR International Series 133. Oxford: British Archaeological Reports.

1991 *Late Quaternary Vegetation in the Near East.* Beiheft zum Tübinger Atlas des Vorderen Orients, Reihe A, Nr. 18. Wiesbaden: Dr. Ludwig Reichert Verlag.

van Zeist, Willem, P.E.L. Smith, R.M. Palfenier-Vegter, M. Suwijn, and W.A. Casparie
1984(1986) An Archaeobotanical Study of Ganj Dareh Tepe, Iran. *Palaeohistoria* 26:201–224.

Vatandust, Rasool
1988 A Preliminary Report of the Conservation and Technical Studies of Some of the Arjan Material (in Persian). *Asar (Athar)* 15/16:72–116.

Veenenbos, J.
1958 *Unified Report on the Soil and Land Classification Survey of Dezful Project, Khuzistan, Iran.* Tehran: Khuzistan Development Service.

Vidali, M.L., Eda Vidali, and C.C. Lamberg-Karlovsky
1976 Prehistoric Settlement Patterns around Tepe Yahya: A Quantitative Analysis. *Journal of Near Eastern Studies* 35:237–250.

Voget, Fred W.

1975 *A History of Ethnology.* New York: Holt, Rinehart, and Winston.

Voigt, Mary M.

1983 *Hajji Firuz Tepe, Iran: The Neolithic Settlement.* Philadelphia: University Museum, University of Pennsylvania.

Voigt, Mary M., and Robert H. Dyson, Jr.

1992 The Chronology of Iran, ca. 8000–2000 B.C. In *Chronologies in Old World Archaeology,* edited by R.W. Ehrich, 122–178. Chicago: University of Chicago Press.

Vollmer, John E., Edward J. Keall, E. Nagai-Berthrony

1983 *Silk Roads, China Ships.* Toronto: Royal Ontario Museum.

Wahida, G.

1981 The Re-excavation of Zarzi, 1971. *Proceedings of the Prehistoric Society* 47:19–40.

Walker, C.B.F.

1981 *Cuneiform Brick Inscriptions in the British Museum, the Ashmolean Museum, Oxford, the City of Birmingham Museums and Art Gallery, the City of Bristol Museums and Art Gallery.* London: British Museum Press.

Wasilewska, A.

1991 To Be or Not to Be a Temple? Possible Identification of a Banesh Period Temple at Tall-i Malyan, Iran. In *Mésopotamie et Elam, actes de la XXXVIème Rencontre Assyriologique Internationale (Gand, 10–14 juillet 1989),* 143–152. Occasional Publication 1. Gand: University of Ghent.

Watelin, L. C.

1931 Essai de coordination des périodes archaïques de la Mésopotamie et de l'Élam. *L'Anthropologie* 41:265–272.

Waters, M.W.

1996 Darius and the Achaemenid Line. *The Ancient History Bulletin* 10.1:11–18.

1999 The Earliest Persians in Southwestern Iran: The Textual Evidence. *Iranian Studies* 32(1): 99–107.

Watson, Andrew M.

1983 *Agricultural Innovation in the Early Islamic World.* Cambridge: Cambridge University Press.

Watson, Patty Jo

1979 *Archaeological Ethnography in Western Iran.* Viking Fund Publications in Anthropology 57. Tucson: University of Arizona Press.

Wattenmaker, Patricia A.

1997 *Household and State in Upper Mesopotamia: Specialized Economy and the Social Uses of Goods in an Early Complex Society.* Washington DC: Smithsonian Institution Press.

Wayman, Michael L., Maurizio Gualtieri, and R.A. Konzuk

1988 Bronze Metallurgy at Roccagloriosa. In *Proceedings of the 26th International Archaeometry Symposium,* edited by R.M. Farquhar, R.G.V. Hancock, and L.A. Pavlish, 128–132. Toronto: Archaeometry Laboratory, Department of Physics, University of Toronto.

Weeks, Lloyd

1999 Lead Isotope Analyses from Tell Abraq, United Arab Emirates: New Data Regarding the "Tin Problem" in Western Asia. *Antiquity* 73:49–64.

Weisgerber, Gerd

1984 Makan and Meluhha—Third Millennium B.C. Copper Production in Oman and the Evidence of Contact with the Indus Valley. In *South Asian Archaeology 1981,* edited by B. Allchin, 196–201. Cambridge: Cambridge University Press.

Weiss, Harvey

1977 Periodization, Population and Early State Formation in Khuzistan. In *Mountains and Lowlands: Essays in the Archaeology of Greater Mesopotamia,* edited by L.D. Levine and T.C. Young, Jr., 347–369. Bibliotheca Mesopotamica 7. Malibu: Undena.

Weiss, Harvey, ed.

1985 *Ebla to Damascus: Art and Archaeology of Ancient Syria.* Washington DC: Smithsonian Institution Traveling Exhibition Service.

Weiss, Harvey, Marie-Agnès Courty, Wilma Wetterstrom, F. Guichard, Louise Senior, Richard Meadow, and A. Curnow

1993 The Genesis and Collapse of Third Millennium North Mesopotamian Civilization. *Science* 261: 995–1004.

Weissbach, Franz

1911 *Die Keilschriften der Achämeniden.* Leipzig: Hinrichs.

Wenke, Robert J.

1975-76 Imperial Investments and Agricultural Developments in Parthian and Sasanian Khuzestan: 150 B.C. to A.D. 640. *Mesopotamia* 10-11:13–221.

1987 Western Iran in the Partho-Sasanian Period: The Imperial Transformation. In *The Archaeology of Western Iran,* edited by F. Hole, 251–281. Washington DC: Smithsonian Institution Press.

Wertime, Theodore A.

1968 A Metallurgical Expedition through the Persian Desert. *Science* 159:927–935.

1973 Beginnings of Metallurgy: A New Look. *Science* 182:875–887.

Whallon, Robert E.

1979 *An Archaeological Survey of the Keban Reservoir Area of East-central Turkey.* Memoirs 11. Ann Arbor: University of Michigan Museum of Anthropology.

Wheatley, Paul

2001 *The Places where Men Pray Together: Cities in Islamic Lands, Seventh through the Tenth Centuries.* Chicago: University of Chicago Press.

Whitcomb, Donald

1971 The Proto-Elamite Period at Tall-i Ghazir, Iran. M.A. Thesis, University of Georgia.

1979 The City of Istakhr and the Marv Dasht Plain. In *Acten des VII. Internationalen Kongresses für Iranische Kunst und Archäologie, München, 7.–10. September 1976.* Archäologische Mitteilungen aus Iran, Ergänzungsband 6:363–370. Berlin.

1987 Bushire and the Angali Canal. *Mesopotamia* 22:311–336.

1988 A Fatimid Residence at Aqaba, Jordan. *Annual of the Department of Antiquities* 32: 207–24.

1991 Pseudo-Prehistoric Ceramics from Southern Iran. In *Golf-Archäologie: Mesopotamien, Iran, Bahrain, Vereinigte Arabische Emirate und Oman,* edited by K. Schippmann et al., 95–112. Buch am Erbach: M.L. Leidorf.

1995 Toward a "Common Denominator": An Archaeological Response to M. Morony on Pottery and Urban Identities. In *Identity and Material Culture in the Early Islamic World,* edited by I.A. Bierman, 47–68. Los Angeles: University of California, Near East Center Colloquium Series.

Whitmore, Thomas M., Brian L. Turner II, Douglas L. Johnson, R. W. Kates, and T.R. Gottschang

1990 Long-term Population Change. In *The Earth as Transformed by Human Action: Global and Regional Change in the Biosphere over the Past 300 Years,* edited by B.L. Turner II, 25–39. Cambridge: Cambridge University Press.

Wilhelm, Gernot

1989 *The Hurrians.* Warminster: Aris and Phillips.

1995 The Kingdom of Mitanni in Second-Millennium Upper Mesopotamia. In *Civilizations of the Ancient Near East,* vol. II, edited by J.M. Sasson, J. Baines, G. Beckman, and K.S. Rubinson, 1243–1254. New York: Scribner's.

Wilkinson, Charles K.

1974 *Nishapur: Pottery of the Early Islamic Period.* New York: Metropolitan Museum of Art.

1986 *Nishapur: Some Early Islamic Buildings and their Decoration.* New York: Metropolitan Museum of Art.

Wilkinson, T.J.

1974 Agricultural Decline in the Siraf Region, Iran. *Paléorient* 2(1):123–132.

1982 The Definition of Ancient Manured Zones by Means of Extensive Sherd Sampling Techniques. *Journal of Field Archaeology* 9:323–333.

1990 *Town and Country in Southeastern Anatolia.* Vol. 1: *Settlement and Land Use at Kurban Höyük and Other Sites in the Lower Karababa Basin.* Publication 109. Chicago: Oriental Institute of the University of Chicago.

1994 The Structure and Dynamics of Dry-farming States in Upper Mesopotamia. *Current Anthropology* 35:483–520.

1998 Water and Human Settlement in the Balikh Valley, Syria: Investigations from 1992–1995. *Journal of Field Archaeology* 25:63–87.

1999 Demographic Trends from Archaeological Survey. Case Studies from the Levant and Near East. In *Long-term Demographic Trends in the Mediterranean Basin,* edited by J. Bintliff and K. Sbonias, 45–64. Oxford: Oxbow books.

N.D. Archaeological Survey of the Tell Beydar Region, Syria 1997: A Preliminary Report. In *Subartu VI,* edited by K. Vandenberghe. Ghent: Brepols. In press.

Wilkinson, T.J., and David J. Tucker

1995 *Settlement Development in the North Jazira, Iraq. A Study of the Archaeological Landscape.* British School of Archaeology in Iraq. Warminster: Aris and Phillips.

Wilkinson, T.J., Belinda H. Monahan and David. J. Tucker

1996 Khanijdal East: A Small Ubaid Site in Northern Iraq. *Iraq* 58:17–50.

Willcox, George

1990 Charcoal Remains from Tepe Abdul Hosein. In *Tepe Abdul Hosein: A Neolithic Site in Western Iran, Excavations 1978,* by J. Pullar, 223–227. BAR International Series 563. Oxford: British Archaeological Reports.

1991 Exploitation des espèces ligneuses au Proche-Orient: données anthracologiques. *Paléorient* 17(2):117–126.

Willey, Gordon R., and Philip Phillips

1958 *Method and Theory in American Archaeology.* Chicago: University of Chicago Press.

Williams, D.

1973 Flotation at Siraf. *Antiquity* 47:288–292.

Williamson, Andrew

1969 Kur River Valley Sassanian and Islamic Pottery: Justification for the Chronological Classification of Sites. Unpublished ms.

1971 Tepe Dasht-i Deh. *Iran* 9:182–83.

1988 Regional Distribution of Medieval Persian Pottery in the Light of Recent Investigation. In *Syria and Iran: Three Studies in Medieval Ceramics,* edited by J. Allan and C. Roberts, 11–22. Oxford: Oxford University Press.

Winter, Irene J.

1977 Perspective on 'Local Style' of Hasanlu IVB: A Study in Receptivity. In *Mountains and Lowlands: Essays in the Archaeology of Greater Mesopotamia,* edited by L.D. Levine and T.C. Young, Jr., 371–388. Bibliotheca Mesopotamica 7. Malibu: Undena.

1980 *A Decorated Breastplate from Hasanlu, Iran.* University Museum Monograph 39. Philadelphia: University Museum, University of Pennsylvania.

1989 The "Hasanlu Gold Bowl": Thirty Years Later. *Expedition* 31(2-3):87–106.

2000 Opening the Eyes and Opening the Mouth: The Utility of Comparing Images in Worship in India and the Ancient Near East. In *Ethnography and Personhood,* edited by M.W. Meister, 129–162. Jaipur and New Delhi: Rawat.

Woolley, Charles Leonard

1954 *Excavations at Ur.* London: Ernst Benn, Ltd.

Woosley, Anne I., and Frank Hole

1978 Pollen evidence of Subsistence and Environment in Ancient Iran. *Paléorient* (4):59–70.

Wright, Henry T.

1969 Archaeological Survey in the Areas of Ram Hormuz, Shushtar and Gutwand. Ms. on file, University of Michigan Museum of Anthropology, Ann Arbor.

1977 Toward an Explanation of the Origin of the State. In *Explanation of Prehistoric Change,* edited by J.N. Hill, 215–230. Albuquerque: University of New Mexico.

1984 Prestate Political Formations. In *On the Evolution of Complex Societies: Essays in Honor of Harry Hoijer 1982,* edited by T. Earle. 41–77. Malibu: Undena.

1987 The Susiana Hinterlands during the Era of Primary State Formation. In *The Archaeology of Western Iran,* edited by F. Hole, 141–155. Washington DC: Smithsonian Press.

Wright, Henry T., ed.
1979 *Archaeological Investigations in Northeastern Xuzestan, 1976.* Technical Reports 10. Museum of Anthropology, University of Michigan and Iranian Centre for Archaeological Research Survey Report No. 1. Ann Arbor: University of Michigan Museum of Anthropology.

Wright, Henry T., and Gregory A. Johnson
1975 Population, Exchange, and Early State Formation in Southwestern Iran. *American Anthropologist* 77:267–289.

Wright, Henry T., Naomi F. Miller, and Richard W. Redding
1981 Time and Process in an Uruk Rural Center. In *L'archéologie de l'Iraq: perspectives et limites de l'interpretation anthropologique des documents,* 265–282. Colloques internationaux du CNRS 580. Paris.

Wright, Henry T., James A. Neely, Gregory A. Johnson, and John D. Speth
1975 Early Fourth Millennium Developments in Southwestern Iran. *Iran* 13:129–148.

Wright, Henry T., and Eric Rupley
2001 Calibrated Radiocarbon Age Determinations of Uruk-related Assemblages. In *Uruk Mesopotamia and Its Neighbors: Cross-cultural Interactions in the Era of State Formation,* edited by M.S. Rothman, 85–122. School of American Research Advanced Seminar Series. Santa Fe: SAR Press.

Wright, Rita P.
1989 New Perspectives on Third Millennium Painted Grey Wares. In *South Asian Archaeology 1985,* edited by K. Frifelt and P. Sørensen, 137–149. London: Curzon Press.

Wulff, Hans E.
1966 *The Traditional Crafts of Persia.* Cambridge: MIT Press.

Yakar, Jak
1985 *The Later Prehistory of Anatolia: The Late Chalcolithic and Early Bronze Age.* BAR International Series 268 (ii). Oxford: British Archaeological Reports.

Yener, K. Aslihan, and Pamela B. Vandiver
1993 Tin Processing at Göltepe, an Early Bronze Age Site in Anatolia. *American Journal of Archaeology* 97:207–238.

Yoffee, Norman
1977 *The Economic Role of the Crown in the Old Babylonian Period.* Bibliotheca Mesopotamica 5. Malibu: Undena.
1979 The Decline and Rise of Mesopotamian Civilization: An Ethnoarchaeological Perspective on the Evolution of Social Complexity. *American Antiquity* 44:5–35.
1988 The Collapse of Ancient Mesopotamian States and Civilization. In *The Collapse of Ancient States and Civilizations,* edited by N. Yoffee and G. Cowgill, 44–68. Tucson: University of Arizona Press.

Yoffee, Norman and George Cowgill, eds.
1988 *The Collapse of Ancient States and Civilizations.* Tucson: University of Arizona Press.

Young, T. Cuyler, Jr.
1967 The Iranian Migration into the Zagros. *Iran* 5:11–34.
1969 *Excavations at Godin Tepe: First Progress Report.* Occassional Paper 17. Toronto: Royal Ontario Museum.
1972 Population Densities and Early Mesopotamian Urbanism. In *Man, Settlement and Urbanism,* edited by P.J. Ucko, R. Tringham, and G.W. Dimbleby, 827–842. London: Duckworth.
1977 Population Dynamics and Philosophical Dichotomies. In *Mountains and Lowland: Essays in the Archaeology of Greater Mesopotamia,* edited by L.D. Levine and T.C. Young, Jr., 387–398. Bibliotheca Mesopotamica 7. Malibu: Undena.
1986 Godin Tepe Period VI/V and Central Western Iran at the End of the Fourth Millennium. In *Gamdat Nasr: Period or Regional Style?,* edited by U. Finkbeiner and W. Röllig, 212–228. Beihefte zum Tübinger Atlas des Vorderen Orients, Reihe B, Nr. 62. Wiesbaden: Dr. Ludwig Reichert Verlag.
1988 The Early History of the Medes and the Persians and the Achaemenid Empire to the Death of Cambyses. In *The Cambridge Ancient History,* vol. 4, edited by J. Boardman, 1–52. Cambridge: Cambridge University Press.

Young, T. Cuyler, Jr., and Louis D. Levine
1974 *Excavations of the Godin Project: Second Preliminary Report.* Toronto: Royal Ontario Museum.

Zadok, Ran
1976 On the Connections Between Iran and Babylonia in the Sixth Century B.C. *Iran* 14:61–78.
1984 *The Elamite Onomasticon.* Supplement 40 to *Annali* vol. 44, fasc. 3. Naples: Istituto Universitario Orientale.

Zagarell, Allen
1975 An Archaeological Survey in the North-east Baxtiari Mountains. *Proceedings of the IIIrd Annual Symposium on Archaeological Research in Iran.* Tehran, 23–30.
1978 *The Role of Highland Pastoralism in the Development of Iranian Civilization.* Ph.D. Dissertation, Free University, Berlin.
1982 *The Prehistory of the Northeast Bahtiyari Mountains, Iran, The Rise of a Highland Way of Life.* Beihefte zum Tübinger Atlas des Vorderen Orients, Reihe B, Nr. 42. Wiesbaden: Dr. Ludwig Reichert Verlag.

Zarins, Juris
1989 Eastern Saudi Arabia and External Relations: Selected Ceramic, Steatite, and Textual Evidence: 3500–1900 B.C. In *South Asian Archaeology 1985,* edited by K. Frifelt and P. Sørensen, 74–103. London: Curzon Press.

Zeder, Melinda A.
1985 Urbanism and Animal Exploitation in Southwest Highland Iran, 3400–1500 B.C. Ph.D. Dissertation, Department of Anthropology, University of Michigan, Ann Arbor.
1988 Understanding Urban Process through the Study of Specialized Subsistence Economy in the Near East. *Journal of Anthropological Archaeology* 7:1–55.
1991 *Feeding Cities: Specialized Animal Economy in the Ancient Near East.* Washington DC: Smithsonian Institution Press.
1995 The Archaeobiology of the Khabur Basin. *Bulletin of the Canadian Society for Mesopotamian Studies* 29:21–32.

1996   The Role of Pigs in Near Eastern Subsistence from the Vantage Point of the Southern Levant. In *Retrieving the Past: Essays on Archaeological Research and Methodology in Honor of Gus Van Beek,* edited by J.D. Seger, 297–312. Winona Lake, IN: Eisenbrauns.

1998   Environment, Economy, and Subsistence on the Threshold of Urban Emergence in Northern Mesopotamia. In *Espace naturel, espace habité, en Syrie nord (10e–2e millénaire av. J.-C.),* edited by M. Fortin and O. Aurenche, 55–67. Bulletin of the Canadian Society for Mesopotamian Studies 33. Québec: Canadian Society for Mesopotamian Studies.

Zeder, Melinda A., and Brian Hesse

2000   The Initial Domestication of Goats (*Capra hircus*) in the Zagros Mountains 10,000 Years Ago. *Science* 287:2254–2257.

Zettler, Richard L.

1992   *The Ur III Temple of Inanna at Nippur.* Berliner Beiträge zum Vorderen Orient. Berlin: D. Reimer.

1997   Introduction. In *Subsistence and Settlement in a Marginal Environment: Tell es-Sweyhat, 1989–1995 Preliminary Report,* edited by R.L. Zettler, 1–10. MASCA Research Papers in Science and Archaeology 14. Philadelphia: University Museum, University of Pennsylvania.

Zimansky, Paul E.

1985   *Ecology and Empire: The Structure of the Urartian State.* Studies in Ancient Oriental Civilization. Chicago: Oriental Institute of the University of Chicago.

1995a   The Kingdom of Urartu in Eastern Anatolia. In *Civilizations of the Ancient Near East,* vol. II, edited by J.M. Sasson, J. Baines, G. Beckman, and K.S. Rubinson, 1135–1146. New York: Scribner's.

1995b   An Urartian Ozymandias. *Biblical Archaeology* 58(2):94–100.

Zohary, Daniel

1999   Monophyletic vs. Polyphyletic Origin of the Crops on Which Agriculture Was Founded in the Near East. *Genetic Resources and Crop Evolution* 46:133–142.

Zohary, Daniel, and Maria Hopf

2000   *Domestication of Plants in the Old World: The Origin and Spread of Cultivated Plants in West Asia, Europe, and the Nile Valley.* 3rd edition. Oxford: Oxford University Press.

Zohary, Michael

1963   On the Geobotanical Structure of Iran. *Bulletin of the Research Council of Israel* 11D, supplement:1–113.

Zwicker, Ulrich, H. Greiner, K.-H. Hofmann, and M. Reithinger

1985   Smelting, Refining and Alloying of Copper and Copper Alloys in Crucible Furnaces during Prehistoric up to Roman Times. In *Furnaces and Smelting Technology in Antiquity,* edited by P.T. Craddock and M.J. Hughes, 103–115. Occasional Paper 48. London: British Museum.

CONTRIBUTORS

Kamyar Abdi
*Department of Anthropology,
Dartmouth College*

John R. Alden
Ann Arbor, MI

Abbas Alizadeh
The Oriental Institute

Lois Beck
*Department of Anthropology,
Washington University*

M. James Blackman
*Smithsonian Center for Materials
Research and Education*

Rémy Boucharlat
Maison de l'Orient, CNRS-Université Lyon

Elizabeth Carter
*Department of Near Eastern
Languages and Cultures,
University of California, Los Angeles*

Robert H. Dyson, Jr.
University of Pennsylvania Museum

Ernie Haerinck
*Department of Near Eastern Art and
Archaeology, University of Gent*

Frank Hole
*Department of Anthropology,
Yale University*

Nicholas Kouchoukos
The Oriental Institute

Michael Kozuh
The Oriental Institute

Wolfram Kleiss
Berlin, Germany

Yousef Majidzadeh
Nice, France

Naomi F. Miller
University of Pennsylvania Museum

Pierre de Miroschedji
*UMR Archéologies et Sciences de
l'Antiquité, Maison de l'archéologie
et de l'ethnologie*

Samuel Nash
University of Pennsylvania Museum

Ezat O. Negahban
University of Pennsylvania Museum

Bruno Overlaet
*University of Gent/Vesalius College,
Vrije Universiteit Brussel*

Vincent C. Pigott
University of Pennsylvania Museum

Holly Pittman
*Department of Art History,
University of Pennsylvania*

D.T. Potts
*Department of Archaeology,
University of Sydney*

Harry C. Rogers
Chester, PA

Michael Rosenberg
*Parallel Program,
University of Delaware*

Mitchell S. Rothman
*Social Science Division LC,
Widener University*

Karen S. Rubinson
New York City, NY

Matthew W. Stolper
The Oriental Institute

David Stronach
*Department of Near Eastern Studies,
University of California, Berkeley*

Mary M. Voigt
*Department of Anthropology,
College of William and Mary*

Donald Whitcomb
The Oriental Institute

T.J. Wilkinson
The Oriental Institute

Henry T. Wright
*Museum of Anthropology,
University of Michigan*

T. Cuyler Young, Jr.
*Department of Near Eastern
and Asian Civilizations,
Royal Ontario Museum*

Melinda A. Zeder
*Archaeobiology Program,
National Museum of Natural History,
Smithsonian Institution*

INDEX